Japan

a travel survival kit

Published by
Lonely Planet Publications,
PO Box 88,
Victoria 3141, Australia

Typeset by
Lonely Planet Publications

Printed by
Colorcraft,
Hong Kong

Illustrations by
Peter Campbell

Photographs by
Ian McQueen

Graphic design
Dover Publications, New York

Design by
Andrew...

National Library of Australia
Cataloguing...

McQueen, Ian
Japan...

ISBN 0 908086 07 5

Japan — a travel survival kit

Published by
Lonely Planet Publications
PO Box 88, South Yarra
Victoria 3141, Australia

Typeset by
Lonely Planet Publications

Printed by
Colorcraft
Hong Kong

Illustrations by
Peter Campbell

Photographs by
Ian McQueen

Graphics from
Japanese Design Motifs
(Dover Publications, New York)

Design by
Andrena Millen

First Published
October 1981
Reprinted May 1982

National Library of Australia
Cataloguing in Publication Data

McQueen, Ian.
Japan — a travel survival kit.

Includes index.
ISBN 0 908086 07 5.

1. Japan — Description and travel — 1945- —
Guide-books. I. Title.

915.2'0448

© Ian McQueen 1981

DEDICATION
To my parents, Edmund C and (the late) Constance A McQueen, and my maternal grandfather (the late) H E Richards, who together gave me interest and assistance in travelling.

Contents

4 Contents

Introduction

It is sad but true that many travellers arrive in Japan not really knowing where to go, what to see, or when to do everything. Japan is so far from all western countries and so expensive to get to, that few people are able to make repeated trips to see what they missed during the previous visit. It is hoped that this book will help you make the best of your time in Japan.

To find the traditional Japan, or what remains of it after the post-war prosperity, improved communications and TV, it is necessary to travel away from the big cities into the countryside, especially the mountain areas that are still somewhat isolated. Good areas are Tohoku (northern Honshu), and Central Japan (Chubu). The Kyoto/Nara area has the largest number of historic remains, beautiful temples and gardens, so should be at the top of any list of areas to visit. Hokkaido, despite its isolation is not a good place to visit for historical remains for it remained largely unsettled until late in the 19th century. It is superb, however, for wilderness scenery and getting away from crowds.

Little remains of the traditional appearance of Japanese towns. The major industrial centres were severely damaged during the war, earthquakes have struck most parts of the country at some time, and the Japanese have been systematically 'improving' what remains. The result is that there are relatively few old buildings, and these are scattered here and there. Towns that have preserved unusually large numbers of old buildings are Kawagoe (Tokyo area), Kitakata and Kakunodate in Tohoku (northern Honshu), the three old post towns Narai, Tsumago, and Magome in the Kiso river valley of Chubu (Central Japan), and the old castle town of Kanazawa (Hokuriku area). Many old thatched-roof houses may still be found in the Shirakawago/Gokayama area of northern Chubu, and along the valley road between Imaichi and Aizu-Wakamatsu, just above Nikko. There are also collections of old buildings (generally wooden structures with thatched roofs) near Kawasaki (Tokyo area), Takayama (Chubu), and Kanazawa, and a few in Sankei-en garden in Yokohama.

Having chosen a district to visit, a suggested way to travel is to book a room in a ryokan or minshuku for a day or two (if starting from Tokyo or other large city with booking offices). It is possible that you will be the first foreigners ever to stay there, and the owners will go out of their way to make your visit a pleasure. After the first day or two you should feel confident enough to set out on your own.

Guided tours are available for many destinations of interest to overseas visitors, but for most people, especially for those on tight budgets, tours are rarely worthwhile. Tour groups must move at the pace set by the schedule; tours often include places of limited interest, or bypass other places of equal interest; and of course tour groups miss the opportunity of mixing with local people and gaining a feel for the life of the average person in the real Japan.

The purpose of this book is to provide detailed information so that visitors to Japan can make their own tours. Information about each place or area the average person in the real Japan.

The purpose of this book is to provide detailed information so that visitors to Japan can make their own tours. Information about each place or area includes details about how to get there, where to find reasonably-priced accommodation, and how to get around the cities, as well as descriptions of interesting things to see.

Getting There

BY AIR

There are seven international ports of entry by air into Japan: Tokyo, Niigata, Nagoya, Osaka, Fukuoka, Kumamoto, Kagoshima, and Naha. The first four are on Honshu, the main island, the last is on Okinawa, far to the south of the main islands, and the rest are on Kyushu, the southernmost of the four major islands.

Tokyo

Tokyo has the largest number of international flights, but nearly all go to Narita airport, nearly 60 km out in the country; getting into central Tokyo takes an absolute minimum of 1½ hours. (Further details are given in the Tokyo chapter.) The only international airline to fly into convenient Haneda airport is China Airlines; most domestic flights use Haneda.

Niigata

Niigata, on the north coast almost due north of Tokyo, is the port of entry from Khabarovsk (USSR) for travellers using the Trans-Siberian railway route from Europe. Only about a third of the passengers from Europe are able to get bookings on the ship from Nakhodka to Yokohama, and the rest must fly into Niigata. The city is easily reached by bus from the airport. Niigata is linked to Tokyo by JNR train in about 4½ hours (by the fastest express).

Nagoya

Nagoya, near the middle of the country, is connected with Hong Kong, Seoul and Manila. The airport is about half an hour away from Nagoya station by regular airport bus. The station is a stop for all Shinkansen (bullet) trains, and there are bus services east to Tokyo and west to Kyoto and Osaka. Narita itself is a commercial city and of negligible interest to a tourist, but there are many attractions within easy reach, so it is a starting point worth considering.

Osaka

Osaka is a good starting point for travel in Japan, for it is close to Kyoto, the premier tourist attraction city in the country, and the trip from the airport is short and simple. Buses from the airport go to various destinations, including Kyoto and the Osaka station area; from Osaka station it is a short trip to Shin-Osaka station, one of the major stations of the Shinkansen, which offers rapid connections as far east as Tokyo, and as far west as Fukuoka, in northern Kyushu.

There are flights to Osaka from Los Angeles, Hong Kong, Singapore, Bangkok, Seoul, Manila, Kuala Lumpur and Teipei.

Fukuoka

Travellers from Antwerp, Brussels, Hong Kong, Seoul, Pusan and Teipei can use Fukuoka (in Kyushu) as a convenient entry point. From there it is easy to circle around Kyushu then carry on through western Japan to Kyoto, Tokyo, etc. Fukuoka is the western terminus of the Shinkansen. There is frequent bus service between the airport and Hakata station. (The station is named Hakata after the city where it is located, across a river from Fukuoka.)

Kumamoto

The rather provincial city of Kumamoto is linked to points in Korea. It is a gateway to the volcano Mt Aso, and Nagasaki is not far away in the opposite direction. A circle around the rest of Kyushu can easily be arranged.

Kagoshima

This is the southernmost city in the main islands, and has several places of interest in and around the city. There is regular bus service between the airport and Nishi-Kagoshima, the main station of the city. From here one can travel up through Kyushu, seeing virtually everything of interest without back-tracking. Flights link Kagoshima with Hong Kong, Nauru, Ponape, Seoul and Singapore.

Naha

The major city of Okinawa, Naha is a good starting point for exploring the numerous islands to the south of Kyushu. There are many flights from Naha to a number of cities on the main islands, as well as boat connections to several cities, like Tokyo and Osaka.

AIR FARES

Air fares are constantly changing, usually upwards, but the following information can be used as a guide.

From Europe

From London you can fly to Tokyo with Cathay Pacific for £215/380 one-way/return, but check this against the cost of a cheap flight to Hong Kong with a separate ticket on to Tokyo. The London-Hong Kong route is very competitive with tickets as low as £100 stand-by.

From elsewhere in Europe there are discount fares from various airlines. For example from Amsterdam, the cheapest fare to Tokyo is f1050/1850 (about £180/320) one-way/return with Biman Bangladesj Airlines. You can fly there with Pakistan Airlines for f1200/2400 (about £210/420) or with Air India for f1400/2550 (about £245/445) one-way/return. The same fares with Pakistan Airlines and Air India are also available from Frankfurt.

From USA

The cheapest trans-Pacific flights, Los Angeles to Tokyo, are US$345 with Korean Airlines, or US$380 via Honolulu with China Airlines. The regular econ-omy fare LA-Tokyo is US$591 one-way.

From Australia

Japan was one of the last major destinations from Australia to get any sort of discount fares. Even so the only 'cheap' fare is an Apex (advance-purchase excursion) return ticket from Sydney with JAL or Qantas. You must pay at least 30 days before departure and must stay away for 14-120 days. No stopovers are permitted.

The fare in each direction is A$400 off-peak, or A$492 in peak season, but only as a return ticket so add the two sector fares together. The peak season ex Sydney is for about five weeks at Christmas and three weeks in both May and August. For the return flight the peak seasons are of similar length but each starts about three weeks later. The rest of the year is off-peak.

If you plan to visit Singapore (or another Asian city, eg Hong Kong or Bangkok) the best deal would be an Apex ticket to Singapore and a separate return ticket from there to Japan. China Airlines are popular with travel agents for this. You can buy the ticket in Australia or wait until you reach Singapore. The total fare is more than the Apex fare to Tokyo but it is a cheap way to get a stopover if you want one.

The standard full-fare economy ticket Sydney-Tokyo is A$834 one-way (no restrictions and unlimited stopovers). For the same price you can also fly on to Nagoya, Osaka and Fukuoka.

Around the world

If you are visiting Japan as part of a longer trip, it is worth considering tickets such as Pan Am's 'Round the World in 80 Days'. For US$1279 economy stand-by or US$1719 advance purchase, you can fly anywhere on Pan Am's northern hemisphere routes for up to 80 days but you must keep going east or west, ie no backtracking. You must start (and finish) in the USA or at London, Istanbul, Bangkok or Hong Kong.

Pan Am also have an extended version of this ticket for Australians at A$1815 standby, A$2349 advance-purchase. This provides travel to and from Honolulu to join the northern routes.

BY SEA

There are no longer any regular passenger liner services between Japan and countries of Europe, North America, etc. Cruise ships stop occasionally, but even these have been becoming less frequent in recent years. The main ports for them are Yokohama and Kobe, and visitors on ships which will stop at both can leave the ship at one and rejoin it at the other.

For cruise passengers with one or two nights in the Yokohama-Tokyo area, suggested places to visit are Nikko, Kamakura, Tokyo. Kamakura, home of the famous Great Buddha, is half an hour from Yokohama station; a couple of hours there is enough to see the Buddha, but more time will allow exploration of some of the temples from which Kamakura is noted. It was once the capital of Japan, so its temples have an illustrious past and are among the finest in Japan. In the Yokohama area, Sankeien Park is one of the finest gardens in Japan. Tokyo is the best place in Japan for shopping. Nikko can be visited in a day trip from Tokyo starting early in the morning, or an over-night stay there can be combined with a visit to a hot spring resort. If your ship will call next at Kobe, you can travel from Tokyo to Kyoto by Shinkansen train, possibly see Mt Fuji from the train tour Kyoto for a while, then go to Kobe to rejoin your ship.

Apart from cruise ships there are a few cargo ships sailing the Pacific which take passengers. Most prefer to take passengers on the entire course to the final destination, so it may be harder to get a booking to Japan on a ship going on to other ports. The best advice is to find a capable travel agent who can find a freighter that will be going to Japan. Fares vary enormously but usually even the cheapest will be considerably more expensive than flying.

Nakhodka & the Trans-Siberian

The only regular passenger service to Japan (apart from the ferry service to/from Korea) is operated by Soviet-owned Far East Shipping Line between Nakhodka (east coast of the USSR) and Yokohama (near Tokyo). It is scheduled to make connections with the Trans-Siberian Railway. There are two ships in regular service, and a third which is used occasionally in the peak summer season. Frequency of sailings ranges from a low of two a month in winter to as many as nine in summer (1980). In addition, each year there are about four return sailings between Japan and Hong Kong by a Soviet ship.

Almost all travellers have had good comments on the ship service, and most have been satisfied by the Trans-Siberian rail trip, although some have been victims of very shoddy treatment (accidental or otherwise) whereby they found it almost impossible to obtain the meals they had paid for.

There are representatives of the Japan-Soviet Tourist Bureau in Tokyo (tel 432-6161) and Osaka (531-7416). The Tourist Information Centre in Tokyo usually has a leaflet giving more details and directions for getting to the Tokyo office.

Korea

There are thrice-weekly (each direction) ferry services between Shimonoseki (at the far west of Honshu) and Pusan, Korea. The Kampu ferry is the least expensive way of getting from Korea to

Japan, the lowest fare is Y8000. Further details of the ferry are given in the section on Shimonoseki, and the Tourist Information Centre in Tokyo has a handout information sheet with complete details.

Many people want to go between Tokyo and Seoul simply to renew visas. If they want to do this as quickly as possible it may be worth flying direct. A three-day excursion ticket to Seoul by air costs about Y10,000 more than the total of fares using the Shinkansen to Shimonoseki and the ferry to Pusan.

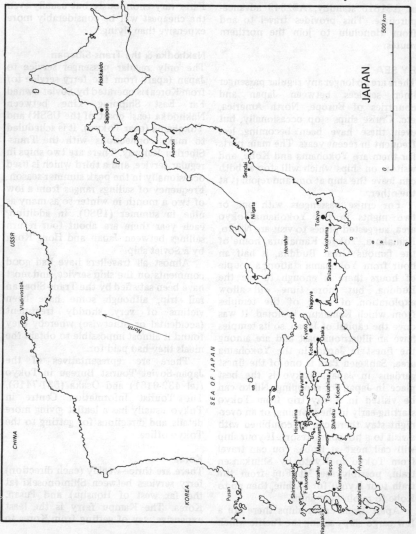

Getting Around

Japan has an immense variety of all forms of public transport. This chapter summarises what is available but cannot give complete details of every train or ferry. Sources of further information for the traveller are mentioned where appropriate.

JIKOKUHYO

The most useful single book for travel by public transport in Japan is called *Jikokuhyo* ('book of timetables'). This invaluable book runs to about 660 pages, with timetables for every form of scheduled transport in Japan — trains, buses, planes, ferries — even cable cars. If there were scheduled stage coaches, they'd be listed too.

There are several editions on sale — some large, some small. The recommended one is the large size ('oki-jigokuhyo') because its maps are more detailed, and it has information on bus lines and ferries, which the small ones do not. It is issued monthly and costs about Y500. It is available from any news stand or bookstore. The entire book is written only in Japanese, but even if you don't read a single Japanese character you can still use it easily.

The secret lies in the maps at the front of the book, which show the entire country, region by region. (Note that they do not follow the convention of having north at the top of the page.) The first group of maps shows every railway line: solid black for regular JNR services, a broken red line with many crossbars for private railway lines.

Bus lines are shown in blue, a hollow blue line for JNR bus lines, a thin solid blue line for private bus lines, and a hollow red line for the few highway (express) buses. A cable car looks like a stretched blue coil spring. Ferries are shown as thin red lines, with the exception of the Aomori-Hakodate (Hokkaido) connection which is shown with a broken black line. The availability of rental cars near the station is shown by a red car symbol.

Areas of touristic interest are shaded in green and have a number in green that corresponds to a brief description at the top and bottom of the page.

The key to using these maps is the number (sometimes with a letter) written in red beside the transportation line. The number refers to the page which has the timetable for that service; the letter, if any, refers to the section of the page. It's that simple.

Although all place names are written only in kanji (Japanese characters), it is easy to match the names of large cities with the names printed in romaji on other maps. There is a railway map with the name of every major station printed in romaji.

Following the maps of various sections of the country are maps detailing the transport facilities in and around Osaka, Nagoya and Tokyo. The final map represents all air services within Japan: the name of the major cities (Tokyo, Osaka, etc) is in a circle and air connections are shown by a straight line drawn to the name of the other city. The colour of the line corresponds to the airline, the names of which are all in Roman letters (eg JAL, ANA, etc). Beside the name of the linked city is a number that corresponds to the sub-section of the airlines section of the book which is located at the very end of the final section. City names are in kanji only.

The book is broken up into about 20 sections, plus bits of information and advertisements scattered among them. In a typical issue (they don't change much in format), the first section gives schedules for Shinkansen, 'L' Limited Express (tokkyu) and sleeper services. The second section shows the most convenient connections for the fastest service over long distances, eg Tokyo-Nagasaki, or Sapporo-Tokyo. Sections 3-18 give the schedule of all intercity services, line by line. Section 19 gives the schedule of all JNR lines operating in the Tokyo-Kawasaki-Yokohama and Osaka-Kyoto-Kobe metropolitan areas. Section 20 is a great catch-all of everything else: JNR highway (express) buses; private transportation of all types (railways, buses, ferries, cablecars) region by region; boat services to and around Okinawa and other southern islands and bus services on the islands; long distance ferry connections; excursion and sightseeing bus tours; airlines (domestic).

INTER-CITY PUBLIC TRANSPORT

TRAINS

The railway network in Japan is by far the best in Asia, and can be ranked among the most comprehensive in the world. Trains in Japan are punctual, range in frequency from adequate to amazing, and in speed from pokey to phenomenal. They include the famed Shinkansen super-expresses, the fastest scheduled trains in the world. Fares are not cheap.

There are both government-operated (JNR) and privately-owned railways that carry passengers in Japan. The government system provides long distance service throughout the country, as well as services around the cities of Tokyo and Osaka. The private lines usually run only comparatively short distances — up to 100 km or so — and are usually regarded as commuter lines. Some private lines run to nearby resort areas. The private lines are discussed in more detail in the section covering intra-city transport.

Stations are usually close to the centre of a city except that in Tokyo stations of private lines are spread around the periphery of the city.

Japanese National Railways (JNR)

The government-operated railway is called JNR in English, but most Japanese know it only as *kokutetsu*, or *kokuden* in Tokyo and Osaka where JNR electric trains serve as commuter transport; 'koku' means 'country' or 'national', 'tetsu' means 'line', and 'den' means 'electric'.

Fares are calculated by distance and the class of service. There is a base fare from point A to point B, to which are added surcharges for the various types of expresses (see below), seat reservation charge, 'Green-sha' (first class), and sleeper/roomette.

The JNTO booklet 'The Tourist's Handbook' can be useful for buying tickets as it has English and Japanese phrases written in the format of an order form.

There are more than 20,000 trains every day throughout Japan, and in a book of timetables (*Jikokuhyo*), JNR train schedules fill more than 330 pages! There is a summary of services printed in English and given out free by the JNTO, 'Condensed Railway Timetable' (407-E). It gives the schedule of all Shinkansen services as well as tokkyu and kyuko (express) trains.

The Tokyo and Kyoto offices of the Tourist Information Centre give out photocopied sheets of the schedule (and required changes of train) for travelling between Tokyo and Kyoto/Osaka by Tokaido line (non-Shinkansen trains). These trains take about 10 hours compared with less than four by Shinkansen, but the fare is less than half. Other sheets from the TIC cover JNR services to and from northern Honshu, including the ferry service (JNR) between Hakodate (Hokkaido) and Aomori (Honshu). The TIC offices are the best sources of information for most travel inquiries.

There are travel information centres at all major JNR stations. At Tokyo station (Yaesu side), the Travel Information Service is clearly labelled in English, and some staff members speak adequate English to be helpful (if you speak slowly and clearly). Travel agencies, like those listed for reserved ticket sales, can also supply information, though they may not have anyone who can speak English.

If you are travelling in the spring, be warned that for many years there has been a nationwide strike of JNR services in the spring nearly every year. It has usually lasted only a few days, but can be a great interruption. Private railways and subways may be struck at the same time.

JNR Services

The basic level is called **futsu** (also called 'kaku eki teisha' or 'kakutei'.) These trains stop at every station (known in North America as a 'milk run'). It is the slowest service and is usually limited to relatively short runs of about 100 km. Around major cities the quality of coaches on such service is good; on country lines the standard may not be so high — there the local trains are called 'donko', a folksy word with a descriptive sound, but a foreigner who uses it will find that the Japanese are amused.

Kyuko means 'ordinary express', and refers to trains that make only a limited number of stops. Except between Tokyo and Yokohama, there is a surcharge for such trains of Y500 up to 100 km, Y600 up to 200 km, and Y800 over 200 km. Reserved seats are available on these trains for an additional Y300-500.

Tokkyu (also called 'kaisoku' or 'junkyu') means 'limited express' and such trains stop only at major cities. They are the fastest trains (other than the Shinkansen) and are used for long distance travel. Surcharges for tokkyu trains are Y1200 up to 100 km, Y1500 up to 200 km, Y400 per additional 200 km up to 800 km, after which it is a

flat Y3100. Non-reserved seats are Y200 cheaper.

Cho-tokkyu is another name for super-expresses like the Shinkansen; they are discussed later.

Tickets can be bought at any JNR station to any other station in Japan. For short distances, there are usually ticket vending machines. For longer distances they can be bought at the ticket window.

For reserved tickets and tickets involving surcharges, tickets should be bought at the Green Window ('midori-no-kadoguchi'). (The name refers to the green colour over the window or the green band around glassed-in offices.) Most stations in Tokyo, and all major stations throughout Japan, have a Green Window. Reserved tickets may also be bought at offices of Japan Travel Bureau (JTB), Kinki Nippon Tourist Corp, and Nippon Travel Agency. Tickets are available a week before the day of boarding at JNR stations and up to a month in advance at the travel agencies.

Shinkansen

The Shinkansen trains have become famous throughout the world as the fastest scheduled surface transport. They have picked up the nickname in English of 'Bullet train', but they are known in Japanese only as Shinkansen ('new trunk line').

The trains run at a maximum speed of 210 km/h (130 mph) and a ride in one is something that should be experienced during a visit to Japan despite the cost that almost matches that of air services to the same destination. The trains run extremely smoothly on continuous welded track set in concrete, so there is negligible sway. It is necessary to look at the speedometer in the buffet car to believe the speed at which it is moving. They are also the safest trains in the world. The Shinkansen runs from Tokyo to Hakata (Fukuoka) in northern Kyushu. A new line is under construction to Sapporo (Hokkaido), including a trip through a tunnel (the longest in the world when finished) under the strait between Honshu and Hokkaido; another will go up the north coast toward Niigata. These lines will not be in service for a few years.

On a clear day, the Shinkansen affords a superb view of Mt Fuji, one of the best available. On one occasion the train actually stopped to give passengers a better view! Don't count on that, though.

The Shinkansen operates only during day and evening hours otherwise it would be leaving passengers at stations in the middle of the night. The longest run, Tokyo-Hakata, takes less than seven hours by the fastest service.

The fastest Shinkansen service is known as Hikari ('light'). The slower Kodama ('echo') service has the same maximum speed, but makes more stops. The Kodama trains operate only from Tokyo to Osaka and stop at 11 stations before Osaka; they take over an hour more than Hikari trains which stop only at Nagoya and Kyoto. The fare is the same. For the two stations beyond Nagoya toward Kyoto, and even for one or two stations back toward Tokyo, it would be faster to go to Nagoya by Hikari on an unreserved ticket and change trains to a Kodama for the rest of the trip.

Beyond Shin-Osaka station (Osaka), there are four Hikari services, with different stops and termini. Two go through to Hakata, the others terminate at Okayama and Hiroshima. Check carefully which one you want for your destination.

As well as the basic Hikari and Kodama services there are also some extra Shinkansen trains with different stop schedules and terminal stations, and during peak travel seasons there are additional trains.

Services are very frequent. A Shinkansen train leaves Tokyo station about every 10 minutes, and Hakata about every 20 minutes. The first trains leave both cities around 6 am. The last train from Tokyo to Hakata leaves at 5 pm, the last for Shin-Osaka at 8.24 pm. To Tokyo, the last one leaves from Hakata at 4.24 pm, from Shin-Osaka at 8.24 pm.

There are both unreserved and reserved seats. Kodama trains are mostly unreserved while Hikari are mostly reserved. In busy travel seasons it is advisable to book a seat, for trains are often full and excess passengers in unreserved sections have to stand just as they do on commuter lines.

Seats can be booked at the Green Window of any JNR station in Japan that has one, as well as at any travel agency; JTB is the best known of these and has offices in almost every city.

Don't look for gourmet meals and high-class dining facilities that should complement the world's fastest trains. One Japanese newspaper columnist has complained of 'awful' coffee, 'the world's worst sandwiches', and dining facilities that are 'a step below most lower class slum eateries'. This exaggeration is a warning not to expect too much. Another complaint is that each train has only one non-smoking car, and the ban is not enforced (Japanese smoke like chimneys).

Seats for the Shinkansen can be reserved in Canada and the USA through JAL offices by passengers who will be flying by JAL to Japan. Tickets can be reserved for trains departing between two days and two months after the date of booking.

In 1979 some European railways were experimenting with trains with a maximum speed of 260 km/h. Shortly afterward it was announced in Japan that the JNR would be running trials at similar speeds. This was probably an attempt to maintain national honour by having the fastest trains in the world.

The current maximum of 210 km/h was originally announced as the practical maximum because wheelslip on the track became appreciable at higher speeds, so it is rather doubtful that speeds will change much.

JNR Fares

As noted earlier, train fares are calculated from a base fare, according to distance, to which are added surcharges for express services, reserved seats, etc. Fares rise with monotonous regularity, and increases are virtually an annual fixture. Shinkansen fares are now almost as high as air fares. For complete up-to-date fares, refer to the JNTO publication 'Condensed Railway Timetable'. Some sample fares are listed below. For journeys over 100 km, student fares are available which give a 20% discount off the regular fare.

From Tokyo to:	Regular	Shinkansen
Shizuoka	2,200	4,100
Nagoya	4,000	7,100
Kyoto	5,300	9,500
Osaka	5,700	9,900
Hiroshima	7,600	13,300
Shimonoseki	8,600	15,200
Hakata	9,000	16,000

Japan Rail Pass & Excursion Tickets

JNR has recently introduced the Japan Rail Pass (similar to the Eurailpass) for use throughout the JNR network. At present it can only be bought from JAL offices in New York, London and Paris. The cost for seven days is Y21,000 (regular class); 15 days, Y33,000; one month, Y54,000. Green car (first class) costs about 45% more. Half price for children uner 12.

For sale in Japan, JNR has excursion tickets (shuyuken). There are four different types, called ippan shuyuken, route shuyuken, mini shuyuken and wide shuyuken. (These are the Japanese terms, the last three using borrowed English words.)

Wide shuyuken This is an all-inclusive ticket for direct travel (no stopover en route) from any place to a distant point, unlimited travel on JNR train and bus services within the designated area, and direct travel back to the starting point. In the north of Japan there are two 20-day schemes for travel in Hokkaido (one for all points in Hokkaido, one for the southern part only, and a variation of the first that includes an air flight in one direction), and another route in Tohoku (northern Honshu) for 10 days. In the south of Japan there is a 'wide shuyuken' for travel anywhere in Kyushu for 20 days by JNR train and bus, with the option of a boat trip in one direction from Beppu (Kyushu) to Kobe/Osaka, or from Beppu to Takamatsu (Shikoku); others offer unlimited travel within Shikoku for 20 days, or unlimited travel in the San-in area (the north coast of western Honshu).

Mini shuyuken This is similar to the wide shuyuken but covers a smaller area and has a shorter period of validity.

Route shuyuken This is for travel along certain designated routes that take in a number of places considering worth seeing. It is valid for 30 days and gives a 10% discount over regular fares.

Ippan shuyuken This is an excursion ticket over a route chosen by the traveller. It must take in two or more designated areas with travel of more that 201 km (train, bus, boat) before returning to the starting point. It is good for 30 days and gives a 10% discount.

There are many options resulting from the number of schemes. It is advisable to obtain copies of the photocopied information sheets from the TICs in Tokyo or Kyoto; the staff there can give further information if required. The same information is available at any JNR or JTB office or from any travel agent, but few of the staff at these places can speak English.

Excursion tickets can be purchased at any JNR station in Japan with a Green Window reservations office as well as at any travel agency.

On round trip tickets for journeys of more than 1000 km one way (JNR train and ferry), the return ticket is discounted 20%.

Groups of 15 or more receive a discount of about 10%.

Economy Coupons are available for JNR trains plus hotels and sightseeing on approved JNR routes.

Special Trains

Steam locomotives ('SL' in Japanese!) can be seen at two places in Japan. JNR phased out its last SL in December 1975, but the clamour of Japanese steam fanatics led them to revive some services on the Yamaguchi line in southern Honshu, the only line where the water towers, etc remained. The service commences in August with runs on Wednesday, Thursday, Saturday and Sunday; from September through December, runs are on Saturday and Sunday plus three national holidays. Trains make one daily round trip, leaving Ogori (one stop on the Shinkansen from Shin-Shimonoseki) at 10 am and arriving at Tsuwano (65 km inland toward Masuda on the north coast) at 12.21 pm, stopping at eight stations along the way; the return trip leaves Tsuwano at 2.16 pm, arriving back at Ogori at 4.09 pm. Speeds reach 65 km/h with types C-57 and C-58 locomotives. Trains have five coaches with a capacity of 400 passengers. One-way fare is Y700. A reserved seat costs an extra Y500 but is recommended; when tickets were first put on sale in 1979, nearly 7000 people applied for tickets for the first month. Tickets are available from travel agents and at any Green Window in a JNR station anywhere in Japan.

The only line in Japan where steam locomotives were never completely phased out is the short (40 km) Oikawa line in Shizuoka-ken. It runs from Kanaya (about 190 km south-west of Tokyo and 12 km west of Shizuoka city) to Senzu. In 1979 it was scheduled for one trip a day each way (Friday, Saturday, Sunday and Monday off season, daily during the summer); up at 11.34 am (arriving 12.53), and down at 2.35 pm (arriving (3.53); Y960 each way.

In 1979 a C-56 type locomotive, built in Japan between 1935 and 1939 was brought back from Thailand where it was used in WW II to haul war supplies on the (in)famous Thailand-Burma railway (known from the film *Bridge on the River Kwai*). The loco will reportedly be used on the Oikawa line.

For further information consult the TIC in Tokyo or Kyoto, or ask someone to look up the schedule in the *Jikoku-hyo*.

Anyone interested in mobile antiques should take a ride on the two surviving cars on a one-km branch line of the Tsurumi electric line between Musashi Shiraishi and Okawa; the Tsurumi line originates at Tsurumi station of the Keihin-Tohoku line (JNR) in Yokohama. The two coaches, about 50 years old, are irreplaceable because they are the only ones in Japan that can be operated singly, and they are three metres shorter than standard 20-metre coaches so they are the only ones that can negotiate the sharp bends and use the short station platforms of this line. The ride lasts two minutes.

FLYING

There are five airlines operating on domestic routes in Japan. JAL (Japan Air Lines — *Nippon Koku)* operates only among Tokyo, Osaka, Sapporo, Okayama and Okinawa. ANA (All Nippon Airways — *Zen Nippon Koku)* and TDA (Toa Domestic Airlines — *Toa Koku Nai Koku)* link a large number of smaller centres with the largest cities; ANA also serves the same trunk routes as JAL, and TDA serves a couple of them. SWAL (Southwest Air Lines — *Nansei Koku*) is a regional carrier serving a number of small islands around Okinawa. NKA (*Nippon Kinkyori Koku*) serves some areas of Hokkaido. (The fact that the initials of four of these represent their names in English, not Japanese, is instructive.)

Domestic air services radiate from large cities, eg Tokyo, Osaka, Sapporo, Nagoya, Okayama and Naha (Okinawa). Thus travel between regional cities is not possible without passing through one of the large airports.

At Tokyo, Haneda airport is used for all domestic flights except for seven a day that link Narita airport with Sapporo, Osaka, Fukuoka and Nagoya.

Listed below are sample air fares (one way). Return fares are 10% cheaper than two one-way fares.

TOKYO TO:

Chitose/Sapporo	Y23,400
Sendai	Y10,600
Nagoya	Y10,700
Osaka	Y14,100
Hiroshima	Y20,300
Fukuoka	Y24,800
Kagoshima	Y27,800
Naha	Y34,600
Nagasaki	Y27,500

SENDAI TO:

Chitose	Y18,700

NAGOYA TO:

Chitose	Y29,400
Sendai	Y17,600
Nagasaki	Y20,100
Kagoshima	Y20,400
Naha	Y31,200

OSAKA TO:

Sendai	Y22,100
Nagasaki	Y16,600
Kagoshima	Y17,100

HIROSHIMA TO:

Kagoshima	Y15,900

KAGOSHIMA TO:

Naha	Y19,900

BUSES

Japan does not have intercity bus services on the huge scale found in the USA, for example. Most long-distance travel is by train (especially the superfast Shinkansen), or by air. The reason for this is that highways are narrow and crowded, cities and towns are incessant, and the speed limit is a maximum of 60 km/h. The only high-speed roads are the expressways linking major cities.

Highway buses (the Japanese name) run on these expressways between Tokyo, Nagoya, Kyota, and Osaka, and some intermediate cities. They normally leave early in the day so as to arrive by early evening, or else they leave near midnight and drive relatively slowly to arrive early in the morning. Compared with trains, buses are more comfortable, with reclining seats and headrests. The highway bus also has toilet service on board.

Many travellers prefer the midnight highway bus between Kyoto and Tokyo because it is less than half the cost of the Shinkansen, and it makes no stops. Also, being able to sleep on the bus saves the cost of a night's accommodation.

During the day, highway buses run only part of the distance between Tokyo and Kyoto/Osaka, and you have to change at Nagoya; only the night bus gives a through service. Many daytime buses make the run between Tokyo and Shizuoka or Hamamatsu. The frequency of daytime runs in each direction is: Tokyo-Nagoya, 14; Nagoya-Kyoto, 24; Nagoya-Osaka, 11.

There is only a single departure time for the night bus on each route, although several buses may depart at the same time. The night bus is popular, so it is advisable to make a booking as far in advance as possible. Reservations may be made up to eight days in advance at any JTB (Japan Travel Bureau) office or at the Green Window of JNR stations.

There are countless bus routes linking country areas with the nearest JNR station, as well as quite long bus routes in areas that are too mountainous or too sparsely populated for railways.

All long-distance, highway, and scheduled country buses are listed in the book of timetables, *Jikokuhyo*. Information in English for Tokyo-Nagoya-Osaka/Kyoto services is available at TIC offices in Tokyo and Kyoto to.

The system of fare collection on scheduled country runs (mostly from railway stations) is the same as is used in some cities. The passenger takes a ticket from a machine at the back entrance; the ticket shows the zone where the passenger boarded. A mechanical sign at the front of the bus shows the fare payable at that point by passengers getting off, zone by zone.

FERRIES
There are many ferries that link up widespread parts of Japan. The word may conjure up the image of a short trip on a small boat across placid and sheltered waters, but many ferries are large ocean-going ships of 10,000 tonnes or so, and voyages may last up to 30 hours. Such ships are equipped with restaurant and bar facilities, and usually have baths as well.

The cost for the lowest priced class is usually lower than competing land transport and is often more enjoyable, with the bonus of an economical 'sea cruise'. The cheapest fare is for an open room with tatami floors that are shared by all passengers. During the busy summer season these may be crowded while at other times they may be nearly empty. There are other classes including private cabins.

The only 'hazard' of the tatami class is that there may very well be several parties of noisy *sake* and *shochu*-tippling merry-makers nearby, particularly after harvest season when farmers have brought in their crops and set off for

their annual vacation. These groups of people are the 'real' Japanese, rustic and simple, quite bawdy and an eye-opener for the person who knows only the prim and proper Japanese businessmen. The drunker they get, the happier they get and the louder they sing. They usually know many folksongs (which all tend to sound alike), and when truly in their cups, their dances become extremely earthy with blatant sexual themes. Even though it may be at the cost of a few hours sleep, this is a good way to get to know another side of the complex personality of Japan and to meet the most genuine people in the country. Any gregarious traveller is sure to get invited to join them.

Many ferries leave at night so you can save the cost of accommodation, but it can mean that the ship passes through well-known scenic waters, eg the Inland Sea, at night. In the summer, however, the sky becomes light as early as 4.30 am.

Many ferries carry motor vehicles — cars and motorcycles. The charge for a motorcycle is approximately 1½ times the 'tatami' class passenger fare. Anyone travelling by bicycle would have no trouble taking the bike along on any boat, especially if it is a collapsible model.

In addition to long-distance ferries, there are many boats operating in the Inland Sea (between Shikoku and Honshu), and between Kyushu and Shikoku. There are also many ships that operate between the main islands and small islands off-shore, and sightseeing excursion boats that cruise for relatively short distances along the coast or loop back to the point of origin. There are also several ships that operate among the chain of islands that extends south from Kagoshima to Okinawa.

Following is a list of the main long-distance ferries, with the cheapest 'tatami' class fare.

OTARU (Hokkaido)
— Niigata	Y5,000
— Tsuruga	Y6,400
— Maizura	Y6,400

SENDAI (Northern Honshu)
— Tomakumai	Y8,600

TOKYO
— Tomakomai	Y11,500
— Kushiro	Y13,000
— Matsuzaka	Y4,800
— Nachi-Katsuura	Y8,800
— Kochi	Y13,500
— Kokura	Y10,000
— Naha (Okinawa)	Y17,400

KAWASAKI
— Hyuga (Kyushu)	Y14,800

NAGOYA
— Sendai	Y9,300
— Tomakomai	Y15,000

OSAKA
— Takamatsu	Y2,300
— Matsuyama	Y4,300
— Beppu	Y5,700
— Hiroshima	Y4,100
— Kochi	Y3,900
— Moji	Y5,500
— Hyuga	Y7,400
— Shibushi	Y9,000
— Kagoshima	Y10,000
— Kokura	Y4,500
— Naha	Y13,000

KOBE
— Oita	Y4,900
— Kokura	Y4,500
— Hyuga	Y7,400

HIROSHIMA
— Beppu	Y3,100
— Hyuga	Y5,100

NAHA (Okinawa)
— Hakata	Y11,800
— Kagoshima	Y10,150

For further up-to-date information on scheduled passenger shipping, there are other useful sources.

Jikokuhyo, the bible of all scheduled

transport in Japan (described earlier), shows ferry routes on maps at the front of the book. Ferries are shown as thin red lines each with a number and a letter which refer to the page and section in which the schedule and fare are printed.

Tourist Information Centres have free information sheets listing a number of boat services, along with fares, scheduled and dock locations. The lists are not complete, however.

The sheet 'Ferry Services in Northern Japan' covers the following services: Sendai-Tomakomai; Tomakomai-Hachinohe; Hakodate-Oma; Fukushima-Miuma; Hakodate-Aomori; Hakodate-Noheji. This sheet does not list services between Aomori and Hakodate and Aomori-Muroran. The former are listed on the TIC sheet 'Transportation for Northern Japan'; the latter are listed in the Hokkaido chapter of this book.

The TIC information sheet 'Coastal Shipping Services' lists mostly ships from Tokyo and Kawasaki. They are: Kawasaki-Hyuga; Tokyo-Kushiro; Tokyo-Tomakomai. It also details services from Osaka/Kobe to Matsuyama and Beppu.

INTRA-CITY PUBLIC TRANSPORT

RAILWAYS — URBAN & SUBURBAN

In the Tokyo and Osaka area, JNR (Japanese National Railways) trains operate as part of the city mass transit system; loop lines circle the central districts of both cities, while other JNR lines and private railway lines act as feeder systems from the outlying areas into the central districts. In Tokyo the loop line is called the Yamanote line: in Osaka it is the Kanjo line. Several other cities are also served by JNR and private railways lines in a similar manner.

The private railway lines usually run

for comparatively short distances, less than 100 km, and link the major cities with surrounding suburban areas or nearby resorts. In the Tokyo area, for example, 11 private railways connect directly to the Yamanote loop line — some even act as continuations of subway lines — and there are many other lines that start from JNR and private railway stations in the suburbs.

In the early days of railway building, the founders discovered that it was good business to build department stores over the large stations, hence many lines bear the name of well-known stores such as Keio, Odakyu or Hankyu, and many lines start from store basements.

In many cases, private railways run virtually parallel to JNR lines and serve the same destinations. The private lines are usually less expensive, sometimes as low as half the JNR fare. (This Alice-in-Wonderland state of affairs seems to come about because government-operated services such as JNR are not required to make ends meet — JNR services certainly don't.) Private lines also have a reputation for better service, cleaner equipment and more polite personnel, but this may not always be true.

Details of the rail services in each city or region are given in the appropriate chapter.

SUBWAYS

There are subway systems in Tokyo, Osaka, Nagoya, Yokohama and Sapporo. They offer a convenient and quick means of getting around these cities because they run free of traffic congestion.

In each city the stations are well marked above ground and can usually be used by foreigners without difficulty because there is adequate information in English. Published maps show the locations of stations. In Tokyo, Yokohama, Osaka and Nagoya, the subways are augmented to greater or lesser extent by private and JNR railway lines.

In Tokyo there are 10 separate lines operated by two independent authorities, so there are complications that can arise when using them. There is an extensive description of the system in the chapter dealing with Tokyo.

Commuter Passes

Passes valid for one, three or six months are available for all forms of public transport in Tokyo and other major cities. A single pass valid for travel on two separate systems (JNR plus subway, for example) can be purchased at the office of either of the destination stations (except for small stations).

BUSES

Every Japanese city of any size has extensive bus services. Unfortunately it is difficult to use them because their destinations are written only in Japanese and the drivers do not usually speak any English. (Buses in Nikko have signs in English because so many foreign tourists use them.) It is necessary to know bus routes in advance before they are useful, which means that only long-term residents will get much use out of them. Buses are also subject to traffic delays, so they are often slower than trains and subways.

Two systems of fare collection are used. In Tokyo and some other cities, the fare is a flat sum paid on entering. The fare is normally marked clearly on the cash box beside the driver. Usually there is a slot at the right side of the box that gives Y10 coins in change from a Y100 coin. There may be two slots on the top of the cash box — the left one is for tickets, the right for coins. If you look unsure, the driver will point to the correct one.

In many other cities, and most country runs, the fare depends on the distance travelled. Passengers enter by the rear door and take a ticket from a dispenser at the right of the steps. On the ticket is a number indicating the fare zone where the passenger boarded. At the front of the bus is an illuminated mechanical sign that shows the fare to be paid if you leave the bus. The fares advance as the bus moves along. Pay at the front when you leave.

Most buses in Japan have recorded messages identifying the next stop, but the announcement is made only in Japanese. There is no system of transfers as is used in North America. A separate fare must be paid for each bus boarded.

TAXIS

Taxis used to be one of the few bargains of Japan. Now their prices match the high prices for everything else. Prices are almost uniform throughout the country.

The flagfall is Y380 for the first two km and Y70 for each additional 405 metres, plus a time charge of Y50 for every 2.3 minutes when the taxi is moving at less than 10 km/h. The flagfall cost is displayed prominently in both windows on the left side of the vehicle, and sometimes in the rear window.

From 11 pm to 5 am there is a surcharge of 20%. That, at least, is the official rate. Because the subways and trains stop running soon after midnight drivers have a sellers market and it is difficult getting a taxi after 10 pm, especially on rainy nights. Drivers expect two to four times the meter fare, and some customers hold up two fingers, etc, to show the bribe rate being offered. A red light sign in the left front windshield indicates an available taxi. A green sign means that a night surcharge is in effect.

Taxis can be flagged down on the street, and there are stands at larger stations. To flag a taxi, it is sufficient to stand at the edge of the road with an outstretched arm, fingers bent slightly downward; never whistle for a taxi. In most cases taxi drivers are polite and patient but it is not unknown for drivers to pass by foreigners and pick up nearby Japanese. Taxis can be summoned by phone in cities; there is a 20% surcharge for this service.

Japanese taxi drivers are not linguists and only very rarely will they understand English. Say your destination in Japanese, if possible, otherwise have it written in Japanese. It is useful also to have the address where you are staying written in Japanese; hotels have cards which are prepared for this purpose. Sometimes the hotel name is different in English and Japanese — eg the Imperial (in Tokyo). Addresses are notoriously difficult to find in Japan, so don't get upset and berate the driver if he takes a long time and has to stop at one or more police boxes to get to your destinations. This is standard operating procedure in Japan.

Tipping is not the practice in Japan unless the driver has performed some unusual service, like helping with heavy baggage, or has spent a long time finding a difficult address. A driver might even refuse to accept the money, although reports of this happening are not so frequent nowadays. Don't try to open or close the passenger side (left) door. It is operated by the driver in most taxis.

RICKSHAWS

There are a few rickshaws in use in Japan. They can be seen every day in the back streets around the Ginza. When traffic is clear, the vehicle moves along surprisingly fast, and surprisingly smoothly. These rickshaws are not for rent by the general public — they carry geisha to teahouses and restaurants where they will entertain in traditional style with songs, dances and stories.

At various places around Japan a few rickshaws have been dusted off and revived as tourist attractions. They are as much a novelty to the modern Japanese as they are to westerners. They can be seen at the charming old town of Kurashiki (near Okayama), at Furukawa (near Takayama), and at Nagasaki.

Rickshaws have their origins in Japan (not China), and the name is a corruption of the Japanese 'jin riki sha' meaning 'man powered carriage'. However, Neil Pedlar, a writer for the *Japan Times*, wrote that the rickshaw was probably invented by an American, Jonathan Goble, who came to Yokohama as a missionary and wanted a carriage for his wife. Further, the rickshaw is a copy of a vehicle called a 'brouette' first used in Paris in 1669!

PRIVATE TRANSPORT & HITCHING

MOTOR VEHICLES

For the person with the yen and the Yen, plus lots of time, there is no better way to see Japan completely and thoroughly than by private motor vehicle — car or motorcycle. A car can be purchased or rented, with or without driver. A motorcycle will be an extremely expensive proposition, but some readers may wish to use one. Because of the time involved in buying (and selling) a vehicle, this will usually only suit people who are staying for several months or more.

Driving Conditions

Roads in Japan are generally as good as they need be. This means that all roads are hard surfaced except for the rarely travelled ones high in the mountains. With the exception of expressways, all roads are narrow relative to the heavy traffic that they carry, and minor country roads are so narrow that one car may have to pull of the road to let another pass. The result is that it is impossible to make good time over long distances. A typical good day's driving will cover 200-250 km, and this will require eight to 10 hours. The main roads are so built up that they seem at times to be one continuous town. Stop lights are very frequent along these

highways and seem to be always red.

Passing slow vehicles is a near-impossibility. Apart from the almost inevitable endless line of vehicles ahead and heavy oncoming traffic, there are few passing zones. Where there are straight and flat stretches, especially in Hokkaido and Tohoku, there will normally be a solid line on the road, indicating no overtaking.

Despite the problems and frustrations, the rewards in the 'good parts' can make driving all worthwhile.

For more pleasant driving conditions and the chance to see a more 'typical' Japan, it is preferable to use the less travelled highways (generally inland). Often they are little slower than the main roads and are vastly more enjoyable. The stretches of open countryside, without the urban blight of much of modern Japan, will make for a much more pleasant trip.

For drivers in a hurry to get from point A to point B, there is no substitute for the expressways. There is quite a large network of these already built and construction is progressing on others throughout the country. (One pessimistic wag suggests that the huge building programme will be completed just in time for them to become the most magnificent bicycle paths in the world as the oil supply runs out.)

Expressways run nearly the full length of Honshu and through much of Kyushu. There are some feeder expressways from country areas, and in metropolitan areas there are several, often parallel to each other though separated by a few km. They are the only way to get through major cities quickly.

Tolls are incredibly high. For a car, from Tokyo to Nagoya (360 km) costs Y4800; Tokyo to Kyoto (510 km), Y6700. This is substantially higher than the bus fare and a good fraction of the cost by Shinkansen. For a motorcycle it is less, but still a large fraction of the cost for a car. Speed limits on expressways are 100 km/h; they are the only roads in Japan with such high limits.

Interchanges ('inta' in Japanese) are well marked in both romaji and kanji, but it is advisable to know the name of the desired exit in advance. For example, on the Meishin expressway (Nagoya-Kobe) the exit for Osaka is not named Osaka, but Toyonaka (which I found out by overshooting and exiting at Amagasaki, a substantial distance farther on). Roap maps show the name of each interchange, but usually only in kanji. Expressway signs in cities are almost exclusively in kanji, so it is essential to know the kanji for your destination before starting out. Signs along city streets are also usually only in kanji.

Fuel is readily available almost everywhere in Japan, the only exception being in remote areas with little traffic. Fuel has always been expensive in Japan, but became even more so after 1973. Regular costs Y90 per litre or more depending on the area. Motor oil is incredibly expensive, up to Y1500 per litre for the highest quality, around Y1000 for good quality.

The single greatest frustration when driving in Japan — even a danger to one's mental health — is the speed limit. Incredible as it may sound, the maximum on highways in open area is only 60 km/h (that's less than 40 mph, for those who haven't yet converted). This limit, laughably low by international standards, is the maximum allowable, and it is often felt by the authorities that this heady speed is rather risky so it is common to find limits as low as 50 or even 40 km/h in open areas in the countryside. Even more ridiculous — going up mountain roads, there are often signs calling for a reduction in speed!

The sad thing about these limits is that they are strictly, if unpredictably, enforced. A speed trap will always be located in the only straight and level section of an otherwise twisty and hilly road, where the temptation is greatest to ease the frustration of being held back by long hills and other lengthy and slow stretches of road.

Offenders are flagged down by a red and white banded pole held touching the road. There is usually an 'office' complete with tables and chairs set up in the wilderness to mass-process the victims, with 10 or more police sitting at the tables writing out tickets. This is why you will only see patrols on main highways, and why driving habits on mountain and winding roads are so bad.

Right of way at an intersection of equal size roads that have no markings goes to the vehicle on the left. Where a small road enters a larger road, all vehicles on the larger road have priority. That at least is the law and it is useful to know the theory, but many Japanese are unsure whether right of way is to the right or left, and in practice there seems to be no clear rule for the right of way. An objective evaluation is that the right of way lies with the bigger vehicle. Not for nothing has the nihonglish word 'dampu' evolved — it means a belligerent and reckless driver, and is a corruption of the English 'dump truck'. This gives a good indication of who are the most dangerous drivers in Japan.

The penalties for driving after drinking are very severe, and can result in on-the-spot cancellation of licence for a year.

International Driving Permits are accepted in Japan. Foreign licences can also be used to obtain a Japanese driving licence without difficulty. Be sure to obtain your licence before coming to Japan because obtaining one is time consuming and extremely expensive. An absolute minumum of 29 hours of instruction (even including minor repairs) is required at Y3300 per hour, or more; most learners require 35-45 hours. The average person has to lay out at least

Y200,000 before getting a licence.

Travellers passing through Singapore on their way to Japan may find it useful to obtain an International Driving Permit there. First obtain a Singapore driving licence (easily done on presentation of your valid driving licence from home). With the Singapore licence, the Automobile Association of Singapore will issue the IDP. Both the licence and the IDP should be endorsed for motorcycles if this is applicable.

The advantage of this system is that the Singapore driving licence can be renewed by mail anywhere in the world, and can be renewed even if the old one has expired.

The Japan Automobile Federation (JAF) has a booklet which details the traffic laws. It is available by mail (within Japan) for Y1120 (including postage) from: JAF, 3-5-8 Shiba Koen, Minato-ku, Tokyo 105. It is available from JAF headquarters (opposite the entrance to Tokyo Tower) for Y1000.

Motorists may wish to consider membership in the JAF. It offers the same sort of road service as similar associations in other countries. Reciprocal benefits are given to members of the automobile associations of Australia, Canada, Germany, Great Britain, Holland, Hong Kong, New Zealand, Singapore and the USA. Membership also gives a discount when buying JAF publications, and members can have strip maps made up for their journeys around Japan. Membership costs Y4000 per year plus a joining fee of Y2000.

Navigation

Finding your way around Japan, especially outside the cities, is not too difficult. International road signs, as found in Europe, are used for information, warning and prohibitions so there is no need to be able to read Japanese. Where words are used on the sign there are also numbers in many cases indicating times,

dates or speeds, so they can frequently be understood.

In the past most directional signs were printed in both kanji and romaji, but in recent years these have been replaced by new ones with kanji only. If a sign in both scripts appears and has your destination written on it, memorize the kanji! You can be sure that at a major intersection the signs will be written only in kanji and if you don't know the characters for your destination you are in trouble. Before setting out on a journey it is a good idea to memorize the kanji for several places along the way so that you can follow road signs. As mentioned earlier, the expressways are well marked in both scripts.

When driving in large cities on ordinary streets, never try to take shortcuts. Except in Kyoto and Sapporo, there are scarcely any two streets that run parallel for more than a few hundred metres, and you can get so completely lost in such a short time that it exceeds belief. If you find you are lost, swallow your pride and go back the way you came, hoping not to encounter any one-way streets. (On several occasions I have had to navigate with a compass!)

Unlike in North America, where road maps are given out free by service stations, in Japan they much be purchased at appreciable cost. There are no maps that are labelled extensively in romaji. The best that you can look for is maps with key cities, and perhaps large towns, marked in both scripts. A further complication is that the city names can be printed in kanji (Chinese characters) while railway stations are shown in hiragana (phonetic symbols representing syllables), so that one cannot be used to locate the name of a place written in the other script.

Maps are available from several sources. The Japan Automobile Federation (JAF), the equivalent of automobile associations around the world, sells a book of maps which cover the entire country. The maps are to a suitably large scale and have many places identified in romaji as well as kanji. Being in a single book and relatively small in size, the maps are convenient to use. The book costs Y2000 (less 10% for members of JAF or any of the nine affiliated foreign associations). JAF also sells a series of individual regional maps at Y450 each. These maps are most easily purchased at the JAF headquarters in Tokyo, across from the entrance to Tokyo Tower. Members of JAF and those with reciprocal privileges can obtain strip maps for individual journeys.

I used the *Hi-Power Map* series for my travels. These have enough place names in both scripts to be useful. They are printed on a paper-like plastic that was not affected by periodic soakings. They are larger and less convenient than a book of maps like the JAF book above, and 10 maps at Y600 each are needed to cover the entire country, so they are not cheap. There are two series of Hi-Power maps — one by region (useful), one by prefecture (requires very many).

A hint on map reading: the legend that explains the meanings of symbols is in Japanese only. Roads marked in pale pink or pale green are unpaved roads, usually high in the mountains; their surface is usually rough, and treacherous for motorcyclists.

Driving Habits

The average Japanese driver is reasonably competent. There isn't the long history of mass motoring in Japan that there is in Europe and elsewhere. Prior to the mid-1960s very few people owned cars and the Japanese car industry was virtually non-existent.

As a result of the late start, Japanese driving for a while was abysmal, but the gross stupidity that seemed prevalent in the early 1970s has almost completely disappeared as a result of improved driver education and police law enforcement. One major exception occurs on mountain roads where every Japanese male driver seems to go silly. Each one seems to think of himself as highly skilled with the trained reflexes of a racing driver. The fact is that the low speed limits prevent them from gaining any experience at high speeds on any kind of road, let alone twisty mountain ones. Almost every driver cuts straight through curves, so it is advisable to sound your horn at every blind corner. Evidence of the bad driving is that there is scarcely a metre of guard rail in Japan that isn't scraped or bent. Bottles of flowers by the roadside, often with a wooden stake or perhaps some personal possessions, are mute testimony to a fatal accident and are a common sight.

The other bad drivers are found in the cities. Again they are young people who race on city streets, often in large numbers and often driving recklessly. In a typical operation, Tokyo police once rounded up 258 persons one late Saturday evening along with 257 vehicles out of 863 that were travelling in 13 groups. Police mobilized 230 patrol cars for the operation. The 'hot rodders' are personally not dangerous, unlike punks in some other countries, but their driving can be a hazard.

Another dangerous spinoff from the low speed limits is that drivers generally have little appreciation of the increased distance required to stop from high speed. Many will drive so they are almost touching the vehicle ahead, and depend on their reflexes alone to save them if a sudden stop is called for.

Truck drivers are the worst on the roads. While many are safe and sane, too many drive in an irresponsibly 'playful' manner, indulging in games of chase, and drive almost touching the vehicle ahead. I have seen a multi-tonne concrete mixer being driven through manoeuvres that I would not want to perform in a sports car. One of the worst smashups in

Japanese road history is believed to have been caused by the driver of a large truck loaded with chemicals playing 'tag' with other drivers. The rear-end collision in a tunnel of the Tomei Expressway (Tokyo-Nagoya) finally killed seven people and destroyed 173 cars in the pileup and fire.

Again, most drivers in Japan are quite all right, but watch out for the crazies.

Importing Vehicles

Motor vehicles (cars and motorcycles) can be imported into Japan for periods of one year on a carnet (explained later), or on a permanent basis if for more than a year. However, it is not a good idea to import a vehicle into Japan. Shipping rates are high, customs clearance and port clearance and other charges will add substantially to the cost, and tax (though not duty) will have to be paid, this being computed on the cost of the vehicle plus shipping charges. In addition to these and other likely charges, many mechanical modifications will have to be made to bring the vehicle into conformity with Japanese safety and anti-pollution requirements. Since Japan has the strictest anti-pollution regulations in the world, this is likely to be expensive. Unless the vehicle can be bought overseas to Japanese specifications, it is better not to bother importing a foreign car. If you must have a foreign vehicle, it is no more expensive to pay the Japanese price for it, incredibly high as it may be (roughly three to four times the domestic price for a USA-made car, for example). The required modifications will bring it into this range anyway. In general it is better to buy a Japanese-made car and leave the overpriced imports to be bought by ostentatious local residents with more money that common sense.

Anyone who wishes to import a vehicle into Japan should contact a Japanese government representative overseas for up-to-date information on regulations. These change — one importer was stuck with nearly 20 cars that were en route at the time of the change and could not be brought into conformity with the new regulations. He dropped a bundle.

Buying

Buying a new vehicle is much less difficult that a second-hand purchase because the price and conditions are more or less fixed, and finding a dealer is easy.

When buying a second-hand car or motorcycle, language may be the main problem because it is necessary to look around, use Japanese newspaper listings, and negotiate with someone who probably doesn't speak any English. For help with this language barrier, contact Tescort in Tokyo and other cities (described later). They can arrange for a Japanese person who wishes to practise his English to accompany you. There is no charge for this service, but it would be a nice gesture to pay for their transportation and a meal or two.

Shaken

For second-hand cars and motorcycles a big consideration in a purchase is *shaken*. This dreaded word in the motoring world of Japan is a combined road tax, registration fee, insurance premium and vehicle inspection. It is an expense every two years and comes due on the same date whether ownership changes or not, thus the time remaining is a large factor in the cost when buying a used vehicle. For my 550 cc motorcycle it was Y50,000, and for a car it can be double this or more, depending on the size of the vehicle.

Exporting a Vehicle

If you buy a car or motorcycle in Japan and wish to take it to another country for a period of less than a year, you can obtain a carnet from the JAF that lets you do so without the problem of paying the duties in cash and trying to get them back when leaving. The carnet is a book of several pages, each of which guarantees that the JAF will pay the duties owed if the vehicle is sold in the other country. The JAF does not do this out of the kindness of its heart of course — you must leave a cash deposit with the JAF equal to the highest amount of duty that would be charged in any of the countries to which you tell them you plan to take the vehicle. For countries like Indonesia the duty rate may be as high as 160% of the purchase price of the vehicle. There is nothing in the carnet that says for which countries the carnet is valid nor the amount of deposit made to the JAF. When you finish your travels in foreign countries, you send the carnet back to the JAF and obtain a refund of your deposit. It is not necessary to belong to the JAF to arrange a carnet.

Worth noting is that a carnet bought in Japan is extremely expensive — the administrative charges are possibly the highest in the world. For five pages (one page per entry into a country) the charge is Y9000; for 10 pages, Y15,000; for 25 pages, Y20,000. Also, some countries near Japan, like Taiwan, Hong Kong, Singapore and Malaysia have, in the past, allowed a Japan-registered motorcycle to enter without a carnet or other formalities. Check with the diplomatic missions of those countries if you plan to go there. Since shipping costs are appreciable, it would be cheaper for anyone planning to travel in the Singapore-Malaysia-Thailand area to buy a bike in Singapore and arrange a carnet there. Not only are the administrative charges lower, but they will probably accept a guarantee letter from your bank in lieu of a cash deposit. A carnet can be arranged through the Automobile Association of Singapore (336 River Valley Road, Singapore 9) for a bike bought in Japan, possibly by

mail; inquire. The only drawback with purchasing in Singapore is that large model bikes are not regular stock items and they have to be ordered long in advance from Japan.

CARS

Generally the only foreigners in Japan who buy new cars are those who will be here for a year or more. Before buying, ask friends if a car is really useful. Within cities, it is often more convenient to use public transport and taxis. Parking places are difficult to find and on-street parking is being actively discouraged by the authorities; commercial parking garages are expensive. Before being allowed to purchase a car, city residents must prove that they have off-street parking space for it.

Many foreigners who have cars find that they don't use them much; they are often more bother than they are worth in the city, and getting into the country takes considerable time, although the expressways do make the job easier. It may be preferable and cheaper to use public transportation to reach a vacation area and then rent a car there. (Details on Car Rental are given later.)

With the advent of the strict anti-pollution laws, domestic models of Japanese cars are generally less desirable than the export models because of the way the added equipment affects the performance. Thus there is now little incentive to buy in Japan and ship home. For people who wish to do this, however, it is possible to buy on a commodity-tax-free basis if the vehicle will be exported. Prices in Japan are not much lower than they are in many foreign countries and with the cost of shipping it might be cheaper to buy in your home country.

Buying a second-hand car can be a money saver for the long term resident, and there are some good buys for someone who wants a car for only a few months of travel in Japan. Buying second-hand involves the same worries as in any country — Japanese used car salesmen enjoy the same reputation for high business principles as do their brethren around the world. However, a used car in Japan is likely to be safer than one bought in the USA or other country where there is no system of compulsory vehicle inspection. As mentioned earlier, *shaken* is very expensive — about Y100,000 for a typical car, and it is a large factor in the price of a used car.

If buying from the owner, have him drive the car for a few minutes to see if he lugs the car in too high a gear. This is a common habit in Japan — how they can ignore the protesting knocking sounds emanating from the engine is beyond comprehension — but this is bad for the bearings and may have caused damage.

Used cars for sale by foreigners are advertised in *Tokyo Weekender*. Such advertisers would be easiest to deal with because of the lack of communications problems, but it is still necessary to negotiate the hurdle of change of registration. Servicemen at American bases often have used cars for sale.

One foreign resident has suggested that travellers who want a cheap car for only a few months of travelling around Japan can buy one at Fussa, a city near Tokyo, which is noted for dealers who specialize in cars that have only a few months of *shaken* left, and that are not worth spending the money to repair when it expires. Such cars sell cheaply, and at the end of the *shaken*, are scrapped. Fussa is to the west of Tokyo and is reached by taking the Chuo line (JNR) to Tachikawa, then changing to the Ome line.

Another suggestion is Kodaira city as a second source of cheap used cars. It is on the Musashi line which is also reached by taking the Chuo line from Tokyo; the transfer station is Nishi-Kokubunji.

MOTORCYCLES

A person who likes motorcycles can have a very enjoyable time touring Japan by bike. There is the individual freedom afforded by any motor vehicle, and a bike has the added ability to get through spaces that can stall a car for long periods when traffic gets snarled. (I once got my bike across construction scaffolding where a road in the mountains had completely slipped away and down the side of the hill.) Another advantage of bikes in Japan is that they can be parked almost anywhere — even on the sidewalk.

Anyone planning to tour Japan by bike should have already learned to ride one and have at least a year of experience elsewhere before considering riding around Japan. You should also have a licence specifically validated for motorcycles. It is best to have an International Driving Permit, although a licence from almost any country can be used to obtain a Japanese licence; if getting an IDP, be sure that it is endorsed for motorcycles. Obtaining a driving licence in Japan is a lengthy and expensive process and should be avoided if possible; if starting from scratch, you must put in time on smaller bikes before being allowed to ride bigger ones.

A car driving licence allows you to ride a motorcycle of less than 50 cc engine size. The next steps, requiring special bike licences in all cases are: under 125 cc, under 400 cc, and over 400 cc. The test for the last is said to be very demanding, requiring the rider to manoeuvre over difficult obstacles and to put the machine back on its wheels if it falls over.

Most bikes in Japan are used for utilitarian purposes like deliveries, and except in metropolitan areas, large bikes (over 250 cc) are quite rare. Although many fire-breathing superbikes are built in Japan, most are exported. There are no Japanese-made bikes for sale in Japan (new) that are bigger than 750 cc.

Some Japanese men buy very expensive foreign bikes and can be seen near Tokyo on weekends, dressed immaculately in costly leathers and always held back by the 60 km/h speed limit and very heavy traffic. It is actually an impressive sight to see a collection of machines like BMW, Moto-Guzzi, Ducati, Norton, and other well known foreign makes, in one small cluster, the value of which may total $200,000.

Not usually seen among other makes, but highly visible, are Harley-Davidsons; the H-D phenomenon is actually worth a trip to Japan just to observe. Some men buy the largest H-D touring machines, load them with every available accessory, then outfit themselves so that they resemble American highway patrol police, right down to shoulder patches and badges on their tailor-made uniforms. (The badges are on sale in shops in Ueon with a choice of cities and states.) The owners then parade their immense machines through the streets of Tokyo and elsewhere. They can't help but make an impression — of some kind.

The optimum size of bike for touring Japan is 250 cc. This is the smallest size that is allowed on expressways, and is the largest allowed on the major streets of Tokyo between 11 pm and 6 am (a crude but effective way of eliminating problems with bike gangs that used to race around the city at night). Best of all, a 250 cc bike is the largest size that is not subject to *shaken*, a very large bienniel expense. (I didn't know about this when I bought my 550 cc bike!). Also the low speed limits mean there is little sense in buying a larger bike than 250 cc.

Many years ago there were no problems with buying a bike in Japan, riding

it while here, then taking it home. However, there are now so many different regulations in various countries regarding lighting, switch operation patterns, reflectors and other things that a domestic model bike cannot be registered in the USA (for example), while the USA export model cannot be driven on Japanese highways. The domestic models could, of course, be modified to meet foreign regulations, but the cost of modifications together with all the shipping expenses, could easily bring the total price up to about the same as you would pay at home.

Also, if you want a large bike, note that the maximum size of Japanese-made bikes sold in Japan is 750 cc. The big 1000 cc (and larger) bikes that many macho males want are just not available from dealers. You will see the very occasional Japanese-made bike larger than 750 cc, and near large cities it is not uncommon to see big foreign-made bikes. Imported bikes may have engines larger than 750 cc, so some Japanese bikes are exported and then re-imported!

Export models that are manufactured in Japan can be bought in Japan and delivered to a shipping compay. They cannot be registered or driven in Japan. Some bikes are being made in the USA and may not be available in Japan at all. If you want a new bike and are travelling through Singapore, it would almost certainly be cheaper to buy one there. There is no duty payable if the bike is exported within a certain period of time, and it couldn't be as expensive to ship from there as it is from Japan.

If you wish to buy a large (over 250 cc) bike new, the best dealers will be in the large cities — Tokyo, Osaka, etc. Large dealers are better able to give discounts, or else may include accessories instead of a price reduction. The dealer can take care of the paperwork for registration, insurance, etc.

Honda has the largest dealer network in the country, followed by Yamaha, then Suzuki. Kawasaki dealers seem comparatively rare. Remember that dealers in smaller centres don't normally work on large bikes so they may not have special parts in stock or carry spares of things that break, like levers or cables.

After considering the cost of a new bike, you may decide to buy a second-hand one and sell it later. Used bikes are rather expensive in Japan. This may seem surprising, because Japan must be the ultimate throwaway society. Generally, things are not reparied, but are discarded at the first sign of trouble, and anything second-hand has little value. But used bikes are expensive, more so than in Australia, for example, and almost certainly the USA as well. My three-year-old Honda 550 with 4000 km on the odo cost Y270,000; the price was Y220,000, and *shaken* added Y50,000.

Prices for used bikes have strange patterns. For example, a used 400 cc bike is not all that much cheaper than a used 750 cc. The reason is that it is very difficult to obtain a licence for bikes over 400 cc. In other words, supply and demand. Similarly, prices of used bikes around 250 cc are also not low because they escape the very high recurring cost of *shaken*.

When buying a used bike in Tokyo, have a look first in the publication *Tokyo Weekender*; its classified advertisements usually include a used bike or two. Since the advertisers are usually other foreigners, there should be no language problem, other than when changing registration, and they should be able to help with that. (You could even run an advertisement in the paper yourself, saying when you will be arriving and what size bike you want. Write to: *Tokyo Weekender*, 55-11 Yayoi-cho 1-chome, Nakano-ku, Tokyo 164). Occasionally used motorcycles are adver-

tised on the bulletin board at the TIC in Tokyo. The personnel might be willing to post a 'bike wanted' advert on the board if you sent it to them. (The address is in the section on Tokyo.) Servicemen at US bases around Japan — there are several within an hour or so of Tokyo — sometimes have bikes for sale.

The largest concentration of used bike shops is in the Ueno area of Tokyo, along the streets parallel to Showa-dori; this runs north-south past Ueno station (JNR) and near Ueno subway station (Hibiya and Ginza lines). The dealers are to the north of the station. Dealers in used bikes in Japan are no more or less honest than their counterparts elsewhere, so caveat emptor.

The Japanese newspapers have classified advertisements, and there are motorcycle magazines with many pages of bikes for sale. As with buying a car, you can get help over the language barrier with aid of one of the people from Tescort (described elsewhere).

Be sure to test ride any bike. There is a 50-50 chance that it will pull to one side — don't reject it immediately, for roughly half the bikes in Japan suffer from such a malady. The most likely cause is simply that the rear wheel has been cocked sideways when adjusting the chain tension — one side has been tightened more than the other; this is easy to check by looking at the index marks on the arm.

If you are touring Japan by bike, it is useful to carry a tyre repair kit and pump. There is nothing worse than getting a flat tyre high up a mountain road; this recommendation is based on personal experience.

When having a bike serviced in a small town, keep an eye on what is going on. I once had an oil change performed in a town in Hokkaido. When I wasn't watching, the 'mechanic' tightened the drain plug in the oil tank with an immense wrench. At the next oil change, the plug didn't come out — the entire bottom of the oil tank broke free!

If possible, bring your own elastic luggage straps, preferably about 60 cm (two feet) long. These are very difficult to find in Japan; the usual type is a skinny and weak cord about three metres long that wraps around and around, but doesn't have much strength. Worth looking for, however, are 'cottage industry' straps cut from old inner tubes. They, too, are long but are very strong and useful. Small local bike shops are most likely to sell them.

Another tip is to put your clothing in individual plastic bags and wrap them with elastic bands when you put them in your pack. Thus, if you get rained on (not uncommon!) your clothes stay dry. Rain gear is useful to carry with you, but it might be cheaper elsewhere. A vinyl jacket and pants costs about Y1500. Helmets are required by law on all but small bikes; even if not required, they should be worn at all times. An HA RS-Z helmet (with chin guard) costs about Y9000 after discount.

Japan is probably no more dangerous than other countries for motorcyclists — possibly less so because the speed limits are so slow — but you must still be careful of a few idiocies that persist. Driving behaviour in Japan has improved immensely since 1970 when I first toured around Japan by bike.

However, motorcyclists will find that drivers in Japan still have no appreciation of the space needs of bikes (or any other vehicles) and will drive close behind, unable to tolerate the sight of clear space ahead of the vehicle in front. They depend on reflexes to keep them out of accidents, and the idea of stopping distance requirements is still an unknown concept. Car drivers will also go to ridiculous extremes to squeeze past a motorcycle, even if there is no space in front of it, passing within inches and totally oblivious of the danger to the rider who might have to make a sudden swerve to avoid something.

Many car drivers do not know the laws regarding motorcycles. Small bikes are required to hug the edge of the road and not exceed 50 km/h. Ignorant car drivers, found in largest numbers in small towns and remote areas, rarely see bikes bigger than 125 cc and they just do not know that the larger bikes have the same right to ride down the middle of the lane that cars have.

Riders must always beware of taxis — they will cut into the curb without warning to pick up a fare, so you must be on the watch for prospective passengers by the roadside as much as the taxi drivers. Other vehicles do the same thing, but not nearly so much.

It seems that this section does little but paint pictures of gloom and doom. Anyone who is objective knows that motorcycling can be dangerous, so it is foolish to hide the hazards, but touring by motorcycle is also one of the most enjoyable ways to see Japan.

Motorcycles are not available for rental for long-distance touring, to my knowledge, but I would be interested to know if there is interest in such a service and could possibly organize something if sufficient interest were shown. Anyone interested could write to me c/o the publisher.

RENTAL CARS

For those travelling on a generous budget, rental cars are useful for sightseeing in relatively out of the way places where the traveller wants to make a number of stops and doesn't want to be tied to the vagaries of public transport. Rates are rather expensive, and road travel for long distances is slow and frustrating, so it is best to use public transport to the area of interest, then rent the car there.

Rental cars are available at many places throughout Japan and they can be reserved from anywhere in the country. Two of the main companies are Nippon Rent-a-Car (associated with Hertz, which allows world-wide reservations) and Toyota. Both have brochures in English, available at their desks at Narita airport, and at offices of JNTO Tourist Information Centres.

Cars of several sizes (and cost ranges) are available, from a small Honda Civic to a Pontiac Firebird Trans-Am 6600. The rate schedules of the two companies are different. Toyota has a flat rental with no charge for distance; Nippon charges base rate plus distance. Either way, the user pays for fuel used. Some typical charges are given below.

	Nippon		Toyota	
	First 24 hrs	Add'l day	First 24 hrs	Add'l day
Civic				
1400	5,000	3,900	5,000	3,900
Corona				
1600	8,260	4,900	11,800	7,000
Crown				
2000	10,500	7,000	15,000	10,000

Nippon rates give a free allowance of 200 km for the first day and 100 km each additional day. After that there is a charge of Y14 per km. There is no distance limit for class S (Civic 1400). Rates for large American cars are much higher, eg Y23,200 for a Firebird Trans-Am, but such cars are totally unsuited to Japanese roads and should not be considered except as a joke. Rates in many areas are higher than those listed.

Toyota rates all give unlimited distance, except in Hokkaido. There the first day is Y500 cheaper but there is a charge of Y20 per km for distances over 200 km per day. Again, there is no distance limit for class S cars (eg Civic 1400).

It is generally possible to rent in one city and leave the car in another, but a rather stiff charge is added, Y2000 for the first 50 km, Y4000 up to 100 km, and Y1400 for each additional 50 km. There are other potential charges (late return penalty, etc), but the above information is adequate for budget estimation. Insurance is included in the rental charge. Cars can be reserved for pickup almost anywhere in Japan through both companies by contacting the following offices:

		Nippon	Toyota
Tokyo	(03)	463-8881	264-2834
Osaka	(06)	345-1671	344-6831
Nagoya	(052)	221-8891	882-1310
Fukuoka	(092)	751-3144	441-1651
Kyoto	(075)	681-0311	
Sapporo	(011)	741-7645	
Sendai	(0222)	25-6951	
Hiroshima	(0822)	43-3794	
Takamatsu	(0878)	61-6723	

Nippon cars can be reserved in North America through the Hertz Worldwide Reservation Centre (toll free 800-654-3131).

Other car rental companies are:

In Tokyo:

ACU Rent-a-Car	(03) 364-2211
Japaren	352-7635
Mitsubishi Rent-a-Car	294-4871
Nissan Rent-a-Car	584-2341

In Osaka:

Japaren	(06) 632-4881
Mitsubishi Rent-a-Car	345-6188
Nissan Rent-a-Car	458-7391

If you really want to impress someone you can rent a Rolls Royce in Tokyo. The rates are a very reasonable Y49,500 for 6 hours, Y59,500 for 12 hours and Y89,500 for 24 hours. Interested persons may phone Mr Hayashida at (03) 485-6064 to inquire if that includes a full tank of gas.

There are also car rental offices at some railway stations. Such stations are indicated in *Jikokuhyo*, the book of timetables (described earlier).

HIRE CARS

Hire cars with drivers can be arranged through the larger hotels that cater to foreign tourists, or travel agencies. They can also be contacted directly in the following cities:

In Tokyo: Imperial Hire-Car Service, tel (03) 264-7441; Kokusai Hire-car Service, 242-5931; Nihon Kotsu Hire-Car Service, 213-6741.

In Kyoto: Kyoto Hotel Hire-Car Service, (075) 211-1818.

In Osaka: Nihon Kotsu Hire-Car Service, (06) 532-5671.

English-speaking drivers are available. The cost of a hire car is about double that of a taxi.

BICYCLES

The person in good health with the time and desire to see Japan in depth and at low cost would be well advised to consider going by bicycle. It offers the maximum interaction with nature and people in the countryside, and the greatest convenience in seeing many cities like Kyoto.

A bicycle is a practical proposition because it can be dismantled and packed in a special carrying bag that may be taken into the passenger compartment of a train or put in a car (if hitching), thus bypassing the long dreary stretches that exist in some parts of the country on the way to the good parts. Because of the huge number of youth hostels and minshuku, reasonable-cost accommodation is available in nearly all parts of the country.

If you already own a good touring bike, you can transport it to Japan by air freight, by mail (if the frame isn't too big), or as part of your checked baggage, either dismantled and packed, or assembled (some airlines).

Japan is one of the world's major bike producers so it could be worthwhile to buy a bike in Japan, either ready-made or order-made. Unfortunately many export models are not sold in Japan, and most domestic models would be on the small side for many foreigners, anyone under 175 cm

(5'9") tall would have a huge number to choose from.

Probably the best buy with the least complication is offered by a foreign resident of Tokyo, Marty Davidson, who imports bikes from Taiwan. They are of adequate quality, are available in gaijin-size models, and are relatively inexpensive, around Y36,000. He can also locate larger domestic and export Japanese-made bikes, and can help in ordering a custom-made bike. His telephone number in Tokyo is 409-5159. (There are too many details that have to be discussed when custom-ordering a frame to permit satisfactory ordering by mail.) He also sells a well-designed carrying bag for taking a partially dismantled bike into a train.

For those who can comfortably use a domestic model, the bikes made by Bridgestone, Fuji, Maruishi, Miyata, Nishiki, Sekine, Silk and Tsunoda, and many others, are well worth considering. The Bridgestone Diamond series is highly regarded by some cyclists.

Brochures of these manufacturers, with photographs of many models, can be obtained by writing to:

Japan Bicycle Promotion Institute
(Att: Mr H Kono or H Ise)
Nihon Jitensha Kaikan Bldg
9-3 Akasaka 1-come
Minato-ku
Tokyo

Tel 583-5444; both men speak good English.

The brochures are in Japanese only, but most of the useful information is in numbers, so this is no problem for anyone familiar with bike specifications.

There are four main types of bike sold in Japan: Camping, Touring (or Randonneur), Sportif, and Racing.

Camping bikes are very strong but heavy and slow. They are built to carry large loads of camping gear over bad roads, and are a common sight in warm weather with loads of everything imaginable slung on everywhere, including bags hung from the axles. It is not a recommended type for overseas visitors.

Racing bikes are equally unsuited to touring, being uncomfortable, twitchy in handling, lacking in comforts like mudguards, fragile (especially the tyres), and expensive.

The Touring and Sportif models are both quite light, typically 11-12 and 12-14 kg respectively. The major difference between them is the gearing. Touring bikes have a wider spread between the two front sprockets and may also have lower low ratios in the rear cluster. Another difference is that a Touring bike will typically have robust and reasonably soft-riding tyres. The end effect is that Touring bikes are a little stronger and able to carry more on rougher roads, while the Sportif types are intended for higher speeds with less luggage.

Road Racer bikes are between Sportif and Racing machines, being light in weight, stripped of extra weight like mudguards, and running on racing tyres, but they cannot be recommended for touring, only for one-day runs.

Many bikes of all the main types are designed for quick disassembly, a definite plus feature. Such bikes are called 'rinko' (short for rinkosha); in catalogues they are usually indicated by a wrench symbol.

Of the many stock bikes available, the Bridgestone Roadman RM-704 (15.5 kg; Y45,800) seems to be the largest stock Touring class bike in Japan, and should be suitable for someone up to 183 cm (6') or more. If you are under about 173 cm there is an extremely wide selection in all classes. The Fuji models FC-T1/2/3 and FC-SI/2/3 are worthy of note because they are the lightest low-priced touring bikes available in Japan.

If you are taking a bagged bike on a train, it is necessary to belong to the Japan Cycling Association. The cost is Y600 joining fee and Y1500 annual dues. There is a Y150 charge each time the bike is taken on a train. Membership may be bought by mail by writing to:

Japan Cycling Association
(Att: Mr Sakon)
Tokyo Cycling Association
c/o Maeda Industry Co Ltd
3-8-1 Ueno
Taito-ku
Tokyo
Tel 833-3967/8/9

If there are difficulties communicating with the JCA, call Mr Kono or Mr Ise at the Japan Bicycle Promotion Institute (tel 583-5444). The JCA has other functions and activities like weekend rides.

A group in the Kansai area (Osaka-Kyoto-Kobe) goes on frequent excursions (weekends and longer) during the seasons of good weather. Members are both Japanese and foreign so foreign visitors will not feel out of place; in fact, they are actively welcomed to join in. The name is simply the Cycle Club; it is a member of both the JCA and the League of American Wheelmen. Visitors who would like to join a ride should join the club in advance so that they can send suitable information in advance. Membership costs Y1000 (international money order or similar) for two years. The club will try to arrange homestays and will even try to meet people at Osaka airport, if forewarned. Write to:

Mark Howell
Daini Kubota Mansion No 203
544 Minbudani
Shioya-cho
Tarumi
Hyogo-ken 654.

If you wish to try out a variety of bikes before buying one, there are two complexes, near Tokyo (Izu-hanto peninsula) and Osaka, with a vast number of rental bikes of different types plus a variety of tracks on which to try them out. The name, in Japanese: 'Cycling Sports Centre!' There is also overnight accommodation (advance reservation recommended), and there are other sports and recreation facilities.

Many second-hand bikes are available, but as with buying anything else, the language problem has to be overcome.

Several bicycle magazines have advertisements. A Japanese friend or someone from Tescort might be willing to assist. Other sources are Police-recovered bicycle sales and suburban 'junk yards' that sell a great variety of second-hand merchandise.

Bikes are available for rent by the day at a number of places in Japan. All the Cycling Inns described in the Accommodation section have bikes for rent at reasonable rates; so do several Youth Hostels. The Youth Hostel Handbook indicates these with a symbol but does not have a central listing of such hostels. Another of their publications, 'Hostelling Way in Japan' does have such a list; the booklet is free on request at the national headquarters in Tokyo. The availability of rental bikes is also shown on the three Cycling Maps described below. (I would be interested to know if readers are interested in being able to rent good-quality bicycles for touring Japan. Letters may be sent c/o the publisher.)

The general road maps suggested earlier for motor vehicles are equally useful for cyclists. In addition, however, there are three maps (of a projected series to cover all of Japan eventually) that have been made up specifically with the cyclist in mind. They show the location of every Youth Hostel, places that rent bicycles (shown by a red bicycle symbol, with telephone number), special bicycle roads and touring routes, 'Koku minshukusha' (accommodation), road gradients — even a star rating system for the difficulty of touring courses. Of all the maps available for touring by road in Japan, these have by far the largest number of places identified in romaji as well as in kanji. The only sad thing is that their coverage takes in only the central third of Honshu. Further maps in the series are intended to cover all Japan eventually.

The maps are printed by the Bridgestone company and are called 'sai-ku-ringu ma-pu' ('cycling map'); English is written on the back of the folder, but the front is only in Japanese. They cost Y650 each and should be available at bookstores. If case of difficulty in obtaining copies, contact the Japan Bicycle Promotion Institute as described earlier.

HITCHING

For saving money and getting to know Japanese people, there is no better way of getting around Japan than by hitching. The Japanese must be the kindest people in the world to thumbing foreigners, and the main difficulty is to avoid taking unfair advantage of them. Tales abound of drivers going hours — even days — out of their way to take travellers to their destinations, all the while buying their meals and sometimes even taking them home overnight. (One friend got picked up by a doctor and ended up with several days free stay at a country club overlooking Mt Fuji, several weeks stay at the doctor's home near Tokyo, and the doctor tried to give him an expensive watch as a going away present! Such occurences are rare, of course, but they are among the strange and wonderful experiences that are Japan.)

The Japanese themselves rarely hitchhike and many drivers are not familiar with the meaning of an outstretched thumb. Many a foreigner has found himself taken to the next town and dropped off at the railway station.

It is useful to make up a large sign in kanji showing your destination, with the addition of the characters for 'homen' which means 'area', otherwise a literal-minded driver may go past believing that only that destination will do, when he is going a slightly shorter distance;

carry stiff paper or cardboard and a felt-tip pen. Another tip is to stand at traffic lights in towns (there are many) and ask drivers if they are going your way. Neighbourhood children may be willing to help. In country areas hitching is no problem because it is easy to reach the highway and vehicles have space to stop.

For straight-through long drives it is hard to beat trucks. They are often going long distances, and drivers frequently try to arrange another lift with a truck going beyond their stopping point. Though they never speak more than a few words of English, they are invariably good natured and interested in their passenger. Often this is their first meeting with a foreigner. It gives them added prestige to be able to show off a *gaijin* in the cab of their truck.

They are usually quite earthy, and the closest inheritors of the ancient Japanese spirit. They are most likely to know and sing traditional folk songs and other elements of the true folk culture, as contrasted with the court culture that produced the refined tea ceremony, kota playing, etc.

To women hitching alone or in pairs who might have some doubts about the whole business, good advice is to stick to trucks with green number plates — they are company owned and the drivers are much more likely to behave themselves.

For women who want to discourage unwanted amorous attentions from Japanese men, there is a message in Japanese at the back of this book.

Another potential risk for western women is the young Japanese male in his jazzed up car who wishes to impress her with his highly developed driving skills and his finely honed reflexes. The fact is that speed limits in Japan are extremely low, only 60 km/h, so he will have had very little experience with fast driving of any kind, especially on twisty roads. However, in the presence of a western woman he is likely to get a bit

silly, especially on mountain roads where young Japanese men drivers go silly anyway.

For rapid travel between cities, the expressways are by far the fastest way to go. The points to remember are, firstly, that the long-distance trucks are like nocturnal animals that come out at night so that expressways are choked with them. Secondly, it is not permitted to hitch at the edge of the road on an expressway.

The best way to get started is to stand before or at the entrance toll gate. Attendants have been known to help by asking drivers if they can give you a lift to your destination.

Once you have a ride, find out where the driver is going. If he plans to exit before your destination, ask him to let you off at the next *sugi no kyukeijo* (or 'rest area') *de orosh'te kudasai.* You can then ask around among truck drivers (they usually stand around in groups talking), or you can stand with your sign near the exit from the parking lot where it leads back to the road. Often your driver will ask around for you so you'll be passed from truck to truck across the country.

You will probably be treated with such kindness that you are sure to want to return the favour in some way. This will be difficult, for they usually refuse to take money and will not let you pay for their meals; usually they will want to treat you! Before setting out, stock up on fruit, candy or *sembe* (rice crackers) and feed them to your driver as you go along; you can leave the rest of the box or package in the cab when you get out. Foreign cigarettes are also very popular (the Japanese smoke like chimneys) — bring them as your duty free allowance.

Be sure to try to talk to your driver, by the way. He will appreciate some attempt at communication even if he speaks no English. If two people are hitching together it is tempting to talk together all the time. If the driver is alone he may get annoyed at being ignored after his kindness in stopping.

The following directions explain how to get to the entrances of the main expressways from the major cities of Japan.

Tokyo (northbound): The Tohoku Expressway (Tohoku Kosoko doro) begins at the city of Iwatsuki, more than 30 km north of Tokyo.

Take the JNR Keihin-Tohoku line from any station between Shinagawa and Tabata to Omiya. Exit from the platform at the end closest to the front of the train; immediately to the left will be stairs down to the Tobu-sen line. Take it to Iwatsuki, the fifth stop. The train fares will total around Y500.

Exiting from the front of the station, walk down the main street until you reach the second large street to the right; ignore side alleys. Walking for 10-15 minutes will take you under the overhead roadway, to the expressway entrance.

Maps show the expressway as being planned to begin closer to Tokyo, so check with the TIC to find out if you can reach the entrance more easily.

Tokyo (southbound): Take the Shin-Tamagawa line to Yoga, the fifth station after Shibuya. Shin-Tamagawa line is a continuation of the Hanzomon subway line and may be entered by continuing along that line, or at Shibuya, where the entrance is close to the statue of Hachiko, the famous dog. At Yoga, the overhead roadway of the Tomei Expressway (Tomei Kosokudoro) is about half a km to the south of the station; there is a police box near the station if directions are needed. Ask, 'kosoko doro wa, dochira?'.

When you reach the roadway, pass under it and turn to the right. A few hundred metres alongside the roadway, a ramp rises to the right up to the entrance; a service road continues straight. You can stand in the vee between the roads (but be ready to run quickly if a car stops because the ramp is narrow and there is a risk of causing an accident), or you can take the safer course and stand farther back on the service road before the ramp splits off. It might also be possible to enlist the help of the toll gate operators.

Nagoya: Take the subway bound for Hoshigaoka or Fujigaoka; the destination is Hongo station but many trains terminate before there at Hoshigaoka. In such a case, change to a later train that goes all the way. The entrance ramps for both northbound and southbound traffic are near Hongo station.

Kyoto: From the front of Kyoto station take bus No 19 or 20, and watch for signs by the roadside for the Meishin Expressway. Get off and select the correct ramp for the desired destinations, Osaka, Kobe and points south, or Nagoya/Tokyo and points north.

Note that it is not worthwhile trying to hitch within the area bounded by Kyoto-Osaka-Kobe; they form one vast conurbation and trying to find your way by road is more bother that it's worth. Trains are much quicker and more convenient, even if you have your own vehicle.

Because of the great buildup of towns around Kyoto, when heading toward the north coast, it is simplest to take the JNR train to Kamioka and start hitching from there.

Customs & Immigration

CUSTOMS

Japanese Customs are quite generous in their allowances, especially for liquor. You can bring in three 760 ml bottles of alcoholic beverages. Other limits are: 400 cigarettes or 100 cigars or 500 g of tobacco, with a maximum combined weight of 500 g; 2 ounces of perfume; and 2 watches of value no higher than Y30,000 each, including any in current use; other goods with a total value of not more than Y100,000. Inspectors are generally lenient, allowing in anything that could be considered reasonable for a person's stay in Japan; luggage often isn't opened unless they are suspicious of the contents.

Even if you don't smoke, it might be worth bringing in foreign cigarettes (US or British are the best). They are very welcome gifts to Japanese smokers, and are a nice 'thank you' for assistance or when hitch-hiking, either the whole packet or one at a time. They are also appreciated by foreigners in Japan who think the local product a bit rough. As for booze, it is expensive in Japan, so bring your limit if you like spirits or if you will be visiting friends who like a nip.

On arrival, a verbal declaration is usually sufficient if there is no unaccompanied baggage. You can send luggage separately (eg by mail) and declare it upon arrival on the form provided. A copy of the form, listing the number of packages that are coming is shown when they arrive, and it is unlikely that duty will be charged on the contents. Parcels arriving without such a customs declaration are subject to duty, although the inspectors are usually not too harsh. Packages of food, and low-value items or gifts usually come through without trouble.

The Japanese authorities are very down on narcotics, marijuana and stimulant drugs. Anyone caught bringing any of these products into Japan can expect no sympathy from the law.

Firearms are very tightly controlled in Japan, any anyone caught smuggling them or ammunition can expect an unpaid vacation.

Pornography is frowned on in Japan, but what constitutes porn may seem rather laughable at times by western standards. The portrayal of pubic hair in any form is a complete no-no. Imported 'men's magazines' are completely sanitized before being offered for sale. Not only are offending areas of flesh disfigured by splotches of a marking pen, but the picture is actually abraded down to bare paper to prevent removal of the ink. Or so it is said: I haven't researched this. Because of the enforced innocence of these magazines, the unexpurgated versions are good conversation/peering pieces. If you bring one in, keep it out of plain sight by carrying it inside a newspaper, or fold the cover over. Most Japanese have never seen Westerners in the nude, so expect some giggles (from men) and have an answer for why a blonde woman doesn't have the same colour hair everywhere.

(Despite the strong censorship on nudity, in Japan you can buy 'comic' books that portray unbelievable scenes of brutality, sexual abuse and sadism, with scenes of sexual encounters painstakingly detailed, though often physiologically inaccurate.)

Selling goods in Japan

Years ago there was a lucrative black market in bottles of foreign whisky, especially Johnnie Walker Black Label which sold then in shops for Y10,000 a bottle. Now the price has dropped to about Y4600 a bottle, so there is not so much profit to be made. In addition, most Japanese are earning very good salaries and don't worry so much about saving a little money, especially if they don't know the seller. If you want to try selling a few bottles bars and other drinking places are said to be good places to try, both customers and the proprietors.

There also used to be a good market for gold Swiss watches (Rolex and Omega especially), but nowadays the Japanese travel abroad a lot and buy their own.

There are other items that would be saleable in Japan, but the amount to be made is rather small. Unusual artefacts may find ready buyers; one person landed carrying a bundle of spears from Papua New Guinea and sold them easily. Top class world-famous goods may find buyers. One entrepreneur was bringing in Fender electric guitars (the latest models not yet available in Japan), and selling them at a good price. Several kinds of old model Japanese-made cameras sell for high prices in Japan, particularly Canon and Nikon rangefinder models. Stores ask very high prices; what they would be willing to pay is another matter.

Some Japanese will pay large sums for expensive foreign-made cameras such as Leica, Hasselblad and Rollei, despite the fact that Japan makes the majority of high quality cameras. This seems to be part of a national inferiority complex that manifests itself in excessive adulation of foreign products simply because they are foreign, a habit going back a century when Japan was opened to the outside world for the first time in 250 years, and when all modern things and knowledge came from abroad. It seems the added prestige of having a foreign model slung around one's neck is worth the extra cost. If you bring one of these cameras into Japan in good condition you could probably sell it but it could take too long to be worth the effort. Professional photographers might provide one market.

ENTRY REQUIREMENTS

Everyone entering Japan must carry a passport with an appropriate visa. If you stay 90 days or more you will need to get an Alien Registration Card. Your passport or registration card must be carried at all times.

Entry to Japan is barred to certain categories of undesirable people, including lepers, paupers (or anyone with insufficient funds), drug users, prostitutes, or anyone who may cause harm to the interests and security of Japan. The latter is a catch all and can be interpreted to suit the authorities.

Japan can deport aliens of some countries without notifying their embassies, but in fact the embassy is usually notified so as to get rid of the problem as quickly as possible.

VISAS

Everyone must in principle have a visa. However, to help tourism, bilateral agreements with some countries mean you don't need a visa if you are from western Europe, the UK or most English-speaking countries, with the notable exceptions of USA and Australia.

Whether or not you need a visa, on arrival in Japan your fate is decided by the immigration inspector who has the final say on whether you are admitted. He may, for example, demand to see a return ticket or proof of adequate funds. He also decides what 'status of residence' to grant you, and your period of stay. The status of residence is identified by a string of numbers, eg 4-1-4; details are given later.

The following countries have reciprocal visa-waiving agreements with Japan: New Zealand (30 days); Canada, Denmark, France, Sweden, and many others (90 days); UK, West Germany, Switzerland, and others (180 days). The periods are nominal periods of stay. For example, Kiwis may get 60 days not 30, simply because the inspector didn't have a 30-day rubber stamp that day.

Visas are waived for people from these countries only if they are entering for tourism. This can include sightseeing, recreation, attending meetings or conventions, inspection tours, participation in contests (athletic and others), visiting relatives or friends, learning cultural arts, goodwill visits and similar non-remunerative activities. Note that 'non-remunerative' excludes any activity that will result in earning income at a later date in another country eg writing a travel book.

Visa-exempt tourists eligible for stays of 90 or 180 days may be granted either 4-1-4 or 4-1-16(3) status. The latter is preferred if you want to stay as long as possible since 4-1-4 status is valid for only 60 days, regardless of nationality. A period of stay can usually be extended twice, eg from 60 to 180 days, but the red tape can be time-consuming so the fewer renewals you need, the better.

Americans, Australians, and other tourists who need visas must apply for them before arriving in Japan. On arrival they will usually get 4-1-4 status with a 60-day period of stay. Again this can usually be extended twice but after that you will have to leave the country eg to Korea, and start again.

(An exception is made for transit tourists. If you are on a cruise ship that will dock at two ports in Japan you may get a transit visa that is valid for up to 15 days for travel by a designated route through Japan to rejoin the ship. Also, sea and air passengers who have onward bookings and the required visa for the next country on their route can obtain up to 72 hours excursion time without visa. In both cases ask your travel agent about the exact regulations and how to obtain the landing permission, for the carrier or its representative must make the arrangements. In both cases an ordinary tourist visa could prevent being unnecessarily restricted.)

When you apply for an extension of stay, the immigration official may ask proof of a ticket out of the country, sufficient funds, and/or a letter of guarantee. Some offices may accept a letter from your bank certifying that you have arranged a line of credit for an amount adequate to guarantee your repatriation from Japan.

LONG-TERM VISAS

For any long-term stay in Japan — more than six months, for example — there are two options. One is to leave Japan at the expiration of the period of stay and return on another tourist visa. This can be done once or twice without problem (although some ports, such as Shimonoseki and Fukuoka, have a reputation for being unco-operative) but it gets harder as the stamps in the passport accumulate. The simplest way around the problem is to obtain a long-stay visa. The type would depend on the purpose, but the most common types are cultural (study of traditional arts, eg tea ceremony, music or dancing, martial arts, or some other aspect of Japanese culture), or student (academic or non-academic). One can also obtain a working or teaching visa that will allow working full time. While it is generally possible to obtain permission to work part-time on a cultural or student visa, for full-time work it might be better to get the appropriate visa.

In any case, it is usually difficult to arrange the foundation for a long-stay visa without actually coming to Japan to make the necessary arrangements in person.

Student and Cultural Visas

For language study, it is much easier to find a school 'on the scene' than by correspondence. For any course of study the institution has to provide letters of guarantee and other documents to satisfy the authorities and they prefer to see the person before committing themselves to this. An exception is study in a recognized academic course, especially at university level, where standards are similar internationally and entry is based on the applicant's academic record. Visas for such study can be arranged from abroad without too much trouble.

If you have to locate a school from within Japan, the usual procedure is to enter, giving 'travel-sightseeing' or 'cultural study' as the purpose of entry, thus obtaining either 4-1-4 or 4-1-16 (3) status. Then find a school or teacher and make the arrangements. The school then prepares the necessary documentation which the student takes to a Japanese diplomatic mission in another country. The Japanese embassy in Seoul is most popular for this purpose. So many foreigners make similar applications that this embassy handles them as a matter of routine, and if all papers are in order, a study or cultural visa will usually be granted in one working day.

Since it is possible for 4-1-16 (3) status to be extended up to three years, anyone eligible for that status could possibly obtain sufficient extensions, 90 days at a time, to complete a year or two of studies without the bother of collecting documents and trekking to Korea. But there is no guarantee this could be achieved. Like everything else involving Japanese bureaucracy, decisions are made case by case. Also there might be difficulty obtaining permission to work part-time under such an arrangement whereas part-time work is possible with a proper cultural or student visa.

Working Visa
In the case of working/teaching visas, it is usually very difficult to arrange employment with a Japanese company from outside Japan unless you are being transferred from another country. So give 'travel-sightseeing' as the reason for entry. Do not say you are looking for

work as that is a prohibited activity on entry and you could be turned back at the port of entry.

Once you have found a job and obtained the required documents (described later), go to Korea and apply for the working visa. This takes about six or eight weeks. During this time you could travel around Korea or return to Japan on a tourist visa.

The embassy in Seoul will give you a receipt of your application but they will not normally inform you whether your application has been approved. You could try leaving a self-addressed card or offer to pay cable fees. Otherwise you must check regularly on the current status. If you remain in Korea, this means checking at the embassy from time to time. If you return to Japan, inquire at the Visa Section of the Ministry of Foreign Affairs (Gaimusho), either in person or by phone (tel (03) 580-3311). With the receipt issued in Seoul, find out the file number being used in Japan (it will be different from the one used in Korea); this can make enquiries much easier. When making enquiries it helps to have the assistance of a Japanese person as the staff speak little English, and besides, foreigners never sound properly obsequious.

Once you have a work visa, remember you still have to pass the Immigration Inspector. An inspector at Shimonoseki (the main port of entry from Korea) once refused entry to a person on the grounds that he did not have enough money, even though he had a new work visa and a job in Tokyo. Shimonoseki has a bad reputation in such matters so it might be worth flying to Osaka or Tokyo where officials seem to be more reasonable.

Other Long-term Visas
Visas that enable a long stay may be issued for other purposes as well and may be useful to some readers, most particularly for Press or Commercial

purposes. In this case it is possible to make all necessary arrangements before entering Japan.

STATUS OF RESIDENCE

The following table lists the main statuses and the nominal period of stay for each.

4-1-4	tourist — 60 days
4-1-5	commercial/management of business — 3 years
4-1-6	student: junior college level and up — 1 year
4-1-7	lecturers/professors (academic) — 3 years
4-1-8	cultural/artistic/scientific — 1 year
4-1-9	entertainers — 60 days
4-1-10	missionary/religious — 3 years
4-1-11	journalist (radio/press) — 3 years
4-1-12	specialized skills/technicians — 3 years
4-1-13	specialized labour (eg specialty cooks) — 1 year
4-1-14	permanent resident — permanent
4-1-15	spouses and children of person in category 4-1-5/6/7/8/9/10/11/12/13 — same as spouse/parent
4-1-16(1)	short-term version of 4-1-5/10/11/12 — 180 days
4-1-16(3)	short-term version of all statuses — up to 3 years; (case-by-case)

The word 'nominal' is used to describe the period of stay because the actual allowable period may be longer or shorter. Thus, a tourist (4-1-4) is given a nominal 60 days, but this can usually be extended for two further periods of 60 days each to a total of 180 days. Periods of stay listed as more than one year usually have to be renewed annually.

The proper term to use is 'extension of period of stay', not 'extension of visa'.

CHANGE OF STATUS

A person entering Japan may only engage in the activity allowed under his or her status, and permission must be obtained from an Immigration office to change activity — or even to engage in the same activity in a different place — or to change status.

For example, permission would be needed for a person with student status, eg 4-1-6 or 4-1-16(3) who wanted to teach English; for a teacher who wanted to change to a different school; for a person on a cultural visa (4-1-8) studying pottery who wanted to take up lacquer-making; or a person wanting to change status from teaching (4-1-7 or 4-1-16(3)) to commercial (4-1-5 or 4-1-16(3)) so as to engage in business.

The good news is that the authorities seem to grant such requests in most cases.

In all cases, though, it is necessary to check before taking on the new activity. There is always the chance that the authorities will check whether the change has already been made, in which the case, a letter of apology might be needed. But it is best to avoid problems in the first place. Failure to obtain prior permission may result in 'unfavourable consideration' of a future request for an extension, or possibly even outright deportation.

Change of status can be obtained in Japan without leaving the country only in the case of status 4-1-5/6/7/8 and 4-1-10/11/12. (Since 4-1-16(3) is frequently given for the same purpose as these it seems logical that holders of that status should also be able to change status, but this remains to be seen.)

A person holding 4-1-4 status definitely cannot change status, nor can holders of status other than those listed above.

Anyone who is leaving Japan to apply for status 4-1-6 (student), 4-1-7 (teaching), 4-1-12 (technical) or 4-1-13 (skilled labour) can speed up the procedure abroad by obtaining from an Immigration Office in Japan a 'Certificate of Eligibility for Status of Residence'. This procedure might be applicable to an application for a cultural visa as well.

RE-ENTRY PERMIT

If you have long-term status and wish to leave Japan for a short time and then return to take up the same activity, you should obtain a Re-entry Permit before leaving Japan. This is not a landing permit, and you must still satisfy the Immigration Inspector at the port of entry, but it does facilitate re-entry and preservation of the original status category. Failure to obtain the permit will almost certainly result in cancellation of the original status.

A Re-entry Permit is valid for up to one year; it will be less if the balance of the permitted period is less. It must be used within six months of issue. Its period of validity (and that of the original visa) cannot be extended outside Japan; if it (or the visa) expires while the holder is abroad, a new visa must be obtained before returning to Japan.

LETTER OF GUARANTEE

For any type of long-term visa, and often for an extension of stay as a tourist, a Letter of Guarantee is required. An acceptable form of letter is shown below.

If possible, the guarantor should be a Japanese citizen who has the financial resources to take on this obligation. To demonstrate this capability, the guarantor is usually required to supply a certificate of employment and a recent certificate of tax payment.

For a working or language-teaching visa, the company or school can provide the letter, and for a press or commercial visa, the guarantee letter would of course be provided by the person's organization.

The Japanese authorities always prefer to have a Japanese guarantor.

In one case, a foreign employee of a very large multinational corporation presented a letter of guarantee from his company, but was asked if he couldn't find a Japanese guarantor. So instead he asked his secretary if she would write a letter of guarantee for him. She did, and it was accepted.

Form Letter of Guarantee

To: Consul-General (Ambassador) of Japan

Letter of Guarantee

This serves to certify that (name, born . . . . at . . . . . . , Nationality, Occupation, etc.,) intends to enter into Japan for (purpose of entry), for (expected period of stay in Japan).

In this connection, I, the undersigned, guarantee the following:

1. Logistic support while he/she is in Japan.
2. Travelling expenses when he/she leaves Japan.
3. He/she will abide by all Japanese laws and regulations.
4. Any other information concerning . . . . will be gladly given.

I should be much obliged if the visa application could be approved at your earliest convenience.

Yours faithfully
(Signature)

Guarantor's address in Japan:
Nationality:
Date of Birth:
Immigration status:
Occupation:
Relationship to applicant:

ALIEN REGISTRATION

All aliens, with the exception of diplomats and US military personnel, must register with the authorities and obtain an Alien Registration Card (ARC) if they remain in Japan for 90 days or more. This includes tourists!

The Alien Registration Card (or your passport) must be carried at all times. You can be asked by police or other authorities to produce it at any time. Failure to be able to show either document will most likely lead to several unpleasant hours in custody while someone else fetches it. The 'offender' is usually not allowed to go and get it, even in the company of an officer, and even if his/her residence is close by. If there is no one else who can get it, an impasse is reached. It is a needless annoyance, but one that could befall any foreigner in Japan.

Obtaining an ARC is simple and costs nothing but does require three photographs — about 5 x 5 cm. It is issued by the municipal office of the city, town or ward (ku) in which you are living. In the case of travellers, the address of a lodging place is acceptable.

An ARC is normally surrendered when you leave Japan. If you have long-term residence status (as discussed above) and intend to return to Japan on a Re-entry Permit, the ARC can be taken with you.

Persons over 14 years of age who are granted a total stay of more than one year must be fingerprinted.

A change of residence within the district must be recorded at the original issuing office. A move to another district requires re-registration in the new district within 14 days.

Much unfavourable comment has been made over the years, observing (probably accurately) that Japan's control and treatment of aliens reflects an element of xenophobia that has existed in the country since it was first opened to foreigners in the 19th century, and probably from much farther back than that. The regulations requiring registration are said to be the strictest in the free world (and the most bothersome); they certainly emphasize the meaning of the Japanese word for foreigner, 'gaijin', which literally means 'outside person'. The elaborate registration procedures emphasize the omnipresent sense of 'us' and 'them' that appears frequently (to the observant) in Japan and Japanese society.

In 1979 Japan signed an international agreement that may eventually result in the abolition of the Alien Registration procedures, but at the time of publication this had not occured.

FURTHER INFORMATION

There are two booklets that give more detailed information on immigration procedures; one is comprehensive, while the other is more abridged but more easily understood.

The more detailed of the two is *Immigration — A Guide to Alien Procedures in Japan.* It is published by the *Japan Times* in cooperation with the Ministry of Justice. It is available at a number of bookstores in Tokyo (and possibly elsewhere), eg Kinokuniya and Maruzen, as well as from the lunch counter in the Tokyo Immigration office. The cost is Y300.

It can be obtained by mail from:

The Japan Times
5-4 4-chome
Shibaura
Minato-ku
Tokyo 108.

The cost for surface postage is an additional Y200 in Japan, or Y300 to any country.

The major shortcomings of this book are because it was written in conjunction with the Ministry responsible for immigration. It may, therefore, be rather vague on some points. Some cross-referencing is needed and it is stronger on how to change status within Japan than it is on the requirements for obtaining visas of different types to get into Japan.

Another source of information about Immigration regulations is the booklet *Now You Live in Japan*. It is a goldmine of information regarding laws in Japan that affect aliens, such as marriage, divorce, citizenship, etc, and it has good, though shortened, coverage of immigration laws. It is available at bookstores and by mail from:

Research Committee for Bicultural
Life in Japan
c/o The Japan Times Ltd
CPO Box 144
Tokyo 100-91

Cost is Y700; Surface postage is Y200 in Japan, Y300 overseas.

IMMIGRATION OFFICES
Tokyo

Tokyo has two Immigration offices one is the nice shiny new (1980) Immigration Service Centre in pleasant surroundings not far from Ikebukuro station; the other is old and dingy in an industrial section near Shinagawa station. Both give the same services, so the one to use depends largely on which is more convenient to reach.

To reach the one near Ikebukuro station, the most difficult problem is finding the correct exit from the station. The correct exit faces a sort-of plaza in front of the Seibu department store, which is located over the station. The station happens to be one of the worst marked in English in the city, but look for a sign pointing the direction of 'Sunshine City' and 'Mitsu-koshi'; that is the correct direction. Another way is to go to the ground floor of Seibu store and go out the East exit, the side where one enters Seibu Ikebukuro station.

The Immigration Service Centre is in the World Import Mart building, just behind the 60-storey Sunshine City building which can be seen from

the station exit. The easiest way to reach it is to walk along the wide tree-lined boulevard stretching out in front of the store as far as the overhead expressway and turn left. After a few minutes, the front of the building will become visible on the far side of the street/expressway. The Immigration office is on the sixth floor of the Import Mart building. (In the same building are an aquarium, laserium, planetarium, a number of restaurants, many shops, and other ways to while away some time.)

The other immigration office (previously listed as the Central Immigration Office) is accessible from the Shinagawa station. Service here has always been friendly and helpful in my experience but other people have not all spoken well of it, so it may be the luck of the draw. Most of the staff speak some English but remember to speak slowly and clearly, and avoid colloquialisms.

To reach the office, take the Yamanote line, Keihin-Kyuko line, or transfer at Sengakuji station of the Asakusa line, and get off at Shinagawa station. (Some trains on the Asakusa line from the direction of Shimbashi go directly and it is not necessary to change lines.) From any JNR platform, exit by the underground passage that is located at the end of the station closest to Hamamatsucho. From the Keihin-Kyuko station, walk out the exit and along the overhead passageway. Walk to the farthest platform, down the stairs to the left and along the platform to the entrance leading down to the same underground passage mentioned earlier. Walk towards the highest-numbered platforms and continue along the tunnel to the end, where you surrender your ticket. This is the east exit. From the exit, walk along the street that leads to the station, cross the pedestrian overpass and the following bridge that crosses the canal. (There is a map at the exit from the station and another at the foot of the overpass.) At the first road after the canal bridge, turn left; this will lead to a large road, and the *Asahi Evening News* building can be seen across the road. The road to the Immigration Office runs to the right of the AEN building.

From the station (east exit) one can also catch a No 99 bus and get off when the AEN building comes into sight, but the walk to the same point takes less than 10 minutes.

On the return, there may be some confusion about the correct ticket machine. Of the machines to the left of the station entrance, the first five are for JNR trains. The sixth one is for Keihin-Kyuko line which runs one stop to Sengakuji (where you can transfer to the Asakusa line) in one direction, and beyond Yokohama in the other. These machines are closed after 6 pm. The machines to the right of the entrance are in two groups; all those outside the building are for JNR, while the left-hand one of the three indoors is for Keihin-Kyoku.

Buses run to Shinagawa station, but they may discharge everyone at the front entrance, making it necessary to buy a platform ticket for the privilege of using the tunnel under the very large railway yard located at Shinagawa. It is preferable to arrive by train.

Local immigration offices

Sapporo	(011)	261-9211
Sendai	(0222)	56-6076
Tokyo	(03)	471-5111
Narita	(0476)	32-6771
Yokohama	(045)	681-6801
Nagoya	(052)	951-2391
Osaka	(06)	941-0771
Kobe	(078)	391-6377
Takamatsu	(0878)	61-2555
Hiroshima	(0822)	21-4412
Shimonoseki	(0832)	23-1431
Fukuoka	(092)	281-7431

Kagoshima	(0992)	22-5658
Naha	(0988)	32-4185

Visa Information

Information on obtaining special visas, like student, working, teaching, etc, should be obtained from the Visa Section of the Ministry of Foreign Affairs (Gaimusho). The immigration offices described above are only for extensions of the period of residence, change of status, etc.

Staff at the Visa Section are helpful. There is no need to fear asking questions regarding visas. They will give out photocopied sheets that list the exact documentation that is required when applying for any kind of a visa at a Japanese representation overseas, and can check the documents to be sure that everything required is present.

The Visa Section office is easily reached from Kasumigaseki station (Hibiya, Marunouchi and Chiyoda subway lines) by taking exit A4 and walking a short distance along the street to the first entrance through the fence. The Visa Section is a small office on the right side of the left-hand building. The phone number is (03) 580-3311.

Information on documentation required for long-term visas should also be available at any Japanese diplomatic representation overseas. Generally one must send (in duplicate): an application form (Form 1C), a photo 45 x 45 mm, letter of guarantee, and documents showing why you wish to stay in Japan, school records, documentation on the institution where you will study/teach, etc.

It is a good idea to take to Japan a 35 mm negative of your photo so that further prints can be made as required.

FOREIGN EMBASSIES

Following are the telephone numbers of the Tokyo offices of some foreign embassies.

Australia	453-0251	Indonesia	441-4201	Singapore	586-9111
Austria	451-8281	Ireland	263-0695	Soviet Union	583-4224
Belgium	262-0191	Italy	453-5291	Spain	583-8531
Canada	408-2101	Korea	452-7611	Sri Lanka	585-7431
China	446-6781	Malaysia	463-0241	Sweden	582-6981
Denmark	496-3001	Netherlands	431-5126	Switzerland	473-0121
Finland	583-7790	New Zealand	460-8711	Taiwan *	583-8030
France	473-0171	Norway	440-2611	Thailand	441-7352
W Germany	473-0151	Pakistan	454-4862	UK	265-5511
Greece	403-0871	Philippines	496-2731	USA	583-7141
India	262-2391				

* See Notes below

Taiwan

Since Japan recognized the People's Republic of China, Taiwan has been doing business under the name 'Association of East Asian Relations' in Tokyo; tel 583-8030. For visas it functions exactly as a consular office. To reach it, take the Hibiya subway to Kamiyacho, walk uphill along the major road (Sakurada-dori) toward Tokyo Tower, then across the large intersection at the top (keeping the Tower to your right). Continue downhill, on the right-hand side of the road. Look for the nine-storey brown T-shaped Heiwado Bldg. The visa office is located on the second floor.

Korea

Many travellers go to Korea from Japan, both for sightseeing and for obtaining Japanese visas. Korean diplomatic representatives are located in the following cities.

Tokyo:	tel (03) 452-7611
Sapporo:	(011) 621-0288
Sendai:	(0222) 21-2751
Niigata:	(0252) 43-4771
Yokohama:	(045) 621-4531
Nagoya:	(052) 935-9221
Osaka:	(06) 213-1401
Kobe:	(078) 221-4853
Fukuoka:	(092) 771-0461
Shimonoseki:	(0832) 66-5341
Naha:	(0988) 55-3381

In Tokyo, visas are not issued at the embassy, but as a separate building about 10 minutes away on foot. The easiest way to reach it is by bus. In all cases, get off at Ni-no-hashi bus stop; it has the same name on both sides of the road. Of the following buses, the first four let off passengers on the same side as the consulate building, the other three on the far side. The building is a tall white structure, about 100 m along in the direction taken by the first four buses after leaving the bus stop.

The following listing gives the bus number, the name of the starting JNR railway station, and the terminal JNR station:

85;	Shimbashi;	Shibuya
10;	Tokyo (S exit);	Meguro
91;	Tokyo (N exit);	Shinagawa
70;	Shinjuku (W exit);	Tamachi
10;	Meguro;	Tokyo (S exit)
85;	Shibuya;	Shimbashi
99;	Gotanda;	Shimbashi

Visas are granted on the spot within an hour except to Japanese who have to wait several days. Cost is the yen equivalent of US$1.50. One photo is required, nominally 6 x 6 cm (but smaller accepted).

WORKING IN JAPAN

Except for employees transferred by a foreign company, it is not usually possible to obtain work in ordinary fields of employment. An exception is a person with a skill not usually found in Japan eg a cook trained in French cooking. For others, it is impossible to get a working visa.

The only jobs open to foreigners are those that require a skill, ability or quality that a Japanese cannot fill. One such example is modelling. Western models, especially girls with blonde hair, are widely used for modelling clothes for well-known department stores. Extraordinary beauty is not necessary for such work.

Teaching English is the most popular occupation, and people with no training in the field are able to pick up work easily. It is a measure of the desperation of the Japanese to learn spoken English that even people who are not native speakers (often with attrocious accents) regularly find work teaching 'English'.

By Japanese law, of course, one is required to have a visa to engage in any remunerative activity in Japan. However, it is no great secret that more than a few people have been known to teach without benefit of governmental blessing. From time to time, schools have been raided and some teachers deported, but there is the possibility that reality tempers enforcement, and the authorities take note of the fact that Japan is very dependent on citizens who are adept in foreign languages and that the educational system fails abysmally to produce them. Without the foreign teachers, there would be a gross insufficiency of native speakers; most Japanese teachers of English at schools are incapable of even an elementary conversation in the language that they are teaching.

Pay at schools averages Y2000 per hour or better, but the problem is that the schools seldom need teachers for more than a couple of consecutive hours. Work is mostly in the evening, and it is often necessary to spend a lot of time travelling between schools.

The easiest place to find teaching work is at schools (private, not academic), though the pay is lower than for private lessons which take time and contacts to arrange. Advertisements for teachers appear regularly in the English-language newspapers, particularly the Monday *Japan Times*, and especially in September and January, when new terms are beginning. The summer is the slackest time because many students are on vacation.

Teaching positions are most easily found in Tokyo, and less easily in other large cities. They are difficult to find in Kyoto because so many foreigners want to live in this historic and cultured city, and there is an oversupply of willing teachers. Those who do live in Kyoto often have to commute to Osaka, an hour train ride, to find work; some even go to Kobe, two hours away.

The preferred accents are, first, North American (northern US and Canadian are best received), and, second, British (no regional dialects, please). Australians, Kiwis and South Africans, etc, will probably have some trouble obtaining work at the 'better' schools unless their accent is closer to British. Sorry, but that's the way it is.

There is a continual need for people who can write or re-write good English. Most translations are first done by Japanese people from Japanese into 'Japlish'; it is the rewriter's job to put this into good, readable English. There are many translation agencies that require rewriters, but this work is sporadic. People who turn out good work can often command higher rates once they have proved their worth. People with the combination of good technical knowledge and the ability to write clear and correct English are especially in demand. At the moment there is a strong demand for people who are knowledgeable in the electronics field, especially computers. Japan has become very prominent in the computer field in recent years, and thousands of pages of instruction manuals have to be translated yearly.

Rewriters who can read Japanese,

particularly those who have a technical background, should have no trouble finding steady work, even on a freelance basis.

Another type of work, suited best to attractive blond women, is working as a hostess in clubs or nightclubs. They can make a good income just from their 'official' duties of talking with customers, but girls who have been hostesses uniformly remark that it is boring; they have to make small-talk with men, most Japanese with next to no English, and it is a continual battle to keep the men's hands in their laps — their own laps, that is.

Those prepared to give special attention outside working hours can make a bundle, so it is said. Apparently the going rate for outside activities can be as much as Y50,000 per night, so a girl can make a lot of money if she has no qualms about how it's made.

Similar sums are rumoured to be made by Westerners willing to perform in live sex shows. There is said to be more need for males, as it easier to find females willing to participate; the work requires a talent that not all men are up to.

Working holiday

In late 1980 an agreement was signed between the Japanese and Australian governments setting up a plan whereby young citizens (18-25; sometimes to 30) of their countries could arrange a working holiday in the country for a period of up to a year, with extension at the option of the authorities. This is the first such agreement of the type entered into by Japan. Australians should obtain further information from Japanese diplomatic representatives.

Facts about the Country

GEOGRAPHY

Japan is made up of four main islands, Honshu, Hokkaido, Kyushu and Shikoku, and hundreds of smaller ones that stretch nearly 3000 km in the temperate and subtropical zones, between latitudes $20^{\circ}-45^{\circ}$; equivalent locations are from Morocco to Lyons or Milan, or from Miami to Montreal. Total land area is 377,435 sq km (147,435 sq mi), about 85% of which is considered mountainous. Mountain ranges divide the country into four zones, the Japan Sea and Pacific Ocean sides of the north-east half, and the Japan Sea and Inland Sea sides of the south-west half, all of which have definite differences in patterns of both weather and customs of the people.

Japan is still young geologically, and volcanic eruptions are not uncommon. The Pacific Plate, one of the huge areas of the earth's crust afloat on the mantle, is slowly forcing itself under the islands of Japan, causing frequent earthquakes, mostly harmless. The volcanoes, 67 of which are considered active, are part of the 'Ring of Fire' that follows a fault line (a junction of two plates) around the earth. Active volcanoes include Usu-zan in Hokkaido, and Aso-zan and Sakurajima, both in Kyushu. Other volcanoes wake up from time to time on Honshu; recently there was an eruption of one that had been thought dead. It is theoretically possible for Mt Fuji to erupt again, although it hasn't done so since 1707, and shows no signs of doing so.

Japan is divided into administrative units that, for the most part, follow natural boundaries. With the exception of Hokkaido and three other units, these smaller units are called 'ken', and are modelled on the French prefectural system. There are 43 ken.

Hokkaido was settled extensively only late in the 19th century and still has a small population relative to its size, so the entire island is a single 'do', or district; this is the last syllable of the name.

Tokyo is a 'to' ('metropolis'), while Kyoto and Osaka and their surrounding regions are both 'fu'; all three compare in size with the smaller ken. When writing the names of the latter cities in Japanese, they are 'Tokyo-to', 'Kyoto-fu', and 'Osaka-fu'.

In addition to the administrative units (ken) there are other traditional ways of dividing the country. The names of these regions, all based on geographical features, are still commonly used by the Japanese. For example, the *Youth Hostel Handbook* is divided up according to one of the two traditional systems, as are most road maps that cover large regions of the country, such as the Hi-Power series referred to elsewhere. (Large scale maps follow ken boundaries.) Several brochures printed by the JNTO follow the old divisions as well, such as Hokuriku and Chubu.

Because the traditional divisions largely follow natural features, similar divisions are used for the chapters of this book. Also, prefectural boundaries are used for detailed description except where attractions overlap ken boundaries.

WEATHER AND CLIMATE

Japan is a long country north to south, so the weather and climate vary widely; there can be blizzard conditions in Hokkaido, sunny, crisply-cool weather in Tokyo and Kyoto, mild Mediterranean conditions in Kyushu, and pleasant warmth in Okinawa. At any time there can be a great difference in conditions from one part of the country to another, and at different parts of the same region, especially in the mountainous areas.

The best time to visit Japan is from mid-September to mid-late November.

By then the heat and humidity of summer have passed, as have the typhoons and rain. Starting in Hokkaido in the north, the weather cools and the leaves change colour in early October in a display of fiery autumn foliage that is among the best to be found anywhere in the world. The change of colour advances southward, earlier in high mountainous regions, more slowly along the coasts, and normally has reached Kyoto by the first half of November. For visiting Kyoto, this is the best two or three weeks of the year, and it is well worth trying to get there at that time. However, the Japanese are fully aware of the beauties of that season, and Kyoto is more crowded then than at any other time in the year, making accommodation difficult to find, so it is worth planning ahead and making reservations months in advance. Within the next couple of weeks the leaves will have fallen throughout the country, and the countryside will have faded to a dull brown, a far cry from the lush greens of summer or the almost-iridescent green-gold of the rice paddies just before the harvest.

Spring has long been touted as the ideal time to visit Japan. It seems that every brochure stresses the beauty of the cherry blossoms (sakura) as the symbol of Japan and gives the impression that this is the only time to visit. The fact is that anyone trying to see Japan at sakura time runs the risk of frustration and disappointment. True, the blossoms are beautiful, and when added to a picturesque Japanese castle, the effect is incomparably lovely. But the blossoms are fickle; for the petals remain on the trees less than a week before fluttering to earth, a symbolic reminder of our temporary existence on earth. The blossoms are prey to wind and rain, both of which are prevalent at this time of year. Fortunately, with the great diversity in climate from north to south, and from coast to mountain, the blossom season extends about six weeks nationwide, advancing in a wave of pink and white from Kyushu north to Hokkaido. Further fickleness of nature means the beginning of the blossom season can vary a few weeks from year to year.

Since sakura are an early blossoming species (though not the earliest, for plums come out in February), their appearance is followed by a period of several weeks while the rest of nature catches up and other greenery appears. This can be a season of windy and unsettled weather, with some beautiful days, some cloudy and some rainy. This leads up to the rainy season, or 'tsuyu' (also called 'baiyu'), which normally begins in mid-June and may continue into early July, during which rain can be expected almost every day. Incidentally, it is a popular belief among the Japanese that there is no rainy season in Hokkaido, but foreign residents who have been there during that time report that a lot of water tends to fall out of the sky!

In general, spring begins chilly and clear in March, and finishes warm to hot and humid in June. In Hokkaido, and in the highlands of Honshu, the temperatures are considerably lower, so that snow may remain on the ground as late as May or even June. There are some mountains where skiing is possible into August. Spring is considered to begin on 1 March not the 21st as in North America.

Summer is hot and humidly uncomfortable in the coastal and lower regions, which includes most major cities. Even in Hokkaido, Sapporo has its hot days but not as many as Tokyo or Osaka, which can be very unpleasant. Despite the heat, summer can still be an enjoyable time to visit Japan. The countryside is lush green, birds and fantastically beautiful butterflies flitter and flutter, and the air is filled with the shrill chorus of cicadas. In Hokkaido and the highlands everywhere summer is generally delightful, with temperature, warm to hot, with low humidity. It is good weather for walking and enjoying the scenery (but a canteen of water will always be a welcome companion).

The summer officially lasts from 1 June to 1 September but the warm weather usually lasts well into October, and it is still pleasant in November. Despite the still scorching temperatures in the southern cities, swimming pools automatically close on the first day of September, and people abruptly cease going to the beach on the same date. (At one time in the past, the entire population even changed from the clothes of one season to those of the next on the same date, regardless of the weather on that day.) Visitors in summer should wear the lightest garments possible; wash-and-wear clothing is very useful. Japanese expect foreigners to be a little strange, so they look tolerantly on the summer 'fashions' worn by some western women whose acres of exposed flesh is a bit unusual. Japanese women rarely even expose their shoulders, so keep that in mind before becoming one of the sights for the locals.

Travellers who plan to spend several months travelling around Japan extensively would be wise to tour Hokkaido and northern Honshu through the hot season of July-August, the southern part of the country (Kyushu/Shikoku) between August and October, and the central part between September and November. For Kyoto aim to be there in mid-November; the period from 10 to 20 November is generally the peak time. Then Kyoto must rate as one of the most beautiful places in the world with its gorgeous combination of beautiful temples set among brilliantly colourful leaves.

Winter is generally a time of clear air, bright sun and cool or cold weather. Snow covers much of Hokkaido, north-ern Honshu and the mountain highlands, often to a depth of several metres. Houses in the snow country may have a separate door at roof level for access during the winter. In lower regions, snow doesn't become a permanent feature until 100-200 km north of Tokyo. Tokyo and the other large southern cities are usually snow-free except for the occasional light falls that usually melts by mid-day, though in 1978 a freak storm dumped 15 cm of snow on Tokyo.

For ordinary touring, winter cannot be recommended very highly. Remember that when visiting temples and many other wooden-floored old buildings, it is necessary to remove your shoes and pad around is slippers so warm socks are a must! Houses are usually not centrally heated, for fuel is very expensive. Youth Hostels often are heated, especially in the colder regions, but an extra fee is levied to pay for the fuel. The large western-type hotels are invariably heated and comfortable; public buildings, such as stores and offices, are generally overheated to the point of being sweltering.

It is said that Kyushu is semi-tropical. While it is a few degrees warmer than Honshu, it is still no tropical paradise, just pleasant, and in the mountain areas it too will be cold and snowy in winter. Okinawa and the Ryuku Islands are the warmest part of Japan; their winter climate varies from cool to warm.

For skiers, winter is of course a good time to visit Japan; conditions and facilities have been described as good but not worth a special trip to Japan just for the skiing.

NATIONAL HOLIDAYS

There are 12 national holidays; the following Monday is generally taken as the holiday if the day falls on a Sunday. On these days, most offices, factories and businesses close, but most stores and restaurants remain open.

1 Jan	New Year's Day
15 Jan	Coming-of-Age Day
11 Feb	National Foundation Day
21 Mar	Vernal Equinox Day (may change some years)
29 Apr	Emperor's Birthday
1 May	May Day (semi-holiday)
3 May	Constitution Memorial Day
5 May	Children's Day
15 Sept	Respect-for-the-Aged Day
24 Sept	Autumnal Equinox Day (date may change some years)
10 Oct	Physical Culture Day
3 Nov	Culture Day
23 Nov	Labour Thanksgiving Day

Two periods to avoid in Japan are around New Year, roughly 28 Dec to 5 Jan, and the week around early May. New Year is the biggest holiday season in Japan, and many people try to return to their family home during this period. Nearly all businesses and many restaurants are closed, busy cities like Tokyo are nearly deserted and most shops are shuttered, so it is the least interesting time to visit Japan except for people with personal connections. In the period from 29 April to 5 May there are no less than four holidays. It is known in Japan as 'Golden Week'. Many businesses give their employees the entire week off and, because the weather is usually pleasant, everyone travels. Or tries to. It is very difficult to obtain reservations on trains and at hotels, and train passengers without reserved seats will most likely have to stand for the full journey.

Although it is not a listed national holiday, be wary of the *Obon* season, a week in mid-August when all Japanese try to visit the graves of their ancestors. Again transport is difficult to obtain. This is, however, an interesting time to visit Japan because there is dancing every night in almost every neighbourhood.

There are busy seasons also when school children go on excursions, but these affect mostly Youth Hostel accommodation in historic or nature areas, and are mentioned in the Youth Hostel section.

Festivals

Japan has a huge number of festivals, many with a known history of hundreds of years, and some that date back thousands, with evidence of religious and folk rites, eg fertility festivals.

The Tokyo Tourist Information Centre has free monthly listings of the festivals in Tokyo and the rest of the country. If you want an idea of what will be happing in the following month, staff can copy the info sheets of the previous year; many dates remain the same from year to year.

Festivals provide an insight into Japan that cannot be gained in any other way, and it is worthwhile trying to plan an itinerary so as to take in as many as possible. With few exceptions, they are an occasion of joy and celebration. The men (and some of the older women) get gloriously drunk and happy, and often invite any foreigners present to join in the fun and sample the contents of the cask of sake just opened. (This can make picture taking later a problem!) A feature of nearly every festival, especially those in the country, is the drumming. The amazingly

primitive rhythm is executed with great skill and precision. The drumming is apparently a carry-over from long forgotten days of the earliest inhabitants of the islands.

Festivals give some of the most lasting memories of Japan for they are a reflection of the true spirit, a renewal of contact with their origins.

HISTORY

Because Japanese records of history don't exist prior to the Nara era (600-784 AD), most knowledge of Japan before that time is based on Chinese records. Archeological excavations have found traces of settlement from 100,000 years ago, but nothing further until a few thousand years ago. The earliest civilization about which much is known has been named the Jomon period, tentatively dated up to the second century BC. There is some evidence of a Polynesian/South-East Asian connection in these people, and possible links between Japanese and Polynesian language structures may have been brought with them. There were probably northern Asian elements present in Japan at this time as well. Jomon pottery has been found throughout much of Japan, as far north as Hokkaido.

The next civilization that has been assigned a name is the Yayoi, identified by a clearly different type of pottery. It is likely that the people were closely related to (or part of) peoples in southern Korea, and that there were close ties of trade between the islands of Japan and the peninsula, nearest landmass to Japan. Bronze and iron were introduced into Japan at this time, although the bronze age was short-lived. In the late fourth century, settlements appear to have been conquered by warriors from Puyo; these were semi-nomadic, horse-riding people displaced from the Manchuria area who gradually had conquered much of the Korean peninsula. Evidence for this is the

sudden appearance of horses and armored warriors, unknown in Japan in the 3rd century, and the commencement of the construction of large tomb mounds in many areas of Japan, a practice previously unknown in Japan but common in Korea.

The native Japanese element probably became dominant around the end of the 6th century and developed into a loosely joined nation governed from Yamato (near present-day Nara). Culture from Korea and China flowed into the country during this time, including Buddhist teachings, the Chinese writing system, and many new arts and crafts. This leads to the dawn of the Nara era (Nara-jidai).

Nara era (600-784)

The most famous organizer of the early Japanese state was Prince Shotoku (shown on the Y10,000 bill). In his lifetime (573-620) he introduced a constitution and concept of the state, promoted Buddhism as a state religion, greatly improved education and culture, and set up an excellent system of state administration. Many temples were built in Nara under his direction. Some still exist, such as Horyuji (Nara). Subsequent rulers continued his program of codification of laws and administration.

This period was the first time that the capital remained in the same location after the death of the ruler. It was a prosperous time, and Nara grew to a large size during this period, much greater than the present city. The Buddhist temples gained so much power and wealth that they were a threat to the ruler, so a later ruler (Kammu) moved the capital to Heiankyo (now Kyoto) in 794 where it remained until 1868.

The first four centuries of Kyoto rule are called the Heian Period (794-1192). The early days were ones of achievement, with cultural delegations from China, conquest of the Ezo (Ainu aboriginal people) in northern Honshu, and syncretion of Buddhist beliefs with those of Shinto to make the former more acceptable by representing Shinto gods as early manifestations of Buddhist incarnations.

During this time the Fujiwara family gained great power, members becoming Prime Minister, regent to the throne, and supreme advisor to the emperor. With their luxurious lifestyle and neglect of administration, corruption grew, civil war broke out between 1156 and 1160, and the Taira family rose to power. In turn, they repeated the luxurious extravagance of their predecessors and were overthrown by the Minamoto (better known as the Genji) in 1185 after a string of battles along the south coast of the country, ending in the battle of Dannoura (Shimonoseki) when the Taira were obliterated. This led to the Kamakura period.

Kamakura era (1192-1333)

The Genji made their government headquarters in Kamakura (near present-day Tokyo) the beginning of military government (bakufu) under a shogun ('generalissimo') which lasted with few breaks until 1868. Military outposts were set up throughout the country with the duties of maintaining order and collecting taxes.

The Minamoto lasted only 27 years, the last one being assassinated, then a Fujiwara was invited from Kyoto to fill the post of shogun, although control remained in the hands of the Hojo family. The imperial capital remained at Kyoto, but the emperor had become a mere figurehead, as he would for most of the period until 1868.

During the Kamakura period the Mongols under Kublai Khan tried in 1174 and 1181 to land at Hakata (northern Kyushu). The first wave was fought off (barely), and defensive walls (traces of which may still be seen near Fukuoka) were built in preparation for the second attempt. The walls helped

somewhat, but a destructive typhoon wrecked the Mongol fleet, decimating its 100,000 warriors. This typhoon was obviously a wind (kaze) sent by the gods (kami), or a kamikaze, a word revived late in WW II when suicidal attacks were made against American ships in a second attempt to save Japan from an invasion.

After the victory over the Mongols, the military could not reward the expectations of its soldiers, and emperor Godaigo took advantage of the unrest to regain power for the imperial throne in his own right.

Muromachi and Azuchi-Momoyama periods (1336-1598)

Godaigo failed to reward his military commanders in proportion to their services, and indulged his courtiers, so forces under the Ashikaga clan drove Godaigo out of Kyoto into the mountains of Yoshino and a new military government was set up in Kyoto (1336) this resulted in two courts for 57 years, after which they joined, with the military government dominant; this was the Kyoto bakufu, which lasted until 1573. The period 1336-1573 is the Muromachi era; the original gold pavilion at Kinkakuji (Kyoto) dates from these times.

The luxury of Kyoto life led to poor administration, heavy taxes, and civil war from 1467 until 1568 when Nobunaga Oda entered Kyoto, but he was assissinated in 1582. The struggle for control of the country was taken over and completed by Hideyoshi Toyotomi. The short period 1573-1598 is the Azuchi-Momoyama era, naed after the castles of Oda and Toyotomi. It is usually called only 'Momoyama'; the name symbolizes a colourful, flamboyant decorative style, quite in contrast with the restrained style that is normally thought of as Japanese. Osaka castle, with its immense foundation stones, dates from this period.

Nagasaki on the southern island of Kyushu; the Portuguese were banned in 1639, and the English and Spanish had been excluded earlier. (The early days of the Tokugawa era are the period fictionalized in the novel *Shogun*; the caracter 'Anjin' was patterned on an actual shipwrecked pilot, Will Adams.)

The following two centuries or so saw a Japan sealed as completely as possible from contact with the outside world. Japanese who left and returned were executed to prevent the introduction of outside ideas. Society was highly organized, with clearly defined classes (nobility, military, farmers, and merchants) with little mobility between classes. Interestingly, the merchants were the lowest class. Incredibly detailed laws decreed every aspect of life, such as the type of clothing that might be worn, the kind of food one was allowed, place of residence, movement, even the position in which one might sleep! Orders of the military leaders were to be obeyed instantly; hesitation or expression of displeasure or question was likely to result in instant death. (This historic fact might give some explanation for the tendency to this day to show relatively little expression and to follow orders without much question.)

The isolation was brought to an end with the arrival of the Black Ships of Commodore Perry (US Navy) in 1853 with a demand that Japan open its doors to trade. Yokohoma and other ports were opened with a few years. The entry of the foreign barbarians was not universally welcomed, and the Choshu clan controlling Shimonoseki shelled ships passing through Shimonoseki Strait, then closed it, resulting in a three-day bombardment and the destruction of the shore installations by British, American, French and Dutch ships in 1864. The Choshu realized that the country had to be modernized to overcome Japan's powerless position.

Emperor Meiji had begun his reign in

Edo era or Tokugawa era (1603-1867)

The time of Hideyoshi Toyotomi led up to the beginning of the best-known period in Japanese history, the Edo (or Tokugawa) era. Ieyasu Tokugawa succeeded in subduing all rivals. He set up a bakufu (military) government in Edo (now Tokyo); the emperor continued to reside in Kyoto, without power. The country was divided into nearly 270 fiefs, each under a daimyo (feudal lords) who owed their power and allegiance to the shogun, Tokugawa.

During this period contact by European traders and missionaries increased to the point where the government felt the foreign influences (particularly Christianity) to be a theat to the stability of the country. Christianity was suppressed with the martyring of many thousands (especially in Kyushu, the center of Catholicism). Only the Dutch were permitted to trade and only through

1852, but was as powerless as his predecessors in face of the Tokugawa. The Choshu joined with the Satsuma clan of Kagoshima (sothern Kyushu) to press for the end of the Tokugawa government and the restoration of the emperor to full power. In the ensuing period of fighting and confusion the shogun stepped down, and emperor Meiji began his amazing reign in 1868. Fighting by elements loyal to the Tokugawa continued in several parts of the country and had to be put down by force, but eventually the emperor was given full powers; This is called the Meiji Restoration.

The Meiji Era and Later (1868-)

During the Meiji era (1868-1912), Japan went from an isolated feudal agricultural nation to one of the world's most powerful and dynamic countries, with a modern navy and army (that defeated Russia in 1905), a network of railroads, industry of all kinds, and a parliament. Every effort was made to modernize all aspects of Japanese life. This resulted, in some excesses as many relics of the past were intentionally destroyed, including many picturesque castles and traditional objects like bronze lanterns; the collection at the British Museum was rescued from a scrapyard by a ship's captain.

The awakened national spirit and expansion had far-reaching effects beyond the Meiji era (1868-1912), the Taisho era (1912-1926), and well into the present Showa era of Emperor Hirohito. The need for raw materials and markets for the growing industrial machine led to wars with China in 1894 and 1937; the former resulted in the ceding of Taiwan to Japanese control. Korea was invaded in 1910, providing the foundation for national antipathy toward Japan that persists to this day.

The world-wide economic depression of the 1930s gave the military the ability to expand its control over the country, resulting in conquests of many Asian countries and the ultimate disaster of W.W II when Hiroshima and Nagasaki became the only cities ever atom-bombed. This was the first time Japan had been conquered in its recorded history. Occupation by Allied forces (mainly American) followed.

Post-war changes have been dramatic, with rejection of military values to such an extent that the armed forces are still held in low esteem. The right-wing militaristic mentality which promoted State Shinto as a national religion has largely disappeared; a small minority still supports it, and loud-speaker-laden trucks blaring nationalistic music and slogans may be seen and heard on the streets of large cities, but are ignored by the general populace. One look at the immature young men strutting on the truck roofs in their uniforms explains why.

Prior to the war, the emperor had been revered as a living god by State Shinto. After Japan's defeat he renounced any claim to divinity. The present Emperor (Hirohito by name, but rarely referred to in this way by the Japanese) is a frail, bespectacled, kindly-looking old man whose main interest (according to information given out by the Imperial Household Agency) is marine biology about which he is knowledgeable and has written books. One has the impression that his was a passive role during the pre-war period and that the military government carried out their actions in his name but without his active participation. Today he is basically a constitutional monarch, like the monarch of Great Britain. His present role is as symbol of the Japanese state; although he is consulted and advised, he has no actual power in governing the country.

The use of war was renounced in the new constitution, although Japan is allowed a Self-Defence Force, which today is among the world's more powerful armed forces.

The country has an elected democratic government; the Diet has two chambers, the House of Representatives and the House of Councillors. The conservative Liberal-Democratic party has held power for nearly all the postwar period. It is a pro-free enterprise party (though the government gives much financial assistance and 'administrative guidance' to important or new industries), and the country is firmly and reliably in the Western camp.

Interestingly, a peace treaty has never been signed with the USSR, partly because that country opportunistically siezed four islands off Hokkaido that had long been Japanese by joining the war against Japan only a couple of weeks before the end and occupying the islands, even though there had never been any agreement among the Allies for this to happen.

The economic miracle that has taken place in Japan is well known and needs little review. It is incredible to the visitor of today to think that all the major cities (except Kyoto, which was spared because of its historic treasures) lay in ruins 35 years ago, and that the Japanese people were on the edge of starvation for several years after the war. Now the country leads the world in many industries such as cars, steel, quality cameras and electronics

Women were given the vote after the war and their place in society has been greatly elevated, although there is still blatant job discrimination in favour of men, and male salaries are as much as double those of women. Women, by and large, are expected to marry and raise children after a few years of work and forget about any nonsense about careers; most are happy to do as expected, and marriage remains the goal of the vast majority.

RELIGION

Shinto ('Way of the Gods') is the so-called native Japanese religion. It has no fixed ceremonies or scriptures, and is basically an animistic belief largely concerned with obtaining the blessing of the gods for future events. Cerem=onies are held to bless babies, children (Shichigosan festival), weddings, and the start of new enterprises; even large corporations take no chances, and enlist the aid of a Shinto priest. It is not uncommon to see a ceremony of blessing a building site before construction begins. Before the war, Shinto was glorified by the state and was used to add a blessing from the gods to the militaristic line that the government was following. State aid was given to shrines throughout the country. After the war, all such aid was cut, and Shinto reverted to its earlier, simpler form, supported only by donations from the faithful.

Before Shinto existed, there was a shamanistic folk faith similar to that in many other Asian countries. It still exists in isolated parts of Japan, such as Osorezan in the very north of Tohoku, and is known as Minkan-Shinko. When Shinto first was introduced, many existing shamanistic deities were given new Shinto names in a (largely successful) attempt to supplant the older religion by absorbings its gods and ceremonies. (In the same way Christianity absorbed many ancient pagan festivals in Europe.)

Shinto shrines, called 'jinja', 'taisha', or 'jingu', are generally identifiable by a torii gate (two uprights and a double cross-bar). Often there is a thick braided rop made of rice straw suspended between the uprights of the torii; it is a 'shimenawa', and is put up after the harvest season. There are normally carved stone koma-inu (guardian lions or dogs) at the entrance, similar to those seen at Chinese shrines. If portrayed correctly, the mouth of one lion is open, the other closed, symbolizing 'Ah' and 'Um', the sounds of birth and death, the Beginning and the End,

from Hindu mythology. The distance between them is the Path of Life, a reminder to those walking between them of the shortness of their temporal existence. (However, most Japanese are unaware of the significance.)

The shrine building is often very simple, although there are customary design elements with symbolic importance in nearly all. Few shrines approach temples in magnificence.

There is often a rope hanging down from a 'rattle' suspended in the eaves. Worshippers shake it to wake up the gods and get their attention, and then clap their hands and make a prayer. This is almost a reflex action with most Japanese, even those who claim to have no religious faith.

It is common for people to follow both Shinto and Buddhist beliefs without any conflict in their minds, for each covers certain aspects of life not touched by the other. Buddhism, with its many sects and voluminous literature appeals more to the intellectual side of the religious nature, while the simplicity of Shinto makes it instantly accessible to all.

The teachings of Buddha reached in the middle of the sixth century from China. Through the centuries, the original teachings of the Buddha in India had already been modified by the Chinese to suit their temperament and culture, and this derivative form which reached Japan was further moulded, so that foreign Buddhists scarcely recognize the Japanese faith in the form that it has taken. Numerous sects have developed through the centuries, even in recent decades, such as Soka Gakkai.

Most Japanese families have some ties with Buddhism, if no other way than burial by a Buddhist priest on temple grounds. The eldest son of most families is guardian of the family altar, an ornately gilded wooden structure in the house-hold place of honour. In it are tablets with the names of deceased family members. Regular ceremonies honour these ancestors, ceremonies which have led to the mistaken belief that the Japanese actually worship their ancestors. During the annual O-bon season (July or August), it is believed that the souls of the deceased return to visit. It is a happy time with public dancing everywhere in the country.

The greatest manifestation of Buddhist belief is the beautiful temple buildings in Kyoto. The significance of the brilliantly gilded figures, altar fittings, etc, will be lost on those not familiar with Buddhist symbolism, but they can still be appreciated as works of art.

People & Language

THE JAPANESE PEOPLE

The origins of the Japanese people are not known with any certainty. There are elements in the language that hint at a Polynesian/South-East Asian connection in very early times, and it seems only logical to assume that various peoples immigrated across the relatively narrow Japan Sea from the Korean peninsula and Manchuria, from Siberia via Sakhalin Island, and from mainland Asia areas, such as China. There are intriguing bits of evidence like tribes in the northern hills of India with several types of food, like sushi, identitical to that in Japan.

There are many dialects spoken in Japan which were originally different languages. It can be proposed that the dialects developed by parallel immigration of numerous ethnic groups with their own language or dialect, each of which had its own rhythm or cadence that was carried over when the vocabularly and grammar of standard Japanese established itself throughout the country (in the same way that numerious British accents developed).

The people of one region often look quite different from inhabitants of another region; Kyushu people would not be mistaken for Tohoku people, for example. Although foreign visitors cannot identify accents they can notice the great variety of facial features around the country.

Many Japanese like to consider themselves as a unique race, different from other Asians, but the fact is that there can be no such thing as an identifiable Japanese race. They have a national culture, but the present inhabitants of the Japanese islands are a mixture of many peoples of Asian origin. In their physical appearances many Japanese are clearly identifiable as such, but as much as 30-50% of the population could be dropped into another country of the region, and would be indistinguishable from the local population. In appearance not only do features differ from person to person and from region to region (for example, some have narrow eyes, while others are almost as round-eyed as Westerners but there is also a large variety of skin colouring, from as dark as Indonesians to whiter than a pale European. However, the Japanese do not remark on these differences much because they all want to believe that they are of the same race, for belonging to the group is very important to individual Japanese.

In addition to the 'mainstream' Japanese, there are also minority peoples. The Ainu (pronounced 'eye-noo') are now found only in Hokkaido though once they lived as far south as about 100 km north of Tokyo. Formerly a hunting and fishing people with an animistic culture, their way of life was destroyed through the centuries by the ethnic Japanese, and they now live much like other Japanese. No one knows the origins of the Ainu; their language seems unrelated to any other in the world, although native Siberian tribes have a similar bear cult. They are also said to be the most hirsute people on earth. Other lesser-known races or ethnic groups, each of only small numbers (Oroke, Gilyak, etc) are also found on Hokkaido.

Within Japanese there is a group who are ethnically Japanese but who, for some reason in history, were made outcasts and have been treated as such ever since. They were formerly called 'eta', and are now 'burakumin' ('village people'). The government is taking steps to improve their lot in life, but most families of mainstream Japanese refuse to let their children marry one; prior to a marriage it is standard procedure to check the background of the other family.

Part of the belief still held regarding the 'uniqueness' of of the Japanese is a legacy of pre-WW II government promotion of Shinto when myths regarding the origins of the Japanese, eg that they were descendants of the Sun Goddess Amaterasu-Omikami, were actually taught in schools. The purpose was to instil a feeling of nationalism. Japanese were encouraged to feel superior to, and separate from, other peoples; this served the ends of the militarists who were pushing Japan into conquest of other Asian countries.

Enough of the past. Japanese today of course have the same human feelings, desires, and many of the same problems and worries as those in other countries. At work and in other formal situations they may seem a stolid people with little spontaneity, personality, 'spark', or dynamism. (Various explanations can be offered for this reticent behaviour: that it has long been a virtue in Japanese society to be self-effacing and stoic, or that in the Tokugawa days, if one questioned an order or even showed hesitation in obeying, it could be grounds for death on the spot.) In contrast, Japanese (men especially) become boisterous when drinking and let this facade slip, for this is the only time when they may voice their honest opinions without fear of retribution.

Although Japanese generally regard themselves as superior to all other peoples, they are extremely kind to foreigners of European extraction; far more so than they are to other Japanese, to non-Japanese Asians or to non-white races, such as Africans. On the other hand some newspapers and magazines, and many films present a distorted view of foreigners, especially regarding Westerners' sexual habits.

Foreigners have a curiosity value to most Japanese. At popular tourist destinations, many Japanese (especially children on a school excursion) seem very outgoing and may even want autographs. They have probably never had the opportunity to see or talk to anyone from another country and they are just curious. Keep this in mind if bombarded with a constant chorus of 'Aro' ('Hello') and try to keep smiling: Foreigners are frequently referred to as 'gaijin'. This, is generally said in complete innocence, and is not meant to be offensive. This is another example of the Japanese tendency to divide everything into 'us' and 'them'. The 'us' can be a family, a school, a company or a department. The 'out' group is 'gai', so a foreign person is a 'gai-jin', an 'outside person'. It can be presumed that white foreigners receive their exalted status because during the Meiji era Japan received nearly all its knowledge from European people (including Americans). Also it was European people who defeated the Japanese during the Pacific War; the Japanese respect a winner.

(The self-indulgent, selfish side of the Japanese nature is recognized by the Japanese themselves; in one survey, they chose it as one category defining their nation, so it is no insult to mention it here. It is apparently an extension of the 'us' and 'them' mentality; everyone looks after one's own group and has little or no concern for others.)

Behaviour in Japan is mainly situational, not determined by a universally acknowledged set of standards. Whereas the average Westerner is generally guided by Judeo-Christian ethnic values of correct behaviour (reflected in 'common courtesy'), such over-riding principles do not exist in Japanese society. One knows how to behave in this or that situation, with people of higher, equal or lower rank, but there is no overall governing principle of doing 'right' on principle. One aspect of this is the exchange of meishi, (business cards) so that each person knows where he stands in relation to the other and can choose his behaviour and language accordingly, for there are completely different verbs for use with people of different status. This seeking of information about another person is a possible explanation for the usual litany of questions that a foreigner tends to be asked on first meeting a Japanese, especially one with a limited knowledge of English. Japanese is not unique, but the way, in having multiple levels of politeness in the language; Korean has even more, and the language of Sunda (Indonesia) has a similar structure of formality.

One of the great achievements of Japanese society is the ability of large numbers of people to live in crowded conditions in peace with each other. Japan is certainly one of the safest countries in the world to live in, and violence is quite uncommon, particularly in comparison with the USA. Japanese society is a system of interlocking obligations, conditioned social reflexes, and formalized responses. This causes a lack of spontaneity, but it provides a lubricant for social interactions to avoid interpersonal frictions. It is rare for Japanese to quarrel (outside the family); even if two people dislike each other, the facade is usually maintained with formally correct ways of speaking so that they can get on with their work or their lives with a minimum of unpleasantness. One of the products of this formality is the 'Japanese smile' that can hide all real thoughts.

Despite the generally peaceable nature of most Japanese, there exists the potential for violence. In the past decade student politics has flared up with occasional violence, mostly limited to radical leftist factions. However, the average Japanese remains an easy-going and relaxed person and not fanatical about anything, just a hard worker who looks forward to moving up the promotional ladder. (Even most student radicals appear to shed their views like a dirty shirt when they graduate and

join a company to become a typical salaryman.)

One of the myths about Japanese behaviour that should be permanently laid to rest is their 'politeness'. As anyone who has travelled by commuter train can aver, the Japanese are not an excessively polite people. Any hint of manners vanishes in the attempt to get into or out of the train. The best summation of Japanese 'politeness' is that 'Japanese are only polite with their shoes off', meaning that they are exceedingly polite to people whom they know well enough to be indoors with (where shoes are removed).

Bowing to show respect is largely a conditioned reflex. Mothers push their children's heads down in a bow before they can even talk. The depth of the bow is more a measure of the rank or business importance of the recipient than a genuine measure of the bower's esteem. Advice to foreigners when respect is called for is to incline the head in a semi-bow, use normal Western courtesy, and don't try to shake hands unless the Japanese person offers a hand first, for they are generally not accustomed to the habit.

In homes, one usually sits on the floor, an uncomfortable position to foreigners for extended periods. Try to keep your legs under you as long as possible; if it is necessary to stretch out, avoid pointing feet at anyone (very rude). Most Japanese will realize that foreigners become uncomfortable and will make allowances for deviation from ideal Japanese manners.

An oft-heard cliche about the Japanese is their 'oneness with nature'. For the most part they (as a group) have no more appreciation of nature than any Westerner. The average Japanese thoughtlessly drops cigarette packets, bottles and cans wherever he happens to be. A depressing number of gardens and other places that should be oases of beauty and tranquility for nature lovers have loudspeaker systems, or else visitors bring portable tape-players. These can destroy any possibility of developing the contemplative mood intended when the structure was built.

The Japanese are also the worst offenders against the endangered species of the world. Pelts of rare animals are imported without a qualm, and ivory is easily available, whereas countries like Canada have virtually banned its import. Japan is among the last countries to hunt whales on a large scale, defending the practice on the specious grounds that it is a needed source of protein and that many people would lose their jobs if it were abolished.

Although, there are many Japanese who practise ikebana (flower arrangement), enjoy the singing of crickets, and refine their mind through the tea ceremony, there is so much publicity stressing these aspects that you can get the impression that everyone is adept in these arts, which isn't true. The average Japanese is probably little more refined than a Western counterpart, and Westerners should avoid coming to Japan with a 'cultural cringe'; there is much to be admired, and there are many things that Westerners can learn from Japan, but it is important to maintain objectivity.

MEETING THE JAPANESE

It is unfortunate that most visitors to a foreign country such as Japan have little opportunity to meet the people who live there. They are always on the move, and there is often the language barrier. Yet it is only through such contact, of course, that a visitor has a chance to learn of their daily life, work, pleasures and problems. Leaving Japan without meeting any of its people, other than hotel employees, etc., is like wearing earplugs to Carnegie Hall or a blindfold to the Louvre. Because of the

education system inflicted on the Japanese (they study only to pass exams, not to learn), most of them have little ability to speak English despite untold hours of instruction at school. The emphasis is all on written, not spoken, work with effect that contact with most people in Japan can be difficult.

There are, however, a variety of programs aimed at introducing visitors to Japanese who do speak foreign languages. Because English is the most widely spoken language in the world it is the one that most Japanese learn. (This is a source of annoyance for many Europeans who encounter Japanese who think that everyone with 'white' skin speaks English.) Through several independent programs in operation around the country, you can visit a Japanese home for a couple of hours in the evening, meet Japanese people who are willing to act as a guide and escort at no charge, attend a wide variety of parties, excursions and cultural activities with Japanese people, simply chat over a cup of coffee in pleasant surroundings, or even stay with Japanese families in their homes around Japan, at no charge.

Home Visit System

The Home Visit Program System is a voluntary program through which Japanese families in several cities receive foreign visitors into their homes. The System is 'semi-official' in that it is publicized in a brochure issued by the semi-government Japan National Tourist Organization (JNTO). Visits are normally arranged for a couple of hours in the evening. Food is not served, but green tea and sweets will usually be part of the evening. Hosts will show guests around the house, if desired, perhaps showing the finer points of Japanese house design (if it is not a modern western type!) and the garden, if there is space for one; Japanese houses are usually rather small. The homes open under this program are often those of well-to-do Japanese so they will tend to be more spacious and elegant than average. The Japanese usually do not receive guests at home because they consider their houses too small and humble.

There is no charge for a visit. It is customary among Japanese to take a small gift to the host or hostess whenever visiting, even among close friends. Flowers, fruit or candy are suggestions. The Japanese participate in the program just for the pleasure it gives the guests and the international contact it gives them.

The program is operating in Tokyo, Yokohama, Nagoya, Kyoto, Otsu (near Kyoto), Osaka, Kobe and Kagoshima. Details about arranging visits are given later in the book in the section covering each city. If possible, obtain a copy of the JNTO publication 'Home Visit System' which contains more information and useful tips. Most hosts speak English but in each city there are some who speak other languages.

Tescort

In the cities of Tokyo, Yokohama, Kamakura, Kyoto, Osaka, Nara and Kobe, members of the volunteer organization Tescort are willing to escort visitors at no charge. They will act as guides, assist with shopping, and generally assist visitors while in their area. The members of Tescort have studied English with the Teijin Education System, a company that produces language tapes; they are happy to act as guides because they have difficulty otherwise coming in contact with English native speakers. Before being put on the roster of volunteers, they are interviewed to ensure that their level of proficiency is sufficient that they will do their best to help as they can. The Tescort office generally introduces male Japanese to male foreigners; there have been unpleasant incidents in the past

with men using the program as a dating or escort service.

The Japanese who act as guides foot their own bills for transport, — food, admittance charges, etc., so visitors should not expect them to go to expensive places. However, some Tescort guides are quite willing to spend a fair amount of money on entertainment (it is very common in Japan), so by prior arrangement this could be the ideal way to go to a better traditional Japanese restaurant or night club and be sure of seeing life as the Japanese see it. It is also an excellent way to go into little intimate bars and clubs that ordinary Japanese frequent but which most foreigners never get to see. Visitors who volunteer to assist with their companion's expenses might find this a good way to enter some of the more interesting and risque forms of evening entertainment — there are many strange and unusual clubs in Tokyo and the other big cities. Also, Tescort people, either singly or in couples might be interested in a weekend trip to a nearby resort or other place of interest to visitors; if they wished to make such a trip, they would pay their own expenses.

There are about 50 volunteers in both Tokyo and Osaka, and lesser numbers elsewhere. For arrangements in the general Tokyo area, contact Mr Araki, tel (03) 478-6577; the Osaka area, call Mr Kira, (06) 445-6116; and around Nagoya, Mr Okuzawa, (052) 581-1872. Usually there are guides who can accompany visitors during the day as well as at night and on weekends; in Nagoya guides are free only on weekends.

Clubs and Organizations

There are several clubs and organizations, primarily in Tokyo, where visitors can meet Japanese people who speak English or other foreign languages while participating in a variety of activities, like parties, studying various traditional Japanese arts and culture, or just getting together for a few hours and talking over a cup of coffee. Most of these activities are best suited to people who will be staying in Japan for several weeks or longer, but there are occasions several times a week when a visitor can just drop in and find someone to chat with. Usually these are local organizations, so they are described separately in the sections on Tokyo, Nagoya and Kobe.

One organization, with operations in more than one city, is the 'parent' of Tescort, called Tesco-ESS. It is a club of foreign residents of Japan and Japanese who have studied English with the Teijin Educational System. It organizes trips to temples, resorts, festivals, etc. every month, and tries to introduce foreigners to traditional Japanese arts, culture, folkways and other aspects of the country. The Japanese members have the opportunity to meet and talk with foreigners, practise their English and learn about foreign culture and customs. Most Tesco-ESS activities are organized in the Tokyo area, but there are some in Osaka, Nagoya and other places. To join, there is a once-only fee of Y1000; after that the only charges are those for individual events, excursions, etc. In Tokyo, tel (03) 404-7003; in Osaka, (06) 445-6111.

Servas

Any one who really wants to get to know the Japanese more than superficially should look into the international organization Servas. If accepted as members of Servas, travellers may stay at the homes of Japanese families in many parts of Japan, both rural and urban, for up to 3 days at no charge, sharing the family's home and life. Anyone looking for a free ride should read no further. Servas travellers staying with Japanese families are expected to spend much of their time talking with their host and otherwise participating in their lives. Only people who have a sincere interest in learning about Japanese family life and exchanging views and experiences would be interested.

Servas was founded in 1948 as a private venture in international relations. Reasoning that person-to-person contact by people from countries around the world is a worthwhile goal, a network of volunteer hosts was put together. In addition to Japan, there are hosts in at least 70 other countries. If it is possible, travelling members are expected to act as hosts on their return to a settled life, although this is not compulsory. Many hosts have never travelled themselves, but open their doors to travellers as their contribution to world understanding and as a way to bring a little of the outside world to them.

It is preferable to join Servas in your home country. Joining requires filling out an application form and appearing for a personal interview in order to ensure that the applicant is sincere in his interest in Servas and its ideals. Regional staff are voluntary, but there are staff and administrative expenses at the local, national and international level; for this reason a contribution of about US$30 (it varies from country to country (is required. For the address of the national offices in your country, write to the international president, Mr Graham Thomas, Servas International Peace Secretary, 80 Bushwood, London E11; send an international reply coupon (or stamps if in the UK). If it is impossible to join Servas before reaching Japan, write as early as possible to Mr Masuo Amano, 21-22 6-chome, Todoroki, Setagaya-ku, Tokyo 158, giving the estimated date of arrival and port of entry, and stating that you would like to participate in the Servas program. If you are accepted there is a joining fee of Y5000.

Communes

Few outsiders are aware of the existence

of several communes in Japan. They have a long history; Itto-en commune in the Kansai area (near Kyoto) dates back to 1905. Travellers interested in communes should write to:

Kibbutz Akan
Shin Shizen Noen
Nakasetsuri
Tsurui-mura
Akan-gun
Hokkaido
Japan

The have published a 230-page book 'Communes of Japan', listed at Y1000. They also issue the 'Journal of the Commune Movement' every month or two. Copies (not free) can be obtained from the above address.

If you have just arrived in Japan and haven't time to correspond with Kibbutz Akan, you could try a phone call to Itto-en Commune, (075) 581-3136. They should be able to give information on the movement and other communes around the country.

Teaching

One of the best ways to meet a cross-section of Japanese people is by teaching English. The system of teaching English in schools is so poor in Japan that private schools are necessary to provide an opportunity to learn from native speakers. Teaching without a proper visa is not legal, of course, but it seems that the Immigration office does not waste too much of its time tracking down illicit teachers.

The only problem with teaching is that you may get any level of student, with beginners who have enough trouble putting five words together correctly, without trying to carry on conversations about Japanese society and culture. However, in free conversation classes with advanced students it is possible to learn a great deal about Japan that

doesn't appear in books. It is interesting that Japanese people will express very open and candid opinions in English (or another foreign language) that will not say in Japanese; there are many constraints on behaviour in Japanese society which are reinforced by the very structure of the language. One also has an opportunity to experience every type of personality, from very open (and contrary to stereotyped image of the Japanese) to girls who are so painfully shy that they refuse to answer questions for fear of making a mistake.

And finally . . . . .

For a different type of socializing, couples visiting Japan have the opportunity to get to know a Japanese couple very intimately, one to one, so to speak, by swinging which has finally reached Japan. There is a magazine which, although it is nearly all in Japanese, has many photos sent in by advertisers who are looking for other couples. The magazine costs Y1500 but it is not necessary to purchase a copy to place an ad. Each month there are usually several couples who would like especially to swing with a western couple, so placing an advertisement should receive replies. There is no charge for placing an ad, and it may be written in English. A photo is not required, but a reply would be more likely if one were included. Advertisers are not named, but are given a code number to which others reply c/o the magazine. Because of the lead times of the publishing business and the time required for mail, anyone interested in this type of cultural exchange program should contact the magazine at least three months before going to Japan.

Single women would almost certainly receive many replies from couples or single men and a single man might hear back, but couples are the most welcome partners.

To write to the magazine, the address is:

SES Inc.
PO Box 641
Shinjuku
Tokyo 160-91

MEN & WOMEN

One of the characteristics of the upbringing of Japanese women is subordination to males, beginning with her brothers. In a relationship, she generally looks after her man. (To may western men first exposed to this coddling it seems like paradise arrived, and many are quite happy with this level of relationship.) Conversely, Japanese males tend to be spoiled from childhood so the result is that Japanese men and western women tend not to be very compatible. This is reflected by the ratio of only one marriage of a Japanese male to a western female to every ten of Japanese women to western men.)

For some Japanese men, there is a prestige in dating a western woman. While this is not the general rule, some foreign women do wonder if they are being asked out for their company or for the prestige they bring. Incidentally, many Japanese men have a very distorted view of western women, especially their moral standards, and expect them to leap into bed with any man. Any woman who suspects this attitude in her Japanese friend, and wishes to dispel it, should easily be able to give a suitable hint in conversation.

Western men looking for the companionship of Japanese women will probably find that the best prospects are well-educated who have studied English. Quite apart from the obvious advantage in communicating with each other, they usually behave more like western women in showing maturity, and are more likely to be interesting people to talk to. Although they are still likely to be shy compared with western women, they usually become much less so after a couple of meetings, especially in private, and may show an openness that she wouldn't show with Japanese in public, though. The average woman is reluctant to show affection or emotional involvement. Many will not even hold hands in public with a foreigner, as some people would assume from this that she is sleeping with him.

Despite the shy demeanour, Japanese women (according to one survey) are less puritanical about sex than women in most other countries. If they care for a man, they consider sex a normal part of the relationship. Although it seems that sex is generally reserved for only one man at a time, a recent trend (according to another survey) is for some office ladies to go to an athletic club on Friday evening for exercise, sauna and shower, they go out for a drink and to find a male partner for the rest of the evening's activities at a hotel; the term for this is 'full course'. Western men interesting in joining in this activity should note that most such ladies speak only a few words of English. Still, you could have a lot of fun with a dictionary or a phrase book.

Many Japanese women would like to meet a western man, either just for friendship, or for a liaison of some sort, perhaps just out of curiosity. (It has happened that a man walking down the street has been stopped by a women and asked to go with her to a 'love hotel' simply because she was curious what a western man was like.) How a man should act with a Japanese women depends very much on the individuals, as it does in any country.

There are various ways to meet Japanese of the opposite sex. In Tokyo, there are several social clubs and coffee shops where people go to chat in English. (See also the 'Meeting the Japanese' section.) There are several places in cities where people gather for drinks and conversation; in Tokyo, Berni Inn, Henry Africa and Charleston are examples. There are also many discos in the large cities; the Roppongi area of Tokyo has several. They are not cheap generally Y3000-4000 entrance charge, which includes some drinks and eats. Their main drawback as meeting places is that the sound levels are so high that it is impossible to talk; many discos and clubs only admit couples.

After meeting a suitably charming young woman (or man) there comes the matter of future meetings. Some families are open-minded and have no objections if their daughter has an 'appointment' (or date) with a foreigner, but others (especially the wealthy and upper-class families) object strongly.

Japanese people in general, by the way, have a reputation for lack of punctuality in keeping 'appointments'. Another incidental bit of information concerns twosomes. There is the distinct possibility that a girl who meets a man casually will keep a second date, but will show up with a girfriend in tow. On further meetings she may appear alone once she knows that there is no danger; Others will continue to show up accompanied.

Couples in Japan who want privacy but have no place of their own to go to be alone have a great range of facilities. Many coffee shops have inky-dark rooms (often downstairs) with two-people booths, high partitions between booths, and discreet waiters. These offer a modicum of privacy for nothing more than the cost of the coffee, and reportedly quite amazing activities have been carried out in the cramped quarters. The next step up the ladder is also a type of coffee shop, but it has individual rooms with a couch and table in each and a door (unlocked). For a moderate fee, couples can stay until 5 am, and the table can be moved to block the door. Beyond this comes the love hotel (about which more is written in the Accommodation section).

Marriage

Marriages in Japan result from love matches, where the couple have met by chance or informally through friends, or from formal arranged introductions, called 'omi-ai'. (Few, if any, result from families getting together and deciding the fate of their children as happens in other societies.)

Formal introductions may occasionally be seen in coffee shops or similar surroundings. The man and woman and their families sit on opposite sides of a table and attempt to make conversation, after which the two have a chance to meet without the onlookers. If they think there might be the basis for a marriage, they arrange to meet again. They soon decide if there is promise in continuing or if they should forget the idea and start over with someone else. Many people have ten or more such introductions. The go-between may be a professional (nakodo), or a maiden aunt or someone else with extra time and many friends. Some Japanese women may begin to get a bit frantic after 26 and put their names before more and more remote acquaintances. Marriages resulting through arranged introductions appear to be as stable and lasting as love matches.

To westerners the reasons for getting married in Japan sometimes seem rather trivial or shallow, more financial than romantic, somewhat akin to arranging a corporate merger than linking two lives. Many couples seem content with an arrangement whereby the husband brings in an income and the wife tends the house, bears and rears the children, with apparently little affection between the couple. In some cases this may be accurate, and in others the couple are not demonstrative but have developed an affection through the years. In most households, the husband dutifully hands over his entire pay packet and is doled out an allowance. Any westerner considering marriage to a Japanese woman should take note of this.

Foreign men and women marrying Japanese are affected differently by Japanese law. When two Japanese marry, the wife's name is removed from her family's register and transferred to that of her husband's family. Because registry is tantamount to Japanese citizenship, foreign spouses may not be put in family registers. Foreign wives may remain in Japan as long as her husband resides there and sends a letter to Immigration authorities whenever her period of stay is due for renewal stating that he wants her to remain. Foreign husbands have no right of residence just because they are married to a Japanese woman. By Japanese law, a wife is expected to reside in her husband's country. A foreign man must have an independent reason for remaining in Japan (work, study, etc, with appropriate visa), or else can be deported with his children, who must take on his nationality by Japanese law. This unequal treatment is in conflict with a constitutional provision of sexual equality and is currently under legal challenge.

Children of mixed marriages often have a difficult time in Japan because their foreign blood sets them apart from the rest of the population in a society which values sameness and uniformity. They may also have difficulty deciding to which society they belong, Japanese or foreign; it is a problem trying to be both, and such children often fail to fit in completely with either, not learning either language perfectly.

Unlike in nearby Korea, it is most unlikely that any Japanese girl would be trying to find a way out of the country by marrying a foreigner, so it isn't necessary to try to figure if the girl's affection is genuine or feigned only to catch a husband. However, one should give careful thought as to how well she would fit in back home.

Sex

Prostitution was declared illegal in 1947. The former red-light districts are no longer official red-light districts but after a history of hundreds of years brothels have just taken a different form. Today, a man with the yen for such things can have his desires accommodated in Toruko (mispronounced 'Turk' of 'Turkish baths'), in a 'Pink Saron', or by negotiating with an obliging hostess at a bar or club.

Although most such establishments are intended for men, there are clubs for women where handsome young men give them total attention and offer similar services. However, they are reportedly equally expensive. (For men contemplating this sort of work the ability to speak good Japanese is a prerequisite.)

For those so inclined, there are hundreds of gay bars in areas like Shinjuku (Tokyo) and in other large cities. There is considerable prestige in having a western boyfriend, so a welcome is assured.

Note: None of this section is intended for encouragement, only for advice. Many clubs (and their female employees) are under control of gangsters. Foreigners with little knowledge of the language are very susceptible to being suckered into exorbitant bills for which payment is extorted by violence if necessary. Any club where large numbers of girls are available is not going to be cheap; even quite legitimate places can be exorbitantly expensive.

Toruko

While a few bathhouses offer legitimate bathing, massage, etc, as the name implies, the majority are designed primarily to satisfy needs deeper than outward cleanliness. Commonly the 'attendant' soaps all of her customer's body, a recent innovation being to apply the soap by first lathering her own nude body and then transferring it to his by acting as a human sponge.

The best-known Toruko areas in Japan are Chiba and Kawasaki (near Tokyo), Gifu (near Nagoya), and Ogoto (on the western shore of Biwa-ko lake, in the Kyoto/Osaka area). Toruko are found throughout the country. They are not, by the way to be confused with sento (local public baths) or onsen (hotspring resorts), although the latter are also noted for catering to male needs or desires. Toruko are for the well-heeled, and can cost up to Y30,000 for high-class services. The help of a Japanese would be almost essential for finding one and obtaining admittance, for foreigners are often unwelcome at such facilities, largely because of the language problem that can give rise to many difficulties and arguments about charges.

Pink Saron

Obviously this is a mispronunciation of 'Pink Salon'. These are bars with hostesses. There is a flat fee for drinks and nibbles (say Y3000), but the tender ministratations of the hostess can become a lot more personal if extra money changes hands. This can run the gamut from a lapful of underwearless hostess unresistant to wandering hands, to 'relief massage' by hand or mouth, or more.

Pink Sarons are plentiful in large cities and elsewhere, usually near large railway stations and indentifiable by garish pink signs and touts standing outside. The interior is very dark to give the hostesses some privacy for their work. Although the touted price is in the Y3000 range, the full treatment will run considerably higher, generally Y8000-10,000.

Hostesses

Hostesses in bars and clubs are there to please their male customers by boosting their frail egos with flattery and flirtation. Although there are bars were the girls merely sit opposite their customers and do nothing more than pour drinks and make conversation, more usually the girls allow the customer to become more physical in the premises and can often be induced to accompany him afterward. It is frequently necessary to pay the establishment a 'ransom' if leaving with a hostess before closing time.

Live sex shows

An amusement that has become popular in recent years at hotspring resort towns, but which may also be found in the larger cities, is live sex shows. A couple performs on stage before the delighted audience. In some cases members of the audience are invited to strip off and join in. As one newspaper expressed it, for the man who is able to function before a crowd, there no cheaper way in Japan to get some action.

Because women of European origin are greatly preferred as partners for such shows, there is sure employment for anyone wishing to partake. Arrest and deportation is a risk of the business, but it seems that the police don't go far out of their way to stamp out such activities.

LANGUAGE

It is very useful to take a course in Japanese before travelling extensively in Japan as few people outside major cities can speak any English, and they never seem to be around when needed. However, even students with a year of Japanese under their belts will probably find that they understand very little of what is said as most language courses seem to have little relationship to the spoken language. When studying, concentrate on the plain or informal forms of verbs; the formal or '-imasu' and '-imashita' forms are seldom unded among people in normal conversation.

There are dialects in various parts of the country. Japanese taught in language courses in normally the Tokyo dialect (Tokyo-ben) which is considered to be the 'standard' dialect; it is taught in the nation's schools and is used on national TV. It will be of negligible use in understanding people in some rural areas such as those who speak Tohoku-ben (northern Honshu) or Kagoshima-ben (southern Kyushu). People of these areas find each other totally incomprehensible, and inhabitants of Tokyo or Kyoto find it equally difficult.

Much is made of the supposed vagueness of Japanese. However, it is not the language itself that is vague but rather the way it is used. Japanese can be spoken just as precisely as English, but to do so would often be considered impolite; the correct thing to do is to speak in circumlocutions and avoid making direct statements of fact that would imply that the speaker has superior knowledge. Actual meanings are traditionally conveyed as much by gestures and tone of voice as by the words themselves although young Japanese are growing up without learning this older system of unspoken communication.

Certainly the language is not simple because of the multitude of verb forms and the many words needed to indicate social distinctions, but it is not difficult to learn a major proportion, perhaps 70%, of the language in romaji (the romanized form). One must learn the written form for the rest because each character (kanji) has at least two pronunciations, *on* (Chinese) and *kun* (Japanese). These multiple readings for kanji cause much difficulty for travellers because names (especially place names) have many ways of being pronounced. As much as possible the correct local pronunciations of place names are used in this book; these may occasionally differ from names in literature printed in Tokyo as these may use Tokyo readings of the kanji. Place names in

Hokkaido are the worst example of this. It all sounds silly but it's true; the average Japanese cannot pronounce the names of a large number of names on a road map.

Important words are written in kanji (Chinese characters) while grammatical endings are written in hiragana, a syllabary of all the vowel and consonant-plus-vowel sound combinations in the language. Yet another complete syllabary is used to transliterate foreign words. Unfortunately they use this method for writing English and so many learn incorrect pronunciations since the syllabary is deficient in l, f and some other letters.

The most valuable basic phrasebook is the *Tourist's Handbook*, available free from the Tourist Information Centres in Tokyo and Kyoto. It has the most often asked questions and a series of answers in both languages, so a Japanese person can point to the correct answer.

If you want to learn the rudiments of the language, one of the best books is *Japanese Made Easy* by Monane, published by Tuttle. For a comprehensive study of Japanese, *Beginning Japanese* by Jorden can be recommended. It is published by Yale University Press.

A few basic phrases are listed on the following pages.

Communicating with Japanese

Except with Japanese who have really mastered English, usually by living overseas, there will be problems with many questions requiring a 'yes' or 'no' answer. In Japanese a 'yes' answer will mean 'Yes, what you say is true', so it is essential to avoid asking negative questions, like 'Aren't you going?' A Japanese will answer 'yes' if he is *not* going, 'no' if he *is* going. It takes a while to get into the habit of asking unambiguous questions.

Another problem is an 'or' question. Even though Japanese has an exact equivalent, they seem to have insuper-

Continued on page 74.

PHRASE LIST
The following phrases may prove useful in daily travels. They are intended for survival, not as a language course. Therefore they are simplified and in some cases barely grammatical, but should be understandable.

yes	*hai; ee*
no	*ie; chigau* (different); *nai/nai des'* (not/ it is not). All mean 'no' but most books only give *ie;* it is too abrupt and rude for use with friends (except as in 'No, you can't pay for this.') The other two forms are heard more often.
how much?	*i'kura?*
how many?	*ikutsu?*
where? (is)	*doko? (des'ka)*
when?	*itsu?*
which one/way?	*dochira?*
where is xxx?	*xxx wa, doko des'ka?*
this xxx	*kono xxx*
that xxx (near you)	*sono xxx*
that xxx (over there)	*ano xxx*
this (thing)	*kore*
that (thing, near you)	*sore*
that (thing, yonder)	*are*
here	*koko*
there (near you)	*soko*
there (yonder)	*asoko*
right	*migi*
left	*hidari*
beyond	*saki*
this side of	*temae*
far, beyond	*muko*
in front of	*mae*
next to	*tonari*
straight ahead	*massugu; zuto* (or *zuuuuuuuto* when spoken by country people!)
today	*kyo*
tomorrow	*ash'ta*
day after tomorrow	*asate*

Numbers
For numbers up to 10, the Japanese have one set of words which can be used alone, and another for use only with a 'counter'. A counter is one of many words, depending on the shape or nature of the object. The with-counter numbers are used to make composite numbers above 10, and in expressions of time. There are too many counters to mention here, so use counterless numbers, or write the number down.

The number goes after the word for the things. When requesting something, put 'o' between the word for the object and the number; eg *Kore o futatsu kudasai* ('two of these, please').

	counterless	with-counter
0	*maru; re*	
1	*hitotsu*	*ichi*
2	*futatsu*	*ni*
3	*mitsu*	*san*
4	*yotsu*	*yon, shi (shi* is a homonym of 'death', so is often avoided.)
5	*itsutsu*	*go*
6	*mutsu*	*roku*
7	*nanatsu*	*shichi, nana*
8	*yatsu*	*hachi*
9	*kokonotsu*	*kyu*
10	*to*	*ju*
11		*ju-ichi*
12		*ju-ni*
. . .		. . .
20		*ni-ju*
30		*san-ju*
49		*yon-ju-kyu*
. . .		
100		*hyaku*
200		*ni-hiyaku*
. . .		
1000		*sen*
5000		*go-sen*
10,000		*ichi-man* (Not *ju-sen;* Japanese count by ten-thousands.)
20,000		*ni-man*
25,000		*ni-man-go-sen*
100,000		*ju-man*
1,000,000		*hyaku-man*

Time
'o'clock' (eg one o'clock)	— *ji (ichi-ji)* (Use with-counter numbers for time.)
minute (for telling time)	— *pun*
hour (duration)	— *jikan*
year (date)	— *nen*
year (duration)	— *nenkan*

Continued on page 74

Telephone

hello	moshi moshi (The caller usually says this first.)
may I speak with xxx?	xxx-san onegai shimasu? (-san = Mr, Mrs, Miss, etc)
isn't here	imasen
extension (eg ext'n 153)	naisen (ichi-go-san) ('With-counter' numbers are used here. See below.)

Post Office

post office	yubin kyoku
stamps	kitte
poste restante (general delivery)	kyoku dome yubin; tome oki
registered	kaki tome
special delivery	soku tatsu
air mail	koku bin
sea mail	funa bin
aerogram	koku shokan mise
money order	yubin gawase
stamped post card	yubin hagaki
letter	kozutsumi

Trains

ticket	kipu
one way	katamichi
return	ofuku, shuyuken
express	kyuko
rapid	kaisoku
local	kaku eki teisha
reserved	shite
unreserved	jyuseki
What track for xxx (station)?	xxx (eki) wa, nan ban sen (des'ka)?
next train/electric train	sugi no kisha/densha

basic charge (all trains)	unchin
limited express charge	tokkyu ryokin
green car (reserved) charge	gurin ryokin
excursion ticket	shuyuken

Youth Hostel

(I am a) member	ka-in (des')
membership card	ka-in sha
Are you a member?	Ka-in des'ka?
Do you have a membership card?	Ka-in sha arimas' ka?
Do you want meals?	Shokuji wa?
evening meal	yu gohan
breakfast	asa gohan
Do you have a sleeping sheet?	Shiitsu arimas'la?
I am a member.	Ka-in des.
May I stay?	Tomare mas'ka?
full	Ippai
Is there a room available tomorrow/the day after tomorrow?	Ash'ta/asate heya wa aitemas'ka?

able difficulty recognizing that there is a choice between A and B. The simplest way around the problem is to say 'Is it A? Is it B?', instead of 'Is it A or B?' The latter is almost sure to get 'yes' as the reply.

Generally, direct statements are not made in Japanese. Instead, the speaker alludes to or suggests a fact so as not to appear superior or presumptuous in suggesting that he knows something that the listener doesn't. Women use this suggestive form to a greater extent than men, which makes their statements less forceful or believable than a similar statement by a man. The existence of 'women's language' and 'men's language' is clearly sexist by western thinking, but is an inescapable fact. Its function is partly to keep women in an inferior position; a woman using stronger forms of expression sounds masculine and quite undesirable.

Because of the circumlocutions often required to bypass a direct statement, misunderstandings can easily occur, with the result that the Japanese language is excellent for maintaining social distinctions but poor for imparting information and knowledge. Younger Japanese today tend not to follow the older conventions of speech and are dropping many of the 'formula' phrases, with the result that older people can have difficulty explaining what they want because the younger ones fail to pick up the cues.

It is a surprise that young Japanese do not speak English better than they do. Most of them have an inability to put together more than one or two sentences of correct English. About 300 hours of instruction is given at junior high school level, nearly 500 hours in senior school, and a further 300-600 hours at university is required to become an English teacher.

Unfortunately a very large proportion of teachers at all levels cannot carry on a conversation in English, and have learned English in the same way as they are teaching it, as a field of academic study. Another problem is that English is mostly taught using the Japanese katakana syllabary to represent English sounds, a purpose for which it is entirely inadequate, having no dinstinction between the letters 'r' and 'l', and misrepresenting several other sounds, which explains the frequent interchange of these letters. (Often quoted is the banner strung across the Ginza when General MacArthur was being proposed for US President: 'We play for MacArthur's erection'.)

The Japanese must have a sense of humour. Why else would the car manufacturers choose the names that they do? Nearly every model has a name which Japanese cannot pronounce correctly, with a copious mix of r's and l's, such as 'Gloria', 'Corolla', 'Tercel', or 'Starlet'.

ROMANIZATION

As a (much appreciated) courtesy to visitors to Japan, many signs are written in romaji (Roman letters). As well as names on road signs, some other Japanese words may appear on signs. Unfortunately there may be difficulty in knowing how to pronounce them because there is more than one system of romanization.

The most common is the Hepburn system, devised more than a century ago and still useful as an aid to English speakers in pronouncing Japanese correctly (but it is of negligible use to speakers of other languages). The other systems are useful in formal studies of Japanese but they are not very useful for general applications because first you have to learn the conventions of the system.

The Hepburn system, with few changes, is used throughout this book. Either it or the Ministry of Education system may be seen on signs in Japan, sometimes both in the same sentence.

The following is a list of the major differences between the two systems; the Hepburn is pronounced like normal English:

Hepburn	Min of Education
shi	si
sha	sya
shu	syu
sho	syo
chi	ti
cha	tya
chu	tyu
cho	tyo
tsu	tu
fu	hu
ji	zyi
ja	zya
ju	zyu
jo	zyo

The use of two systems of romanization (both of which Japanese know) leads to mistakes as a result of carelessness or ignorance. One common mistake is interchanging 'a' and 'u' because they sound the same to the Japanese (compare the sounds of the vowels in 'a cup'). Because 'n' and 'm' are also interchangeable, the word 'damper' (meaning shock absorber to British) gets written 'dunper'. Sometimes, also, one sees 'thu' instead of 'tsu' or 'tu'; thith ith a mithtake ath the 'th' thound doethn't exthitht in Japanethe.

Facts for the Visitor

INFORMATION
Japan National Tourist Organization (JNTO)
The best single source of information on Japan is the JNTO. This is a semi-official body set up to distribute tourist information and otherwise encourage travel to Japan.

The JNTO has prepared a large number of excellent pamphlets and other publications that provide a great deal of useful information for travel in Japan. Recently, with the sharp rise in the value of the yen there has been a drop in the number of foreign travellers in Japan, so the JNTO has begun preparing information specifically slanted toward the budget traveller. JNTO publications are available by mail from their many overseas offices. These are listed at the end of this section.)

Within Japan, the JNTO operates three Tourist Information Centres (TICs). Two are located in Tokyo, (in Yurakucho district and at Narita Airport Terminal), and one in Kyoto. (The exact location of each office is described in the section dealing with each place.) In addition to the JNTO publications, the TIC have a large number of typewritten information sheets about various topics such as campgrounds. These can be photocopied for anyone who is interested in a specific subject. Each TIC has an index of sheets available . Staff of the TICs are also goldmines of information.

While TICs can provide information on any aspect of travel in any region of Japan, they do not make bookings or reservations. These services are available at offices of travel agencies. The best known travel agent is the Japan Travel Bureau, another semi-official organization, which has offices in every major city throughout Japan. They also have offices overseas.

Unfortunately these three Tourist Information Centres are the only places in Japan that are equipped to give a full range of travel information in foreign languages. Information offices in other cities are there to provide information on the local area only, and there is usually no one who can speak any language but Japanese.

Publications
The following are useful general information booklets or other publications offered by JNTO/TIC. The number in brackets is the JNTO code number, and the letter is the initial letter of the languages in which it is available: English, French, German, Spanish, Portuguese, Italian and Chinese.

Your Guide to Japan (101-E, F, G, S, P, I, C)
A 24 page booklet containing a wealth of general information about Japan — history, weather, geography, accommodation, transport, culture and the arts, sightseeing; it summarizes the information presented in this guide in much more expanded form.
Japan Traveller's Companion (105-E)
A 24 page booklet containing more specific information than the above publication, with information on transportation, accommodation, sports, embassies.
The Tourist's Handbook
A booklet of useful phrases in an interesting layout that makes communication less of a problem.
Tokyo (222-E, F, G, S, P, C)
Kyoto-Nara (224-E, F, G, S, P)
Nikko (221-E, F, G, S)
Northern Japan (Hokkaido and Tohoku) (211-E)
Fuji-Hakone-Izu (223-E, F, G, S)
Central Japan (Kanto, Chubu, Kinki) (214-E)
Western Japan (Chugoku, Shikoku) (212-E)

Southern Japan (Kyushu, Okinawa) (213-E)

Other JNTO publications on specific topics such as accommodation and transport are listed in the appropriate sections of this book. The JNTO-issued *Tourist Map of Japan* is useful for overall itinerary planning; it also has large scale maps of many cities in Japan.

Other Sources
The commercial publication *Japan Visitor's Guide* has some useful information and maps that may be useful supplements to those mentioned in this guide, but it is best to wait until arrival in Japan before obtaining a copy. It is distributed free at the Tokyo TIC and possibly at other tourist centres.

JNTO offices Overseas

USA	45 Rockefeller Plaza, New York, N.Y. 10020 tel (212) Plaza 7-5640.
	333 North Michigan Ave, Chicago, Ill. 60601. Tel (312) 32-3975.
	1420 Commerce St., Dallas, Texas 75201. tel (214) 741-4931.
	1737 Post St., San Francisco, Calif. 94115. tel (415) 931-0700
	624 South Grand Ave., Los Angeles, Calif. 90017. tel (213) 623-1952.
	2270 Kalakaua Ave., Honolulu, Hawaii 96815. tel (808) 923-7631.
Canada:	165 University Ave, Toronto, Ont. M5H 3B8. tel (416) 366-7140.
England:	167 Regent St, London W. 1. tel 734-9638.
Australia:	115 Pitt St, Sydney, NSW 2000. tel 232-4522.
Hong Kong:	Peter Bldg, 58 Queen's Road, Central. tel 5-227913.
Thailand:	56 Suriwong Road, Bangkok tel 233-5108.
Switzerland:	Rue de Berne 13, Geneve. tel 318140.

Germany: Biebergasse 6-10, 6000 Frankfurt a/M. tel 292792.

BOOKS
The following short list of books can be recommended as an introduction to Japan, the country, people and language, as well as for specialized aspects of travel. There are hundreds of books about Japan available in Japan, and a healthy number in foreign countries; any competent bookstore would list its listings and could order what it didn't stock.

People and Society
The Japanese, Jack Seward (Lotus Press, Tokyo)

More about the Japanese, Jack Seward (Lotus Press, Tokyo)

The Tourist and the Real Japan, Boye de Mente (Charles E Tuttle)

All three books are getting on a bit in years, but nearly all their comments are still valid except for costs and economic commentary.

Japanese Society, Chie Nakane (Penguin Books). Rather turgid and exhaustingly exhaustive at times, it gives a thorough examination of the social structure of Japan.

The Chrysanthemum and the Sword, Ruth Benedict. The 'classic' book on Japanese society; although Japanese thinking has changed somewhat since it was written during WW II, it is still a good guide to what makes Japanese society function.

Japan: The Coming Economic Crisis, Jon Woronoff. An excellent dissection of the Japanese economy, how it works and potential problems; of interest for it looks at Japanese society as much as for its economic analysis.

The Land of the Rising Yen, George Mikes (Penguin Books). Although published in 1970, this book in the inimitable Mikes style gives a witty and perceptive look at the country and people better than any five sociology and history books combined.

History

Japan from Prehistory to Modern Times,
   John Whitney Hall (Charles E Tuttle)
The Japanese, Reischauer

Language Instruction

Japanese Made Easy, T A Monane
   (Charles E Tuttle)
Beginning Japanese (Parts 1 and 2),
   Eleanor Harz Jorden (Yale University Press)
The former is a normal-size paperback
and gives adequate instruction for
basic conversation as used for travel.
The latter is a pair of larger paperbacks and is much more detailed in
vocabulary and explanations of usage,
and thus better suited to a formal
course of study.

Bookshops — Tokyo

Jena Bookstore is one of the major
sellers of English and other foreign-
language books. It is on Harumi-dori,
not far from the Tourist Information
Centre and on the same side, towards
the railway bridge.

Other bookstores with English
language publications are Maruzen department store near Nihonbashi, Yeasu
bookstore near Tkoyo station (Yaesu
side), Kinokuniya bookstore in Shinjuku, Kitazawa and the Tuttle bookstore in Kanda, Books Horindo (and
one other) at Takadanobaba, and some
in the arcade of the Imperial Hotel.

TIME

All of Japan is in the same time zone,
9 hours ahead of GMT. Because of its
eastward position, day begins in Japan
ahead of nearly all major populated
areas except New Zealand and Australia.
Day begins excessively early in summer,
with sunrise 4.30 in mid-summer, and
very short evenings. Japan does not
use Daylight Saving Time.

When it is 12 noon in Tokyo the
time in other places is:

Hong Kong	11 am
London	3 am
America, east coast	10 pm*
America, west coast	7 pm*
Hawaii, Alaska	5 pm*
Sydney, Melbourne	1 pm
New Zealand	3 pm

(* previous day)

The 24-hour system is used for
writing nearly all times in Japan, whether
railway timetables, or notices in restaurant windows. To convert a time later
than 1300 (1 pm) to the 12-hour
system, simply subtract 1200; thus
1730 hours is the same as 5.30 pm. For
am times no arithmetic is necessary:
0900 simply means 9 am. The system
is more convenient than having to write
am and pm continually.

HEALTH

Food and water

It is very unlikely that anyone will
become ill in Japan as the result of eating or drinking. Food sold is of high
standard, and tap water can be drunk
anywhere in the country. The digestive
troubles that one expects in most of
Asia are virtually unknown. Food from
mobile stalls, often seen at night near
railway stations, is safe to eat. (A
murder case in 1978 made headline
news when the hands of the victim were
cut off and boiled for a day in the
cooking pot of one of the mobile stalls
in an effort to destroy the fingerprints.
Customers apparently noticed no difference in flavour. This sort of thing is
rare.)

Medical

The standards of health care in Japan
are good, as reflected in the life expectancy of about 73 years for men and 78
for women (1972 figures), both the
highest in the world. Medical personnel
are generally trained to high standards
and many Japanese doctors would rate

highly in any country. Likewise, there are many good hopitals with up-to-date equipment and facilities.

The other side of the coin is that Japan has its full share of quacks and unqualified practitioners who, if they got through medical school at all, it was more through money and influence than by merit. (A case came to light in 1980 of a non-doctor owner of a hospital who had ordered numerous hysterectomies based on his improper and unqualified use of a diagnostic instrument.) Thus, if any serious procedure, like an operation, is suggested, be sure to get a second opinion even if the first doctor complains about losing face. Better his face than your health and wealth.

Hospital charges tend to be very high, and there is the occasional tendency to keep patients longer than necessary in order to increase the income, especially at hospitals that are privately owned by doctors. There are several hospitals (especially in large cities) that were founded by various Christian groups: their approach to medical care would be most familiar to Westerners, and anyone needing hospital care should try to contact them. Also in large cities there are several Western doctors with whom foreign patients will be able to talk more easily. In Tokyo their names, and those of hospitals are available, from the Tourist Information Centres.

If you need shots against any diseases, the least expensive place is the Tokyo Port Authority or the health facility at Narita airport; contact the TIC for further information. If obtained through a private doctor they will be much more expensive.

Dental

Japanese dentists are equipped with the most modern equipment available in the world, and much dental research of a high standard is carried on in universities, yet as a nation with a very standard of living, the Japanese have shockingly bad teeth. This is probably the result of carelessness on the part of the toothowners more than a reflection on the standards of dentists. Nevertheless the only filling I ever had in Japan was very poorly done according to my dentist in Australia. This sample is probably not typical, but it indicates that not all are overly competent. None are cheap; the Japanese have national health insurance costs, so they don't mind Y5000 and up per filling.

Costs

It is advisable to have your own medical insurance because costs in Japan are extremely high. Foreign residents of Japan may be eligible for Japanese health insurance, but this varies from one locality to another. Being a doctor or dentist is one of the most lucrative professions in Japan. This is reflected in the fact that prospective students at some medical schools must make a 'gift' to the college of up to Y40 million before they are admitted, and the average total cost for six years of study is Y19 million. This, of course, means that only the children of wealthy parents will get into those schools, and the patient has to pay off that scandalous 'bribe' for entry. (Being Japan, however, this practice will probably continue ad infinitum; service for the general good is not a generally admired concept in this country.)

Contraceptives etc.

The main methods of contraception in Japan are the condom (known in Japanese as 'condom' or 'skin'), tablets that are inserted prior to intercourse (two such as brands being CCC and Sampoon), gels and foams that are introduced similarly, and the diaphragm; the latter is the least popular. The message is that contaception is the responsibility of the male, and few Japanese women will be prepared for spontaneous sexual activity, (even though an indeterminate but appreciable fraction of the female population most certainly is active). Abortion is readily available at low cost with no difficulty for both Japanese and foreign women, and is a common method of preventing unwanted births. Probably as a result of this factor, Japan has a very low rate of population increase (less than 1%).

The Pill is generally not available to Japanese women; they must have a medical examination every month if they are able to get a prescription. Women using the Pill who will be travelling or living in Japan have three courses of action. One is to bring an adequate supply to last through their Japan travels. Another is to arrange to have the prescription filled by mail from home. The third is to bring the prescription (a wise policy in any case) with the dosage and composition listed in detail; large pharmacies in major cities can then match the prescription to a Japanese-made Pill. Foreign brands are not imported. In Tokyo, the American Pharmacy in Yurakucho (close to the TIC) can do this.

Familiar brands of sanitary protection will be found only at pharmacies like the American Pharmacy that cater to foreign clientele; Tampax is the only familiar brand distributed nationwide.

Mental Health

If you get the 'coming unstuck' feeling, or need someone to talk to for any reason such as advice and help in personal matters, there is a small choice of agencies who can help.

Tokyo English Lifeline (TELL) offers confidential and anonymous counseling by telephone; they can also refer callers to other agencies that might be able to help. In Tokyo, the number is (03) 264-4347. Another useful organization is Tokyo Community Counseling Service; it refers callers to trained professional counsellors in a variety of fields; tel (03) 403-7106.

Tokyo Tapes offers an extremely useful and comprehensive range of tape-recorded information. Callers phone and request one or more tapes by number. For a listing of tapes by number, tel (03) 262-0224 and ask for take 302. The listing is also available from Tokyo Tapes, 610 Homat Commodore, 5-13-28 Roppongi, Minato-ku, Tokyo 106; and from the sponsoring organizations, the Franciscan Chapel Center, St Alban's, St Paul's Lutheran, Tokyo Baptist or Tokyo Union churches.

Toilets

Most toilets in Japan are the Asian squatting type. These are supposedly physiologically the best kind, and are personally hygenic because no part of the body comes in contact with it, but many Westerners find them uncomfortable and undignified to have to use. But unless you continually travel first class, at some time it will be necessary to use one, so be forewarned.

Except for the most primitive rural toilets, there will be an oval porcelain fixture with a raised 'cup' at one end. Flush models will have a bottom; those over a septic tank will be bottomless. You are meant to squat over the fixture facing the cupped end. (If you are getting on in years or very heavy, make sure you can stand up from a squatting position. Some people can't and the result could be very embarrasing.) Most public toilets have no paper, so it is wise to have your own when travelling away from familiar territory. There are often dispensers for tissues at the entrance. Where paper is provided, it is almost uniformly of extremely poor quality. When squatting, be careful not to let money or other things fall out your pockets; some people completely remove their trousers to avoid such an occurrence.

All western-style hotels, some ryokan,

most large and modern office buildings and department stores have clean, western-style facilities. Some westerners make mental notes of their location and plan a daily visit to one.

In private homes, youth hostels, ryokans, minshuku, and other residential places, there will be a separate pair of slippers at the entrance to the toilet area. Take off the house slippers and into the toilet ones. Never forget to change back again when leaving, and never wear the house slippers into the toilet — both are social gaffes without peer. It all becomes instinctive after a while.

Don't be surprised or shocked at the sight of men urinating in public, especially at night after coming out from an evening of drinking in bars. Even in daylight it is not unknown to see one facing a wall. Women do not indulge themselves in the same way except in the country where customs are a little less polished.

MONEY

The unit of Japanese currency is the yen. There are coins of 1, 5, 10, 50 and 100 yen, and banknotes of 500, 1000, 5000 and 10,000 yen.

The value of the yen has changed a lot in recent years, generally getting stronger (ie more expensive) relative to other major currencies. At the time this book was published, the approximate rates were:

US$1 = Y230	Y1000 = US$4.35
£1 = Y430	Y1000 = £2.33
A$1 = Y260	Y1000 = A$3.85

In terms of actual purchasing power in Japan, compared with what a US dollar will by in the US, the 'true' exchange rate is closer to 350-500 yen to the dollar. Its official value is pushed up by continuing demand for the products of Japan's few really efficient industries such as electronics, cars, motorcycles,

optical goods, ships and steel. Most other products including food are very expensive, the result of small-scale and inefficient production. Rice, for example, could be bought in the US or Australia for a fraction of the price charged in Japan. However, since it is the products in demand overseas that determine the demand for the yen, this knowledge will be only academic and the exchange rate will probably stay around 200-220.

Only yen may be spent in Japan. It is against the law for foreign currencies to be used. Unlike in many other countries in Asia, the US greenback is not a second currency, and the average shopkeeper would not recognise one.

Foreign currencies can be changed only at banks with a sign 'Authorized Foreign Exchange Bank', or at a few authorized stores that have a large tourist trade; they will have a similar sign posted. In metropolitan areas, authorized banks are thick on the ground, but don't get short of yen out of town. Both cash and travellers' cheques may be exchanged at such banks. The currencies of the following countries may be exchanged in Japan: Australia, Austria, Belgium, Canada, Denmark, Netherlands, France, Germany, Hong Kong, Italy, Norway, UK, Portugal, Sweden, Switzerland and the USA. Travellers' cheques of the following countries can be exchanged: Australia, Canada, France, Germany, India, Italy, UK, Switzerland and the USA. While these currencies may be exchanged for yen, don't walk into a bank in a small city and try to exchange Canadian banknotes, for example. The bank will only accept them for clearance and send them to its head office, a process that would take several days.

The currencies of Korea and Taiwan are worthless in Japan; be sure to convert them in their home country before arriving in Japan. If going to Korea, convert your yen to US$; they receive a premium on the black market (quite open in Seoul — just ask among other travellers), whereas Japanese money is worth little more than the official rate.

Travellers' cheques for yen are said to be of little more use than foreign currency. Banks are unwilling to cash the 'paper' of another bank, accepting them only for collection, so unless there is a branch of the bank that issued the yen cheques, you may have trouble trying to cash them. The major banks that issue travellers' cheques often don't have branches in the secondary cities, so check carefully where they can be cashed.

There are two ways to avoid carrying large amounts of cash. The first method, and probably the simplest, is to open a Post Office savings account. With such an account you can withdraw money from almost every post office in Japan during normal business hours. Since there are far more post offices than banks, this method is most useful. An account can be opened at any but the smallest post office; certainly there is no problem at the central post office, Tokyo (near Tokyo station). The magic words are 'Yubin chokin-o hajimetai'. That should be enough to open an account.

The second method is to open a passbook savings account with a bank that has branches throughout the country. Many banks use the invisible signature system, so money can be withdrawn at any branch as long as the passbook isn't lost. (Mitsubishi Bank's Marunouchi branch, near Tokyo station, has staff who speak enough English to take care of the procedures.) Be warned that any bank transaction is slow, typically 10-15 minutes for a withdrawal. Keep in mind also that many of the big banks, such as Mitsubishi, have very few branches outside the major cities; it might be better to use one that has branches spread more widely.

It is not well known that one can open a US dollar savings account in Japan. This is probably of greater use to residents than visitors. It allows easy transfer of money in and out of Japan without having to exchange it each time. Banks might be unwilling to open an account for a stranger, but by looking around, there should be no trouble finding a branch willing to help. Interest rates paid on dollar accounts are usually higher than for yen accounts, but a tax of about 20% is deducted, and some banks deduct a handling fee of 1/10 of 1% per transaction (or a minmum imum charge of Y750 to 100, whichever is greater). The Bank of America in Marunouchi is said not to have such charges.

Transferring Money

Many travellers find it necessary to transfer money urgently from home while travelling. The path of transferring money to Japan can be smooth, or it can be fraught with difficulties, so it is useful to know what can go wrong.

If there is no rush to have money sent, the simplest way is to have a money order sent by mail. The money order should be payable in yen, and could be bought in a bank or post office, depending on the country of origin. A money order can also be carried by hand and is a cheap way of transferring money to Japan without carrying a large amount of cash, and it saves the 1% commission charged for travellers' cheques. While most mail gets through in Japan, it would be safer to send a draft by registered mail, especially if it is to a Poste Restante (General Delivery) address.

Money can be sent directly from an overseas bank to its correspondent bank (or branch, if it has one), either by mail transfer (slower but cheaper) or by cable transfer (faster but at a price). However, from my own experience, I could not advocate transferring money between banks. On two occasions funds were meant to be transferred from the National Bank in Australia to the main branch of the Mitsubishi Bank in Kyoto; instead they went to the Daiwa Bank in Tokyo. It would be a good idea to talk to with someone in your home bank before setting out, asking their advice on the best method of transferring money.

Despite the use of computers, and other technology, the Japanese banking system is slow and inefficient in some fields. Transferring money to and from Japan is more expensive than in many other countries. Service charges seem to pop up out of nowhere; for example a few hundred yen can be taken out of a money order received from overseas as a 'cashing charge'.

If remitting money out of the country, banks charge Y1500 per money order, and preparing it will take several days except at the bank's main branch. (Remittances to the USA are somewhat less costly, and are prepared on the spot, at the Bank of America.) If there is no rush, smaller sums can be transferred out at lower cost by the post office, but they send the remittance, a process which takes up to a month. The charges increase in stages; beyond Y200,000 the fee is the same as for a bank transfer (or higher).

It may be cheaper to buy US banknotes and send them by registered mail; the exchange rate is different for purchasing banknotes and for drafts, however, so compare costs before acting.

In recent years the foreign exchange regulations have been relaxed greatly. For the amount of money that most travellers are likely to be dealing with, there are effectively no restrictions in changing money in either direction. An exchange receipt is given with each transaction. Up to Y3,000,000 may be exchanged without documentation, but if your exchange dealings are in this range, it is wise to hold on to the receipts.

American banknotes may be purchased over the counter (though with the inevitable wait) as long as the bank has them in stock. This is generally true but I was once told that the bank had no notes available even though the woman ahead in line was exchanging dollars for yen; when I requested those, I was told that they had to be sent to the New York office.

Credit Cards

Several international credit cards can be used in Japan. These include Diner's Club, American Express, Master Charge and Visa Card; inquire before leaving home if you have a card from another large credit card organization. Establishments accepting credit cards have signs prominently displayed. Usually the places that accept them are high-priced, aimed at the expense account or wealthy traveller. When using credit card you are unlikely to obtain a discount of any size because the shops must pay a commission to the card company.

POSTAL

The Japanese Post Office is generally reliable and efficient, though its charges are among the highest in the world. Occasionally letters go astray and don't get delivered. It is important to remember that the average Japanese has very little experience in reading romaji (Roman letters), especially handwriting, so always write clearly or print addresses, especially names.

In Tokyo, postal information is available in English by telephone at (03) 241-4891. However, there may be some problems in communication.

Main post offices are open from 8 am to 8 pm except on Sundays and afternoon of national holidays. Smaller post offices close at 5 pm or 6 pm and on Saturday afternoons and Sundays. The Central Post Offices at Tokyo and Kyoto are open 24 hours a day, Sundays and national holidays.

Sending Mail

Any post office will accept ordinary letters (airmail or surface) for delivery anywhere. Registered letters and parcels for overseas must go through major post offices.

In Tokyo there is a special post office for overseas mail. It is called, naturally enough, Tokyo International Post Office (Kok'sai Yubin-kyoku in Japanese). They know all regulations regarding foreign mail. It is located in Otemachi and is shown on the TIC's Tokyo guide map. In theory one can obtain information in English by phone, tel 241-4877.

Overseas Postage Rates

The table below lists typical postage rates for the following destinations.

1: Oceania (inc. Australia, New Zealand)
2: South-East Asia (inc. Singapore, Thailand)
3: USA and Canada
4: Western Europe

Region	1	2	3	4
Airmail				
Aerograms	100	100	100	100
Postcards	70	70	80	90
Letters				
(up to 10 g)	100	100	120	140
Small packets				
(up to 80 g)	190	190	230	270
Parcels				
up to 500 g	1750	2100	1800	2200
add'l 500 g	450	700	750	700
Surface Mail				
Postcards	60	40	60	60
Letters				
(up to 20 g)	90	60	90	90
Small packets				
(up to 100 g)	110	110	110	110
Parcels				
up to 1 kg	1350	1600	1300	1650
add'l kg	200	250	400	300

Domestic Postage Rates

First class
letters (teikei) (up to 50 g): Y60
letter-cards: Y50

Second class
Post cards: Y30
Reply-paid postcards: Y60.

Miscellaneous

The maximum size for regular letters (domestic mail) is 12 x 23.5 cm; for postcards it is 10.5 x 14.8 cm. The minimum size for both is 9 x 14 cm. Some stores sell under-sized stationery so check before buying if it looks small.

International Postal Reply Coupons (kosai henshin kitteken) can be bought if it is necessary to pre-pay postage from a foreign country. One coupon is adequate for postage for a minimum cost letter by surface mail from nearly every country in the world. The coupons cost Y140 each. This cost is extremely high, several times the actual cost of postage from overseas countries, so it may be cheaper to send money order for postage.

For wrapping parcels, most post offices supply free twine. If you need cardboard boxes, most grocery stores and many other shops discard them every day.

Airmail envelopes should not be used for domestic mail. There may be a surcharge for coloured envelopes as they require special handling. Stickers may be attached to postcards as long as they don't appreciably add to the weight or thickness.

Philatelists may be interested to know that Japan, like every other country, regularly issues commemorative stamps (kinen kitte). These are sold at every post office in the country on the day of issue, but they usually disappear quickly on the same day. After that, they can be purchased (until sold out) at Tokyo CPO, near Tokyo station, Marunouchi side. The philatelic counter is at the end of the building nearest the station and is open until 4 pm. Stamps available are displayed on a board.

Receiving Mail

Mail can be sent c/o *Poste Restante* (General Delivery) to any post office in Japan, but preferably to the Central Post Office is usually very close to the main railway station. Things to note are: (1) letters are held for only 30 days before being returned to the sender; and (2) the Japanese seldom use the service and most people don't know that it exists, so postal clerks in smaller post offices may even be unsure where to look for such letters, so there is a risk that they will go astray.

At the Post Office, ask for either 'tome oki' or 'kyoku dome', and have your passport or other identification ready. As this method is not totally reliable, it is preferable to use one of the following mail drops.

American Express offices hold mail for customers. They can ask for proof that you are a customer, but this can simply mean someone who has bought their travellers' cheques. Mail is normally held for only 30 days, but they will hold it longer if it is marked 'Please hold for arrival'.

The addresses of branches that hold mail are:

TOKYO
   c/o American Express
   Halifax Building
   16-26 Roppongi 3-chome
   Minato-ku
   Tokyo 106.

OSAKA
   c/o American Express
   Kita Hankyu Bldg 3rd floor
   1-4-8 Shibata
   Kita-ku
   Osaka.

OKINAWA
   c/o American Express
   Awase Shopping Center
   241 Aza Yamazoto
   Okinawa-shi 904

To reach the Tokyo office, take the subway to Roppongi, and leave the platform at the end nearest the rear of the train when coming from the Ginza direction. After exiting, turn left and leave the station. At street level, turn right, walk past the 'Almond' coffee shop (a well known rendezvous), across the little street that goes downhill, and turn right on the main thoroughfare. After a 5-10-minute walk, the large American Express sign will be visible on the left side of the street.

In Osaka, the office is near Osaka station.

Embassies Some embassies will hold mail for their passport holders, but they may normally return it after 30 days, unless it is marked 'Please hold for arrival'.

The embassies of Australia, Canada, South Africa, New Zealand and USA will hold mail; but the UK embassy will not. (Embassies and their addresses are listed elsewhere in this chapter.)

Banks Some banks will hold mail for their customers. For example, the Royal Bank of Canada will but First National City Bank would not. Inquire from another branch for your bank's policy.

Hotels and Youth Hostels will hold mail for their customers. Some unscrupulous people have had their mail sent to one even though they weren't staying there, but this isn't a practice to be encouraged. Hotels are usually quite safe places to have mail sent to, but Youth Hostels vary. In my own experience mail has arrived safely, but a friend had her mail sent to one Youth Hostel and when her letters were finally turned over to her, every one had been opened. This is probably not typical.

TELEPHONES

Japanese phone numbers have nine or ten digits, usually in three groups. The first group is the area code and is only used when dialling from another zone. For some peculiar reason brackets are often written round the second group, not round the area code as is commonly done in other countries. The latter method is sometimes used in Japan and is used in this book.

Local calls in Japan cost Y10 for three minutes. There are several kinds of public (pay) phones. The most common type is red, sometimes with a gold band. It can hold six Y10 coins and uses them one at a time and returns unused coins. It can be used for local or inter-city calls. These are found in many shops, stations, etc. There is a smaller sort of red phone, only for local calls, which takes one coin and cuts off after three minutes.

Pink pay phones are found in private homes, and operate exactly as large red ones.

Yellow phones are the same as large red phones, except that they can hold up to ten Y10 coins and nine Y100 coins; they are the most useful for inter-city direct-dialled calls.

Blue phones are also identical to large red ones in function, but rarely have slots for Y100 coins.

Below is a list of representative rates from Tokyo, giving the number of seconds per Y10. Day rate applies from 7 am to 8 pm.

	Day	Night
Kyushu, Hokkaido; Okinawa	2.5	4
Hiroshima, Shikoku	3	5
Kyoto, Osaka, Kobe, Nara	4	7
Sendai, Nagoya, Gifu	5	9
Kamakura, Yokosura	21	21
Yokohama	38	38

Emergency numbers for use anywhere in Japan are: Police 110; Ambulance 119. However, the person answering will probably speak only Japanese. Yellow and blue phones can be used for making emergency calls without coins.

International

Calls can be made to any country. Direct dialling is available for some calls but it is probably better to ask the operator. For information on overseas calls, tel (03) 270-5111.

To place a call dial:

0051	from	Tokyo, Osaka
(06) 945-1122	from	Kyoto, Kobe
0988-54-0011	from	Okinawa

From other areas, tel 03-211-4211 for calls to Asia, or 03-211-5511 for calls to other areas.

A 3-minute call to North America, Europe, Australia or New Zealand costs Y2430. Person-to-person rates are higher. Some calls may be cheaper on Sunday. Reverse-charge calls can be made.

TELEGRAMS

Within Japan, telegrams can be sent in Roman letters from major post offices and offices of the telegraph company, NTT.

Overseas telegrams can be sent to most countries of the world, and are accepted in Roman letters at telegraph, telephone or post offices. Hotels catering to foreign customers can also help. The number of KDD Information Centre, Tokyo, is (03) 270-5111.

Rates within Japan are Y600 for the first eight words plus Y80 per additional word. For overseas telegrams, representative rates per word are:

Australia, New Zealand	Y150
Europe (Western)	192
Canada	108
USA	118

Any group of 10 letters is accepted as one word so words may be run together to economize if the recipient can successfully separate them, but remember that letters can get mistransmitted.

Rates given are standard rates for an Ordinary Telegram, minimum seven words. Letter Telegrams go at half these rates but delivery is more leisurely. (Also there is a minimum length so that up to 17 words it is cheaper to send by Ordinary Telegram.) Urgent Telegrams are charged at double the Ordinary rate.

ADDRESSES

Visitors to Japan should know from the outset that it is almost impossible to find a place just from the address. Even Japanese find it very difficult.

Addresses are not by street. In fact, most streets have no name at all; only the most major avenues have names, and even then some Japanese may not be familiar with some of these. Addresses are by district (area), not by street (linear). The smallest district is the 'chome', usually only a few blocks in area. Within the chome, each building has a one-digit or hyphenated two-digit number, eg 4-4. What makes the system interesting is that until 1955, the numbers were assigned by chronological order of construction, not by location!

The next larger unit may have one of several names: 'cho', 'machi' or no

name at all. Next comes 'ku' which is the equivalent of a ward. In Tokyo, well known ward names are Chiyoda-ku, Chuo-ku (Central Ward), Minato-ku (Harbour Ward) and Shinjuku-ku. For example, an address of the form '1-2-3 Nishi Meguro' means the same as '2-3 Nishi Meguro 1-chome'; the '2-3' refers to the building number.

Published maps are available that show the breakdown of every chome, building by building, but few foreigners bother with them. It is common, however, for any business, store, etc, to print a small map on its business card ('meishi') or advertisements, showing the location relative to the nearest railway or subway station.

There was an effort during the Occupation to assign numbers and letters to the major thoroughfares of Tokyo, but this effort at rationalization of the non-system was definitely not appreciated, and was dropped when the Japanese were given full control of their own affairs.

The names of cities are properly followed by the suffix 'shi', as 'Yokohama-shi'. The word means city, and is tagged on to distinguish between cities and prefectures ('ken') of the same name; there is an Okayama-shi and Okayama-ken, for example. The cities of Tokyo and Osaka, by the way, are special administrative districts known as '-fu'; they are not properly '-shi'. In the countryside there are many '-mura' or villages. Another word found often in addresses in the countryside is '-gun' which corresponds to 'county', one step smaller than '-ken'.

Japanese addresses sometimes have commas in the middle of a line. When the whole address is printed on a single line, this can be confusing to a reader who is unfamiliar with the system.

TIPPING

Japan has the distinction of being one

the few developed countries where tipping is not generally expected, even at places like restaurants, hotels, etc. If a service charge is expected, it will automatically be added to your bill (another way of saying it is compulsory); this may be found at hotels and restaurants. Quite separate from the service charge, by the way, is the 10% tax which is incurred if restaurant or bar bills exceed Y1200.

Only at expensive nightclubs, which are a western type of import, is tipping of waiters normal. Even nightclub hostesses do not expect tips if you pay the hostess charge and buy her drinks; this will amount to plenty, in any case! (Tipping hostesses is common practice if a man is trying to get on her good side for a future conquest.)

Porters at stations and airports (if you can find any) receive Y100-250 per piece of luggage, depending on the place and the size of the bags. At facilities frequented by foreigners, like international airports, there is often a sign in English stating the fee expected.

LAUNDRY

Anyone staying at hotels or ryokan can have their laundry done by the hotel. Dry cleaning shops and depots are common in every suburban area. Travellers using Youth Hostels, etc, will have to do their own washing, in many cases in a wash basin or sink using cold water (not very pleasant in unheated washrooms in mid-winter!). A manicure brush is useful for scrubbing.

The coin-operated washing machine reached Japan a couple of years ago and is very popular, so their numbers will only increase in the future. They are usually operated in conjunction with 'sento' (neighbourhood public baths) because they have the facilities for heating copious quantities of water. Many Youth Hostels have washing machines for the use of their guests.

ELECTRICITY

Electric service everywhere in Japan is 100 volts AC, an odd voltage used nowhere else in the world except Korea (and they're changing to 220 V). North of an imaginary east-west line just south of Tokyo, the frequency is 50 Hz (cycles); south of the line it is 60Hz. Most 117-volt equipment such as shavers and hair dryers, designed for use in North America, will work satisfactorily, if a little slowly or with reduced heat output.

RADIO

The only regular broadcasts in English are those of the Far East Network (FEN) or the American armed forces. While they are slanted toward the interests and tastes of people in the services (very heavy on pop music and sports), they also have hourly newscasts, and have an hour-long news, sports and commentary segment between 6 and 7 pm on weeknights. Those who missed out on, or who want to relive, the golden days of radio can hear rebroadcasts of '40s and '50s broadcasts such as The Whistler, Amos 'n' Andy. Listening areas and frequencies (kHz) are: Tokyo (810); Sasebo, Kyushu (1566); Iwakuni, near Hiroshima (1575); Misawa, northern Honshu (1575); and Okinawa (650). Tokyo area programs are listed daily in the *Japan Times*.

There are a few minutes of news in English each day on NHK, the government broadcasting organization.

The Japanese AM stations are heavily biased toward pop music, Japanese style, although there is a substantial amount of the Western variety as well. Program notes are published in the English-language dailies.

FM fans will find a limited number of stations in large cities like Tokyo and Osaka. They broadcast several hours a day of classical, pop, jazz and 'easy listening' music. The FM frequencies used in Japan are 76-90 MHz, below the international standard FM band 88-108 MHz found on most radios, so a special radio tuned to the local bands, or a converter, is necessary to pick up the broadcasts. If you want to buy good Japanese hi fi gear to take home, buy the foreign frequency model and use the converter while in Japan.

TV

Most programming in Japan is in Japanese only. Imported programs and films are dubbed. However, there are some prgrams which can be picked up on cable TV (to some apartment buildings and most hotels catering to foreigners) which can be heard with their original soundtrack. American service people living on or near base can pick up cable broadcasts all in English. A new development in the electronics field is multiplex broadcasting of TV soundtracks. With an adaptor, it is often possible to receive the original soundtrack of the film or program instead of the dubbed version, though there may be some lack of continuity if segments have been cut.

Watching the Japanese programs, even if one can't understand a word of the dialogue, can give many insights into modern Japanese life. The role of women is clearly seen on one program after another — they are usually there only to provide a little scenery and to say 'hai' ('Yes!') in obsequious agreement with every statement of the male who is, by definition, the most important and intelligent person on the screen.

FILMS

About 90% of the colour film sold in Japan is for prints. Slides are not popular and slide film can be hard to find in some areas.

Kodak, Fuji and Sakura print films all give good results and are sold everywhere in Japan. Prices are identical. They can all be processed in the same way, but Sakura is not as widely distribed overseas as the other brands so processing in other countries could be difficult. Films come in 12, 24 and 36-exposure rolls for 35 mm as well as all other standard sizes like 110.

Colour prints are of good quality and reasonable cost. Discount prices can be as low as Y32 for standard-size prints.

For colour slides, Fujichrome has a good reputation and is available in ASA 100 and 400 speeds. It can be processed in Kodak E-6 (Ektachrome) chemicals and has good colour-shift stability. Other Japanese films may fade after several years and in my opinion their colours are not as pleasing. Kodachrome is also available; it has excellent stability and good colours.

The following are some typical discount prices for films (full list prices can be considerably higher): Kodachrome, Y725; Ektachrome 64, Y805; Fujichrome 100, Y725; Kodacolour II, Y550. (All prices are for 36-exposure rolls.)

With any sort of film, remember when you go through customs that most luggage is x-rayed. This is said not to affect films but to avoid any chance of ruined films, pack them together, eg in hand luggage, and get it inspected by hand.

If you are going to Korea, take all your film with you as non-Korean film is either unobtainable or more expensive than in Japan.

Processing

Japanese films can be processed quickly at any camera shop; some offer same-day processing, but I wonder if the quality of the work will be as good if it is so rushed.

Kodak films can be sent for processing by any camera shop in the country.

For faster service than the usual four to eight days for slides, take your films to the Kodak depot in the Ginza and ask for fast processing; they can have films back in two days.

For one-day service, go to the professional service depot in Aoyama (Tokyo). To reach it, take the Chiyoda subway line to Omote-sando and look for signs to Aoyama-Gakuin. Find exit B2 and follow it to the surface; about 10 metres along that lane, on the left, is a building with a small parking area in front of it. The Kodak depot is on the ground floor of that building in room 111. They speak little English, but processing will automatically be on a one-day basis.

Kodak slide films are sold without processing which is relatively expensive, around Y1300 for a 36-exposure film. To avoid the high cost, you could take the films out of the country, or buy prepaid processing 'mailers' in counties where they are less expensive, eg Hong Kong or USA. These valid for use in Japan. You could also use Kodachrome that has the processing charge included in the purchase price; this type is available in Hong Kong and other countries. (Japan, by the way, is one of relatively few countries where Kodachrome can be processed.)

The address to which mailers and processing-prepaid Kodachrome film should be sent is:

Far East Laboratories, Ltd.
14-1, 2-chome
Higashi-Gotanda
Shinagawa-ku
Tokyo

BUYING

Even back in the good old days when a US dollar was worth more yen and price tages were lower, there were relatively few bargains in Japan. The only good buys (price wise) were in cameras and other optical goods, electronics prod-

ucts (radios, hi fi gear, etc), watches, motorcycles, cars and oil tankers.

Well, you can forget the oil tankers now — the Koreans are building them cheaper.

As for the other goods, prices have gone up with inflation, as they have everywhere, and the value of the yen has skyrocketed, so that there are even fewer 'bargains' today if the word means only low prices. However, the quality of manufactured goods has continued to improve, with features undreamed-of only a few years ago, so possibly the products of today are better value because they can do more things better, more effeciently, more easily, or quicker.

It comes as a surprise to many Americans, and possibly other Westerners, to find that many Japanese-made goods cost more in Japan than they do at home. The main reason is that the distribution system in Japan is notoriously long and complex, with many links in the chain, each of which tacks on its markup. Foreign importers can usually buy in huge volume and distribute the goods more efficiently and therefore more cheaply. Even where import duty is applied prices can be lower than in Japan, especially considering the sales taxes in Japan that can push up the price by 10-35%.

Japan's distribution system is actually a form of social welfare. Many of the people employed in sales and distribution have relatively few skills, do not work for companies that can pay large retirement pensions when they retire, and are actually surplus to the task of distributing the goods, but are supported by the system as a type of tax.

A large number of Japanese goods sold overseas are made for export only and are never seen on the domestic market. (An example is the miniature cast-iron grill called a 'hibachi'; this has never been used in Japan and can only be found in stores selling to US service people.) So if a friend at home asks you to buy a particular product, in most cases you would be advised to refuse politely. Even if a product is sold in Japan, unless it is something common, like a camera, that is available everywhere, you might spend long hours trying to track it down, only to find that it is cheaper back home.

One of the big surprises about Japan is that much of their industry is small in scale and inefficient, with the result that many goods made in Japan are actually very expensive, much more so than in other countries. The large assemblers of components, like the car manufacturers, buy many of their parts from very small companies that may have only a few pieces of machinery and depend on long working hours by family firms to survive financially.

There are many hand-made artistic and decorative items still being made with the exquisite attention to detail for which Japan has long been famous. They exhibit the best workmanship imaginable — flawless lacquerware, hand-forged swords and knives, incredibly beautiful hand-woven fabrics and textiles — the list goes on and on. Naturally, the prices for time-consuming hand labour will make these items costly, but the quality of the work justifies the price. The coexistence of the finest of centuries-old artistry with some of the world's most modern mass-produced goods is one of the fascinations of Japan.

While Japanese stores are usually very competitive with each other, especially for items like cameras and electronic goods, there is very little bargaining, and certainly none of the camel-market haggling of some countries. Japanese regard this with contempt as bad manners. However it is possible that a store clerk, after quoting a price, might add an accessory to sweeten the deal.

When shopping for a camera, or other expensive item, it is generally not a good idea to go with a Japanese friend. Because the Japanese have little tradition of bargaining they tend to pay the first price asked. If you are with a Japanese friend, and the price you are offered with him is not as good you have seen elsewhere, just postpone the purchase politely. Don't bluntly say that you can get it cheaper elsewhere, for things aren't done that way in Japan; say you'd like to think it over.

Customs Inspection at Home

Travellers should determine what they are allowed to take back to their home country without incurring duties. Check with your embassy if you are in doubt.

Americans should take note of US trademark regulations. In addition to the dollar limit on what can be brought back duty-free (now $300), many goods of foreign origin are registered with the US Customs service by trademark. These companies have the right to limit the volume of private imports of goods bearing that trademark; some companies totally ban private imports, while other companies place no restrictions on such activities. Items made in Japan that fall into this category include cameras, binoculars, lenses, and hi fi gear. The booklet 'Trademark Information' can be picked up at the US embassy in Tokyo, or ordered by mail from: Department of the Treasury, US Customs Service, Washington DC 20229, or the US Government Printing Office, Washington DC 20402.

Tax-free Buying

Most goods sold in Japan have a national sales tax of 10-35% imposed on them; list prices and price tags in most shops include this tax. Foreign tourists can purchase many types of goods free of this tax. A card is stapled into your passport at the time of purchase and is removed by Customs at the port of departure. You may be asked to show that you have the item in your possession so as to ensure that the goods are taken out of the country.

Only some stores, generally located in popular tourist areas, offer goods on a tax-free basis; many of these, such as camera shops, will have a prominent 'Tax Free' sign. An individual item must have been registered for sale tax-free to allow its sale on that basis. Thus, a shop selling to the domestic market would not stock tax-free items and would not be able to sell items in stock on a tax-free basis.

The tax-free price is not the lowest possible price; it is only the starting point for negotiations. For items such as cameras, one can obtain a further discount of 5-25%, depending on the brand and the store.

Remember, too, that the discount available from some shops selling at domestic, with-tax ('kazei') prices, can be much greater than the saving at tax-free stores, especially for cameras.

Although tax-free ('menzei') purchasing is intended for tourists and other short-term visitors, those on working visas may be able to buy tax-free during the first six months or when planning to leave Japan.

Cameras

Cameras and lenses are among Japan's best-known products, with a reputation for quality at reasonable prices. Despite increases in the value of the yen, the industry has almost eliminated all international competition in 35 mm cameras, and it dominates most of the other camera markets.

Japanese-made cameras are often slightly cheaper in Hong Kong and Singapore, but the difference in price is not enough to lose sleep over.

The lowest prices in Japan are to be found in Tokyo, especially in Shinjuku, a sub-city with many large stores of all

kinds. Some shops in the Ginza area sell at very reasonable prices but others are fully aware that many well-heeled foreign tourists pass by their doors, and feel no need to reduce their prices excessively.

The Yodobashi and Sakuraya stores in Shinjuku are close to the Takano Building and are easy to find from the station once you are above ground on the east side. Both are brightly lit, and the store jingles repeat incessantly and loudly.

As with most purchases, you should compare prices carefully if you want a bargain. Make sure you are comparing identical equipment, ie the same model with the same lens. Check tax-free prices but remember that they are not always the lowest as some stores offer bigger discounts on the with-tax prices.

Visitors may be surprised to find that many brands of Japanese-made photographic equipment are not available in Japan. (This is true of many other Japanese products.) For example, one company may make the lenses sold under several different names; the only private brand lenses normally available in Japan are Komura, Sigma, Tamron and Tokina. Some companies put different name plates on the same model in different markets, and some models are never sold in Japan (eg the Konica T-4).

If you buy a camera, it is wise to check immediately that it is giving correct exposure and is functioning correctly. Servicing is faster and much easier in Japan than elsewhere.

The best way to check it (other than the simple check of operating the shutter on all speeds at the store) is to run a roll of colour slide film (Kodachrome 25 or Kodachrome 64 film can be highly recommended) through the camera and check if the pictures are satisfactorily exposed. Test pictures should be taken of normal subjects that are evenly lighted and don't contain large areas that are very bright or very dark. If the camera has shutter speeds that can be varied manually, use the full range of them and make a record of the setting for each shot to match them later. If only the aperture can be varied (aperture priority models), use the full range available. If you buy extra lenses, test them all, using the full method just described.

Electronics & Hi Fi

Hi fi stores in Japan, especially in Tokyo, are a gadget-lover's paradise. But before rushing in with a bulging wallet, be warned of thse pitfalls.

First, electronic products, like many other Japanese goods, are often cheaper in other countries, whether it's the US discount stores, duty-free stores, Hong Kong or Singapore. In other words, know your prices. (Admittedly, the very latest models may not be available elsewhere.)

Next, remember that most electronics goodies are heavy, bulky, or both. This makes them prohibitive as checked air luggage. The weight limit for parcel post is only 10 kg (22 lb), and sea freight or express charges are not cheap. (Sea freight expenses just for crating something, hauling it to the docks, and customs inspection amount to about Y20,000; then there is the actual shipping costs and customs duties at the other end. The cheapest way to send a single item is by air freight.)

If you still want to buy, you will find that many items on display are made for Japan only. Japan's power supply is 100 volts (an odd value used almost nowhere else in the world) at a frequency of 50 or 60 Hz depending on the region. Low-power equipment may work satisfactorily on 117 V (as in North America) but with no guarantee against damage. The frequency affects motor speeds. (In Australia, UK and Europe supplies are usually 230-240 V at 50 Hz.)

Japanese TV channels and some other specifications are different from other countries. Also their FM radio band (76-90 MHz) is different from most of the rest of the world (88-108 MHz). Because the local models are not usually exported, getting service and parts could be a problem. Many Japan-only models have export equivalents with adjustable settings.

If you are buying FM *stereo* equipment, note there is a specification called the 'stereo de-emphasis time constant'. In Australia, UK and Europe it is 50 microseconds; in North America it's 75. The modification is simple, but would cost a serviceman's time to change. It would be simpler to buy the right model from the beginning; some have a switch at the back that allows selection between the two.

Only a few 'Tax Free' shops specialize in selling the export models. Several shops in the Ginza area stock a few types of electronic equipment, especially portable items like tape recorders and portable radios, along with camera gear, but the range is usually limited and the higher quality models may be a little rare. Prices tend to be higher than in the 'discount' areas because Ginza real estate is the most expensive in the world.

Best place in Tokyo to buy domestic models of electronic equipment is Akihabara (the name means 'Autumn Leaf Field'), but remember that not much Japanese equipment is usable off-the-shelf in other countries. You can get there by JNR Yamanote line; Akihabara station of the Hibiya subway line exits onto a street parallel to and one block away from the electrical area so it is necessary to walk under the JNR tracks to get there. In this district there are dozens, if not hundreds, of shops of all sizes selling everything electrical that is made in Japan.

Records

Records make a good souvenir of a country, but unfortunately records in Japan are very expensive usually over Y2000 for an LP. Some Japanese music is very much an acquired taste, particularly the screechy *gagaku*, but other types of music can be appreciated by almost any western ear for its often-haunting beauty. Most pleasing is the music of the *koto*, a long, thin stringed instrument played while seated on the floor, and the *shakuhachi*, or Japanese flute. The koto and shakuhachi are often combined and complement each other. One of the most beautiful of all Japanese compositions is 'Ko jo no tsuki' (or 'Moon over Castle Ruins'), another is 'Sakura, Sakura'. Both should be enjoyable for any listener, and are included on almost every disc of traditional Japanese music. (The first was actually composed in the 19th century after the influence of western music had hit Japan, so it is not traditional in style at all.)

Clothes

Bring everything from home that you will have to wear, or stop off in Korea on the way. First, clothes are very expensive in Japan and secondly, it is difficult for most westerners (both men and women) to find anything that fits. Tailor-made clothes are very expensive. Also, while fashion sense has improved immeasurably in the recent past, the styles tend to be a little different from those that Westerners are accustomed to.

Men's shoes generally available fit a foot no longer than 25 cm. For women, the largest sizes are proportionately smaller. Below is a list of equivalent shoe sizes.

Japan	USA	UK	Europe
23	5	3	36
24	6	4	37
25	7	5	38
25.5	7½	6	39

If you want to buy shoes despite their high prices (starting at Y6000 for cheapies), try branches of Isetan department stores; in Tokyo, there is also Big Shoes Akasaka (3-21-18 Akasaka, near Akasaka-Mitsuke subway station).

Women should bring all the underwear they will need. About 80% of bras in Japan are 'A' cup and finding larger sizes can be a problem. Again, try Isetan department stores; in Tokyo, there is also 'Silver Doll' on Aoyama-dori opposite the Peacock supermarket (tel 402-1894).

Antiques

The post-war days when Japanese antiques were sold for a song are long gone. The song has become an operatic chorus with full orchestral backing, and prices for almost anything really good will be from high to astronomical. They are high enough that Japanese buyers have been going overseas for a number of years and buying back Japanese items at foreign auctions. If you don't know your Japanese antiques, it is best to avoid spending large sums. If you see something that you really like, then buy it, but remember Japanese dealers know the value of their merchandise. Prices can vary, depending on how the dealer sizes up the customer.

There are regular flea markets in Tokyo and Kyoto where stallholders set up business. The chances of finding a treasure are quite remote for these people are not as naive as they might let on. One warning: if you wish to examine a piece of pottery or glassware, ask the stallholder to hand it to you. The occasional unscrupulous one carefully assembles the pieces of a broken item so that it collapses as soon as anyone touches it, so the customer then has to pay for it.

Eyeglasses

Glasses are expensive in Japan. It is better to get them in Hong Kong, Singapore or Korea, but if this is not possible, lower than usual prices are available at a type of 'self-service glasses supermarket'. The company, Megami Drug, has several branches in Tokyo (perhaps elsewhere); tel (03) 735-0022 for information.

Calculators

There are no cheapie calculators such as you find in Hong Kong and Singapore. Even simple ones rarely cost less than Y3000. Instead of cutting prices, manufacturers have added gimmicks like musical tones, or have gone in for ultra-small sizes. Cutesie cases in pink or other colours, decorated with little animals, are made for the local market and indicate what is very popular with young Japanese women. Many models combine the functions of calculator, clock and timer since the electronic chip of all such devices is similar.

Watches

Japan has a good name in watches. The names Seiko and Citizen have become well known around the world. The trend is, as in electronics, toward higher quality, more features (or gadgetry), higher fashion and higher prices. Convention mechanical watches are generally rather expensive. Many electronic watches are also up-market items with high prices, but some calculator companies like Casio offer a range of electronic timepieces at reasonable prices. With the advent of electronic watches, the industry has been turned topsy-turvy and they are marketed through electronics distributors as well as jewellers, and can be bought at the same discount shops as cameras and electronic products. Places to look first (in Tokyo) are the Akihabara electrical area, and the Shinjuku discount camera stores and nearby shops.

Books

The Japanese printing industry produces some of the finest quality colour printing in the world. Many books are published in English every year, including books of photographs of Japan and works on other subjects related to the country. These can make good souvenirs of a visit to Japan.

Maruzen and Kinokuniya sell English-language books in a number of cities. In Tokyo there are also Jena and Yaesu stores, the Tuttle shop (which displays titles of that publishing company), plus stores in the arcades of most of the large international hotels; the arcade in the Imperial Hotel probably offers the greatest selection.

Lacquer (makie)

Japanese lacquerware is one of the most beautiful souvenirs of the country. Every region produces many different objects — bowls, vases, plates, wall plaques, trays — so the total variety is great. Some cities known for lacquerware are Kyoto, Kanazawa, Wajima and Kamakura. Quality objects can be found in most large department stores as well as specialty shops. Prices of the finest pieces, with flawlessly smooth finish, gold designs, etc, can run into the hundreds of thousands of yen, but smaller and less pretentious pieces can be had for a couple of thousand.

Cloisonne

This is produced by soldering fine wires to a metal base to trace the outline of a pattern, then filling in the spaces with material that fires to a glassy finish. Cloisonne is a favourite purchase in Japan.

Damascene

A steel base is criss-crossed with fine lines, then pre-cut patterns of gold and silver foil are beaten onto the base. The base is corroded with nitric acid, lacquer is baked onto the entire surface, then the pattern is polished out. The revealed gold and silver may then be engraved further.

Dolls

Delicate Japanese dolls make a beautiful decoration in any home. There are several styles of doll made in Japan, such as Hakata clay figurines and the more familiar kimono-clad women with fine porcelain faces and hands. The latter vary in fineness of sculpturing, so it is wise to compare several. Department, specialty and tourist shops sell them.

Pearls

The process for culturing pearls was devised by a Japanese (Mikimoto), and they remain one of the favourite purchases in Japan. Mikimoto is still the world leader in fine pearls, but many other companies also produce good quality pearls.

In the Ise area (not far from Kyoto/Nara) you can see how the oysters are induced to produce pearls, and the largest number of the gems that you are ever likely to encounter in your life. It is a good opportunity to see the range of colours available before buying: gold, silver, grey, black and white. It wouldn't hurt to check prices in Tokyo in advance to see if they are better at the source, but be sure that you have exactly the same specifications of size of pearl(s), number, colour, etc, so that the comparison is valid. The value of pearls varies with rarity, of course, so large pearls, and some colours are worth more. Because of increasing pollution off the coast of Japan, producers are now harvesting the pearls earlier, so more small pearls are being produced than before. Whether new growing areas in other parts of the world will maintain the supply of large pearls, or whether large ones would be a good investment is hard to say.

Americans buying pearls should note a quirk in the law that sets a 2½% duty rate on unknotted strings of pearls, but 27½% for knotted strings.

Cars, Motorcycles & Bicycles

Information regarding the purchase of vehicles is given in the 'Getting Around' chapter.

Swords (katana)

Japanese swords are the finest weapons of their kind ever made anywhere in the world. Because of the great skill and workmanship (described under Seki in the Central Honshu chapter), good swords have very high prices, often millions of yen. They are like jewels made of steel. Few foreigners can appreciate the fine details of a good sword, such as the pattern in the grain of the steel of the blade, consequently they do not attach the mystique to a sword that the Japanese do and would not wish to pay the high prices demanded. 'Swords' selling for Y10,000 or so are nothing but toys, pieces of ordinary steel shaped like a sword and chrome-plated to give the outward appearance of the mirror-like side of a real sword, and are only for yokels.

Although a sword is both expensive and not very useful in daily life, give thought to buying a knife for carving turkey. The process used produces knives that take an incredibly sharp edge. Prices for good ones are quite steep, Y20,000-30,000, but an adequate one with a 30 cm blade can be bought for Y5000 or so. Many shops sell them. For example, in Tokyo there is one

A Shamisen players at Takanawa Prince Hotel's annual cherry blossom festival, Tokyo

B A pilgrim at Asakusa Kannon temple, Tokyo

C Traditional Japanese archery at Ueno, Tokyo

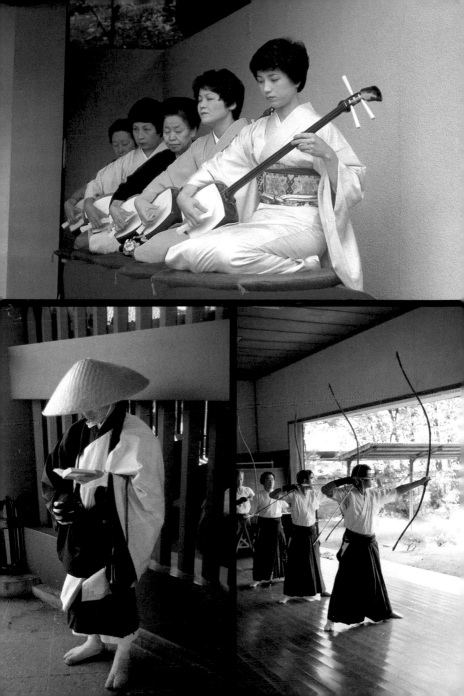

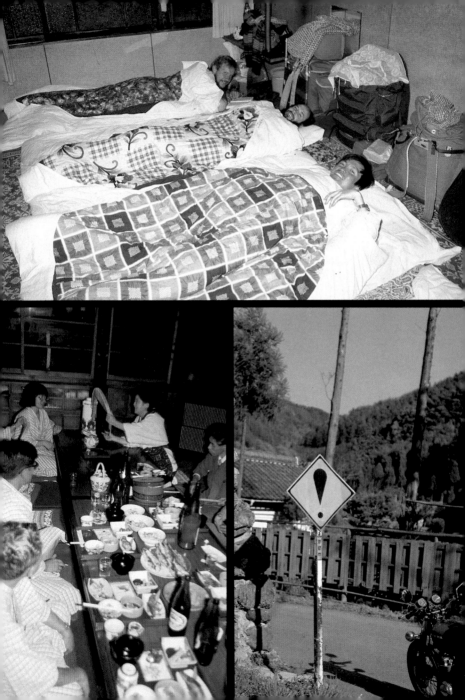

on Chuo-dori in the same block as but opposite Kabukiza, and another in Shinjuku between Takano and Mitsukoshi department store.

Kimono

Although the kimono (pronounced ki-mo-no, with equal stress on all syllables) looks beautiful on Japanese women, it does not adapt well to being worn by taller western women. Even Japanese women must take many hours of lessons to learn how to put on and wear a kimono correctly. So-called kimono sold in tourist shops have only a passing resemblance to the real thing. If it is emblazoned with images of Mt Fuji, shrines, temples, cherry blossoms and Tokyo Tower, you can be sure it isn't the real thing.

Unfortunately, the beautiful cloth for kimono is too narrow to make into western style of clothing, and can usefully be employed only for wall hangings or similar purposes (where it would get more exposure than if worn). Good kimono cloth is extremely expensive. It may be seen in any large department store; some smaller shops sell nothing but cloth and accessories.

Another material to consider for wall hangings is the sash (obi); some of them are also very attractive, and costly.

Incidentally, although the style of all kimono looks the same to untrained eyes, there are several styles for wearing

A *Typical scene in a youth hostel: sleeping on tatami mats, covered with a warm furon (a type of quilt)*
B *Evening scene in a minshuku, this one in an old thatched farmhouse at Shirakawa-go (Gifu-ken)*
C *A comment on driving conditions in Japan*

to various occasions. The most readily discernible is the length of the sleeves: formal kimono have very long sleeves.

Used kimono, often of very beautiful cloth and patterns, may be bought in stores in Tokyo and Kyoto; ask at the TIC offices for information.

Model equipment

For another kind of enthusiast, there is a large variety of radio-controlled (R/C) and other equipment for model aircraft, boats and cars. Specifications may vary from country to country. Some manufacturers (eg Futaba) make only equipment that meets USA specifications, while others (eg Kyosho) manufacture special models for the American market.

There are several hobby shops that can provide such equipment. One where some staff speak English is Aile Ken 4, not far from Roppongi station.

It is advisable to know prices back home before buying in Japan; the savings may not be large enough to make it worthwhile, and the guarantee is valid only in the country of purchase.

Engines are a good buy compared with their price in many foreign countries. The best known manufacturers are Enya and OS who specialize in larger sizes; Fuji and G Mark are known mainly for smaller displacement engines. There are also some specialty manufacturers who make unusual configurations, some of which are never seen outside Japan.

Radio-controlled model cars have become very popular in recent years, some powered by batteries, others by engines. A large variety of models is available.

Exquisitely detailed miniature railroad equipment is sold in Japan, particularly HO and N scale. Some locomotives sell for as much as Y150,000 each and are miniature masterpieces of the model maker's art. More reasonably priced model equipment is also available. Two places to look are Tenshodo and Itoya, both in the Ginza area.

DANGERS AND ANNOYANCES

Japan is one of the safest countries in the world for foreigners and locals alike. It is safe to walk on the streets of almost any section of any city or town in Japan at any time of night or day without risk of assault, mugging, or worse. There are a few areas that might be risky, populated by derelicts, and the rougher of the day-labourers ('jikatabi', so named for their split-toe shoes) who often drink to forget their unsatisfactory life, but these areas are far from the usual tourist beat. At one time gangs of youths were robbing intoxicated celebrants in the very expensive Ginza entertainment area, but the police soon put a stop to them and anyway they were more of a threat to Japanese than to foreign visitors. One reason for this is that Japanese generally carry more cash for entertainment than westerners do; also geisha entertainment is too expensive (and too boring) for the average foreigner. Attacks on foreigners are rare in any case, partly due to general respect for (white) foreigners (often unwarranted!).

For theft of personal belongings, such as cameras, Japan is one of the lowest-risk countries in the world. Probably the riskiest places are those with large numbers of tourists, such as the airports. Generally throughout Japan, particularly away from the large cities, one could leave a suitcase unattended for hours and find it on returning. There are even tales of absent-minded persons leaving cameras on park benches and returning hours later to find them still there, but this isn't recommended. The average Japanese is just very honest. Lost goods are very likely to be turned in to the police or transport authority, so if you leave

something valuable behind on a train, don't give up, for there is a very good chance that it has been turned in.

The remarks on theft and honesty do not apply to umbrellas; these will disappear without a trace if left in an unlocked drip-tray on a rainy day. Also, bicycle owners should lock their bikes.

Even if you are sharing your room at a youth hostel, it is usually safe to leave your belongings unattended. Japanese hostellers regularly leave their cameras or other valuables lying on their beds.

Burglaries are quite common in the big cities, although they are rarely reported in the English-language papers, so take all the usual precautions applicable in any city. In small towns you may find that the locals don't bother locking their doors very much, but don't be insulted if they start locking up when they hear that a foreigner has moved into the neighbourhood!

One of the main lessons that the rest of the world could learn from Japan is how to get along with other people in crowded surroundings. Most of the misunderstood ways of the Japanese people, as seen by foreigners, come about from this accommodation process. What may seem to be insincerity on the part of a Japanese could be cross-cultural misunderstanding. Japanese have a trait of talking and acting in such a way as to maintain the greatest degree of harmony, even if it means not telling the truth. In the case of two Japanese, they both know it is not the truth, but they see it as a way to avoid saying something unpleasant to each other, and both try to maintain the required harmony. In other words no Japanese who is functioning within the constraints of his society will look for trouble, especially with foreigners. Very occasionally, a Japanese, after an overindulgence in alcohol and xenophobia, has been known to try to attack a foreigner, but by the time the booze has diminished his ability to function effectively, so such a man is likely to be nothing more than an annoyance.

If, by the way, things ever come to the physical stage, there are two things to remember. First, usually no one will come to your aid. In Japan one just does not get involved in the affairs of anyone other than family or acquaintances. Secondly, if the police are involved, any foreigner present is automatically suspected of being the culprit, and is likely to be arrested even if he is an innocent bystander.

Much of the misunderstandings between Japanese and foreigners is a result of misinformation. Many books and movies present a very distorted view of Westerners especially their sexual habits, so sometimes women travellers get openly propositioned. Usually ignoring the advance or walking away will be sufficient to discourage the man. (Conversely, to be fair, many western men have an equally distorted view of Asian women and their habits.)

For women who want to discourage unwanted amorous attentions from Japanese men, there is a message in Japanese at the back of this book.

A hazard of a different nature is the lighted cigarette. Japan seems to have a very high proportion of smokers so in crowded areas such as busy streets or stations, watch out or you may get a hole burnt in your clothes.

Natural Hazards

Like most countries of the world, Japan has mosquitoes. Not in huge swarms but enough to make it advisable to use insect repellent. Their bites are relatively innocuous. Mosquitoes occur from summer into late November.

Japan has many popular swimming beaches and every summer weekend there are numerous drownings. Don't take chances. There are no trained lifeguards so try to swim with a 'buddy'. Some beaches have a dangerous undertow.

There are two kinds of poisonous snakes in Japan, both deadly. All the main islands are the habitat of the mamushi, while the habu is found only in the islands south of Kyushu, between Kagoshima and Okinawa. Like most snakes, they will usually try to escape from people if not cornered or startled; snakes are deaf so they cannot hear people's approach in advance and hide, although they can feel vibrations in the ground.

The mamushi usually grows to a length of 70 cm or so, has a diamond shaped head with a moderately thick body, and is covered with a pattern of dark circles with lighter centers. The habu is larger, up to 2 meters long and has the stronger venom of the two. It is found both in trees and in grass, has a diamond-shaped head, and a pattern of diamonds on its body.

Earthquakes

Earthquakes are common throughout Japan. Most quakes are very mild, a mere tremble, and not enough to cause any damage.

The most famous disaster was the Kanto earthquake of 1923 that killed about 40,000 people in the Tokyo and Kanto area. Buildings of that day were mostly flimsy wooden structures, and many of the deaths were the result of their collapse or ensuing fires. All buildings in the Tokyo area must now be built to resist earthquake damage, so an equally strong one would probably have a lower death toll despite the vast increase in population.

In case you are caught in a strong quake, the best actions to take are: (1) Do not use elevators. (2) Stand near a supporting pillar or in a doorway, and far from the centre of a room; the former will be the strongest part of the structure, and the centre of a room is the part most likely to collapse. Ducking under a desk or table is a good second-best, and better than no protection from falling debris. (3) Get outdoors if possible, and move as far as possible away from buildings.

Doors

Paling into insignificance as a hazard after earthquakes is the warning that anyone taller than 175 cm must be on constant guard for low doorways. Until recently the Japanese were a very short people and doorways were made to suit. Sliding doors (shoji) seem to have a uniform height of 180 cm. Train entrances are also low. (Young Japanese today are much taller, probably the result of better diet.)

ZEN STUDY & MEDITATION

Some visitors to Japan may wish to participate in Zen studies and zazen meditation. Most temples and instruction centres in Japan will accept those who speak Japanese or are already familiar with the practices of Zen meditation. Otherwise foreigners are generally not welcomed unless they have an introduction from a responsible Zen teacher. However, there are few places that do welcome foreigners; these have been established specifically to introduce foreigners to Zen and its practices, so these are the best places in Japan to begin. Most of these activities are in Tokyo and the surrounding area.

Tokyo (Metropolitan)

The Zen Centre has the most regular programs. There is zazen meditation every Monday, Wednesday and Friday from 6 to 7.30 pm and every Tuesday, Thursday and Saturday from 9 to 10.30 am. In addition, there is special instruction session for newcomers to Zen every Saturday from 2 to 4 pm.

Once a month Rev Matsunaga, the priest under whom the Centre is operated, visits Tokyo and delivers a lecture. For information on the Centre, call Ann Sargent, (03) 404-5755.

Zen seminars are given in English every Saturday by Rev G Nishijima at one or two locations in the Tokyo area. These are usually publicized in the 'Announcements' section on the back page of the *Japan Times*. For information, call Rev Nishijima at (03) 866-4171 ext 44 (business hours), or Mr H Saito, (03) 581-0261 ext 5141. A modest Y200 fee is charged for each lecture.

Tokyo Area

Zen training sessions extending over Saturday and Sunday are held monthly (usually) at Jokuin temple at Higashi-Matsuyama in nearby Saitama prefecture (Saitama-ken). This temple has been specifically set aside for instructing laymen; participants are not required to have had any prior training. Instructions are given in both English and Japanese. This is a moderately rigorous course, and requires rising at 4 am for meditation. A fee of Y2000 is charged including overnight accommodation and three meals.

For further information, contact Gaynor Jenke at (03) 981-8469 (in English), or the temple, (0493) 23-9815 (in Japanese only).

There are several other temples in the Tokyo area where you can participate in zazen. However, no English is spoken at most of these so best to go with someone who can translate. Two such temples are Eiheiji-Betsuin in Tokyo and Sojiji in Yokohama. These, and all other Zen activities described so far, are of the Soto sect. For information on these temples, and Zen activities in general anywhere in the Tokyo area, it is best to use the willing assistance of Ann Sargent or Gaynore Jenke.

Elsewhere in Japan

Eiheiji temple is one of the two main temples of the Soto sect in Japan. Eiheiji is famous throughout Japan. It is located near Fukui which is on the east shore of Lake Biwa, not too far from Kyoto. Its magnificent and historic buildings and setting on a mountainside make it a target of thousands of sightseers each year, along with the many who wish to study Zen. Foreigners are invited to participate in the activities of the temple and may arrange accommodation there. It is necessary to arrange this in advance. Contact: Sanzenkei, Eiheiji, Eiheiji-cho, Yoshida-gun, Fukui-ken. This should be done well in advance of a proposed visit in order to give time for making arrangements.

Jofukuji on Shikoku is a small, local temple that also functions as a Yoth Hostel (7404 in the YH Handbook). The younger priest is friendly and speaks good English. He welcomes visitors who wish to join him informally in meditation. It is a 'family'-type temple and no advance arrangements need to be made for Zen participation although, like any Hostel, it may be booked up at any time, so it is advisable to check ahead to be sure there is space. The temple is located on the side of a valley, peaceful at any time, very pretty in November when the leaves change colour. The address: Jofukuji, 158 Ao, Otoyo-machi, Nagaoka-gun, Kochi-ken. Tel (08877) 4-0301.

Kaiohji once offered a course for female foreigners. Anyone who is curious can make inquiries. The temple is located in Katsuura, on the Kii Peninsula which is between Nagoya and Osaka, not too far from Kyoto/Nara. The address: Kaiohji, Katsuura, Nachi-Katsuura-cho, Wakayama-ken. Tel (07355) 2-0839.

Kyoto can offer no temples where foreigners can receive instruction in English. Several temples used to allow foreigners to join in meditation, but too many became restless and disturbed others. An introduction from another priest would be best to obtain admittance to temples in Kyoto. For further information, contact the Tourist Information Centre in Kyoto, they may be able to help.

For complete information on all the temples in Japan that will accommodate foreigners, send Y500 in stamps plus a self-addressed stamped envelope to: John Stevens, Mukaiyama 3-15-16, Sendai 982.

ZEN SECTS

There are two main Zen sects in Japan, Soto and Rinzai. Differences between them are minor. In zazen, Soto practitioners face a wall while in Rinzai they face the room; Rinzai uses more koan (riddles) than Soto; and Soto sessions last longer, typically 40-50 minutes against 20 or so for Rinzai.

The Rinzai sect is more active in giving classes for laymen, but these are almost exclusively in Japanese; the Soto sect seems to have more programs in English.

A good introduction to Zen is *Zen Mind, Beginner's Mind*, by Shunryo Suzuki, a Soto priest. There is a very large selection of Zen books at English language bookstores in Japan, especially in Tokyo (Kinokuniya, Maruzen, etc).

SPORTS

Sumo

Not well known to foreigners except for its 'fat wrestlers', Sumo is a very Japanese sport and interesting to watch. Two men face each other in an earth circle and grapple when they both feel ready. The loser is the first one pushed or thrown out of the cirlce or who touches the ground with any part of his body other than his feet. The action lasts between a second and a couple of minutes.

There are six basho (tournaments) per year according to the following schedule: early January (Tokyo); mid-March (Osaka); early May (Tokyo); early July (Nagoya); mid-September (Tokyo); mid-November (Fukuoka).

Seats cost from the mid-hundreds to the mid-thousands, but the best view is that on TV, broadcast live from 4 to

6 pm, with a summary of all 15 bouts late in the evening.

Baseball

The Japanese are as baseball-mad as the Americans, and fans of the game might enjoy seeing a game while in Japan. The players are good, although it is admitted that the US leagues are at a higher level yet.

Skiing

Japan offers good skiing if you live here, but it would not be worth making a special trip for. Information on ski areas and resorts is available from the Tourist Information Centre. Some are mentioned in general descriptions of the areas, later in the book.

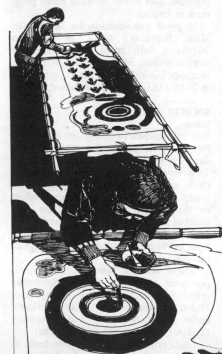

WEIGHTS & MEASURES

Japan uses the metric (SI) system so you will find kilograms, litres, metres and Celsius temperature measurement. For those who are still unfamiliar with these measurements the following rules of thumb may help:

A metre is a bit more than a yard (about 10% more). Three metres is close to 10 feet so a 300-metre mountain is about 10,000 feet high.

A centimetre is a bit under half an inch and one inch is about 2.5 cm, so one foot is close to 30 cm.

One kilometre is close to 5/8 of a mile, and a mile is 1.6 km.

For areas, one hectare (ha) is about 2.5 acres.

One kilogram (kg) is a bit more than two pounds (about 10% more). The luggage weight limit on most airlines is 20 kg or 44 lb.

For temperatures, to convert Celsius (known in some parts as Centigrade) to Fahrenheit, a simple rule is to double and add 30. (To be precise you multiply by 9/5 and add 32).

One litre (1 l) is close to 35 British fluid ounces or 34 US fluid ounces; or about one US quart; or about 1¾ British pints. Four litres is slightly over one US gallon and a bit under a British gallon.

Accommodation

The travel industry is well established in Japan and there is accommodation of almost every type throughout the country. Most of it is designed for Japanese tastes so that outside the major cities which are visited by tourists and foreign businessmen, the facilities are mostly Japanese style and western-style accommodation will be less common. Even when facilities are billed as western in style they may not live up to foreigners expectations. Large hotels in the metropolitan areas are well up to international standards (and prices).

There is no equivalent in Japan of the cheap Chinese hotels of South-East Asia. The cheapest room in Japan is around Y1000 and most are higher. This chapter deals mainly with low-priced accommodation in the various ports of entry (sea and air). After you have been in Japan for the first traumatic day or two you should begin to understand the 'system' enough to rely more on local sources of information for making your way around.

The Japan National Tourist Organization (JNTO) has prepared several booklets and brochures on accommodation. These are available at the Tourist Information Centres operated by the JNTO. One JNTO publication worth mentioning is 'Reasonable Accommodation in Japan' (Code Number MG-12). This lists economical places to stay in 26 cities around Japan. 'Reasonable' in this case means Y3500 and up per person. Accommodation prices quoted in Japan are nearly always 'per person'.

If you arrive in a town without having booked a place to stay, the local railway station usually has an office that gives help in finding accommodation. However, listings at stations often lack the lowest-cost places. There are usually many ryokan near a station of any size. Family-owned ryokan have lower rates than commercial ones; If

wandering in search of a ryokan, look for large numbers of shoes at the entranceway. Also, the entranceway will usually be quite wide and open, unlike the average rather secluded entrance to a house. People at small tobacco shops or other local businesses can often give help in finding a ryokan or minshuku.

HOTELS

Hotels as they are known in the West, with beds, familiar furniture and amenities, can be found in the major cities, especially cities where foreigners go frequently for business, as well as in popular resort and tourist areas. In smaller centres a 'hotel' is likely to have a mixture of western and Japanese style rooms and with an equal confusion about what is expected in service. The quality of facilities and service in Japan can vary from internationally acceptable levels in the major centres to something much less pretentious (but nearly as expensive) in more remote area. In this book some hotel accommodation will be listed in the sections covering larger cities.

A good listing of over 250 hotels of internationally acceptable standards, along with nearly 160 ryokan, is contained in the JNTO publication 'Hotels and Ryokan in Japan' (305-E). The places listed usually have air conditioning or central heating and other modern facilities. Prices for rooms of various sizes are listed along with the contact adress and the means of getting there.

The Tourist Information Centres at Narita airport and central Tokyo, and at Kyoto also have detailed information on hotel and other accommodation throughout Japan.

BUSINESS HOTELS

This type of accommodation has appeared in Japan in recent years. It is intended primarily for travelling businessmen who want respectable and clean accommodation without the high cost of luxury hotels. It achieves economy by eliminating frills like room service — each floor has vending machines for drinks, etc. Costs vary from Y2000 to Y5000 for a single; doubles cost somewhat more. There are many such hotels in commercial cities around the country.

RYOKAN

To sample the best of Japanese life try to spend at least one night at a ryokan. Unfortunately the name covers a wide variety of facilities. At its best, the ryokan embodies the best of Japanese hospitality and elegance, providing a simple but flawless traditional Japanese style room with high quality furnishings and the best in food and service. The senses should be pleased or soothed in all ways including visually, so a good ryokan should have a beautiful garden, not necessarily large, but definitely elegant. Unfortunately, there are many places called ryokan that do not live up to such expectations, but if the facilities are of high standard then the time spent there can provide some of the best memories of Japan.

There are 80,000 or so ryokan scattered around Japan. Many of these are rather ordinary and of little interest. Some will not let you stay, not because of racism, but because they are very exclusive — even Japanese cannot book into them unless introduced by someone of high enough position who ensures the ryokan that the visitor is worthy of being allowed to stay there. Other ryokan do not want foreigners to stay because bad experiences in the past with foreigners who did not know how to behave, did not understand the system, or made demands that the staff were not able to meet. (In general, Japanese are convinced that their way of life is completely beyond the understanding of foreigners, and that for-

eigners of any kind will just not fit in.) If you can make yourself understood in Japanese many more ryokan will be open to you.

The JNTO has prepared two booklets containing listings of ryokan that are accustomed to or prepared to accept foreign visitors. These are 'Japan Ryokan Guide' (303-E), and 'Hotels and Ryokan in Japan' (305-E). Each booklet has a section giving further details on what a ryokan is like and explaining how a guest should behave. These booklets are available from JNTO offices and the Tourist Information Centres in Tokyo and Kyoto. Another booklet 'Enjoy Japanese Life at Ryokan' is published by the Japan Ryokan Association, and also describes the features of the ryokan and how to enjoy them. It is available at the Tokyo TIC.

Bookings can be made in every part of the country at any travel agent, especially JTB. Also, at every railway station of any size there is an information office (ryoko an nai jo) that has listings of all accommodation in the surrounding vicinity. They can make reservations on the spot, but it is rare to find anyone who can speak English at these offices.

MINSHUKU

Short-time visitors to Japan usually have little opportunity to see the inside of a Japanese house. Even fewer stay overnight. However it is a simple matter to arrange to stay at a minshuku a family home that takes guests. There are minshuku (pronounced much like minsh'ku') in every area with tourist attractions, such as historic towns, coastal villages, hot spring resorts, ski areas, etc. Most towns and villages have one or two and there are thousands scattered throughout Japan, operated by local people such as fishermen, farmers and townspeople.

Some minshuku are interesting in themselves and are an actual attraction to visitors. At Shirakawa (Gifu Pref.) there are many huge old thatched roof houses in an isolated valley. Some of the houses are minshuku, and afford the opportunity to spend the night in a very unusual farmhouse, even by Japanese standards, one that may be a couple of hundred years old.

For travellers not on an absolutely bare-bones budget, minshuku are the best places in Japan to stay to gain an impression of what the real Japan is like.

Where guest houses abroad may be rather impersonal affairs, in a minshuku the guest is made to feel like part of the family. It is the best sort of place to experience the warmth of ordinary Japanese. Foreigners are rare, and you may be the first ever to stay at a particular home. The hosts may have a few misgivings at first because many Japanese have never met or seen a foreigner, but if you can reassure them that you won't use soap in the bathtub then they will relax and there will be no problems. The big problem may be that they are too kind — there are many stories of hosts pouring drinks all evening (at no charge) because of the honour of the visit!

Minshuku are not hotels so there is minimum 'maid service'. Guests make their own beds at night and put the bedding away in the morning, provide their own towels, etc. Charges are relatively uniform throughout Japan, about Y3500 per person per night, including supper and breakfast. It is possible to negotiate a reduction if meals are not needed, but they are often local delicacies and it may be one of the few opportunities to sample typical Japanese cooking.

If you who have no knowledge of Japanese but who would like to stay at a minshuku you could try contacting Tescort (see 'People & Language') and ask if any members would be interested in accompanying you on such a trip (at their own expense). Such an excursion would give them the opportunity to practise their English while give you a personal guide to take care of the language troubles and to explain what you are seeing.

Travellers on their own can easily find a minshuku from a railway station of any size. There is usually an information office (an nai jo) with listings of minshuku and other accommodation in the surrounding area. They will phone ahead and make bookings, also giving warning that foreigners are on the way.

Travellers who begin their excursion from Tokyo can make reservations by computer. There are several offices in Tokyo that can do this, but the most convenient one to use is Travel Nippon because they speak English. It is located close to the TIC office in Yurakucho. The address is:

Travel Nippon
2-2-1 Yurakucho
Chiyoda-ku
Tokyo
tel (03) 572-1461

It is located on the 5th floor of the Rakucho Bldg and is open Monday to Saturday from 9 am to 5 pm. To find the office, stop by at the Tourist Information Centre and get directions from there.

A very good leaflet in English describing minshuku and how to act at one (folding bedding, eating, etc) is available from:

Japan Minshuku Association
New Pearl Bldg Rm 201
10-8 Hyakunincho 2-chome
Shinjuku
tel 371-8120

and possibly through the Tourist Information Centre. Accompanying it is a listing of a large number of minshuku in nearly all regions of the country that are better prepared than the average minshuku to take foreign guests; a map shows their general location.

YOUTH HOSTELS

Budget-watching travellers in Japan usually stay in the Youth Hostels. There are over 500 of them, scattered nearly everywhere in Japan that people normally want to go. They are clean and respectable, and they are reasonably priced (by Japanese standards, anyway). There is usually no other accommodation at prices as low, although some ryokan and minshuku may be in a similar price range.

To stay at most youth hostels in Japan you need a valid membership card issued by a Youth Hostel association belonging to the International Youth Hostel Federation (IYHF). It is best to buy a membership card in your home country, but if this isn't possible, then an International Guest Card (IGC) can be purchased from national headquarters in Tokyo or from the prefectural head office. The price is approximately US$9. About 73 hostels, detailed below, do not require a YH membership card, a foreign passport is adequate.

The International Guest Card is also available as a replacement in case a card is lost. The purchase price (less Y100) will be refunded (within Japan) after a replacement card has been received from the original issuing office and shown at the Tokyo head office.

Despite the name, there is no age limit who may use the hostels. There are, however, more regulations than at other accommodation. Until recently these regulations included curfew at 9 pm.

Hostels were closed between 10 am and 3 pm and hostellers were segregated by sex. Some of these restrictions have now been eased. A regulation sleeping sheet is required at nearly every hostel. These can be rented at each hostel, but the cost soon mounts up so it is better to make your own. The design has been standarized internationally, and every YH association has the specifications. Alternatively, one can be delivered in Japan by mail for Y550 and Y300 respectively. Only a few hostels permit a sleeping bag to be used.

The best listing of hostels by far is the (Japan) Youth Hostel Handbook. Anyone planning to stay at more than a couple of hostels would be well advised to buy it, either by mail or on arrival. It is written mostly in Japanese, but there is adequate explanation in English and profuse use of symbols so that foreigners can use it easily. It lists every hostel in Japan by district (with maps to show general locations), with a code number and the address in both Japanese and romaji. There is also a detailed map and access information for each hostel, the telephone number (for booking or assistance in finding the hostel), the number of beds, costs of meals and heating, dates when open, and the type of hostel.

This last bit of information is very valuable. There are eight types of hostel in Japan: built and managed by the JYHA (51), built privately (107), built with government subsidy (municipal) (75), managed by other youth organization (55), private house (61), temple (76), shrine (7), ryokan (144). As a general rule it is best to avoid JYHA hostels. While they often have the best physical facilities, too often the staff tend to be unfriendly, officious or even rude. No doubt there are good JYHA hostels, and perhaps it is unfair to judge them by a few, but Nara YH (5501), for example, has had a poor reputation as far back as 1970. (The number in brackets is the code number used in the Handbook to identify hostels. There is another hostel in Nara that is more friendly so check the numbers to get the right one!) In balance it should be noted that at least one municipal hostel, Nikko YH, also had some rather rude staff who even turned members out of bed at 6.45 am even though they didn't plan to eat the hostel breakfast. Given the opportunity, it is preferable to stay at other types of hostels, especially the temples, shrines, private homes and ryokan. Staff there are usually friendly and the atmosphere relaxed. (I have met one hosteller who planned his travels so that he can stay exclusively at temples.)

Hostellers staying at Buddhist temple hostels may be wakened abruptly at 6.30 by drumming. This happens Jofukufi (7404), a Zen temple in a particularly beautiful valley setting on Shikoku island. The priest there speaks English and invites visitors to join in zazen meditation.

As a general rule visitors may use the 75 municipal Youth Hostels without having a YH card — a passport is adequate. Such hostels are described in the Handbook as 'built with government subsidy'. Useful ones to know about are Hinoyama YH at Shimonoseki (port for the ferry from Pusan, Korea), and both Nagai YH and Hattori-Ryokuchi YH at Osaka. There is no such hostel at Kyoto or Tokyo.

In Tokyo the Handbook is sold at the national HQ, a 10 minute walk from Ichigaya YH (described in the Tokyo section). Hours are 9 am to 5.30 pm weekdays, 9 am to 4 pm Saturdays.

The Youth Hostel Handbook is sold by many hostels around the country and at the national headquarters in Tokyo (not far from Ichigaya YH). The Handbook can also be ordered and sent by mail to a Poste Restante address. The Handbook can also be ordered and sent by mail to a Poste Restante address. The Handbook costs Y350; postage

within Japan is Y300, or Y370 by surface mail to other countries. Airmail postage to Australia, New Sealand or South East Asia is Y590; to North and Central America, Y730; and to Europe, Y870.

The national HQ also has a free booklet 'Hostelling Way in Japan'. It has much more information on hostel rules, rail fares, a list of hostels with bicycle rentals, distances between cities and other information, but its prices may be out of date.

There is also a free JNTO booklet 'Youth Hostels in Japan'. It lists every hostel in the country by region, but it lacks maps for locating them, either overall or detailed. Only the name is written in Japanese, not the address which can make it difficult if you need assistance in finding the hostel.

The third, and least satisfactory, listing of hostels in Japan is the 'IYHF Handbook Vol II' which lists hostels in Africa, America, Asia and Australasia. This booklet, Y600 in Japan, lists less than half the hostels in Japan, gives no instructions in Japanese, and is not detailed in its descriptions of locations. For travel in Japan it is a waste of money but it might be useful for travel in the other countries which it covers.

Generally very little English is spoken at any of the hostels or at the head office. If corresponding with the head office, always send International Postal Reply Coupons for the return postage. YH associations everywhere operate on tight budgets and cannot afford to pay return postage. An alternative if the postage will be high is to estimate the cost and remit it by postal or other money order.

During the busy seasons (New Year holidays, March, late April to mid-May, July and August) it is advisable to make advance bookings. This is most easily done by computer bookings in Tokyo and Osaka. In Tokyo booking offices are located at:

Shinjuku: Keio Dept Store-6fl
Yurakucho: Sogo Dept Store-2 basement (near the TIC)
In Osaka there is one location:
Shinsaibashi: Sogo Dept Store (near Osaka station)

It is necessary to pay a Y200 deposit (credited to the cost of the room) per person per overnight, plus a booking fee of Y50. The offices in Tokyo are open daily except Thursday from 10 am to 6 pm.

An alternative to computer booking is the use of return postage paid postcards. Blank ones are available from post offices but it is much simpler to use pre-printed ones that have spaces for all the required information. These cost Y80 for ten from the head office. Postage in Japan is Y140.

If you cannot book ahead it will usually be possible to get a bed at most hostels throughout the year with the possible exception of the most popular areas during the school holidays. The most popular areas are Kyoto/Nara and resorts, especially those in the mountains. To check on vacancies the simplest way is to telephone ahead a day or two in advance and make a booking. Japanese hostellers usually don't mind making the call for foreigners. Another reason for planning ahead is that some hostels inconveniently take holidays that are not listed in the Handbook.

If you are planning to eat the hostel supper, it is essential to phone ahead, or else arrive early enough to permit the cook to prepare the extra food. Hostel meals are adequate nutritionally, but very few are gastronomic delights.

Many hostels have 'members' cooking' (jisui), which means that hostellers have the use of a gas cooker and pots and pans. The gas is usually metered so it can be a contest to try to finish cooking the meal with one 10 yen coin. There is a small charge, Y20-30, for the

use of the kitchen. There are many kinds of food that can be easily prepared, like fruit, vegetables, meat, fish and poultry. There is a wide variety of canned food, and everything is of good standard. The instant food revolution has also hit Japan with a fury, and there are many things, especially noodle dishes, that can be prepared quickly.

Staying at Youth Hostels offers other advantages in addition to the relatively low cost; in particular there is the opportunity to observe what Japanese homes and people are like. Although the hostels are institutional in nature, and many buildings are modern structures with not a hint of Japanese origin in them, many others are like enlargements of the traditional Japanese house. They may have the soft tatami mat floors, sliding shoji doors, and many typical architectural details, like the tokonoma (alcove) with a painting, scroll or other decoration. The bath will be like that of an average home (probably larger in scale), and hostellers sleep on mats laid out on the tatami. The modern buildings usually have furnishings to match, and usually have western style bunk beds.

Staying at hostels also gives the opportunity to meet a number of young Japanese and find out what makes them tick. While few can coverse in depth in foreign languages, it is usually still possible to carry on simple coversations. One feature immediately noticeable to westerners is the general lack of social mingling of sexes. To overcome this there may be a 'meeting', the Japanese word used to describe an hour-long get-together in the evening. This can include information such as a talk about the attractions of the nearby area, transport facilities, etc, followed by party games which serve the purpose of breaking down the barriers of shyness. Most westerners opt out unless dragooned into attending, for it is all in Japanese. During the summer there are often unscheduled and informal activities, like bonfires, and fireworks, or playing traditional games. There may also be less traditional pastimes such as guitar playing, or disco dancing to the music of a portable cassette player.

Most hostels are goldmines of information on attractions in the surrounding area. There are usually bulletin boards covered with train, bus and boat schedules and other useful information. Usually is all in Japanese, but you should be able to get some help in reading it.

Virtually all hostels have posted rules and hours for eating, bathing, lights out and getting up. At busy hostels these are usually rigidly adhered to, but during the off-season, or when there are few people staying there, the rules may be relaxed greatly, especially for foreigners who often receive differential treatment everywhere in Japan. In recent years several rules have been relaxed at the 75 or so municipal hostels: curfew has been extended from 9 pm to 10.30 and lights out from 10 pm to 11 pm. A radical departure from the past is that alcohol is allowed in some hostels as long as the drinkers do not disturb other guests. Whenever possible, married couples will be given rooms together in these hostels. (The curfew is no hardship, by the way, except in large metropolitan areas, as Japanese towns go to sleep early.)

Bath hours usually have their rules too. At some hostels you can take a bath at any time during the evening, while at others one may not use the bath outside the prescribed hours even though the tub is sitting unused and full of water that will go to waste. (It is almost impossible, by the way, to take a bath or shower in the morning. To do so would run counter to centuries of tradition.

Being public institutions, municipally-owned hostels often have magnificent locations on prime real estate. Hinoyama YH at Shimonoseki commands a superb view of the Kanmon Strait that separates Honshu from Kyushu, and the new and graceful suspension bridge that spans the gap. Other hostels are situated close to places of natural beauty. Ura-Bandai YH (1606-Tohoku) is only a short distance from an emerald-green lake and numerous other smaller ponds of similar intense colour. It also features a good view of the jagged top of Mt Bandai. There are many other hostels around the country with equally fine settings.

If you stay at a Youth Hostel where you must share a room with Japanese hostellers, you may find that you have to fight a guerilla action to get a window open for fresh air during the night, even in mid-summer. There seems to be a perpetuation of the idea held in medieval Europe that night air is somehow dangerous and must be shut out at all costs, even on a hot night in an eight-bunk small room. The modern hostels with solid concrete walls and close-fitting doors and windows are the worst in this respect. The older, more traditional buildings are sufficiently draughty that this isn't much of a problem (though they are cooler in winter!). Another possible inconvenience if there is a group of young people in the same or an adjoining room, is that they are likely to wake up early, between 5 and 6 am, and start talking and giggling among themselves, quite oblivious of the fact that other people might want to sleep.

The polite way to ask them to be quiet is to say 'Shizuka-ni sh'te kudasai', or for a much stronger effect just say 'shizuka-ni!' in a firm tone.

PENSIONS

The word 'pension' has been borrowed from the French and in Japan refers to accommodation of a somewhat rustic lodge-type building. There is a strong association with sports, usually in fairly remote country areas. Many are located near ski hills, and may have other sports facilities like boating, swimming, tennis, walking trails, table tennis, cycling and so on.

Pensions are generally operated by younger people so the spirit of the places is more open and unrestricted than Youth Hostels, while the facilities are more elaborate and luxurious than those of a minshuku and more homey than a hotel. Prices are higher than those of a minshuku: the cheapest run about Y3400/5400/7900 single/double/triple plus Y1500 for dinner, while more expensive ones run up to Y5200/7200/9700.

The pension idea is very recent, dating only from around 1973, but already there are over 200 around the country from southern Kyushu to Tohoku. The pensions are not especially set up for foreign guests, but anyone with a sense of fun and adaptability will be able to get by and enjoy the features offered.

The pensions are listed, often with photos or sketches in a booklet *Pension '80* (revised annually) available at bookshops for Y700. It is written only in Japanese but there are sufficient numbers that you should be able to understand the important features, like price. In addition, the Tourist Information Centres in Tokyo and Kyoto can give further information and assistance. Bookings can be made through the following offices, though the help of a Japanese-speaking friend will probably be needed: Tokyo tel (03) 295-6333; Osaka, (06) 448-2641; Sendai, (0222) 65-0534; Fukuoka, (092) 471-7555.

TEMPLES
There are a number of Buddhist temples where visitors can stay overnight. At some temples the visitors may participate in prayer and religious observations such as zazen meditation. At others the accommodation can be regarded just as a room — usually traditional tatami style — that happens to be on temple grounds. Most temples are very graceful structures, and representative of what foreigners think of as the traditional Japan, so it is a good idea to stay at a temple at least once during a vist to Japan.

It is easy to find a temple that accepts guests. At least 75 function as Youth Hostels (along with their religious purposes, of course); these are all listed in the YH Handbook with a symbol. A few temples are modern concrete structures that lack the grace of the traditional wooden temple buildings, some of which embody the finest skills in Japanese woodworking. In the following, numbers in brackets are those in the YH Handbook.

Many temples are quite historic. Zuiryuji (3207, Takaoka) is about 350 years old and has several very large buildings. Other temples are set in beautiful surroundings. For example Jofukuji on Shikoku (7404) is on a hillside overlooking a valley. Jofukuji is a zen temple and one of the priests is a young man who speaks good English and invites people who stay there to join him in zazen meditation. Because it is a 'family' temple it is small, and no advance arrangements need to be made to stay overnight or to join him in meditation, though a phone call would be prudent, as with any hostel.

There are five temples in the Kyoto area that accept lodgers. They are: Enryaku-ji (on Mt Hiei — the number one temple of the Tendai sect with a history of 1200 years), Myoren-ji (noted for its beautiful garden), Komyo-ji Shokubo, Daishin-in (a former detached palace of the Emperor Hanazono that was later rebuilt as a Zen temple), and Inari Taisha Sanshuden. The last named is actually a shrine, not a temple; it is the most important of the many Inari shrines throughout Japan, and is noted for the huge number of torii gates — over 1400 — that have been placed along paths that wind up the mountain.

The prices (accommodation only) range from Y1500 to Y3500. Some offer meals as well. To stay at any of these temples it is best to make arrangements through the Tourist Information Centre in Kyoto. They will also give any further information that may be necessary.

In the area around Koya-san (reasonably close to Nara) there are more than 50 temple lodgings available, virtually covering the mountain. Koya-san is very important in the Buddhist history of Japan and is very popular with pilgrims so accommodation may be hard to obtain. Costs are Y4500 and up with two meals. Reservations can be made through the JTB, or through:

Koyasan Tourist Association
Koyasan
Koya-machi
Into-gun
Wakayama-ken
tel (07365) 6-2616.

CYCLING INNS

There is a small network of cycling inns which have been set up specifically for bicycle travellers, both those on their own bikes and those who rent bikes at the inns. The facilities and costs are similar to those of Youth Hostels, except there is usually a workshop for bike repairs as well. The buildings are all new within the last few years. It is hoped to have one every 100 km or so, but at the moment there are only 19.

The inns have been built in regions of natural beauty that invite exploration by bike; often there are specially constructed cycle paths that are separate from regular highways. In many cases it would be worth a trip to the area for sightseeing. Rental charges are reasonable, as low Y200 for four hours plus Y50 per additional hour, to a maximum of Y250 per hour.

Information about locations and bike rentals in a booklet issued by the Japan Cycling Association called *sai-ku-ring-gu*

te-mi-na-ru ('cycling terminal'). Although it is in Japanese only, approximate locations are shown on a sketch map at the front. Detailed addresses and specific information on how to get there from the nearest railway station is given with the description of each inn and its facilities. Copies can be obtained from the JCA. It may be easier to contact the Japan Bicycle Promotion Institute first as they have English-speaking personnel who can give information and assistance. Write to:

Mr H Konno or Mr H Ise,
Japan Bicycle Promotion Institute
Nihon Jitensha Kaikan Bldg
9-3 Akasaka 1-chome
Minato-ku
Tokyo.
Tel 583-5444.

KOKUMIN SHUKUSHA (PEOPLE'S LODGINGS)

People's Lodgings are accommodation and recreation facilities in a number of popular resort and natural park areas throughout Japan. They have been built by local authorities under the guidance of the Ministry of Health and Welfare as a means of bringing a vacation in pleasant surroundings within the reach of most Japanese. The room charge of about Y3400 per night with two meals is lower than that of most ryokan.

The Lodgings are open to anyone, Japanese or foreigners, and no membership in any organization is required. During the summer and busy travel seasons they tend to be fully booked, or it may be necessary to share a room. Otherwise, anyone showing up at the door will be given a room and couples will be put together, if possible.

Bookings are most easily made through JTB which issues vouchers for reserved rooms, but this system is in effect for only about 70% of the Lodgings and it takes about a week. Bookings can also be made privately by mail or phone, providing you can speak or write Japanese. The Tourist Information Centres have a complete listing of all Lodgings in Japan; it runs to several pages and is not a published booklet, so it is necessary to inquire in person.

KOKUMIN KYUKAMURA (VACATION VILLAGES)

The Vacation Villages are intended mainly for stays of several days for workers who want a quiet, relaxing rest. They are primarily in quiet areas, sometimes near famous resort or sightseeing areas, sometimes in rather remote regions. There are 27 throughout Japan; 19 have camping grounds with good facilities and about half have sporting facilities. Rates run from Y1500 per person for room only to about double that. Usually two or more different menus are available at different prices.

The Villages have not been used much by foreigners, and there is no quick booking system available. There is an office in Tokyo, but the simplest way is to go to the Tokyo Tourist Information Centre, explain your travel plans, and ask their advice (though Staff at the TIC state that the villages 'are not suited to all'.

SEISHOMEN RYOKAMURA (YOUTH VILLAGES)

The Youth Village program is one of fairly recent origin (late 60s). The Villages are located in remote areas, and are located in actual villages or towns (or nearby) that have been losing population and which are in danger of becoming ghost towns. There are 40 to 50, and all are in remote areas. They may be a good way to see life in remote Japan.

Often there is a central lodge plus a very simple camping ground. Rates are similar to those of minshuku, Y3500-4000 with two meals.

As with the Vacation Villages (described above) it would be best for any foreigner who is interested in staying at a Youth Village to contact the TIC in Tokyo and discuss travel plans. They can make suitable recommendations and suggestions. Staff at the TIC warn that hosts at the Youth Villages are not familiar with foreigners so a little knowledge of Japanese would be useful.

CAMPING

Camping has not caught on in Japan to the same extent that it has in western countries because there isn't the same reliance on car transport as there is elsewhere. However the number of camp grounds increases yearly. A complete list of campgrounds is available for reference at the TIC in Tokyo. It runs to 20 typewritten pages so it is not available for mail distribution. It is best to wait until arrival in Tokyo then get the information direct from the TIC.

Camping facilities vary from spartan to ultra-elaborate, with prices to match. Some have only tent sites and a source of fresh water, while others have bungalows and cottages as well. Most grounds are open only in July and August. (Summer is, by definition, only those two months, even though the weather is warm, though sometimes rainy, through June and all through September and often well into October.)

Most travellers will probably find it a nuisance lugging camping gear around. Many young Japanese set up their tents in almost any open space in the country. This is forbidden in national parks, and the intensive cultivation of land makes it difficult to find open and flat space in many areas, but tents in vacant fields are a common sight. Probably the campers ask permission before setting up tent; this could pose a problem for someone not able to speak Japanese.

LOVE HOTELS

There is yet another type of public accommodation available throughout Japan, though it is less written about than, for an example ryokan. This is the

Love Hotel. (The Japanese usually refer to it as 'Abec Hoteru', 'abec' being the closest pronunciation possible to 'avec', the French word for 'with'. These places rent rooms for short periods but they may be used purely as overnight accommodation, as long as you are aware of their peculiarities.

The busy period is during the day and the early evening; business generally begins to slacken off in the later evening, and they will usually rent rooms for the night for little more than the short-time charge of earlier in the day. So if you can wait until quite late in the evening (the exact time varies), you can obtain quarters that are usually pleasant and clean, though you will probably also have to vacate quite early in the morning; the exact time should be clearly determined in advance, for it may be necessary to pay the hourly rate for every hour of extra sleep-in. Many love hotels have facilities rather out of the ordinary, such as floor-to-ceiling mirrors, often with a mirrored ceiling too, for good measure. The decor may resemble the harem of a sultan, or equally lush and plush places. A common feature is a colour videotape recorder for instant replay of the action.

Once you learn to recognise the word 'hoteru' in Japanese you will find them everywhere. Outside, a sign usually shows two prices — one for a 'rest' (about an hour), the other for a 'stay' (which normally means overnight). The price is quoted for one room, not per person as is the case at most other types of accommodation.

Entry to the 'hoteru' is the ultimate in discretion. After passing through a narrow entrance, the customers can no longer be seen from the street and usually the person admitting them is out of sight behind a curtain. After the use of the room, the fee is paid to an anonymous hand. One never sees the staff, and supposedly vice-versa. Customers never see each other, by the way; each room has a separate entrance for the maximum privacy. Outside the cities, there are also 'moteru' for the motorized trade. While Japan does have motels as the term is used in western countries, the majority are of the type just described. There is usually no mistaking one type for the other, for the love hotels and love motels are often the very picture of bad taste, with garish pink neon signs bordering the roof, flashing signs, and outlandish architecture. One had the shape of a ship, while another in the Gotanda section of Tokyo is known throughout the country for its pseudo-feudal castle architecture, complete with turrets and other gewgaws.

OTHER ACCOMMODATION

Servas

Travellers who are sincerely interested in meeting Japanese families and interacting with them have the opportunity to stay in Japanese homes free of charge through the international organization Servas. As described elsewhere in this book, this program should not be looked on as a cheap way to travel, for people who stay with families are expected to participate in some aspects of daily life, exchange ideas (where the language barrier doesn't intrude), and 'relate to' their hosts.

Communes

There are several communes scattered around Japan, some of which welcome guests. These, too, are described earlier in the book.

HOUSEHUNTING

For those who plan to remain in Japan for a considerable period of time and who wish to have their own accommodation, here are some tips and general information on househunting in Japan.

Costs

Housing in Tokyo and other metropolitan areas is very expensive; in smaller places prices are considerably lower. In the metropolitan areas, a single room, about three metres square, may be found for less than Y20,000 a month, but any reasonable accommodation (solo) with a minimum of facilities (kitchen with sink, gas outlet, bath/ shower, toilet) and close to central Tokyo will usually cost at least Y40,000, and is more likely to be Y10,000 — 20,000 higher. Places with a shared toilet and bath are less expensive, and there are some bargains to be found if you can spend a long time looking. These prices refer to normal 'everyday Japanese' accommodation; for apartments and houses corresponding in size and facilities to those found in the USA, Canada or Australia, the rents are astronomical, from Y250,000 up to Y1 million a month.

Room sizes are measured by the number of tatami mats that do or could fit. There are actually at least three 'standard' sizes of tatami in use in Japan, but one mat is roughly a metre wide and two metres long. A small room is 3 mats (san-jo), a medium one 4½ (yo-yo han), and a large one is 6 mats (roku-jo). Larger rooms do exist, but are not common. Room types are listed as either Japanese-style (wa), with tatami, or western-style (yo), with a concrete or wooden floor, probably covered by carpeting. In Japanese-language listings, it is common to see such abbreviations as 2LD, 3LDK, etc. The digit is the number of rooms, 'L' is 'living room', 'D' is 'dining room', and 'K' is 'kitchen'.

Apartment buildings and houses constructed of concrete have higher rentals than wooden buildings because of the greater strength and earthquake resistance.

It is usually necessary to have a bundle of money on hand before moving into your own accommodation. First, there is a month's rent in advance. Second, there will usually be a deposit (Shikikin), repayable when leaving, less costs of repairs, etc; this range from two to four months' rent. Third almost invariably there is 'key money' (reikin), which is nothing but a bribe to get the place; this is most commonly two months' rent, occasionally one, and rarely none. This money is not returned. (It may be possible to get around the initial outlay for key money by arranging to pay a higher monthly rent.) Fourth, there is frequently a maintenance fee, which may vary from a reasonable Y1000-Y3000 per month to Y10,000 or more at ritzy adresses. Finally, there are separate charges for gas, water, electricity and telephone, all which are expensive. Telephone installation charges are high compared with North American rates.

Location

Before settling permanently at one address, it is advisable to stabilize your activities so as to optimize the location. Tokyo is a huge city and, despite quick train service, commuting long distances can waste a lot of time. Remember though, that express service can make a place farther out of the city a better choice than one closer to the centre of town. After settling into a job or routine, ask others about the best or preferable residential areas. In Tokyo, for example, everyone wants to live in Roppongi/Azabu because they are close to downtown and the area has the brightest of night lights. The Hiroo and Shibuyg are well regarded, while Ebisu, Gotanda and other areas can be equally convenient and less expensive even if they are not quite as fashionable: Check access to subways, JNR lines or bus lines (but remember that buses don't run after about 9 pm); optimum for this are Shibuya, Ebisu, etc, which are junctions of two systems.

Finding Accommodation

After deciding on one or two areas of

interest, the next step is to find listings of places available. The most common ways are agencies, newspaper ads, bulletin boards and words of mouth.

Near almost every railway station, and elsewhere in most districts, are rental agencies (fudoya) with listings of apartments, houses and rooms for rent in that district. The agent (fudoya-san) will ask about the type of accommodation required, number and sizes of rooms, and any other feature desired, then hill will prepare a list of places that might be suitable, taking clients to see them until one is found that is satisfactory. His charge for each placement is usually one month's rent. Add this to all the other charges listed earlier and you may have to lay out seven months' rent before moving in. Fudoya-san rarely speak much English except for the ones who look like used car salesmen and specialize in the horrendously expensive rental market catering to foreign executives on large living allowances.

Newspaper advertisements for accommodation are usually for high-priced executive-style places, but occasionally there are reasonably priced places. (I once found a small but adequate studio-style apartment with modern facilities through an ad in the Japan Times. The rental of Y55,000 wasn't exorbitant considering it was close to Ebisu, there was no agent's fee, deposit was only two months' rent, and key money was only one month.) Newspaper ads appear daily but the *Japan Times* on Friday has the most comprehensive Tokyo listings.

Bulletin boards may have ads for apartments, houses, rooms, sub-lets, 'house-sitting' arrangements, or shared accommodation. Look for them at supermarkets in areas with a large foreign population, or at the Tokyo TIC, Com'inn and International 3F Club.

In large cities there are usually regular English-language news-sheets that may have listings of apartments, etc. The *Tokyo Weekender* has a sizeable section of classified ads including accommodation. Occasionally there are some moderately-priced apartments listed by their owners (so there is no agent's fee).

Eating & Drinking

FOOD

Travellers in Japan will encounter few difficulties in finding palatable food at reasonable cost. Western food is available at the large tourist hotels and restaurants in the larger cities, but it will be very expensive and cannot be considered when travelling on a budget. If you want to eat at moderate cost you must eat as the locals do.

Japanese food is not spicy so there is no problem for delicate tongues or stomachs. The weird foods that you may have read about, such as grasshoppers or chocolate-covered ants, are just as strange to the average Japanese as they are to foreigners. Yes, the Japanese do eat raw fish (sashimi), but it must be fresh to be eaten in this style. (If it seems a strange practice, remember how Westerners eat oysters.) Sashimi has a weak flavour with no 'fishy' taste or smell, on the other hand, sushi (raw fish or other ingredient with rice) is very tasty. The only other common food that foreigners might find repulsive is natto: fermented soybeans that look, smell, taste and feel like something moist that was forgotten on a back shelf for too long.

Some typical Japanese dishes are:

Sashimi: slices of raw fish of various kinds.

Sushi: raw or cooked fish, vegetables, egg, etc, on or in rice.

Tempura: batter-dipped and deep-fried fish and vegetables. (This is of Portuguese origin; accent is on the first syllable.)

Sukiyaki: vegetables, meat, shirataki (like vermacelli), soya sauce, sake, sugar, water, tofu (soy bean curd), all cooked together at the table.

Jingis Khan: similar to sukiyaki, but the pot has a dome in the centre surrounded by a trough; vegetables are cooked in broth while meat is cooking on the dome.

Domburi: a bowl of rice with added chicken, egg, meat, etc.

Okonomiyaki: a type of pancake usually cooked on a griddle at the table by the diners themselves various ingredients are mixed into the batter, eg shrimp, squid, beef.

Fish is the major source of protein. Beef is outrageously expensive, the result of deliberate and scandalous government policy to protect small and inefficient domestic producers who raise only one or two animals on miniscule plots of land. (And to protect the farmers' votes.) Imported beef is sold and resold (often without leaving the freezer) until it sells in shops for the going rate, approximately ten times the original purchase price. (Some of these profits have been reported to find their way into the pockets of politicians.) Similarly, the price of rice is much above the world level because the government buys everything produced at a fixed and high price.

Beef is not a traditional item of the Japanese diet. Until the country was opened to barbarian Westerners in the 1860s the Buddhist Japanese would have been horrified at the thought of killing an animal so that it could be eaten. The famous Kobe and Matsuzaka beef are a relatively recent innovation in the diet. The meat is tasty and tender (and very very expensive), but very fatty (marbled) in the eyes of a lean-meat eater.

Those who know Japanese cooking from expensive restaurants in Western countries will find that the cuisine of such places owes as much to showmanship as to Japanese origins. A 'hibachi steak' has never existed in Japan; a hibachi is a large ceramic 'urn used to hold charcoal for heating. The method of serving is also different. Unless cooking facilities are limited, Japanese food is served all at once so that you a full choice at any one time; it doesn't normally arrive in dribs and drabs as the chef prepares the next item on the griddle. Food served at an expensive restaurant will be as much a treat for the eyes as the tongue. Vegetables are sliced in intricate shapes and everything is decoratively arranged. Of course less pretentious restaurants for budget eaters are much more basic and utilitarian.

Western cutlery is available at most restaurants but it is advisable to know how to use chopsticks. Japanese chopsticks (ohashi) are shorter than the Chinese variety. In less expensive restaurants they are usually joined together and must be broken apart. (About 350 million pairs of chopsticks are used in Japan each month!)

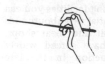

Using chopsticks

Place first chopstick between base of thumb and top of ring finger. (Bend fingers slightly.)

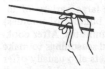

Hold second chopstick between top of the thumb and tops of middle and index fingers.

Keeping the first chopstick and thumb still, move the other one up and down by middle and index fingers.

Choosing a meal is no great problem even though staff rarely understand English. Some restaurants in metropolitan areas have menus in English but the majority have listings only in Japanese. However most restaurants have very realistic wax replicas of various dishes, so you can always summon a waitress and point to what looks good.

Typical Japanese cooking centres on a bowl of rice (gohan), usually has a

bowl of miso shiru soup (based on soybeans and a good source of protein), features one or more kinds of vegetable, plus a portion (generally small) of fish or meat. More economical dishes are based on noodles, either soba (white flour noodles) or ramen (buck-wheat noodles). Semi-western food may be found in many towns. Typical offerings are hamburger steak, macaroni and spaghetti dishes, pilaffs, dorias and gratins, usually with a choice of bread or rice as there is a mistaken belief that these are equivalent. Interestingly, rice served with such dishes comes on a flat plate and is called rice, not gohan.

There are many kinds of specialty restaurant in Japan. Typical is a robatayaki. Generally rustic in decor, they display the raw materials that are available, like whole fish, potatoes, etc; customers pick out the one they want and it is cooked for them. If you want to visit such a restaurant, it is invaluable to have a Japanese companion.

For simple meals while on the move, some suggestions include tempura and onigiri. In most towns there will be a tempuraya with freshly cooked pieces of fish, vegetables, meat (called 'katsu', a corruption of the word 'cutlet') and croquets (potato cakes) on display on trays in their window. They are tasty and filling (if a bit calorie-laden because of the deep-fat frying), and not expensive.

A very traditional food for lunches is onigiri, basically a ball of rice with a piece of fish or vegetable in the center; the outside is wrapped in a sheet of crisp seaweed. The tastiest is sakae, salmon.

Japanese pastries rate very well by international standards, according to a pastry lover. But beware of the object that has every appearance of a jelly donut. It has the same shape, the same colour, the same texture. Many an innocent has bitten into one and been shocked by . . . . . curry! An only-in-

Japan invention. (To ask, the word 'curry' is the same in both languages.)

Etiquette

It is polite to slurp noodles; it makes them taste better. Otherwise Japanese table manners are not so different from Western. Sake or beer are often drunk with meals but wine is a comparative newcomer and is not common.

Economy Eating

Nearly all department stores and large office buildings have restaurants in the basement and offer reasonable cost meals, especially at lunchtime. You can order individual items, but the cheapest way is to order teishoku, the day's set lunch; it will usually be on display. A typical teishoku will have a bowl of rice, miso shiru soup, a plate of vegetables, and meat or fish, salad, and dessert.

Near most railway and subway stations, there are usually restaurants of many types such as simple noodle shops where everyone stands, Korean barbecues, semi-western style restaurants, sushi shops, coffee shops (kisaten) and others. Simple meals begin around Y500-600. Places catering mainly to drinkers often prove more costly because each item ordered, such as a skewer of meat, is served and charged for separately, and is regarded more as a snack to accompany the drinks than as a meal in itself.

The pizza chains Shakey's and Pizza Hut, as well as Trecca in Kyoto, offer a real bargain between 11 am and 2 pm every day except Sundays and holidays — all the pizza you can eat for a fixed price (only Y500 in 1981). The nutritional value is suspect, but it is certainly very filling and there's lots of cheese.

For breakfast, most coffee shops offer 'morning service', which includes toast and sometimes an egg for the usual price of a cup of coffee alone. Visitors are always shocked at the price of a cup of coffee at coffee shops, usually

Y250 to 350. The usual excuse for the high cost is that you are paying for the space and congenial surroundings. You can stay all day for the price of a single cup, and young people often have coffee-shop dates.

If you have cooking facilities you can economize. Residential neighbourhoods have vegetable, fruit and meat shops, and supermarkets have spread widely since their introduction in the late 1960s. As well as eggs, meat, fish, chicken, vegetables, cheese and milk, etc, you can get a large variety of instant ramen (dried bundles of noodles) that cook in a few minutes. After cooking add the provided seasonings to make a broth. Supermarkets also usually offer a good selection of prepared food such as sushi, tempura (meat, fish, squid, vegetables, etc) and croquets (potato with or without corn, curry, etc.)

For those on a super-tight budget, bakeries slice the heels off loaves of bread, and you can get a bag of them at little or no cost. Peanut butter and jam are available. Jam from Soviet satellite countries is good; probably that from Bulgaria is the best. Much of the domestic product lacks enough fruit.

For more detailed information, a good inexpensive book is *Eating Cheap in Japan.*

BOOZE

Alcoholic beverages of all kinds are expensive in Japan compared with most western countries. At neighbourhood shops beer costs Y215 for a 633 ml bottle, while a 500 ml can from a vending machine costs Y200 or more. Alcoholic drinks of all kinds are sold in local shops without restrictions, and beer, sake and whisky are usually available at almost any eating establishment. Beer is the favourite alcoholic drink in Japan. Japanese beers are well regarded by beer connoisseurs, and are generally brewed in a German or Czech style. Well-known brands are Kirin, Sapporo, Suntory and Asahi.

Imported whiskies and wines are available, especially in larger cities, but there are few bargains. Johnnie Walker Black Label sells for Y4600 and up, nearly always higher (760 ml bottle); Red Label costs Y2900 or more. The locally-made Suntory Black Label is said to compare well with imported Scotch and costs less. Brandy and cognac are incredibly expensive in Japan. If you like them or have a Japanese friend who likes them, be sure to bring it in duty free.

Japanese wines have not reached very high levels of quality and most of the best-known widely advertised brands are very ordinary. It is only in recent years that the Japanese have developed much appreciation of wine and there is no tradition of making or drinking it, so the efforts that have produced high quality beer, sake and whisky haven't yet reached the wine industry. Because of costs in Japan it is said that there is no incentive to make necessary investments for improved processing facilities and that wines can be imported cheaper. There is a limited selection of wines from many countries on sale in the metropolitan areas; prices are seldom below Y900. The Australian wines selling in this range have been the standard lines of good and reliable quality, but not outstanding, and sell for about double their home price —

for Japan that is a remarkably small ratio.

Sake
This is pronounced like 'sah-kay', not 'sah-key'. It is the traditional Japanese drink and is very pleasant with Japanese food and on its own. Sake is served hot in small 180 ml flasks from which it is poured into tiny cups. The flask is called a tokkuri and is usually a decorative item made of pottery; it makes a good memento of Japan, along with a set of cups (sakazuki).

Sake is brewed from a mash of rice that has been cooked with water and fermented, so it is more like beer than wine, except that the alcohol content goes as high as 17%, more than many wines. It is certainly possible to get drunk on it, but it is not as potent as much folklore would lead one to believe.

There are several grades and types of sake. The highest grade is tokkyu (shu). Next comes ikkyo (shu), then nikkyu (shu). Sake from different regions of Japan has different characteristics and tastes, so these designations do not indicate the flavour, only the quality. In addition to the standard types of sake, other types are made like amazake (sweet sake) and otoso (sake with suspended rice solids). The are worth trying; some may be seasonal.

In shops, sake is sold in large 1800 ml bottles, as well as in smaller sizes. The size is a traditional measure called issho. At festivals a common sight is a large wooden keg of sake, opened by simply smashing in the lid, with the contents handed out freely in a square wooden box with neatly dovetailed leakproof joints. These boxes are of 180 ml capacity, and were the traditional way of measuring granulated solids, like rice, as well as liquids. These boxes (masu) make good souvenirs of Japan; the 180 ml size is called ichi go.

In a classic case of coals to Newcastle, a joint venture in California will be producing a million litres of sake annually, with about 3000 bottles going to Japan each month. This will be a mere drop in the bucket compared with total Japanese consumption, but is an interesting trend. Rice in California costs only a fraction of the Japanese price so the venture seems likely to succeed.

Other drinks

Another alcoholic drink, becoming more popular these days is *shochu*. It is a distilled liquor made from rice, wheat, sweet potatoes, sugar cane — anything containing sugar that can be fermented.

The Kagoshima area of Kyushu is the shochu capital of Japan, though it is made in many areas. The distillation process is a copy of brandy-making that was introduced by foreign missionaries in the late 1500s, and shochu was once the beverage of feudal lords and the upper classes.

Earlier this century, shochu was popular throughout Japan, but at the end of the war the materials for high quality shochu were not available and bootleggers blended it with anything on hand, including highly poisonous methyl alcohol. From then on it gained a bad reputation as a low-class drink associated with jikitabi (manual labourers nicknamed for their split-toed boots) who get blotto on it regularly.

In recent years new processing methods have been introduced so that most of the impurities that cause bad hangovers have been eliminated. Good shochu is little more than alcohol and water, 25-35% (50-70 proof); the strength will be marked somewhere on the label. The leading brand is Jun ('purity'). It is very low in price, Y590 for a 720 ml bottle, a fraction the cost of whisky.

A popular home-made drink, based on shochu, is *umeshu*, which translates as plum wine. It is made by soaking green, sour plums in shochu to which has been added lots of rock crystal sugar. The process is started in late June or early July, and lasts at least three months. The result is delicious but very sweet and potent.

For the greatest power in the smallest volume, it is possible to buy pure ethyl alcohol (99.9%+) without prescription at drug stores. It is called *musui etanoru* (ethanol), and a 500 ml bottle costs about Y850. (Warning: this must be considerably diluted; drinking it straight will constrict the throat so much that it may cause death.)

DRINKING CUSTOMS

When drinking beer, sake, etc with a Japanese person, the proper etiquette is to fill his glass or cup after he has filled yours. While he is pouring, hold your cup or glass up so that he can fill it more easily. If you don't want any more, put your hand over the glass. If you are new at the game, the Japanese may think you aren't familiar with the 'rules' and may fill his own glass. This is normally considered bad manners, and the Japanese say 'toku shaku', meaning who fills his glass with one hand and drains it with the other; in other words, an alcoholic. Before he can pour anything into his glass, take the bottle from him and fill his glass. This may result in a mock fight, but the gestured will be appreciated.

When drinking in company, it is an honour for the senior person to offer his cup to a guest, then fill it. The guest then rinses the cup and returns it to its owner, and fills it for him. Actually, among the Japanese it is the inferior who offers the cup to the superior, but in the case of visiting foreigners the normal practice may be reversed — or the host may be implying that the guest is the honoured superior in this case. In any event, it is an honour if the occasion arises.

When drinking with Japanese people, particularly those who are making a good salary, it will be difficult to pay any share of the bill. Customarily one person, often the most senior, will pick up the tab and pay everything. It is necessary to think up some way to repay the favour at a later date.

With students and other people who are not very wealthy, the bill is usually split up according to who had what. As a foreigner you may sometimes have trouble paying your share, but if you are drinking among friends they will not put up a fuss — it is only strangers who want to give the foreigner a good impression who will insist on paying the whole shot.

Getting drunk is one of the few safety valves open to Japanese to escape the manifold duties and obligations that they must continually observe. Because of this, almost any behaviour while drunk is excused. Consequently, hordes of faceless salary men, who show little individuality or personality during working hours, get quite thoroughly smashed quite frequently, sometimes nightly. They sing loudly, sometimes perform dances that can only be described as bawdy, and carry on in a manner thought quite un-Japanese. Getting drunk is a very popular activity in Japan, and getting blotto with a group is almost a ritual, helping to cement interpersonal relations with co-workers, etc. Records in China mention that the Japanese were much given to drink at festivals 2000 years ago, so the process has a long history.

Virtually the only (though common) ill-effect of this excess drinking is that many drinkers don't know their limit and cannot hold their liquour (literally). Having lost their inhibitions, they may vomit on streets, railway platforms, and even inside railway cars, especially on Friday and Saturday nights. If you see people avoiding one end of a train car, you can suspect that that is the reason.

DRINKING PLACES

There are two main types of drinking establishments in Japan; those strictly for drinking (usually with music and pleasant surroundings), and those for drinking with pleasant female companionship, ie hostesses.

Bars, pubs and other drinking places range in price from reasonable to astronomical. The appearance of the place does not necessarily give an accurate indication of the prices to be paid. A place that looks expensive probably will be; nightclubs and similar places are guaranteed to take a huge bite out of a wallet. However, looking modest or even rundown is no guarantee that it will be cheap; some simple-looking places are extremely expensive, either because of special service, atmosphere, or whatever that appeals to Japanese on huge expense accounts. There are stories of innocent gaijin (westerners) walking into such joints, ordering a single beer and being presented with a bill for Y18,000!

To avoid such overcharging, stand bars are the answer. Many are operated by large companies in the liquor business, like Suntory and Tory. Otherwise the safest course as soon as you enter an unknown bar is to ask the price of a drink and check if there is a cover charge; some places charge a couple of thousand yen as soon as a customer sits down. A favourite lurk of even better quality places is a dish of peanuts or other nibbles (called a 'charm' in Japanese) that the customer is obliged to pay for at a price equal to a couple of drinks. Foreigners can sometimes get away from this racket by politely indicating that they don't want it and feigning lack of understanding about the system.

Places with hostesses are always going to be much more expensive than those for drinking only. Customers are charged for the time that girls sit with them. Anyone going in only to drink, without benefit of hostess, would probably be unwelcome. Hostesses are part of the Japanese system of male ego-boosting; they flatter and flirt, and act as a listening post for the man's frustrations in life. (Often these women are available for other outside activities, usually on paid basis, but sometimes on a purely friendly basis if she likes the customer. Boye de Mente's book *Bachelor's Japan* gives some specific advice on this topic.)

The services offered by hostesses range from sitting opposite the customer and doing nothing but pour drinks, sitting on the customer's lap without benefit of undergarments and doing everything. The latter type of place is usually garishly decorated with bright lights (often pink), and are further indentified by touts outside who try to entice customers in. Such places are never cheap.

Beer halls are popular and relatively inexpensive places for a drink. They can be recognized partly by the prominent jugs and bottles of beer in the window, although many restaurants also offer beer and have similar window displays; there is often a rather thin line between a restaurant and a beer hall, for both serve food as well as drinks.

Almost any restaurant of any size will offer alcoholic drinks with the meal, particularly beer and sake.

The words for large, medium and small mugs of beer are dai, chu, and ko.

During the warm months, many department stores open beer gardens on the roof, often with live entertainment. Prices are reasonable, the heights of the building gives relief from the hot air at ground level, and it is a good place to see Japanese having a good time. There is usually elevator service to the roof.

For economical drinking, with a simple list of drinks such as sake and beer, and simple decor, sometimes scruffy, sometimes pleasant, investigate the 'workingman's nightclub' or *aka chochin*. These are found in many places, and almost invariably near stations. The name literally means 'red lantern' which is what will be found outside the establishment to identify it.

Tokyo

INTRODUCTION

Tokyo is one of the most populous cities on earth, the centre of government and commerce in Japan. It is difficult to put an exact number on the actual population because in the central part it varies by nearly two million between day and night. The actual Tokyo administrative area is 2031 sq km and includes many sub-cities, and adjacent Kawasaki and Yokohama from one vast conurbation with Tokyo itself. Thus, while the population is quoted around 12 million, it totals close to 15 million when the adjacent areas are included.

It is a commercial, administrative and industrial city that can be enjoyed for shopping and entertainment, but it has relatively little of historic or sightseeing interest; what did exist was largely destroyed by the 1923 Kanto earthquake or wartime bombing. It is better to go to such places as Kyoto, Nara, Kamakura, Nikko, etc, for sightseeing. Tokyo is a very interesting place in which to live because then you have time to explore it slowly and at depth.

GETTING THERE

As well as the many international flights arriving in Tokyo, most of them at Narita airport, there are also many domestic flights linking Tokyo with other cities in Japan. Domestic flights nearly all land at Haneda airport which is far more convenient than Narita. (Details about Narita and how to get to the city are given later.) Numerous rail lines of JNR connect Tokyo in all directions. The fastest service with points along the south coast as far as Kyushu is the Shinkansen (bullet train). Other Shinkansen services are under construction to the Tohoku area (northern Honshu) and the north coast (toward Niigata). Many regular trains run parallel to the Shinkansen routes;

they are slower and less expensive. Shinkansen trains stop only at Tokyo station, while regular services normally stop at some other stations.

The many private railway lines that start at various points around the Yamanote loop line reach as much as 100 km into the surrounding countryside.

Buses from Tokyo station run along the Tomei expressway to Nagoya, where transfer can be made to another bus to Kyoto or Osaka. Buses leave every night at 11 pm for a direct run to Kyoto and 10.20 pm for Osaka; both arrive the following morning around 8, allowing an early start for sightseeing while saving the cost of a night's accommodation. Seats recline and are reasonably comfortable. The fare, while nominally quite a bit below that of the Shinkansen, is pushed up Y1500 if reservations are made, a necessity during busy travel seasons.

Yet another way to or from Tokyo is by ferry. Boats sail from Tokyo as frequently as once a day for Tomakomai and Kushiro (Hokkaido), Matsuzaka (near Nagoya), Nachi-Katsuura (Kii peninsula, below Nara), Kochi (Shikoku), Kokura (northern Kyushu) and Naha (Okinawa). There is also daily service between nearby Kawasaki and Hyuga (south-east Kyushu).

Hints for hitching out of Tokyo are given in the 'Getting Around' chapter.

Further information on any scheduled transportation is available at the TIC or any large travel agency. JNR has an information office in Tokyo station, Yeasu side.

GETTING AROUND

Tokyo has a comprehensive public transportation system. Although large and complex, it is easy to use once it is understood, and is the cheapest way to get around the city. Comprising the system are suburban feeder buses, 11 private railways, 10 subway lines in two seperate (though linked) systems, JNR train lines, and city buses. The major shortcoming is that there is no system of free transfers between systems; a seperate fare is required for each.

Note that your ticket must be kept through the ride and surrendered at the end of the journey. Try to avoid the peak periods 7.30-9.30 am and 4.00-6.30 pm; there are 1.7 million people on the move, and they all will seem to be in your coach.

JNR TRAINS

The government-operated JNR (kokutetsu in Japanese) runs several lines in the Tokyo area. Most important is the Yamanote loop line that circles the city in both directions, and the Chuo and Sobu lines that cross the city. Other lines feed into these. Fares are charged by distance, minimum Y100. Tickets can be sold by vending machines. Fares are given on a large map over the machines but you need to know the name of the station in kanji (Japanese script). This can be obtained from JNTO's 'Tourist Map of Tokyo'. Most stations have maps of stations but in romaji (Roman letters) only; to ask for one say 'Kokuden no chizu-o kudasai'.

One way around the fare problem is to buy a minimum fare ticket and pay the difference at the 'Fare Adjustment' window at the destination. A perplexed look will usually elicit help.

Ticket machines may sell a single value of ticket or have a row of buttons to choose from (two rows, actually; the bottom one is for children's tickets). The machines give change, so it is safe to insert coins in excess of the fare.

If you put coins into the wrong machine and realize the mistake before pushing a fare button, you can get the coins back by pushing the button

marked とじ) (ナ じ" (torikeji). If you buy a ticket for a fare higher than required, etc, take it immediately to the Fare Adjustment window or push the one marked よび" だし (yobidashi) and ask for a refund. (This is the button to push if the machine jams and keeps your money.) You cannot get a refund of excess payment at the end of the journey.

Commuter passes are available and permit an unlimited number of trips between any two stations in the Tokyo area (and all stations in-between). They can be issued to include on other transportation system, such as a subway line or bus route. Passes are available for one, three or six months.

Note that it is often quicker to reach a destination by using a combination of JNR and subway than to use one system exclusively, but it will be more costly because separate tickets are required for each.

At any JNR station in Tokyo it is possible to buy a ticket to any station in Japan. The fare on the Yamanote (loop) line is included in the ticket so the fare is the same from anywhere in the city.

Every JNR station in the Tokyo area (and generally throughout the country) is identified by signs over the platform in romaji (Roman letters) as well as Japanese, but they are rather high and difficult to see when standing. They are few in number, so watch carefully when entering a station. At the lower left of the sign is the name of the following station, and at the right is the previous one. On each platform, hanging overhead near the edge of the platform and at right angles to the tracks will be a small sign giving the names of major stations ahead along that line; there is usually one sign in romaji.

In stations served by several lines, there is nearly always a sign in romaji giving the destination of trains from each platform. In larger stations like

Tokyo and Shinjuku there are illuminated colour-coded signs giving the destinations and platforms; the colours correspond to the colours of the trains. Even if the signs are only in kanji, the colours can be followed.

If you overshoot your station just get off and take a train going the opposite direction; usually this requires only a walk across the platform, but not always.

Yamanote line

Yamanote trains are green.

The Yamanote line circles the central part of Tokyo. Trains run in each direction at very frequent intervals through the day, tapering off later at night. Like all trains in the Tokyo area, service stops soon after midnight.

There are 29 stations around the loop, a circuit of which takes about an hour and gives a good introduction to the city. Three of the stations are the starting points for JNR intercity trains. Trains from Tokyo station (which is a copy of Amsterdam station) include the super-express Shinkansen through Osaka to northern Kyushu, plus other, slower, services to points along the south coast. Ueno is the station for northbound services, while Shinjuku is the starting point for trains to the Matsumoto area north-west of Tokyo.

All the private suburban railways begin at their own stations adjacent to stations of the Yamanote line.

Special day-excursion tickets are available, valid for unlimited travel for one day within the bounds of the Yamanote line. It is called a 'free kipu', a mixture of English and Japanese that is quite common.

Chuo line

Chuo line trains are orange.

Trains of the Chuo line begin at Tokyo station and give rapid east-west service across the city to Shinjuku, stopping only at Kanda, Ochanomizu, Yotsuya and Yoyogi en route. Beyond Shinjuku on the way to Takao, many km west of the city, there are two types of service, express (kyuko) which stops at only four stations before Takao, and local service that stops at 17.

Sobu line

Sobu line trains are yellow.

Trains of the Sobu line begin at Chiba, along the coast to the east of Tokyo and run into the Tokyo area. There are two types of service. Expresses run between Shinagawa and Chiba, skipping most stations, while local trains pass through Akihabara and cross the city parallel to the Chuo line to Shinjuku, then continue to Mitake, some distance to the west of the city. The last common station before branching to Shinagawa or Akihabara is Kinshicho. Sobu line trains stop at all stations across the city; passengers in a hurry to one of the intermediate stations take the Chuo line as far as possible, then transfer to the Sobu line.

Keihin-Tohoku line

Keihin-Tohoku line trains are blue.

Trains of this line run from below Yokohama into Tokyo and beyond to the north. From Shinagawa to Tabata they run alongside the Yamanote line and either line may be used over this distance.

Yokosuka & Tokaido lines

Yokosuka (pronounced Yo-kos'ka) line trains are blue and cream. Tokaido line trains are orange and green.

These lines overlap the Yamanote line from Tokyo (their terminus) to Shinagawa, but they function as expresses and stop only at Shimbashi, Shinagawa and Kawasaki before reaching Yokoshama; they offer the fastest service to Yokohama.

Beyond Yokohama the lines separate.

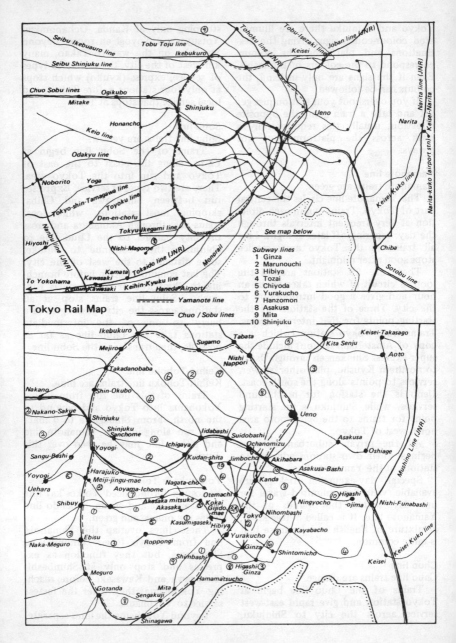

Tokyo Rail Map

Subway lines
1 Ginza
2 Marunouchi
3 Hibiya
4 Tozai
5 Chiyoda
6 Yurakucho
7 Hanzomon
8 Asakusa
9 Mita
10 Shinjuku

------- Yamanote line
======= Chuo / Sobu lines

See map below

TOKYO STATION

Track	Line
1/2	Chuo: west to Shinjuku, etc.
3	Keihin-Tohoku: to Omiya and points north.
4	Yamanote: counter clockwise to Ueno, Shinjuku.
5	Yamanote: clockwise to Shinagawa, Gotanda.
6	Keihin-Tohoku: to Shinagawa, Yokohama, Ofuna.
7/8	Shonan Densha: to Zushi (local service along Tokaido/Yokosuka line).
9/10	Yokosuka: to Yokohama, Kamakura, Yokosuka.
12/13	Tokaido: to Yokohama, Atami, Shizuoka, Nagoya.
14/19	Shinkansen: to Nagoya, Kyoto, Osaka, Hiroshima, Hakata (Kyushu).

SHINJUKU STATION

Track	Line
1/2	Chuo: west to Matsumoto (long distance).
3	Chuo-kaisoku: east to Tokyo (morning peak period only).
4	Chuo: east to Tokyo (regular service).
5	Chuo: west to Kofu, Matsumoto (long distance).

Track	Line
6	Chuo: west to Takao.
7	Chuo/Sobu: east to Ochanomizu, Akihabara, Chiba (local service).
8	Yamanote: counter-clockwise to Shibuya, Shinagawa.
9	Yamanote: clockwise to Ikebukuro, Ueno.
10	Chuo/Sobu: west to Mitaka (local service).

UENO STATION

Track	Line
1	Keihin-Tohoku: north to Omiya.
2	Yamanote: counter-clockwise to Ikebukuro, Shinjuku.
3	Yamanote: clockwise to Tokyo, Shinjuku.
4	Keihin-Tohoku: north.
5/6	Takasaki: north to Shin-Etsu area (local service).
7/8	Takasaki: north to Shin-Etsu area (express).
9	Takasaki: north to Shin-Etsu area (local service).
10	Joban: north (express).
11/12	Joban: north to Toride (local service).
13	Tohoku: north.
14/17	Tohoku: north (express).
18/19	Tohoku: north.

Yokosuka line trains continue to Kamakura and Yokosuka (pronounced Yokos'ka), while Tokaido line trains continue all the way west to Nagoya.

Because the major stations are large and confusing, the table above lists platform numbers and destinations at some key stations.

SUBWAYS & PRIVATE RAILWAYS

The subway lines criss-cross the city largely within the bounds of the Yamanote line, but also extend to the east of the city. Some lines extend a considerable distance outside the bounds of the Yamanote line, and many lines feed directly into private railway lines.

At least one subway line connects with each of the 11 private lines. In some cases the transfer involves a short walk, but in many cases the subway coaches continue along the tracks of the private line so that at the terminus you only have to cross the platform to catch a connecting train. An increased fare, however, is levied whenever the train crosses the bounds of the other system. All lines connect with the Yamanote line at least once, and several lines allow transfer to the Chuo or Sobu lines.

There are 10 subway lines operated by two separate authorities. Seven are privately owned Eidan lines (Marunouchi, Chiyoda, Ginza, Tozai, Hibiya, Yurakucho and Hanzomon), and three are municipally owned Toei lines (Asakusa, Mita and Shinjuku, sometimes called Toei No 1, 6, and 10, respectively). The Tozai and Chiyada lines are operated by JNR.

Transfers between lines of either the Eidan system or the Toei system can be made using the same ticket, but a transfer from one system to the other requires either a special ticket or two separate tickets; the cost is the same in either case. At stations serving both systems, there may be a dozen or more different ticket machines, including some that also sell tickets for transfer to private railways.

Transfers from JNR lines to subways always require an extra fare, and the stations are usually separate. Transfers to the JNR-operated subway lines (Tozai and Chiyoda) can be made at some JNR stations such as Nakano just by walking to a different platform.

When transferring from one line to another, the stations may be some distance apart, but joined by a concourse. If you have a transfer ticket you should keep it when leaving the first station.

As with JNR stations, fares are shown on maps above the ticket machines. Again, names are usually only given in kanji so it helps to have a map with the Japanese subway names. Even with a subway map written in romaji, you should be able to calculate the fare by counting the number of stations.

Each subway station along the way is clearly identified in romaji, and signs give the direction to follow to make a transfer. Signs are clearly marked in words and in symbols, colourcoded by the line's colour, and are posted on walls, pillars and overhead. (Station names on private railway lines are often not marked in romaji, but most newcomers don't need to use those lines, so this will not be such a great problem.)

Some of the combinations of subways and private lines are potentially very useful; for example the Toyoko/ Hibiya combination. The Toyoku line offers a convenient service at reasonable cost between Yokohama and Tokyo, where its terminus is Shibuya. At Naka-Meguro you can get off and continue by Hibiya subway simply by crossing the platform. At the other end of the Hibiya line, the nominal terminus is Kita-Senju, but many Hibiya line trains continue to Kita-Kasukabe on the Isezaki line.

Similarly, some trains of the Asakusa subway line go far beyond their nominal limit of Oshiage and run to various termini including Narita airport station. (This is the most economical way to get to Narita, and for many it is also the most convenient and quickest.) At Sengakuji station of the Asakusa line, some trains (from platform 1) go south through Shinagawa and on to Kawasaki, Yokohama, Yokosuka and the bottom of the Miurahanto peninsula.

Timetables are posted on large signs over platforms. The two columns on the timetables are for weekdays (Mon-Sat) and Sundays/holidays; the symmetrical kanji is weekdays (heijitsu), the other is holidays (kyujitsu). Being able to read the timetable is also useful for determining the last train home late at night. A departure time marked in red is an express, but sometimes an express is marked by a symbol above the time. Other symbols above the number may indicate the station at which the train will terminate. So by using the JNTO map of Tokyo (which has station names in both scripts) it is possible to determine which trains go to Narita airport, etc.

Commuter passes are available for travel between any two stations in the Tokyo area as for JNR trains; periods are also one, three and six months.

A Western fast food has arrived in Japan
B Commuting in Tokyo's rush hour; note the gloves
C Signs in Tokyo's Akihabara area

Commuter tickets, kaisuken, are also available for travel between two specific stations; they give 11 rides for the price of 10.

STREETCARS

There is a single surviving tram line in Tokyo, running from Ikebukuro to Oji (on Keihin-Tohoku line), not a generally useful route.

BUSES

There is a large network of bus routes throughout the greater Tokyo area. They mostly act as feeders to railway and subway lines, often through incredibly narrow streets. Most routes are laid out between large JNR stations. Buses generally stop running soon after 9 pm.

The drawback of the buses is that the destination signs are only in kanji and the drivers rarely speak English. However, since the destination signs are nearly always the name of a station, you can find the kanji for them by checking the names of stations of the JNTO Tokyo map. At bus stops there is a sign with the name(s) of the destination station(s), and a route map.

Buses are, of course, subject to the delays of Tokyo's heavy traffic, so bus travel is slow in the morning and afternoon peak periods.

Traditionally the fare is paid when entering the bus. The fare is marked on the cash box (Y110 in 1981) and the money is dropped through a slot. Strips

of tickets are also available. A new system is being introduced, and is used in many other cities and on country runs. Passengers enter by the back door and take a ticket from an automatic dispenser. A number on the ticket shows the fare zone where the bus was boarded. As the bus proceeds a sign at the front of the bus indicates the fare for tickets from various zones. Passengers then pay when they exit by the front door.

Buses are most useful to residents who have time to establish what lines are most useful to them. At least one map, 'Great Tokyo Detailed Map', (Nippon Kokuseisha, Y680 at bookshops), shows bus routes.

NARITA AIRPORT

Nearly all international flights to Tokyo arrive at Narita airport (Narita Kuko), located 66 km out in the countryside east of Tokyo. A minimum of 1½ hours is required to get from there to central Tokyo, making it one of the world's most inconveniently located airports. A high speed rail service was included in the 'planning' stage, but less than 1% of the land was ever purchased, and the present 'system' for getting into Tokyo was assembled from existing rail lines plus a new bus service. (The authorities would prefer that the public not know, but there is a blocked-off station for the planned rail service beneath the terminal building.) Narita 'errport' (as it has been called) is Japan's contribution to the world's collection of vast projects started on half-vast ideas. It would have been better to have enlarged the existing and infinitely more convenient Haneda airport. Japanese opposition to Narita airport continues with occasional sabotage and other disruptive tactics by radical 'student' groups. For this reason you may meet a police check when entering the airport. These security measures account for the high airport tax of Y1500.

A *Many shops use 'English' words in signs with no rhyme or reason*
B *The ubiquitous game of pachinko*
C *Typical Tokyo sidestreet*

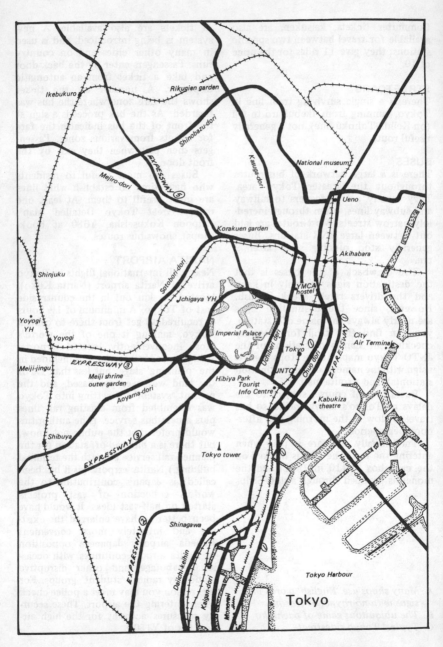

Tokyo

Faced with the problem of coping with Narita airport, how do you use it? First, fly China Airlines if possible and use Haneda airport, avoiding the problem in the first place. Unfortunately this isn't possible for everyone (CAL is heavily booked, as one might expect).

Narita airport has well-signposted routes through quarantine/health, immigration, and customs checks. (Details of immigration and customs regulations are given earlier in the book.)

Before leaving the customs hall be sure that you have Japanese currency. It can be purchased at a window at the centre of the row of exit doorways from the hall, before exiting to the arrival concourse. The only other money changers are on the fourth floor. Yen is the only currency which can be used in Japan. It is illegal (and impossible) to use any other currency, including US greenbacks.

The arrival concourse (ground floor) is the first place where incoming passengers can be met by friends, but it would be an act of friendship to arrange to meet them in Tokyo because of the inconvenience and cost involved in getting out to the airport. There are north and south wings of the terminal, so be sure that 'meeters' know the flight and airline so that they can be at the right place.

Before heading into Tokyo, stop at the Tourist Information Centre (TIC) which is operated by the semi-governmental Japan National Tourist Organization. This and two other TIC offices (in Tokyo and Kyoto) are the only places in Japan which have comprehensive information in English. The airport TIC is tucked away almost out of sight at the junction of the central block and the south wing on the side nearest the runway; it is sometimes omited from airport directories. Other 'information centres' in the centre of each wing are generally useless because most of the staff do not speak English.

The TIC has the full range of information and publications of the Tokyo office, including up-to-date listing of low-cost accommodation in Tokyo and Kyoto. (They do not, however, make bookings.) Of immediate use will be 'Tourist Map of Tokyo' (405-E), 'Map of Tokyo and Vicinity', and 'Tokyo' (222-E); the last is available in several languages.

Another useful booklet is the free commercial publication 'Narita-Tokyo Guide Map'. Its format changes from time to time, but it usually has interesting sightseeing information, maps of Narita, Chiba and some important districts of Tokyo, a subway map and schedules of transportation to Tokyo.

The TIC is open from 9 am to 12 noon and 1-8 pm on weekdays, and on Saturday mornings. Unfortunately the JNTO doesn't recognize that travellers arrive seven days a week so it is closed on Sundays, and on Saturday afternoons.

The Japanese National Railways (JNR) counter at the centre of the central block gives information on JNR services, makes bookings and sells tickets. There are usually English-speaking personnel on duty. Next to the JNR counter is an information and ticketing counter for the Keisei rail line, one of the two most convenient ways of getting into Tokyo. Reservations for the Skyliner can be made here.

On the other side of the JNR counter are counters for Toyota and Nippon (Hertz) car rental agencies. No one in his right mind would try driving in Japan on first arrival, but brochures could be useful for future reference. (Further information on car rentals and road conditions is given elsewhere in this book.)

LEAVING THE AIRPORT

There are several ways of getting from Narita airport into Tokyo: taxi, rental car, JNR train, airport bus, and Keisei train. Only a couple are really worth considering. A taxi would cost a small fortune of Y12-15,000, and a hire car about double this. JNR trains are costly, infrequent, slow, and leave only from JNR Narita station, a longish bus trip from the airport. They can be recommended only if you are going to the Chiba and Boso-hanto peninsula area. Buses for the JNR Narita station leave from in front of the central block. More information is available at the JNR information counter.

Airport Bus

The airport bus (frequently and misleading referred to as a 'limousine') is one of the two convenient convenient ways to get into central Tokyo. The fare is Y2300 (half price for children and handicapped). The bus runs nonstop from the terminal to Tokyo City Air Terminal (TCAT), located in Hakozaki, a section of Tokyo about 2.5 km from Tokyo station.

The chief advantage of the bus is that it departs from the front of both north and south wings (near the end), so baggage does not have to be carried far from the customs area. Bags are carried on the same bus and claimed at the end of the ride in the TCAT building.

A shortcoming of TCAT is that it is in the middle of nowhere, not close to public transport, so you have to take a shuttle bus to Tokyo station (a further Y190), or go to the nearest subway station, a 10-15 minute walk. The shuttle bus is well marked. To reach the subway station, exit from the front entrance of TCAT (under the expressway), turn right, cross the street and walk straight along the broad street. The entrance to Ningyocho station is on the right side of the road. The station is served by both Hibiya and Asakusa lines.

Another disadvantage of the bus is that the fare is about three times the cost of the basic Keisei rail service. Also,

the bus is subject to traffic tie-ups. The trip to Hakozaki takes an average of 80 minutes; this can be as low as 60 minutes in early morning, mid-day and late evening, or it can stretch to nearly two hours.

At the airport terminal the exits for the bus are clearly indicated, but the word 'limousine' is used in all signs.

A taxi from TCAT to places in central Tokyo will add at least Y1000 to the bill; this can double or triple for more distant destinations.

There is also a shuttle service to Haneda airport. The fare is Y2500 and the trip takes about two hours. The buses (again called 'limousines') leave from the same places as TCAT buses so make sure you get the right one. (See below for further details about Haneda airport.)

Airport bus to Tokyo hotels

A new bus service was announced in 1980, to run between Narita airport and a number of hotels in six central Tokyo areas, with three to five runs per day, depending on the area.

Scheduled departure times from Narita airport for each area (and the hotels serviced) are as follows.

Akasaka area: 8.10 am, 10.30 am, 1.55 pm, 8 pm, 9.45 pm. (Hotels: Okura, Tokyo Hilton, New Otani, Akasaka Tokyu, New Japan.)

Ginza area: 8 am, 10.15 am, 2 pm, 7.40 pm, 9.30 pm. (Hotels: Ginza Tokyu, Ginza Daiichi, Shimbashi Daiichi, Shiba Park, Tokyo Grand.)

Tokyo station area: 7.45 am, 10.20 am, 1.50 pm, 7.20 pm, 10.10 pm. (Hotels: Tokyo station, Marunouchi, Palace, Imperial, Tokyu Inn, Tokyo Prince.)

Shinagawa area: 7.55 am, 9.55 am, 1.55 pm, 7.30 pm, 10 pm. (Hotels: Miyako Tokyo, Shinagawa Prince, Pacific Tokyo, Takanawa Prince, Miyako Inn.)

Palace area: 8.10 am, 2 pm, 9 pm. (Hotels: Tokyo Station, Grand Palace, Fairmont, Diamond, Asakusa Prince.)

Shinjuku area: 8 am, 2 pm, 8.10 pm. (Hotels: Century Hyatt, Keio Plaza, Sunroute Tokyo, Shinjuku Prince.)

Departures (at the time of writing) are not nearly as frequent as for the bus to TCAT, but it would be much more convenient for travellers to the hotels listed if they arrive at an appropriate time. The bus service is intended only for hotel guests, but whether they actually check for reservations is for the traveller to determine.

The exact place of departure was not announced at the time of writing, but would be from the ground floor of north and south wings like all other Tokyo-bound buses. Up-to-date information on schedules is available by telephone at (03) 574-7871. Fare is Y2300.

Airport bus to Yokohama

By far the most convenient service to Yokohama is the bus to Yokohama City Air Terminal (YCAT), located close to Yokohama station. On average there are two buses per hour. The schedule is printed in Narita-Tokyo Guide Map, available at the TIC office. Fare is Y2600, and travel time is about two hours.

Train services from Narita Airport

Most travellers will find the train services from Narita-kuko station the most economical and the most convenient, provided carrying baggage is no problem. In contrast with the bus service, transfers to public transport within Tokyo are simple. The main complication of the train services is the multiplicity of terminal stations. Also it is hard to find information in English about train services out of Narita-kuko station except for the fast Skyliner train; others which could be more convenient are hardly mentioned.

The tracks out of the station are

those of the Keisei line. Of the more than 80 trains a day, at least 60 go to Keisei-Ueno station at Ueno in the north-east part of Tokyo, where transfer can be made to JNR trains and Ginza and Hibiya subway lines. About 14 trains a day go to the south-west side of the city. Some trains from the airport station terminate at the intermediate stations: Takasago, Tsudanuma and Sakura; they are of no use to Tokyo-bound travellers.

Of the trains to Ueno, nearly 30 are non-stop expresses called the 'Skyliner' (Japanese name). They leave from tracks 1 and 2. Seats are reserved. This is the fastest service to Ueno, but there is a surcharge of Y500 on top of the regular fare of Y740. They leave at half-hour intervals and take 60 minutes. The slower Tokkyu (special express) takes 75 minutes to Ueno, the still slower Kyuko (express) 90 minutes. (Early and late in the day there are some very slow local trains to Ueno that stop at every station. If you are catching a train after 9.55 pm it is best take a Skyliner; the last one leaves at 11 pm.)

Approximately 14 trains a day do not go to Ueno, but switch off at Aoto, pass through Oshiage, and join the Asakusa subway line. They terminate at Nishi-Magome, on the south-west side of the city. These trains are very useful because they pass close to the central Tokyo (the Ginza area), and connections may easily be made to other lines: to JNR at Asakusabashi, Shimbashi and Gotanda; to Hibiya subway line at Ningyocho and Higashi-Ginza; to Ginza subway to Asakusa, and to Mita subway at Mita. (Also, at Sengakguji, you can transfer to the Keihin-kyuko line which goes through Kawasaki and Yokohama to the Miura-hanto peninsula.)

The last of these trains leaves at 5.21 pm, but if you want to go to destinations in the southern part of Tokyo after this time don't give up hope. Take any Ueno-bound train (other than a

Skyliner), and get off at Aoto (past all the intermediate stations listed earlier, and after crossing a long bridge across a river). Walk across the platform to track 1 and catch the next train. This may run through to Sengakuji or beyond, or it may stop after six stations, at Oshiage. If it stops, take a train from track 1 to Nishi-Magome or track 3 to Kawasaki and Mokohama.

A timetable of Keisei services is printed in the 'Narita-Tokyo Guide Map', and on a pillar facing the ticket machines at the airport station, another is posted at Keisei-Ueno station. In each case, the type of service is indicated on the timetable; at the station, a blue dot is a Skyliner, a red circle a tokkyu, and a red triangle a kyuko.

Narita-kuko station is about one km from the airport. There are shuttle buses that leave regularly from the front of both north and south wings, close to the centre block. The trip takes about six minutes. The fare is Y130.

Tickets can be bought at the terminal (near the Keisei counter) and at the station. If going by Skyliner a reserved ticket must be bought at the counter or the reservations office at the station. Tickets for ordinary trains may be bought from vending machines at either place; those obtained at the terminal include the shuttle bus fare. Buy a minimum price ticket and pay the difference at the final station. Be sure to keep your ticket to surrender at the end.

At the station, machine No 2 issues tickets for the switch to the Asakusa line from its left side (labelled 'Toei Line'), and for the Keihin-kyuko line from its right ('Keihin Line'). Machines 3-8 issue tickets only for Keisei trains. Machines 3 and 4 accept Y1000 notes and give change; the others accept only coins and give change. They are to the right at the foot of the stairs; tracks are to the left.

From Tokyo to Narita

Begin your trip to the airport about four hours prior to departure time to allow for travelling, check-in, and security checks. As with travel from the airport to Tokyo, the only methods which can be recommended are train to Narita Kuku (Airport) station or the airport bus.

As described above, the two train routes that end at Narita Kuko station come from Keisei-Ueno station, and from stations along the Asakusa subway line.

Keisei-Ueno station is close to Ueno stations of JNR railway and of Hibiya and Ginza subway lines. From the JNR station, easiest access is to leave the train platform by the overhead passageway located at the south (Ginza) end, walk along the passage toward track No 1, exit, cross the road, turn left and walk down the hill; to the right and about 50 metres along is the entrance to the underground Keisei station.

Skyliner tickets can be bought in advance at JTB offices and Keisei-Ueno station, as well as at the airport terminal and station buildings.

If you are travelling from the central and south-west parts of Tokyo, the service by the Asakusa subway line is the most convenient, for it allows easy transfer from JNR trains and from Hibiya and Ginza subway lines, as described earlier. About 20 trains a day of the Asakusa line continue past the usual terminus at Oshiage, and go all the way to Narita Kuko station. Ask in advance at one of the Asakusa line stations for the schedule of trains that will go to the airport, or check the time-table on the platform; the symbol for an airport-bound train is ⊃.

If you catch a train going only as far as Oshiage, switch to another train to go to Aoto; from there you can catch a train going to Narita Kuko station.

Some trains passing through Aoto go only as far as intermediate stations so inquire about the terminus. If a train happens to go only as far as Narita (city) station, walk to platform 5 and wait for a train to the airport station, the next stop.

From Narita Kuko station there is a regular shuttle bus to cover the short distance to the terminal.

The airport bus runs non-stop from Tokyo City Terminal (TCAT) to the front of the terminal. Many (but not all) airlines allow complete check-in at TCAT so you don't have to touch your baggage until the flight destination. For these airlines, a bus is assigned to each flight and if it is delayed in traffic the plane is held until its arrival. Check-in time at TCAT is usually three to four hours ahead of departure to allow for such eventualities. At TCAT everything is self-explanatory with clear signs indicating the way to the departure level (upstairs).

Apart from taxi (not cheap), there are two ways to reach TCAT. The least expensive and simplest is by subway to Ningyocho station (Hibiya or Asakusa line). From the Hibiya line, exit from the end toward Kayabacho and look for signs 'For Tokyo City Air Terminal'. This will lead to a street-level exit. Turn left and walk 10-15 minutes to the overhead expressway under which TCAT is located.

The other way to reach TCAT is by shuttle bus that leaves every 20-30 minutes from in front of the TDA office opposite Tokyo station (Yaesu side, the side remote from the Post Office). If you arrive at Tokyo station by Marunouchi subway line you have to walk via an underground passage from the Post Office side of the station. The walk from the train or the subway (especially the latter) to the shuttle bus is nearly as far as from Ningyocho station to TCAT, so you might as well go to Ningyocho in the first place.

Remember, though, that if you are at Ningyocho station you can catch a train on Asakusa line direct to the airport. The time taken is about the same and the train fare is about Y1500 cheaper. You will of course have to check in your luggage at the airport this way, not at TCAT, but you won't have to carry it any further than you would lugging it from the station.

In addition to the numerous buses from TCAT, Cathay Pacific has its own buses four times a day to connect with its flights. They depart from Ginza Tokyu Hotel at 7.30, 8.30 am, 12.45 and 2.20 pm. Fare is Y2000; advance booking is recommended.

After check-in at the airport, turn in any certificates for tax-free purchases just before the immigration clearance. Duty-free liquor, etc can be bought in the terminal building or after passing through Immigration. Before boarding there is an x-ray security check at hand buggage. Although signs state that the amound of x-ray exposure will not damage film, it may be advisable to request a visual inspection instead, unless you have a lead film bag. A polite request will usually be met, eventually. It helps to have all cameras and film in a small bag that can be easily separated from other baggage.

HANEDA AIRPORT

Because of the running contretemps between the governments of Taiwan and (mainland) China, Taiwan's national airline, China Airlines, was denied the dubious privilege of using Narita when Japan recognized the Peking government. China Airlines have been crying all the way to the bank ever since because they have the most convenient service into Japan of any airline. They have several flights a week from Taipei and the US west coast, but advance bookings are required because of the airline's popularity.

Nearly all domestic flights use Haneda.

Central Tokyo is easily reached from Haneda airport by the monorail. The way from the terminal to the monorail station is clearly marked. Tickets are available from vending machines; the machines give change. The terminus is at Hamamatsucho, on the south side of Tokyo, which is also served by JNR trains of the Yamanote and Keihin-Tohoku lines.

Transfer between Haneda and Narita airports can be made most conveniently by shuttle bus. The trip takes about two hours and costs Y2500. Buses operate between 8.40 am and 8.30 pm. For connections between flights at the two airports it is wise to allow 4½ hours.

To get to Haneda from Narita, a determined budgeteer with a sense of adventure and lots of time could save about half the bus fare by taking a Nishi-Magome-bound train as far as Shimbashi, or a Keisei-Ueno-bound train to Ueno, then transferring to a JNR train (Yamanote or Keihin-Tohoku line) as far as Hamamatsucho station (one stop from Shimbashi; many from Ueno) where the monorail to Haneda airport begins. Using this route you would have to carry your luggage, and allow at least three hours. Also, don't take a Skyliner to Ueno, otherwise much of the cost saving would be lost. The route from Haneda to Narita would be the reverse of the above; the route via Shimbashi would be the faster.

INFORMATION
Tourist Information Centre (TIC)
The Tokyo TIC is operated by the Japan National Tourist Organization (JNTO). The only other TICs are at Narita Airport and at Kyoto. These offices are the best sources of information in Japan for travel and sightseeing. They have many free informational pamphlets and brochures, including the official JNTO publications and some private or commercial publications. The TIC also has files bulging with miscellaneous information on every imaginable subject, and the helpful staff can give verbal information on any aspect of travel and sightseeing in Japan. They have typewritten information sheets on a variety of specialized topics and can make photocopies of these.

The TIC is open Monday to Friday 9-12 noon and 1-5 pm, and 9-12 noon on Saturday. It is closed on National Holidays. Tel 502-1461.

The Tokyo TIC is located near the Ginza area of Tokyo on Harumi-dori, about 200 metres from Mitsukoshi Department Store on the way to Hibiya-koen (park). From Mitsukoshi you can see the railroad bridge (used by Shinkansen and local trains) down Harumi-dori; the TIC office is just beyond the bridge, on the left. It is clearly marked with a large illuminated sign with yellow letters 'TIC' on a black background.

Access from JNR trains: If travelling on the Yamanote or Keihin-Tohoku lines, get off at Yurakucho station. Walk to the end of the platform in the direction of Shimbashi station and look for the sign 'For Hibiya Area'. Note the Sogo Department Store on the right (it has a Youth Hostel booking office in the basement) and exit from the station on that side. Then turn left and walk along the street, keep to the right of the elevated railway tracks. At the major road (Harumi-dori), the TIC office will be clearly visible across the street.

Hibiya line: Get off at Hibiya station and leave the platform at the end closest to Ginza station (next stop). Walk up to the exit and double back between the exits (there's one on each side of the passageway). Watch for a sign on the wall to the left for the Imperial Hotel and follow it to the sign for Exit 4/5. Take Exit 4, walk up the steps, and the TIC sign will be visible about 50 metres ahead.

Chiyoda and Mita lines: Get off at Hibiya station on each line. Both stations are located some distance from the Hibiya line's Hibiya station, but they are all connected by underground passages. After exiting from the platform, follow signs for the Hibiya line. This will lead to a long passage that has an entrance to the Hibiya line at the near end. Walk past this along the passage as indicated by signs 'Passage for Ginza'. Exits 4/5 will be to the right.

Publications available from the TIC include:

Tokyo, a JNTO pamphlet (222-E), describing many of the attractions of the city, including a good overall map and subway map (in English only).

Tourist Map of Tokyo, a well-detailed map of the part of Tokyo most likely to interest visitors, as well as detailed maps of some important sections of the city. Its subway map is usefully labelled in both kanji and romaji; the map 'Communications Network' details all rail lines, both JNR and private, for a considerable distance into the surrounding area.

Your Guide to Tokyo, a publication of the Tourist Section of the Tokyo Metropolitan Government. It gives information on many attractions of the city.

Map of Tokyo & Vicinity, also a JNTO publication, gives good coverage of the area near Tokyo, particularly to the west, where it takes in the Fuji-Hakone-Izu area.

Tour Companion, a commercial weekly paper aimed at tourists, also available at hotels, airline offices, travel agents and some supermarkets frequented by foreigners. It is a superb source of information on events for the following week or two, with details of festivals and cultural/entertainment offerings in the Tokyo area. It also lists phone numbers of embassies and airlines, and has information on movies, gallery showings, concerts, etc. There is also space devoted to shopping, restaurants, night spots, etc. It is a commercial publication, so its listings should be regarded in that light.

Tokyo Weekender Billing itself 'a forum for Foreigners in Japan', the Weekender is aimed more at residents than travellers, but it has a couple of sections of interest to those passing through, and is very useful for those staying a while. Some of the articles are occasionally so frank that they seem almost anti-Japanese. There are also thorough rundowns during the six annual sumo tournaments, no-nonsense film reviews, and classified ads. It is released Fridays, and can be picked up at the TIC, most large hotels, the American Pharmacy, many supermarkets and pubs or restaurants catering to foreign clientele (mostly in Roppongi and Akasaka).

The Tokyo TIC also has brochures on a number of areas of Japan such as Osaka, Kagoshima, Fukuoka, and others, so it will pay to look carefully at their racks for English-language material on areas where you plan to travel.

Telephone information services give recorded information on current festivals and cultural events in the immediate Tokyo area. The numbers are 503-2911 (English), 503-2926. For specific inquiries during business hours, dial 502-1461.

SIGHTSEEING

Although a centre of power since the early 1600s, there is little of historic or visual interest in Tokyo. This is partly because Kyoto continued to be the imperial capital with the figurehead emperor, his court, and the elaborate structures (such as temples) that went with it, while Tokyo was more a military and governing centre that did not attract such grandiose construction. It is also because the great 1923 Kanto earthquake and wartime bombing flattened much of the city.

Tokyo definitely is an interesting city to visit, but more for shopping and sampling the offerings of a modern city that combines many good features of East and West than as a place for sightseeing.

Ginza Area

Located close together are the Imperial palace grounds and Ginza, the highest class shopping district in Japan with several department and other stores.

The Imperial palace can be reached from Hibiya stations of the Chiyoda, Hibiya and Mita subway lines, Nijubashi-mae station of the Chiyoda line, Otemachi station of the Mita, Marunouchi and Tozai subway lines, Tokyo station of the Marunouchi line, and Tokyo and Yurakucho stations of the JNR Yamanote and Keihin-Tohoku lines. The actual palace grounds may not be entered except at New Year and on the Emperor's birthday, 29 April. However, you may walk through the East Garden (Higashi-Gyoen), walk parallel to some of the high, walled embankments, and view Nijubashi bridge from the Palace Plaza area.

The circumference of the palace, several km, is a well-known jogging course, with distance markers (free map available at the Imperial Hotel), but few would find it a particularly interesting walk except in cherry blossom season when the many trees on the north-west side are lovely.

A better walk from the palace is along Harumi-dori the few blocks to Ginza intersection, identified by the Mitsu-koshi department store.

Along the way, on the right and before passing under the railway bridge, is the Tourist Information Centre. Farther along Harumi-dori is the famed Kabukiza theatre (for Kabuki plays).

The cross-street at Ginza is Chuo-dori ('Centre Boulevard'). To the right are many more stores. The energetic could turn left for a lengthy but interesting walk with many large and small stores along the way.

Chuo-dori has many interesting little shops of a specialized nature, some of which give a little insight into Japan, old and new. These include stores selling dolls, fans, antiques, etc, and a cutlery shop where a workman can sometimes be seen assembling knives and tools by hand in the same way it was done a century ago. (Japanese knives of traditional manufacture are extremely fine cutting instruments and would make a practical souvenir.) Another shop that may be encountered is a zori-ya where an elderly craftsman hand-makes zori, the dress sandals that are worn with a kimono.

Chuo-dori passes Maruzen department store, and leads up to Akihabara. An hour of steady walking would take you from Ginza to Akihabara which is a good area for buying electrical goods. (See the 'Buying' section for more details.) To get there faster you could get the subway at Nihonbashi, Mitsukoshi-mae, or Kanda to Akihabara.

Chuo-dori is blocked to traffic in the Ginza area on Saturday and Sunday afternoons and shoppers stroll at will. Tables are set up for eating. Exotic Western food is available at McDonalds.

Meiji-jingu shrine

Meiji-jingu is possibly the finest shrine in Japan and well worth a visit. It was built early in this century to honour emperor Meiji who reigned during the eventful period 1867-1912, when Japan changed from a self-isolated feudal country to a world power, largely under the wise guidance of this emperor.

The shrine grounds are extensive and heavily wooded, offering a respite from the bustle of the city. Its broad paths lead to the main shrine building, a simple building of traditional style and the finest of materials and craftsmanship. Because of its exalted status among the shrines of Japan, it is a popular place for blessings for various events, and you can often see such ceremonies being performed by priests in traditional costume.

The entrance to the shrine is close to Harajuku station (Yamanote line) or Meiji-jingu-mae station of the Chiyoda line.

Gardens and Parks

There are several gardens of traditional style in this generally parkless city. Rikugien garden offers pleasant strolling, as do Koishi Korakuen and Kiyosumi gardens. All are gardens of the traditional Japanese type, low-key but peaceful and beautiful. There are other parks (listed in the JNTO pamphlet on Tokyo), but they can be recommended more for their oasis function than as attractions per se. All the parks are particularly enjoyable in the summer when the shrill semi (cicadas) may be heard; indeed, they may be loud enough to make conversation difficult. Their 'me-me-me-me' sound is one of the memories of Japan.

Museums

There are many good museums in Tokyo. A good listing is given in the JNTO pamphlet on Tokyo. The Sunday *Japan Times* and the 'Tour Companion' list attractions at museums and galleries for the following week.

Lookouts

There are several tall structures for viewing the huge expanse of Tokyo and even distant Mt Fuji during the clear weather of the cool months. Admittance to the 52-storey Sumitomo Building in Shinjuku (west of the station) is free; the Tokyo Tower (a copy of the Eiffel Tower, but slightly taller) and other buildings offer views also, but there is a charge. They are listed in the JNTO pamphlet.

Shinjuku

This is one of the major shopping and entertainment areas of Tokyo. It has several top name department stores, and is the only district of Tokyo with tall buildings. Its entertainment appeals to a younger crowd such as office workers and young professionals, in contrast to the older and wealthier crowd that frequents the Ginza and Akasaka areas on expense accounts. Shinjuku is known for its many bars, pubs and other drinking and eating places. The drinking places include 'pink salons', gay bars and there are many love hotels to cater to liaisons. Advice from a local resident is indispensible before entering the 'floating world' otherwise you can get stuck with horrendous bills. The raunch is mostly located north-east of the station. The respectable stores and businesses run along Shinjuku-dori and several other main streets near the station.

Asakusa Kannon temple

This temple and its five-storey pagoda are always highly touted in any brochure on Tokyo, but I am less enthralled. The present buildings are post-war concrete reconstructions. The temple is very active with worshippers praying for some sort of assistance, lighting bundles of incense and catching the smoke to rub on afflicted parts of their bodies to relieve an ache or pain, and enjoying themselves. The approach is lined with shops selling every manner of tourist junk. (The shopping street, Nakamise, is often described in terms like 'street of gaily decorated souvenir shops'.)

The temples of Kyoto are much more beautiful and representative of Japan, so you can safely skip Asakusa Kannon if Kyoto is on your agenda. An exception is the festival in early March that is definitely worth going to see; it features a dragon dance and a procession of costumed children.

The Asakusa area is popular for theatres and other types of entertainment for 'plain folks' Japanese.

Geihinkan

Otherwise known as Akasaka Palace, this curiosity is worth mentioning only in passing. It is a copy of the Palace of Versailles, with fine interiors and graceful construction features of its inspiration. Unfortunately only a few visitors (selected by lottery) get to visit it during the summer for a few days.

Zojo-ji

This was the temple of the Tokugawa family. The modern building is of no interest, but anyone lacking the chance to visit Kyoto might be interested by the old gate fronting Hibiya-dori, between Onarimon and Shiba-koen subway stations. It dates from 1605 and has details typical of such gates at Kyoto.

Festivals

There are many festivals in Tokyo every month. Details are given on handout photocopied sheets from the TIC. They also cover the rest of Japan. Major festivals are given front-page coverage in the weekly publication 'Tour Companion' which is available at the TIC and major hotels. Some of the festivals are quite fascinating and may even feature firewalking.

Other Sights

On Sunday afternoons in warm weather the Harajuku area, specifically the broad boulevard Omote-sando, is the gathering place for thousands of young people who show off their latest fashions, skateboard down the slope, shop, and set up tape players to provide music for dancing. Some of the clothes and make-up are quite wild and give a window on one segment of Japanese youth.

For exploring the 'real' Tokyo, Jean Pearce's *Footloose in Tokyo* is useful. It describes walking tours in the vicinity of the stations of the Yamanote line. A similar activity would be to take one of the private lines a few stops, get off at a suburban station, and just wander

around. This would give a feel for the flow of daily life of ordinary people — children, shopkeepers, and housewives (older ones in household kimono and white apron). Look around a market and see how goods are displayed — individual piles of five cucumbers, each decoratively arranged, etc.

Near Tokyo

It should be kept in mind that Kamakura, Yokohama and several of the attractions of the area near Tokyo can be reached in an hour or so and can be considered as part of the Greater Tokyo collection of things to see. This includes Sankei-en garden in Yokohama (one of the best in the country), the many attractions of Kamakura, and the Japanese Farmhouse Museum in Kawasaki.

There are many interesting side trips that can be made out of Tokyo, some as day excursions, others for one or more overnights. Possible day trips with the area include Kawasaki, Yokohama, Kamakura, Hakone, Mt Fuji, Kawagoe, and Chichibu-Tama National Park. These are all included in the following chapter.

A worthwhile day-trip (hurried) or overnight (leisurely) is to Nikko, which is described in a later chapter.

MEETING JAPANESE

Of the cities in Japan, Tokyo offers the greatest number of ways for meeting Japanese people who can speak English and would like to talk with visiting foreigners. They have relatively few opportunities to speak English with native-speakers, and they welcome the chance. (Actually, they are willing to spend large sums of money for this questionable privilege.) The following describes ways in which visitors can gain an insight into what the Japanese people are really like and to find out more about the culture, etc, of Japan. For those who will be staying a while, it is also the chance to make lasting friends. (See also the 'Meeting Japanese' section earlier in this book.)

Home Visit

It is possible to visit a private home for a couple of hours in the evening under the Home Visit Plan. The organization office is the TIC in Yurakucho; the phone number is (03) 502-1461. There are nearly 60 host families; languages spoken include English, French, German, Italian and Chinese.

Tescort

Members of the Tescort will gladly act as unpaid companions to visitors to Tokyo, accompanying them sightseeing, shopping or whatever. For an introduction to a Tescort guide in Tokyo and the surrounding Kanto area (including Yokohama), phone Mr Araki at (03) 478-6577. If the person who answers does not speak English well, say 'Tescort' clearly, and you will passed on to someone who does.

International 3F Club

One of the most useful organizations in Tokyo to know about, whether you are staying for a few days, or for months or longer, is the International 3F Club, '3F' for short. (The name makes perfectly good sense to the person who thought it up, and it is not for us to pass judgement on the selection of 'Freedom, Friendship and Forward Action' as a theme.)

The club provides opportunity to meet a large number of English-speaking Japanese in congenial and informal surroundings, at the twice-weekly meetings (Monday, Friday 6-9 pm) of the 'Friendship Salon'. Many tables are set up in a large room, and a visitor may sit anywhere and talk with anyone about anything. There is unlimited coffee and visitors are entitled to one free drink at the bar. You do not have to be a member of 3F to go to the Salon.

By the fact that they speak a foreign language and are interested in foreign contact, the Japanese members are not completely typical of the general population, and they may be more outspoken and candid than average. This makes them more interesting to know, and it is possible to learn a great deal about modern-day Japan and Japanese by talking with them for an evening or more. As with any group of people, not all are conversational wizards, and some are complete bores. On the other hand while the Club is not intended as a dating service, it is almost impossible to avoid meeting someone nice. More than one romance has blossomed as the result of a meeting at 3F.

(Many foreigners have heard about the Club and gone to the Salon blatantly 'on the make'. Some from rigidly controlled societies, have propositioned girls or shown an offensive degree of attention to a girl. Japanese girls are usually reserved, if not shy, in public.)

In addition to the Friendship Salon, there is a similar meeting on Wednesday night at the same time, but the tables are divided into different language groups, and there are no free bar drinks that night.

To get to the Salon, take the Marunouchi subway line to Hongo-Sanchome. There is only one exit; turn right after surrendering your ticket and walk along the narrow lane out to the main road, then turn left. Walk down the gentle slope, across another main road and continue; at the bottom of the grade is the only tall building in the immediate area. It is graced by a pachinko parlour on the ground floor, and there is a soba (noodle) stand at one corner. Walk between the soba-ya and the corner of the building to the outdoor walkway and follow it to the back of the building; enter and take the elevator to the third floor. (In warm weather go to the tenth floor and walk up to the penthouse.)

The activities of 3F Club do not end with the Friendship Salon; it also organizes a huge number of activities for its members, approximately 100 per month. These include classes in traditional Japanese crafts, dinner parties, get-togethers of a social or cultural nature, and weekend excursions to a wide variety of places, like temples, ski resorts, hot springs, scenic places, etc. They are an excellent way to meet people and to have a good time.

The Salon is open to all but to participate in the other activities it is necessary to join the Club. For foreigners it is a reasonable Y6000 per year (Y10,000 for a family), plus a charge for each activity. For the Japanese the cost is exorbitant, but they pay it willingly. Full information can be obtained by writing to:

The International 3F Club
Bunkyo Centre Bldg 10 fl
37-13 4-chome
Hongo
Bunkyo-ku
Tokyo 113.
Tel 812-7700 or 811-5855 (ask for Patricia in the afternoon).
Or just go to a Salon meeting and ask.

Com'inn

Com'inn (short for 'Communications Inn') is one place in Tokyo where you can go almost any day of the week and be sure of meeting Japanese who can speak English (in varying degrees) and who would like to meet visiting foreigners. It functions like an informal coffee house, with the added facilities of a library of paperbacks, English-language newspapers and magazines, games, musical instruments, a cassette deck and turntable, even a TV and videocassettes. Some people drop in daily because the atmosphere is friendly and genuine and the surroundings are pleasant. It tends

to be very crowded on Saturdays and Sundays.

Hours are 3-10 pm Monday to Friday, 1-10 pm weekends. It is closed on the third Wednesday of each month. Tel 993-3371.

They also organize some dances, film nights, excursions, and other events, but not on the scale of 3F Club.

Access is by JNR Yamanote line or Hibiya subway line to Ebisu station. From the station it should be possible to see the Mitsui Bank facing a small plaza. Facing the front of the bank, walk left to the first corner and down the sidestreet. Just past the next intersection, on the left, will be a sign at street level indicating 'Com'inn' (in romaji) on the 5th floor; there is also an illuminated sign at the 5th floor level.

Tesco-ESS

Tesco-English Speaking Society, or Tesco-ESS for short, is a club established and financed by Teijin Educational System, a commercial company which produces English instruction materials. ESS was established to permit contact between students who had used its materials, and English-speaking foreigners. The benefit is the opportunity to talk with Japanese people, and to enjoy a number of programs like skiing trips, cultural evenings, weekend excursion to historical or scenic areas, parties, dances and other social get-togethers that have as their theme the introduction of traditional Japan (and a bit of the modern one as well) while breaking down the barriers of shyness and insularity among the Japanese.

Like most of the activities of 3F Club, most of Tesco-ESS will appeal more to people remaining in Tokyo for a period of time. The number of activities is smaller than those organized by the 3F Club, around five or ten per month, but the joining fee is a once-only Y1000. The address is:

Tesco-ESS
Aoyama Bldg
1-2-3 Kita-Aoyama
Minato-ku
Tokyo 107.
Tel 479-6577 (Mr Araki).

Others

Another social/coffee place is CIDA club; it also offers the choice to meet people, has organized outings and parties, etc. Access is from Takadan-obaba station of the Yamanote JNR line and the Tozai subway line. Tel 208-9338 or 200-1461.

Other means of meeting Japanese people include using clubs and organizations with international ties. Many service clubs, like Lions International, have branches in Japan and might be able to arrange introductions.

Tokyo Toastmasters meet on the first three Thursdays of the month at 6.30 pm in the Otemachi area, and English-speaking guests are welcome. Tel Mr Izumi at 503-3901, or Mr Mori at 271-3258.

Yokota-Fussa Toastmasters meets every Friday at 11.30 am at Yokota Officers Club, some distance to the west of Tokyo, accessible by train. It has been organized by and for the military, but any English-speaking guests are welcome. Tel Yokota Air Base at (0425) 52-2511 and ask for Andrepont (ext 225-8345), or Ohta (0426) 23-1460.

To learn Japanese arts, the Tokyo Baptist Church organizes classes in ikebana, shiatsu, Japanese conversation, wood-carving, etc. Contact Mrs Mock at 467-3051 or the church at 461-8425.

Ikebana International offers classes in Ikebana (flower arranging). Call Michiko Marini at 464-3938 (evenings only).

Jewish visitors to Tokyo are welcome at the Jewish Community Centre. Call 400-2559 or 400-6866 (Mr Aviner), John Eliel at 552-4027, or Mr Bornstein

at 584-7711, all during office hours.

Otemachi ESS (English Speaking Society) is a group of informed Japanese who speak English and meet Saturdays for conversation at the Chiyoda-ku (ward) area. Information is available from Mr(s) Adachi, tel 483-3081.

Mensa: Call Kimiko Fisher at 408-3366 for information on activities.

Tokyo Newcomers Club is intended for ladies in Tokyo, and offers a variety of activities. For information call Suzie Tachibana at 470-2869 or Katherine Crouch at 446-9087; they advertise frequently on the back page of the *Japan Times.*

All Japan Feminist Assosication: For all women who wish to meet and discuss feminist issues (in English). Contact: Anne Blasing, Fuji-so, 2-7-1 Haramachi, Meguro-ku, Tokyo 152; tel 712-0794, 5-9 pm.

After the novelty of eating and drinking only in Japanese has worn off, many visitors want places where they can eat or drink at reasonable cost and have a chance to speak normal-speed English again. The following are some suggested places.

Berni Inn is a small chain of pub-restaurants styled on an English pub (complete with darts, and fish and chips). The best known branch is in Roppongi, near Seryna restaurant; there is another branch in Roppongi, plus others elsewhere. *Henry Africa* has at least two branches, in Roppongi and Harajuku. Drinks are reasonable in cost, and the surroundings pleasant. At Roppongi there is unlimited fresh popcorn. *Charleston pub* in Roppongi offers reasonable cost drinks, music, and all-night hours.

All the above are good places to meet people and learn of other places to try.

SHOPPING

Tokyo is probably the best in Japan for shopping for Japanese antiques, handicrafts, optical and electronic goods. (For further information on 'technological' goods see 'Facts for the Visitor'.)

Even if you are not in the market for anything in particular, a walk through one or two large department stores, floor by floor, is recommended. Many items made and used in Japan are interesting to look at or to take home as an unusual souvenir. Some are definitely gadgets or gimmicks, while others are artistic and decorative. Pottery and other decorative items are well worth a look.

There are many shopping arcades selling export models of electrical goods and tourist-oriented souvenirs (some of high quality, others junk). Information about the location of such places may be found in 'Tour Companion' and other tourist give-away material, although only advertisers are given mention. Inquiries about specific items can be made at the Tourist Information Centre.

If buying a camera or lens, it is a good idea to get a price from Sakuraya or Doi camera shops in Shinjuku before laying out money. Stores in the heavily-touristed Ginza area vary widely in their prices.

Of the stores in Shinjuku, I would try Sakuraya and Doi first. These two stores are well set up to sell at either a domestic price or a tax-free price. Nearby Yodobashi (famous among the Japanese for its low prices) has been unsatisfactory in tax-free sales in my experience. Note, however, that it is sometimes possible to make a better deal paying the discounted domestic price than the tax-free price.

Yodobashi and Sakuraya camera shops are located near the Takano Building, while the Doi and main Yodobashi shops are near the Highway Bus Terminal. These locations are on opposite sides of the Shinjuku station/department stores complex, one of the poorest laid out and most confusing

station buildings in existence (and the world's busiest). Routes between the two sides are via the underground passage in which the subway station is located, or by the roads to the north and south of the station. Refer to the JNTO 'Tourist Map of Tokyo'.

Generally the lowest prices in the country are to be found in Tokyo, as well as the greatest selection of lenses and accessories. Never buy a foreign-made camera in Japan — the prices are outrageous (as is true for most imported goods).

For buying other Japanese-made articles, check out the Akihabara area for electrical goods. Goods for export are to be found in shopping arcades which seem to be located close to all the major hotels in Tokyo. The best-known one is possibly International Arcade, which is located more-or-less under the railway tracks in the Yurakucho area, on the same side of Harumi-dori as the TIC (very close to the latter). Check out several, for stocks appeared to be limited any time I had a look.

For some items, like dolls, that also appeal to the Japanese, it is wise to check out what the department stores have in stock.

Several flea markets are held regularly in the Tokyo area.

— Tokyo Flea Market, Nogi-jinja shrine near Nogizaka station: second Sunday of the month (third in case of rain).
— Roppongi Antique Fair, in front of Roppongi Roa Building, near Roppongi station: third Friday and Saturday of the month.
— Shibuya Junk Fair, Seibu parking lot on Koen-dori: date fixed each month (call Mr Tsuzaki, tel 462-0111).
— Arai-Yakushi Antique Charity Fair, Arai Yakushi-jinja shrine, near Arai Yakushi station, Seibu-Shinjuku line: first Sunday and Monday of the month.

ENTERTAINMENT

Kabuki, a very Japanese form of theatre with its spectacular costumes, highly stylized acting, and fantastic stage effects, is worth seeing during a visit to Japan. The plot is often thin or incomprehensible, but it is worth seeing for the visual effects along.

Performances are given most days at the Kabukiza theatre beginning at 11.30 am and 4.30 pm. The theatre is located close to Ginza crossing along Harumidori, and is easily reached from Higashi-Ginza subway stop where signs in English give directions. It is essily recognized by its traditional architecture. The lowest cost tickets are Y1000 (less 10% with a foreign passport), ranging up to Y6500. The cheapest balcony seats

give a sufficiently good view for an introduction to the art. Enquire also about makumiken tickets for around Y500 which allow you to sit through an act.

English-language program notes may be purchased and give a detailed description of the action which is nearly incomprehensible otherwise.

The National Theatre, Kokuritsu Gekijo, sometimes presents Kabuki too, as well as other traditional performing arts like bunraku and traditional dances.

Noh drama, much more restrained and refined than Kabuki (and more somnolent) is often presented in Tokyo at a variety of theatres.

Bunraku puppet performances are given several times a year at the

National Theatre. (For notes on Bunraku, refer to the Osaka section.)

The weekly tourist publication 'Tour Companion' gives current information on Kabuki, Bunraku and Noh performances as well as for theatre and movie performances. Also, the TIC has a bulletin board where reviews or summaries of the cultural presentations are posted.

FOOD

The incredible variety of eating places in Tokyo range from modest stand-up noodle shops to the most posh restaurants and nightclubs serving international dishes at international prices.

Reasonably priced restaurants of many kinds are found near most JNR stations in the metropolitan area and many subway stations, especially on the little side streets. There is an especially large number of eateries in the areas around Shinjuku and Shibuya stations and the Yurakucho/Hibiya/Ginza area (on the TIC side of the street).

For a super-filling lunch, the *Shakey's Pizza* and *Pizza Hut* shops around the city offer all the pizza you can eat for Y500 from 11 to 2 daily except Sundays and holidays.

ACCOMMODATION

Youth Hostels There are two Youth Hostels within Tokyo. Best known, most easily reached, and the lower in cost is *Ichigaya YH*. It has 128 beds, eight to a room. Room cost is Y1000, breakfast and supper extra. Tel (03) 262-5950 or 261-6839.

Near Ichigaya station it is easily reached by JNR from Akihabara on the Sobu line, and from Tokyo or Kanda stations via the Chuo line as far as Ochanomizu and changing to the Sobu line. Continue in the same direction to Ichigaya station. The Youth Hostel is a hulking grey building at the top of the rise, easily visible from the exit of the station. A side-benefit of this hostel is

that it is close to the national Headquarters.

It is also accessible by the Yurakucho subway line, although this is probably the most awkward line to transfer to. At Ichigaya station, leave the platform from the Kojimachi end and follow the signs 'To JNR Lines' and 'Exit for Kudan' to Exit 3. For the Youth Hostel headquarters, exit from the Iidabashi end of the platform, follow the signs 'Exit for Ichigaya'. It is only a couple of minutes on foot.

The other hostel is *Yoyogi Youth Hostel*, located in one of the dorms constructed for the Tokyo Olympics. It is a little more complicated to reach. First go to Shinjuku station, then change to the Odakyu railway and go to Sangubashi, the second stop. The hostel can also be reached via Harajuku JNR station or Meiji-jingu-mae or Yoyogi-koen stations of the Chiyoda subway line, but these require longer walks. Tel (03) 467-9163.

There are also Youth Hostels at Yokohama and Kamakura, both within an hour of Tokyo.

Okubo House After the Youth Hostels, the best known place to stay. Originally a workingman's dormitory, it now also houses foreigners, some of whom stay there for months. The cost is about the same as a Youth Hostel, about Y1200, but there are fewer restrictions, eg curfew isn't until midnight. (You can bang on the door after 12 and be admitted, but you will be looking for new accommodation the next morning; late arrivers usually go to a nearby all-night coffee shop and wait until morning.) The long-term residents make it a good source of information for travel, finding jobs, etc. Most of the accommodation is bunk beds, eight to a room, but there are some small tatami-matted rooms for couples or women. The staff sometimes seem gruff, but they are good people, and will usually allow travellers to leave small amounts of baggage there while they travel around Japan.

A hint: take a bath as early as possible, for many of the Japanese residents seem to have never heard that you should wash before entering the tub; they hop in after a perfunctory rinse with a single bucket of water, then sit and rub their bodies earnestly with the result that the water is quite dirty by the end of the evening. (The same people squawk loudly if a foreigner hops in similarly; foreigners are automatically dirtier.)

An enduring memory of Okubo-House is the nightly performance by Mosquito-san.

Okubo House is easily reached by taking a Yamanote line train (JNR) to Shin-Okubo station (one stop north of Shinjuku). Leave by the only exit, turn left, and left again at the first little side-street, parallel to and almost beside the tracks. Okubo House is on the right, almost at the end of the street. It is closed from 9 am to mid-afternoon.

Telephone reservations are taken (361-2348), but their English is minimal so speak simply and clearly. There are many restaurants nearby, and Shinjuku is only 15 minutes away (or a short train ride).

English House Accessible from Mejiro station (Yamanote line), this is an upward step from Okubo House for many long-termers. Although a little more expensive (Y1700-1900 single, 3000 double), it offers cooking facilities and more congenial surroundings, and you can stay through the day. Tel (03) 988-1743.

Kimi Ryokan A little more costly that Okubo House, but with more pleasant surroundings. It has 40 Japanese style (tatami) rooms at Y2400/3800/4400 for singles/doubles/twins, and there is an associated business hotel next door at Y2200, with a discount for longer stays. There are cooking facilities. It is close to Ikebukuri station which is

reached by Yamanote JNR line or Marunouchi subway line. Tel (03) 971-3766.

Yoshida House Time-consuming to reach but inexpensive, this private home has several rooms available at Y1300 a day, with long-term reductions. Cooking facilities are available. Access is by Seibu line from Ikebukuro station, getting off at Toshi-mae station. Tel (03) 926-4563.

Ryokan Yashima Another reasonable-cost ryokan, rates are Y3000/4000/4500 single/double/twin. Access from Shin-Okubo station (Yamanote line). Exit and turn left, pass the police box and turn left down the street with a pharmacy on the next corner. Kimi Ryokan is located partway down, on the left side. Tel (03) 364-2534.

Other reasonably priced places are listed below with rates (per night) and means of access.

Shin Nakano Lodge. Tel 381-4886. 4-bed room Y3000 per bed; 2-bed room Y3500 per bed. Subway: Shin-Nakano.

Tokyo YMCA Hotel. Tel 293-1911. Single wo/bath Y4200; twin wo/bath: Y7400. Subway: Kanda or Awajicho.

Japan YWCA Hostel. Tel 264-0661. Women only. Single wo/bath Y4000; twin wo/bath Y8000. JNR: Ichigaya.

Tokyo YWCA Hostel. Tel 293-5421. Women only. Single wo/bath: Y3600; twin wo/bath: Y6800. JNR or subway: Ochanomizu.

Tokyo YWCA Sadohara Hostel. Tel 268-7313. Single wo/bath Y3300; twin w/toilet Y7500. JNR: Ichigaya.

Asia Centre of Japan. Tel 402-6111. Single wo/bath Y3200; twin wo/bath Y4400. Subway: Aoyama-Itchome.

Mr Tom Oshidari's Home Tel 712-6064. Four furnished rooms with shower: Y2500 per person. Bus from Gotanda Station.

Yayoi Kaikan. Tel 823-0841. Single w/bath Y3850; twin w/bath Y6270. Subway: Nezu (Chiyoda Line).

Tokyo Green Hotel, Awajicho. Tel 255-4161. Single w/bath · Y5000; twin w/bath Y800. Subway: Awajicho (Marunouchi Line).

Tokyo Green Hotel, Suidobashi. Tel 295-

4161. Single w/bath Y5000; twin w/bath Y8000. Subway: Suidobashi (Toei Mita Line).

Tokyo Hotel. Tel 494-1050. Single w/bath Y4800; twin w/bath Y9000. JNR: Gotanda.

Ryogoku Pearl Hotel. Tel 625-8080. Single w/bath Y4800; twin w/bath Y8000. JNR: Ryogoku.

Ahihabara Pearl Hotel. Tel 861-6171. Single w/bath Y5000; twin w/bath Y8000. JNR or Subway: Akihabara.

Hotel Sunlight. Tel 356-0391. Single w/bath Y4800; twin w/bath Y8000. Subway: Shinjuku-Sanchome.

Business Hotel Suehiro, Honkan. Tel 734-6561. Single Y3800; twin wo/bath Y6000; JNR: Kamata.

Business Hotel Suehiro, Bekkan. Tel 732-4101. Single wo/bath Y3800; twin wo/bath Y6000. JNR: Kamata.

Central Hotel. Tel 256-6251. Single wo/bath Y4800; twin wo/bath Y7200. JNR: Kanda.

Akasaka Shampia Hotel. Tel 583-1001. Single w/bath Y5200; twin w/bath Y8800. Subway: Akasaka.

Tokyo Station Hotel. Tel 231-2511. Single wo/bath Y5800; twin wo/bath Y8580. JNR: Tokyo.

Shibuya Business Hotel. Tel 409-9300. Singles Y5200; double Y6800; twin Y7880; all w/bath. JNR or subway: Shibuya.

Business Hotel Heimat. Tel 273-9411. Single w/bath Y4530; twin w/bath Y8000. JNR: Tokyo.

Keihin Hotel. Tel 441-7236. Single w/bath Y5560; twin w/bath Y8800. JNR: Shinagawa.

Hotel Ohgaiso. Tel 828-3181. Single w/bath Y4840; twin w/bath Y8250. Subway: Nezu. JNR Ueno.

Hokke Club Tokyo-Ten. Tel 822-3111. Single wo/bath Y3900; twin wo/bath Y6600 (Without breakfast). Subway: Yushima or Ochnomizu.

Hotel Satoh. Tel 815-1137. Single w/bath Y5400; twin w/bath Y8800; Japanese-style w/bath Y6600 for one person, Y8800 for two persons. Subway: Suidobashi or Korakuen.

Ginza Capital Hotel. Tel 543-7888. Single w/bath Y5560; twin w/bath: Y8800. Subway: Tsukiji.

Accommodation near Narita Airport

Because of the time required to get to Narita from Tokyo, an early morning flight demands a very early departure from the city. Some travellers may wish to overnight close to the airport. Suggested places are Chiba and Narita.

Several ryokan, hotels, etc, are located near Chiba station. Chiba is linked with Narita (city) station by JNR services; from there a shuttle bus goes to the airport. The following are close to Chiba station and are listed in ascending order of cost. (Further information on Chiba and Narita accommodation is available at the TIC offices.)

Chiba Kyozai Kaikan. Tel (0472) 48-1111.

Business Hotel Takane. Tel (0472) 41-8051.

Chiba Keisei Hotel. Tel (0472) 22-2111.

Chiba New Park Hotel. Tel (0472) 42-1111.

Chiba Grand Hotel. Tel (0472) 41-2111.

Business Hotel Chiba. Tel (0472) 46-2332 (located farther from the station).

Accommodation close to Narita city is more costly that that at Chiba.

Business Inn Kinoshita. Tel (0476) 22-0800.

Hotel Tsukuba. Tel (0476) 24-1234.

Ryokan Ogiya. Tel (0476) 22-1161.

Ryokan Wakamatsu Honten. Tel (0476) 22-1136.

Hotels close to the airport are considerably more expensive, though of higher quality that those at Narita city.

Holiday Inn Narita. Tel (0476) 32-1234.

Narita View Hotel. Tel (0476) 32-1111.

Narita Prince Hotel. Tel (0476) 33-1111.

Hotel Nikko Narita. Tel (0476) 32-0032.

Narita International Hotel. Tel (04769) 3-1234.

Narita Airport Rest House. Tel (0476) 32-1212.

Near Tokyo

The region around Tokyo offers some of Japan's more interesting attractions, including Kamakura, Mt Fuji and the Chichibu-Tama National Park. This chapter follows an arc around Tokyo from the south-west to the south-east.

WEST FROM TOKYO

There are several individual attractions and interesting areas to the west of Tokyo. Many can be visited as day trips or weekend outings, or en route to Kyoto and other destinations in western Japan.

Although generally industrial/ commercial in nature, Kawasaki and Yokohama have an attraction or two each, and the many interesting sights of the historic city of Kamakura are only a short distance beyond Yokohama. South of Kamakura is the Miura-hanto peninsula, and west of the city lies Odawara, gateway to the Izu-hanto peninsula, the Hakone area, and Mt Fuji. Going west from the Hakone/Fuji area takes you along the south coast (generally heavily urbanized and uninteresting); going north leads inland via Matsumoto and very much more interesting and less-travelled regions. The following section describes each in turn, with optional routes.

KAWASAKI

Kawasaki is a typical Japanese industrial city with virtually nothing of interest to visitors, with one notable exception, Nihon Minka-en.

Getting There

Kawasaki can be reached by train from Tokyo on the Yokosuka or Tokaido lines, from Shimbashi or Shinagawa stations: these lines continue to Yokohama (the next stop). You can also use the Keihin Kyuko line from Shinagawa station (or from Sengakuji station on the Asakusa subway line). From Kawasaki the Yokosuka line (with blue and cream cars) goes to Kamakura.

There is a daily ferry service between Kawasaki and Hyuga (Kyushu). The trip takes 20 hours, leaving Kawasaki at 6.30 pm, leaving Hyuga at 7 pm. Minimum fare is Y11,600. To a destination much closer, there is also service from Kawasaki across the bay (Tokyo-wan) to Kisarazu on the Boso-hanto peninsula.

Nihon Minka-en

The name means Japan Farmhouse museum. It is a collection of traditional thatch-roofed buildings (17 at the time of writing, with more on the way) that have been moved to this peaceful forested site from many places around Japan. The oldest dates from 1688. It offers a very convenient way to get a glimpse of how Japan looked in centuries past. A pamphlet in English given at the entrance explains the origin, use, and unusual points of each building. Visitors are free to wander through the interiors of many. The second floor of one building is a museum of traditional farming implements, utensils and tools, plus some armour and weaponry. (Closed Monday; no entry after 4 pm.)

Access from Tokyo is by Odakyu line from Shinjuku station to Muko-ga-oka Yuen station; the express from track 5 takes about 30 minutes. From the south exit (minami guchi), look for the monorail (same word as in English) and follow along to the right; continue straight at the main road where it turns left. From the station it takes about 15 minutes on foot. (From Muko-ga-oka Yuen, the Odakyu line continues west to Odawara.)

To go to Kawasaki, backtrack one stop to Noborito and change to the JNR Nanbu line going south to Kawasaki.

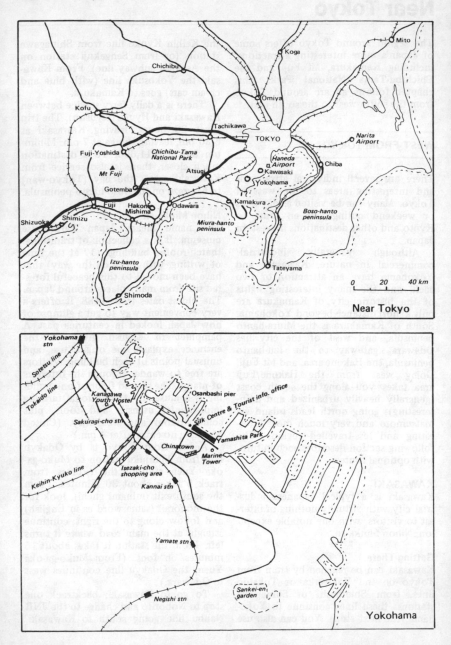

Near Tokyo

Yokohama

(At Muko-ga-oka Yuen you can get a single ticket that permits the transfer to the JNR line; tickets are issued from the leftmost of the three groups of vending machines — buy any ticket and pay the difference later.)

Other attractions

Kawasaki is known for its 'toruko' red light district (named Horinouuch), and its many love hotels. It is one of the three or four best known such places in Japan.

Kawasaki has one other attraction, an interesting annual festival, **Jibeta-matsuri**. This festival (matsuri) honours Kanamara-sama (deities of the metal phallus). It is based on a fable of a maiden (beautiful and rich, of course) who had an unusual and terrible affliction, being 'inhabited' by a sharp-toothed demon which bit off the phallus of two successive grooms who tried to do their wedding night duty. A divinely inspired blacksmith got and took the girl with the aid of an iron phallus that de-toothed the demon while deflowering the girl. And everyone lived happily ever after, including the Kawasaki businessmen who have revived the festival, which also honours the gods of business, growth, prosperity, reproduction, etc, all being various forms of the same fertility. Whatever the motives, all have a good time as phalluses are carried in procession and local smiths re-enact the forging operation. It is no orgy, just a good-humoured celebration of the joys of sex.

The festival is held on 15 April beginning with music in the early afternoon, a parade of the sacred palanquin and masked persons carrying phallic offerings (4-5 pm), followed by the forging (5-6 pm), then an outdoor banquet.

The festival is held near the Kawasaki Taishi station. From Tokyo take the Keihin Kyuko line to Keihin Kawasaki station, then transfer to the Kawasaki

Taishi line downstairs. The Taishi station is about 10 minutes away. From the station (there is only one exit) cross the street outside, turn right and walk about 50 metres.

YOKOHAMA

Yokohama is the port city for Tokyo, and is about 20 km away. It has become the second largest city in Japan, (about 2.7 million in 1978) but both Tokyo and Yokohama have expanded toward each other and now form one vast conurbation. Being a commercial city there is little for the sightseer. Its large office buildings are much the same as those anywhere.

Yokohama has a short history by the standards of Japan. Before 1850 it was only a sleepy fishing village. With the signing of the treaty forcing Japan to open its doors after 250 years of seclusion, Yokohama was made one of six ports open to the world, and was the port for Tokyo. At the time it was an ugly expanse of mud, and was chosen by the Japanese officials to keep the unwanted and unclean foreigners as far from the capital as possible in conditions less than pleasant. It has improved somewhat since.

GETTING THERE

Most people visit Yokohama from Tokyo. Details of train services, etc, are given below. If you are going there direct from Narita or Haneda airports, the most convenient service is by airport bus which connects with Yokohama City Air Terminal (YCAT), a few minutes from Yokohama station. Fare is Y280 (Haneda) or Y2600 (Narita). Travel time is scheduled at two hours, but extra time should be allowed for traffic tie-ups. There is an average of two buses per hour. When departing, luggage may be checked in at YCAT and not touched again until the destination, and planes are held back for delayed buses if passengers check in at YCAT. (See below for details on how to get to YCAT from the station.)

For connections between Yokohama and Narita airport, it is cheaper but more time-consuming to use trains instead of the airport bus. This involves taking a train from Narita to the Asakusa line (see Tokyo chapter for details), then change to Keihin-Kyuko line at Sengakuji (see below).

Yokohama is a port of call for cruise ships, and is served by regular sailings to and from Nakhodka (USSR) at the eastern extremity of the Trans-Siberian Railway. Passenger ships arrive at the modern and pleasant International Port Terminal located on Osambashi Pier.

After clearing Immigration and Customs, passengers walk to the mainland. At the entrance to the pier is a small square; on the right side is a map of Yokohama and the first of many indicators pointing the way to Sakuragicho station (from which trains can be caught to Tokyo); on the left is the nine-storey Silk Centre Building.

Train Services from Tokyo

To reach Yokohama from Tokyo or Narita Airport there are five rail services — three JNR and two private lines, Toyoko and Keihin-Kyuko.

From the central Tokyo area and areas near JNR Tokyo, Shimbashi or Shinagawa stations, the fastest service is by JNR Tokaido or Yokosuka lines. They leave at frequent intervals and stop only at Kawasaki before reaching Yokohama. Trains on the Keihin-Tohoku line stop at all 12 stations from Tokyo to Yokohama.

From points near Eidan (private) subway lines, the most convenient and cheapest way to go is probably by the Toyoko line. It starts from Shibuya. (You can transfer here from Ginza subway or JNR Yamanote lines, but separate

tickets must be used, and this increases the cost.) A direct transfer (without changing platforms) can be made from the Hibiya subway line at Naka-Meguro, and some other stations along the line.

From stations on the Toei (Asakusa and Mita) subway lines, go to Sengakuji and transfer there to the Keihin-kyuko line to Yokohama. Many trains leaving Narita Airport station have the marked destination 'Nishi-Magome'. For Yokohama, take one of these trains to Sengakuji and transfer to the Keihin-kyuko line.

GETTING AROUND

Yokohama has a subway system but it is of little use to the newcomer.

There is also an extensive network of buses but this too is of more interest to residents than travellers passing through. There is a map available of all the routes, but it is written only in Japanese. It is available at subway stations and probably at the city office, since buses and the subway are city operated.

Buses terminate on both sides of Yokohama station, by the main entrances. Buses from the port, Sankei-en, Chinatown, etc, stop at the east side where there is an overpass over the highway. An underground passage connects the east exit (Higashi-guchi) of the station with the west exit (Nishi-guchi, also called Chuo-guchi).

TRAIN SERVICES

Yokohama station is very large with many platforms, and very few destination markings in romaji. There are two major entrances, east (Higushi-guchi) and west (Nishi-guchi); they are joined by a broad underground passage.

Tracks 1 and 2 are for Keihin-kyuko trains (private line). Track 1 trains go west to Yokosuka and the Miura-hanto peninsula. Expresses are marked with green or red kanji on the front and side of the trains, locals in black.

Trains from track 2 run to Kawasaki

and Tokyo. Some terminate at Shinagawa, but many continue to Sengakuji where they switch onto the tracks of Asakusa subway line and run at least to Oshiage. Some run all the way to Narita airport.

Tracks 3 to 10 are JNR services.

Track 3 is Keihin-Tohoku line which becomes the Negishi line after another stop; it provides local service as far as Ofuna, a station on the Yokosuka line.

Track 4 is Keihin-Tohoku line which provides local service to Tokyo. It stops at all 12 stations along the way and costs the same as the much faster Yokosuka and Tokaido lines; in the Tokyo area it runs parallel to the Yamanote line for many stops. This is the line to take for connections with the Shinkansen, which leaves from Shin-Yokohama station. Go one stop to Higashi-Kanagawa station and transfer for a Yokohama-sen line train bound for Hachioji; the third stop is Shin-Yokohama. Keihin-Tohoku trains are blue.

Tracks 5 and 6 are Tokaido line services west to Odawara, Atami and Nagoya.

Tracks 7 and 8 are Tokaido line services to Tokyo, stopping en route only at Kawasaki, Shinagawa and Shimbashi, the latter two being stations in the metro Tokyo area. This is one of the fastest services to Tokyo. Tokaido line trains are orange and green.

Track 9 is Yokosuka line (pronounced Yo-kos-ka) service west to Kamakura, Zushi, Yokosuka and Kurihama, at the south-east side of the Miura-hanto peninsula.

Track 10 is Yokosuka line service east to Tokyo, making the same stops as the Tokaido line trains and giving equally fast service. Yokosuka line trains are blue and cream.

Tickets for all JNR services can be purchased from vending machines in the underground passageway or at the west exit, (on the right when entering the station). In case of doubt about the fare, buy the cheapest ticket and pay the difference at the other end. JNR services are more expensive into Tokyo than either the Keihin-kyuko or Toyoko lines.

There are two tracks in this area of the station, those of the Toyoko (or Tokyo-kyuko) line. Its trains run to Shibuya station in Tokyo, convenient for people headed for the west side of Tokyo; transfers are easy there to the Yamanote loop line, two subway lines leading into the city, and a couple of private railway lines heading west. Transfer to the Hibiya subway line can easily be made at Naka-Meguro, you simply cross the platform and take the next train (although the fare jumps because it is a change of system). There are many expresses between Shibuya and Yokohama through the day, but they are only about 10 minutes faster; expresses have red kanji on signs on the trains and on timetables.

Track 1 of the Toyoko line serves trains that go only two stops, to Sakuragicho.

Track 2 of the Toyoko line serves Shibuya-bound trains.

Tracks of the Toyoko line can only be reached from the West Exit area. When entering the station turn left before the large entrance that leads to the stairs down to the passageway. Tickets for the Toyoko line are sold by vending machines to the left. In case of doubt, buy the cheapest ticket and pay the difference at the other end.

To get to the Yokohama subway, follow the passage toward the west exit, climb up the stairs and turn left. Continuing down the passage to the end leads to an open area and exit to the right; the subway entrance is just outside and is identified in English.

Straight ahead at this exit is the entrance to the Sotetsu line that runs west and intersects the Odakyu line to Odawara and area.

Yokohama City Air Terminal (YCAT), is easily reached from the east exit of the station. A shuttle bus runs from stop No 1 about three to five times an hour. Fare is Y110 and the trip takes only a few minutes. In early 1981 daark blue minibuses were being used, identifiable by the letters YCAT on the side. If you don't have to carry luggage it is about a 15-minute walk. Turn left from the front of the station and walk until you see New Japan Motors (a Ford dealer) across the wide road. YCAT is across the road and down the side street.

From the Port

To get to the Yokohama station from Osambashi Pier at the port, you can walk, get a bus, or go by train from a nearer station.

Buses No 8, 20, 58 and 81 go to Yokohama station via Sakuragi-cho station; buses 11, 21 and 22 terminate at the latter. To get to the bus stop from the pier, walk straight ahead past the Silk Centre Building (on the left) to the first major cross street (the Post Office will be to the right on it). The bus stop is a little along the street from the far right hand corner.

Near the map across from the Silk Centre Building is the first of a series of signs showing the way to Sakuragi-cho station, a simple 20-30 minute walk. If you follow the signs to a tree-lined avenue you can walk along that to Yokohama Park and through there to Kannai station. Both stations are on the Negishi (JNR) line, a local line with trains to Yokohama station.

INFORMATION

Beside the Silk Centre Building (at the port, facing the harbour) is the Kanagawa Prefectural Tourist Information Centre. It has a good selection of useful information for Yokohama and for travel elsewhere in Japan. Tel (045) 681-0506.

There is a free handout 'Map of Tokyo and Yokohama', published by Sanyo, but at the time of writing it is badly out of date, it does not show the subway system or Sankeien Park. It is also confusing because north is to the right and is not indicated.

Home Visit

If you wish to visit a Japanese home in Yokohama for a couple of hours in the evening, arrangements can be made at the Tourist Information Centre, at the Yokohama International Welcome Association (ground floor, Silk Centre Building, tel 641-5824), or at the Silk Centre Hotel (tel 641-0961). (Details about the Home Visit Program are given earlier in the book.)

Tescort

Visitors who would like an English-speaking Japanese to accompany them around Yokohama, Tokyo, Kamakura, Nikko or other nearby tourist attractions should contact Tescort in Tokyo; tel (03) 478-6577 and ask for Mr Araki. (Details about Tescort are given elsewhere.)

ACCOMMODATION

There is a Youth Hostel at Yokohama, about 10 minutes from Sakuragi-cho station. From the station you can see the 'Golden Centre' Building (that's the name in Japanese if you have to ask anyone), and there is a wide street on the far side of it. Walk to the right along that street, keeping the elevated railway tracks to the right, past two small side-streets to the left until you reach a short, steep incline leading up to a steep cobblestoned street to the left and a traffic bridge to the right. Turn left up the hill; the Hostel is on the right, about 100 metres up.

If you want to stay overnight in a typical Japanese lodging, eg a ryokan or minshuku, you can get help in making bookings at the Tourist Information Centre. Also there is an office for minshuku reservations and information located on the balcony beside the Sky Building, at the end of the elevated passageway from Yokohama station to one of the bus stations.

There are several hotels in Yokohama.

Note that Kamakura is about half an hour away from Yokohama (or an hour from Tokyo) and may be a preferable place to stay. Kamakura was once the capital of Japan and has a number of interesting temples and is home of the well-known bronze Daibutsu (Great Buddha); it should be on the itinerary of any traveller to Japan.

SIGHTSEEING

The attractions of Yokohama are limited and most are located quite close to each other: Yamashita Park (along the harbour front), Marine Tower, Port Viewing Park, Chinatown and the Silk Centre Building. A convenient bus ride away is Sankei-en Park.

The **Silk Centre Building** houses a permanent display of all aspects of the silk industry, from raw cocoon to beautiful fabric. To get there from Yokohama station, the simplest access is by bus from the depot beside the Sky Building, opposite the East Exit. Bus 26 passes in front of the Silk Centre. Buses 8 and 58 pass nearby; get off at the Post Office.

From the Silk Centre, it is a simple walk along **Yamashita Park** to the very visible **Marine Tower**. On a clear day it is possible to see distant Mt Fuji; this is more likely in the cooler months or following a day of strong winds. From Yokohama station, buses 8, 26 and 58 pass nearby.

An alternative to Marine Tower for viewing the harbour (though not Mt Fuji) is the **Port Viewing Park**. The road up to it can be found easily from the vicinity of the Tower. This area is known as the Bluffs and has been the prestige residential area, especially for foreigners, since Yokohama was opened

to the outside world. Near the tower is **Chinatown,** the only one in Japan, known for its restaurants and shops selling Chinese products and curios.

After the Tower, catch a No 8 bus to **Sankei-en Park** (get off at Sankei-en-mae stop). This is one of the nicest garden parks in Japan — in my opinion it is far more attractive than the 'Big Three' at Mito, Kanazawa and Okayama. It is not old — it dates from the late 19th century. It was built by Tomitaro Hara a wealthy silk merchant. It is laid out around a large pond, with walking paths circling it and branching off to other places. Wooded hillsides totally obscure the ugly reality of the surrounding 20th century. One of the side paths leads to the Inner Garden which is laid out in the traditional Japanese style and is an excellent example of the landscape gardener's work. Within the Inner Park are several historic buildings which have been moved here from other parts of Japan; a short explanation in English is found by each.

Elsewhere in the park, on the highest hill, is an old three-storey pagoda in excellent condition and representative of such buildings. This one dates from the 15th century and was moved to the park in 1914. A nearby lookout gives a good view of the harbour, on a clear day you can see Mt Fuji but the scene is spoiled by a tall smokestack.

Near the pagoda is another noteworthy building, the **Yonohara farmhouse**, a huge thatched-roof building. It dates from 1750, and is held together only by straw ropes — there are no nails in it whatever. This one was moved in 1960 when a nearby dam was about to cause it to be flooded. The only other similar buildings are in the farther reaches of Japan so take this opportunity if you can.

To return to Yokohama station, or the vicinity of the Tower or Chinatown, take a No 8 bus going in the same direction as the one which got you to the park. Get off anywhere near the Tower and you'll find it easily. The closest railway station is Ishikawacho on the Negishi (Keihin-Tohoku) line.

BEYOND YOKOHAMA

KAMAKURA

Now a resort town for day-tripping Tokyoites and residence of many more fortunate citizens, Kamakura was effectively the capital of Japan from 1192 to 1333 when the *baku* military government of the Minamoto family gained the upper hand in Japan. During that period it became very prosperous, but it subsequently declined to a regional government centre, and finally lost all special status in 1603 and became a quiet backwater.

Kamakura is the most interesting single place in the Tokyo area to visit for historic remains, the best-known of which is the famous Kamakura Daibutsu (Great Buddha), but there are other sights as well.

Two useful leaflets are available from the Tokyo Tourist Information Centre — 'Kamakura' (MG-6) and 'Fuji-Hakone-Izu-Kamakura'.

Getting There

Kamakura is easily reached in just under an hour from Tokyo station (tracks 9 or 10), Shimbashi and Shinagawa stations in metro Tokyo, or from Kawasaki or Yokohama (track 9) on the Yokosuka line. From Yokosuka it is the fourth station.

Sightseeing

Kamakura is a good starting point for the area. It is the starting point for buses as well as the Enoden railway line to Fujisawa via the beach resort town of Enoshima. A day pass ('furii kipu') for unlimited travel for a day on city buses is available for Y500,

but visitors generally will not use it enough to make it a bargain. (Passes are sold at the ticket office close to the police post, to the left when exiting the station on the bus terminal side of the station.)

Finding your way around on foot in Kamakura is very simple because of the large number of signposts in English that point the direction and give the distance to the next attraction (usually a temple or shrine). Every point of interest has a plaque at its entrance giving the history and points of major importance/interest. The following route takes in the major places of interest.

Daibutsu The most famous single sight in Kamakura is the great bronze figure of Buddha (Amitabha). It sits in the open, looking with half-closed eyes on the rise and fall of Kamakura as a seat of power. The seated figure is more than 11 metres tall, plus pedastal, and weighs nearly 100 tonnes. The pose and position of the hands represent the Budhist symbolism for steadfast faith. The expression on the face is one of great serenity, and it is a work of art, far superior to the larger figure at Nara.

The figure was cast in 1252 and was originally protected by a temple, but a tidal wave in 1495 swept this away, and the figure has been in the open since. The tidal wave must have been monumental as well, for the Buddha is nearly one km inland!

(The temple has a welcome facility: clean toilets, with a western style one and toilet paper as well!)

Access is by bus No 3 or 7, both of which serve Daibutsu-mae stop; an alternative is bus No 8 to nearby Hase Kannon temple.

Hase Kannon Temple This is an interesting temple to visit before or after Daibutsu. It is famed for a huge nine-metre figure of Kannon, Buddhist

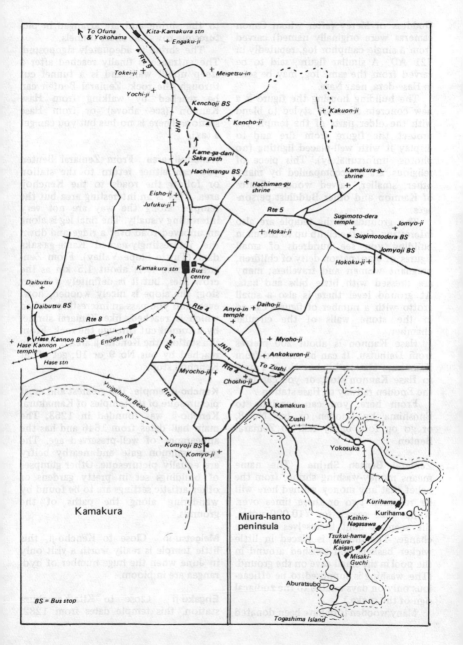

To Ofuna
& Yokohama

Kita-Kamakura stn
Engaku-ji

Rte 9

Tokei-ji

Meigetsu-in

Yochi-ji

JNR

Kenchoji BS

Kakuon-ji

Kencho-ji

Kame-ga-dani
Saka path

Hachimangu BS

Eisho-ji

Kamakura-gu
shrine

Jufuku-ji

Hachiman-gu
shrine

Rte 5

Sugimoto-dera
temple

Jomyo-ji

Hokai-ji

Sugimotodera BS

Jomyoji BS

Kamakura stn

Bus
centre

Hokoku-ji

Daibutsu

Rte 8

Daibutsu BS

Rte 4

Anyo-in
temple

Daiho-ji

Rte 2

Hase Kannon BS

Enoden rly

Myoho-ji

Hase Kannon
temple

JNR

Ankokuron-ji

Hase stn

Rte 4

To Zushi

Myocho-ji

Rte 2

Chosho-ji

Yuigahama Beach

Komyoji BS

Komyo-ji

Kamakura

BS = Bus stop

Kamakura

Zushi

Yokosuka

Kurihama

Keihin-
Nagasawa

Kurihama

Tsukui-hama
Miura-
Kaigan

Misaki-
Guchi

Aburatsubo

**Miura-hanto
peninsula**

Togashima Island

Goddess of Mercy (after whom Canon cameras were originally named) carved from a single camphor log, reputedly in 721 AD. A similar figure, said to be carved from the same log, may be seen in Hase-dera, near Nara.

The building housing the figure is a new concrete structure styled to blend with the older parts of the temple yet protect the figure from fire and to display it with well-placed lighting (no photos, unfortunately). This piece of religious art is accompanied by many other, smaller, carved wooden figures of Kannon and other Buddhist personages.

The grounds of the temple are also interesting. On the climb up to the main building you see hundreds of small figures of Jizo, patron deity of children, pregnant women and travellers; many are dressed with little bibs and hats. At ground level there is also a small grotto with a number of figures carved in the stone walls of the circular chamber.

Hase Kannon is about 200 metres from Daibutsu. It can be reached from Kamakura station by bus No 3, 7 or 8 to Hase Kannon stop, or you can take the Enoden railway to Hase station.

From here, you can continue to Enoshima by Enoden or bus No 8, or go on foot or by taxi to Zeniarai Benten.

Zeniarai Benten Shrine The name means money-washing shrine, from the belief that any money washed here will be returned two or three times over. While some search for Y10,000 notes, the sceptics limit themselves to loose change. The money is placed in little wicker baskets and swished around in the pool in the small cave on the ground. (The washing is supposed to be efficacious only on days related to the zodiacal sign of the snake.)

Many wooden torii have been donated

to the shrine and are arranged in picturesque rows like short tunnels.

The shrine is adequately signposted. The entrance is finally reached after a steep uphill walk and is a tunnel cut through the rock. Zeniarai Benten can be reached by walking from Hase Kannon (see above) or from Hase station. There is no bus but you can get a taxi.

Kenchoji area From Zeniarai Benten you can either return to the station or follow the roads to the Kenchoji area. This is an interesting area but the temples along the way are not very interesting visually. The final leg is along an unpaved road over a ridge and down the interestingly-named Kame-ga-saka dani (Turtle Slope Valley). From Zeniarai shrine it is about 1.5 km as the crow flies, but it is definitely a longer slog; the slope is nicely wooded, however, and you pass an interesting ryokan which is reached, like Zeniarai shrine, by a tunnel cut through the rock. From the station, the Kencho-ji area is quickly reached by bus No 9 or 10; get off at Kenchoji stop.

Kencho-ji temple The greatest and most picturesque of the temples of Kamakura, Kencho-ji was founded in 1253. The main hall dates from 1646 and has the appearance of well-preserved age. The great sanmon gate and nearby belfry are equally picturesque. Other glimpses of buildings set in pretty gardens or other artistic settings are to be found by wandering along the paths of the grounds.

Meigetsu-in Close to Kencho-ji, this little temple is really worth a visit only in June when the huge number of hydrangea are in bloom.

Engaku-ji Close to Kita-Kamakura station, this temple dates from 1282, but virtually all the old buildings have been destroyed, many by the great 1923 Kanto earthquake. The great san-mon main gate is impressive, carvings of lions and dragons, and there are glimpses of beauty here and there, but the effect is not maintained, and the main building is made of unromantic concrete. It superficially resembles Kencho-ji in lay-out, but has less to offer.

There are other temples nearby that may be explored if leisure allows, but all are low-key. Downhill from Kencho-ji is a side entrance to Tsurugaoka Hachiman-gu shrine.

Hachiman-gu shrine Occupying the place of honour in Kamakura, the shrine is built on a hillside overlooking the city and a long boulevard that leads to the sea. (The boulevard is divided by twin rows of cherry trees that attract throngs in spring.)

Hachiman is the god of war, so it was natural for the military government (the baku) to dedicate the shrine to him. The present site was first used from 1191, the successor to an earlier one founded elsewhere in 1063. The present colourful orange buildings date from 1828. The small museum in the main buildings house armour, swords, masks and other historic items.

At the foot of the staircase leading down from the shrine is a Noh stage from which a long stone-paved walkway leads to the front entrance; it is always crowded on weekends and holidays. To the left is the Kamakura Municipal Museum (Kamakura Koku-hokan) which displays a number of treasures of the Kamakura and Muromachi periods (1192-1573) that belong to various shrines and temples in the area. Near the main entrance to the grounds, to the right, is the Prefectural Modern Art Gallery. Also near the entrance is the steep taiko bashi (Drum Bridge) a sort of practical joke in stone for it is so

steep that one cannot walk up and over. A running start should be enough to carry you over, and is reputed to grant a wish.

Hokuku-ji temple Access is across Hana-no bashi bridge, an ordinary con-crete structure, but note the colourful carp in the stream below. The temple is not noted for its buildings, but for the beautiful bamboo grove behind that is interspersed with numerous historic gravestones. At the teahouse in one corner you can sit and contemplate the small but attractive garden behind the grove.

Hokoku-ji is a zen temple, and zazen meditation is held at the garden before 8 am every Sunday; anyone may partic-ipate.

Hokoku-ji can be reached from Hachiman shrine or the station by No 5 bus to Jomyoji stop.

There are several other temples and shrines along the same road, including thatched-roof Sugimoto-dera which is the oldest temple in Kamakura, but most are of historical interest only and have little visual appeal unless you are familiar with (and interested in) Japan-ese history.

Komyo-ji temple This temple is usually nearly deserted, yet it is one of the most worthwhile destinations in Kamakura for visual appeal. The temple dates from 1243, although the main building is a modern concrete structure (but of traditional appearance). What sets it apart from other temples in Kamakura is its karesansui garden of rock, gravel and greenery, located at one side of the temple,and another garden consist-ing of a lotus pond (best from late summer) and other picturesque elem-ents, all arranged in front of an attract-ive building. Unlike most other temples, there is no charge to see either. To get there, take a No 2 bus from the station.

Other attractions of the temple include a large and old-looking sanmon gate, a bell tower with some of the finest wood carvings in Kamakura, and a number of interesting tombs. Although many other temples in the city have extensive burial areas, this is the only one with a memorial for pet animals; look for a large monument on the right with food dishes left out.

ENOSHIMA

This is a popular beach resort town west of Kamakura. Because it is close to Tokyo it gets extremely crowded in summer weekends.

The main beach is Higashi-hama (higashi = east); on the Katase (or west) side of the Katese River is Nishi-hama beach (nishi = west), accessible by Katase-bashi bridge. Also on the Katase side is an aquarium and Enoshima Marineland.

In the harbour is Enoshima, the island that gives its name to the area. It offers the hillside Enoshima shrine (reached by steps or escalator), various recreation facilities, and scenic views at Chigogafuchi (including two nearby caves). Enoshima-jinja shrine has a nude statue of Benten, the Indian goddess of beauty and the only female among the Japanese seven deities of good luck. There is an observation tower that gives a good view of Mt Fuji in one direction and Oshima Island in another. The latter (described later in this chapter) can be reached by ferry from Shonan Harbour, on the north side of the island. Enoshima island is easily reached by a footbridge.

To get to Enoshima from Kamakura, you can go by Enoden train or bus No 8 from Kamakura station. There is also the monorail from Ofuna on the JNR Yokosuka line.

To continue from Enoshima to the Hakone/Izu/Fuji area, take the Enoden line to Fujisawa and transfer to the JNR to go to Odawari or Atami. (This area is described later in this section.)

MIURA-HANTO PENINSULA

This peninsula projects into Sagami-wan Bay between Yokohama and Kamakura. The east side is mainly industrial and commercial and includes Yokosuka Naval Base, the largest US naval base in Japan. The west side and south-east coast is largely beach and resort territory.

A bus from Zushi station runs down the west coast to Misaki station; it passes beaches, the Emperor's walled-in villa at Hayama, and several pleasant views of the sea and pleasure craft. During clear weather (winter, late autumn) Mt Fuji is clearly visible.

Aburutsubo

Aburutsubo has one of the finest aquariums in the East. It is named 'Sakana-no-kuni' ('Fish World'). As well as displays of live fish, it has a dome onto which films are projected to give the impression of being underwater. Buses run between Misaki-guchi station and the aquarium; the trip takes about 15 minutes.

Jogashima Island

Located at the far south-west tip of the peninsula, Jogashima has preserved a picturesque cape as parkland, sparing it from a 'development' and encroachment of urban sprawl. The shore is made of strangely twisted rocks, apparently of volcanic origin. There are several small pools, some with colourful small fish. Anyone wanting a peaceful place for a picnic or just for relaxing by the sea would enjoy it. It is a good destination for a day-trip to escape Tokyo, or even for a longer stay for a traveller with extra time. It was almost deserted during my late-September visit, but it might be more crowded in summer. There is a Youth Hostel nearby.

Buses run to Jogashima from Misaki-guchi station. The trip takes about 30 minutes.

Miura-kaigan coast

Above the 'bulge' at the bottom of the peninsula is Miura-kaigan (coast), known for the very long Shonan-hama beach, with good white sand and temperate water. Access is by Keihin-kyuko railway to any of the three stations: Miura-kaigan, Tsukuri-hama, and Keihin-Nagasawa; local buses run along the coast. There are many minshuku and ryokan along the beach.

From Kurihama, a ferry crosses to Kanaya on the Boso-hanto peninsula (on the opposite side of Tokyo-wan bay); service is approximately every 35 minutes through the daylight hours.

FUJI-HAKONE-IZU   AREA

Some of the finest scenery in Japan is located close to Tokyo, and is easily reached. The centre piece is Mt Fuji, while the other areas offer views of Fuji and attractions of their own. This section begins with a description of the Hakone area, followed by the Izu-hanto peninsula and finishes with the area around Mt Fuji.

HAKONE AREA

Hakone, and its nearby attractions, is the closest resort to Tokyo, and thus is very popular with Japanese holiday-makers. Because of its popularity with the local population, it is also heavily promoted for visiting foreigners, perhaps over-promoted.

The major attractions of the Hakone area are good views of Mt Fuji, Ashi-no-ko late, some interesting historic remains, and other views of the terrain created by volcanoes. Be warned, though, that much of the beauty and interest of the area comes from having Mt Fuji as backdrop, and this mountain is notoriously bashful in spring, summer and early autumn, often totally obscured by cloud even from close up. Thus, the later in the season, the better the chance of seeing the undisputedly superb form of Mt Fuji. Japanese visitors may not be too concerned with missing the view, but foreigners who may have only a short time in Japan should plan their itinerary accordingly.

For further information, the Tourist Information Centre in Tokyo has copies of the JNTO publications 'Hakone' (MG-7), and 'Fuji-Hakone-Izu-Kamakura', as well as the Hakone city brochure 'Hakone'.

Getting There & Getting Around

Odawara is of little interest but makes a convenient starting point. It is most easily reached from Tokyo by the Odakyu line from Shinjuku. The fastest service (75 minutes) is by Romance Car (a Japanese name), a non-stop express. An express from track 5 takes 20 minutes longer and is Y400 cheaper but usually involves a change of trains, whereas most Romance Car trains go direct to Hakone-Yomoto station, the most useful destination. The schedule is complex so get advice from the Tourist Information Centre.

There are two daily buses from Shinjuku station (west exit) to Hakone-Yumoto and Moto-Hakone. There are many daily buses from Shinjuku to Tomei-Gotemba, Sengoku and Togendai.

Summary of bus services in the Hakone area:

Kojiri/ Sengoku/ Tomei Gotemba/ Gotemba station — many.

Moto-Hakone/ Hakone-machi/ Jukoku-toge/ Atami — many.

Hakone-machi/ Odawara — three a day.

Hakone-en/ Kojiri/ Owakundani/ Hakone-Yumoto/ Odawara — many.

Moto-Hakone/ Hakone-machi/ Mishima/ Numazu — many.

Odawara/ Miya-no-shita/ Gora — many.

From Odawara

Instead of returning to Tokyo from Odawara, you can take one of the many

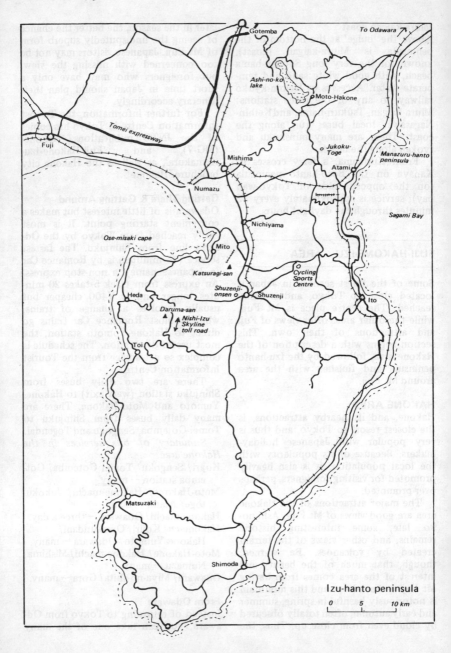

Izu-hanto peninsula

0   5   10 km

regular buses from Moto-Hakone and Hakone machi to Atami, Mishima, or Numazu, all gateways to the Izu peninsula, or one of the many buses from Kojiri-Sengoku to Gotemba, which is a gateway to Mt Fuji and the surrounding area. The former passes via the scenic Jukoku-toge ('Ten Countries Pass') area along a ridge that offers a superb view of Mt Fuji in good weather, while the latter also gives a superb view of Fuji as it clears the mountain range between Hakone and the area surrounding Mt Fuji.

ODAWARA TO GORA

Odawara's main attraction is a reconstruction (1960) of Odawara-jo castle; it preserves the outward appearance of the ancient castle but is not 'authentic' despite its realistic appearance.

Odawara has little else to offer but it is also the starting point for the Tozan railway which climbs a ridge to a point high above (but not overlooking) Ashi-no-ko Lake. The switch-back train takes you to Gora, and a cable car continues from there to Sounzan and then down to the lake. The journey can also be done by bus, direct from Hakone station to Sounzan. Going by bus avoids the frequent long wait for the cable car but traffic on the road can make it a slow trip, especially in weekends. One bus goes through Miyanoshita so it is possible to change there if you want to use both.

Hakone-Tozan Railway

This two-car train, resembling a municipal tram, is well-known among Japanese. It starts from platform 12 at Odawara station (accessible from tracks 7 and 8). The little-train-that-could struggles valiantly against the steep 8 in 100 grade, making stops at Hakone-Yumoto and Miyanoshita (among others) on its way to the terminus at Gora; there are three switch-backs along the way.

Miyanoshita

The only (low-key) attraction here is the Fujiya Hotel, a five-minute walk uphill from the station. It was the first western style building to be constructed in the Hakone district (1878), and has since added wings that are more modern, giving an interesting blend of American Colonial and Japanese architecture. The main building has the mustiness of age, and is now like a dowager who has known better days. It will appear largely to those of a nostalgic frame of mind who wish to see how expatriates once spent their summers — the library and its old books are still there, as is one billiard table; a number of modern electronic games look out of place.

You can have coffee in the first-floor lounge overlooking the pond and garden; prices are reasonable. In the lobby there is a display case with a large number of miniature figures playing 'native' instruments; the anomoly is that all the figures portray Indonesians! At basement level there are commercial exhibits of electronic and photographic equipment that have not been changed in 10 years.

There are several walking trails from Miyanoshita, such as that to Sengen-san.

Chokoku-no-mori

This is the stop and the Japanese name of Hakone Open-air Museum, where sculptures are arranged around a garden. Some people speak highly of it. Much of it is visible from the right side of the train as it passes. The garden and several other attractions are largely aimed at the day-tripper Japanese market enjoy such 'exotic' Western things.

Those getting off the train here can continue on foot to Gora, the terminus, or take a later train.

GORA TO ASHI-NO-KO LAKE

Gora, the upper terminus station of the Tozan line, is the base for a cable railway up to Sounzan.

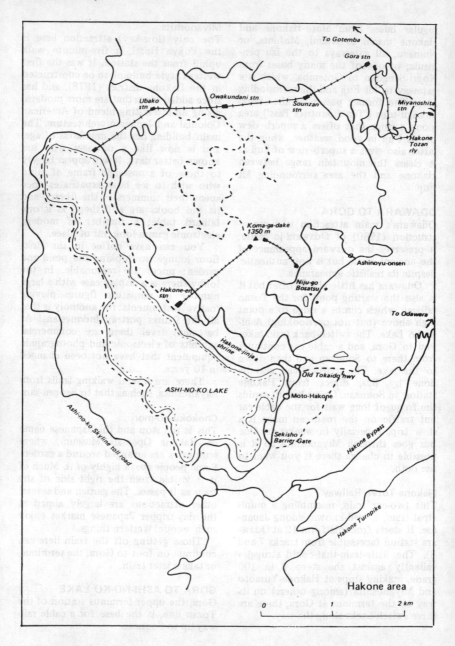

Hakone area

0   1   2 km

Sounzan

This is the base station for a four-km cable car system of many gondolas, each holding 10 passengers. The line rises to Owaku-dani station, passing over Souen-jigoku en route where steam jets noisily high into the air. It then continues almost level for a long span, finally descending to Togen-dai beside Ashi-no-ko lake.

You can buy a ticket only as far as Owaku-dani, and then decide whether to take the cable car the rest of the way down to Togen-dai on the shore of the lake, or to take a bus to Kojiri, not far from Togen-dai. (The extra cost of buying two separate tickets for the cable car is negligible.)

Owaku-dani

The name means Valley of the Greater Boiling. (There is also one of Less Boiling, the Kowaku-dani, but it is so much lesser than it is of negligible interest.) The 'Greater' is the crater of old Hakone-san volcano.

The road from Owaku-dani station leads upward; on one side is the bus stop (for the bus to Kojiri as well as in the opposite direction), and on the other is the entrance to a path that meanders among the traces of activity of the old volcano. Steam pours out of the ground in several places, and grey mud boils endlessly at another. The hot water is used at one place to hard-boil eggs which can be purchased; chemicals in the water turn the shells black. Each attraction is explained in English on an etched aluminum plaque.

Near the cable car station is the modern Natural Science Museum (Shizen Kogaku-kan) that explains the geology of the area, as well as the wildlife.

Continuing by cable car takes you on the longest cable car ride in Japan. It lasts several minutes, first crossing a rolling highland, then descends to the lakeshore at Togen-dai.

From here there is the choice of cruise boats (including one made to resemble a galleon) to Moto-Hakone and Hakone-machi via Hakone-en. An alternative is to walk the short distance to Kojiri and take a bus to Hakone-en, then a boat the rest of the way.

AROUND HAKONE-EN

The main attraction of Hakone-en is the recreation centre with its bowling alleys, swimming pools, golf, etc. It also has camping facilities. An 'International Village' has reproductions of houses of 29 nations, each containing arts and crafts of the country. The recreation centre will be of very limited interest to short-term visitors (other than for camping), but may be of greater interest to residents who want a day excursion; it is intended primarily for Japan visitors.

Hakone-en is the base station of a cable car to the top of Koma-ga-take mountain (1327 metres). If the weather is clear, the summit offers a superb view of Mt Fuji and Ashi-no-ko lake. From there you can circle back down to Moto-Hakone.

The ascent lasts eight minutes. After looking around, catch a bus going toward Hakone-Yumoto and take it as far as the T-junction with the main road at Ashi-no-yu town. Then walk or take another bus going to the right (toward Moto-Hakone) to the historic stone carvings of Buddha and Jizo.

Rock carvings   Visible on the left side of the road are several carved stone monuments; get off the bus as soon as they come into view. The religious significance of these pagodas is largely lost on non-Japanese. Behind them is part of the old road between Tokyo and Kyoto.

A very short distance along the road, a small lake (Shozin-ike) comes into view. On the right side, at the bend in the road, a path leads down a few metres to a large rock covered with 25 carvings of Buddha; this is named Niju-go Bosatsu. Some are very artistically executed and all are in remarkably fine condition considering their exposure to the elements from the time of the Kamakura era (1192-1333).

On the left, about 100 metres along the road (just past halfway along the lake) is a large and benevolent figure of Jizo, the Buddhist patron saint of travellers, children and pregnant women. The figure is about two metres tall and was carved primarily for the benefit of the farmer in this very difficult mountain terrain. There are several smaller and less interesting figures near by. Together they are known as Roku-do Jizo.

From here, take a bus at the stop on the side nearer Jizo-sama and ride it down to lake level; get off at Seki-sho bus stop at the entrance to Hakone-machi town (at the top of a downgrade) and walk along the short street running off the main road toward the lake. This leads to Seki-sho barrier gate.

Seki-sho Barrier Gate   During the Edo era under the rule of the Tokugawa military government (1600-1868), travel was tightly controlled to prevent the movement of arms and men. Local governors (daimyo) were compelled to spend part of each year in Edo (Tokyo), effectively as hostages, and there was frequent movement of parties of daimyo and their retainers along this road.

The main checkpoint on the Tokaido highway between Edo and Kyoto was Hakone Seki-sho, built in 1619; all travellers had to produce 'passports' at this point. The barrier stood until 1869. An exact reproduction was built in 1965 across the road from the original site, and wax figures dressed in period costumes show how things looked at that time.

A short distance up the road (or along the lake shore) is a small museum, **Hakone Shriyo-kan**, housing materials related to the gate. Most are unintellig-

ible to foreigners and of little interest, but there are some firearms, armour, etc. The same ticket gives admittance to both the museum and the barrier display.

Hakone Detached Palace Garden   This is next to the museum and has pleasant walks through a small forest, but it is special interest. During clear weather, this area offers a good view of the upper part of Mt Fuji complete with reflection in the lake.

Suginami-ki   Just a short distance beyond the garden is the entrance to a half-km section of the old Tokaido highway that runs parallel to the modern road. It is lined with majestic cryptomeria (cedar) trees planted in 1618 to provide shade for travellers. The trees make a very pleasant walk to Moto-Hakone town. From the shore at Moto-Hakone, near the bus station, you get the best view of Mt Fuji in the area.

Hakone-jinja shrine   A short walk from Moto-Hakone, and a longer distance (nearly two km) from Hakone-en and the Koma-ga-take cable car base station, lies Hakone-jinja. The present main building dates from 1667, though the shrine is believed to date from the eighth century. The buildings are not particularly noteworthy as shrines go, but the path is lined with venerable cedars, and the shrine is set among equally huge trees, dating from the 17th century. The atmosphere verges on mysterious.

There is a picturesque torii gate in the lake just off-shore. Be satisfied looking at it from a distance for it is made of practical but unromantic concrete.

The shrine festival takes place on 31 August when lanterns are set adrift on the lake as part of Obon ceremonies.

Old Tokaido Highway   A short distance up the hillside road from the lakeside bus terminal (by the large torii) in Moto-Hakone is the beginning of a stretch of the original Tokaido road. A pedestrian overpass leads up to it. Because of the hill, the road was paved with stones for a considerable distance to make walking easier and to prevent rain from destroying the path.

Most people will be content with a look and a photo at the beginning, but a walk of about 20 minutes takes you to a coffee shop and restaurant in a traditional style building which also houses a few Edo era exhibits. Buses return to Moto-Hakone, and also go to Odawara (opposite direction), but service is not frequent, about two an hour until mid-afternoon.

Accommodation

There are many hotels, ryokan and minshuku of all price ranges in the many hotspring resort towns and other centres in the area. The most famous is the *Fujiya* at Miyanoshita, the oldest hotel in the area (described earlier), while the most luxurious might be the *Prince* beside the lake. As for all accommodation in Japan, reservations may be made in advance through any travel agent in the country.

There is a Youth Hostel at Sounzan, very close to the base station of the cable car to Owaku-dani, tel (0460) 2-3827.

IZU-HANTO PENINSULA

The Izu-hanto peninsula is probably the most popular seaside recreation area for Tokyoites. There are some interesting historical sites and some nice scenery, but it is low key and the resorts are crowded during the summer season. It is better regarded as an excursion destination for Tokyo residents and of secondary interest to short-term visitors.

For additional information, the Tokyo Tourist Information Centre has a pamphlet 'Fuji-Hakone-Izu-Kamakura', and the information sheet 'The Izu Peninsula' (MG-2).

A suggested way to see Izu-hanto is to take a bus down the east side from Atami to Shimoda and back up the west side to Numazu and Mishima. Trains of the Izukyu line run as far as Shimoda, but about half the distance is in tunnels, while buses pass closer to the water and give better views.

Atami can be reached from Tokyo by JNR trains, either regular Tokaido-sen or Shinkansen (Kodama only); the latter is faster but more than double the fare. Both lines also pass through Odawara. There is also a frequent bus service from Hakone along a scenic route over the mountains.

Atami

This is a favourite of honeymooners (largely of the weekend type) and other hotspring lovers, but will be of limited interest to most Western visitors for there is little more than countless hotels stretching up the hillside. The Art Museum (Atami Bijutsu-kan) has a good collection of Japanese arts, such as wood-block prints, lacquerware, etc.

Ito

Like Atami, this is another town of resort hotels.

At the mouth of the Okawa river there is a monument to Will Adams, a British pilot who was shipwrecked off the coast in the 1600s. He served as the model for Anjin, the main character in the novel *Shogun*, and in reality did found a shipyard that built two ocean-going European-style vessels.

Between Ito and Shimoda there are many pleasant views, though none can be singled out for special attention; it's just an enjoyable trip.

Shimoda

At the south-east end of Izu-hanto peninsula, Shimoda is a major summer resort for Tokyo residents.

As well as the train and bus services

along the east coast, Shimoda can also be reached by bus down the middle of the peninsula from Mishima and Shuzenji to Toi and Matsuzaki.

Shimoda has an important place in Japanese history. It was here that Townsend Harris, the first American diplomat to Japan, took up residence in 1857 in accordance with provisions of a trade treaty signed in 1854 after the American 'Black Ships' under Admiral Perry forced the country to end centuries of self-imposed isolation from the rest of the world. There is a large model of one of the side-wheel ships at Shimoda station.

Ryosen-ji A treaty between the US and Japan was signed here on 25 May 1854, supplementary to one signed earlier at Yokohama. However, the temple is much better known for its interesting collection of erotic statuary (which a JNTO publication coyly describes as 'Buddhist images symbolizing ecstasy'). The phallic symbols (and female equivalents) range from life-size upward. Although the exhibits don't match the heroic proportions of items displayed at Tagata-jinja (near Nagoya) or Beppu (Kyushu), they do include some examples of erotic statuary from India and Tibet.

The 'story' of Okichi is portrayed in a series of pictures hung inside the temple. According to the Japanese version of the story, Okichi was compelled to act as mistress to consul Harris while he resided in Shimoda; Harris's side of the story is that he was offered a girl and haughtily refused. Who can say which version is true? (The Japanese have a long history of slanderously maligning foreigners so their version may be more suspect.) Elsewhere in Shimoda is Hofuku-ji temple, built for the repose of the soul of Okichi.

Ryosen-ji is a 10-15 minute walk from Shimoda station. A rather vague map of the town is available at the station.

Gyokusen-ji temple was the residence of Harris and the first foreign consulate in 1857; he resided here for about 1½ years. It is about two km from the station on the east side of Shimoda at Kakisaki village (accessible by bus from the station).

Of greatest curiosity value is a monument to the first cow slaughtered in Japan for food, erected by Tokyo butchers. There is also a plaque commemorating Jimmy Carter's visit in 1979. The temple is well marked in English by a roadside sign on the sea side of the road. Monuments and plaques on the site give all necessary information.

At the edge of the sea, opposite the road leading to the temple, is a tiny shrine set at the bottom of a picturesque wind-sculpted large rock. A similar rock face can be seen beside the road nearby.

Accommodation There are countless minshuku, ryokan and hotels around Shimoda, but the town is very crowded during the summer, and asking for a room at one after another can be a waste of time. There is an accommodation centre at the station and another across the road from it. Each will phone and arrange a room. (Similar assistance may be found at all resorts and at stations in most centres.)

Yumigahama Beach
This is probably the best beach in the Shimoda area, accessible from Shimoda by bus in 20 minutes. There are also other beach areas closer to town, on the way to Kakisaki.

Iro-Misaki Cape
The southernmost tip of the peninsula is noted for its high perpendicular cliffs. It is accessible from Shimoda by bus in 40 minutes, but a boat ride from Shimoda gives a better view. Boat info is available at the station.

West Coast

The west coast has fewer resort towns than the east coast and so offers more enjoyable travelling. The west coast also has of the peninsula's single most scenic place, Dogashima.

Dogashima

The geological structure of this area is sedimentary rock that is banded in clear layers. Erosion or physical separation has resulted in large numbers of huge rocks jutting out of the sea. It is scenic from the shore, but can be seen much better from a cruise boat out of Dogashima.

Most of the coast north from Dogashima offers attractive views of the sea. Buses run north as far as Heda, then turn east inland toward Shuzenji, so anyone wishing to continue around the coast to Mito would have to hitch across the gap between Heda and Ose.

North-west Corner

The north-west corner of the Izu peninsula offers excellent views of Mt Fuji over Suruga-wan bay in clear weather (generally late autumn and the winter). Suggested places are:
— the top of Katsuragi-san, easily reached by cable car from Izu-Nagaoka town (accessible from Mishima via Nagaoka station);
— the beach at Mitohama (near Mito);
— along the coast between Mitohama and Ose-Misaki cape;
— the top of Daruma-yama, accessible by Nishi-Izu Skyline toll road, or by hiking from Shuzenji-onsen via Heda-toge pass, one of the best hiking trails on the peninsula.

An unusual sight along the coast between Mito and Ose is the old Swedish luxury passenger ship *Stella Polaris*, permanently berthed and serving as a floating hotel.

There is a boat service several times a day between Numazu and Matsu-zaki, stopping at Heda and Toi.

Mito

Of interest here is a natural aquarium formed by nets stretched between rocks. Dolphins and great turtles may be seen.

North Central Area

Shuzenji-Onsen

This town takes its name from Shuzen-ji temple which was founded in the ninth century. It is a typical hotspring resort town with many hotels/ryokan using the hot water.

Unusual is a hot spring, Tokkonoyu, that bubbles forth at the edge of the small river that passes through the town. A roofed, slatted-wall bath house has been built around a small pool of comfortably warm water. For those not too shy disrobe and hop in, there is no charge. (People in the pool can see out quite well, but those outside are not able to see in well enough to get much of an eyeful. Something unusual for the adventurous.)

There is a Youth Hostel on the hill behind the town.

Shuzenji-onsen is reached by bus from Shuzenji station, the terminus of Izu-Hakone Tetsu-do railway from Mishima. Shuzenji is the transfer point for bus travel through the middle of the peninsula from Mishima to Shimoda. There is also service to Ito and other points on the peninsula from Shuzenji; further information is available in Jikokuhyo or from tourist information sources.

Cycle Sports Centre

Less than half an hour from Shuzenji by bus is one of two cycle centres in Japan. There are several courses and tracks of various types and lengths, and hundreds of bikes for rent. It is well suited to people who want to try a variety of bikes before purchasing, and also offers a weekend recreation centre. It has reasonable cost accommodation.

Nirayama

Near this town is the oldest

private house in Japan, Egawake, approximately 700 years old. It was the residence of the hereditary administrators of the Izu area, so is large and has a nice garden, canopied by a number of tall old trees.

Access is by bus from Nirayama station of the Izu-Hakone railway line between Mishima and Shuzenji.

WEST & SOUTH OF IZU/FUJI

West and south from the Izu-hanto/ Fuji area the road and train lines run very close to the coast; the inland area is inhospitable mountains with very few settlements. Other than a couple of attractions around Shizuoka and Shimizu there is little of interest to anyone except students of Japanese industrialization. Unless you want to go directly to Kyoto, there is little incentive to take this route, for Route 1 is incredibly busy and very slow to travel on with numberless stoplights and continuous conurbations. Only trains and vehicles on the Tomei expressway move quickly.

To see some of the 'real' Japan with rural areas, mountain scenery, relatively unspoiled areas, and some historic remains, including one of the nation's finest castles, it is better to consider travelling through the Hakone and Fuji areas to Matsumoto (via Kofu).

Mishima The Izu-Hakone railway, to Shuzenji, begins here. There are also several daily buses to places in the Mt Fuji area.

Okitsu This was the 17th stage on the old Tokaido highway from Edo (Tokyo) to Kyoto. There is still an inn (honjin) that was designed to accommodate daimyo (feudal lords) during their periodic travels between Kyoto and Tokyo. The old inn is still functioning as a ryokan.

Seiken-ji temple has a very nice landscape garden; it is about 1 km west of the station.

Fuji The name of this city sounds inviting, but the place isn't. The only attractions are paper mills and other industries. On a clear day there is a good view of Mt Fuji from trains and motor vehicles passing the city.

Shizuoka/Shimizu Area

On the south side of Kunozan hill near the coast and between Shimizu and Shizuoka (accessible from both cities by bus) is **Tosho-gu shrine**. Ieyasu Tokugawa was interred here before being finally laid to rest at the magnificent and famous Tosho-gu shrine at Nikko. The shrine, accessible after a climb of more than 1100 steps, is elaborately decorated.

Nihondaira This is a plateau atop Udo hill, one valley away from Kunozan hill. You can get to the top by a cable car that begins near Toshogu. Also, buses run across it via Nihondaira Parkway (Japanese name) between Shizuoka and Shimizu stations. From the top there is an excellent view of Mt Fuji in one direction, and the bay and Miho-no-matsubara in another.

Rinzai-ji A couple of km to the north of Shimizu station is the temple, known best for its beautiful garden. Nearby is Sengen-jinja shrine. Its festival is 1-5 April.

Toro In the general area of Rinzai-ji is this site of an ancient settlement of 17-18 centuries ago, discovered in 1943. Excavations showed it covered an area exceeding 16 hectares; the Archaeological Museum on the site shows relics dug up.

Oikawa Valley has one of only two steam-powered train lines left in Japan, the Oigawa hon-sen private railway line. (The other steam line, the JNR Yamaguchi-sen in the far west of Honshu reverted to special steam runs after being completely dieselized.) Every day there is one run in each direction between Kanaya and Senzu. The train leaves Kanaya at 11.34 am (arriving 12.53), Senzu at 2.35 pm (arriving 3.53 pm). The steamer is quite ancient — more than half a century old by appearance.

The trip through the river valley (Oi River) from Kanaya is pretty, and at Senzu you can continue on a different line where the cars are pulled by a miniature diesel loco. This one really twists and turns, passing over deep chasms and climbing ever higher. Its terminus, Ikawa, is a popular starting place for climbing in the South Japan Alps.

There is a small Youth Hostel a short distance from Kanaya.

There is little of interest west of this area until Nagoya (described in a later chapter).

MT FUJI AREA

Every visitor to Japan wants to see Mt Fuji, or Fuji-san as the Japanese call it (*never* Fuji-yama!). It is the symbol of Japan recognized universally and is truly one of the world's most beautiful mountains and a spectacular sight no matter how many times you see it.

Visitors should be forewarned, however, that Fuji-san is very bashful in spring, summer and early autumn, and is usually totally obscured by cloud cover, even from close up.

There are several places that offer superb views of the mountain (some of which have already been described): from the Shinkansen as it passes near Fuji city; from the Tomei expressway; from Nihondaira, near Shizuoka; from several places in the north-west corner of the Izu-hanto peninsula; from several places in the Hakone area; from Nanao-

toge pass, between Hakone and Gotemba.

There are also clear views from many points along the roads that nearly encircle the mountain, chiefly between Yamanaka-ko and Sai-ko. West of Saiko the view is not as good because of a 'shoulder' at the base of the cone which diminishes the symmetry seen from other directions.

Getting There & Getting Around
The two main gateways to the Mt Fuji area are Gotemba and Fuji-Yoshida (and nearby Kawaguchi-ko).

Gotemba is conveniently reached from Tokyo by the Odakyu line from Shinjuku station; expresses (four a day each way) take less than two hours. Somewhat slower is JNR service, by Tokaido line to Kozu, changing to the Gotemba line; there are many trains every day.

There are four express trains of the Odakyu line from Shinjuku that run past the terminus of most Odakyu trains and go directly to JNR Gotemba station. These take 94-110 minutes. Other Odakyu services are by regular express to Shin-Matsuda (about 80 minutes), then transfer to JNR services to Matsuda (a further 45 minutes).

There are also expresses operated by JNR, four from Tokyo (taking about two hours) and one from Shinagawa (about 10 minutes less). There is also a regular Tokaido line service from Tokyo via Yokohama to Kozu (90 minutes) and transfer to the Gotemba line to Gotemba (75 minutes).

Buses run several times a day from Shinjuku station (west exit) along the Tomei Expressway to the Hakone area, stopping at Tomei-Gotemba bus stop, about one km from JNR Gotemba station, on their way to Sengoku and Togendai. There is a good view of Mt Fuji for much of the latter part of the distance to Gotemba (in clear weather).

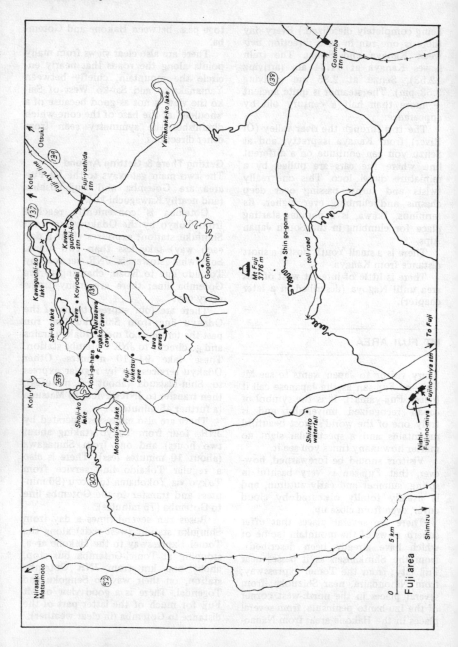

For Fuji-Yoshida and Kawaguchi-ko, there is a private line from Otsuki; a JNR service goes from Shinjuku to Otsuki. There is also a bus from Hamam-atsucho and Shinjuku stations to Kawaguchi-ko, Yamanaka-ko and Motsuji-ko.

There are about 20 buses a day covering the route between Mishima, Gotemba, Fuji-Yoshida and Kawaguch-iko, at 20-50 minute intervals. From Gotemba, the road climbs for several km to the tableland surrounding much of Mt Fuji, and the mountain comes into clear view near Yamanaka-ko lake.

There are many buses through the day (approximately every 30 minutes) from Gotemba station to Shin Go-gome (New Fifth Station), one of the two major starting points for climbing the mountain, and the one best served by buses. The last one leaves about 9.30 pm.

Summary of main bus services in the Mt Fuji area:

Fuji-Yoshida/Kawaguchiko/Sai-ko — 10 a day

Fuji-Yoshida/Kawaguchiko/Koyodai/ Motoso-ko — 11 a day

Motoso-ko/Shiraito waterfall/Funino-miya — nine a day (some continue to Fuji station)

Kawaguchiko/Go-gome — few

Gotemba/Shin-Go-gome — many

Mishima/Shin-Go-gome — some

Fujinomiya/Shin-Go-gome — summer only

Shinjuku/Tomei-Gotemba/Sengoku/ Togendai — several

Shinjuku/Kawaguchiko/Yamanaka-ko — many. Some buses start from Hama-matsucho station; some finish at Shoji-ko/Motoso-ko

Shinjuku/Shin-Go-gome — few

After visiting the Mt Fuji area, there are several possible destinations for further travel. For the Izu-hanto penin-sula there is a bus from Shin Go-gome to Mishima, or a train or bus to Numazu

from Gotemba station; to Hakone (Kojiri), there is a bus from Gotemba station; to Kofu and Matsumoto, a bus from Kawaguchi-ko station.

AROUND MT FUJI

There are several routes you can take. There is no single optimum. Buses circle Mt Fuji in both directions. The main places on the circuit are Fuji-Yoshida, Fuji Go-ko (the Fuji five lakes), Fujino-miya, the 7th station of Mt Fuji, and Gotemba. This route is described below.

Fuji-Yoshida This city, not far from Kawaguchi-ko town, has no attraction other than its annual festival 31 August, but it is a transport centre. Buses leave here for Kofu (via Kawaguchiko) and there is a train to Otsuki. Buses from Kawaguchiko pass through here on their way to Gotemba and Mishima.

From Fuji-Yoshida there is bus service to Go-gome, the older Fifth Station and once the only main starting point for climbing Mt Fuji. There are only a few scheduled buses. The sched-ules change with the season, so it is advisable to check with the TIC or *Jiko-kuhyo* for the latest information. This side is a popular starting point for people with their own vehicles, so it should be possible to hitch a ride in from Fuji-Yoshida.

Kawaguchi-ko lake This is the second largest of the five lakes, and is a popular resort with Tokyo residents. There is a superb view of Mt Fuji and the lake from atop nearby Tenjo-san mountain; it is accessible by a cable car that begins quite close to Kawaguchiko station.

Also of interest is the museum, Fuji Hakubutsu-kan, in front of Fuji Lake Hotel. It has exhibitions related to the people, geology, etc, of the area and is noted for the Amano collection of erotic items from bygone days. (This is a good opportunity to see some aspects of the large role of fertility symbols, etc, in the lives of the Japanese not so long ago. The very earthy element in much of Japanese society is not so apparent nowadays as it once was.) The museum is 10 minutes walk from Kawaguchiko station.

The next attractions lie along the road west from Kawaguchiko. Buses run only about once an hour so it might be worth trying to hitch. Taxis are also available. (Kawaguchiko is on the bus route between Fuji-Yoshida and Kofu.)

Yamanashi-ken Visitors' Centre This is the Japanese name for a museum of material relating to the natural history of Mt Fuji. It is about 15 minutes on foot from the station.

Fujikyu-Highland amusement park This is mostly of interest to residents rather than visitors (except visitors with children). It is most easily reached from Fujikyu-Highland station of the Fuji-Kyuko railway line. It is no coincidence that 'kyu' appears in the names of the railway and the park; the latter is an attraction that draws users to the railway.

Sai-ko lake This is a picturesque lake, less developed than Kawaguchi-ko and Yamanaka-ko; it still preserves much of the wilderness look. There is an excellent view of Mt Fuji from the west end.

A vantage point near the lake is Koyodai (Maple Hill), along one of the roads from the main highway.

Saiko Youth Hostel is close to here and offers pleasant surroundings with a good view. It is about two km off the main road so you may have to walk or hitch to it. (The only time I went there, it was closed, taking an unannounced 'holiday' not listed in the Hostel Handbook, a habit all too common around the country.)

Shoji Panorama This is the Japanese name for a scenic lookout on Eboshi-

san mountain that takes in a superb view of Mt Fuji over the Aoki-ga-hara Jukai ('Sea of Trees'). It is a climb of about an hour from the road. Inquire locally about bus services; none is listed in *Jikokuhyo*.

Aoki-ga-hara The 'Sea of Trees' is an area of wild forest. The Shoji trail to Mt Fuji passes through it, but general exploration is not encouraged because it is easy to get lost, and minerals prevent a compass from functioning. It is well known among Japanese as a place where people intentionally get lost and die.

Narusawa Ice Cave & Fugaku Wind Cave The former (Narusawa Huoketsu) is not made of ice, nor is the latter (Fugaku Fuketsu) made of wind. Both are lava tubes (or caves), formed when lava from a prehistoric eruption of Mt Fuji cooled on the surface and still-molten material flowed out below the surface, leaving the still rough and jagged inner surfaces. Both are cold, even in mid-summer, so a sweater is welcome. There are no stalagmites of stalactites; they are features only of limestone caves.

The entrances to both are quite close to the main road (Route 139), and each has a bus stop; the caves are about 20 minutes apart on foot.

There are several other such caves in the area, including Fuji Fuketsu cave on the Shoji trail which has a floor of solid ice.

Shoji-ko lake The smallest of the five lakes and regarded as one of the prettiest. If you have the time you could climb to the summit of Mt Eboshi for a look from Shoji Panorama. The climb takes about 90 minutes.

Motosu-ko lake This is the westernmost and the deepest of the five lakes that stretch around the north side of the mountain. It is of little interest to short term visitors. Buses run between here and Fuji-Yoshida once an hour.

Shiraito This is a very pretty and unusual waterfall. The drop is not great, only a few metres, but the falls make a semicircle of considerable length. The name translates as 'White Threads', which the countless rivulets resemble. It is accessible by bus from Motosu-ko lake. (Nearby is another waterfall, Otodome-no-taki.)

Fuji-no-miya The city is of no interest, except that it is one starting point if you want to walk the entire distance to Mt Fuji. The usual procedure is to take a bus from the station to Go-gome (fifth station) and climb from there, but these buses run only from mid-July to mid-August. Several buses a day go from the station to Motosu-ko lake.

Gotemba The city is of negligible interest for itself, but it is one of the two major gateways (with Fuji-Yoshida) to the Mt Fuji area. It has the best public transport to the mountain for climbing.

CLIMBING MT FUJI

The most common way to climb Mt Fuji is to go by bus or car to Go-gome ('Fifth station') on the north side of the mountain or Shin-Go-gome ('New Fifth Station') on the south side. From these starting points, the climb is little more than five km and takes somewhat over five hours.

To Go-gome, there are a few buses daily from Kawaguchi-ko. Sing-Go-gome is served very much more frequently from Gotemba, and from Mishima and Fujinomiya (in the season only). There are also several daily buses direct from Hamamatsucho and Shinjuku stations in Tokyo.

Formerly people climbed during the day, but now increasing numbers of people begin climbing well after dark and continue through the night, watching the sunrise from the top or flank of

the mountain. There are huts at various places along the upper reaches of the major trails, but they are crowded and do not have a reputation for cleanliness. By starting around midnight or a bit earlier, you may avoid the need to stop for a sleep.

Although the experience of watching the sunrise from the summit is often spoken of, the fact is that in early morning the top is often enshrouded in mist and visibility is not good until later in the morning. One guide who has made the climb many times (from the north side) recommends watching the sunrise from the eighth station (Hachigome).

The descent can be made more quickly on the north side than the south because a large patch of the mountain side is covered with volcanic sand, and you can slide down it very quickly. This is called *sunabashiri* ('sliding on sand').

Anyone in reasonably good health can make the climb, and there is no danger of getting lost because there is a continual stream of climbers. The official 'season' is July and August; during this period there are few risks from the weather. Earlier and later there can be sudden changes, storms or blizzards, and several climbers perish each year while climbing at other times with inadequate clothing. Mt Fuji is 3776 metres (12,388 feet), so it becomes very cold at the top.

In olden times, before buses went to points high up the sides, it was customary to walk the distance from the railway stations, and then climb to the top. Several trails still exist, but nowadays these would be better regarded as hiking paths for a day's outing (without climbing). The best known such trails are the Yoshida trail from Fuji-Yoshida station, the Kawaguchi trail from the town of that name (it joins the Yoshida trail at the sixth station), the Shoji trail from the Shoji-ko lake area (which passes Fuji-fuketsu cave along the way), and Gotemba trail from Gotemba. There is also a circular trail around the mountain about half-way up.

The following description of climbing Mt Fuji is reprinted with kind permission of Jean Pearce who writes a regular column in the *Japan Times*. (Her columns have been collected in two books, *How to Get Things Done in Japan*, volumes 1 and 2; she has also written *Footloose in Tokyo*.)

I know what I should have been doing a year ago. I should have been jogging every morning, doing deep knee bends and running up the subway steps in preparation for what everyone should do once but never twice — climb Mount Fuji. But I know now how to answer this question: What should I take along on the climb?

You don't need much of anything, but you must be a stoic if that is your choice. We climbed in the heat of late July but it was freezing after the sun went down. You can have a year's variety of weather — it rains, the sun beats down, you'll be groping in the mists. Be sure to have a cover-all plastic raincoat. After the storm, you can put it between the layers of your clothing when you get cold to seal in your body warmth, if you have any. And beware of the sun. Have a hat to shade your face and wear long sleeves. Even on a hazy day. Fujisan's sun can inflict a painful burn.

You can buy lemons, hard-boiled eggs, soft drinks, beer and sake, and such standard foods as soba and oden. Prices are high but remember, you didn't have to carry them. Take along foods that don't spoil easily such as cheese, cucumbers, nuts, chocolate and sliced meat, and a bottle of water. Put a wet oshibori (small towel) in a plastic bag. You won't find running water. Toilet facilities are adequate, but don't expect them to be clean, or to flush.

Take gloves. Climbing Fuji is not a stroll; you'll be pulling yourself along with a chain over some rocky areas. You'll want them if you come down by way of the lava slide in case you fall. Cinders can leave scars with the persistence of a tattoo. Have a backpack so your hands will be free, and outer clothing with plenty of pockets for immediate necessities like tissue and money. For your feet, sturdy hiking boots and two or three pairs of wool sox.

Accommodations are cozy, your own futon on your own tatami mat in friendly proximity with a hundred or so other hikers. If you don't have reservations at the top, stop early to be sure of space, and don't necessarily believe the resthouse keeper who tells you there is room at the next station. He does not know. Some like to sleep a few hours along the way and finish the climb the next morning before dawn. Since dawn usually arrives about 4.30 am, it seems easier to me to do it all in one piece.

Be prepared for an early morning at the summit as well. Someone will likely be pulling off your covers at, say, 3 am (that's morning?) and if you don't get up then, attendants will be back for your futon some 10 minutes later. The room must be readied for breakfast service for the morning climbers who are just arriving.

There are 10 stations, but don't be lulled by that statistic as you look up and count. You can't see the top from the bottom, and there are a number of resthouses between each official station that can delude the unwary.

Climbing the mountain on the same day I did — I climbed with a group from the Press Club and recommend that you find companions — were four blind men, two boys with their bicycles (later I saw them riding around the summit), a one-legged man, an 88-year-old lady and a gentleman of 93. Not everyone gets to the top, but it is worth all the exertion you can extend to make it.

I don't believe there is a mirror on all of Fujisan, except perhaps a sacred one in the shrine at the top. But it doesn't matter. You won't care after a while. At one stop I saw a woman powdering her nose. It looked pretty silly.

The best season to climb Mt Fuji? There isn't one. Climb it early in the official season (it begins on 1 July and ends on 31 August) and it's bitterly cold; later you'll likely have rain, perhaps a typhoon and pathways lined with discards of earlier climbers, though it wasn't the huge garbage heap that I expected, thanks in part to the tractors that, unseen, ply the back slopes carrying up supplies and returning at least some of the empty bottles. You will still marvel at the old men who jog up the mountains with three cases of beer and a dozen litre-bottles of sake on their backs for their resthouse concession; their sons, if they stay on the mountain, hire the tractor.

Oh yes, on the way back, it took us 4½

hours by bus from the fifth station to the highway at the foot of the mountain, normally a 20-minute drive. Sturdy climbers make the summit in less. When you climb Mt Fuji be prepared for anything. Ganbatte!

NORTH OF MT FUJI
From the Mt Fuji area there are many further destinations. Those to the east, south and south-west have been described earlier. It is easy to continue north-west through Kofu to Matsumoto and the many other interesting destinations described later in the Central Honshu chapter.

Kofu can be reached from Fuji-Yoshida and Kawaguchiko by bus (many times through the day) or by train with a transfer at Otsuki.

SAITAMA-KEN

This section covers the Chichibu-tama National Park, Kawagoe and Sakitama kofun-koen. Other attractions of Saitama-ken are included in descriptions of the Nagano-ken and Tochigi-ken (Nikko) areas in later chapters.

Chichibu-Tama National Park
The park is divided into two sections, Chichibu and Okutama, in parallel valleys. Both offer pleasant nature walks, and are especially popular with Tokyo residents, for each can make a day trip out of the city. A hiking trail extends between the two sections of the park.

Okutama
This section is easily reached by JNR Ome line which begins at Tachikawa (on the Chuo line).

Ome The attraction here is the JNR Railway Museum (Ome Tetsu-do koen). Around the main building are several steam locos formerly in service with JNR. The museum has moving displays of model trains. Meals are available in an elegant old dining car. The museum is in Hikawa-koen to the north of the city, a 15-minute walk from Ome station.

Hinatawada The general appearance of the town is scenic, with a low mountain looming over it. The town is famed for plum blossoms which bloom and attract many visitors in late February and early March. An interesting festival is held at this time. The best known groves are Yoshino Bai-en, less than one km from the station.

A walking trail extends beyond the Yoshino area via several low mountains (Sampo, Hinode, and Mitake). The trail passes close to Mitake-jinja shrine (described later).

Mitake Mitake keikoku (gorge) is visible from the train before you reach Mitake station; it can also be seen on foot from the path along either side of the river. The best way to see it is to get off the train at Sawai station (one before Mitake) and walk to Mitake.

Mitake-san mountain (930 metres) is well forested with tall cedars and other trees. A cable car runs close to the top; the base station can be reached by bus or on foot. The cable car gives easy access to Mitake-jinja shrine; this intersects the Yoshino — Hatonosu trail.

The main building of Mitake-jinja is about a century old, but the shrine has a history of about 1200 years. The shrine festival, Hinode-matsuri, takes place on 8 May and has a procession of mikoshi and people dressed in samurai armour.

Hatonosu The gorge here, Hatonosu-keikoku, can be seen from the train or on foot.

Okutama Terminus of the railway, it is the point of departure by bus for Nip-

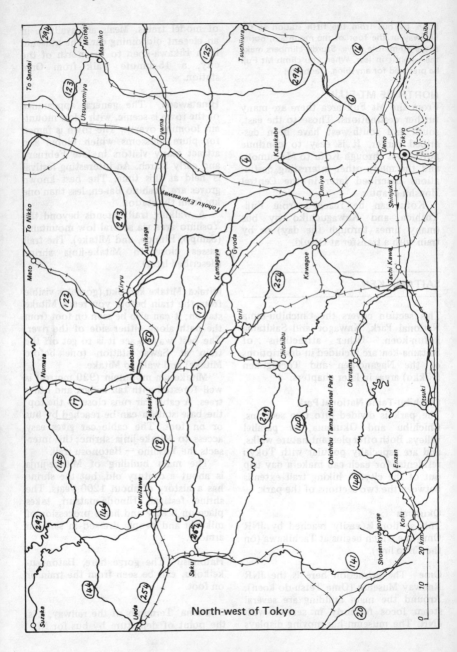

North-west of Tokyo

para cave and Oktama-ko lake.

Nippara shoyudo is the largest cave in the Kanto area; it is lit for about 280 metres to allow exploration. The area is pretty in late October when the leaves change. It change. It is about 40 minutes from Okutama by bus.

The south shore of Okutama-ku lake, created when the Tama river was dammed to provide water for Tokyo, still has natural terrain on the south side; the north shore has typical Japanese tourist facilities and about 6000 cherry trees that are usually at their best around mid-April. The lake can be reached in 20 minutes by bus from Okutama station.

Further information on the area may be found in the JNTO publication 'Okutama' (MG-5), available at the Tokyo Tourist Information Centre.

Chichibu

The Chichibu part of the park offers pleasant scenery and hiking trails. It is particularly popular with Tokyo residents for it can easily be reached from the city as a day trip.

There are two approaches into the park area: Chichibu-tetsudo railway and the Seibu railway. The former passes along the river valley and is intersected by the Seibu line near Ohanabatake station. The Chichibu line can be reached by changing at Yorii from the Tobu line (from Ikebukuro station, Tokyo), or at Kumagaya from the JNR Takasaki line (from Ueno station, Tokyo).

By Seibu line from Shinjuku station (Tokyo) the trip takes 1½ hours limited express, longer by local train. By JNR it takes about two hours, and slightly less by the Tobu line.

The Chichibu line route (described below) takes in more, and is the only way to reach Mitsumine-guchi, the innermost station.

Nagatoro area Several attractions are accessible from stations near Nagatoro.

Near Nogami station is Nagatoro Sogo hakubutsukan, a small museum of rocks and fossils. A similar museum is Chichibu Shizen kagaku-kan (Natural History Museum), five minutes from Kami-Nagatoro station.

Nagatoro is noted for the nearby scenery, including sheer rock faces and interestingly-shaped rocks, including a 'rock garden', a famous rock formation near the river. It is about five minutes from Nagatoro station. The area is beautiful in spring when blossoms deck a line of cherry trees, stretching 1½ km from Nagatoro to Kami-Nagatoro; likewise in summer when azaleas bloom, and in autumn when the coloured leaves appear.

An excellent view of the area may be had from Hodo-san. A cable car goes to the top; its base station is easily reached by bus from Nagatoro station. Hodo-jinja shrine is close to the upper station.

Kami-Nagatoro A boat ride through rapids of the Arakawa river is available from either end of the Oyabana-bashi bridge, taking 25-30 minutes. The terminus is Takasago-bashi bridge.

Chichibu area The main attraction of the city is Chichibu-jinja, 200 metres west of the station, one of the three most famous shrines of the area (along with Hodo-jinja at Nagatoro, and Mitsumine-jinja). It is noted for large buildings and its tall, old trees. Its night festival of 3 December is well-known through Japan for the procession of lantern-lit floats.

The Municipal Folk Museum (Chichibu Shiyaku-sho Minzoku hakubutsukan) has good displays of articles traditionally used by people of the area in their daily life. It can be reached quickly by taxi or on foot in 40 minutes.

There are two pleasant hiking trails, a relatively short one near Buko-san, and another that joins the Chichibu and Okutama areas.

The starting point of the shorter trail is Yokoze station of the Seibu line. It climbs to the top of Buko-san (1336 metres), passes the entrance to Hashidate stalactite cavern, then descends to Urayama-guchi station (Seibu line). In addition to picturesque 'normal' mountain scenery, the area around the cavern has a Karst-type topography with large outcroppings of limestone that resemble sheep or tombstones when seen from a distance. (Similar terrain may be seen in west Honshu and north Kyushu, and are described in the appropriate sections of this book.) The cavern may be explored.

The hiking trail to Okutama, called Oku-Chichibu Ginza, stretches between the two sections of the park. From the Chichibu end it begins at Mitsumine-guchi station (terminus of the Chichibu line). You climb to Mitsumine-san on foot or ride the cable car. Mitsumine-jinja can be visited along the way; it has a history of about 2000 years. When Buddhism and Shinto were intertwined, it was the centre for aescetic yamabushi pilgrims and priests of the Tendai sect of Buddhism; some may be seen today, and halls on the grounds serve priests and pilgrims as well as climbers and hikers.

The trail is about 10 km long, and passes along the ridges that stretch between mountains. The trail splits between Shira-iwa-san and Kumotori-san, one fork going to Nippara, the other toward Okutama-ko lake. The trail is well signposted, and there are several lodges and huts along the way.

Points along the route are listed in detail in the JNTO publication 'Chichibu' (MG-4), available at the Tokyo Tourist Information Centre. Many areas like this that offer good hiking are covered by detailed maps that may be purchased at map specialists in large cities. They are often only in Japanese, but the general features can be readily understood.

KAWAGOE

Of the cities and towns in Japan, Kawagoe possibly has the largest number of old buildings still in use. The main street has many shops in heavy-walled, tile-roofed structures more than a century old. For a glimpse of 'old Japan', a visit can be recommended.

In addition to walking around the town looking at the charming old buildings, Kita-in temple is worth a visit to see its attractive main building and garden, visible from an open elevated corridor. Nearby is the garden of Gohyaku rakan, 500 statues of Buddhist characters (about 40 cm tall) in a variety of poses. They are a little unusual and of moderate interest.

From Tokyo, the most convenient access is by the Seibu line from Shinjuku, for its terminus (Hon-Kawagoe) is closest to the centre of the city. Alternatives are the Tobu railway (Tojo line) from Ikebukuro (Tokyo) to Kawagoe station, or by JNR from Ueno station (Tokyo) to Omiya, with a change of train to the Kawagoe line, to Kawagoe or Kawagoe-machi stations.

SAKITAMA KOFUN-KOEN

The Kanto plain has been settled for more than 2000 years, as shown by excavations of ancient relics throughout the region. One of the three largest clusters of ancient tomb mounds in Japan is to be found near Gyoda, consisting of eight burial mounds plus a museum of artefacts dug up in the area.

Sakitama kofun-koen (Sakitama Tomb Park) is reached by taking a JNR train (Takasaki-sen line) from Ueno station to Fukiage station, then changing to a bus bound for Gyoda (via Sama). The stop is Sangyo-doro; from there, the park is a 15-minute walk.

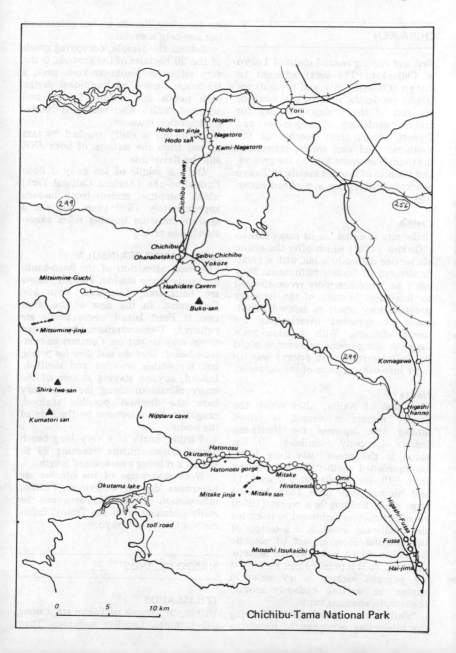

Chichibu-Tama National Park

CHIBA-KEN

East and curving around south of Tokyo is Chiba-ken. The areas adjacent to Tokyo (Chiba-shi city and beyond) are largely residential suburbs and much of the rest of the peninsula is used for market gardening of vegetables and flowers. Apart from beaches of the south-east and east coasts, attractions for tourists are quite thin on the ground, and the area of interest mainly to Tokyo residents looking for a weekend excursion.

CHIBA

Chiba city is noted for its many toruko ('Turkish baths') which offer the ultimate service of brothels but with a greater element of fantasy fulfillment. They can't be wholeheartedly recommended to foreigners because of the language problem may result in refused admittance or apparent overcharging for special favours. With suitable male Japanese companions, however, it might be an interesting (but pricey) way to delve into other aspects of the Japanese.

Narita

The city of Narita, after which the nearby airport is named, is famed among the Japanese for Narita-san temple (properly Shinsho-ji). It has stood at the present site since 1705, but succeeded another elsewhere dating from 940. Its pagoda dates from 1711 and Niomon gate from 1838, but the large main building is a recent (1968) concete structure fashioned to resemble the traditional wood. It is a temple of the unusual Shingon sect of esoteric Buddhism which is known for aescetic practices, so it is possible that you could see pilgrims bathing in icy water in winter, or walking endlessly around the temple, chanting sutras.

Visitors have a good chance of seeing the interesting ceremony of blessing a car for safety. Results are not guaranteed but any help is useful.

Behind the temple, occupying much of the 20 hectares of the grounds, is the very attractive Narita-san-koen park, a landscape harden of traditional design with ponds and artfully formed and arranged 'hills'. Also nearby is Narita-san historical museum.

Narita-san is easily reached by taxi or bus from the stations of both JNR and the Keisei line.

Only a couple of km away is Boso Fudoki-no-oka (Ancient Cultural Park) which comprises ancient tomb mounds approximately 1500 years old, and a modern museum housing relics excavated in the area.

BOSO-HANTO PENINSULA

The main attraction of the Boso-hanto peninsula is the seaside. Popular resorts are Shirahama, Tateyama, Hoto and Katsuyama. In the area of the latter two is Pearl Island where pearls are cultured. Demonstrations by women divers may be put on. Contrary to common belief, they do not dive for pearls, but for edible seaweed and shellfish. Indeed, anyone staying at one of the many minshuku along the coast may have the freshest possible seafood, caught in the afternoon by the lady of the house.

Farther north is a very long beach named Kujukurihama (meaning 99 Ri Beach, a ri being a measure of length).

Note that some of the beaches are hazardous due to undertows. Further information about this area can be easily obtained from the Tourist Information Centre in Tokyo.

NANPO ISLANDS

IZU ISLANDS

Within the bounds of Tokyo are, among other things, two live volcanoes. They

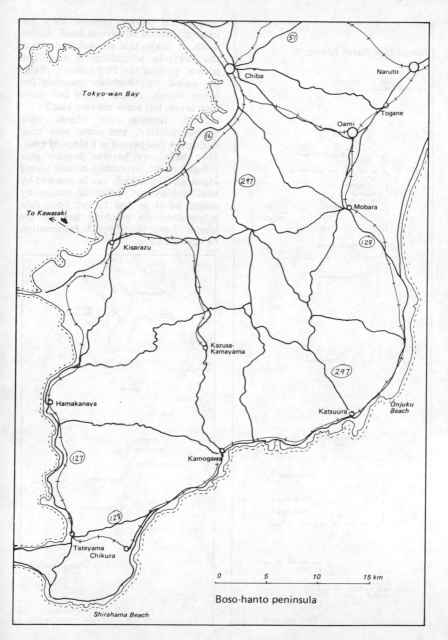

Boso-hanto peninsula

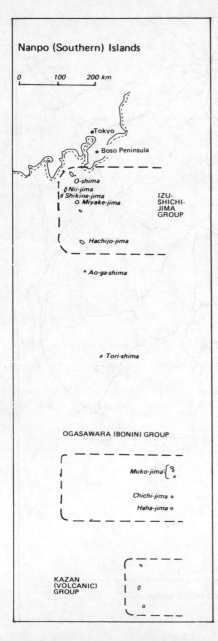

Nanpo (Southern) Islands

present no danger because they are located on two of several small islands south of Tokyo that are included within the Tokyo-to administrative area. The islands, part of the Fuji volcanic chain, are called Izu Shichi-to, meaning Izu Seven Islands. (There are in fact more than seven, but some are very small.)

Until recently the islands were relative isolated, and some were used during the Edo period as a place of exile. They have now become popular as a holiday resort, especially among young Japanese. The islands can be reached by boat and by air. Schedules change by season so it is best to get up-to-date information on reaching any of the islands from the Tourist Information Centre in Tokyo.

Izu Seven Islands

Oshima

This is the largest of the islands (91 sq km); the name means 'Big Island'. Its high point (literally and figuratively) is Mihara-yama (758 metres) which last erupted in 1957 and is still smoking.

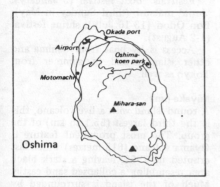

Activities on the island include swimming at several beaches, going to the top of the volcano (on foot or by bus from Okada or Motomachi), and visiting the 'Hawaiian' Botanical Garden of tropical and subtropical plants which grow in the mild climate.

The town of Saki-ichi and nearby area are known for old houses and customs which differ from those on the mainland. There is a distinct dialect on Oshima (and the other islands). The dark costume with a white pattern is unlike a kimono; an 'apron' substitutes for the obi (sash), and the headdress indicates if a woman is single or married.

Bus service makes travel simple. There are two tour buses each day at 7 and 9 am from both Okada and Motomachi.

For accommodation there are about 120 minshuku, 70 ryokan, two youth hostels, and five campsites. Advance reservations are suggested.

Because it is close to Tokyo, and easily accessible by boat from Tokyo, Atami, Ito and Inatori (near Shimoda)

and perhaps Shimoda in season, and by air from Tokyo, it is crowded during the summer.

Toshima

This tiny island (4.2 sq km) is the smallest of the group. It is round and of volcanic origin, but the fires have gone out. There is almost no flat land on the entire island, 60% of which is given over to growing camellias from which fragrent oil is extracted. They bloom in late February and early March. There is one concentration of population in the north, a few hundred people who make their living from the camellia oil business. Accommodation is limited, four minshuku and one ryokan. Access is by boat from Oshima.

Nii-jima

This island (23.4 sq km) is rather enlongated with a volcanic peak at each end and long beaches on each side. Swimming is excellent at several places. Maehama (on the west) offers the best swimming and white sand, but it is very crowded in season; there is a campsite to the north. In the area is a museum, hotspring, temple and a cemetery from the days of the exiles. Habushi-ura beach has very high cliffs (up to 250 metres); but it is better for surfing than swimming. Another beach is Awai-ura.

The main town, Honmura, is reached by boat from Oshima and Tokyo.

The houses on the south of the island are interesting because they are constructed of lightweight volcanic rock that is mined in the area; they are known for their unusual architecture. Objects carved of the rock are on sale, as is locally-distilled shochu.

Accommodation is plentiful with about 235 minshuku and seven ryokan, but reservations are recommended in the summer because this island (along with Shikine-jima and Kozu-shima) has become very popular in recent years as a boy-girl meeting place.

Shikine-jima

Despite its diminutive size (3.8 sq km), this island offers more than its share of interesting attractions. The scenery along the rugged shore is pleasant, with 10-30 metre cliffs encircling the island; inland it is mostly flat. Most of the population is found in fishing communities to the north-east, like Nobushi and Kohama.

Shikine-jima and Nii-jima were once the same land mass, but tidal waves in 1688 and 1704 separated them.

There are several beaches around the island, with a variety of surfaces, from rock to sand. There are two beaches where hotspring water gushes out to form a natural (and free) onsen. The water of both is too hot to enter directly, but at Ashizaki one may bathe at the seashore where the 60°C water mixes with the sea. At Jinata the sea mixes with the hot water only at high tide and cools the 80°C water enough to be enjoyable. Play it by ear as to whether a swimsuit is needed.

This was one of the penal/exile colonies, and some traces of those days remain.

Bicycles can be rented at shops, but the island is small enough to walk around easily.

On the island are about 100 minshuku and five ryokan, so there is plenty of accommodation, but reservations are suggested in the summer because it is a popular place with young people.

Shikine-jima can be reached by boat from Nii-jima.

A festival is held around 24 January for the return of souls of sailors lost at sea. In mid-June there is a sea festival.

Kozu-shima

This gourd-shaped island (18.5 sq km) has a dead volcano in the centre. Most of the population lives on the west side; fishing, farming and catering to tourists are the main activities. The island is noted as a good place for fishing from the rocks; swimming is good at Takowan, a white sand beach. Climbing the central peak is a popular activity.

Bus transport is good in summer, and bicycles can be rented.

There are about 200 minshuku and five ryokan.

Festivals: boat festival (5 January); 'Juria' matsuri (third Sunday in May); Bon Odori (13-16 July); shrine festival (1-2 August).

Access is by boat from Oshima and other islands, and in summer from Tokyo as well.

Miyake-jima

A round island with a live volcano, this is the third largest (55.1 sq km) of the group. The most prominent feature is Oyama volcano (815 metres) which last erupted in 1962, leaving a stark black area resembling a collapsed sand castle. Much of the island is surrounded by cliffs 20-30 metres high. Activities include swimming and inland hikes through the forests.

The main beach is Miike-hama; it is unusual for its black sand. It is the centre of seaweed harvesting, and there is camping nearby, but it tends to be crowded and littered in season. Less crowded is Okubo-hama. Swimming is good, and there is a campground nearby.

There are two small lakes, an unusual feature on such an island. Shin-Myo-ike dates only from 1763 following an eruption. It is less than one sq km in area

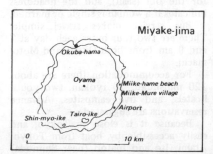

(the Japanese name means 'pond'), and it is largely surrounded by cliffs 70-80 metres high. The water is salty, and mysteriously takes on seven different colours through the day. One can climb to the rim and look down onto the water. The other lake, Tairo-ike, is only a smidgen bigger (1.2 sq km) but much older, 2000 years or so. It contains fresh water and is used as a water supply reservoir, so swimming, camping, etc are banned. Although the island has a nearly-tropical climate, the lake has many qualities of a mountain lake, an interesting contrast on such a small island.

Festivals: boat festival (2 January); shrine festival (8 January); ajiisai (a type of blue flower) festival (mid-June).

Accommodation is plentiful, as on the other islands: 130 minshuku, 12 ryokan, and a youth hostel.

Access is by boat from Oshima or Hachijo-jima, or by air from Tokyo.

Mikura-jima

Although this smallish (20 sq km) circular island is only 20 km from Miyakejima (an hour by boat) there is only infrequent service, six or seven times a month. It is rugged, with cliffs 100-300 metres high around the periphery, and has a dead volcanic peak in the middle. There is not a single stretch of level road on the island and there is no public transport. All the population lives on the north side. There is a 100-metre waterfall on the west side.

There are 12 ryokan, adequate for the few who can wait out the period between boats; camping is not allowed.

Hachijo-jima

The most southerly of the Izu group, this is the second largest (71 sq km). It is characterized by two volcanic peaks, Higashi-yama (Mihara-sen) in south-east and Nishi-yama in the north-west, and cliffs along most of the rugged coast. It has a mild and wet climate year-round

Hachijo-jima was the outermost of the islands used for exile, and some relics may be seen, such as ruins of mansions. Tourism is a relative newcomer to the island, and some old customs may still be found. A local type of cloth, ki-hachijo, is still woven and coloured with vegetable dyes from local sources. It is one of the souvenirs of the island. (Others are sake, and shell and coral products.)

The scenery can be seen by rented bicycle or bus tour beginning at Hachijo shi-yaku-sho (city hall) daily at 9.30 am. Another attraction is Jiyugaoka-yuen park, where bullfights are held twice daily. Like those on Shikoku, Okinawa, some other islands of Japan, and as far away as Indonesia, the fights are not against man, but between two bulls, a test of strength; the winner pushes the other out of the ring.

The exiles festival is held on 28 August.

There are nearly 100 minshuku and 22 hotels or ryokan on the island.

There are boats from Tokyo, and also air flights from Tokyo and Nagoya.

Getting There

Summary of boat services:

To Oshima (Motomachi or Okada) from Tokyo/Yokohama, Atami, Ito, and Inatori.

Oshima(Motomachi) — Toshima — Nii-jima.

Shimoda — Nii-jima.

Nii-jima — Shikine-jima — Kozu-shima.

Oshima (Okada) — Miyake-jima — Hachijo-jima.

Summary of air services:

Tokyo to: Oshima, Miyake-jima, and Hachijo-jima.

Nagoya — Hachijo-jima.

OGASAWARA ISLANDS

South of the Izu Islands is another group, the Ogasawara Islands. These too are part of Tokyo-to administrative district and extend as far south as Okinawa.

The islands can be recommended for getting away from it all; access is only by ship from Tokyo (generally twice a week), and they are beyond TV and regular radio range. The climate is semi-tropical, slightly cooler than Okinawa. Small palm trees grow, and there are frequent showers. Whereas the Izu islands offer a good weekend excursion for swimming and meeting the opposite sex, the Ogasawara Islands are better for quiet exploration and adventure.

The main islands are named after family members such as Chichi-jima (father), Haha-jima (mother), and Ani-jima (elder brother). The first two are the main islands; Ani is a small island just above Chichi-jima. Muko-jima is a cluster of small islands to the north. To the south are the Kazan (Volcano) islands, which include Io-jima (better known as Iwo-jima), famed as a battle site in WW II and memorialized in the photo of Marines raising the US flag atop 185-metre Suribachi-san (a posed shot, by the way). Tourists are not permitted on Io-jima because large areas still have live ordnance from the fighting, and the remains of many Japanese soldiers lie entombed in the caves where they died. Only Chichi and Haha are regularly populated.

Chichi-jima

This, the largest island, offers peaks up to 600 metres but it also has beaches and good swimming. It is small enough to walk across in two hours, or around in a day; roads are good and there is a bus service. Bougainvillea and hibiscus give a tropical air.

There are three beaches, one of which is sandy, another of which has some coral. Skin-diving can be recommended at many places around the island, especially between Chichi-jima and Ani-jima because of the many fantastically coloured tropical fish; they are not afraid of people and come close. There are also turtles and rays. Scuba and less complex diving equipment is available for hire. You can also rent a boat and circle the island, stopping to dive where desired. It is reminiscent of the Barrier Reef of Australia. From shore, throwing bread on the water results in 'instant fish'. The water is a darker blue than that of the Okinawa area, and is not as clear.

On the west side, the rusting hull of a small ship is a relic of the war. There are also caves around the shore that were used for defence purposes; some are now used by fishermen for storage, and others are blocked by gates.

There are minshuku on the island, but they tend to be crowded, and generally do not serve meals, so you have to eat at restaurants or buy food at a local store. The few shops close by 6.30 pm, and the hottest nightspot, a coffee shop, is closed by 10 pm.

Because the island was under US control for a long time, many people can communicate in English, and there are several US-style buildings, a curiosity to the Japanese.

Access is from Tokyo to Futami-ura. There are one or two sailings a week in each direction (depending on season); the trip takes a little over a day. Further information is available at the Tourist Information Centre, Tokyo.

Northern Honshu

North of Tokyo are some of Japan's best attractions. A few are man-made relics, but most are natural scenic beauties or curiosities. Perhaps most interesting, especially for the traveller with some time to spare and an interest in the 'real Japan', is the legacy of folkways. The northern part of Honshu, called Tohoku ('north-east'), was late in being developed, and in this respect it still lags far behind other parts of the country. This is to the disadvantage of the people who live there (although the area produces a large percentage of Japan's rice), but to the distinct advantage of foreign visitors who want to see at least some aspects of Japan as it used to be. (There are, of course, modern amenities, so there is no hardship involved when travelling in the area.) I would rank the Tohoku area with the Noto-hanto (Ishikawa-ken), Gifu-ken and Nagano-ken areas as the best in Japan for independent exploration. More folklore, dances and tradition survive concentrated in these areas than in most other parts of the country.

This chapter describes a route northward along the east coast and through some of the centre, and a southbound route along the west coast and other parts of the centre. This covers the maximum of territory with a minimum of backtracking and also allows description prefecture by prefecture, since their boundaries follow the same geographical features used for laying out this itinerary. You can also go to Hokkaido and then resume the route without missing anything.

IBARAKI-KEN

Tokyo is on the edge of the Kanto plain, one of the largest areas of flat terrain in Japan, which is why it was one of the most prized fiefs in feudal times. The plain is intensively populated in all directions outside Tokyo. One of the few attractions of the Kanto area is at the city of Mito.

MITO

The main drawcard of this city is Kairakuen, a garden traditionally rated by the Japanese as one of the three finest in Japan. I have visited it on two occasions, and had the same reaction both times — a feeling of acute disappointment. The garden is, for the most part, little more than open lawn, with clusters of trees or bushes. It seems ironic that two of the most celebrated gardens in Japan (the other is Korakuen in Okayama) are noteworthy primarily for their vast expanses of lawn; perhaps it is this novelty that reaps such a rating. There are many other gardens in the country that would be better examples of what foreign visitors are looking for in Japanese gardens.

The Kairakuen garden was completed in 1843. Of interest within its grounds is Kobuntei, a building (reproduction) where Nariaki — one of the lords of Mito, formerly the home of an important branch of the Tokugawa family — used to meet learned men, relax, and compose poetry. The building is well made of fine materials, and is a good example of the simplicity and refined restraint of Japanese architecture. It is surrounded

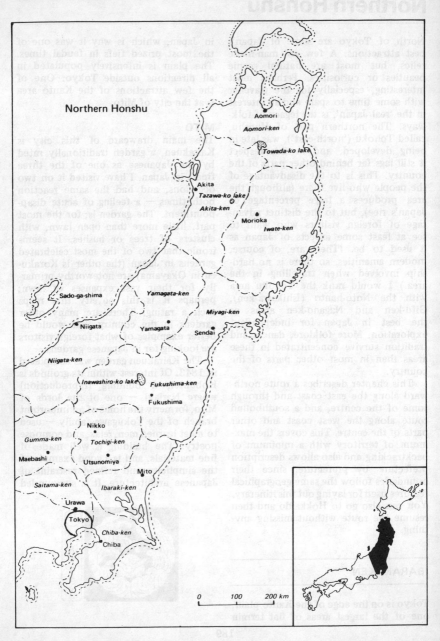

Northern Honshu

Aomori
Aomori-ken

Towada-ko lake

Akita
Tazawa-ko lake
Akita-ken

Morioka
Iwate-ken

Sado-ga-shima

Yamagata-ken

Miyagi-ken

Niigata
Yamagata
Sendai

Niigata-ken

Inawashiro-ko lake
Fukushima-ken

Fukushima

Nikko

Gumma-ken
Tochigi-ken

Maebashi
Utsunomiya

Saitama-ken
Mito

Urawa
Ibaraki-ken

Tokyo

Chiba-ken
Chiba

0   100   200 km

by tall trees, and the atmosphere is very peaceful. Even the shrilling of semi (cicadas) in the summer only adds a note of ruralness, in contrast with the commercial appearance of the surrounding city.

TOCHIGI-KEN

The main attractions of Tochigi-ken are the pottery town of Mashiko, ancient Buddha statues at Oya, the incomparably beautiful and ornate Toshogu shrine at Nikko, mountain scenery, and the start of the valley with possibly the most thatched-roof houses in Japan.

MASHIKO

Of the several historic pottery centres of Japan, the most accessible from Tokyo is Mashiko, a couple of hours to the north-east. A visit to Mashiko can conveniently be combined with a trip to Nikko, as they are in the same general area.

The pottery of Mashiko is made entirely from local materials — from clays to glazes. They do not lend themselves to elaborate techniques, so the results are rather simple and seem to me (who professes neither deep knowledge nor interest in pottery) almost a trifle crude. However, to potteryophiles this equals native charm, and the sometimes rough surfaces, simple designs and frequent asymmetry are all to be treasured. The properties of the clay could be improved with additives, but the potters prefer to use only natural materials. If you like pottery, you will enjoy a visit to Mashiko. It is also interesting for those who would like to learn something about traditional Japanese methods of making and firing pottery, for there are large numbers of 'climbing kilns' and a visit to one is easy to arrange.

The town of Mashiko owes its fame to Shoji Hamada, who found here a town of potters who had been turning out serviceable but simple and repetitive designs since 1852. He settled in the town, absorbed their traditions and then built on them, establishing his own kiln in 1930. As his fame spread, it reflected back to the town which had nurtured him. Adding to Hamada's and Mashiko's fame was the English potter, Bernard Leach, who lived and studied here for several years before returning to his homeland to spread the Mashiko influence.

Getting There

Mashiko can be reached from Tokyo by JNR, going to Oyama from Ueno station, transferring to the Mito-sen line to Shimodate (fifth station), and then changing again to the Moka line. Mashiko is the seventh station. It is also accessible by road.

Sightseeing

The town is filled with shops selling the local wares, so it could take a week to explore it thoroughly. A good starting place, then, is the Hamada 'home', which houses a small museum and other attractions.

The Hamada Home

This is made up of thatched-roof houses moved from elsewhere in the area plus two stone gura (storehouses) of the type found throughout the region. The gura house the Mashiko San-kokan (Reference Collection Museum), a collection, in effect, of odds and ends that Hamada collected during his travels outside Japan. There are few treasures, and little of his own work. I found the place more interesting for the old farmhouses that Hamada had brought to this place in 1943. The largest one was built in 1850, and houses furniture and other things brought back from abroad. Although visitors cannot enter the house, you can look in through the doors and windows and admire the massive pillars and crossbeams of the

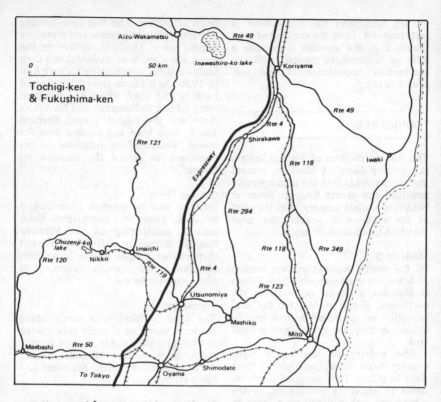

Tochigi-ken
& Fukushima-ken

building itself, which is a fine example of a traditional house of this area. Houses of this type use no nails in their construction, so they can be dismantled and moved easily. The roof is unusual because bamboo poles are used at the peak to anchor it in place (again typical of the region). There are other buildings of the same type elsewhere in the grounds, one lived in by Hamada's widow.

Shimaoka Pottery

Adjacent to the Hamada grounds is the Shimaoka pottery, also well worth visiting. While many of the kilns used here are small oil- or gas-fired units, the famous kilns of Mashiko are the traditional nobori-gama wood-fired climbing

kilns, two of which are in the grounds of the Shimaoka pottery. There are always some foreign students working in the village, and they are often willing to give a guided tour or direct you to other kilns. The kilns have several chambers arranged up a hillside. Firing begins at in the lowest chamber, with the gases climbing and preheating the other chambers. When the first chamber is thoroughly fired, fuel is then added to the second chamber and the first allowed to burn out. This sequence is repeated until all chambers have been fired. Be-

A *View of Mt Fuji*
B *Rice harvesting, Noto peninsula*
C *Daibutsu (the great Buddha) at Kamakura, near Tokyo*

cause of the size of the kilns and the fuel consumption, many of the large kilns are fired only three or four times a year. It is an awesome sight as the flames and sparks shoot high over the stacks at the top of the hill.

There are many of these kilns scattered around the hillsides and they can be found easily enough, but the distances become appreciable. A look at the Shimaoka kilns will probably be adequate. If you are able to arrange a visit, try to look at the carpentry of the new Shimaoka building as well, for it is a fine example of the best of traditional Japanese woodworking skill. A crossbeam of untrimmed tree trunk is supported on two poles, each of which has its end shaped to match the shape of the crossbeam, and vertical supports for shelves are keystoned into notches so that they support without nails. The new house took more than a year to build, all the work being done by one family of carpenters.

As for finding pottery to buy, there is no problem whatever. There must be few towns in the world with so many shops selling the stuff — some by recognized potters (at high prices), and much at very reasonable prices, turned out by the large number of anonymous workers who make the bulk of the output. Everything, however, is hand-made. Those interested in weaving should look for the Higeta Workshop.

OYA

At Oya, near the city of Utsonomiya, there are ten Buddha images carved in relief in the rock wall of a protective overhang. The temple building of Oya-ji extends back into the shallow cavern, protecting the images. It is believed that

A Nihon Matsuri festival, Tokyo
B Dragon dance at Asakusa temple, very much of Chinese origin
C Typical summer festival, in Tokyo — carrying a mikoshi (portable shrine)

they date from the early Heian period (794-897 AD) and are the oldest stone statues of Buddha in Japan. Near the temple is an unmissable (27 metres) concrete statue of Kannon (goddess of mercy), finished in 1954.

Visible in the surrounding countryside are the quarries and nibbled-away hills that are the source of soft stone (tuff) used in structures such as the granaries (gura) throughout the region and beyond Nikko. Many small workshops can be seen where the stone is cut into building blocks.

Getting There
The easiest way to reach Oya is by bus from Utsunomiya station; the trip takes about 25 minutes.

NIKKO
Nikko is one of the 'must-sees' of Japan, to be included in even the shortest visit. Adjacent to the town are some of the most beautiful buildings in the world, ornately coloured, and covered with gold leaf. The surrounding area is also famed for natural scenery — waterfalls, a lake resort, forests and volcanic mountain peaks.

Getting There
From Tokyo there are two train lines, JNR and Tobu. The latter is the more convenient, for there are many more trains each day, they are quicker, and the fare is lower. Tobu trains leave from Tobu station in Matsuya department store in Asakusa, not far from Asakusa station of the Ginza subway line. There are more than 35 trains per day, ranging from the 2½-hour kaisoku (rapid) at Y900, to the 1¾-hour tokkyu (special express) at Y1700.

Further Information
The trip to Nikko is so popular that the Tokyo TIC has prepared free notes that give much useful and up-to-date information on trains, accommodation

and sightseeing. Be sure to get them before leaving Tokyo.

Accommodation

As befits one of the most popular tourist destinations in Japan, there is no shortage of accommodation in Nikko. It is wise to book ahead through a travel agent (eg JTB or the minshuku association) to be sure of a room. Much available accommodation is of the high-quality, high-cost type. There are, however, two youth hostels. Nikko Youth Hostel does not enjoy a good reputation among those who have stayed there in recent years: the staff have been petty and officious, enforcing rules as if they were the ten commandments and having everyone out of bed at 6.30 am whether or not they planned to eat the hostel breakfast. (Grudgingly, it must be admitted that an early start does mean you can get several hours sightseeing in before the rains begin.) Nikko Daiyagawa Youth Hostel, not far from Shinkyo bridge, is reputed to be much nicer (though it has only half as many beds).

Sightseeing

The term 'sensory overload' was invented just for Nikko, particularly the Toshogu and Taiyuin shrines, as well as for lesser shrines in the area. Superlatives become exhausted before the sightseeing does: you should allow a full day to absorb it all. The best way, if time permits, is to spend a night in Nikko, thus giving yourself two part-days. Keep in mind that during the summer it frequently rains extremely heavily for an hour or two from about midday, so try to get an early start.

Rinno-ji temple

At the top of the hilly main street stands the Sacred Bridge (Shin-kyo), an orange structure blocked to traffic. Follow the road around to the left of the hill, to the footpath up the hill. This leads to one corner of the compound of Rinno-ji temple. The major point of interest of this temple is Sambutsudo (Temple of the Three Buddhas), the largest temple in the Nikko mountains. It houses three gilded wooden statues (five metres tall) of Kannon (a Buddhist saint with 11 faces and 1000 arms), Amida-Nyorai, and the Bato-Kannon (believed to be the incarnation of animal spirits).

The large avenue at the left side of Rinno-ji is named Omote-sando ('main approach'), and it leads to Toshogu shrine, the most important single attraction at Nikko. To the left of the path is a five-storey pagoda, 32 metres tall, built in 1818. At the entrance to the shrine is a tall granite torii gate.

There is a basic fee of Y230 for admittance to Toshogu shrine, Rinno-ji temple and Futaara-san shrine.

Toshogu shrine

Entry to this shrine is through Otemon, also called Nio-mon gate, with its statues of the guardian Deva kings (Nio-sama). The decorations are but a hint of what is to come. From the gate, the path bends to the left. The decorated buildings encountered on the right are the lower, middle and upper storehouses. On the upper storehouse are noted relief carvings of elephants, carved by a sculptor who had never seen an elephant, only drawings. To the left of the path, opposite the middle storehouse, is the sacred stable, the only unlacquered building in the compound. Overhead are various carvings of monkeys: second from the left is a famous panel featuring the three monkeys in the 'see, speak, hear no evil' poses. Carvings of monkeys were reputed to fend off diseases in horses. Visitors can feed the sacred horse (which obviously relishes the tidbits) by purchasing a small dish of carrot slices.

Facing the upper storehouse, and to the left of the bronze torii, is the Kyozo (Sutra Library), which houses nearly

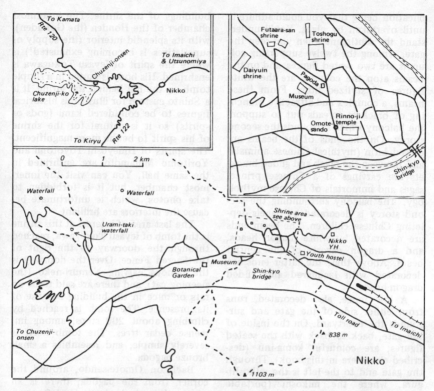

7000 volumes of Buddhist sutras (sacred writings). Beside it is the sacred fountain where Japanese visitors rinse out their mouths to purify themselves before proceeding farther. The water is safe to drink.

Yakushido temple The next flight of stairs leads to the middle court. The similar buildings on each side are the belfry and the drum tower. Beyond the drum tower is Yakushido, the only Buddhist-style structure in the shrine. Yakushido is famous for its Crying Dragon (Naki-ryu), a ceiling painting in an inner chamber. Admittance to this inner shrine requires a separate ticket, which may be paid for when first entering Toshogu. Visitors stand on a

marked spot, clap their hands together, and the echo sounds like the reverberating roar of the dragon. The painting is quite recent, for the roof was destroyed in a fire in 1961, along with a very famous painting by Yasunobu Kano (1607-85).

Gate of Sunlight (Yomeimon) Returning to the courtyard and climbing the next set of steps, one comes to the most beautiful gate in Japan and one of the most elaborately decorated structures on earth. Yomeimon (Gate of Sunlight) contains a wealth of intricate carvings, gilt and lacquer work, the details of which would be worthy of display in isolation. The Japanese nickname is Higurashi-mon (Twilight Gate), the implication being that you could admire it until overtaken by night. You'll understand the sentiment when you seen the gate. Among the twelve supporting columns are two seated figures, and on the beams atop the columns are the white figures of stylized lions. From these beams, a complex and attractive branching of brackets spreads out to support the balcony which surrounds the second storey. On the ends of the beams are carved kirin (mythical Chinese animals) and between the black and gilded brackets are carvings of a Chinese prince, sages and immortals of Chinese mythology. The balcony surrounding the second storey is decorated by panels depicting Chinese children. The beam ends are decorated by white dragon heads, and a dragon cavorts of the central beam. Above that, the rafter ends are decorated with lacquered and gilded dragon heads.

A low fence, also decorated, runs from either side of the gate and surrounds the courtyard. On the inside of the gate, back to back with the seated figures, are colourful koma-inu (described elsewhere in this book). Through the gate and to the left is the mikoshigura, where the mikoshi (portable shrines) are stored. These shrines are carried in the two annual festivals (17-18 May, and 17 October). Kaguraden, in the courtyard, is the stage used for performances of Kagura (sacred shrine dances).

The closed gate facing the courtyard is Karamon (Chinese gate). White predominates, in contrast with the fantastically brilliant colours and gold leaf of the other buildings and structures. The door panels are decorated with carvings of various flowers and bamboo, and the pillars with dragons. The figures around the support beams depict Chinese celebrities.

Karamon gate and the Sacred Fence (Tamagaki) surround the Haiden (oratory) and Honden (main hall), the central buildings of the shrine. The innermost chamber of the Honden (the Gokuden), with its splendid interior (the supply of superlatives is becoming exhausted!) is where the spirit of Ieyasu Tokugawa is enshrined. His body is buried in a simple tomb on the hill behind the shrine. It is a Shinto custom for illustrious historical figures to be considered kami (gods or spirits) so it is natural for the shrine of his spirit to be the more magnificent. The spirits of Hideyoshi Toyotomi and Yoritomo Minamoto are enshrined in the same hall. You can visit the innermost chamber, but it is forbidden to take photos, which is unfortunate because the interiors are brilliant.

The last area of interest at this shrine is the tomb of Ieyasu Tokugawa, reached through the doorway to the right of the Sacred Fence. Over the doorway is the famous carving Nemuri-neko (the sleeping cat), and there are said to be no rats or mice in the building because of its presence. The tomb is reached by climbing about 200 steps, among immense cedar trees. The tomb itself is severely simple, and resembles a small bronze pagoda.

Back on Omote-sando, around the corner from the pagoda, there is an avenue through the trees. On left, close to the pagoda, is the shrine museum, which houses a good collection of armour and other relics, and has exhibits showing how the buildings are constructed, how the wooden beams are protected by multiple layers of lacquered cloth, and so on.

Futaara-san shrine Further along the path, away from Omote-sando, is Futaara-san shrine. It is of lesser interest, and is best left to see at the end (if you have any energy or interest left).

Daiyuin-byo
This is the shrine to Iemitsu (1604-51), who constructed Toshogu in honour of his father, Ieyasu. It is somewhat

smaller than Toshogu, but almost up to its standards in beauty. (I think that the Haiden and the Honden are even more beautiful than the equivalent buildings of Toshogu.) In addition, it is possible to stand back some distance to take in their beauty and gain some perspective, as well as to photograph them, whereas the buildings of Toshogu are closely surrounded by a wall and photography is prohibited.

Approaching Daiyuin-byo, you first walk through Nio-mon (Deva king gate) with its guardian statues. You then pass a small garden, and can see the sacred fountain ahead and to the right. Turning left, you climb the stairs to Niten-mon (Two Heavens Gate), named for the two Buddhist deities Komokuten and Jikok-uten. On the other side of the gate are the Gods of Wind and of Thunder; the former is holding shut the opening of the bag of winds.

After climbing more stairs, you pass through Yashamon (named for its four figures of Yasha, a Buddhist deity), and arrive at the middle court with its belfry and drum tower. Between the middle court and the inner shrine is a Chinese gate, beautifully decorated and flanked by the sacred fence. Time and weather — it snows profusely in Nikko — take their toll of the decorations, and they must be continually repaired or repainted. The intricate carvings of birds were re-touched in 1978, so should stay colour-ful for several years.

Inside the inner shrine is the oratory (Haiden), from which a passageway leads to the inner main hall (Honden), both interiors being richly decorated with carvings and gold leaf. To the right of, and behind, the main buildings is a walkway that leads to the tomb itself, a simple structure by comparison.

Nikko Museum and Botanical Garden

Beside Hanaishi bus stop (en route from Nikko station to Chuzenji), is Nikko Botanical Garden. A short distance back toward town is Tamozawa villa, a for-mer imperial residence, which is now a museum. Set in a quiet garden, the buil-ding is constructed of the finest mater-ials, and is a good example of good Japanese architecture, although it is much larger than most wooden buildings in Japan.

Festivals

Nikko is noted for several annual fes-tivals. On 17 October and 18 May, there is a great procession of hundreds of people dressed in samurai armour and other costumes of the Tokugawa era. Mikoshi (portable shrines) carry the enshrined spirits of Ieyasu, Hideyoshi and Yoritomo. This is a big even and always crowded, but worth seeing for both the glimpse of pageantry and the feel of bygone days that it gives. On 17 May, the Ennen-no-mai (Longevity Dance) is also held, in front of Sambut-sudo, with two priests in elaborate costume performing ancient dances.

On 5-6 August there are very popular folk dances (Waruku-Odori) during the O-bon season which honours the souls of ancestors. Similar dances are held in communities throughout Japan at this time, but the Nikko dance is particularly famous.

Other days with festivals are 17 May (at Sambutsudo), and 14 and 17 April (Futaara-san jinja shrine).

NIKKO TO CHUZENJI

A few km beyond Nikko, the road twists upwards to Chuzenji-ko lake, a popular summer resort. On the way, the bus stops at Akechi-daira, a lookout and the base station for a cable car that leads up to Tempodai (three minutes). This is a higher lookout with a much better view (in clear weather), taking in Kegon-no-taki waterfall. The source of the water is Chuzenji-ko lake, which can be clearly seen, backdropped by the conical peak of Nantai-san (2844 metres). From Tempodai there is a trail

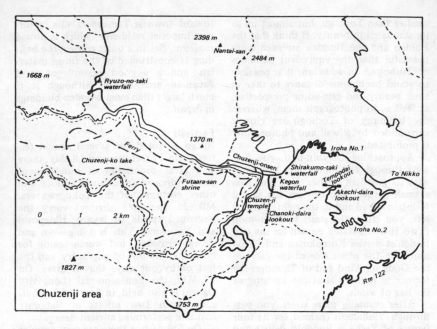

Chuzenji area

(for those who wish to take the cable car only one way) that leads to a ridge surrounding the lake (possibly the rim of an old volcano). A 30-minute walk leads to Chanoki-daira, the top station for a cable car which leads down to a point close to Kegon falls. (A handout map/brochure of the area is available from the Nikko Youth Hostel.) On the many walks in this area you will find enough points of interest to last for several days.

Chuzenji-onsen

This is an extremely popular and very crowded town, especially in summer (when the weather is pleasantly cool) and in autumn (when the leaves are beautiful). Although the time for the bus trip up from the station is nominally 50 minutes, this can be doubled or tripled on busy weekends and holidays The lake can be toured by regular excursion boat from various points: either

by circling the lake (50 minutes, Y450) or crossing it from the town to Shobugahama (20 minutes, Y240). South from the town, on the shore of the lake, is Chuzen-ji temple, which is worth a visit. The principal attraction is a 1000-year-old tall wooden statue of Kannonbosatsu. The carving, made from a single tree, has far fewer than 1000 arms, and the 11 faces are worked into a crown on a single benevolent visage. The present temple dates only from 1902, when it was moved from a point west of Chugushi shrine when the buildings were washed away. A booklet in good English explains other details of the temple.

Chugushi-jinja shrine This is the middle-shrine of the three that make up Futaara-san (the first is at Toshogu). A museum here has a reasonably good collection of armour and swords, as well as portable shrines. The collection is similar to those of many Japanese museum. A trail begins in the shrine grounds and leads to the peak of Nantai-san, a four-hour climb.

Kegon-no-taki waterfall Kegon waterfall drops 100 metres from an escarpment into a wide basin below. The falls are not visible from the surrounding cliffs, so the best view is from Tembodai (as described earlier). A lift takes you to the foot of the falls, where the full power of the plummeting torrent can best be appreciated.

Shirakumo-taki ('white cloud') falls This waterfall, one of many in the area, is located a short distance from Kegon falls. The best vantage point is Kasasagi-bashi bridge, which crosses the ravine near the mid-point of the plunge.

IMAICHI

Travellers going to Nikko from the Utsunomiya or Tokyo direction by train might wish to consider getting off at Imaichi first, and then taking a bus to Nikko (13 km away) instead of going all the way by train. The reason is that the road is lined for much of the distance with thousands of tall, straight cedar trees. They were planted by a feudal lord over a period of years. He lacked the money to contribute a sumptuous structure when the shrine was being built. About 13,000 trees still stand, and although the narrow avenue is crowded with traffic during the summer season (especially on weekends), it still retains its stately dignity. Check with the TIC in Tokyo about schedules and bus connections to ensure that there won't be a long wait in Imaichi. Remember that noon rain!

Thatched-roof houses

Route 121 runs north from Imaichi to Aizu-Wakamatsu (in Fukushima-ken). Along this road is the largest concentration of thatched-roof houses I encountered during 30,000 km of road

travel around Japan. The road follows a river valley for much of the journey: the scenery is nearly always pleasant and often rustic, with many old houses, although many changes have taken place within the past 10 years and it is much a part of modern Japan.

Tajima A little more than halfway up the valley lies the town of Tajima. It has a museum of folk craft, housing items that were used in daily life. One traveller rated it better than the similar but more famous museum at Kurashiki in Okayama-ken. Ask for the Mingei Hakubutsukan.

OZENUMA

A little farther into the hinterland beyond Nikko (westward) is the very popular swamp of Ozenuma. Swamps don't usually sound exciting, but this one is a bit special. It is set on a plateau 1400 metres high, with a generous amount of pretty scenery, wildflowers and unspoiled nature, including a lake that reflects nearby low mountains that have patches of snow into late spring.

Trails of logs are laid out as hiking tracks through the swamp. They are usually wet and slippery, so take appropriate footwear.

The entry road branches from Route 120 at Kamata, about 50 km from Nikko by bus; from there it is another 25 km or so, also by bus. From Tokyo, access is by train to Numata and by bus from there. There are many buses every day, and at least 9 per day to Tokura. There is a youth hostel at Tokura, and other accommodation facilities in the area.

GUMMA-KEN

From Nikko you can travel on through Numata in Gamma-ken. This region is described in the next chapter.

FUKUSHIMA-KEN

AIZU-WAKAMATSU

This city was the site of the strongest castle in Tohoku (north-east Japan) at the end of the feudal era. At the time of the Meiji restoration, the local lord resisted in favour of the Tokugawa who had ruled Japan for about three centuries. Imperial troops battled the garrison for a month, and the castle was destroyed. There is a realistic replica of the castle in the city today, but there are still authentic castles extant else-

where, so this is not of great interest. There are, however, several attractions nearby.

Inawashiro-ko lake

Because the land near Aizu-Wakamatsu is so flat, the best view of the lake is to be had from the mountain Bandai-san, described below.

Kitakata

This town is located a short distance north of Aizu-Wakamatsu. It is noted for the very large number of old rice storehouses scattered around the town, and walking around the streets is an enjoyable way to spend a few hours. There is a large map posted near the station, and handout maps may be available at the information centre at the station. To the west of Kitakata both road and rail lead to Niigata.

BANDAI AREA

The area of Bandai-Azuma National Park, near Aizu-Wakamatsu, includes some of the prettiest, most interesting and accessible mountain scenery in Japan. There are several volcanic peaks in the area, mostly dormant or extinct. In 1888, a series of colossal explosions literally blew the top off Bandai mountain, hurling the rock in a general northward direction over an area of 70 sq km. This 'instant excavation' changed the topography of the entire area, burying 11 villages and killing nearly 500 people. The rock blocked the former course of the Hibara and Nagase rivers, creating dozens of lakes, ponds and swamps, each one said to be a different colour. The colours range from deep emerald to jade and turquoise, possibly due to copper minerals, for this once was copper-mining country.

Bandai-san, now a group of peaks, is much like part of the rim of a crater. Its northern side still has the vivid, jagged scar of its eruption, for there was no lava flow to change the appearance. The

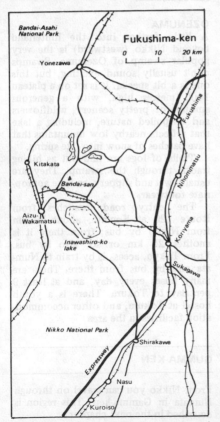

Fukushima-ken

0   10   20 km

Bandai-Asahi
National Park

Yonezawa

Fukushima

Kitakata

Bandai-san

Nihommatsu

Aizu-
Wakamatsu

Koriyama

Inawashiro-ko
lake

Sukagawa

Nikko National Park

Shirakawa

Expressway

Nasu

Kuroiso

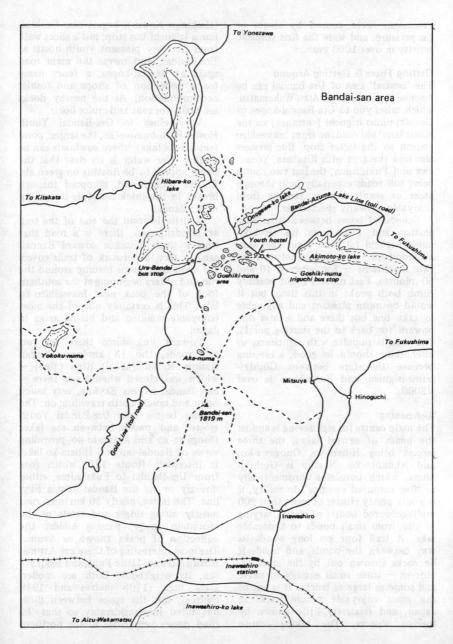

To Yonezawa

Bandai-san area

Hibara-ko lake

To Kitakata

Onogawa-ko lake

Bandai-Azuma Lake Line (toll road)

To Fukushima

Youth hostel

Akimoto-ko lake

Ura-Bandai bus stop

Goshiki-numa area

Goshiki-numa Iriguchi bus stop

Yokoku-numa

Aka-numa

To Fukushima

Mitsuya

Hinoguchi

Gold Line (toll road)

Bandai-san 1819 m

Inawashiro

Inawashiro station

Inawashiro-ko lake

To Aizu-Wakamatsu

explosions were caused by steam or gas pressure, and were the first volcanic activity in over 1000 years.

Getting There & Getting Around

The 'central' area of Ura-Bandai can be reached by bus from Aizu-Wakamatsu, which takes you to Ura-Bandai-kogen or Goshiki-numa-iriguchi (entrance) via the 'Gold Line' toll road; or from Inawashiro station to the latter stop. Bus services also link the area with Kitakata, Yonezawa and Fukushima, the last two routes being toll roads especially built through areas of scenic beauty, ranging from enjoyable to nearly spectacular.

Scheduled buses between Aizu-Wakamatsu and Fukushima via Goshiki-numa-iriguchi (at least 7 per day) stop at Jododaira — which lies between the two mountains — for between 40 and 60 minutes. Fast movers could possibly climb both peaks in this time, but it would be more pleasant and enjoyable to take one bus there and a later one onward (or back to the starting point). The area is popular with sightseers, so hitchhiking should be good, a blessing because the fare between Goshiki-numa-iriguchi and Fukushima is over Y2000.

Sightseeing

The main centre for sightseeing is amidst the heads of several lakes, the three largest being Hibara-ko, Onogawa-ko, and Akimoto-ko. Nearby is Goshiki-numa, which translates unromantically as 'five coloured swamps'. In reality, it is a very pretty cluster of more than 200 multi-coloured bodies of water, varying in size from small ponds to a sizeable lake. A trail four km long wends its way between the ponds, and beside it lie rocks thrown out by the great explosion — some small enough to move and some as large as trucks. It is one of the most enjoyable nature walks in Japan, and relatively little known by foreign visitors. The hiking course

(Haikingu Koosu), begins near Goshiki-numa-iriguchi bus stop, just a short walk from the very pleasant youth hostel at Ura-Bandai, and meets the main road again at Bandai-kogen, a fancy name for a collection of shops and tourist accommodation. At the nearby docks are boats for rent and cruise boats.

Very close to Ora-Bandai Youth Hostel is Bishamon-ike, the largest pond (actually a lake) where rowboats can be rented. The water is so clear that the boats appear to be floating on green air. In the background, glimpsed through breaks in the thick forest, is the stump of Mt Bandai.

A little beyond the end of the trail at Bandai-kogen, there is a road that runs a short distance toward Bandai-san. In fact, a network of trails covers the mountain, some leading around the rim and others beginning at the southern foot of the peak near Inawashiro-ko lake. This is certainly one of the most enjoyable walking and hiking areas in Japan.

Toward Fukushima there are two toll roads, the 13 km-long Bandai-Azuma Reiku ('lake') Rine ('line') — which was closed when I was there — and Bandai-Azuma Skyline, very much open and much worth travelling on. The former begins near Ura-Bandai Youth Hostel and passes between the lakes Onogawa-ko and Akimoto-ko, providing views of Bandai-san and Hibara-ko lake. It intersects Route 115, which goes from Ura-Bandai to Fukushima, either directly or via the Bandai-Azuma Skyline. The latter, nearly 30 km long, runs mostly along ridges and crests of the mountain range, passing amidst the collection of peaks known as Azuma. The most interesting of these are Azuma-Kofuji (Azuma-Little Fuji), and Issaikyo-san, its neighbour. Both are moderately high (1705 metres and 1949 metres), but the space between them has filled in considerably so that the road passes very close to the northern rim of Azuma-Kofuji. You can climb up in less than 10 minutes, and look or climb down into its crater, probably the most accessible one in Japan.

On the other side of the road is Issaikyo-san, an active volcano that jets steam with a continuous roar. Anyone who is the least bit energetic can scramble to the top in 30 minutes or so, and be rewarded by a superb view over the conical-cratered top of Azuma-Kofuji, the rapid drop to the valley floor, and Fukushima city.

From Jododaira to Fukushima, the road and scenery are all downhill (literally and figuratively), and the road through the valley to Sendai has little of note.

MIYAGI-KEN

SENDAI
The largest city in northern Honshu, Sendai was flattened during the war and has been rebuilt like any typical commercial city, with many large buildings and straight streets in the central area. Foreigners there say it is a pleasant place to live, for the mountains are an hour in one direction and the sea an hour in the other. But short-term visitors will find only a small number of attractions, mainly the grounds of the former castle (Aoba-jo), Osaki-Hachiman shrine and a garden.

A guidebook prepared by foreign residents gives good sightseeing and other information on Sendai and vicinity. Its title is simply *Sendai*, and it should be available at Maruzen bookstore, Sendai station and downtown hotels. Price is Y1300.

From Sendai, long-distance ferries ply daily to and from Tomakomai (Hokkaido) and Nagoya. Departures are at 11 am and 9.30 pm, the lowest fare is Y6800, and the trips take 22½ hours and 16½ hours respectively. The terminal can be reached by train or bus from Sendai station; further information is available at the station.

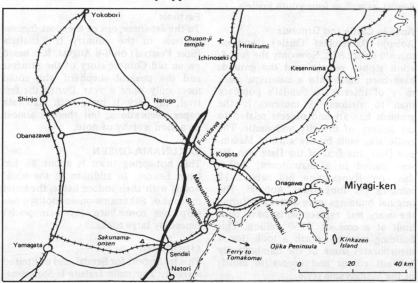

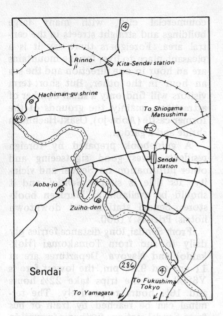

Sendai

Accommodation
There are many hotels and ryokan in Sendai, as well as four youth hostels.

Aoba-jo Castle and Grounds
Aoba-jo (Green-leaf Castle) stood on this hill until 1872. Now only the foundation stones remain, and the grounds have been made into a municipal park m re of interest to Sendai's populace than to visitors. A museum in the grounds has art and objects related to the history of the city and castle. The castle was built by the warlord Masamune Date, the first of the Date clan. He was buried in a mausoleum, Zuihoden, on Kyoga-mine hill, about 15 minutes on foot from Aoba-jo. The original buildings were destroyed during the war, but replacements have been built at a cost of Y750 million. This building may be worth a look, for it incorporates some of the flamboyantly brilliant colour and decorative motifs of the Momoyama style.

Osaki-Hachiman-gu shrine
The main building of this shrine survives from 1607, and is one of the National Treasures of Japan. It is a genuine Momoyama-era structure, and is beautifully decorated with much use of gold leaf and colour. Like Toshogu in Nikko, it is not at all in the restrained style that is usually thought of as 'Japanese', although the outlines of the building are typical.

Rinno-ji temple
The garden here is noted for its artistic layout, with a pond as the focus, and a stream, clusters of bamboo and other natural beauties arranged around the undulating grounds.

Saito Ho-onkai Museum of Natural History
Featured here are geological and paleontological specimens of the area, including some dinosaur skeletons. However, the museum is rather small, as is the number of exhibits in relation to the Y300 admittance charge.

Festivals
To the Japanese, one of the most famous festivals in the country is Tanabata (Star Festival) on 6-8 August. It is based on an old Chinese story of the princess and the peasant shepherd who could meet only once a year. During the festival, the city is hung with elaborate paper decorations, but there is almost no action worthy of note.

SAKUNAMA-ONSEN
This hot-spring town is about 28 km from Sendai. In addition to the usual hotels with their indoor baths, the hotel in front of Sakunama-onsen-motoyu bus stop has rotemburo (open-air pools) fenced by large rocks.

SHIOGAMA
This is the port for Sendai, and of limited interest. The main feature is Shiogama-

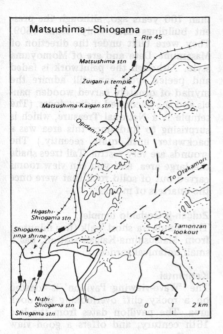

jinja (shrine), a large structure mostly painted orange and white, although inner buildings are built in a traditional manner with very simple lines and natural wood. In the grounds is a museum of historic relics and exhibits related to whaling, which used to be carried out here. The shrine is on a wooded hill near Shiogama station.

MATSUSHIMA

About 40 minutes by train from Sendai lies famed Matsushima Bay, which is dotted with more than 250 small islands covered with twisted pine trees. Some of the islands are inhabited, while others are little more than dots in the water. The area is regarded as one of the traditional 'big three' of Japanese natural scenery (along with Amanohashidate, north of Kyoto, and Itsukushima, near Hiroshima). It is certainly pretty and worth seeing, either by regular cruise-boat from Matsushima or Shiogama, or on foot around Matsushima.

There are several ways to view the bay. Four famous vantage points are spread around various headlands, islands and high areas. Tamonzan hill is accessible by boat from Shiogama harbour near Hon-Shiogama station, or by land. Closest to Matsushima-kaigan station (the main station for sightseeing around the bay) is Ogidani, accessible by bus and some walking. Farther out is Rikuzen-Tomiyama station, from where one walks up to Daigyoji temple (about 20 minutes). The other lookout is Otakamori on Miyato-jima island, which is reached by boat en route through the islands. Since Matsushima Youth Hostel and a hotel are located nearby, one can combine an overnight stay with this view and the boat trip. Nearly all attractions are within 10 minutes of the station.

Information

All attractions of Matsushima-kaigan (coast) are within a few minutes of the station of that name. When leaving the station, turn left at the road and follow it around the bend to the boat docks and an information office. They can give details (though probably only in Japanese) for boats around the bay, to Otakamori, etc, and their handout map should be adequate for finding your way around.

Getting Around

There are several boats every day around the bay, from here to Shiogama, and to Otakamori. At least two boats a day leave for the latter, at 9 am and midday, taking 65 minutes for the trip. The return boat leaves at 10.05 am and 1.05 pm. There are also boats between Otakamori and Shiogama, leaving the latter at 9 am, 11 am and 2 pm, and the former at 10.30 am, 12.40 pm and 3.45 pm (the trip takes 70 minutes). There may be extra sailings on weekends.

Accommodation

There are more than 40 ryokan around Matsushima-kaigan, and youth hostels on Miyato and Kinkazan islands. Matsushima Youth Hostel on Miyato Island can be reached from Nobiru station, or by boat to Otakamori and then bus (or walking) the three km to the hostel. From the dock, go left past Otakamori-kanko Hotel and continue to a very definite fork in the road. The right fork goes along the seawall of a beach, while the left fork passes by the hostel. (The beach has nice sand, but is incredibly littered and has much broken glass, so cannot be recommended, unfortunately. One place mentioned for swimming is Katsura-shima Island, 30 minutes by boat from Shiogama.)

Zuigan-ji temple

This Zen temple was established more than 700 years ago, although the present buildings date 'only' from 1609. They were built under the direction of Masamune Date and are of Momoyama style. Although the paintwork is faded and peeled, you can still admire the myriad of ornately carved wooden panels and the decorated sliding doors. (The temple is a National Treasure, which is surprising to find since this area was a backwater until quite recently.) The grounds are very restful. Tall trees shade the large area, and you can view rooms carved out of solid rock that were once the quarters of monks.

Zuigan-ji Godaido temple

This temple, a short walk (five minutes) from Matsushima-Kaigan station, has a small botanical garden.

Kanrantei

The 'Wave-viewing Pavilion' is located on a rocky cliff overlooking the dock area. The pavilion dates from the late 16th century, and offers a good view over the water.

Matsushima Museum

Located next to Kanrantei, this houses exhibits of armour and other items of the Date family.

Oshima Island

Also close to Matsushima-kaigan station, this is a small, scenic island connected to the mainland by red-lacquered Togetsukyo bridge.

Festivals

On 15 August, the Matsushima-Toro-Nagashi festival is held at Matsushima-kaigan.

Thousands of tiny lanterns are set adrift from the beach, starting at about 7 pm, after which there is a fireworks display. The festival is part of the Buddhist observances of the Festival of the Dead (Obon), which is held throughout Japan.

KINKAZAN

This island is located off the east coast of Miyato Island. The name means Gold Flower Mountain, which seems to originate in the sparkle of mica in rocks on the island.

Various visitors have ascribed a mysterious mood to the island, and mentioned the peace at night, especially when staying at the youth hostel, which is located at Koganeyama-jinja (shrine). The shrine itself is one of the main attractions of the island, and is surprisingly large for such a remote place. The island is covered with dense bamboo groves and forests, and monkeys and deer roam free. From behind the shrine a path leads to the top of the mountain, where there is another shrine. The walk to the top takes about 15 minutes. There may be an early-morning service at about 6.30, featuring sacred dances by shrine maidens, with traditional music and chanting by the priests.

Getting There

Kinkazan can be reached by boat from one of three ports. Eight ferries a day leave from Ayukawa, and four a day from Onagawa. Only one boat a day goes from Ishinomaki (9.40 am), returning at 1.10 pm, so the other ports are preferable. Onagawa is on the JNR system, and seven buses a day run from Ishinomaki to Ayukawa.

INLAND ROUTE

To travel north from Sendai, one follows Route 4. It is slow, crowded and not very interesting, but *shi kata ga nai*, it can't be helped. To go to Narugo and its nearby geyser, turn off on to Route 47 at Furukawa, or take the train.

NARUGO

This town, actually the collective name for a series of hot-spring resort towns, has numerous ryokan and hotels catering to the hot-spring crowd, as well as an unmemorable (but adequate) youth hostel. The town is not particularly noteworthy — basically a string of buildings up one side of a hill and down the other — but some very attractive lacquerware is produced, and the town is famous for Narugo-kokeshi dolls. Kokeshi are severely simple, with a cylindrical (lathe-turned) body, round head, and rudimentary painted features. The Narugo dolls 'cry' when the head is turned, one explanation (veracity not guaranteed) being that families made them years ago to honour the souls of girl babies that had been abandoned because there was not enough food to support them (being less-useful females). Many dolls are made in shops along the main street and you can watch the process.

Onikobe-onsen

One of Japan's few geysers, and probably the highest-spurting, is located at Onikobe-onsen (another collective name for several onsen, meaning 'ogre's head'). About 14 km above Narugo, the geyser can be reached by bus from Narugo station (there are at least nine per day), and you should ask to be let off at Onikobe kanketsu-sen-onsen. From the stop, the small park surrounding the geyser is down a side road.

The geyser is 'artificial' to the extent that a hole was bored to tap the underground pool, but the eruption (every 30 minutes or so) is entirely natural. Water shoots at least 15 metres into the air for several minutes. Close by is a swimming-pool full of warm water, that can be used by those who have already paid to see the geyser.

Narugo-kyo gorge

About three km outside Narugo, near Nakayama-daira-guchi, this gorge offers a pleasant walk along a small river (about four km). There are no places of particular note — it's just a pleasant walk, best made with company rather than alone. A bus is available from Narugo station.

IWATE-KEN

HIRAIZUMI

This ordinary looking town is a former centre of culture as well as containing the most historic temple in northern Japan. Nearby are two interesting gorges, and beautiful views of typical farmland with some of the largest and finest farmhouses in Japan.

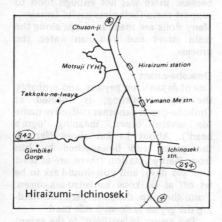

Chuson-ji

This temple was founded in 1105 to accompany a fortress in Hiraizumi built by the Fujiwara family. Of the more than 40 buildings then standing, only two have survived. One, Kyozo, is not particularly noteworthy, but the other, Kon-jiki-do, is a marvel of finely executed ornate decoration. Kon-jiki-do ('golden hall') was originally protected by an outer structure, but recently a new concrete building was put up around it to provide a climate-controlled environment. At the same time, it was

restored to its original splendour, using authentic materials from the same sources as the ones used initially. The exterior is lacquered black, and there are large panels of mother-of-pearl and gold leaf. Inside are three altars, each with 11 Buddhist deities (three Amida, six of Jizo and two of Ten). The building is small (only 5.5 metres square) but you can stand for a long time admiring it through the protective plate-glass. The remains of three of the Fujiwara rulers lie under the central altar.

The grounds of the temple are very restful, set at the top of a large hill that overlooks fertile farming country. An avenue of tall trees lines the stone-paved road from the entrance. A walk of 10-15 minutes, including stops to admire wood carvings and other details along the way, brings you to the concrete building that shelters the Kon-jiki-do. The entry fee also covers the nearby Sankozo Museum.

The entrance to the walkway is the drop-off point of buses that run from Ichinoseki station (the next large town) and stop at Hiraizumi station on the way. There are many buses throughout the day, usually at 20-minute intervals.

Motsu-ji

During the era of the Fujiwara, this was the largest and greatest temple in northern Honshu. All the buildings, however, have been destroyed over the years, and nothing but foundation stones and Oizumi-ga-ike pond and garden remain from that era, although there are some picturesque buildings of more recent vintage around the grounds. A large sign illustrates the size and splendour of the original buildings.

The temple grounds and pond would be very peaceful, except for several PA speakers with recorded messages, two of which can usually be heard at any one time. Why silent signs could not do the job has yet to be explained, for the Japanese boast one of the highest

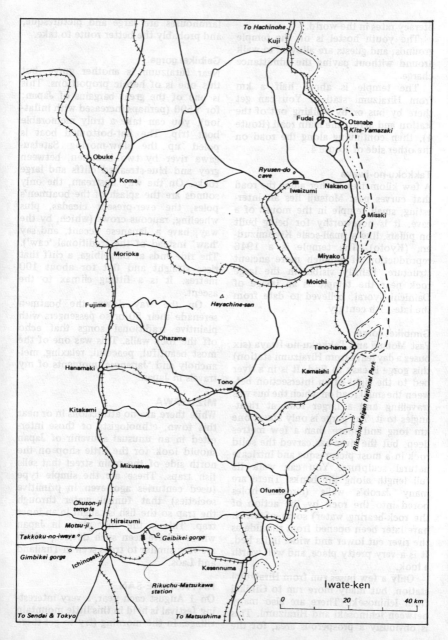

To Hachinohe

Kuji

Fudai

Otanabe
Kita-Yamazaki

Obuke

Koma

Ryusen-do cave

Iwaizumi

Nakano

Misaki

Miyako

Moichi

Morioka

Hayachine-san

Fujime

Ohazama

Tano-hama

Hanamaki

Kamaishi

Tono

Rikuchu-Kaigen National Park

Kitakami

Mizusawa

Ofunato

Chuson-ji
temple

Hiraizumi

Motsu-ji

Takkoku-no-iwaya

Geibikei gorge

Gimbikei gorge

Ichinoseki

Kesennuma

Rikuchu-Matsukawa
station

Iwate-ken

0   20   40 km

To Sendai & Tokyo

To Matsushima

literacy rates in the world.

The youth hostel is on the temple grounds, and guests are allowed to walk around without paying the admittance charge.

The temple is about half a km from Hiraizumi station. You can get there by bus or by walking out of the station and across the main road (Route 4), then continuing along the road on the other side of Route 4.

Takkoku-no-Iwaya

A few kilometres farther along the road that curves past Motsuji lies an interesting, small temple in the mouth of a cave. It is noteworthy for being built on pillars, like a small-scale Kiyomizudera (Kyoto). The temple is a 1946 reproduction of a much more ancient structure. Faintly visible in the large rock near the temple is an image of Dainichi-Nyorai, believed to date from the late 11th century.

Gimbikei gorge

Past Motsuji and Takkoku-no-Iwaya (six buses a day leave from Hiraizumi station) this gorge is easy to find. It is in a river bed to the right of an intersection between the small road on which the bus was travelling and a larger road at right-angles to it. The gorge is only about one km long and more than a few metres deep, but the river has carved the solid rock in a most picturesque and intricate natural sculpture. You can walk its full length along the banks. There are many Jacob's wells (circular holes bored into the rock by the action of the rock-bearing water) some of which have later been opened from the side as the river cut lower and wider in its bed. It is a very pretty place, and well worth a look.

Only a few buses run from Hiraizumi station, but many more run to Gibikei from Ichinoseki. There are also many between Ichinoseki and Hiraizumi. This is obviously a prosperous area, for the farmhouses are large and picturesque, and probably the better route to take.

Geibikei gorge

Near Hiraizumi is another gorge, but this one is of heroic proportions. This is one of the great bargains of Japan: for Y500 (perhaps increased with inflation), you can take a truly memorable boat trip. The flat-bottomed boat is poled up the slow-moving Satetsugawa river by two boatmen, between grey and blue-streaked cliffs and large rocks. On the way upstream, the only sounds are the splash of the boatmen's poles, the ever-present cicadas, plus wheeling, raucous crows (which, by the way, have a Japanese accent, and say 'haw' instead of the traditional 'caw'). The ride ends at Daigeibiga, a cliff that rises straight and flat for about 100 metres. It is a fitting climax to the ascent.

On the way down, the boatmen serenade their 50 or so passengers with plaintive traditional songs that echo off the rock walls. This was one of the most beautiful, peaceful, relaxing, melancholy and 'Japanese' moments of my travels in Japan.

MIZUSAWA

While there are no attractions in or near this town, ethnologists or those interested in an unusual souvenir of Japan should look for the little shop on the north side of the main street that sells fish traps. These are the simple type (used centuries ago even in primitive societies) that funnel water through the trap so the fish is caught in an inner trap. This is the only place in Japan where I have seen such devices, which are very similar to traps seen in Thailand and Laos.

HAYACHINE-SAN

On 1 August each year, a very interesting festival is held in this little mountain village. In the morning (try to get there by 9 o'clock), there is a procession from a small shrine in the hills to the main shrine of the village. Most fascinating are the shishi, townspeople dressed in lion costumes that are topped with very large wooden masks of lion heads. The heads are beautifully carved, and the lower jaw is hinged. Twenty or more shishi parade along the road, the heads and connecting costumes held high overhead so that the 'animals' are much taller than a man, and the jaws clack resonantly in unison with the music. The effect is truly eerie, and except for the onlookers, you feel as if you have been dropped into a supernatural and surrealistic world. After the procession, the heads are put on display in the front room of each house. The doors are left open so that visitors can admire the family treasures.

In the afternoon there are performances of a very rare type of theatre, yamabushi-kagura, stories acted out in dances. Prior to the war, farmers in Tohoku used to regularly act out these very energetic masked dances/dramas in their farmhouses during the winter nights, a tradition hundreds of years old. Now, with the TV era, the performances are limited to this annual festival.

Performances are given on a stage in the courtyard of the shrine. The best seats are in front of the stone steps in front of the shrine building. The music, drumming and cymbals, is quite primitive, somewhat reminiscent of Balinese music. At the same time, Sumo wrestlers perform in a ring in a nearby field.

In the evening, another performance is given in a large house in town in exactly the informal manner that the plays were staged during the long winter nights. To see this, it is advisable to make arrangements to stay overnight at a local home, for it finishes late and there is no public transportation.

I was told that similar performances of yamabushi-kagura are given three times a year at Otsugunai-jinja shrine,

less than 20 km away, on 16 March, 16 September and 16 December. Make inquiries if you are interested.

TO THE COAST
The coast can be reach from this area by train from Ichinoseki or Hanamaki, by Route 284 from Ichinoseki to Kesennuma, or Routes 107 or 283 from Kitakami or Hanamaki.

TONO
Tono is a special little town east of Kitakaham and Hanamaki, on the road towards Kamaishi on the coast. Its populace has decided, as much as possible, to retain traditional small-town values and appearance, so they have rejected industrialization, etc. It might be of interest if you want to visit a relatively unchanged town.

COASTAL ROUTE
Northward from the Matsushima area, one can continue along Route 45. The road runs close to the sea for much of the way, but there is little in the way of coastal sights until Miyako. At Kesennuma you reach the beginning of Rikuchu-Kaigan National Park. A boat cruise is available from Tano-hama around a large protrusion of land to Miyako, passing many small bays, fjords and reefs. The cruise costs Y2000.

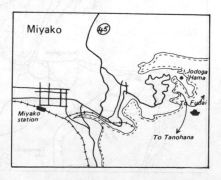

MIYAKO

The central attraction of this town is Jodogahama beach, 20 minutes by bus from Miyako station. It is famed for its white sand, pine-covered dunes, and large rocks jutting from the sea. The starting point of cruises north and south is near the beach. There are ryokan and two youth hostels at Miyako.

From Miyako there is a boat cruise north to Otanabe. Like the other cruise it costs Y2000 but is more scenic for the coast becomes more spectacular as one goes north, culminating in the cliffs at Kita-Yamazaki that rise 100-300 metres out of the water. These cliffs are, by the way, accessible by bus from Otonabe, but the view is more awe-inspiring from a boat.

If you take the northern cruise, you will dock at Fudai and can then go south to Nakano and turn inland to visit Ryusendo cave.

From Fudai (or Ryusendo), you can continue northward along the coast to Hachinohe. You can also reach this city by Route 4, if you go back inland and then travel northward through the central valley. Your choice of route will depend upon the time available, and the time of year.

Ryusendo cave

This is one of the three major caves in Japan. Visitors are permitted 300 metres into 16, passing stalagmites and stalactites. Ryusendo can be reached by bus from Iwaizumi (which is served by JNR via Moichi). Buses also run directly from Morioka and from Komoto, on the coast. There are ryokan and min-shuku at Iwaizumi and at other tourist spots in the area.

AOMORI-KEN

This is the northernmost part of Honshu and is of interest mainly for access to

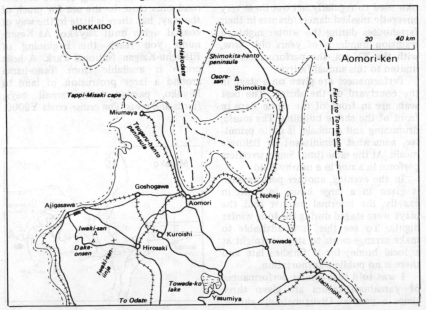

Hokkaido. If you are travelling up the east coast, Hachinohe is the first ferry port; others are Aomori, Noheji and Oma.

From Hachinohe to Aomori there is little of interest (except for the unusual sight of North American-style barns, also seen in Hokkaido) so the ferry service from Hachinohe to Tomokomai is a convenient way to bypass the rest of northern Honshu and the not-so-interesting part of Hokkaido. Details of ferries are given below.

Shimokita-hanto Peninsula

The eastern horn of northern Honshu is quite flat and rather bland. There are beaches all along the inner coast, but they collect everything that is floating on the sea and so are littered with plastic waste. With the exception of festival time at Osore-san, most visitors would come here only to take the ferry from Oma to Hokkaido.

Osore-san

This mountain has been regarded as sacred since the 9th century. Entsu-ji temple was built on its flank on the north shore of the small lake Osoresan. The landscape around the lake is desolate, stark and white, the result of minerals deposited from underground by hot springs. The temple is associated with mediums who attempt to contact the dead. This is the main purpose of the annual festival (20-24 July), when blind women act as mediums, go into trances, and attempt to contact the souls of departed members of worshippers' families. These activities take place in tents set up on the temple grounds, and are the only remnant in Japan of shamanist rites. (Similar practices are still widespread in Korea, and those are almost certainly the same rites that were formerly practised in Japan.) The temple is nominally Buddhist, but Japanese Buddhism is rarely recognized as such by Buddhists from other coun-

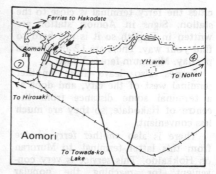

tries, and this set of beliefs is called Minkan-shinka.

Accommodation

The youth hostel can be reached from Aomori station by bus 1, getting off at Sakaimachi-ichome. It is associated with a temple, and faint drumming may be heard in the morning.

Festivals

Aomori is famous for its Nebuta festival, (3-7 August) in which very large floats move through the streets at night. The floats are unusual, huge three-dimensional representations of men and animals that are lit from inside. The sight is memorable. An explanation of the origin of the festival is given for Hirosaki, which has a similar festival called Neputa.

FERRIES TO HOKKAIDO
Hachinohe

There are two ferries a day to (and from) Tomokomai (Hokkaido), leaving Hachinohe at midday and 10 pm. Minimum fare is Y2400, and sailing time is nine hours. The ferry terminal is reached by shi-bi bus from Hachinohe station. The destination stop is Shin-san-kaikan-mae.

Aomori

This is the most convenient port for getting to and from Hakodate. In both cities the ferry terminal is close to the station. Signs in Aomori station are written in English so it is not hard to find your way. There are 12 JNR ferries per day. Minimum fare is Y850.

Ferries also leave from another terminal west of the city, and dock at a terminal some distance from the centre of Hakodate, so they are much less convenient.

There is also another ferry service from this latter terminal, to Muroran on Hokkaido. This service is very convenient for reaching the popular Shikotsu-Toya area of Hokkaido. The principal disadvantage of this service is the awkward departure and arrival times (6 am arriving at 7.30 pm, or 9 pm arriving at 4.30 am) — quite acceptable to truck drivers, the main customers, but less convenient for others. Minimum fare is Y2100.

Noheji
Ferries sail between this town and Hakodate (10 per day). The terminal is a couple of kilometres west of town, and can be reached by bus from Noheji station. At the Hokkaido side, the ferries dock some distance from the centre of Hakodate, which makes it preferable for foot travellers to go via Aomori.

Oma
Ferries cross each way between Oma and Hakodate three times a day. However, the boat docks at the same awkward-to-reach terminal as mentioned

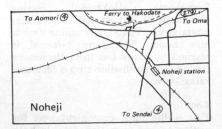

for Noheji, which again makes it easier for foot passengers to use the JNR service from Aomori, which lands at the heart of Hakodate city. Sailing times are usually 7.30 am, 1.25 pm and 6.25 pm, but it is best to check in advance in Jikokuhyo or elsewhere. The dock at Oma is easy to find, for it is a small town.

NORTH-WEST COAST
Miumaya
During the summer months, a ferry crosses from here to Fukushima, in Hokkaido.

Tappi-Misaki Cape
Located at the tip of the western 'pincer' of northern Honshu (Tsugaru-hanto peninsula), the cape has sheer cliffs, eroded rocks, and grottoes. It can be reached from Miumaya station by bus in less than one hour.

Kamegaoka
Stone-age remains have been excavated near here, and are on display at Kamegaoka Archeological Museum.

Fukaura
The attraction of this area is the seashore: cliffs, caves and grottoes eroded by the action of the sea.

Juniko
The name means 'twelve lakes', and this plateau is dotted with more than 30 lakes, 12 of which can be seen from the top of Okuzure in the centre of the plateau. It can be reached by bus from Juniko JNR station, on the coast (summer only).

AOMORI TO TOWADA-KO
The shortest route to the area around Lake Towada, recommended if you are in a hurry, is the direct road south. The view is of pleasant woodland areas, but there are few exceptional scenes. A pleasant stop is at Suiren-numa, a small

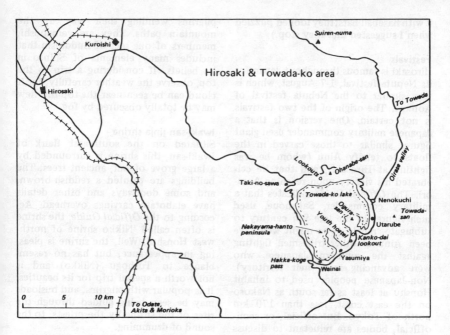

Hirosaki & Towada-ko area

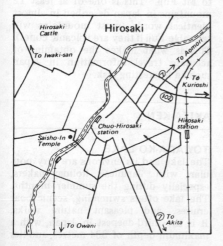

Hirosaki

pond backdropped by four mountain peaks, still snow-patched in late July. The area is at its best in autumn. There are at least 11 buses a day.

For those in less of a hurry, the route south via Hirosaki is more interesting.

HIROSAKI
Hirosaki-jo castle
This is a lovely castle dating from 1610. In any season the gardens are pretty; during the cherry-blossom season (usually late April to early May), they are truly beautiful.

Saishoin temple
Standing in the temple grounds is a give-storey pagoda dating from 1672. Although many people believe that Japan is full of such pagodas, they are, in fact, relatively rare and therefore worth a visit. (I was saddened to see young boys knocking stones against

it with baseball bats; they looked puzzled when I suggested that they stop.)

Festivals

Hirosaki is famous throughout Japan for its Neputa festival, 1-7 August, which is very similar to the Nebuta festival of Aomori. The origin of the two festivals is not certain. One version is that a Japanese military commander used giant figures similar to those carved in the floats to terrify Ainu (whom he was fighting at Hirosaki), and that he celebrated his victory upon reaching Aomori. The *Official Guide* indicates that a military commander, Sakanoue, used such figures in the late 9th century to subjugate 'rebels' (who might well have been Ainu or other tribesmen fighting against the southern Japanese who were advancing into their territory). Non-Japanese peoples used to inhabit Honshu at least as far south as Nakoso on the east coast, less than 170 km north of Tokyo. But official, or semi-official, bodies are reluctant to discuss such matters in Japan.

These two festivals, along with ones at Hayachine-san (1 August), Yamagata (6-8 August) and Akita (5-7 August), make early August an excellent time to visit this part of Japan, especially since its climate is cooler and less humid than that of southern regions, particularly in mountain highland regions.

Buses are available from Hirosaki or Kuroishi to Kenokuchi and Yasumiya on Towada-ko lake (described later).

SIDETRIP TO IWAKI-SAN

The cone of this 1625-metre dormant volcano dominates the flat countryside west of Hirosaki. It can be climbed in about four hours (7.3 km) from Hyakuzawa-onsen, or can be approached the easy way by bus and chairlift. Five buses a day go from Hirosaki station to the top of the mountain (sancho) from where the chairlift begins. On the mountain, one may see white-garbed pilgrims wending their way up the mountain paths. They are yamabushi, members of one sect of Buddhism that includes many elements of Shinto in its beliefs. If considering a trip to the top, observe the weather carefully, for if cloud can be seen near the top the view may be totally obscured by fog.

Iwaki-san-jinja shrine

Situated on the south-east flank of Iwaki-san, this shrine is surrounded by a large grove of tall, ancient trees. The buildings are painted a reddish-brown, and some doorways and other details have elaborate carvings overhead. According to the *Official Guide*, the shrine is often called 'Nikko shrine of northwest Honshu'. Well, the shrine is pleasing in appearance, but has no resemblance to Toshogu (Nikko) and is not worth a special trip for its beauties. It is popular with pilgrims, and busloads may be seen being guided through the rites of the shrine by the priests, to the sound of drumming.

Similarly, Iwaki-san's description, also in the *Official Guide*, is 'The mountain is often called Tsugaru-Fuji because of its remarkable resemblance to Mt Fuji.' This is one of at least 12 mountains in Japan described in almost identical words (most mountains will resemble Fuji if they are volcanic cones). This is what makes the obtaining of accurate travel information in Japan such an interesting task.

AKITA-KEN

TOWADA-KO LAKE

The lake and its environs are very popular with Japanese holiday-makers, especially during the summer months. The lake offers swimming, scenic boat cruises, and pleasant nature walks. It is the third-deepest in Japan, with a maximum depth of 334 metres, and lies

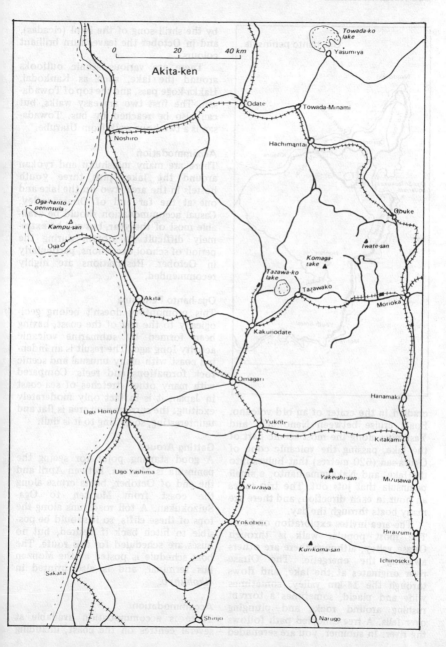

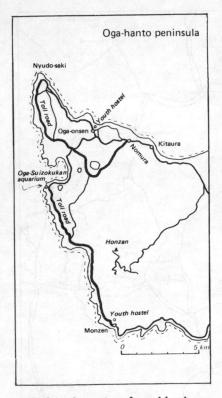

Oga-hanto peninsula

Nyudo-saki

Toll road

Youth hostel

Oga-onsen

Kitaura

Nomura

Oga-Suizokukan
aquarium

Toll road

Honzan

Youth hostel

Monzen

0   5 km

cradled in the crater of an old volcano. Boats cruise between Nenokuchi and Yasumiya along the most scenic part of the lake, passing the volcanic cone of Ogura-san (620 metres) that bulges into the lake, and Nakayama-hanto, a small peninsula that juts out. The trip takes an hour in each direction, and there are many boats through the day.

The area invites exploration on foot. The most popular walk is through Oirase valley, although there are others awaiting the energetic. The Oirase river originates at the lake, and flows through the 14-km valley, sometimes wide and placid, sometimes a torrent rushing around rocks and plunging over falls. A tree-canopied path follows the river. In summer, you are serenaded by the shrill song of the semi (cicadas), and in October the leaves turn brilliant colours.

There are various scenic outlooks around the lake, such as Kankodai, Hakka-koge pass, and the top of Towada-san. The first two are easy walks, but can also be reached by bus. Towada-san is a two-hour walk from Utarube.

Accommodation

There are many minshuku and ryokan around the lake, plus three youth hostels in the area, two on the lake and one at the far end of Oirase valley. Casual accommodation should be available most of the year, but will be extremely difficult to obtain during the period of school excursions, particularly in October. Reservations are highly recommended.

Oga-hanto Peninsula

This promontory doesn't belong geologically to the rest of the coast, having been formed by submarine volcanic activity long ago. The result is an indented coast with many unusual and scenic rock formations and reefs. Compared with many other stretches of sea-coast in Japan, it is in fact only moderately exciting: the surrounding area is flat and uninteresting, so getting to it is dull.

Getting Around

A good starting point for seeing the peninsula is Monzen. Betwen April and the end of October, boats cruise along the coast from Monzen to Oga-Suizokukan. A toll road runs along the tops of these cliffs, so it should be possible to hitch back if desired, but no buses are scheduled for this route. The boat schedule is posted at the Monzen bus terminal, and is also printed in *Jikokuhyo*.

Accommodation

There is accommodation available at several centres on the coast, including

Oga city and Monzen. Oga Choraku-ji Youth Hostel at Monzen is more pleasant than usual. It is part of a temple (which has been there for 1200 years), and an alarm clock is unnecessary because drumming, which is part of the religious ceremony, begins at 6.30 am.

At Oga-onsen there are a number of ryokan and minshuku, plus another youth hostel.

Sightseeing

Oga-suizokukan is an aquarium that is worth a visit. In addition to the commonplace ocean fish, it has some truly wierd and wonderful creations of nature that outdo anything that a Walt Disney Fantasia cartoonist could turn out — some incredibly beautiful, others equally ugly. Most fish are identified in English (or Latin), but one enormous seal (possibly a sea lion?) was not. There are also several alligators, crocodiles and large turtles.

A very unusual sight near here, and also seen at Monzen, are dugout boats still in everyday use (with outboard motors). The availability of large trees in the area make them very practical.

From Oga-suizokukan, one can continue by bus to Nyudo-saki cape via Oga-onsen. From the cape, a toll road runs along another stretch of cliff and between two small deep green lakes, ending at Nomura. At the cape, and elsewhere, you can see masks and costumes of ogres (called 'namahage'). On New Year's Eve, groups of young men in similar costumes visit homes where they are formally received by the master of the house, pause to honour the family shrine, and then walk around the house shouting 'Any good-for-nothing loafers here?'

AKITA

This city is noteworthy only for its famed annual Kanto festival (5-7 August) when young men balance tall bamboo poles that support as many as 40-50 lighted paper lanterns on cross-bars.

TAMAGAWA-ONSEN

South of Towada-ko and below Kazuno, the road splits into Route 282 (which goes to Morioka) and Route 341, which passes through the Hachimantai plateau (Towada-Hachimantai National Park). There are several hot-spring resort towns in the area. Just a little off Route 341 lies Tamagawa-onsen, one of the most typical of these traditional hot-spring resorts. Nearly all the buildings are simple and old wooden structures, built close to the springs. Typical is the large old bathhouse which ones 'walks past to reach the ravine that is the source of the hot water. It has several pools, and mixed bathing is still the practice, as could be seen through the open windows. (The resort is, like many such hot-spring towns, more of a health clinic.) In the ravine, there is one stream which has some of the most unusual water anywhere: it is brilliant orange. Further upstream, a violent bubbling and boiling marks the emergence of the many gushers of hot water. One was throwing water half a metre into the air, and a workman said that it boils two metres high in winter.

Water from the different streams is sluiced separately to various pools, each of which is believed to be efficacious against specific ailments. Some streams are laden with yellow minerals that precipitate out as the water cools, and this water is led into settling chambers where the minerals are collected for sale.

A common sight up in the ravine is one or more people lying on straw mats. The earth is hot (potatoes cook if buried a short distance underground), and people believe the heat to be healthful. Nearby is a small concrete pool, perhaps three metres square, in the open air. It is filled with hot

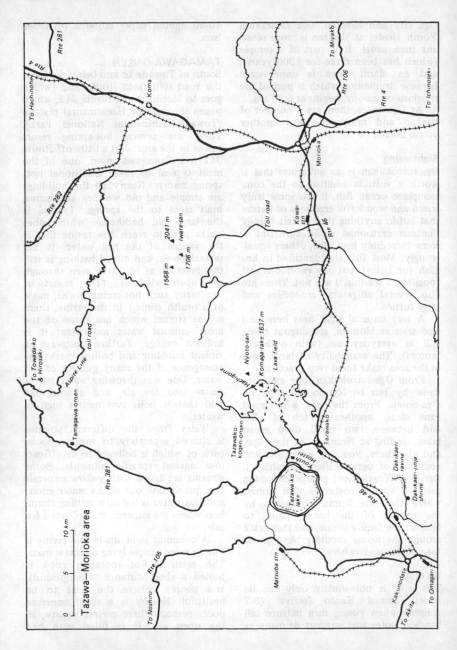

Tazawa—Morioka area

0   5   10 km

water, and is free to the public.

Getting There
Tamagawa-onsen is linked by eight buses a day to and from Hachimantai station, and seven a day to Tazawa-ko station. There is a reasonable amount of traffic for hitchhiking.

A toll road, the Aspite Line (Japanese name) leads across the mountain range from Route 341 toward Routes 282 and 284, past several peaks. However, the scenery can be described as no better than pleasant, a bit disappointing if it is you who is paying the toll. It will be enjoyable if you happen to be going that way, but it is not worth a special trip.

TAZAWA-KO AREA
In the area around this lake are several interesting individual attractions, such as the lake itself, nearby mountains and plateaus, Kakunodate town, Daikakiri gorge, and the general countryside. It sticks in my mind as one of the most pleasant areas visited in Japan while researching this book.

Tazawa-ko lake
This is a classic caldera lake, and the round shape of the old crater is apparent. The swimming is good, and the water shallow for some distance offshore, but it does plunge to 425 metres the deepest in Japan.

Accommodation
There are several ryokan, hotels and minshuku around the lake, so accommodation is no problem. There is a very pleasant youth hostel near the lake. The evening meal is sukiyaki, and the large dining-room becomes the scene of a big party. Definitely light years ahead of most hostels and worth a trip for.

TAZAWAKO-KOGEN PLATEAU
Located a few kilometres from the lake,

the plateau offers some of the most interesting and scenic nature walks in Japan. The scenery ranges from highland scrub (low trees and bushes) to a dormant volcano that erupted recently. There are several trails, the most interesting of which is Koma-ga-take mountain and vicinity. The scenery is quite outstanding (if the highland area is not fog-bound), and the walking and climbing are within the range of anyone except cardiac patients. Koma-ga-take erupted in October 1970 an event which I actually witnessed. The tens of thousands of tons of rock hurled out then now lie in a 'river' of rough-textured boulders that stretches down one side of the hill. Exploring it may be interesting to more than a few people, for the forms and shapes of the lava are fascinating. Sometimes hot gases blasted past the surface of rocks, giving them a rippled surface. Others were torn asunder while hot and taffy-like, and the strings of then-sticky rock can still be seen, looking like stretched bread dough. The eruption was fascinating to watch. Following one explosion, gases shrieked from the earth like a hundred jet engines, then rock from underground slowly collected at the entrance, finally sealing the tube. For many minutes the air was silent until, as amazed onlookers watched, a dome began to form and smoke began to rise over it. Finally, when it had reached a height of about four metres and a diameter of perhaps 10, the pressure became too much and the dome shattered, hurling fragments high into the air. Toward dusk, the red glow of rock chunks could be seen as they traced arcs in the air. The cycle repeated itself again and again.

The easiest way to reach the top is by bus from Tazawa-ko station (of which there are three a day) to Hachigome ('Eighth Station'), and then walking for about 40 minutes up a clearly marked trail. Two other trails start lower down, one beginning at the road near Seishonen Sports Centre, the other at the top of a string of three lifts; the base of the bottom lift is called Mizusawa Daburu Rifuto (double lift). There is some road traffic and hitching is possible, but waiting time is unsure. The first route takes you to the rim of a bowl that looks down on a couple of mini-cones and the high 'bump' of Me-dake (the peak that erupted in 1970). Its black top and, to the right, the river of boulders ejected at that time can't be missed. On the rim of the bowl is a small hill, on the left side of which is a path that leads down to the foot of Me-dake and the floor of the small, green valley, as well as the mini-peaks. On the other side of the hill is a long trail down to the lava river and Me-dake. (Me-dake means 'female peak'; there is also an Odake (male peak). By pre-Shinto custom, all natural features came in matched pairs, or a male and female aspect could be found when there was only a single feature.)

The last bus leaves Hachigome at 3.50 pm (in years past, at least), which puts a crimp in extended walks if you plan to take the bus back down. There are two other trails down, but to find them it is better to have used them to climb up as well, for there are unmarked forks that can lead one astray (as I can certify). It is advisable to carry food and a lot of water, for there are no sources and the climbing generates a healthy thirst.

The region around Tazawa-ko is ideal for exploration by those with their own transport, although buses do cover several routes. The farmland is good and the people prosperous, so the houses (some with thatched roofs) are large and handsome. Residents take pride in their homes and the surroundings, and one of the delights is the sight of long stretches of flowerbeds along the roadside. There is a youth hostel at Matsuba that looks nicer than usual (it

is a private home), but it was full when I visited the town.

KAKUNODATE

This town is very unusual, and offers a good chance to see daily life in pleasant surroundings. Although located in the far north, relatively a cultural backwater, it preserves a number of 350-year-old samurai houses in surroundings of tall, old trees, quite unlike almost any other place in Japan. The old houses stand mostly on a single street, not far from the station, where there is a large map posted as a guide. The houses are open to the public for a reasonable fee, and are interesting for the glimpse into the past that they offer. Most have simple but elegant tree-shaded gardens, and are built with the best materials. It is interesting how little different the construction of these old houses is from that of modern but traditional style houses.

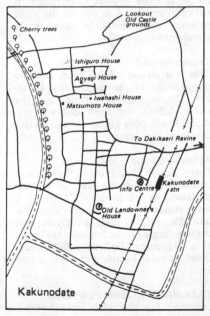

Kakunodate

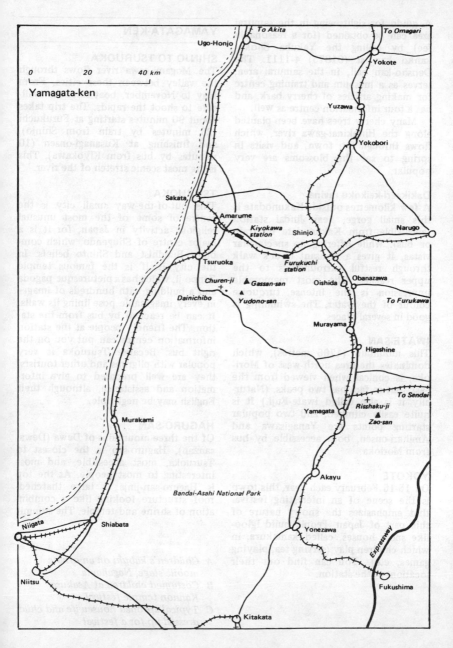

Yamagata-ken

0   20   40 km

A guide for sightseeing in the samurai area can be obtained (for a reasonable fee) by calling the Yakuba Shoko-kanko kan at (01875) 4-1111. The Densho-kan hall, in the samurai area, serves as a museum and training centre for making articles of cherry bark, and has a tour information centre as well.

Many cherry trees have been planted along the Hinokinai-gawa river, which flows through the town, and visits in spring to see the blossoms are very popular.

Dakikaeri-keikoku ravine

A few kilometres outside Kakunodate is this small gorge, near Jindai station (accessible from Kakunodate by train or bus). While offering no spectacular vistas, it gives a pleasant hour's walk through restful surroundings to the upper reaches. The most memorable impression is the intense turquoise colour of the water. The swimming is good in several places.

IWATE-SAN

This mountain (1706 metres), which dominates the area north-west of Morioka, is conical when viewed from the east, but in fact has two peaks. (Naturally it is also called Iwate-Fuji.) It is quite easily climbed, and two popular starting points are Yanagisawa and Amihari-onsen, both accessible by bus from Morioka.

YOKOTE

On 15-16 February each year, this town is the scene of an interesting festival that emphasizes the snowy nature of this part of Japan. People build igloo-like snow houses, called kamakura, in which children play (serving tea, playing games, etc). You can find out their locations at the station.

YAMAGATA-KEN

SHINJO TO TSURUOKA

The Mogami-gawa river flows through the valley between these cities. From May to November, boat rides are available to shoot the rapids. The trip takes about 90 minutes starting at Furukuchi (20 minutes by train from Shinjo), and finishing at Kusanagi-onsen (10 minutes by bus from Kiyokawa). This is the most scenic stretch of the river.

TSURUOKA

This out-of-the-way small city is the centre of some of the most unusual religious activity in Japan, for it is a major centre of Shugendo, which combines Buddhist and Shinto beliefs. In the city itself is the famous temple Zenpo-ji, which has a picturesque pagoda and a building with hundreds of images in every imaginable pose lining its walls. It can be reached by bus from the station. The friendly people at the station information centre can put you on the right bus. Because Tsuruoka is very popular with pilgrims and other tourists, they are well prepared to give information and assistance, although their English may be negligible.

HAGURO-SAN

Of the three mountains of Dewa (Dewa-sanzan), Haguro-san is the closest to Tsuruoka, most accessible, and most interesting to most people. At the top is Haguro-san-jinja, a large thatched-roof structure looking like a combination of shrine and temple. The summit

---

A Children's kabuki on an ornate mobile stage, Nagahama

B Costumed children at Asakusa Kannon temple festival

C Typical aproned housewife and child dressed up for a festival

can be reached by bus from Tsuruoka station via a toll road. On the mountain can still be seen the tiny huts used by pilgrims when they visited for prayer, fasting and other forms of religious penance. The more interesting and pleasant way to reach the summit is the traditional way, climbing on foot up the long stairway through a continuous grove of huge, tall and ancient trees. From the village of Haguro, near the bus station, there is a gateway that leads to steps down to the valley below. This is one of the nicest forest glades in Japan: tall trees line the walking paths, and there are several small shrines, a small waterfall, a picturesque bridge. Only the omnipresent semi can be heard. The path leads to a five-storey pagoda, then to the base of the very long stairway that leads to the top. (I counted the steps on my first visit in 1971, but can remember only that there are more than 1000.) At one time this was the only way to go; for the person with the time and the health, it still is. Anywhere on the mountain there is a good chance of seeing pilgrims, yamabushi, dressed in white and carrying rosaries and bells. During the day, you can sometimes hear the sound of a conch-shell blown by priests as part of their religious observations.

Accommodation

Many temples and homes at Haguro offer accommodation. Help can be obtained at the station if you wish to stay pilgrim-style. The youth hostel is several kilometres down the coast, accessible by train from Tsuruoka station.

A *Cherry blossoms at Heian-jingu*
B *Autumn at a Kyoto temple*
C *Pagoda of Sojiji temple near Monzen, Noto-hanto peninsula*

GASSAN & YUDONO-SAN

Together with Haguro-san, these form the three sacred mountains of Shugendo. Gassan is the main peak, with Yudono-san as an outcropping on one flank. At the top of Gassan is Gassan-jinja, to which pilgrims and others climb in summer. Climbers are advised to take warm clothing, for it gets cold even in mid-summer. A toll road runs to the top of Yudono-san. Probably the most fascinating (if a trifle morbid) sights are the mummies of two aescetic priests who were voluntarily buried alive in chambers on the mountain. Both are on display, one at Dainichibo, the other at Churen-ji. Both temples can be reached by bus from Tsuruoka station, to Oami, from where you walk inland for about one km. (You may need to ask for directions.)

Dainichibo The mummy here is always open to view in a passageway that encircles the temple. Photos are permitted, and some light enters by windows. The mummy (mirabutsu) is that of a man who ate no meat or grain, living (if that is the word) on nuts, grass-roots and seeds. His purpose was to remove from his body all substances (like fats) that could rot, and when he reached the age of 96 (in 1783) he was buried by his disciples. They dug him up after three years and three months, dried his body and put him on display (his wish was for people to look on his body and be inspired to understand Buddhist ideas).

Churen-ji Only a kilometre or so away from Dainichibo, at Churen-ji is the second mummy. However, this one is kept in a glass case in the main hall, and special arrangement must be made to have the drape removed. This man was an itinerant preacher who travelled around Tohoku and Kanto. In 1821, during an epidemic in Tokyo that was causing blindness, he went there, prayed and, as an act of atonement, tore out one eye and threw it into the Sumida river. He was known as the 'priest of the eye'. In 1829, at the age of 62, he was buried at Churenji, and dug up after his death.

YAMAGATA

The town itself is of little interest, but those interest in studying traditional Japanese society would find this a good place to visit or live in. Each section of town has a traditional industry or craft, and many crafts are still performed as daily work. The father of one of my friends makes his living by hand-forging and polishing agricultural shears. He makes one to two pairs a day, and sells them for Y20,000 each.

Festivals

The city's main festival is Hanagasa-matsuri (Floral Sedge Hat Festival), on 6-8 August, when thousands of townspeople in costume dance through the streets at night.

YAMADERA

The main attraction of the Yamadera area lies several kilometres out of town. Yamadera ('mountain temple') is properly known as Risshaku-ji. The buildings are scattered around the heavily-wooded mountainside. Some are perched at the edge of precipices, and look as if they will topple at any time. It takes two to three hours of climbing on foot to visit the various temples. The place is best visited with a friend, for the exploration can become boring alone. Access is from Yamadera station, which is reached by bus or train from Yamagata or Sendai.

ZAO-SAN

This mountain is best known for its winter skiing. At that time of year, trees become coated with snow and ice, giving them fantastic shapes. Toll roads make travel through the mountain area easy.

YONEZAWA

Formerly a castle town of the Uesugi family, the small town is now noted for the tombs of 12 generations of the family. They resemble 12 small wooden shrines laid out in a row beneath tall trees. A bus runs from Yonezawa station. From Yonezawa, a local road leads to Nishi-Azuma Skyline toll road, which leads to Bandai-san and area (described in the Northward segment). At the northern entrance to the road is a chairlift to the Tengendai plateau, which a friend describes as 'not worth while'. Route 121, which goes over a mountain range from Yonezawa to Kitakata and Aizu-Wakamatsu, is a twisty gravel road in paris, with no buses listed, and little traffic. Also accessible from the area, both from a short distance above Yonezawa, and from Kitakata or Aizu-wakamatsu, is the west coast. From the last two cities, Route 49 goes directly to Niigata, a gateway to Sado Island.

NIIGATA-KEN

NIIGATA

Located on the Japan Sea coast north-west of Tokyo, Niigata is an international port of entry, and one of the ports for sailing to nearby Sado-a-shima island.

To the east it is about 120 km by road (Route 49) or rail to Aizu-Wakamatsu (Fuku-shima-ken), a good starting point for a trip northward. Tsuruoka (Yamagata-ken) is straight up the coast, but the terrain is uninteresting all the way, for Niigata lies in a large, flat area (that produces more rice than any other prefecture). The trip south-west is also unexciting. Travellers

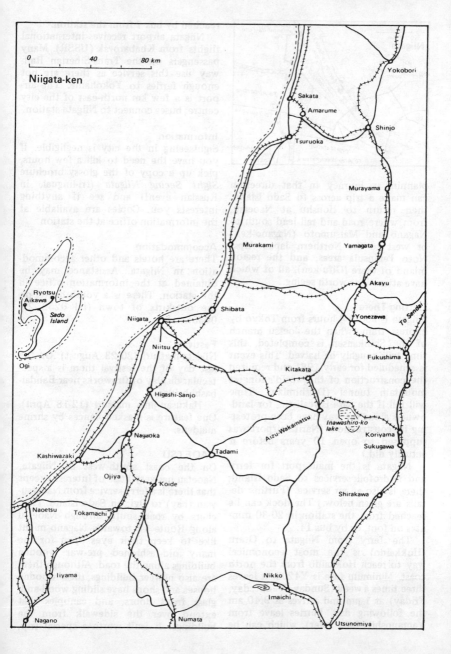

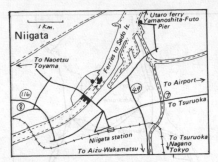

planning a journey in that direction can make a trip across to Sado Island, then return to Honshu at Naoetsu, from where road and rail lead south to Nagano and Matsumoto (Nagano-ken) or west to the Northern Japan Alps / Noto Peninsula areas, and the region inland of there (Gifu-ken), all of which have attractions worth seeing.

Getting There
Niigata is about 4 hours from Tokyo by express train. When the Joetsu branch of the Shinkansen is completed, this time will roughly be halved. This event is scheduled for early 1981 and required the construction of the world's longest mountain tunnel (Daishimizu). Time will tell if the date is realistic, for land-owners along the way have been protesting its construction. (Narita airport was supposed to open 10 years before it actually did.)

Niigata is the main port for ferry and hydrofoil services to Sado Island; there is also an air service. (Further details are given below.) The dock can be reached from the station in 20-30 minutes on foot, or by bus 14.

The ferry from Niigata to Otaru (Hokkaido) is the most economical way to reach Hokkaido from the north coast. Minimum fare is Y4200. It leaves three times a week (Sunday, Wednesday, Friday) at 1 pm and arrives at 9.40 am the following day. Ferries leave from Yamanoshita-futo (pier), which can be

reached by bus 7 from the station.

Niigata airport receives international flights from Khabarovsk (USSR). Many passengers on the Trans-Siberian Railway use this service as there are not enough ferries to Yokohama. The airport is a few km north-east of the city centre; buses connect to Niigata station.

Information
Sightseeing in the city is negligible. If you have the need to kill a few hours, pick up a copy of the glossy brochure *Sight Seeing Niigata* (tri-lingual, in Russian even!) and see if anything interests you. Copies are available at the information office at the station.

Accommodation
There are hotels and other accommodation in Niigata. Assistance may be obtained at the information office in the station. There is a youth hostel on the outskirts of town (tel 0252 29-0935).

Festivals
Niigata-matsuri (20-23 August). On the last day of the festival there is a spectacular display of fireworks near Bandaibashi bridge.

Hakusan-jinja matsuri (12-18 April). One feature is masked dances by shrine maidens.

NAOETSU
On the coast south-west of Niigata, Naoetsu has very little of interest except that there is a ferry service from Naoetsu-wan (bay) to Ogi, on Sado Island. Travellers by road south through Naoetsu along Route 18 towards Nagano might like to keep their eyes open for the many old-fashioned pre-war wooden buildings along the road. Although there are also neweer buildings, these wooden houses and shops have sliding wood-and-glass front doors, and canopies that extend over the sidewalk from the buildings. It isn't worth a special trip,

but is worth looking for because it gives a glimpse of something that has vanished almost everywhere in the rush to plate glass and brick.

SADO ISLAND

Sado-ga-shima Island is the fifth largest of the islands of Japan. The main attraction is its remoteness. Despite the large number of sightseers annually (about one million), the people of Sado continue much as they have for decades, or even centuries, though with accommodation to modern times. It is like most island communities — the people are friendlier, and the pace of life slower. These are not things that a visitor can see, of course, but if you have a feeling for 'atmosphere' you should enjoy a visit.

Getting There & Getting Around

The main town is Ryotsu, a small-townish port city, linked to Niigata by hydrofoil (eight per day) or ferry (four per day). Hydrofoils travel at up to 80 km/h and the trip takes about 60 minutes. The fare is Y2200. The car/passenger ferries are slower (2½-3 hours) but cheaper (lowest fare Y900). The last ferry leaves Niigata at 9.10 pm.

There is also one ferry a day between Niigata and the small town of Akadomori.

There are four ferries a day between Naoetsu and Ogi, another ferry port on Sado. Lowest fare is Y1000. Travellers who plan a trip (on Honshu) between Niigata and Naoetsu would find a circling route Niigata-Ryotsu-Ogi-Naoetsu (or vice versa) more enjoyable (time permitting) because the Niigata-Naoetsu trip is dull.

From 25 April to 31 August there is an exciting hovercraft service twice a day in each direction, linking Ogi with Suzu and Nanao on the Noto-hanto peninsula (Ishikawa-ken). From then until 15 October, the service is once a day.

Buses run between the major centres on the island, so there is no problem getting around. Tour buses also run, offering tours lasting from four to eight hours. They leave from Ryotsu and Ogi, another ferry port.

Sightseeing

The island is made up of two long, oval-shaped mountain ranges with a fertile valley sandwiched between them. Ryotsu is at the north-east end of the valley. Starting from here, one route (along the south side of the valley) first passes Honma-ke Noh theatre, where performances of local dances and folk theatre are given during the summer. Check locally about these performances.

Konpo-ji temple

This is located in a forest setting, 30 minutes from Ryotsu by bus.

Myosen-ji temple

This has a 21-metre high pagoda, and also has a forest setting.

Mausoleum and Museum

A little further on is the mausoleum of emperor Juntoku, who was exiled here for 22 years in the 13th century. Nearby is a museum of relics of Juntoku and the priest Nichiren (a famous name in

Japanese history) who was also exiled here centuries ago.

Ogi

This city lies near the south-west corner of the island. It is the other major port for boats to Honshu.

In Ogi harbour there is a chance of seeing 'washtub' boats — perfectly circular, flat-bottomed boats made in the manner of staved barrels. They were once a common sight around the island, where they were used for harvesting seaweed and shellfish. Their main use these days is as a tourist attraction. If you see one, you can hire a ride.

Other routes to Ogi are by circling south-west along the coast from Ryotsu, or by crossing the hilly spine of the southern range by one of three small roads. One source indicates a bus service on all, while another shows buses only on the western route across to Akadomani and around the eastern tip. Inquire locally. There is definitely a section of the south coast without buses.

Past Ogi, toward Nansenkyo, there are many old houses built over 200 years ago. Along the way is the Ogi folkcraft museum (mingei hakubutsukan). The coast becomes rugged around the Nansenkyo-Sawazaki area, then becomes quite gentle until the far side of Mano-wan bay, past Sawada. Sado is of volcanic origin, and the rock outcroppings have the weird shapes typical of once-molten lava, aided by the erosion of the sea. There are many pleasant vistas.

Aikawa

This was formerly the major gold-mining centre of Japan, once the largest producer in the Orient. Its miners were often prisoners, many of whom died here. Now the gold is nearly gone. Visitors can tour one of the mines, Sodayu-ko, started about 360 years ago. Most of its passages are low and

narrow. Mechanized displays (robots) show how the mining was done by hand.

Continuing up the coast, one passes more pretty coastal scenery, with the Sotokaifu-kaigan coast the most attractive. Much of the coast is of indented bays. The east coast is much more tranquil, and not as interesting.

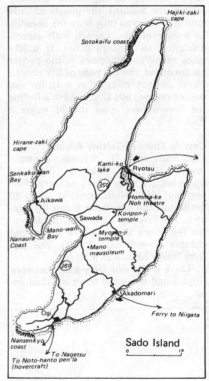

Sado Island

Hokkaido

Hokkaido is the northernmost major island of Japan. It was settled quite late in Japanese history, so it has little of historic interest — its strong suit is natural beauty and outdoor activities. It is also of interest for being the home of aboriginal peoples who are not related to the Yamato Japanese who comprise almost the entire population of Japan.

Much of Hokkaido has a strong flavour of eastern North America. In the river valleys, where most of the population has settled, the terrain features broad, rolling valleys flanked by low wooded hills. Also, because the climate of Hokkaido is colder than that of the south islands, traditional farming methods and crops did not succeed, so foreign experts (mostly American) were brought in as advisers. With them came large farms, dry-land crops, barns, silos and cows (a rarity elsewhere). It is all very exotic to the Japanese, but of limited interest to foreign visitors. The areas of greatest interest to travellers are the coastal, mountain and lake regions where the characteristic Hokkaido scenery, much of volcanic origin, can be enjoyed.

History and Peoples

Hokkaido was long a frontier region of little interest to the central governments in the south of Japan. The major groups of inhabitants were native peoples of various origins (mostly unknown), including the Ainu, Gilyak and Oroke.

Not much is known about the Ainu. It seems that their languages have no known relatives elsewhere in the world, although there are tribes in Siberia with similar shamanist forms of worship based on a cult of the bear. Also, there are Ainu living on Sakhalin Island. Until recently, it was thought that they were a Caucasian race, but now no one is sure. One person observed that Ainu and Navajo music is similar.

It has also become known that they are recent arrivals in Hokkaido, having come only about 800 years ago, displacing an even more mysterious people who seem to have occupied the island for much longer. It appears that Hokkaido has been occupied for about 23,000 years. Ainu used to live on Honshu as well; in 724 AD their territory extended to within 78 km of present-day Sendai, and it is quite possible that they lived farther south in earlier times. They were a peaceful people, and were no match for the more aggressive Yamoto Japanese, so they were slowly pushed back into the remoteness of Hokkaido.

Up to the end of the last century, they lived a life of hunting and fishing, and engaged in small-scale agriculture of dry-field crops (no rice). By the last decade of the century the encroaching settlements of southern Japanese had almost destroyed the Ainus' way of life, and they were a dispirited people seemingly on the way to extinction. The central government adopted an enlightened policy and assimilated them into the mainstream of Japanese life. As a result, they have adopted Japanese names, language and customs, so that they would be difficult to identify. In Japan, there is discrimination against those who are 'different', so most Ainu do not advertise the fact that they are of Ainu descent. There are perhaps 15,000 full-blooded Ainu left in Hokkaido. The only Ainu wearing traditional garments do so for the benefit of visiting tourists. They may be seen at Shiraoi, Noboribetsu-onsen, Asahikawa, in the area around Akan-ko, Kutcharo-ko, and wherever tourists gather.

No one speaks any of the Ainu languages (except, perhaps, for a few elders) but many place names are of Ainu origin. This can cause problems,

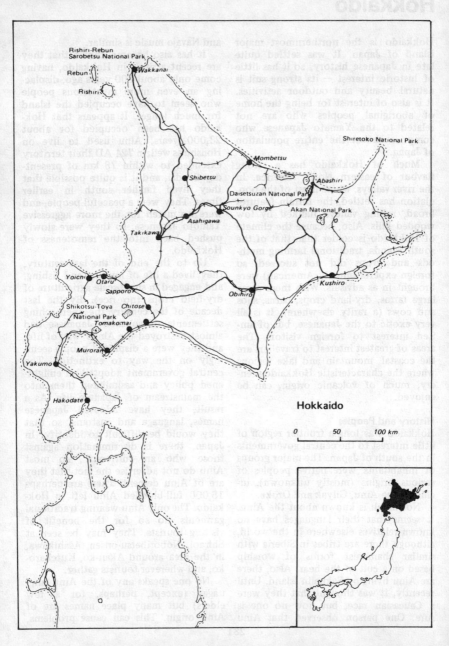

Rishiri-Rebun
Sarobetsu National Park
Rebun
Rishiri
Wakkanai

Shiretoko National Park

Mombetsu

Shibetsu

Abashiri

Daisetsuzan National Park

Sounkyo Gorge
Akan National Park

Asahigawa

Takikawa

Kushiro

Yoichi
Otaru
Sapporo

Obihiro

Shikotsu-Toya
National Park
Chitose

Tomakomai

Muroran

Yakumo

Hakodate

Hokkaido

0   50   100 km

because nearly all are written in kanji, and even southern Japanese are unable to read many place names correctly. Many of the pronunciations do not even appear in kanji dictionaries.

The Gilyak were a hunting and fishing 'people, like the Ainu, and were largely found in Sakhalin. They also lived along the lower Amur River on the mainland, and are a Mongolian race.

The Oroke lived on Sakhalin and were nomads who lived on their reindeer herds. They are a Tungus people, and are related to the Orochi of the Amur River delta region. They were not originally inhabitants of Hokkaido, but the takeover by the USSR of Sakhalin after World War II caused several Oroke to move to Hokkaido, and about 30 of them are scattered around the island. One of them recently opened a small museum at Abashiri.

Getting There

Since Hokkaido is an island, it is accessible only by plane and ship. Work is under way to build the Sei Kan tunnel under the Tsugara Straight for a Shinkansen-type super-express train from Tokyo to Sapporo, but because the tunnel will be 54 km long, it is not scheduled for completion until 1982. Travel time between the cities will be about 5 hours and 40 minutes.

The main airport is at Chitose, and it serves nearby Sapporo.

Visitors with only a few days for Hokkaido should note that a ferry runs from Aomori (northern Honshu) to Muroran, which is very close to the Toya-ko Shikotsu-ko area, one of the two most popular and interesting regions for travellers in Hokkaido. Similar savings in time can be effected by using ferry connections between the other ports.

There are several ferry lines. Listed below are the main ferry ports in Hokkaido, and the cities in Honshu with which they connect.

Hakodate — Aomori, Noheji and Oma. Of these lines, detailed below, by far the most convenient is the JNR ferry from Aomori.

Aomori Two ferry lines connect Hakodate with Aomori: JNR and Higashi Nihon Ferry (HNF). The more convenient by far is the JNR, for its terminal in both cities is very close to the station. JNR ferries have 10 sailings a day in each direction, between 12.15 am and 7.50 pm from Hakodate, and between 12.10 am and 7.25 pm from Aomori. Sailing time is four hours. HNF has 12 sailings a day in each direction, virtually around the clock from Hakodate, and between 12.05 and 9.30 pm from Aomori. Sailing time is four hours. (Note that schedules may change from year to year, and that some ferries offer 'express' service by travelling a little faster.)

At both Hakodate and Aomori, the HNF terminal is some distance to the west of the city and is inconvenient to reach. If you arrive by HNF at Hakodate, you can reach the JNR station by taking the road from the terminal, turning right at the first T-junction, left at the next corner and continuing to intersect a major road. The bus stop is across the road and to the right. The name of the stop (written only in Japanese) is Hokodai (Hokkaido University). Nearby is a midget submarine named Kuroshio. Take bus 1 to the station. See the sections on Accommodation and Hitching for further information from this point.

Noheji HNF has 12 sailings a day in each direction to this small city, virtually around the clock. Sailing time is 4 hours 40 minutes. The terminus is a few kilometres to the west of the JNR station; a bus service makes the connection.

Oma HNF has six sailings a day in each direction to this small town at the north of the Shimokita Peninsula. Times are between 5 am and 5.50 pm from Hakodate, and between 7.30 am and 8.30 pm from Oma. Sailing time is one hour 50 minutes. The sea distance is shorter and the fare is slightly less than from Aomori, but balancing that is the longer land distance to reach Oma.

Muroran — Aomori. There are two ferries a day in each direction, at 6 am and 9 pm (from Aomori), and 6.50 am and 3.50 pm (from Muroran). Duration is about 7½ hours. These are about the most inconvenient times conceivable, unfortunately.

The ferry terminus ('Ferry Noriba') is easy to find, and is one km from the JNR station. Buses leave from the station as well.

Tomakomai — Nagoya, Tokyo, Sendai and Hachinohe.

Nagoya Two or three per day; 42-hour trip; cheapest fare Y13,700.

Tokyo One per day; 30-hour trip; cheapest fare Y10,500.

Sendai One per day; 16-hour trip; cheapest fare Y6800.

Hachinohe One per day; 8-hour trip;

Kushiro — Tokyo. This port gives easy access to Akan National Park. There is a ferry twice a week from Tokyo, operated by Kinkai Yusen Ferry. The trip takes 33 hours; cheapest fare is Y11,500.

Otaru — Niigata, Suruga, Maizura (west coast of Honshu). These services are run by Shin Nihonkai Ferry. Suruga and Maizuru are quite close to Kyoto. From Niigata there are three sailings a week in each direction; duration is about 20½ hours. From both Suruga and Maizuru there are four sailings a week in each direction; duration is 32 hours from both ports. Several classes are offered; the cheapest is tatami mats shared with your neighbours (quite acceptable behaviour!). The cheapest

fare from Niigata is Y4200 and from the other two ports, Y5300.

Fukushima — Miumaya. This is a small port south-west of Hakodate. (Some maps show it as Oshima-Fukushima.) Between June and August there is a ferry service from Miumaya on the Tsuguru peninsula. Check with the TIC in Tokyo for times, or find a timetable of the Higashi Nihon Ferry company.

HAKODATE

Hakodate is primarily the port of entry to Hokkaido from Honshu.

Hitching

If you wish to hitch to Sapporo and else-where immediately, it is necessary to get to Route 5. If arriving by HNF, get off the bus at Gas-gaisha-mae, which is near a large gas holder. Just before reaching it, the road from the ferry terminal follows an overpass that curves to the left and intersects a major road at right angles; that is Route 5.

From the station, take tram 10 to the end of the line (going to the left when leaving the station); it passes Gas-gaisha-mae along the way. From Gas-gaisha-mae, tram 20 runs along the same route.

Accommodation

There is one youth hostel in Hakodate; it is several kilometres from the station in the hot-spring town of Yunokawa ('hot water river'), a suburb of Hakodate. From the station take a tram 5 or 8 and get off at Yunokawa-onsen (the second-last stop on the line). Be sure to get a 5 going the right way; 8 ends at the station. (Trams 2, 3, 6, 10 and 20 go as far as the car barns, one stop before Yunokawa-onsen, which would add over half a kilometre to the distance to the hostel.)

The hostel is located amidst resort hotels, and its bath is fed with the same

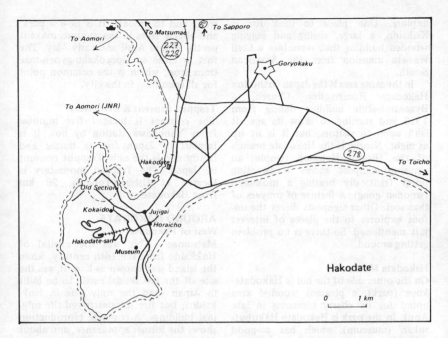

To Aomori
To Matsumae
To Sapporo
227
228
Goryokaku
To Aomori (JNR)
Hakodate
278
To Toicho
Old Section
Kokaido
Jujigai
Horaicho
Hakodate-san
Museum
Hakodate

0   1 km

naturally hot (and *very* hard) water, so you can enjoy the privilege without the cost of a resort hotel. The hostel tends to be quite full on weekends. If you arrive early in the day, consider staying at the Onuma area, about 25 km away. It is scenic and pleasant.

Hakodate-san
The city of Hakodate is dominated by (Mt) Hakodate-san (335 metres), a large hill of volcanic origin at the end of a small peninsula that forms a natural shelter for ships. The view of Hakodate at night from this hill is considered the finest night view in Japan; a carpet of coloured lights stretches into the distance.

It is possible to walk up, but it is easier to take the cable car ('ropeway') which runs to the top from a base station partway up the hill. The base station is easily reached from tram stops Horaicho or Jujigai on lines 2 and 10, or the latter stop only on lines 3, 5 or 6.

The old section
The first impression of Hakodate is that it is an unattractive city, but its appeal grows. It has character, something which most Japanese cities lack. In the port area and on the hillside at the base of Hakodate-san are many old and often decrepit buildings, distinguished because they are American or European in style. The area is charmingly seedy and thus receives no publicity from tourist organizations that would rather have tourists look at their sterile, concrete, new buildings. The old section is very interesting to wander around in.

There is no particular street to see: each one has its quota. Trams 3 and 6 pass by a number of such buildings near the harbour terminus, and the streets of nearby hillsides are a good area to explore. One place to look for is Kokaido, a large, ageing and sagging wooden building that resembles a Civil War-era mansion from the American South.

In the same area is the Japan Orthodox Hakodate Resurrection Church, a Byzantine-style building dating from 1916 and starting to show its age. It isn't open to visitors, but it is lit up at night. Nearby is the Hakodate branch of the Higashi Honganji temple; an amusing signpost shows a sweating priest frantically beating a mokugyo (wooden gong), a feature of prayers of that sect. Other signposts direct the on-foot explorer to the places of interest just mentioned. So there is no problem getting around.

Hakodate Museum

On the other side of the hill is Hakodate-koen (park), a pleasant wooded area noted for its cherry blossoms in late April. In the park is Hakodate Hakubut-sukan (museum) which has a good collection and a modern display of arte-facts of the aboriginal races that inhabit(ed) Hokkaido. If you have time to see only one museum in Hokkaido, this would be a good candidate. It is close to the last two stops on tram line 2, and not too far from the junction stop Horaicho (line 10).

Goryokaku

This is an interesting fort, the only one in Japan built in a European style (fin-ished in 1864). It is shaped like a five-pointed star, a design which allows defenders to rake all approaches with gunfire. It was the scene of a siege of more than a month in 1868, when sup-porters of the Tokugawa shogunate res-isted the Meiji restoration. A small museum inside the walls has relics of the battle, and a small tower allows a view over the area. The walls themselves are low, perhaps five metres high, and there is no superstructure, only the walls and the moats. It is now a park, and cherry trees in the grounds make it pretty in late April and early May. The fort is close to Goryokaku-gyoen-mae tram stop, which is the common point for all tram lines in the city.

Trappist convent & monastery

The convent is located five minutes from Yunokawa station by bus. It is famous in Japan for its butter and candy and is the only Trappist convent in Japan. The Trappist monastery is located at Oshima-Tobetsu, 26 km from Hakodate.

AROUND HAKODATE
West of Hakodate

Matsumae This was the capital of Hokkaido from the 16th century, when the island was known as Ezo. It was the site of the last feudal castle to be built in Japan (and the only one in Hok-kaido), but fire has destroyed the orig-inal buildings. A concrete reproduction shows the former appearance, and about 5000 cherry trees make the place one of beauty from late April.

East of Hakodate

Mt Esan This is an active volcano (618 metres) with steaming vents at the sum-mit and an oval crater. It can be climbed in about an hour, and access to the base takes about 2¼ hours by bus from Hak-odate.

North from Hakodate

The view from either the train or road (Route 5) leaving Hakodate is typical of the valley scenery anywhere in Hok-kaido — broad rolling farm land inter-spersed with numerous towns. After 25 km or so, road and rail pass through a tunnel and the scenery changes abruptly. One is suddenly confronted with the very scenic lake Konuma, which reflects the squat volcano Komagatake. This is the entrance to Onuma Kokuritsukoen (National Park), a very pleasant place

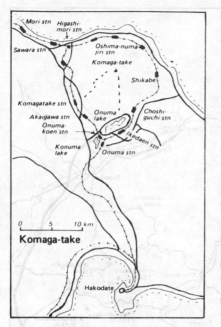

Komaga-take

to spend a day or two. Travellers arriving at Hakodate might consider making their way here for the first night in Hokkaido instead of Hakodate.

Koma Visible for the next 20 km or so, Koma consists of three peaks (Sahara, Kengamine and Sumidamori). It is an ugly brown ulcer on the green countryside, but is nevertheless very scenic. Originally conical, explosions have blasted the top off, leaving an elongated flat and sloping top.

Mt Higure As well as the view over Lake Konuma, the best lookout is considered to be Konuma Hill, and another is the top of Mt Higure (313 metres). It is an easy walk to the top, where one finds three smaller craters within the large horseshoe-shaped outer rim (which is two km east-west and 1.5 km north-south, sloping towards the sea). Any of the three youth hostels in the area will

have information on the best routes. It is also possible to circle the mountain by train; from the sea side, one can see distant Mt Yotei across the bay (weather permitting).

HAKODATE TO OSHAMAMBE
As Komagatake falls behind, the road and railway run parallel to the shore of Uchiura Bay for the next 70 km or so to a point slightly beyond Oshamambe. They are seldom far from the water, and travellers with the time to stop will find beachcombing in this area probably the best in Japan because the bay seems to act as a collection point for anything floating in the area. Stop anywhere distant from habitation, and the beach is almost sure to be littered with glass fishing floats that have been washed ashore. I stopped at random three times, and each time found more than 20 floats within half a kilometre of the starting point; carrying them all became a problem! It appears that they are replenished regularly, because a beach picked over on the way north had another 25 or so by the time of the return trip just a month later. Their origin is a mystery — fishermen in Hokkaido use plastic floats in the small sizes. The glass floats are all hand-made.

The road passes through many fishing villages; draped everywhere are fishing nets, with fishermen making repairs. On flat areas you can often see large pieces of kombu, an edible seaweed, laid out to dry.

OSHAMAMBE TO SAPPORO
There are two suggested routes between these two cities. One follows the railway and Route 5 inland in a loop northward, while the other continues around the bay, then cuts inland and touches on the Lake Toya-ko area before continuing through mountainous terrain to Sapporo. The first passes mostly through river valleys and, near Sapporo, a dismal succession of unappealing towns, but it

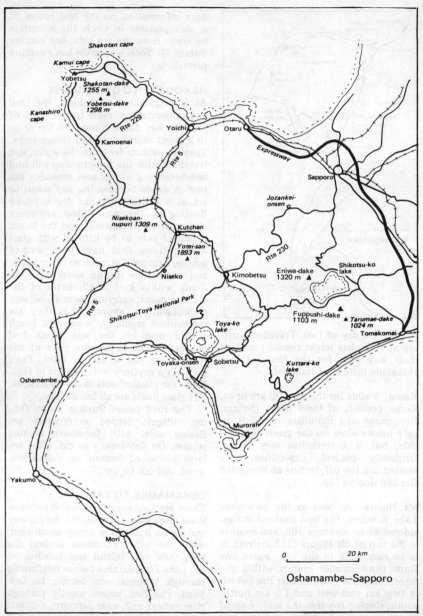

Oshamambe—Sapporo

0   20 km

offers the option of a looping sidetrip through Shakotan Hanto (peninsula). The second route passes through much more attractive scenery for most of its length.

The traveller who has adequate time, and who plans to circle back to the Toya-ko area, can combine the best of both these routes by taking the first to Yoichi, circling the Shakotan Peninsula to Iwanai, then cutting over to Kutchan and Kimobetsu, and carrying on from there by the second route to Sapporo.

Oshamambe to Kutchan

Both road and rail run parallel through this succession of river-valley farmland. Between Niseko and Kutchan it skirts Mt Yotei, an impressive conical volcano (1893 metres), now extinct. The top is mostly lava-covered, but the lower sections are pleasantly wooded. Climbing Mt Yotei is popular with the Japanese, and it is not particularly difficult. (Most 'mountain climbing' in Japan is simply a matter of putting one foot in front of the other for a long enough period.) One popular route is via Hirafu station by bus to Lake Nangetsu-ko from where one begins the climb. The walk up takes about four hours, plus an hour at the top to walk around the three cauldrons. For up-to-date information try the Niseko Youth Hostel (in Kutchan).

Mt Nisekoan-Nupuri (1309 metres), also near Kutchan, is rated as one of the four best ski areas in Hokkaido. There are nearby onsen for relaxing in afterward. (Kombu-onsen is noted for its autumn leaves.)

Kutchan to Yoichi

Yoichi is best regarded as the gateway to the Shakotan Peninsula. The town has an aquarium, and offers tours of the Nikka Distillery (near Yoichi Station: Monday to Saturday).

Shakotan Peninsula

The Shakotan Peninsula is noted for its rugged scenery — cliffs rising out of the sea as high as 250 metres, and the peaks of two mountains, Yobetsu (1298 metres) and Shakotan (1255 metres). Two capes mark the tip of the peninsula, Kamui and Shakotan; the former is noted for a huge rock rising abruptly about 40 metres from the sea. A road goes only partway around the tip of the peninsula, to Yobetsu; from there a boat goes around to Kamoenai, which is linked by bus with Iwanai. From Iwanai one can return to Yoichi, thus completing a circle, or go to Kutchan, Kinobetsu and other destinations.

Yoichi to Sapporo

The short distance between these two cities includes the best sand beach in Hokkaido (at Ranshima) as well as shorter stretches of beach at irregular intervals. There are several traces of prehistoric dwellers in the area. Oshoro Stone Circle is a rough circle of large stones about one metre tall; it is located on Ranshima-Kawa river, south-east of Ranshima station. Other indications of settlement are to be found in the area, such as traces of a dwelling, pottery, tools, Oyachi Shell Mound, a fort and a cave with over 200 pictographs on the walls (both in the Fugoppe area, estimated to be about 1500 years old).

Mt Tengu, three km south-west of Otaru station offers good skiing.

As noted earlier, Otaru is a ferry port with services to and from Niigata, Suruga and Maizuru. Also there is an overnight boat from Otaru to Rishiri Island off the far north coast of Hokkaido. More details on that are given later.

To Sapporo via Lake Toya-ko

This route continues around the shores of Uchiura Bay, then turns inland to Lake Toya-ko and continues through

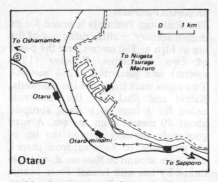

Otaru

To Oshamambe

Otaru

Otaru minami

To Niigata
Tsuruga
Maizuro

To Sapporo

0   1 km

highland scenery to Sapporo. It is by far the more scenic route, and is recommended for travellers in a hurry or for those who will be going in this direction only once. From Toya station (on the bay) there is a regular bus service to Toya-ko onsen on Lake Toya-ko. (The many attractions of the Toya-ko area are described in detail in the section on Shikotsu-Toya National Park, because this area logically fits in with Noboribetsu and Lake Shikotsu-ko.)

From Toya-ko, Route 230 climbs to a plateau, passing areas of forest land with broken-top trees, smashed by rock ejected in the 1977 eruption of Usu-san. As the road climbs beside the lake, one gets a superb view of Nakajima, a cluster of small volcanic islands poking up in the middle of Shikotsuko (Nakajima means middle island(s)). Other points of interest are Uzu-san, probably steaming profusely, and Showa Shinzan. Once on the plateau, the road leaves the lake, and the view of Yotei-san begins to dominate the landscape. From there to Sapporo the road passes through a very pretty mountain and farming area, with few built up areas.

The road passes through Jozankei-onsen, one of the best known spas in Japan. Previous notes on Japanese onsen apply equally here, and mixed bathing, formerly the custom here, has gone the way of the auk. At best it is worth a walk around the town; autumn is the best time for such a tour for the leaves are beautiful.

SAPPORO

A rarity among Japanese cities, Sapporo is laid out with streets at right angles, and has an address system that makes sense to foreigners. (This is true for many other cities in Hokkaido.) The reason for this is that Sapporo was founded only in 1869 when the Kaitakushi (Commissioner of Colonization) was stationed there to establish the city as the capital of Hokkaido. Like other 'instant cities', it lacks soul and the element of disorder that gives older cities their character. The somewhat sterile atmosphere is offset partly by many parks and gardens, and foreigners there find it a pleasant place to live, but as a tourist goal it is rather low-ranking. It is at its best when the bright lights of the Susukino district give it a magical touch. Those with a larger budget will find that it has the best night-life north of Tokyo, with more than 3500 bars and cabarets.

The main street, O-dori is famed for its great width (105 metres), but this is a deceptive statistic because most of the space is occupied by a park-like boulevard. This is a popular place in summer when visitors sit around, usually huddled under the inadequate number of trees. (Why do planners love huge open spaces which become intolerably hot under the summer sun? This is a query for many countries, not just for Sapporo.) At the east end of the boulevard is the TV tower (147 metres) which gives a good view over the entire city.

Getting There & Getting Around

In addition to the JNR and road connections, Sapporo is easily reached by air from other parts of Japan. The actual airport is at Chitose, about an hour away by bus. (The JNR bus ter-

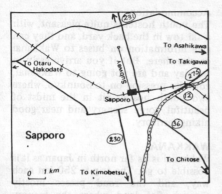

Sapporo

To Asahikawa

To Takigawa

To Otaru
Hakodate

Sapporo

To Chitose

To Kimobetsu

0   1 km

Museums

A number of museums are located in the gardens, the best-known being the Batchelor Museum of Ainu artefacts (named after an English minister who lived in Sapporo for 40 years). The house was moved to its present location after his death, and displays his collection of items of daily use. The style of the display is very old and obviously hasn't been touched in years, but the collection is good and worth seeing (if one is interested in the way of life of these non-Japanese peoples). Most labels are in Japanese only, unfortunately. To get to the museums, one must first pay admittance to the garden, and each of the buildings has a separate fee. One of the buildings has only a tatty collection of stuffed animals and birds of Hokkaido; to be sure of seeing only the Ainu museum section, ask, 'Kore wa Batchelor no Ainu hakubutsukan des'ka?' (The animals include the collection of Blakiston, another Englishman who noted the difference in distribution of animal and plant life between Honshu and Hokkaido.)

minal is beside the station.) The city of Tomakomai is only a short distance beyond Chitose, and it is the port of entry of ferries connecting with Tokyo, Sendai and Hachinohe in Honshu.

Sapporo has the nicest subway in Japan. Like those in Paris and Montreal, it runs on rubber tyres and so is quiet. Stations are marked in romaji at the station, but next and last stations are labelled only in Japanese.

Accommodation

There are three youth hostels in the Sapporo area. By far the most convenient to reach is the one near the station.

Information

The first move is to pick up a map from the tourist information centre in the station. They have a good one showing the points of interest and subway lines, and the text gives enough information for most travellers. The JNTO map of Japan also has an adequate Sapporo map on the back.

The Botanical Garden

The Botanical Garden has about 5000 species of plants from Hokkaido and the rest of the world. It is a pleasant place for a picnic or strolling.

Other attractions

The Clock Tower Building This is the only Russian-style structure left in Hokkaido, the clock of which has been a Sapporo landmark since 1881.

Maruyama Park and Maruyama Natural Forest Remnants of natural forest that provide recreation grounds and ski slopes in winter.

Mt Moiwa This provides a lookout over the city. It is accessible by cable car from near Ropeway Iriguchi Mae subway station.

Festivals

Sapporo is probably best known for its Snow Festival, the first weekend of

February, when O-dori boulevard is built up with huge ice sculptures of people, famous buildings and mythological figures.

Shopping

The main shopping area is Tanuki-koji (Badger Alley), an eight-block long arcade. Also well known is the underground shopping arcade that stretches from the TV tower under the boulevard and then turns to run to Susukino. It reflects the cold winter climate.

ASAHIKAWA

Asahikawa is a city at a decision crossroad: from it you can make a sidetrip north to Wakkanai, or proceed east to the major attractions of that area.

In the Chikabumi district of the city is the Ainu Kinenken (memorial hall), combining a reasonably good museum with a large number of souvenir stands that sell Ainu handcrafts, mostly identical wooden bears and statuettes of Ainu people. Many Ainu live in the area. One or two people, often old, may be dressed in traditional costume and delegated to satisfy tourists' cameras. Dances are performed (when a tour bus turns up). If you are going to Noboribetsu, Akan or Shiraoi, it is not worth seeking out Chikabumi.

Accommodation

The youth hostel is quite pleasant, with a ski tow in the back yard, and they can give information on buses to Wakkanai or elsewhere. But if you arrive early in the day and are not going to Wakkanai, consider pressing on to Sounkyo, where two youth hostels sit in the midst of beautiful gorge scenery and near good hiking territory.

WAKKANAI

Wakkanai is as far north in Japan as it is possible to go. The trip is 250 km each way, and the road passes mostly through flat land where the scenery consists mainly of spreading farms, barns and silos, and possibly even a farmer on horseback (he would be doing it for recreation — modern farming machinery is the rule here).

Wakkanai is reminiscent of Reykjavik in Iceland. The houses are low, with brightly coloured roofs in red, green and blue. The landscape in the area around Wakkanai is quite different from that of most of Japan — it is windswept, with low scrub and few trees along the coast. In late summer the grass is a picturesque golden colour, and you have a feeling of splendid isolation obtainable in few places in Japan. Those who like the romance of the Hebrides will enjoy the atmosphere of the coast near Wakkanai, especially to the north and west around Cape Noshappu-misaki. In late summer, the light has a particular 'northern' quality, giving a characteristic mood and atmosphere. The main industry of the district is fishing, and that, too, gives a distinctive atmosphere.

RISHIRI & REBUN ISLANDS

A very popular excursion with the Japanese is the boat trip from Wakkanai to the islands of Rishiri and Rebun. Although close together, the two islands have a totally different history. Rebun has been there for millions of years, and was formed by an upthrust of the earth's crust. Rishiri, on the other hand, is a 'youngster' only a few hundred thousand years old, formed when a submarine volcano built itself above the ocean surface. The picturesque cone of Rishiri-san (1719 metres), now gullied by eons of rain, remains as a reminder of the eruption. The attraction of the islands is their unspoiled nature — the scenery, seabirds, wildflowers in profusion and the magnificent isolation.

A road runs around nearly-circular Rishiri, and bus transport is available. 'Hiking courses' (Japanese term) are set out and connect the major points of interest around the island. Scenic spots include the view of Rishiri-san over the small lakes Hime-numa and Otadomari-numa, and many seascapes and capes that jut into the sea.

Rebun is very low, but nonetheless offers scenic views near Nishi-Uedomani, the view of Tadoshima Island from Cape Sukoton-misaki, and the towering rock Jizo-iwa.

Getting Around
Roads and transport facilities are not overly developed on either island, but they are adquate. Hiking is enjoyable and, since the islands are small, can be used for much sightseeing. On Rebun, one can take the bus one way and hike back in one day. There are almost sure to be Japanese young people doing this, and they usually are happy to have an extra person tag along. Many will be camping.

Getting There
Access from Wakkanai is by Higashi Nihonkai ferry; two boats a day go to Oshidomari (Rishiri) each way, likewise for Kafuka (Rebun), and there is one a day to Funadomari (Rebun). Other ferries of the same line link Kafuka,

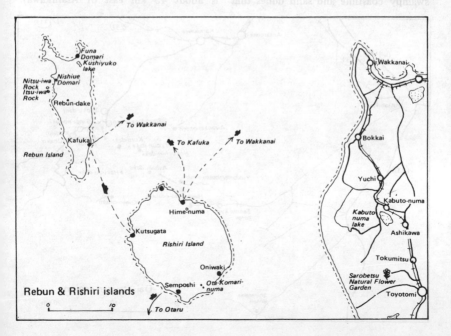

Rebun & Rishiri islands

Kutsugata and Oshidomari. There is also an overnight boat between Rishiri and Otaru (near Sapporo), which might be of interest to those who wish to see the northern islands and the tip of Hokkaido, but don't relish the return trip by land from Asahikawa, since it is not the most exciting for scenery.

Further information on the boat connections is available at the TIC in Tokyo or at the information centre at Sapporo station.

Accommodation

There are three youth hostels on Rebun, two on Rishiri. Rishiri Choritsu Youth Hostel is reported to be not overly clean.

National Park

The two islands of Rebun and Rishiri are combined with a part of the mainland to form Rishiri-Rebun-Sarobetsu National Park. Sarobetsu is an area of swampy coastline and sand dunes that

is known for the beauty of its wild-flowers. It can be reached by bus from Wakkanai to Bokkai, or by train to Bokkai (the northernmost point of entry), or to Toyotomi, from where a bus is available (through the middle of the park) to Wakasakanai. The most important part is Sarobetsu Gensai-kaen (Natural Flower Garden); it is about 15 minutes from Toyotomi station. Forget it in the spring; the area floods annually.

DAISETSUZAN NATIONAL PARK

Daisetsuzan Kokuritsu-koen is one of the best-known scenic areas in Hokkaido and would rank just behind Akan and Shikotsu-Toya parks as an attraction. For those who enjoy pleasant hiking it is superb, and it is very popular among the Japanese for this reason. The entrance to the park is 16 km east of Kamikawa on Route 39 (Kamikawa is about 45 km east of Asahikawa).

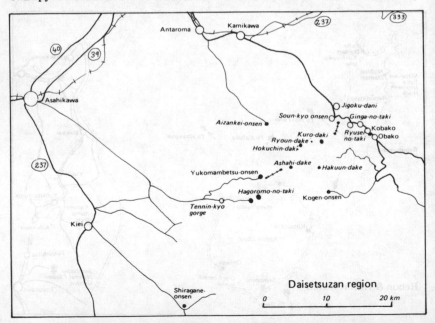

Daisetsuzan region

From Kamikawa ('upper river') onward, one gets occasional glimpses to the right of a group of volcanic peaks which are collectively known as Daisetsuzan. The most pronounced peak is the sloping cone of Asahi-dake ('Sunrise Mountain', 2290 metres), the highest peak in Hokkaido. Climbing and hiking are popular summer activities in this area, skiing in winter.

Soun-kyo gorge

The single most scenic attraction of the park is Soun-kyo (gorge) a canyon on the Ishikari river extending 24 km from the entrance to the park. Rock walls rise sharply on both sides of the road, and outcroppings of jagged rock jut from cliff faces. In the middle of the gorge is the hot-spring resort town of Soun-kyo-onsen, with a number of resort hotels and two youth hostels. It is a base for climbing and hiking through Daisetsuzan.

About three km farther along the gorge are two of the most picturesque waterfalls, Ryusei-no-taki and Ginga-no-taki, which are close to each other but separated by huge Tensho-iwa ('Heavenly Castle Rock').

Near the end of the gorge are Kobako and Obako ('small box' and 'large box'), closely enclosed sections of the gorge where you tend to feel as if at the bottom of a box. The walls of the 'boxes' and much of the gorge are columnar basalt, lava that cooled into large crystals. Australians from Melbourne will find the gorge like a hundred Hanging Rocks laid side by side. The way in which both were formed is similar.

Exploring Daisetsuzan

The area known as Daisetsuzan (Great Snow Mountain) consists of a number of volcanic peaks, all about 2000 metres high. They do not require scaling gear or great skill, but invite exploration for the terrain is easy to walk through,

being basically undulating plateau that fills in the area between the various peaks that make up the mountain. The view is one of small craters (some steaming), wildflowers, the crater of Daisetsuzan, and open spaces with no signs of civilization. A network of trails makes walking easy.

The best-known trail runs from Soun-kyo-onsen to Yokomambetsu-onsen; it can be walked in a day with little effort. From Soun-kyo-onsen, a cable car runs a good part of the way up the side of Kuro-dake ('Black Mountain', 1984 metres). From there, the path is easy to follow past Ryoun-dake (2125 metres), to the upper station of the Daisetsuzan Asahi-dake ropeway that leads down to Yukomambetsu-onsen. This resort has a nice youth hostel which offers a good view of Asahi-dake, as well as other accommodation.

Continuing on along the path without descending the ropeway leads to Hagoromo waterfall, Tennin-kyo-onsen, and Tennin-kyo gorge. Tennin-kyo ('Heavenly Maiden') gorge is similar to Soun-kyo, but its sides are less steep and the cliff faces have crumbled more. Hagoromo-no-taki, a beautiful waterfall, is located a few hundred metres from Tennin-kyo-onsen: it is a cascade of seven falls set in a high ravine that is studded here and there with trees. Tennin-kyo-onsen and Yukomambetsu-onsen are about four km apart. The road joining them passes through Tennin-kyo, and both onsen are linked to Asahikawa by bus.

There are many other trails across the plateau of Daisetsuzan (nicknamed 'the roof of Hokkaido'). A short one runs from Soun-kyo-onsen to Aizankei-onsen, while a slightly longer one goes to Kogen-onsen; both are shorter than the hike to Yukomambetsu/Tennin-kyo-onsen. A bus service is indicated to Kogen-onsen, but not to the former.

Further information is available locally, especially at youth hostels.

SOUN-KYO TO OBIHIRO

Route 273 runs south to Obihiro, and is mentioned only as a shortcut for those pressed for time who wish to circle back to Shikotsu-Toya National Park. Part of the road is rough gravel. The preferred alternative is to continue on toward Bihoro and the attractions of the Akan-ko — Kutcharo-ko — Mashuko area; the following brief section only details the route to that (and other nearby) areas.

SOUN-KYO TO SHIRETOKO PENINSULA

After leaving Soun-kyo, Route 39 continues eastward through Onneyu-onsen, Rubeshibe, Kitami and Bihoro. The fields around Kitami are planted with peppermint (claimed to be the world's best), and at Rubeshibe Youth Hostel there is a well-preserved steam engine of the type used in Hokkaido into the early 1970s. Otherwise there is little of interest along the way. Like many roads that pass through the valleys of Hokkaido, this one is simply a means of getting from place to place and must simply be endured.

Bihoro to Akan National Park

Those with a limited amount of time will head for Akan at once; it ranks with Shikotsuko-Toya National Park as one of the two most scenic and interesting travel destinations in Hokkaido. It is discussed in detail in a later section.

The most direct route would be Route 243, which goes to Teshikaga, more or less in the middle of the park. You could turn off it at Lake Kutcharoko. This gives an excellent view over the lake from Bihoro-toge (mountain pass). Another route is via Route 240 to the west entrance of National Park, but it would probably cause a considerable amount of backtracking.

Bihoro to Abashiri

Abashiri is a fishing port with some re-

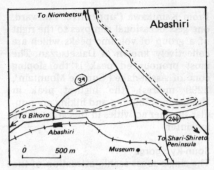

mains from the recent and prehistoric past. The Municipal Museum in Katsuraoka-koen (park), one km southeast of the station, has a good display of Ainu artefacts from the area, plus pottery and stone tools excavated at nearby Moyoro Shell Mound (north-east of the station on the left bank of the Abashiri river), relics of aboriginal dwellers who predated the Ainu.

Late in the summer of 1978, Daahennieni Gendaanu, one of about 30 Oroke people living in Hokkaido, opened a museum to keep alive the memory of his people, nomads who lived by herding reindeer. (There are still Oroke living on Sakhalin Island.) The Oroke word for the museum is Jakkadohuni; it may be known in Japanese as Oroke Kinenkan. It should be worth visiting.

North of Abashiri are two lagoons, Notoro and Saroma. In this area is shown (on the map in the TIC brochure on Northern Japan) the intriguing entry 'Coral Grass Gregarious Spot' but, alas!, there is no further explanation. (It might refer to an unusual red plant that grows on swampy ground; in September the fields are quite bright red.)

A word of advice: If the Abashiri Youth Hostel address continues to be Higashi 1-chome, Minami 5-jo, avoid it like the plague. It is dark, cramped, and has the most primitive and smelly toilet 'system' (located adjacent to the eating area) that can be imagined. Use the hostel at Gensei-kaen (next section), or go slightly further north or south to one of the others if possible.

Abashiri to Akan National Park

There are two suggested routes to follow: one is direct, while the other circles around the Shiretoko Peninsula. Both offer better scenery than the route back through Bihoro.

East of Abashiri along Route 244, the first attraction is Gensei-kaen (Natural Flower Garden). This is a strip of coastal sand dune that is heavily overgrown by wildflowers which bloom in late June and early July, and are the target for swarms of Japanese photographers. It begins at Kitahama and continues along the road for about 30 km to Shari.

Before Shari, about 25 km out of Abashiri, at Hokuto, the road turns off to Koshimizu and then on to Kawayu and Teshikaga. Kawayu is the centre of many of the attractions of Akan National Park.

Instead of turning off for Koshimizu, you can continue along Route 244 to Shari and beyond (on Route 334) to Utoro on the untamed Shiretoko Peninsula. Beyond Shari, one can look inland and see the jagged cone of Shari-dake (1545 metres), and later, the rounded outline of Kaibetsu-dake (1419 metres). Shari-dake is also visible along much of the length of the direct route.

SHIRETOKO PENINSULA

Shiretoko is an Ainu word meaning 'end of the Earth', and it lives up to its name. The end of the peninsula is a national park, the most 'primitive' in Japan. There is a small number of hiking trails, and roads go along both the north-west and south-east coasts, but not to the tip. A single road crosses it, from Utoro to Rausu.

From the middle to the tip there are three major mountains, Rausu-dake (1661 metres), Io-san (1563 metres) and Shiretoko-dake (1254 metres). At the base of the peninsula is Kaibetsu-dake, and between it and Rausu-dake is a smaller peak. Io-san is one of the most unusual volcanoes on earth, for when it erupts it emits pure sulphur. In its eruption of 1936 (the most recent), more than 15,000 tons of nearly pure sulphur poured out. The volcanoes (all but Io-san are extinct) are a continuation of the chain that extends through the Kuril chain to Alaska; on Hokkaido, this is the Chishima volcanic zone.

It is almost impossible, however, to see the mountains while travelling along the road, which passes so close to the base of the hills that it has often been hacked out of the rock. The best way to see the beauty and splendour of the peninsula is by boat.

The cape is famous for its rugged cliffs that rise as much as 200 metres from the sea and stretch up to 10 km without a break. The cliffs are noted for their black and white stripes, layers of volcanic rock alternating with sedimentary rock. Time, wind and water have sculpted them into many fanciful shapes which resemble real objects and beings.

Also visible from the boat around the tip, along the shore, are huts used by fishermen and gatherers of kombu (giant kelp, a delicacy) during the summer, as well as small rivers that tumble over cliffs into the sea.

Hot springs There are several places along the shores where hot-spring waters collect in pools near the water's edge, making natural rotemburo (open-air pools). One is located near Kamuiwakka-no-taki waterfall. These are popular, especially with young vacationers. There's no charge; just take your clothes off and hop in.

Walks One place that rewards hiking is

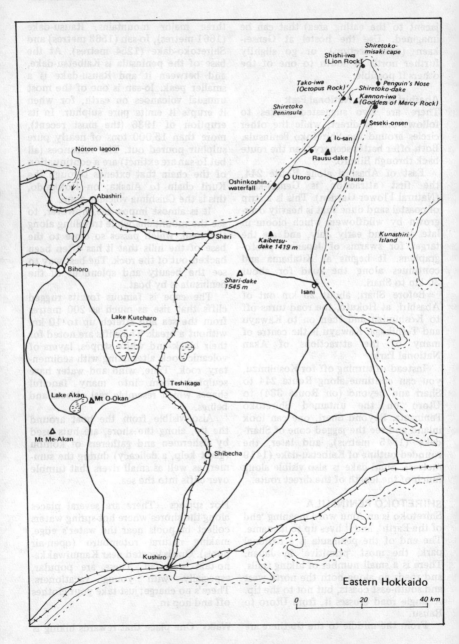

Eastern Hokkaido

0   20   40 km

the Shiretoko-Go-ko (five lakes) area near Iwaobetsu. Another destination is Io-san and its two large craters and fuming vents. The four-hour hike begins near Kamuiwakka waterfall. Visible on the sea-bottom near here is yellow sulphur from the 1936 eruption. Information on other trails can be obtained locally; youth hostels are usually invaluable for such help.

Accommodation

There are five hostels on the peninsula, three near Otoru (Utoro, Utoro-onsen, and Iwaobetsu), and two near Rausu. There is also one each near the north and south bases of the peninsula (Shibetsu and Shari — the former has a Genghis Khan supper similar to that described later for the Shikotsu-ko hostel).

Getting There

From May to September, two boats a day go in each direction around the tip of the peninsula, between Utoro and Rausu. In recent years, such boats have left at 6.15 am and 10.45 am, but make inquiries on the spot to check if the schedule has changed. There are also return boat excursions from Utoro just to Shiretoko-misaki. (This takes only 90 minutes, instead of the four hours or so of the complete trip around the tip.)

Kunashiri Island

This, along with the islands of Etorofu, Shikotan, and the Habomai group, was seized by the USSR two weeks after the end of World War II. This was contrary to the Yalta Agreement, and there is no legal basis for the occupation because the islands had always been indisputably part of Japanese territory. The issue is very much alive in Hokkaido, and you can see numerous signs that show the map of Hokkaido and the occupied islands, a reminder of the Soviet action. Residents of the peninsula

would like to have access to the rich fishing grounds around the islands, but this is not likely to eventuate, because the Soviets have been increasing their presence there in recent years. Kunashiri can be seen from a boat, or from parts of the south-east coast of the peninsula.

AKAN NATIONAL PARK

This area is one of the two major scenic regions of Hokkaido. The attractions can be divided into two areas, those centred around Kutcharo-ko (lake) and those around Akan-kohan.

KUTCHARO-KO AREA

The attractions of this area are remnants of a gigantic volcanic crater, the bounds of which are now difficult to discern (the present body of water is only a small part of the former huge lake). In subsequent geological eras, the level of land has changed, and new, smaller, volcanoes have popped up. A good centre of operations is Kawayu railway station.

Kawayu-onsen

This is a typical hot-spring resort, full of hotels (most rather costly), and the streets lined with souvenir shops, most of which have captive bear cubs or Ainu wood carvers as the attraction. There is a youth hostel in the town, which is three km from Kawayu station.

Kutcharo-ko

This was originally a caldera lake, but its circular shape has been changed beyond recognition by the intrusion of later volcanoes. The water is a scenic and unusual green due to the very high mineral content, but the nearby terrain is almost at the same level so the colour is not so apparent. The best view can be obtained from high ground like Bihoro-toge (pass) on the road from Bihoro. The lake is a pleasant place to relax, and the hostel on its shore uses the baths of the

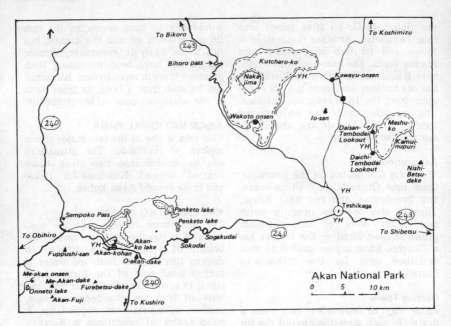

Akan National Park

0   5   10 km

neighbouring hotel, so one has the advantages of a visit to a resort without the painful cost. The bath is quite memorable, with continually overflowing hot water in a pool four metres square and about knee-deep; smooth pebbles on the bottom give an unusual feeling underfoot. Large windows give a view out over the lake toward Mokoto-san (1000 metres). On my first visit to this hotel in 1970, hostellers were accommodated in the resort hotel itself, but it is not sure if travellers late in the season still get this treatment.

Wakoto-hanto

A small bump on the map at the south end of the lake indicates this mini-peninsula, little higher than water level. Hot-spring water rises from below and feeds open-air baths at Wakoto-onsen; at Sunayu it warms the sand of the beach (Sunayu means 'hot sand'). There is a camping ground on the peninsula,

as well as others along the shore. There may be performances of Ainu dances at Sunayu during the summer.

Mashu-ko

Nearby is the remarkable and beautiful lake Mashu-ko. Situated partway up the side of a sprawling mountain, its water was clear to a depth of 34.8 metres in 1978 (41.6 metres in 1911). It is, however, extremely difficult and dangerous to try to reach the water's edge. Like many other calderas, the walls of the old volcano that encloses it rise very steeply, giving negligible foothold. It is better to be content admiring its incredible blue colour from the two observatories, the one nearer the town of Teshikaga (Dai-ichi-Tembodai) gives the better view, showing part of the crater in the peak of Kamuinupuri on the far side of the lake. Both observatories (the other is called Dai-san Tembodai) give a good view of the entire lake, which appears to fill two separate craters that have linked. On a sunny day, when the blue colour is most intense, the view is quite unforgetable, one of the most memorable in Japan. Dain-san Tempodai is 14 km from Kawayu station; the other is a little farther on. There is a regular bus service in the area linking Kawayu station to Teshikaga station via Mashuko. Depending on the month, there are five to eight buses a day. Hitching should present no problem, and would get around the problem of inflexible bus schedules.

Io-san

This active volcano emits volumes of steam that can be seen 10 km when arriving by road from Koshimizu. From two ravines in the side of the earth-brown mountain, sulphurous (smelly!) steam issues forth, gently wafting from some vents, violently jetting from others with a great roar. Around these holes, vivid yellow needles of sulphur have crystallized out of the steam. Io-san means 'sulphur mountain'.

For the ultimate in natural foods, you can buy eggs cooked by the heat of the earth in one of the little saucepan-size pools that boil endlessly; look for the old women near the base of the ravines.

AKAN-KO AREA

The area around Lake Akan (Akan-ko) is noted for scenic beauties, mountains, Ainu people, and a weed that acts like a submarine. Like Kutcharo, Akan-ko is located in the remnants of a huge volcanic crater, the shape of which has also been changed beyond recognition by subsidence, and the incursion of smaller, volcanic peaks. The size of Akan-ko was originally much greater, but the intrusion of O-Akan-dake broke it into the present Akan-ko and two smaller lakes, Panketo and Penketo. On the east shore is an area of bubbling

mud called Bokke — which describes the plurp sound of the bursting bubbles (to Japanese ears, at least).

Akan-kohan

The focal point of the lake is the hotspring resort town of Akan-kohan. In it are an Ainu kotan (village) where Ainu can be seen living their 'ordinary daily life'. As mentioned elsewhere, the Ainu have been completely absorbed culturally by the ethnic Japanese, and almost no one knows more than a few words of the original Ainu languagues. However, this is at least a chance to see what they look like and to obtain a small idea of the old ways. They may also be seen at shops in town, carving an endless succession of wooden bears.

Marimo weed

Another attraction is this curious weed. Not just any old garden-variety weed, mind you, but one that acts like a submarine, with the ability to rise and sink in the water. Marimo is actually an intertwined mass of hair-like green algae that have formed into spongy spheres up to 15 cm in diameter. Other species live in Lake Sakyo (in Aomori-ken) Lake Yamanaka near Mt Fuji, and in some lakes in Siberia, Switzerland and North America, but it is quite rare elsewhere. The Akan variety is the largest, and is considered the most attractive. In the past, so many people were taking marimo home as a souvenir that there was danger that they would be wiped out, but they are now under government protection.

All excursion boats on the lake stop at a small island on which a marimo sanctuary has been built, and visitors can see them lying on the bottom of concrete tanks, doing their thing. In Akankohan, there is a glass tank containing many marimo at the town information office (located beside the police station on the short street across the road from the Akan Kanko Hotel).

On 10 October each year there is a 'traditional' Ainu festival in honour of the marimo, which dates back at least beyond 1970. Supposedly it celebrates Ainu legends about the marimo, but publicity photos show Ainu elders carrying a type of tray used only in Shinto observations. Since Shinto is foreign to the original Ainu culture and worship, one may judge the genuineness of the festival. Still, it is a chance to see some Ainu and dances.

O-Akan & Me-Akan

The most prominent peaks in the vicinity of the lake are both easily climbed and offer beautiful views as a reward. Closer to the town is O-Akan-dake, the trail to which begins at O-Akan-onsen; ask for 'O-Akan Hiking Course'. The summit is 10.7 km from the onsen. Me-Akan-dake probably offers the more beautiful and unusual scenery from its summit, a wierd view of extinct and active volcanic cones, steam jets, and the overall impression of being on the moon. It can be climbed from either Akan-kohan-onsen or from Me-Akan-onsen, which is 20 km west of Akan-kohan. From the former the summit is 10.7 km, but from the latter is only 2.2 km.

Lookouts

There are two well-known scenic lookouts on the road (Route 241) between Teshikaga and Akan-kohan. Sogakudai ('Two Mountains Lookout') gives a good view of Me-Akan-dake and O-Akan-dake, while Sokadai ('Two Lakes Outlook') overlooks (need it be said?) two pretty lakes, Penketo and Panketo. The whole area is at its finest in autumn when the leaves turn into masses of reds, oranges and yellows.

Getting Around

The area is very popular with Japanese tourists, so there will be no trouble arranging transport to the various attractions.

Accommodation

There are three youth hostels near the lake, as well as others in the general area, plus many hotels of varying prices (tending toward the high, this being a resort town).

Getting There from Kushiro

Akan is readily accessible from Kushiro, due south on the coast. Routes 38 and 240 lead to Akan-kohan, and the JNR line leads to Teshikaga and Kawayu. Kushiro is of little interest as a tourist destination, but it is served twice weekly by a ferry direct to and from Tokyo, operated by Kinkai Yusen Ferry. The trip takes 33 hours and the cheapest fare is Y11,500.

The attractions of the largely industrial city include the sanctuary for rare red-crested white cranes at Tsuruoka (20 km west of Kushiro station). The number of resident cranes is small, but several hundred come to feed in the winter. The other attraction that the local authorities promote is Harutai-koen (park) with its lake and an Ainu 'village'. These would be best regarded as something to see while waiting for a train or boat connection.

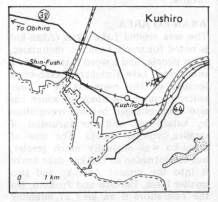

WEST FROM AKAN NATIONAL PARK

This route includes some of the prettiest countryside in Hokkaido, and leads to Tomakomai, a port for ferries to Honshu and gateway to Lake Shikotsu and Shikotsu-Toya National Park.

Akan to Tomakomai

The first destination along Route 241 is Obihiro, an unexceptional town with a nice youth hostel very close to the station; the staff rush out with banners to greet and send off hostellers. Beyond Obihiro, Route 38 leads to Tokachi-Shimizu; from there one branches onto Route 274 as far as Hidaka and then to Route 237 to Tomikawa on the coast. From Hidaka one has the option of the JNR line to Tomakomai.

The road from Tokachi-Shimizu to Hidaka (Nissho Highway) passes through almost total wilderness and offers many lovely views of the Hidaka mountains as the road snakes up and down and over crests, as well as glimpses of the green Saru river as one nears the coast. It is a contrast with most roads in Hokkaido, which follow along valley floors. About 15 km before Tomakomai is the town of Biratori, known for its large Ainu population, but it is similar

in appearance to any other Hokkaido town. From Tomikawa, it is another 45 km to Tomakomai.

TOMAKOMAI

This port and industrial city is the gateway to the attractions of nearby Shikotsu-Toya National Park. It is close to Chitose airport (which also serves Sapporo, 65 km away), and is the terminus for ferry services from Nagoya, Tokyo, Sendai and Hachinohe.

From Tomakomai ferry terminal, bus 41 runs to the station and vice versa; from there you can make bus and train connections to other parts of Hokkaido. The same bus goes to the ferry terminal, but service in infrequent, so a taxi may be necessary if you are rushing to catch a boat.

Sidetrip down the coast

At the bottom of the peninsula is Cape Erimo and Erimo Prefectural Park. The tip of the cape is noted for 60-metre cliffs that become a line of rocks and reefs protruding several km out into the ocean like a line of sentinals. The cape is desolate, swept clear of vegetation by

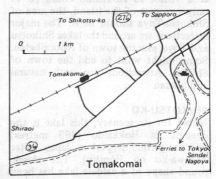

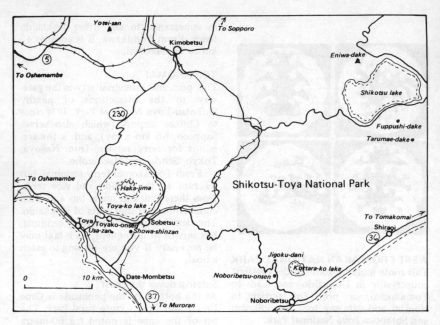

To Sopporo

Yotei-san

Kimobetsu

To Oshamambe

(5)

(230)

Eniwa-dake

Shikotsu lake

Fuppushi-dake

Tarumae-dake

To Oshamambe

Haka-jima

Toya-ko lake

Shikotsu-Toya National Park

Toya Toyako-onsen Sobetsu

Usa-zan Showa-shinzan

To Tomakomai

Shiraoi

0   10 km

Date-Mombetsu

(36)

Jigoku-dani

Kottara-ko lake

Noboribetsu-onsen

(37)

To Muroran

Noboribetsu

winds, and is usually blanketed by
thick fog in summer.

SHIKOTSU-TOYA NATIONAL PARK

If a visitor to Hokkaido could go to
only one part of the island, the area of
Shikotsu-Toya should be it. The major
attractions are around the lakes Shikotsu
and Toya, plus the town of Noboribetsu.
Some might want to add the town of
Shiraoi. Attractions are both natural
and human.

SHIKOTSU-KO

Noted for its scenery, this lake is the
deepest in Hokkaido (363 metres)
and the second-deepest in Japan (after
Tazawa-ko on Honshu). The classic
round shape of a caldera lake has been
intruded on by the cones of Mt Eniwa-
dake (1320 metres) on one side and
Mt Fuppushi-dake (1103 metres) on
the opposite shore. The altitude of
the lake itself is 248 metres. Boat

cruises are available on the lake from a
point near the bus terminal. Swimmers
should take note that the bottom slopes
gently for the first 10 or so metres from
shore, then plummets sharply to a maximum depth of 363 metres.

Eniwa-dake   The low cone of this
volcano is the most prominent feature
of the lakeshore. It is easily climbed and
makes a good day's excursion. The starting point is Poropinai, accessible by a
toll road along the lake (beginning near
the bus terminal) or by boat from the
same place in Shikotsu-kohan. The
climb to the crater top takes about
three hours and gives a view as far as
Sapporo (on a clear day), as well as
Lake Okotampeko on the far side and
the other mountains around the lake.

Fuppushi-dake   The outline of this low
mountain is visible across the lake from
Shikotsu-kohan.

Shikotsu-ko lake

Tarumae-dake Behind Fuppushi is this unusual volcano. In its eruption of 1909, a dome of lava 450 metres across and 100 metres high formed in the central crater. It varies in its activities these days: sometimes it shows few signs of life, but much of the time it sends plumes of steam into the sky, and it erupted in February 1979 and May 1978. The rim of the crater can be reached by a 40-minute walk after a bus ride from the town of Morrapu (partway around the lake from Shikotsu-kohan). There may also be service directly from Shikotsu-kohan.

Accommodation
The Shikotsu-ko YH is very close to the bus terminal, as are numbers of more expensive resort hotels. The hostel is pleasant, and is noteworthy for its evening meal which is vastly superior to the usual hostel fare: it is Genghis Khan, a filling and tasty Hokkaido specialty of mutton and vegetables cooked at the table on special domed burners. This is a very inexpensive way to try the dish; in summer it is prepared on tables outdoors under a row of tall pines, and the mood is one of a giant

party. The hostel is famous throughout Japan among members for this, and for its later entertainment when the dynamic housemother leads everyone in dancing.

Getting There
Shikotsu-ko is easily accessible from Tomakomai and Chitose; in both cases buses run from the railway station. The trip takes less than an hour.

TOYA-KO AREA
The remaining area of interest in the Shikotsu-Toya National Park is found around Lake Toya. In addition to the beauty of the lake and its central islands, there is much evidence of past and on-going volcanic activity. Toya-ko lake is another circular caldera, much larger than Kuttaro-ko. In its centre are the islets that collectively comprise Nakajima (middle island); they are remains of the volcano whose crater forms the basin of the lake.

Accommodation
The shore of the lake has been heavily built up with tourist hotels, and it is a popular summer retreat from the heat of Honshu. Swimming and boating (commercial cruises available) are popular activities. The town of Toya-ko-onsen is the largest centre on the lake, and has several deluxe resort hotels. The two youth hostels are about four km out of town on the road toward Sobetso,

Getting There
Toyako-onsen is linked eight times a day by bus with Muroran and Noboribetsu-onsen, the latter by a scenic mountain pass. The JNR station on the coast is called Toya, but the town of Toya is on the lake, several km inland and you have to take a bus from the station. (Toya town and Toyako-onsen are on opposite sides of the lake)

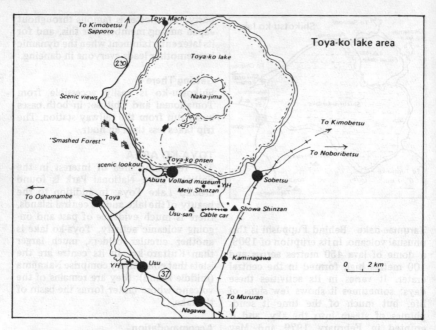

Toya-ko lake area

To Kimobetsu
Sapporo
Toya Machi

(230)

Toya-ko lake

Scenic views

Naka-jima

To Kimobetsu

"Smashed Forest"

To Noboribetsu

scenic lookout

Toya-ko onsen

Abuta Volland museum
Meiji Shinzan
HY
Sobetsu

To Oshamambe
Toya

Showa Shinzan
Usu-san
Cable car

0   2 km

Kaminagawa

HY
Usu

(37)

To Mururan

Nagawa

and are only a few hundred metres apart.

Getting Around

There is a regular bus service around the
lake and surrounding area. Bicycles can
be rented near the bus station and at
Toya Kanko-kan Youth Hostel, and are
a very convenient means of getting
around.

Lookouts

An excellent view of the lake, Toya-ko-
onsen and Usu-zan can be had from the
lookout beside the road to the coast
(Abuta). From the T-junction near the
bus station and police station, it is 1.6
km up the hill.

Other good views can be found by
following the road clockwise around the
lake (Route 230 to Kimobetsu). From
the same T-junction, the road goes at
lake-level for a short distancce before
beginning to climb to a broad plateau.
Just over six km up the hill (one km

above the entrance to the Toya Country
Club) there is an excellent view over
the lake. On the plateau there are other
good views of the lake and its islands,
and visible inland is the tall cone of Mt
Yotei. Beyond the red barn-like
restaurant/bus stop, the road goes
inland and the lake is lost to sight.

There is a road down to Toya town
(at lake-level) a little farther on, and
from there is a road circling the lake,
back to the youth hostels and hotels.
However, the road down is loose gravel
and risky on a bike, and the view from
the lower road is rather so-so.

Showa Shinzan

'New Mountain of the Showa Era' is
one of the most remarkable pieces of

A *Interior of an old farmhouse at
Nihon Minka-en, Kawasaki*
B *Old lady and one of the character-
istic walls of Kurashiki*

rock on Earth. On 28 December 1943, earthquakes hit the area around Toya-ko. Near Sobetsu, to the south-east of the lake, the formerly flat farmland begain to rise and formed a hill nearly 25 metres high during the next two months. Within the hill, a bulge formed and slowly moved northward. Between late June and late October, many volcanic eruptions took place, and seven craters formed around the hill, which continued to grow. By November, the hill had reached a diameter of 800 metres, and the climax began when a tower of hardened lava started to rise through the crust of the earth. By September 1945, it had reached an altitude of 408 metres above sea-level, a respectable 150 to 200 metres above the surrounding terrain. There it sits today, a chunk of colourful yellows and browns, bare of vegetation and issuing steam from many crevices.

At the base of Showa-Shinzan is a museum relating to the volcano, and the Ainu Memorial Hall (Ainu Kinen-kan), which contains some memorabilia of the native peoples. Also here is the base station of a cable car that used to go to the top of neighbouring Usu-san. As a result of the 1977 eruption of that volcano, however, service was suspended until things settled down. On the road that leads to Showa Shinzan from the lake, where it skirts the east side of Usu-san, the surface has subsided in some places while the edge has been raised more than half a metre in others. It seems that Usu-san is rising at a rate of 15-30 cm each year.

A friend once said that he feels a sort of affection for sharks, tidal waves and volcanoes, for they remind man just how powerless he is against nature. A realization of the immense forces at

work lifting this huge chunk of rock should do the job of pushing any ego back into place. The rock showing above the surface weighs at least 100 million tons!

The road to the 'instant mountain' turns off the Sobetsu highway about four km out of Toyako-onsen, just beyond the youth hostels. There are buses from Toyako-onsen to Showa Shinzan.

Usu-san

This volcanic mountain overlooking the town of Toyako-onsen is the mother of all recent geological disturbances south of Lake Toya, and is known for its frequent eruptions. Showa Shinzan is one of its offspring; another was Meiji Shinzan in 1910, a much less spectacular production. To maintain its reputation, Usu erupted in August 1977, and for more than a year afterward there were a dozen or so perceptible earthquakes (of short duration), plus about 200 a day measurable by seismograph. This was its most spectacular eruption, as photos on sale around Toyako-onsen clearly show. Most subsequent activity has been confined to blowing out great volumes of steam and gas. An immense cloud of black ash and soot was blown about 10,000 metres skyward, and 30 cm of fine ash fell on Toyako-onsen, causing some buildings to collapse, burying crops, forcing the evacuation of the populace, and causing a giant headache for those who had to clean up the mess. Chunks of rock hurled out during the eruption damaged much of the forest land near the town, and broken tree tops and stripped branches along the roadsides remain as silent witnesses to the event.

In late July 1978 Usu again erupted, sending another cloud of ash and dust high into the air, to the delight of visitors (including myself), and the annoyance of the townspeople who had to clean up the thick layer of fine dust

A *Interior of Tagata-jinja shrine, typical of any large Shinto shrine*
B *An Ainu elder, Noboribetsu*
C *Shinto priest at Meiji-jingu shrine*

that settled on Toyako-onsen. At that time, supposedly more than 80 per cent of the volcanic energy had been dissipated, so it is unlikely that activities will be as spectacular in the future.

Prior to the eruption there were hiking trails around the rim of the summit, and there were two cones, O-Usu ('Great Usu', 725 metres), and Ko-Usu ('Lesser Usu', 611 metres), plus a small lake. The recent eruptions will probably have changed the topography and possibly the altitudes in the area. The land at the north and east feet of the mountain has been rising noticeably. For example, at Toya-Kanko-kan Youth Hostel all the window frames and doorways have been pushed out of square, the baths are no longer level, walls are cracked, and parts of the building have lifted relative to others. Up the hill, a hospital stands in ruins and the ground has risen a metre in places.

Museum
Near the bus station is a newly opened museum, the Abuta Volcano Science Museum (but ask for Abuta Kazan Kagaku-kan), identifiable by a small wooden fishing boat in the car park in front, visible as you descend the hill from Toya station on the coast. This museum should not be missed. It has videotapes of the 1977 eruption and the aftermath, a car damaged by ejected rock, a seismograph recording earth tremors as they happen and, most interesting of all, a projection room with a model of the volcano complete with 'pillar of smoke'. To the accompaniment of actual recordings of the eruption, 'lightning' flashes through the plume and the floor shakes with terrifying realism, simulating the earth tremors and explosions that actually took place. The museum also has an excellent display of relics from the area, and an exhibit of items used until recent times by people in their daily work.

NOBORIBETSU-ONSEN
If a foreign visitor were to sample only one hot-spring resort in Japan, this would be a good choice. It is one of the few that a foreigner can enjoy fully, for onsen are usually sampled only by staying at a hotel and taking delight in purely Japanese things (which may be difficult to understand, appreciate, or learn in time). In Noboribetsu, however, the famous baths are open to the general public, and are among the most magnificent and largest in Japan. There are also other attractions in and around the town to add to its interest.

The town is a few km inland from the coastal town (and railway station) of Noboribetsu-shi. It is built on the slope of a hill, with the bus stations partway up. Akashiya-so Youth Hostel is a short distance down the hill from them; other youth hostels are located in the town.

Going up the hill, you pass numerous hotels and streets lined with souvenir stalls, patronized by numbers of Japanese tourists, many dressed in the yukata of their hotels. The souvenir stands all sell wood carvings of bears and repres-

Noribetsu-onsen area

entations of Ainu people (some of fancifully beautiful maidens). The only glimpses of originality are a few anomalies like a Vishnu-on-Garuda, as seen everywhere in Bali, or a large and incongruous Polynesian-appearing figure (carved by a Japanese who read many books on folk-art). Some of the carvings are well done, and would be classed as sculpture if they were not all so nearly identical.

The Baths

Continuing up the hill, the road levels off, and where it branches to the left stands a large brown hotel. This is the Dai-ichi Takimoto Hotel, famous for its enormous bath room, and one experience that a visitor should not miss.

The entrance, for non-guests of the hotel, is to the left of the hotel. After undressing, you enter the bath room (take your own towel). The first surprise is the immense size of the cavernous room, at least 100 metres long and half that in width. There are nearly 20 large pools, plus a small number in the women-only section, all of differing size and shape, and containing water of different mineral content and temperature. At the far end is a shallow wading pool that has the only cool water in the place — it is good to know about!

There are numerous fonts where you can sit and wash before taking the waters. The little squirrels gush drinking water; drink frequently to avoid exhaustion from dehydration.

The second big surprise is that there are people of both sexes in the pools. This is one of the few places in Japan where the custom of konyoku (mixed bathing) still prevails.

The correct decorum is to hold your towel in front to cover the 'nether regions'. It is not polite to stare, although some Japanese men were sitting around the women-only section peering intently; that is definitely Not

Good Form. It also shows the development of the Peeping Tom in Japan, something quite unknown when the human body was no mystery. It is advisable to go with a friend mainly because it becomes boring after a while with no one to talk to, despite the sheer physical pleasure of the baths. Western women would be well advised to go in with a western man to establish 'ownership' — in that way no peepers will cluster around their pool as *might* happen to women alone.

But by all means go! — the American girl who went with me thought it one of the most pleasurable experiences of her visit to Japan. The bath closes to non-guests at 5 pm (it should be possible to stay on after that time, and it seems possible to arrange to go in the evening by approaching the front desk.)

Jigokudani

Beyond the baths, a further 150 metres or so up the hill, is the unusual and beautiful Jigokudani (Valley of Hell), so named for the evil smell and noise of the steam and boiling water that pours forth from the earth. The colourful valley is a ravine with small hills and gullies; the yellow earth has been stained in bands and patches by the minerals that have been deposited by the water over the centuries. The valley is the source of the hot water used in the baths of the town, and different pools have different kinds of water. At maximum flow, it can exceed 75,000 litres per minute, a householder's dream.

The path through the valley (no admittance charge!) begins above the car park at the end of the main street through the town. The dangerous areas are roped off: if you broke through the crust, you could be scalded to death before being rescued. Pleasant thought! The sense of 'hell' is very appropriate; down in the valley is a Buddhist shrine to ward off evil.

Oyunuma

The path through Jigokudani hooks sharply to the left; at that point is a small gravel path, labelled in Japanese only as leading to Oyunuma. It leads up to a gravel road, across which is the lookout which overlooks the boiling pond. Oyunuma ('hot water pond') is an intriguing large pool of muddy water that boils continuously. It sits in what is believed to be the crater of an extinct volcano, and is simultaneously scenic and ugly.

Besides the path are some small stone statues with cloth bibs and a sad story. These are figures of Jizo, the protector of children (as well as travellers and pregnant women). One of his responsibilities is the souls of dead children, and sewn to each bib is the name of the dead child whose soul is to be helped in the underworld. Areas of subterranean activity like Jigokudani are obviously entrances to hell.

The road crossed while walking to the lookout leads to Lake Kuttara (to the right); to the left it leads back down to the car park at Jigokudani.

Kuttara-ko

This is a classic caldera lake — almost perfectly round with the surrounding shore rising steeply to an almost level rim. On a crystal-clear sunny day, the water is an intense sapphire blue, said to be even deeper in colour than that of famed Mashu-ko. (On a hazy day — judge from conditions over Noboribetsu — only the outline of the lake will be visible and the water will be a characterless grey, making a trip to the lake a disappointment.)

From the lookout over Oyunuma, it is about three km to a lookout over Kuttara-ko. It is a further 2.5 km down to the bus terminus/rowboat rental/restaurant at the edge of the lake. Buses leave Noboribetsu-onsen at 10 and 11.40 am and 1.20 pm, stopping at the lake for five minutes. Taxi, hitching and walking are alternative ways of getting there.

Kumayama

Overlooking Noboribetsu-onsen is the high hill Kumayama ('Bear Mountain'). A trip here can be recommended, although it is rather pricey (¥1000 return by cable car, 10 per cent discount with a Youth Hostel voucher). There used to be a trail up, but it is now blocked, and finding any alternative would be quite time-consuming. The main attraction (to foreigners) is a reproduction of an Ainu settlement, with five or six buildings built in the traditional Ainu style — grass thatch over a wooden framework. The bottom building houses a small museum.

Four times a day (10.30 am and 3.30, 7.30 and 8.10 pm), in the second building from the bottom of the slope, a number of aged Ainu re-enact several of their traditional dances, chants and ceremonies. These are centred on the bear: in traditional times a bear was raised from a cub, then ceremoniously killed, thus releasing the soul of the dead Ainu believed trapped within. Nowadays a bewildered bear cub is 'shot' with a blunt arrow that does it no harm. Yes, it is for the tourists, but there is no other way to get a glimpse of their former culture. No photos may be taken during the ceremonies, and it is unlikely that anyone will pose for photos afterward. This is annoying after paying a considerable sum to see them, but they are probably heartily sick of cameras . . . . . and who can blame them?

To guarantee a good seat, be at the base station of the cable car more than half an hour before a performance (especially in the busy summer season) to be sure of getting a car up the mountain in time.

Another attraction of the mountain is a large enclosure full of very large and dangerous Hokkaido bears. They are bored by their existence of sitting around on unyielding concrete, and have devised many tricks to cadge biscuits from visitors. Although these bears lead a much better life than those in cages at Shiraoi, both places exemplify a definite shortcoming of the Japanese — their disregard for animals. Another building houses a Bear Museum that shows and tells everything that you ever wanted to know about bears — including a photo of a mating couple — but the text is in Japanese.

Minor entertainment at the top of the mountain also includes goose races. The view from the top over the sea, neighbouring mountains and Kuttaro-ko is very good on a clear day.

The base station of the cable car is reached by walking up a short sidestreet off the main street in Noboribetsu and either walking up a flight of steep steps (past a number of souvenir shops) and following the path, or taking a chair lift that runs parallel to it. (The distance is so short that this is only for the very tired.) The base station is just a short distance away in the large building.

SHIRAOI

This is a town, about 20 km from Noboribetsu on the way to Tomakomai, in which about 3000 Ainu have settled. It was originally known for its reproduction of a small Ainu village (kotan) but is now more famous for its commercialism. To get in to see five or so Ainu-style buildings, the bored, frustrated and pitiable bears in tiny cages, and a five-minute performance of chants and dances by a few Ainu women who look as if they'd rather be elsewhere, you first pass through a very large and very modern building full of stall after stall of the Ainu souvenirs (all staffed by ethnic Japanese).

The redeeming features of the place are a well-presented modern museum of Ainu artefacts and life-size reproductions of daily activities in traditional times, plus an excellent booklet, *Shiraoi &*

Ainu. This gives a vast amount of information about the traditional way of life, far more than is available from sources other than scholarly journals, and presented from the Ainu point of view (which often is quite different from that appearing in official Japanese publications).

Compared with this village, however, the 'settlement' on Kumayama is *much* less commercialized, and gives a better view of the Ainu customs. Shiraoi's advantage is a good, modern large museum, and the excellent publication already mentioned. Comparing the cost of transport to Shiraoi and the admittance charge there, Kumayama is not much more expensive to visit, and would normally get the nod as the better place to visit.

Shiraoi can be reached easily from Tomakomai or Noboribetsu, by train or bus. The bus stop (Shiraoi-kotan) is right in front of the village; from the train station, you walk along the road to Tomakomai for about 20 minutes until you see a large archway over a side road.

MURORAN

At the tip of the peninsula is the city of Muroran. Other than the annual festival (28-30 July), and the cliffs of

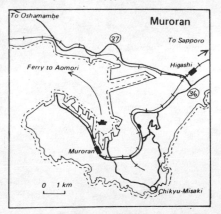

Chikyu-misaki, the sole attraction of this dark steel-producing city is that it is the terminus of a ferry line to Aomori. For anyone with limited time but who wishes to sample a little of Hokkaido, this ferry is invaluable because it allows you to skip Hakodate and the long (about 150 km) and rather dull .trip from there to Shikotsu-Toya National Park. From Muroran to Toyako-onsen (Toya station) it is no more than 50 km by bus (eight per day) or train, and Noboribetsu-onsen (Noboribetsu station) is only about 25 km away by bus (also eight per day). There is also a train service to Noboribetsu town, on the coast, then on to Tomakomai and Sapporo. All trains for Toya, and about half of those for Noboribetsu/ Tomakomai/Sapporo leave from Higashi-Muroran station, three stops from Muroran station.

Central Honshu

This section covers much of what is traditionally regarded as Chubu, or central Japan. For the traveller who wants a feel for the 'real' Japan, this is one of the two or three best regions of the country to visit. Much of the area was, until only a few years ago, quite isolated, and some places were cut off during the winter except for boats on narrow ·rivers. As a result, many folk traditions that have disappeared elsewhere still survive quite strongly. The region also offers much natural beauty, historic remains, and some of the most interesting festivals in Japan.

The areas covered here are Nagano-ken, Gifu-ken, parts of northern Aichi-ken, Fukui-ken, Ishikawa-ken and Toyama-ken, plus the eastern shore of Biwa Lake (north of Kyoto). The route followed begins in the north, as a continuation of the description of the Northern Honshu section. It starts with the alps area of Toyama-ken and Nagano-ken, then across Gifu-ken to Fukui-ken and Ishikawa-ken, then circles back near the starting point.

NORTHERN JAPAN ALPS

This region has the highest mountains in Japan, several over 3000 metres. (Keep in mind that 85 per cent of Japan is considered mountainous.) The mountains are widespread, and Nagano-ken is known as the 'roof' of Japan. There is also, of course, a southern alpine region, but description has been omitted because it is not as accessible as that in the north.

The alps overlap Toyama and Nagano prefectures, and some areas are accessible from both directions. Many peaks require mountaineering skills (for further information, consult *The National Parks of Japan* by Sutherland and Britton,

and the JNTO *Official Guide*) but there are three routes into the mountains that can be followed by anyone. One is most easily reached from Toyama (or via the north coast from Niigata/Naoetsu), one runs between Toyama and Shinano-Omachi (Nagano-ken), and one lies between Matsumoto and Takayama.

FROM KUROBE & TOYAMA

The least complicated trip into the alps is a train ride through the Kurobe Gorge (Kurobe-kyokoku) on the Kurobe-kyokoku railway. The starting point for the 20-km run is Unazuki-onsen. The train passes through gorges as deep as 2000 metres, and is specially designed for sightseeing, with open-sided carriages consisting of little more than seats and a roof. The trip takes 40 minutes each way, and there are 12 trips daily in season (1 May to 30 November). The fare is Y1550 return, and there is no onward journey. There are several stations along the way, so it would be possible to walk through some of the gorge. It would be best to ride in and get an idea of the practicality of walking back through particular sections. Unazuki-onsen is easily reached from Kurobe (on the coast), or Toyama (same railway line); it can also be reached by road.

Although the above trip is easily made, probably the most popular journey in the alps passes through territory that was the province only of alpinists until recent times. The Tateyama-Kurobe Alpine Route takes in the peaks of the Tateyama group, centered around Tateyama itself (3015 metres). The route runs between a point near Toyama (Toyama-ken) and Shinano-Omachi (Nagano-ken), and is enjoyed by many partly for its variety of transport (including train, bus, cable-car and trolley bus). The drawback is cost: transport alone comes to more than

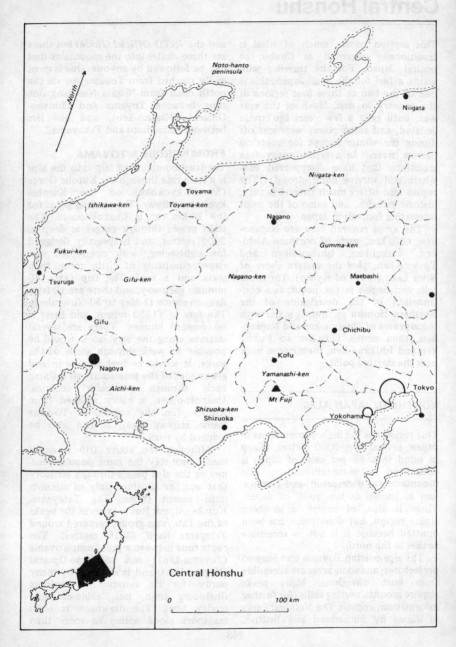

Central Honshu

0   100 km

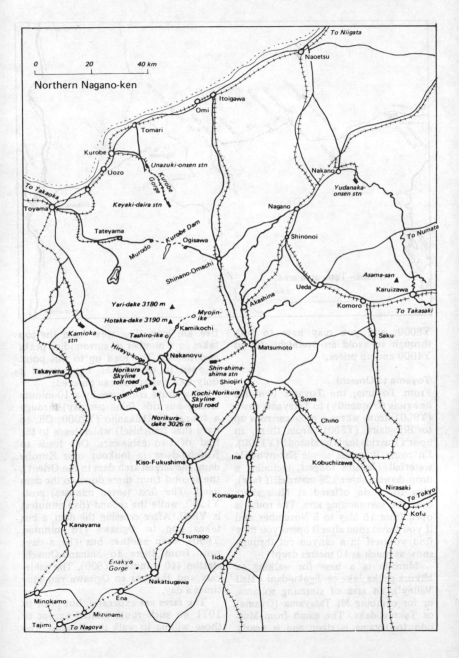

Northern Nagano-ken

0   20   40 km

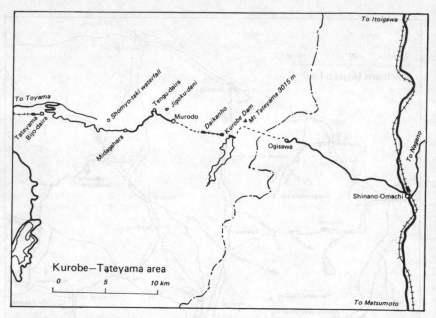

Kurobe—Tateyama area

0   5   10 km

Y8000, and you may have to rush through to avoid an overnight stay at Y4000-and-up prices.

Toyama to Omachi

From Toyama, the Toyama Dentetsu line runs (frequently) to Tateyama town (Y950), from where a cable-car runs up to Bijo-daira (Y550). From there, an hour's bus ride leads to Murodo (Y1200). En route it passes scenic Shomyo-taki waterfall (Japan's longest, including a drop down a sheer 126-metre cliff face), plus the vista offered at Midagahara over the surrounding area. The route is open from 15 May to 5 November, and if you travel soon after it opens you may find yourself in a canyon cut through snow as much as 10 metres deep!

Murodo is a base for walking to Mikura-ge-ike lake or Jigoku-dani ('Hell Valley'), an area of steaming solfaras, or for climbing Mt Tateyama (Oyama) or Tsurugi-dake. The climb from Murodo to Oyama is steep and is nearly

five km long. The view from the top takes in a number of surrounding peaks and valleys. The road up to this point is open to all vehicles, but beyond it only foot passengers can proceed.

The route continues by a 10-minute trolley-bus ride (nine per day) through a tunnel to Daikanho (Y2000; Oh, to have that franchise!) which leads to the first of two cable-cars. One leads to Kurobe-daira (a lookout over Kurobe dam, the largest arch dam in the Orient), the second from there down to the dam itself. The first (seven minutes) costs Y1200, while the second (five minutes) is Y880. After crossing the dam, a bus takes you to Ogisawa (16 minutes, Y800), then another bus (10 a day) runs from there to Shinano-Omachi station (40 minutes, Y600). The cable-cars and the bus to Ogisawa run nine times a day.

The fares are expensive, but prior to 1971 no such route existed except to those willing to walk the distance. The

Tokyo TIC has an information sheet with up-to-date prices and times.

NAGANO-KEN

Omachi is located on Route 148, which runs north to Itoigawa and south to Matsumoto through a river valley. Nagano and its nearby attractions are situated in another parallel valley, separated by a chain of mountains. There are two small, local roads across to Nagano.

NAGANO

The city of Nagano lies in a valley hemmed in by mountain ridges on two sides. Nearby are the best skiing areas in the Tokyo vicinity, such as Shiga Heights; snowfalls in the mountains can reach as much as 15 metres over a winter. This is the area written about by Nobel Prize winner Kawabata in *Snow Country*.

Zenko temple

The main attraction of Nagano is Zenko-ji temple, which draws several million visitors a year. It houses historic statues that are shown only every seven years (the next showing is several years away) and the rest of the time they are concealed. A totally dark tunnel passes beneath the altar, along which people grope their way hoping to touch the 'key of Paradise' that is supposed to guarantee easy entry to Heaven. There is nearly always a service in progress for the benefit of visiting pilgrims, and the interior is richly decorated with Buddhist motifs. It is one of the better temples in Japan to visit for a glimpse of the ceremonies of one branch of Japanese Buddhism.

Yudanaka-onsen

Into the mountains from Nagano (about 25 km north-east) is the hot-spring resort town of Yudanaka. It has open-air pools which are famous from photos of snow-covered monkeys sitting in the pools keeping warm in winter.

Beyond Yudanaka, one can continue by the Shiga-Kusatsu Kogen toll road to Kusatsu, then cross to Nikko and Oze-numa via Numata. Since there are so few individual attractions in Gumma-ken, this route description is split between this section (as far as Numata) and that on Tochigi-ken (Numata to Nikko).

KUSATSU (GUMMA-KEN)

This is one of the best-known hot-spring towns in Japan, with more than 130 ryokan in the central part of town. Yuba (Hot Water Field), the origin of the hot water, gushes, boiling, from the ground. Sulphur precipitates out of the water as it cools, is collected, and sold as yunohana (hot-spring flowers), a home remedy.

The main (public) bath is named Netsunoyu (Heat Bath), and is famous for its exceedingly high temperature. It is so hot that (reputedly), a 'drill master' has to enforce discipline to ensure that bathers stay in for the prescribed time. Anyone who stays in accommodation with Japanese people knows that they can withstand water that would boil a lobster, so this must really be hot!

Kusatsu is also a ski resort, and has several pleasant walking paths nearby.

SOUTHERN NAGANO-KEN

There are two major routes south from Nagano. One goes via Karuizawa, and the other passes through Matsumoto and then down one of two river valleys.

KARUIZAWA (GUMMA-KEN)

Much touted in tourist literature as the 'ideal' resort, Karuizawa is in fact a high-fashion summer resort more of interest to residents of Japan who are seeking an escape from the city. It is largely for the rich, as indicated by the

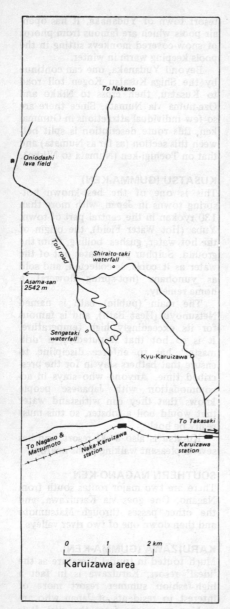

To Nakano

Oniodashi
lava field

Shiraito-taki
waterfall

Asama-san
2542 m

Sengataki
waterfall

Kyu-Karuizawa

To Takasaki

To Nagano &
Matsumoto

Naka-Karuizawa
station

Karuizawa
station

0   1   2 km

Karuizawa area

fact that more than 250 shops based in Tokyo and Yokohama have branches here, so it has aspects of a shrunken, transposed Tokyo. In summer it is extremely crowded. The city is divided into several parts, the main area being Kyu-Karuizawa. The station is two km away.

Asama-san

The backdrop of the town is Asama-san, a conical volcano that is still active. Its last major eruption was in 1783 when awesome amounts of lava poured forth. The field of this lava, Onioshidashi, can be seen easily by taking a bus (55 minutes) from either Karuizawa or Naka-Karuizawa stations. Asama-san can be climbed quite easily from several starting points, the favourite two being the same two stations. It is advisable to check before climbing, because the volcano still erupts from time to time, and climbing is banned when it is active.

There is a good view of Asama-san, as well as the surrounding countryside from Usui-toge (pass), which can be reached on foot in 30 minutes. Kumano-jinja shrine is nearby. The pass itself was part of the old Nakasendo highway between Kyoto and Tokyo. (Some old towns along this route that retain much of their original appearance are described in the section of Nagano-ken covering the Kiso river valley, following.)

A 30-minute walk from Karuizawa station leads to Shiraito falls, 3 metres high and spread along a width of 70 metres.

About 300 species of wild birds inhabit the sanctuary near Hoshino-onsen. They can be watched from two observation huts or from the 2.4 km walking path.

Accommodation

There are many hotels, ryokan, min-shuku, villas, camping grounds and two youth hostels around Karuizawa.

Information
More information on Karuizawa is available in the JNTO pamphlet *Karuizawa-kogen*, available at the Tokyo TIC (and possibly at Kyoto).

MATSUMOTO
Matsumoto is a city situated in the basin of mountain ranges. It possesses one of the finest castles in Japan, and this alone makes it worth visiting. Streets nearby are narrow and winding, typical of castle towns.

Matsumoto Castle
Matsumoto-jo (castle) is the most easily reached feudal castle in the region around Tokyo. The trip can be made in four hours from Shinjuku station (Tokyo). The castle stands an imposing six storeys above its surrounding moat, and is unusual among Japanese castles because it is black, rather than the usual white. Its nickname is 'Crow Castle', a joke to the Japanese, for the renowned white castle at Himeji (Japan's finest) is known as 'White Egret Castle'. The original castle on this site was built in 1504, but the present structure is from a somewhat later date. However, it is important enough to rate as a National Treasure. Swans swimming in the moat add a note of grace to its beauty. In the compound of the castle is the Japan Folklore Library which houses an exhibit of 60,000 items of history, archaeology, folklore and geography.

The castle is a little over one km north-east of the station, substantially closer to Kita-Matsumoto station. The TIC in Tokyo has an information sheet that gives more details on transport, sightseeing and accommodation in Matsumoto.

Getting There
From Tokyo the easiest and quickest way to get to Matsumoto is by JNR train from Shinjuku station (track 1). There are local trains plus expresses and limited expresses, a total of 19 per day. The local is slow, but there is little difference in speed between the other two (the limited express takes 15 minutes longer than the express's 3¾ hours). Since the express costs Y4600 vs Y3500 for the limited express, there is little justification for taking the faster train. There is an information sheet (photocopied) available at the TIC Tokyo with updated fare and schedule information.

Other train lines run from Nagano/Naoetsu, and from the north coast (Itoigawa). From mid-May to mid-October, there is a complicated connection by train and two buses through the mountains to Takayama. I haven't used it, but it might be quite scenic.

KAMIKOCHI
Some people believe that this highland basin west of Matsumoto is the nicest single area in the northern alps. It is reached by private railway from Matsumoto to Shin-shima-shima, from where buses run (up to 15 a day, depending on season) to Kamikochi directly, turning off the highway (Route 158) at Nakan-oyu.

To Nagano (JNR)

To Ueda

0   1 km

(143)

Matsumoto

(19)

(147)

To Itoigawa

Matsumoto castle

Kitamatsumoto stn

To Takayama

Matsumoto station

Local line to Shimashima

JNR

(19)

To Shiojiri

Several trails begin at Kamikochi. A well-known one leads to Kappabashi, a famed suspension bridge across the Azusa-gawa river. From the bridge one obtains a beautiful view of Mt Hotaka, and nearby is a rock sculpture of Walter Weston, a Briton who was the first alpinist to explore the Japan alps in the last century. Prior to this, the alps were regarded as sacred or inhabited by evil spirits, and avoided. Other attractions, apart from the general pleasant mood, fresh air and views of the area, are Tashiro-ike and Taisho-ike ponds, and Myojin lake. A three-hour walk from Kamikochi passes Myojin lake, Tokusawa, and Yokowao. Trains continue beyond here to nearby high peaks, such as Yari-dake (Spear Mountain, the 'Matterhorn' of Japan), but scaling them is for the experienced only. Every year, dozens of Japanese are killed in falls from slopes.

Mt Norikura

This is the most accessible peak in these alps, despite its 3026 metre height, for a toll road runs most of the way to the top, crossing an alpine plateau en route. Buses via the Norikura Skyline go as far as Tatami-daira (2½ hours from Kamikochi; less from Nakanoyu or Hirayu-koge), from where a three-km hike (90 minutes) leads to the top.

Information

The TIC in Tokyo has an information sheet on this area.

KISO REGION

Along with very enjoyable scenery, the Kiso river valley (south-west of Matsumoto) is worth visiting to see three villages that have remained relatively unchanged since a century or two ago. Narai, Tsumago and Magome were located along the old Nakasendo highway between Kyoto and Edo (Tokyo). Every year there were grand processions of daimyo (feudal barons) along this road between the two cities. Their retinue often numbered in the thousands (at least one of 30,000 was recorded), a measure of the power and wealth of the baron. Because the distance between the cities was great, there were post stations where travellers could rest overnight. To meet the exalted demands of their guests, the ryokan (inns) had to be of high standard: some of these fine buildings are still standing, and a visit to one or all of these towns is highly recommended. Apart from a few collections of old buildings that have been gathered from other parts of the country, there are relatively few places in Japan where one can see more than one or two old buildings in any one place. In these towns, one can see a large number side by side, with only relatively few newer buildings interspersed. These towns retain their old appearance mainly because they were bypassed when the railways were built late in the last century. Their future is assured because of the interest (belated) by the Japanese in their past, and they are popular destinations for Japanese sightseers.

KISO-HIRASAWA

If you travel south from Matsumoto and Shiojiri, this is the first town of interest along the valley. It is noted for the production of lacquerware, and there is a lacquer museum near the station.

NARAI

One station (JNR) away from Kiso-Hirasawa is one of the 62 post towns used by travellers along the Nakasendo highway. The old buildings are easy to find, for they line the main street and are located only a few minutes on foot from Narai station (turn left when leaving the station). The majority of the buildings fronting the street are old, although there is a larger proportion of newer structures than in the other two towns. However, Narai is less accessible, so there are fewer fellow sightseers to contend with and you can enjoy the atmosphere a little better.

There are several buildings open to the public, and money would be well spent visiting a few. On the same side of the street as the station is an historic inn, described by two Danish architects who had been studying Japanese architecture as 'one of the most beautiful buildings in Japan'. Diagonally opposite it is the former house of a merchant, now a minshuku (Y3700 per person). It is before the museum, which is on the same side of the street. The inn's construction and materials are of the highest quality: note the deep brown of the wooden floors and the fineness of the costly wood, the size and layout of the garden, and the spacious interiors. The well-off people of those days lived very well.

KISO FUKUSHIMA
During the Tokugawa era this was the most important barrier gate of the Nakasendo (Middle Way) road that linked Kyoto and Tokyo. Here, the 'documents of travellers were inspected to verify that they had permission to journey. Life was very strictly regulated in those days (down to such details as to what kind of clothes one might wear, and even the position in which one had to sleep!), and most people were not allowed to leave their appointed work or home village. Some mementoes of those days survive in the form of old buildings and exhibits in museums.

Yamamura Daikan Yashiki This was formerly the residence of the Yamamura family, high officials in the Kiso region; it is 15 minutes on foot from Kiso-Fukushima station.

Kiso-Fukushima Kyodo-kan This is a museum of historic artefacts and materials related to the Nakasendo road and

the barrier gates; it is five minutes by bus, or 25 minutes on foot from Kiso-Fukushima station.

Kozen-ji temple One of the three largest temples in the Kiso region, the temple is known for its Kanuntei garden. It is close to both of the attractions listed above.

Festivals
21 July-16 August: Kiso Odori, folk-dances of the Kiso region.

22-23 July: Mikoshi Matsuri, procession of portable shrines.

ONTAKE KOGEN
This plateau is one hour from Kiso-Fukushima station by bus, and is noted for wildflowers in spring and autumn, skiing in winter.

NEZAME-NO-TOKO
Some distance below road-level is this small but pretty 'miniature' gorge, an outcropping of large rocks through which the river has carved its way through the ages. There is a large area where buses can park (the place is only five minutes or so from Agematsu station); the entrance is to the north of the parking lot. I inadvertently avoided paying the admittance fee by walking down a service stairway between the two large buildings. The name means 'place that opens sleepy eyes', but we have to allow the namers some poetic licence; it's attracting but not outstanding — worth visiting if you have the time.

ONO-NO-TAKI
About 10 minutes by bus from Agematsu station is this cascade some 10 metres high.

SUWARA
A short walk from Suwara station (two stops from Kiso-Fukushima) is Joshoji temple. It was founded by the Kiso

family in the 14th century, although the present buildings date 'only' from 1598.

TSUMAGO & MAGOME

Both these post towns have preserved much of their original appearance. It would be difficult to choose between them, so why not visit both? The walk between them takes about 2½-3 hours, and passes along the old Nakasendo road. The walk from Tsumago to Magome is recommended because the road is generally downhill in that direction. Tsumago is laid out almost on the level (there is a bit of a gap between two sections of the town), while Magome is strung out down the side of a steep hill. In Magome, the Wakihontin Okuya, a building shaped like a castle (built 1877), has an exhibition of material regarding the old post towns.

Accommodation

There are buildings open to the public in both towns, and several have been converted to minshuku so travellers can stay overnight. The towns are very popular with tourists, so it is likely that reservations will be necessary (refer to the section on Minshuku for information on bookings from Tokyo).

Festival Tsumago-matsuri is held on 23 November, and takes the form of a procession of townspeople dressed in the style of ancient times as a re-enactment of one of the processions of the daimyo who travelled along the Nakasendo road in feudal times.

Getting There

Both Tsumago and Magome are linked with the city of Nakatsugawa by regular bus service (Meitetsu line). From Nakatsugawa station, it takes about 30 minutes to Magome, and a bit over an hour to Tsumago. There is also a direct bus connection to Magome from Nagoya; the trip takes about two hours. If you are coming from Matsumoto or

Shiojiri, Nagiso is the closest station to Tsumago.

TENRYU RIVER VALLEY

Another route from Shiojiri southward is through the Tenryu (Heavenly Dragon) river valley to Iida via Komagome along Route 153, or by the parallel JNR line. The scenery is pleasant enough to make the trip enjoyable, although there are few points of special note. At Ina, the grounds of the former castle Takata-jo are very pretty in the cherry-blossom season (probably a couple of weeks later than in Kyoto, Tokyo, etc).

Tenryu-kyo

The major attraction of the river valley is the scenic Tenryu-kyo gorge, accessible from nearby Iida. Tenryu-kyo station (JNR) is near the gorge, but the most enjoyable way to see this and other parts of the Ina valley is by boat through the Tenryu rapids. There are at least two points of departure. The longest trip (20 km) is from Ichida (JNR) station, while a shorter trip (12 km) can be made from Benten (10 minutes by bus from Iida station).

SOUTHERN GIFU-KEN

The attractions of Gifu-ken can be divided into two general groups, those located in the mountain highlands where historic isolation has preserved many traces of 'old' Japan, and several cities in the south which have always been more in the mainstream of Japanese life. Some attractions of bordering prefectures are also included here, either access is easier from Gifu-ken, or there are no neighbouring attractions that would otherwise draw you to the area.

The city of Nagoya, one of the largest in Japan, is easily reached from many centres in this area. However,

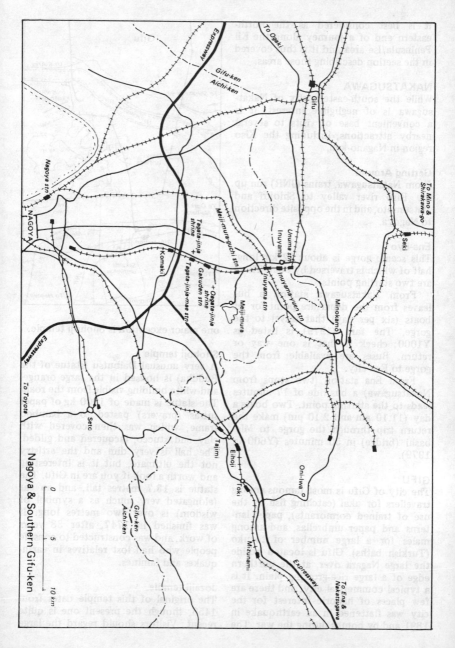

Nagoya & Southern Gifu-ken

it is best considered as the north-eastern end of a journey along the Kii Peninsula/Ise area and it is thus covered in the section describing those areas.

NAKATSUGAWA

While the south-eastern city of Nakatsugawa is of negligible interest, it is a convenient base of visits to several nearby attractions, including the Kiso region in Nagano-ken.

Getting Around

From Nakatsugawa, trains (JNR) run up the Kiso river valley to Shiojiri and Matsumoto, and in the opposite direction to Nagoya.

Ena-kyo

This scenic gorge is about 12 km long, half of which is traversed by boat. There are two starting points.

From Nakatsugawa station a bus leaves from the departure point for jet boats (six per day) that travel to the gorge. The fare (1979) is listed as Y1000; check if that is one way or return. Buses are available from the gorge to Ena city.

From Ena station (two stops from Nakatsugawa) a bus ride of 17 minutes leads to the starting point. Two boats a day (11.10 am and 2.10 pm) make the return trip through the gorge, to Miebashi (bridge) in 50 minutes (Y600 in 1979).

GIFU

The city of Gifu is most famous among travellers for ukai (catching fish by the use of trained cormorants), paper lanterns and paper umbrellas, and among males for a large number of toruko (Turkish baths). Gifu is located beside the large Nagara river, at the northern edge of a large rice-growing plain. It is a typical commercial city, and there are few places of historic interest for the city was flattened in an earthquake in 1891 and by bombs during the war. The

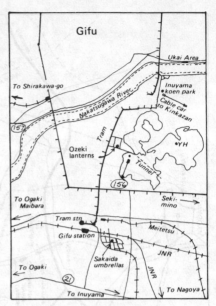

one major exception is Shohoji temple.

Shohoji temple

A very unusual Daibutsu (statue of the Buddha) is housed in the large orange-and-white building visible from the road. The statue is made of 1000 kg of paper sutras (prayers) pasted to a bamboo frame, which was then covered with clay and stucco, lacquered and gilded. The hall is very dim and the artistry not the ultimate, but it is interesting and worth a look if you are in Gifu. The statue is 13.7 metres tall, and an ear (elongated very much as a symbol of wisdom) is over two metres long. It was finished in 1747, after 38 years of work, and was constructed to console people who had lost relatives in earthquakes and famines.

Jozaiji temple

The original of this temple dates from 1450, though the present one is quite recent. Visitors should regard the large structure simply as a neighbourhood temple and watch daily life go by around it; it is popular as a playground for toddlers and their ever-watchful mothers.

Kinkazan

The backdrop to Gifu is Kinkazan (Silver Mountain). On it are located Gifu Youth Hostel and a concrete reproduction of the castle that stood at the peak until the earthquake of 1891. The new castle (1956) houses a small prefectural museum. Exercise freaks can walk up from the city or from the hostel, or the lazy can take the cable car ('ropeway') from Gifu-koen (park), but the castle and mountain are very much 'something else to do' and not attractions of great merit. The castle looks very pretty (and *very* high up) at night when it is floodlit.

Ukai (cormorant fishing)

From 11 May to 15 October there are nightly displays on the Nagara river (just above Nagara bridge) of the ancient 'sport' of using trained cormorants to catch fish. The birds are kept on a leash, and a ring around the neck prevents them from swallowing any but the smallest fish. The action takes place at night when the ayu (river smelt or sweetfish) can be attracted to the surface by a torch blazing over the bow of each ship (there are usually several). One fisherman (usho) in each boat, dressed in mediaeval grass-skirted costume, controls several birds, pulling in each one as it makes a catch, taking the fish from the bird, and putting it back in the water for another dive.

Large numbers of people can see this spectacle at any one time because there are more than 130 covered boats of different sizes (capacity of 10 to 30 persons). Tourists normally go out an hour or two before the fishing starts and dine (meals by prior arrangement), drink, sing and set off fireworks. It

becomes a grand party, and probably more than a few revellers are unable to focus by the time the boats and birds appear. The sightseeing boats are usually lined up, and a 'showboat' of women dressed as geisha moves up and down past them while the women perform traditional songs and dances. After a suitable period of time, the fishing boats make their passes up and down.

People wishing to take pictures should keep a few things in mind. The fishing performance lasts only 20-30 minutes, and the boats pass by quite quickly. A powerful flash is needed because the distance to the boats will be at least three or four metres, often considerably more.

The cost per person is around Y1600, and bookings can be made at any hotel, tourist agency or at the boat office just downstream of Nagara-bashi bridge. The phone number is 0582 62-0104, but it will be necessary to call in Japanese.

The fishing can be seen almost as well from the east shore of the river (nearest town) in summer the water is low and you can walk out over the stony river bottom to the main channel near where the boats pass. The added advantage of this is that you can watch later as the fishermen touch shore, remove the leashes and neck-rings, feed the birds with their hard-earned supper, and put them back into their basket-cages, load them into trucks and disappear into the night. There is no Ukai when the river is muddy following heavy rains or during the full moon, because the torches cannot attract the fish.

Crafts

Gifu is the best-known centre in Japan for both paper lanterns (chochin) and paper umbrellas (kasa). Paper lanterns were made here as early as 1597. One of the best-known lantern factories is Ozeki; it is located in the Oguma-cho area of the city near the main shopping street, on the road leading up to the tunnel through Kinkazan.

Visitors are allowed to walk through and watch the interesting process. The lanterns are made by winding bamboo or wire around a form made up of several pieces of wood that lock together to give the shape. Paper is pasted to the bamboo strips, and after the paste has dried, the form is dismantled and removed through one end of the lanter. Sometimes the paper is pre-stencilled with a design, while other lanterns are hand-painted at the end of the process. The factory can be recognized by the symbol of a flattened 'O' superimposed on a 'Z' on the building.

There are no large umbrella-manufacturers, just small shops (eg Kaida Kasaten) and home workshops, so it is more difficult to see them being made.

Accommodation

There are two youth hostels in Gifu. The only one I know first hand is Gifu Youth Hostel, perched high on Kinkazan mountain, which gives it a good location but makes it difficult to reach. The simplest way to get to it is by chairlift, that takes you to within a couple of hundred metres of the hostel. However, I have been in Gifu several times and have never seen the lift actually moving. (Remember it is only a chairlift, so travel lightly.) Near the base of the chairlift is the beginning of a path leading up to the same place. The nearest tram stop from the station is Yanagase.

An alternative is to take a trolley in the direction of Nagara-bashi bridge, get off at Shiyakusho-mae stop, and follow the road uphill to the tunnel; there is a path to the right that leads up to the hostel. At the stop beyond Shiyakusho-mae, after a sharp right-hand turn, there is another path which also leads up the hill. This stop is close to both the Daibutsu and the base station for the

cable-car to the top of the mountain. Any of the walks will take 20-30 minutes. Orienteering fans will find a kindred spirit in the hostel manager, Mr Nomura.

At the other end of the cost scale, there are many resort hotels bordering the far side of the river, upstream from Nagara-bashi bridge. They tend to be expensive (Y10,000 and up) which is not uncommon for hot-spring resorts.

There are also several business hotels in Gifu. The phone numbers for two are: (058) 65-4111 and 51-2111. Prices range upward from Y3210 single, Y7190 double.

Festivals

On 5 April is Inaba jinja festival, and on 11 May is the opening of cormorant fishing (fireworks at night). On the last Saturday of July and the first Saturday of August is the All-Japan Fireworks contest, held on the Nagara river just above Nagara-bashi bridge.

Getting There

Gifu is linked to Nagoya by JNR (Gifu station) and Meitetsu line (Shin-Gifu station), as well as to Gifu-Hashima by bus. (Both Nagoya and Gifu-Hashima are on the Shinkansen). Gifu is linked to Ogaki and Maibara by JNR, and to Inuyama by both JNR and Meitetsu line (from Shin-Nagoya station). A railway that begins as a tram service on the major cross-road in the city (Route 156) leads to Seki and Mino.

YORO-NO-TAKI

Yoro waterfall is a 32-metre high cascade located in a scenic little tree-lined ravine. The nearby area has been made into a nature park with picnic facilities, etc. The water plummets into a natural pool and visitors may, it is said, take a natural shower. (Take your own soap.)

The name Yoro translates as 'filial piety', and has an interesting history. It is said that Shonai Minamoto was extremely faithful to his aged father, and spent his hard-earned money from wood-cutting for sake to keep the old man happy. On one occasion, the water near the waterfall is said to have come out tasting like sake, a reward from his filial piety so that he would not have to spend all his money for the bottled type. The story dates from 717. Access is from Ogaki via the Kinki Nippon railway (25 minutes from Ogaki station) to Yoro station from where a bus (seven minutes) leads to the park.

INUYAMA

Inuyama (Dog Mountain) on the Kiso river, is known for its castle, river scenery, shooting the rapids, and cormorant fishing (ukai).

Inuyama Castle

Inuyamo-jo is the oldest castle in Japan, dating from 1440. It is a pretty white structure, scenically located on top of a cliff overlooking the Kiso river. It is open to the public, and close to the entrance is a small shrine where worshippers (usually older people) come, clap their hands to get the attention of the gods, make their prayer, and leave.

The castle and shrine are a short walk downstream from Inuyama-yuen station of the Meitetsu line (from Nagoya to Gifu); Inuyama station is some distance away. From Gifu by JNR, the terminal station is Unuma at the other end of Inuyama-bashi (bridge). The bridge is the only place where I have seen a train caught in a traffic jam: both cars and trains use the same bridge.

Jo-an

One of three finest teahouses in Japan, Jo-an is located in Inuyama close to Inuyama-jo. A teahouse is supposed to be the ultimate in restrained refinement, so you may concentrate on the elegant simplicity of the utensils used, and the grace of the person preparing and serv-

ing the tea. Jo-an is a rather austere, low-key building set in pleasant surroundings. With this background information, it can be appreciated for its inherent worth and purpose, but as a sightseeing attraction, it is not everyone's cup of tea (so to speak).

Kiso River

The river (Kiso-gawa) has several scenic spots along its banks in the Inuyama area, especially where the castle overlooks the water, and where a mysterious rock looms out of the water just upstream of Inuyama-bashi (bridge) and Inuyama-yuen station. This area of the Kiso has been dubbed as 'Nihon Rhine' (the Rhine of Japan), but only the strange rock fulfills this impression, as it would be a perfect home for water nymphs or Lorelei. (It would do so better, however, if some garish buildings had not been stuck on to its flanks; but such is the way that things are done here.) The general area is very attractive, however, because the banks have been preserved as a nature park, thus sparing the 'benefit' of development with hotels, restaurants, etc. Rocks along the shoreline make a walk upstream from Inuyama-yuen station an enjoyable excursion, forested hill on one side and the river on the other.

Shooting the Rapids

A popular activity in this area is shooting rapids on the Kiso river for about 13 km down to Inuyama. It is perfectly safe, enjoyable, and a year-round sport (weather permitting), though more pleasant in warm summer sunshine. This is probably the best place in Japan for shooting rapids. Long, flat-bottomed Kiso-kudari boats, guided by two or more boatmen with poles, make the descent in about two hours. In recent years engine-powered boats have made an appearance; they take about half the time.

There are two starting points in the

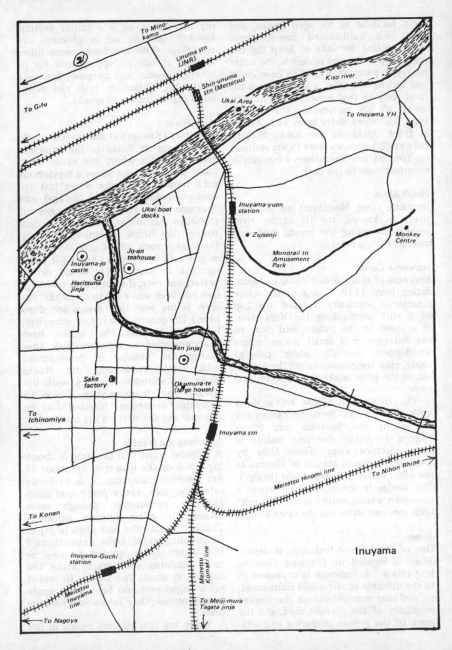

vicinity of Mino-Kamo city, one on each side of the river. One is at Mino-Ota city (part of Mino-Kamo) on the north bank, accessible from Gifu by JNR. On the south bank the starting point is Imawatari, accessible by Meitetsu Hirome line from Inuyama station to both north and south docks, while buses from Nagoya go only to the south docks (five minutes), but a bridge joins the two sides. There are several companies offering tours, so check to be sure of getting the type of boat you want; more of the traditional boats leave from the south docks. The (1979) cost: adults, Y2100; children, Y1000. Highpoints of the trip are at Kaniai, the rocks at Sekiheki, Rhine-yuen, and the park area along the shore at Inuyama. Rhine-yuen is another starting point for boat rides, and is reached from Sakahogi station on the Meitetsu line from Gifu. (The starting points near Mino-Kamo are probably better, however.)

Ukai

Inuyama is another of the several places in this region that feature ukai (described in detail under Gifu). At Inuyama, boats carrying spectators to the fishing area leave from the bank of the river downstream from Inuyama-yuen station, at the row of hotels. Most boats leave an hour or two before the fishing begins (soon after dark), which is rarely later than 7 pm even in mid-summer (just about the only benefit of the refusal of authorities to introduce Daylight Saving Time).

The overall scene can be viewed quite well from the shore on the Unuma side upstream of the bridge, but the boats anchor off-shore and the row of spectator boats is between the shore and the fishing boats. (One gets a better view from the shore at Gifu, and probably at Uji, near Kyoto.)

The cost for boat rental will be about

Y1800. Reservations can be made by phone (0568 61-0057), or through hotels and travel agencies in the area.

Accommodation

There are many hotels and ryokan in Inuyama, including a number just downstream of Inuyama-yuen station. The youth hostel is about 800 metres upstream of this station, and a further 400 metres uphill. It is quite pleasant (bar the usual noisy PA system), and a bargain the second-cheapest youth hostel in Japan, Y400 in 1979.

Meiji-mura

Within the boundaries of Inuyama is an open-air museum of more than 50 buildings and other memorabilia of the era of the Emperor Meiji (1868-1910), who regained the power of emperor from the Tokugawa who had ruled for about 300 years. He pushed Japan into the modern age after three centuries of almost total isolation from the rest of the world. The innovations of his rule ran the gamut of every aspect of Japanese life, and within 10 years of his taking power there was a railroad operating in Japan, quite an advance on horses and hand-carried palanquins.

To most Westerners, the items in the museum have symbolic rather than inherent interest. Most of the buildings, for example, are 19th-century Western in style, and rather commonplace in appearance; to the Japanese, they are somewhat exotic. Of world renown is the lobby of the old Imperial Hotel (Tokyo), a famed design of Frank Lloyd Wright.

Meiji Village is most easily reached by taking the Meitetsu-Komaki line from Nagoya or Inuyama to Meiji-mura-guchi station, from where it is a 12-minute bus ride (or four-km walk). There is also a direct bus service from Nagoya (60 minutes) from Meitetsu bus centre near Nagoya station.

Fertility shrines

The next two stations along the Komaki line from Meiji-mura-guchi are located near two shrines devoted to fertility, both of crops in the area (a rich rice-growing valley), and human. There are shrines of this sort scattered around Japan, but these are the best-known and the most accessible in the country.

Oagata-jinja This is the female shrine, and houses several natural phenomena, like a cleft rock, that resemble the female genitalia. It is a popular place of veneration for women about to marry and those who want children. The shrine is reached from Gakudan station (after Meiji-mura-guchi), by turning right when leaving the station and walking across the tracks and up the road for 10-15 minutes toward the forested hills.

Tagata-jinja This is the male shrine. In the small building to the left of the main building is a quite amazing collection of phallus carvings of all sizes, from a few centimetres to one about two metres long, all donated by grateful parents. The shrine is close to Tagata-jinja-mae station, the next after Gaku-den. Souvenirs are on sale at both

shrines, but the object venerated at Tagata-jinja in vastly easier to portray, so its trinkets are more striking.

Shrine festivals

Tagata-jinja has a very interesting festival each year on 15 March. Anyone with a healthy sense of humour, as have the thousands of Japanese and a few foreigners who attend each year, will definitely have something to talk about and show pictures of when they return home. A carved wooden phallus about 3 metres long is carried in happy procession from another shrine about a kilometre away, and is accompanied by Tengu (a Shinto deity with a very long nose) and several women carrying smaller carvings similar to the main attraction. The procession moves slowly along the small road behind Tagata-jinja, starting early in the afternoon. In the morning, sake casks are broken open and the contents distributed, and the people carrying the mikoshi (portable shrine) make frequent stops during the procession to partake of it. The owners of every field they pass also give them libations, so by the time they reach the shrine (about 3 pm or later) and carry the mikoshi into the main building, the bearers are thoroughly sloshed and have to be guided in the right direction.

There is usually a sign at the shrine indicating the parade route. The procession used to pass along the main road, but has now been relegated to the back road, so its format will likely remain unchanged unless the puritanism of the police increases.

Oagata-jinja also has a festival, but its format has been changing. Up to 1978 it took place on the morning of 15 March, but in 1979 it was moved to the following weekend. In 1978, the procession featured a number of pretty young women (brides-to-be?) on decorated floats, as well as the shrine's mikoshi, a discretely covered tree-root

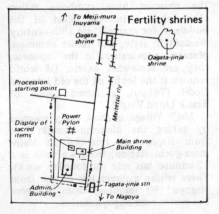

that serves as a female symbol. If you are interested in this festival, it might be possible to get further information at the TIC in Tokyo.

MIZUNAMI

Paleontologists passing through this town might find the Fossils Museum of interest.

TAJIMI

About 80 per cent of the porcelain for the Japanese market, and more than half of the porcelain exports, are produced in Tajimi at more than 1300 pottery plants. Those interested in pottery could probably arrange to visit one of the plants. Those interested in studying pottery should refer to the notes on Pottery in the General Section.

ONI-IWA (Ogre Rock)

Travellers between Toki and Mino-Kamo might wish to stop off for a look at this interesting gigantic granite formation rising from the edge of the river near Oni-iwa onsen (hot spring resort).

SEKI (GIFU-KEN)

This small city has been known for centuries as the centre for production of many of the finest swords in Japan. To this day there are still many people in the city who make their living solely from this craft, including 12 swordsmiths, plus polishers and other assistants. There is little if any other point of interest in Seki besides the swordsmiths, so it is worth using a little space to describe the fascinating process by which the swords are made.

Seki swordsmiths

The Japanese sword is the finest weapon of its kind ever created anywhere in the world; it is the ultimate expression of the swordsmith's art. It is unfortunate that their only raison d'etre is killing, for they could truly be described as

jewels in steel. When making a sword, a balance must be struck between hardness (for cutting) and resiliency (so that it does not snap in service). To accomplish these conflicting goals, Japanese swordsmiths use two processes together: they combine different kinds of steel in the blade, and the tempering (heating and cooling the steel quickly to bring it to the correct degree of hardness) is varied over the width of the blade so that the back remains soft, while the cutting edge is hard. This process takes a long time: a swordsmith is permitted by law to make only two swords per month, and it is not likely that he could make swords of quality in much less time than this. The work is quite fascinating (at least to engineers and those with mechanical interests), and most steps of the process can be seen at Seki.

It is generally very difficult to see the process of making swords, for the smiths are busy and do not relish a continual stream of sightseers. Fortunately, however, demonstrations (open to the public) are given six times a year at Seki city, on the first Saturday of each of the odd-numbered months. They are given in a corner of the grounds of Kasuga-jinja (shrine), where a workshop has been set up duplicating the equipment found in a traditional smithy. Kasuga shrine is straight down the street leading from the town hall. If you are seriously interested in sword-making, and are not in Seki at demonstration time, there is a city official (Mr Shigeru Matsui) who speaks a little English and *might* be able to arrange an introduction to a practising swordsmith. (Modern smithies, however, are equipped with power-operated machinery, unlike the demonstration smithy.) Mr Matsui's phone number is 05752 2-3131; it might be advisable to have a Japanese-speaking friend make the call.

At the Kasunga-jinja demonstration, a master dressed in traditional costume is accompanied by several apprentices (also dressed in traditional costume). The first 'striking' is the most spectacular, for the spongy mass of steel sends out a spray of sparks in all directions as it is heated in the fire by the master smith and then mashed into a cohesive blob by the apprentices. The process of heating and beating is repeated a couple of times, until the metal has become a small bar about 60 x 200 mm and 20 mm thick. Water is poured on to the anvil, and the red-hot bar is struck on top of it which prevents the metal from oxidizing. This slab is then cut with a chisel, and then folded back on itself.

Now follows the most important stage. The smith rolls the glowing metal block in a small pile of black carbonized rice husks. When the metal is completely smothered, in black, he pours a brown liquid over both sides, and returns the metal to the fire. The liquid is a type of clay, and protects the carbon from burning in the fire. When the metal reaches red hot temperatures again, the carbon is actually absorbed into the surface of the metal.

The rest of the process is a repetition of the above. The number of times this is repeated determines the carbon content of the finished steel and thus its potential hardness. For the hardest steel, to be used for the edge of the blade, the metal is folded 20 to 25 times. Softer steel for the inner structure of the blade may have only 10 to 12 doublings, and steel for the side plates (and back, if one is used) might have 12 to 15 foldings.

During the demonstration (from 10 am to 4 pm) there is time to make only a couple of the required pieces of steel. When all the pieces are available, they are forged together into a single mass which is then beaten out into the rough shape of the finished sword. The individual pieces made for the edge, core, sides, etc, keep their relative positions through the beating stage, and the boundaries can be seen when the sword is polished. The final stage (shaping and straightening a previously-made sword) are usually shown during the demonstration.

After the sword has the proper shape, two stages remain, tempering and polishing. To enable the edge to be tempered to a high hardness while keeping the back relatively soft, the blade is covered with clay so that only the edge is exposed. The clay is often made wavy so that varying widths of the edge are exposed. After heating, plunging the blade into water, and polishing, this pattern appears, and is one of the signs of beauty looked for in a sword. (The parts of the sword protected by the clay do not cool so abruptly, so they can revert to softer forms of steel to some extent.)

An interesting finale to the demonstration is a display of the use of some finished swords. Bamboo poles are set up, and swordsmen dressed in traditional costume show how effortlessly the swords can cut off pieces of bamboo. (In olden times it was customary to show the sharpness of a new sword by demonstrating through how many condemned criminals it could cut.)

Other craftsmen in Seki make the elaborately decorated handles, handguards, etc, while most factories in the city make knives and other cutting utensils.

If you're thinking of picking up a sword while in town, you may want to know the price so that you can save up. In 1979, a sword of the type being made and demonstrated would sell for Y6,000,000.

Cormorant fishing (ukai)

During the season mid-May to mid-October, there is ukai at Seki as well as at the better-known centres of Gifu and Inuyama. There are several ryokan and minshuku around the city, including at least two minshuku that are operated by cormorant fishermen. Thus it is possible to stay at one of the houses and have dinner on a boat for an all-inclusive price of Y7000 to Y8000 (which is rather high by minshuku standards, even including Y1800 or so for the performance). Two such fishermen are Mr Adachi (tel (05752) 2-0799) and Mr Iwasa (tel (05752) 2-1862).

Getting There
Seki is easily reached from Gifu by the train that begins service in Gifu as a tram but continues far into the country parallel to the road to Seki and Mino. By JNR, one could go from Nagoya, Inuyama, Minokamo or Takayama.

NORTHERN GIFU-KEN

Because of the isolation of this highland area until very recently, many customs and other remnants have survived which make it one of the most interesting areas of Japan to visit. There are two major river valleys, and both have many places of interest. One extends northward from Seki along Route 156 to the isolated Shirakawa/Gokayama area, famous for large thatched-roof houses; the other runs north from Minokamo along Route 41 (or from Nakatsugawa along Route 257) to Takayama. There are sufficient road links in the northern region to allow you to travel across from one valley to the next, through pretty mountain scenery.

SEKI TO THE SHOKAWA VALLEY
The scenery along this road is pleasant for most of the journey, with typical small farms and farmhouses, few towns, and few signs of rampant modernization.

The only town of note is Gujo-Hachiman.

Gujo-Hachiman
There isn't much to see here, but the town is famous for its celebrations of Obon, when large numbers of townspeople dance in the streets every night throughout August, and in late July and early September as well. This 'madness' is known as Gujo Odori, and is famous throughout Japan. The peak nights are around 13-16 August, but other nights would be equally good for a visit.

Shiratori
This is the road junction with Route 158 to Fukui. There is pleasant mountain scenery, and the area is described in the section on Fukui-ken.

SHOKAWA VALLEY AREA
There is a very interesting region along the Shokawa river valley, south of Takaoka (Ishikawa-ken). It includes Shirakawa-go, Gokoyama and other villages.

The area was settled in the 12th century by survivors of the Keike (Taira) clan who were defeated in the great battle of Dan-no-Ura (near Shimonoseki) with the Genji (Minamoto) clan for control of Japan. The Taira fled to this remote area to escape slaughter by their foes.

The area was still considered remote as late as 1961, when construction of the Miboro dam brought it to greater attention. Even until 1978, the only communication during the winter was by boat along the river. Nowadays there is year-round bus service. The description of this region overlaps Gifu and Toyama prefectures, which has made it difficult to obtain information on the area as a coordinated attraction, because prefecturally-prepared travel literature tends to studiously ignore attractions even a kilometre outside its boundaries.

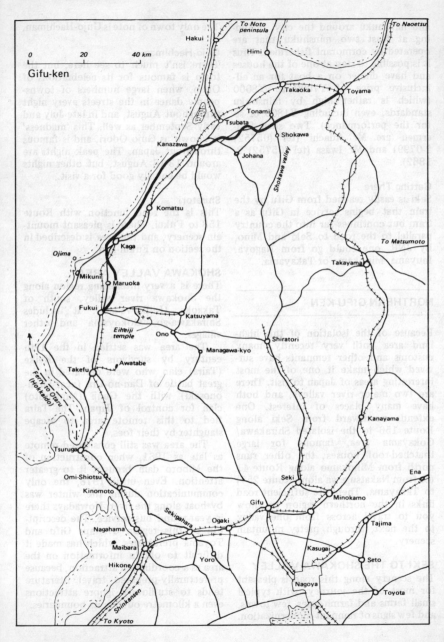

Gifu-ken

0   20   40 km

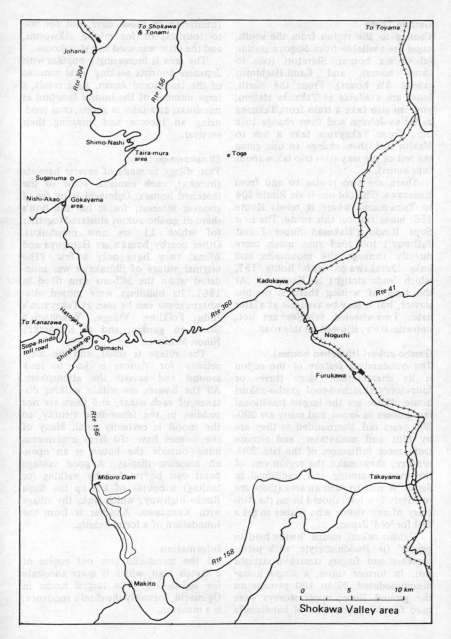

To Shokawa & Tonami

Johana

To Toyama

Rte 304

Rte 156

Shimo-Nashi

Taira-mura area

Toga

Shirakawa-go

Suganuma

Nishi-Akao

Gokayama area

Kadokawa

Rte 41

Rte 360

To Kanazawa

Hatogaya

Noguchi

Supa-Rindo toll road

Shirakawa-go

Ogimachi

Furukawa

Rte 156

Miboro Dam

Takayama

Rte 158

Makito

0   5   10 km

Shokawa Valley area

Getting There

Coming to the region from the south, buses are available from Nagoya station (about six hours), Shiratori (two to three hours), and Kami-Hachiman (about 3½ hours). From the north, buses are available at Takaoka station; you can also take a train from Takaoka as far as Johana and then change to a bus. From Takayama take a bus to Makito and then change to one going the rest of the way (this trip takes about four hours).

There are two routes to and from Kanazawa. The old one is via Route 304 to Taira-mura, where it meets Route 156; buses run on this route. The new Supa Rindo ('Hakusan Super Forest Pathway') toll road runs much more directly through the mountains and links Shirakawa-go with Route 157, which leads straight to Kanazawa. At the time of writing there is no bus service, but it may be available at a later date. Two-wheeled vehicles are not, unfortunately, allowed on this road.

Gassho-zukuri (thatched houses)

The outstanding feature of the region is its characteristic large three- or four-storey thatched-roof gassho-zukuri house. These are the largest traditional farmhouses in Japan, and many are 200-300 years old. Surrounded as they are by hills and mountains, and remote from most influences of the late 20th century, they make the region one of the most charming and traditional in Japan. A visit to such an area (there are relatively few left) should be on the itinerary of any visitor who wishes to get a feel for 'old' Japan.

Gassho-zukuri means 'hands held in prayer' (ie Buddhist-style, with palms together and fingers stretched straight up). In former times, a single house accommodated 30 to 100 persons on the ground floor; upper storeys were used for the production of handicrafts (utilitarian in those days, not for sale to tourists) or for raising silkworms, and the attic was used as a storehouse.

The area is increasingly popular with Japanese tourists seeking what remains of the traditional Japan. As a result, a large number of the houses function as minshuku and take in guests, thus producing an income and ensuring their survival.

Shirakawa-go

This village is made of several hamlets (buraku), each contains some of the thatched houses. Ogimachi is by far of greatest interest, for it has the lion's share of gassho-zukuri clustered together (of which 11 are now minshuku). Other nearby buraku are Hatogoya and Iijima; they have only a few. (The original village of Shirakawa was inundated when the Miboro dam filled in 1961. Its buildings were moved elsewhere: some can be seen at Takayama's Hida Folklore Village, Yokohama's Sankei-en garden, and at Kawasaki's Nihon Minka-en.)

The village is small, and the main activity for visitors is just to look around and savour the atmosphere. All the houses are within walking distance of each other, and there are rice paddies in the immediate vicinity, so the mood is certainly rural. Many of the houses have old farm implements hung outside the house as an open-air museum display. A good vantage point can be reached by walking (or taxiing) a couple of km up the Supa Rindo highway, which links the village with Kanazawa. Another is from the foundation of a former castle.

Information

All the minshuku give out copies of a sketch map, which is quite adequate for sightseeing. The largest house in Ogimachi, formerly the chief's residence, is a museum.

Accommodation

One of the most memorable experiences of a visit to Japan would be a night spent in one of the many gassho-zukuri coverted into minshuku. Although modern amenities have been added, the traditional appearance of the exterior has been retained in all cases, and the common-rooms often have the original hearth over which is suspended a pot-hook. All guests eat together and, if my experience at the Juemon was typical, the lady of the house keeps everyone company, pours beer and sake for them (ordered separately), and even sings folksongs of the region and performs local folk-dances.

Departing from the usual practice of this book, I have listed below the names and phone numbers of almost all the minshuku in Ogimachi. In the July-August season this area is very popular, and it is advisable to phone ahead to be sure of having a place to stay. (None of the proprietors speak English, so you will need a Japanese person to phone for you. It might be possible to book through an agency in Tokyo or other large city, or in Toyama or Gifu at the station.) The number in brackets is the approximate age of the house, the charge is uniform in all minshuku (Y3200 with two meals in 1979, plus Y200 for heating in cold weather).

Juemon (05769)	6-1053	(300)
Yosobe	6-1172	(230)
Nodaniya	6-1011	
Kidoya	6-1077	(200)
Gensaku	6-1176	(170)
Magoemon	6-1167	(280)
Iicha	6-1422	(200)
Koemon	6-1446	(200)
Furusato	6-1033	(150)
Yoshiro	6-1175	

The hostess at Yosobe seemed extra-pleasant and friendly, but the people in charge of the last two minshuku did not seem very interested or helpful so these seem less recommendable.

While it's not a gassho house (only a country farmhouse) some travellers have had only the highest praise for a minshuku they stayed in near Shirakawa-go; it is Minshuku Osugi/Okubo/Shirakawa-mura (tel (05769) 6-1345).

A few km above the buraku of Shirakawa-go is another small cluster of gassho houses to the west of the road and down near the valley floor. There is a minshuku advertised on a sign at road level (Toichin-sa; tel (07637) 3632), but the surroundings are not as picturesque as at Shirakawa-go.

Other villages

Gokayama A little farther north, across the boundary into Toyama-ken, are the gassho houses of Gokayama (which is technically part of Kami-Taira, or 'upper Taira' village), beginning at Nishi-Akao. There are so few that they can be identified by name. First comes the Iwase family house; a little further on, at Suganuma (Kami-Taira), one finds the houses that make up Gokayama Seishonen Ryoko Mura (Youth Tourist Village) which offer accommodation. Near the Tourist Village is a road that turns off and runs inland to the west: this leads to Etchu Gokayama Youth Hostel, itself a gassho house (tel 07636 7-3331). Another house (Murakami family) can be found at Kami-Nashi (Upper Nashi), a hot-spring town. At Shimo-Nashi (Lower Nashi), you can see traditional Japanese paper (washi) being made at Goka-shi Kyodo Kumiai (Goka-city Paper Producers' Cooperative).

Toga You can also find gassho-zukuri in the Kami-Momose section of Toga village. I haven't been there, but saw a newspaper photo showing five thatched houses close to each other. Being not so well known (the newspaper article was the only reference I saw), as well as being more remote, it may be less touristy. I can't give any information on accommodation, but there is a reasonable chance that there is at least one minshuku. Getting there may not be too easy: one map shows a good road direct to the village from just above Furukawa/Takayama, with a minor road linking that road to Inokuchi, a little above Taira; another major map gives no hint of such a road.

MINO-KAMO TO TAKAOKA

North from Shirakawa-go along Route 156 and branching to Kanazawa on Route 304, you pass through some very pretty countryside. Continuing along 156 toward Takaoka after the fork to 304 is less memorable but still enjoyable. Routes 41 and 257 north meet just a little below the town of Gero.

Gero

This is a typical hot-spring resort, basically a collection of concrete hotels that feature the mineral-laden water, mostly for therapeutic benefits. There are no attractions for the casual visitor, except that travellers with time to spare could check out one travel publication's mention of a village of gassho-zukuri houses transplanted here from Shirakawa-mura when it was flooded by the waters of Miboro dam. (I cannot guarantee its existence.) Those in a hurry can rely on the existence of houses still at Shirakawa-go, and a 'village' of houses transported to Takayama.

Another attraction of Gero is the Chubu Sangaku Archaeological Museum.

Zenshoji

One stop above Gero is Zenshoji station; nearby is Zenshoji temple, the largest in the Hida region. Hida is the name given to the region generally above Gero to beyond Takayama.

TAKAYAMA

The city of Takayama ('High Mountain') is often called Hida-Takayama. It has been a prosperous area for several centuries, and there is a tradition of cultured living that one would not expect to find in an isolated river valley. Several fine old houses and other buildings survive in the city; these and other attractions make wandering around the city interesting and pleasurable, and make Takayama one of the most worthwhile places in Japan to visit.

Information

Your first stop should be at the information booth in front of Takayama station to pick up a copy of their English-language booklet *Hida-Takayama*. It lists all the places of interest to visitors, with a brief description of each, and locates them on a map. If you are starting from Tokyo, you should also obtain from the TIC a copy of their photocopied information sheet on Takayama; it has more detail on train connections, accommodation, etc.

Getting Around

Since the city is laid out with streets at right-angles (a rarity in Japan) it is easy to find one's way around Takayama. The city is small enough that the energetic can see it on foot. An alternative is a bicycle: you can rent them from at least two shops on the main street near the station. One is to the left when leaving the station, on the opposite side

A Rickshaws can still be found, especially at tourist destinations
B Young women in their best kimono at the Furukawa Matsuri festival

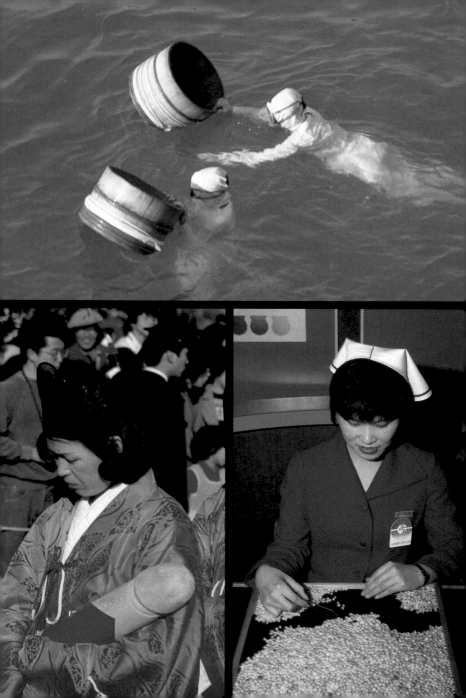

of the street, and the other is farther along the street on the same side. The rental is Y1500 per day.

There is a regular bus service that goes to or near most of the attractions of the city and circles back to the station. A 'free pass' (the Japlish term) costing Y770 is available; it gives unlimited travel for two days, and can be bought at the station. Buses run every 20 minutes between 9 am and 4.40 pm.

Hida Kokubunji temple

This is the oldest temple in the Hida region, originally founded in 746. The main hall is about 500 years old.

Kusakabe Folkcraft Museum (Kusakabe Mingei-kan)

The house itself, dating from 1880, is a fine example of the residence of a wealthy merchant (Kusakabe family) of that era. The interior features heavy beams of polished wood, and other details matching the elegance of the rest of the building. There is also a collection of folkcraft items from the region (closed Wednesdays from December to February).

Yoshijima House

A neighbour of the Kusakabe house, this building was the residence of the Yoshijima (Old Island) family, also wealthy merchants. The two are among the finest houses in Takayama. Yoshijima House is closed Tuesdays from November to February.

A *Diving demonstration by ama who collect edible seafish and seaweed*
B *Tagata-jinja fertility festival*
C *Sorting pearls by colour, Mikimoto Pearl Island*

Shishi Kaikan

This is an exhibition of the elaborately carved and ornately lacquered wooden lion-heads used for dances during processions.

Hachima shrine

This is the site of the autumn festival (described below). In the grounds is Takayama Yatai Kaikan, an exhibition hall containing four of the 23 elaborately decorated festival wagons (yatai) arranged as you would see them in a procession during the spring or autumn festival. It gives at least an impression of the magnificence of the festival to those who are unable to see the real thing.

Higashiyama Teramachi

This name comes from the row of ten temples at the foot of Higashiyama ('East Mountain'); teramachi means 'temple town'. (The youth hostel at Tenshoji temple is in this area.)

Hida Fubutsu-kan

This is a museum showing artefacts related to the way of life in the Hida region.

Hachiga Folk Art Gallery (Hachiga Minyoku Bijutsu-kan)

This building houses the folk-art collection of the Hachiga family.

Hirata Memorial Hall (Hirata Kinen-kan)

Art objects belonging to the Hirata family, descendants of a wealthy merchant, are displayed in this museum.

Kyodo Gangu-kan

This museum houses about 2000 traditional toys from different regions of Japan.

Municipal History Museum (Takayama Kyodo-kan)

This building, built in 1876 and formerly a storehouse, belonged to the Nagata family and now houses many items of

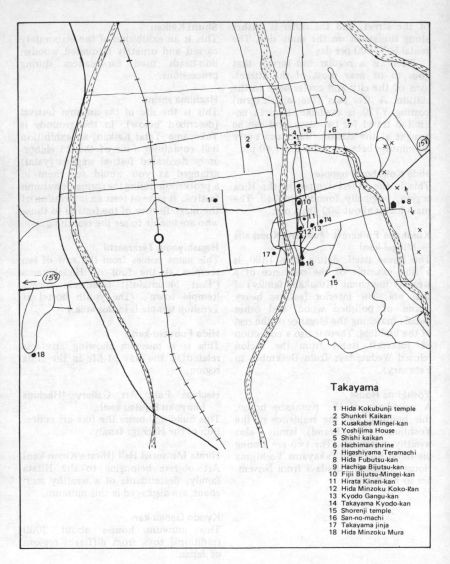

Takayama

1 Hida Kokubunji temple
2 Shunkei Kaikan
3 Kusakabe Mingei-kan
4 Yoshijima House
5 Shishi kaikan
6 Hachiman shrine
7 Higashiyama Teramachi
8 Hida Fubutsu-kan
9 Hachiga Bijutsu-kan
10 Fijii Bijutsu-Mingei-kan
11 Hirata Kinen-kan
12 Hida Minzoku Koko-Kan
13 Kyodo Gangu-kan
14 Takayama Kyodo-kan
15 Shorenji temple
16 San-no-machi
17 Takayama jinja
18 Hida Minzoku Mura

local history as well as a famous Enku statue. The latter is one of many well-known statues roughly sculpted with a hatchet by the itinerant priest Enku.

Shorenji temple

This temple (main building dating from 1504) is built in a unique ancient style and is famous for the elegant curved shape of its roof. It was moved here from Shirakawago when the Mihoro dam was built in 1961.

San-no-machi

A row of old houses and shops lines both sides of Kami-San-no-machi street. Many are restaurants, coffee shops or souvenir shops (the owners have to make a living, too), but the overall impression is like that of a century or so ago. The buildings with the large spongy-looking 'ball' hanging from the eaves are old sake warehouses, where various kinds of sake are still on sale. Takayama has been known for more than a millen-eum for its carpenters and woodworkers, so have a look at the small chests, trays, bowls or even just chopping-blocks, that are on sale in the shops.

Takayama Jinya

This imposing building was the residence of the local governor in the Tokugawa era. Formerly, it was the heart of a complex of buildings (shown in outline in the pamphlet given at the entrance); now most are gone, except for eight samurai barracks and a garden behind the main building. Closed Wednesdays.

Hida Folklore Village (Hida Minzoku Mura)

This is a large park on the edge of the city, where many traditional farmhouses (mostly thatched) and other buildings up to 500 years old have been moved and set up around a pond. (Because the buildings were held together with ropes and not nails, they could be dismantled and reassembled without damage.) The reservation includes houses from a number of districts in the mountains around Takayama, including the Shira-kawago area. A pamphlet in English describes the salient points of the various buildings. This is probably the best park of its kind in Japan in terms of both the buildings and the setting: in the distance are the mountains that surround Takayama, and the impression in the immediate vicinity is that of being in a functioning village. (Parks on a similar theme are to be found at Kawasaki, near Tokyo, Kanazawa, and on Shikoku.) The park is a couple of kilometres from the station and can be reached by bus, taxi or on foot.

Other

There are also a number of museums and exhibitions worth visiting. They include the following: the Shunkei Lacquerware Hall (Shunkei Kaikan), Fujii Folkcraft Museum (Fujii Bijutsu Mingei-kan), and the Hida Archaeology Museum (Hida Minzoku Koko-kan).

Festivals

Takayama is justly famous throughout Japan for its spring and autumn festivals, two of the most magnificent and inter-esting in the country. Huge, incredibly ornate festive wagons (yatai) are put on display for most of the day, and are later pulled through the streets. The tradition of building them began a couple of centuries ago, as a supplica-tion to the gods to protect the inhabit-ants of the city from a plague that was ravaging the country. Their prayers seemed to be successful, and the custom continued (a sort of preventive medic-ine?); the carts became more magnificent as a spirit of competition among wealthy merchants developed. Since Takayama was a wealthy town, the best materials and construction could be afforded. A booklet is on general sale that gives the history of each yatai; some are nearly 300 years old. During the rest of the year, the wagons are stored in yatai-gura, tall concrete storehouses with no windows and very tall doors, that can be seen around the town. As mentioned earlier, there is a permanent display of four yatai during the rest of the year at Yatai-kaikan, on the ground of Hachiman shrine.

Details of the wagons (which are hard to describe since they resemble nothing known in Western countries) include intricate wood carvings that form panels and pillars of the structure, antique tapestries of European origin, and other embellishments. In additon, there is a small number of mechanical 'dolls' that perform amazing movements and tricks, all controlled by wires and push-rods; the ingenuity of their designers deserves greater recognition. A typcal doll 'walks' out along a beam, rotates and bows to the audience, pivots around completely a couple of times, then releases a shower of flower petals. One even has a couple of acrobats that swing from perch to perch.

During the display of the wagons, performances of the dolls are given from time to time (indicated on a board near the wagons). It pays to arrive early for a performance to get a good pl'ace, because the crowds are very heavy.

The spring Sanno-matsuri is held on 14-15 April near Hie-jinja (shrine), and the autumn Yahata-matsuri on 9-10 October. There is a total of 23 yatai (wagons), but only 12 are shown at the spring festival, and the other 11 in the autumn. There are also parades of people in various feudal costumes. An interesting feature is one of the musical instruments, a circular metal pan that is struck with a wooden mallet to yield a peculiar 'ging' sound; it seems to be found only in this district.

Accommodation

There is a youth hostel in Takayama, Tenshoji-temple (tel (0577) 32-6345). However, it was not the most pleasant I encountered: the house-mother had a love affair with the PA which, like most hostel PA systems, had only one setting — full blast. At 10 pm (lights-out) she continued for 15 minutes to tell her charges to go to sleep, etc, while they were all lying in bed in the darkness waiting for her to keep quiet!

As might be expected in a town that is very popular with Japanese sightseers, Takayama has plenty of minshuku and ryokan. One is at the information booth in front of the station. There is an agency down the street to the left after leaving the station, and another located at the far side of a large department. store opposite and to the right of the station. Both are signposted only in Japanese, but the Kanji for 'minshuku' are prominent and can be recognized easily.

The phone number of the Takayama Minshuku Association is (0577) 33-8501/2; that of the Takayama Ryokan Association is (0577) 33-1181. Have someone call in Japanese, as it is unlikely that anyone will understand English. There is also a Kokumin-shukusha (Peoples' Lodge): tel (0577) 32-2400; Y3400 with two meals in 1979. The cheapest hotel is the Meiboku (tel (0577) 33-5510), which cost Y4000 in 1979. The Hida and Green hotels are more expensive: tel (0577) 33-4600 and 33-5500 respectively.

Getting There

Takayama is easily reached by JNR train from Nagoya, Osaka/Kyoto, and Gifu (the local train from Gifu is cheapest). There is also a bus service to and from Gifu year-round; and from mid-May to mid-October from Matsumoto, by a complicated route of two buses and a train via Shimajashima. From the north there is JNR service to and from Toyama, and possibly a bus service. Highway 41 is a major road linking Nagoya with Toyama and there is quite heavy traffic, so hitching should be no problem.

FURUKAWA

About 15 km above Takayama is the small city of Furukawa ('Old River'). It has a number of old houses, and the appearance of some of its streets is, overall, perhaps more traditional that

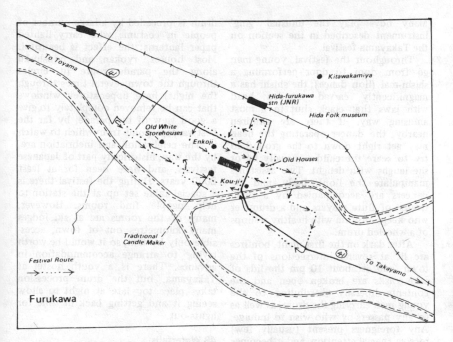

Map labels:
To Toyama
Kitawakamiya
Hida-furukawa stn (JNR)
Hida Folk museum
Old White Storehouses
Enkoji
Old Houses
Kou-ji
Traditional Candle Maker
Festival Route
To Takayamo
Furukawa

those of Takayama. It is a pleasant place to walk around, and there is a chance that a rickshaw will be available for short rides.

Festival

Furukawa is probably best known for its annual festival, which is well worth trying to see. Furukawa-matsuri is held on 19-20 April. The feature is a night procession of a huge drum on which two men sit back-to-back and swing their hammers down to strike both ends in unison. The festival dates back 1500 years, so I was told, to the time when drums were used to scare boars away from the crops.

The festival lasts two days, and it is advisable to see all of it. During the day, there are processions of the nine yatai (festive wagons similar to those at Takayama and Kyoto). The wagons are elaborately decorated, though they are

not as large or imposing as those in the other two cities. Two of them also have ingenious mechanical dolls which are on display on the second day of the festival (times for their performances are posted beside the yatai-gura). In 1978, the times for the kirintai (a kirin is a mythical dragon) yatai were 1.30 and 3.30 pm, while those of the seyutai yatai took place at 10 am and 3 pm. The dolls are at least 150 years old (ca 1820) and are marvels of design skill. They are similar to those described for the Takayama festivals, and similar dolls can be seen at one of Nagoya's festivals.

During the processions of the first day, many townspeople in old costume accompany the wagons. Children are dressed at their best (as they are for the more crowded Takayama-matsuri), and it is a splendid chance to photograph them dressed in very beautiful kimono.

Many boys play the unusual 'ging' instrument described in the section on the Takayama festival.

Throughout the festival, young men go from door to door performing a shishi-mai (lion dance); the shishi has a magnificently carved wooden head with jaws that clack shut in a most amusing way. If there are children nearby, the dancer operating the head may get right down to the ground to try to scare the child — usually he or she laughs with delight. Two assistants manipulate the lion's body, and the dancers are accompanied by a small troupe of flute players and a drummer who keeps rhythm with healthy wallops of a wheeled drum.

After dark on the first night, bonfires are lit at several intersections of the town, and at about 10 pm the lids of sake casks are broken open and the contents liberally distributed to the young men carrying the drum, as well as to any passers-by who wish to indulge. Any foreigners present (usually few) receive special attention, and it becomes a problem keeping sober enough to see the rest of the festivities, let alone take pictures. The fires and sake help to keep the young men warm, because they wear nothing but haramaki around their middles and a loincloth and the nights are cold (nearby ski-grounds still have large patches of snow on them). After they have become sufficiently soused, one after another demonstrates his balancing skills by scaling a bamboo pole and lying on it, all his weight held by the small circle of the pole pressing into his belly.

Not long afterward, the procession with the large drum begins. The drum (at least 1.5 metres in diameter), the two drummers and at least 10 other people carrying lanterns, are supported on a large structure of bamboo poles and beams that is carried through the streets on the strong shoulders of many (usually inebriated) young men. The drum is preceded by a large number of people in costume who carry lighted paper lanterns; the effect is beautiful. Most houses, ryokan and minshuku along the parade route (it circles through the town several times through the night) have upper-storey windows that can be removed completely to give a good view of the parade, by far the best vantage point from which to watch it. The celebration and inebriation are, by the way, historically part of Japanese festivals, and have been for at least 2000 years. During the festival there is a special table set up at the station to help people find rooms. However, many of the rooms are at ski lodges many kilometres out of town, accessible only by taxi, so it would be worth trying to arrange accommodation in advance. There is a youth hostel at Takayama, but the drum procession takes place too late at night to allow seeing it and getting back in time for lights-out.

48 Waterfalls

Between Takayama and Furukawa there is a turn-off (signposted in Japanese) pointing the way to 48 Waterfalls (Yonju-hachi taki), about eight km off the main road. They are a pleasant, low-key bit of scenery — the water flow and the drops are moderate — but they provide a pleasant walk relatively remote from humanity (most of it, anyway).

SHIGA-KEN — LAKE BIWA

HIKONE

Little mentioned in tourist literature, this small city can be reached from Kyoto or Gifu in an hour, and is worth a visit to admire its pretty feudal castle overlooking Lake Biwa, and one of the loveliest gardens in Japan. Both can be reached by a 10-minute walk

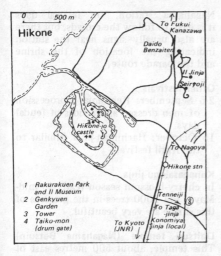

Hikone

0   500 m

To Fukui
Kanazawa

Daido
Benzaiten

Ii Jinja

Seiryoji

Hikone-jo
castle

To Nagoya

Hikone stn

1 Rakurakuen Park
  and Ii Museum
2 Genkyuen
  Garden
3 Tower
4 Taiko-mon
  (drum gate)

Tenneiji

To Taga
-jinja
Konomiya
jinja (local)

To Kyoto
(JNR)

along the road leading from the front of Hikone station.

Hikone Castle (Hikone-jo)

The castle, perched scenically atop the only sizeable hill in the area and close to the waters of Biwa-ko (lake), was finished in 1622 and is one of relatively few original castles remaining in Japan. The main building is a National Treasure, and several of the towers and gates are rated almost as highly. One of the towers functions as an art gallery, and displays many art works and arms of the Ii family, the owners. (Tall people: watch your heads on the beams!)

Two of the original three moats remain and their banks give good views of the walls and castle itself. Cherry trees line the banks, and during the cherry-blossom season (usually early to mid-April) the castle and grounds are one of the most beautiful places in Japan. Graceful swans swimming in the moat add a note of serene beauty.

A booklet in English is usually available (free) when entering the castle; it gives a good description of the various features of the castle and other attractions of Hikone. (If the booklet, *How to*

See Hikone in Japan, is not available at the castle or Genjyuen garden, ask at the city office.)

Genkyuen Garden

Located just north of the castle moats is Genkyuen, a landscape garden patterned on the garden of the same name in China, dating from 1678. Although it is not as famous as the 'Big Three' gardens, I consider it far more attractive than any of the others and one of the loveliest in Japan. This view was shared by a Japanese garden lover I met while strolling around the central pond: according to her, it is beautiful in all four seasons. If you take bread, you can feed the colourful carp in the pond. The admittance ticket for the castle also includes the garden.

Other

Other attractions in the Hikone area include Taga-jinja (shrine) and its garden, nearby Konomiya shrine and garden, Ryotanji temple and its highly regarded Zen-type rock garden, Seiryoji temple, Daido Benzaiten temple, and Tenneiji temple. These are all described in the city office publication mentioned earlier.

Festivals

Early April: Sakura-matsuri (Cherry Blossom Festival).

22 April: Taga-jinja matsuri.

1 August: Fireworks display.

8 August: Hikone Bayashi (dance) in the centre of the city.

Autumn: Shiro-matsuri (castle festival), a procession of children in costumes of feudal days.

Getting There

Hikone is served by JNR trains, and is one station away from Maibara, a major railway junction on the Shinkansen and Tokaido main line towards Kyoto/Osaka. It is about an hour away from Kyoto.

NAGAHAMA

The name means 'Long Beach'. This is not a very interesting town except during the Nagahama-matsuri festival, 14-15 April, and possibly during another festival in October.

Nagahama-matsuri

This festival is one of the more interesting in Japan, and is worth trying to see if you are anywhere remotely near the city at the time. The festival features 12 yatai, which are used as portable stages on which children in costume present Hikiyama-kyogen, (a type of comic drama). The stages are covered with miniature roofs of the same graceful shape and construction as those on temples, and the wagons are decorated with elaborate carvings, gilt, even Gobelin tapestries showing European soldiers and believed to have been brought from Belgium in the 16th century.

On the evening of 14 April, the yatai are gathered in lantern-light at Hachiman shrine. The next day, the yatai are moved from the shrine into positions on the city's streets, and performances of the kyogen are given, each one lasting 20-30 minutes. Then the wagons are moved ahead to a new position (replacing the wagon that had been standing there), and another performance begins. The process is repeated throughout the day.

Watching the moving of the wagons is as interesting as the plays themselves, for each yatai weighs many tons and is little narrower than the small streets through which they process. The wheels cannot be moved, so the wagons must be manhandled sideways with the use of long levers — more than one protruding advertising sign gets knocked off each year, even at the second-storey level, for the carts are at least five to six metres tall.

Hachiman-jinja is a 10-15 minute walk from the east exit of the JNR Nagahama station. On festival days it is easy to follow the crowds, but there are also usually signs near the station indicating the location of the shrine and the parade route.

Other festivals

2-5 September: Kehi-jinja, a procession of men dressed as warriors of feudal days.

15 October: Hachiman-jinja (similar to the April festival).

Kanagasakigu-jinja

In cherry-blossom season (early to mid-May), the 2000 trees in the grounds of this shrine are very beautiful.

Daitsuji temple (Nagahama Betsuin)

This temple, about 500 metres east of the station, is designed in the rather flamboyant Momoyama style, and dates from 1586.

Getting There

Nagahama is three stations north of Maibara, a major junction on the Tokaido main line and the Shinkansen.

FUKUI-KEN

FUKUI

The city of Fukui, while of little intrinsic interest, is a centre for visiting several interesting nearby attractions.

Eiheiji temple

One of the most famous temples in Japan is Eiheiji, less than 20 km southeast of Fukui. Founded in 1244, it is one of two head temples of the Soto sect of Zen Buddhism (the other is Sojiji in Yokohama, near Tokyo). The temple is very beautifully located at the foot of a mountain amongst trees up to 600 years old; the buildings, about 70 in number, climb up the hillside. As

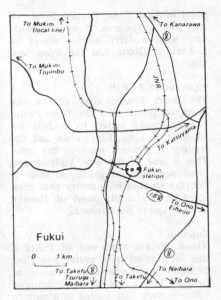

Eiheiji, most of it along scenic river-banks.

Kuzuryu gorge/Managawa gorge

Both of these gorges, noted for their scenery, are in the vicinity of Ono. The former is close to Echizen-Shimoyama station (JNR), and it is likely that buses run to the latter from Ono station (JNR).

TAKEFU/IMADATE

Imadate is a town not far from Fukui that is noted for paper-making — not machine-made, but traditional washi hand-made paper. There are about 120 establishments making paper in the district, about half in the village of Otaki. The process of paper-making is illustrated at Washi-no-Sato-Kaikan (open daily except year-end). Paper and paper products are on display and for sale.

Paper-making is a cottage industry carried out by many families. To see one of these workshops (kojo), contact the Washi Kumiai (Papermakers' Cooperative) who will then arrange a visit. The Kumiai also sells paper of the area. Paper-makers use mostly traditional methods, although almost all use dryers rather than depending on air drying. A major exception is Ichibei Iwano, son of a former 'living national treasure', who makes paper used for woodblock prints. These hand-made papers are not cheap, but they require a large amount of hand labour and justify the asking price.

Getting There

Access is from Takefu (18 km south of Fukui by JNR) by a local train line, the Nan-etsu-sen. The destination is the final station, Swatabe, which is in Imadate.

Accommodation

A ryokan which sounds above average is the Suya; it has a nice garden with a

well as being a large, functioning Zen temple, with shaven-headed monks silently meditating, the natural beauty makes this worth a visit. A pamphlet in English is given at the entrance, and gives a good description of the main buildings set on 33 sq km of grounds.

The temple authorities allow foreign visitors to stay at the temple and participate in Zen meditation. (Refer to the notes on Zen meditation earlier in the book.) At Eiheiji, visitors are expected to follow the same discipline as Japanese participants, starting with meditation at 3.30 am. Arrangements should be made in advance by writing to: Sanzenkei, Eiheiji, Eiheiji-cho, Yoshida-gun, Fukui-ken.

The temple is reached by Keifuku Dentetsu railway or by bus, both from Fukui. The train is caught most easily from the east side of Fukui station (behind the building). A bike path is under construction between Fukui and large thatched-roof teahouse; prices are from Y5100 with two meals.

ECHIZEN TOGEI MURA

Echizen Pottery Village, also not far from Fukui, was set up to preserve and continue the tradition of ceramics that has existed here for centuries. Echizen is one of the 'Six Ancient Kilns' and has been a pottery-making centre since the Kamakura Era (1192-1333).

Many potters of note have their workshops in Togei Mura; their work can be seen at the associated showrooms, as well as in shops in the town, and most potters have no objection to visitors in the workshops and studios. Other pottery, both modern and historic, is on display at Fukui-ken Ceramics Museum (Fukui-ken Togeikan) nearby (open daily except Monday, the third Wednesday of the month, national holidays, and the New Year period). Local kilns are described in a booklet available at the museum, but the help of a Japanese-reading friend will be needed.

Pottery Lessons

Amateur potters can take single lessons or a course at the pottery school (Togei kyoshitsu) in the village. It is usual to make arrangements in advance (tel 07783 2-2174), but students may be enrolled on the spot if there is space. The school is located beside the Togeikan and has the same holidays.

Getting There

Echizen Togei Mura is in the Ozowara section of the Miyazaki-mura (village), and is easily reached from Takefu station by bus in less than a hour. You can get to Takefu from Fukui by JNR, or from Maibara, 55 minutes to the south. There is also direct service from Kyoto/Osaka.

TSURUGA

A city on the coast nearest the northern point of Lake Biwa, Tsuraga is one of two ports in the area (along with Maizura) with a ferry service direct to Hokkaido (Otaru, not far from Sapporo).

NORTH OF FUKUI

The entire Echizen coast all the way north to and around the Noto Peninsula is ideally suited to cyclists because it is quite flat terrain and the scenery is pleasant most of the time. This is one of the least built-up and developed parts of Japan, so there is not the amount of industry that characterizes the south coast of Honshu from Tokyo to Shimonoseki.

Tojimbo

About 30 km north-east of Fukui is this focal point of a pretty coastline. Tojimbo is a small-scale version of Britain's Land's End, an outcropping of volcanic rock that cooled in a pattern of roughly hexagonal pillars rising sharply out of the sea for 25-30 metres. Since the rock is an extension of the land, it is easy to scramble over it; cruise boats leave from a cove between outcroppings. It is impossible to photograph without including several dozen tourists, for it is a very popular destination. Tojimbo is most easily reached by taking a tram-train from Fukui to Mikuni-minato station, then changing to a bus for the last two km.

Ojima Island

A couple of km up the coast is a small forest-covered island called Ojima, which is joined to the mainland by a bridge. Visitors to the island are greeted by a shrine and torii gate.

Coastal scenery

A little farther up is a stretch of very pretty coast (not spectacular, but pleasant, with rock outcroppings). The rest of the coast up to Kanazawa is pleasant, though not outstanding. Of interest are the houses which face the coast: their roofs are often weighted with rocks, and in the autumn (the only time I have travelled in the area), there are boards and other forms of protection against winter winds in front of the houses.

Accommodation

Of the hostels in the area, I found Youth Hostel 3404 (in Fukui) to be rather institutuional. More pleasant, though some distance out of town, is Gankeiji Youth Hostel, which is a large functioning neighbourhood temple near Kaga. The temple's history goes back several hundred years (though the present buildings are comparatively recent), and the house-mother is exceptionally kind and pleasant. There are some minshuku right on the northern coast, overlooking the water, which would probably be a particularly nice place to spend a night.

Maruoka Castle

Maruoka-jo is one of the oldest castles in Japan, dating from 1575. It is quite small and not particularly notable — of greatest interest to castle aficionados. It can be reached from Maruoka station by bus in 15 minutes.

ISHIKAWA-KEN

KANAZAWA

This city is a favourite of Japanese tourists, and has much to recommend it to foreign visitors (who are still quite rare, for this part of Japan is off the usual track for foreigners). This part of Japan is relatively little industrialized, so there has been less of the tear-down-and-rebuild activity that has destroyed so much of the heritage of Japan. It also escaped bombing during the war, the only large city other than Kyoto to do so: many old buildings have survived,

and old neighbourhoods are almost unchanged from their appearance of decades or a century ago.

Strangely, being so far from cultural influences like Kyoto (the area is heavily covered with snow in winter, and transport was difficult for much of the year in former times), the city has historically been a centre of culture and learning. A major factor is that it is one of the richest rice-growing areas in Japan, and another is that the Maeda clan who controlled the city and region valued education and a cultured life. They spent the wealth of the largest feudal land tenure wisely, and encouraged such crafts as lacquerware and weaving, encouraged artisans to settle, and established traditions that survive today.

Kanazawa owes this preeminence to Lord Toshiie Maeda, who captured the city in 1583 from warrior-general Sakuma. The latter had taken it three years from Buddhist priests of Oyama Gogo temple (formerly located on the site of the present castle) who had controlled the city and region for more than a century. During the next 300 years, Maeda and his successors brought about prosperity and established the fine buildings and traditions of the city.

A large proportion of the attractions of Kanazawa date from the days of the Maedas. Since they were mostly for the benefit of that family, they are generally located near Kanazawa Castle, and can be seen on foot (though it does involve a healthy amount of walking). Most are located around an irregular loop encircling Kenrokuen garden, which is across the road from Kanazawa Castle. This makes the castle a good starting point: it can be reached by bus in 15 minutes from Kanazawa JNR station (about 2.5 km away); the stop is 'kenrokuen-sh'ta'.

Kanazawa-jo

Little remains of the former imposing

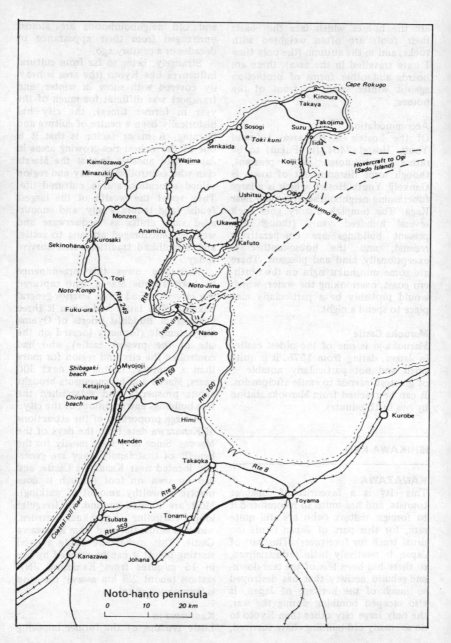

Noto-hanto peninsula

0   10   20 km

castle because a series of fires in the last century. That of 1881 destroyed all the major buildings except Ishikawa-mon gate, parts of the walls, moats and the armour (sanjuken nagaya). The site of the castle is now the campus of Kanazawa National University (to be relocated in the near future). In one corner of the grounds is Oyama-jinja shrine.

Oyama-jinja The gate of this shrine is very unusual in design and history, and is unlike that of almost any other shrine in Japan. It was designed in 1870 by a Dutchman, a scientist who was teaching in the city during the Westernization period. The top two storeys of the gate strongly suggest two squared arches, one atop the other, of traditional Chinese design. Similar (rare) arches may be found in the Karamon of the innermost shrine Toshogu shrine in Nikko, and another in Nagasaki at Kofukuji (nicknamed the 'Chinese' temple). Filling the top arch is a stained-glass window (the coloured glass actually had a purpose, for it was used as a lighthouse to guide ships on the Sea of Japan). The shrine itself dates from 1599 and was built to honour Toshiie Maeda, the founder of the Maeda clan; it was moved to its present site in 1873.

Gyokusen-en garden This was the garden of the Nishida family, and is laid out in a circular style around a pond.

Ishikawa-ken Handicrafts Museum (Ishikawa-ken kanko Bussan-kan)
Ishikawa-ken is famous for several handicrafts: some of Japan's finest lacquerware, cloth weaving and dyeing, pottery-making, as well as wood-carving and others. This museum makes it possible for visitors to see some of the crafts actually being performed. Master craftsmen give demonstrations daily in lacquerware, carving of wooden heads for shishi (lion dolls), gold-beating, kaga yuzen (fabric dyeing), and kutani pottery-making. An excellent pamphlet in English gives sufficient explanation of the crafts to understand the processes. Demonstrations are given on the third floor. There are restaurants and shops selling a wide variety of handicrafts native to the area. In addition, there is a tourist information office at the entrance: their map of Kanazawa is a typical handout map and is very stylized, not to scale, and north is off to the left; beware! (Closed Wednesdays in winter.)

Kenrokuen Garden
This large landscape garden (10 ha) dates from 1819 and is considered by the Japanese as one of the three finest landscape gardens in Japan. Roku means 'six', and Kenrokuen combines the six features considered essential to fine gardens: vastness, solemnity, careful arrangement, coolness (water), age, and pleasing appearance.

The garden is spacious and encloses two ponds with several pleasing views. It is, to me, by far the most attractive of the 'Big Three' gardens. However, although Kenrokuen is certainly worth seeing, for some viewers it does not quite live up to its advance billing. The north entrance to the garden is across the road from Ishikawa-mon gate, but there are also other entrances.

Other
Seisonkaku On the south edge of Kenrokuen is situated Seisonkaku, a beautiful two-storey mansion built by one of the daimyo for his mother. It is a fine example of Shoin-zukuri architecture. In addition to the design and workmanship of the house and garden themselves, there is an exhibit of many items used by the Maedas. (Closed Wednesdays).

Ishikawa Prefecture Art Museum (Ishikawa-ken Bijutsu-kan) A very
short distance from Seisonkaku, this

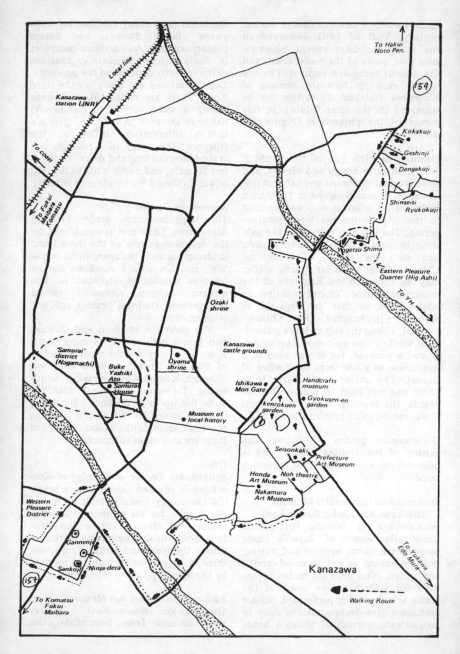

Kanazawa

museum is most worthy of note for its collection of kutani pottery.

Prefectural Noh Theatre (Nohgaku Bunka Kaikan) Noh plays are performed here frequently, mostly by amateur groups, but there is a regular professional performance on the first Sunday of every month (some sources claim the third Sunday, so be sure to check!) Performances last from 9 am to 5 pm. The theatre dates from 1972; inside is the stage which was salvaged from the old Noh theatre that stood beside the town hall. The theatre is just a short distance south of Seisonkaku. (Closed Mondays.)

Honda Memorial Art Museum (Honda Zohin-kan) Also located near Seisonkaku, at the top of the hill, this museum houses a collection of items used by the Honda family, the chief retainers under the Maeda.

Nakamura Memorial Art Museum (Nakamura Kinen Bijutsu-kan) Close to the Honda Museum, this is a large Japanese-style house that belonged to a wealthy sale dealer named Nakamura. He donated the house and his collection of Oriental art (including fine lacquerware and utensils for the tea ceremony) to the city. (Closed on Tuesdays and the day after national holidays.

Museum of Local History (Kyodo Shiryo-kan) This museum has a variety of exhibits local archaeology, folklore and history, including one relating to the processions required of local daimyo to Edo (Tokyo) in feudal times, which often involved thousands of people. The building looks incongruous, for it is a Western-style red-brick structure built in 1891 as a high school at a time when Westernization was in full swing. Note that on the map included with the information sheets available at the Tokyo TIC, this is labelled 'History Museum'. (Closed Mondays).

Samurai district Not far from the Museum of Local History is Nagamachi, an old samurai town. There are several typical narrow crooked streets lined with packed-earth, tile-topped walls that keep out curious eyes. Walking through the little lanes gives at least a little impression of olden times. Most of the houses, however, are actually from the Meiji era (1868-1910), rather than genuine samurai-built houses. One genuine samurai house which has been restored and is open to the public as a museum is Buke Yashiki Ato (closed Wednesdays). Another old house, Saihitsuan, is used for demonstrating yuzen, the traditional method of hand-painting patterns on silk for kimono (closed Thursdays in winter). For a look over two former samurai gardens, have a coffee at either Kaga-no-niwa or Nokore (both closed Thursdays). The reason why there are not many samurai houses is that, while the Japanese like to admire the buildings, they are not very comfortable to live in.

Oyama-jinja shrine After visiting the samurai area, and shopping in the many stores along the nearby main street, one can return full-circle to Oyama shrine, or leave it to the last for a visit along with a more leisurely look at the handicrafts-making displays at the handicrafts centre.

Higashi (geisha) district
This is one of two 'old' districts of Kanazawa that are popular with visitors because they preserve much of the atmosphere of former times. According to one story, the Maedas decreed that geisha areas and temples be placed on the banks of both the Agano and Sai (west) rivers, so that invaders would be distracted by one or the other. More likely it was a way to minimize their effect on daily life, just as Tokyo had

the Yoshiwara area for its geisha houses. The main attraction is just wandering along the back streets among the old houses and temples. Visitors are allowed in to one of the geisha still-functioning houses: the Shima (usually open 9 am-5 pm; closed Mondays). Another has been converted into a minshuku, the Yogetsu (Y3700 with two meals).

Termachi

This is the second of the 'old' districts. The geisha houses are no longer mentioned, but the temples still remain, including one of the most unusual in Japan, Myoryuji.

Myoryuji Dubbed Ninja-dera (Ninja temple), this is not only a temple but also a type of fortress with labrynthine secret passages, hidden traps and exits, etc, that would serve to hold off invaders while the daimyo escaped. Myoryuji was the Maeda family temple. There are tours lasting 20 minutes, but the temple is so popular that it is generally necessary to make reservations (tel 41-2877, in Japanese); on Sundays and holidays it may be impossible. The best time to go is mid-afternoon. If there are not many people scheduled for a tour, it may be possible to squeeze in without a reservation. Some of the guides may speak English. (Closed 1st and 13th of each month, and New Year.)

Edo-mura

Of interest to many will be Edo-mura, a 'village' of Edo-era (17-19th century) buildings that have been moved here from different places in Japan. Some of the buildings are luxurious mansions and houses, while others give an idea of the less-exalted conditions of the ordinary people. The village is well done, but the number of buildings is rather small (about 20) in view of the rather high admittance charge (Y650 in 1979).

Included in the price, however, is admittance to nearby Danpuen, a small village concentrating on crafts; a mini-bus goes every 20 minutes between the two villages. The village rather suffers in comparison with the similar park in Takayama, but it is worth seeing if you don't have to pinch pennies. Access is by Hokuriku Railway bus 12 from Kanazawa station of Yukawa Onsen; Edo-mura is a short walk away, uphill.

Home Visits

To arrange a visit to a private house in Kanazawa, tel 20-2075.

Getting There

Kanazawa is easily reached by train from Tokyo, Nagoya, Kyoto, Osaka, etc via Maibara (on the Shinkansen); or by plane to nearby Komatsu airport.

Accommodation

There are two youth hostels in or near Kanazawa. One of these is the cheapest in Japan (Y300) but it is so far out in the country that it is not worth trying to find; it also has a very early (and noisy) morning. reveille.) There are many hotels, ryokan and minshuku (especially in Higashi); bookings can be made at the station. There is a very interesting inn/restaurant in a 150-year-old farmhouse, Zenigame, a few km out of town toward Edo-mura (tel 35-1426; Y6000 overnight with two meals).

Festivals

There are many festivals through the year. Most are small neighbourhood affairs, but there are some very large and well-known ones as well.

10-16 February: performances of dek-umawashi (a kind of puppet theatre unique to the area) at the community centre of Oguchi; access by bus 47 bound for Shiramine, getting off at Higashi Futakuchi. Performances are at night, so it is advisable to take the 5 pm bus, and make prior arrangements for accommodation with a village family by calling Mr Zenzai (tel

076196-7120).

19-20 April: Gokoku-jinja Spring Festival, featuring dances by shrine maidens.

15 May: Shinji Noh performance, given outdoors at Ono Minato Jinja (in Kanaiwa) for the benefit of the gods; a 370-year-old ritual.

13-15 June: Hyaku-man goku matsuri celebrates the entry in 1583 of Toshiie Maeda, first lord of the Maeda clan, into Kanazawa. (Other sources say 12-14 June, so check in advance.) The main feature is a procession of people in colourful feudal costumes, which takes place on the last day. Other activites include folk-dancing in the evening, geisha show at Kanko Kaikan, tea ceremony at Kenrokuen and Seisonkaku, and martial arts displays. The festival name literally means 'hundred ten-thousand goku': one 'man', or 10,000, is the awkward unit still used in counting beyond 1000; a goku (or koku) is five bushels. The name is usually translated as 'Five Million Bushel Festival' — from the annual rice harvest of one million goku, the richest in Japan.

24-25 July: at Ono, three mountain demons (villagers in bright costume) spend two days going from house to house exorcising demons with flutes and drums. Ono can be reached by bus 61 from Musashi.

1-3 August: Ono-minato-jinja Matsuri, held in Kanaiwa town and famous for its carved wooden floats.

15 August: Obon dances at Hatta village (night); its Sakata Odori is one of the few in Japan in which old costumes are worn, and music is live and not recorded.

October: through the month there are local shrine festivals.

19-20 October: dances by shrine maidens, at Gokoku shrine.

15 November: Shichi-go-san (7-5-3) festival, celebrated everywhere in Japan. Go to Ishiura-jinja to see children dressed in beautiful kimono.

Information

At the Tokyo TIC, pick up their photocopied information sheets, which give useful additional information on accommodation, etc. In Kanazawa, there is a travel information office in front of the station (to the left when exiting), as well as the small office at the handicrafts centre (Kanko Bussan-kan). There is a large guide-map in front of the station. If you do get lost, you will probably have no trouble getting assistance: I have never experienced so many offers of help as in Kanazawa when I stopped to consult my maps.

If you really want to experience all that Kanazawa has to offer, try to find a copy of Ruth Steven's guide book *Kanazawa: The Other Side of Japan*. It is a labour of love and describes everything in the city that is worth seeing, in a lighthearted and informative manner. Its first printing sold exceptionally well (Kanazawa residents bought thousands!) so it is difficult to predict its availability. It should be available in Kanazawa, but if you see a copy in Tokyo, snap it up and read ahead to have an idea of what you really want to see.

FROM KANAZAWA TO THE NOTO PENINSULA

Of historic interest betwen Kanazawa and Hakui are two large and venerable houses, Okabe-ke, and Kita-ke, the homes of local governors in the Tokugawa era. In addition to administering the law, these officials collected taxes in the form of rice. Both houses (which are about 10 km apart) have collections of relics from that age; Okabe-ke is somewhat larger, and is accessible by bus from Kanazawa station. (I didn't stop at Kita-ke, but there is probably also a bus service to there as well.) Okabe-ke is close to Menden station

(JNR); Kita-ke is close to Minami-Hakui station.

There are several good beaches along the strip of coast from Kanazawa to Hakui. One is Chirihama, a little north of Kita-ke, and another is Shibagaki, between Keta-jinja and Myojoji. Beaches are accessible via roads passing under the seaside toll road that runs from near Kanazawa to Hakui.

Keta-jinja

There is nothing of interest at Hakui itself, but just a short distance north is Keta-jinja (shrine), which faces the sea and is set in a picturesque grove of trees. It is near Noto Ichi-no-miya bus stop of Hokoriku Railway Bus Line, and is 13 km from Hakui station.

Kyojiji temple

Only a short distance north of Keta shrine is one of the great temples of the region, Myojiji. It is located a bit inland, and its five-storey pagoda looks out over the surrounding flat countryside. The view of the pagoda at the top of a long flight of stone steps is quite memorable and beautiful, except for the inevitable wires draped right across the middle of the scene and which will appear in any photo. (This was only one of dozens of views around the country spoiled by these wires.) The temple was established in the 13th century, although most of the present buildings date 'only' from the 1600s. There is the usual Japanese-language handout, and another one that explains in perfect English the history of the temple and each of the main buildings.

NOTO-HANTO

The Noto-hanto peninsula contains some of the most pleasant scenery in Japan. There are still large rice paddies, farmers working diligently, and typical rural scenes that look much the same as they have for decades. It is an area highly

recommended for a tour and visit. Cyclists will enjoy it in particular, for there are relatively few hills, yet the scenery is pleasant most of the time (usually mutually exclusive conditions, for industry and cities tend to concentrate on the valley flats).

The outer (soto) coast of the peninsula is much more rugged and scenic than the calm inner (uchi) shore. The finest scenery begins just above Kanazawa, and continues around to the eastern tip, Cape Rokugo, while there are also pleasant though less dramatic views past the cape down to Nanao on the east coast.

Getting Around

There is a frequent and convenient bus service to all the places of interest around the Noto Peninsula, making it the recommended means of transport. In brief, there are special sightseeing buses around the north-east end of the peninsula between Wajima and Anamizu/Ushitsu, plus regular buses that cover the following steps: Kanazawa-Togi; Togi-Monzen; Monzen-Wajima; Wajima-Ushitsu; and Monzen-Anamizu.

Trains run Hakui-Nanao-Wajima, and Nanao-Takojima. There is a JNR service to Wajima and Takoshima (a little east of Suzu), but for the loop around the peninsula, there are only buses. Since Wajima is more or less in the middle, it is not a useful starting point.

As there are many places to see and visit, and because the land is relatively level all around the peninsula, it is one of the best areas of Japan to explore by bicycle. Cyclists and other independent travellers should have detailed maps to enable them to follow little roads closest to the coast. The preferred direction of travel is clockwise, the Kanazawa area being a good starting point. In that way, the sun will be to your left or behind you through the most scenic parts.

Accommodation
There are 12 youth hostels around the peninsula, nine peoples' lodges, and probably hundreds of minshuku as well as hotels and ryokan. The hostels are listed in the Youth Hostel handbook, the JNTO booklet on hostels, and on the photocopied information sheet *Noto Peninsula* given out at the Tokyo TIC. One hostel I found very pleasant was the Noto-Katsurazaki Youth Hostel, right beside the water near Kafut station.

Information
The information sheets from the TIC in Tokyo are very useful for train, bus and boat schedules, and should be picked up for up-to-date information.

Noto Kongo
About 15 km above Myojiji, a small road turns off Route 249 to Fukuura and the shore. Between Fukuura and Togi is a 14 km stretch of coast known as Noto-Kongo, noted for its scenic formations of eroded rock. Most noteworthy are Gammon, a grotto 54 metres deep and 15 metres wide, and Taka-no-su (Hawk's Nest), a rock that rises 27 metres and projects far over the sea. Buses run along this coast, leaving from Hakui (50 minutes away), or Sammyo (30 minutes). Boat cruises lasting about 20 minutes leave from Fukuura.

Seki-no-hana
Above Togi a small road turns off Route 249 and runs to and along the coast, rejoining the main road farther along. The scenery is pleasant most of the way; the high-point is Seki-no-hana. This road is along the regular tourist route between Togi and Monzen.

Monzen
Near Monzen is Sojiji temple. Surprisingly located in this remote area, it was the national headquarters of the Soto sect of Zen Buddhism (founded in 1321) until 1818, when most of its buildings were destroyed in a fire. After that, the headquarters were moved to Sojiji in Yokohama. The present buildings are attractive, especially in summer when the cicadas are singing loudly (as is true of all parts of Japan where there are trees in which they can perch). Sojiji and Monzen are accessible by bus from Anamizu (on the uchi coast) as well as being on the regular bus run around the soto coast. The temple is a five-minute walk from Monzen bus station.

Sojiji is a functioning Zen temple, and visitors may obtain accommodation and participate in meditation. It is best to make reservations in advance by writing to: Sojiji, Monzen-machi, Fugeshi-gun, Ishikawa-ken. Tel (07684) 2-0005. It is said not to be possible to obtain accommodation on the spot. Costs range from Y3500 to Y5000.

Monzen to Wajima
Inveterate sea-coast buffs armed with a sufficiently detailed map can find roads along parts of the coast between Monzen and Wajima, but the area isn't generally famous for scenery. Your own transport would be useful, though there are buses along the main roads. There is a 5.5 km hiking trail along the coast (no road, so it is still quite primitive) between Minazuki and Kami-Ozawa. The former can be reached by bus from Monzen, the latter likewise from Wajima.

WAJIMA
This small city on the northern coast is noted for its large-scale production of good-quality lacquerware (on sale everywhere in town). About one person in four of Wajima's population is engaged in some aspect of the lacquerware craft.

There are several places where one can see the process of lacquerware-making. In the area near the harbour, countless little shops turn out chopsticks with interesting patterns, the result of repeated dipping. The best single demonstration of the whole process can be seen at the main store of Inuchu (daily except Sunday). It can involve 18 or more steps, from forming the wood to the addition of layer after layer of lacquer, interspersed with careful polishing to make the finished product gleaming-smooth, a true work of art and more demanding than the better-known craft of pottery making. Somewhat directed toward the tour-bus trade (but also good) is Wajima Shikki Kaikan (which also has a small museum of lacquerware on the second floor). Wajimaya store also has demonstrations.

Markets

Every day (except the 10th and 25th of the month) there is both a morning market (asa-ichi) and an evening market (yu-ichi): the former from 8 am to midday at Honcho-dori of Kawai-cho, the latter on the grounds of Sumiyoshi-jinja from 4 pm to 7 pm. Goods sold include handicrafts and other tourist items as well as food.

Other

In the grounds of Sumiyoshi-jinja is an interesting museum, Omatsuri-kan, containing local folk-art and objects related to the major Wajima festivals. At Kiriko-kaikan there is an exhibition of floats used in festivals around the peninsula, along with a short film of a festival. Sodegahama is a pleasant beach near Wajima.

Diras In the winter months, women divers operate off the coast looking for shell-fish and edible seaweed (in the warmer months they migrate to nearby Hegura Island). In former times, these women dived wearing only a loincloth, but those days are far gone.

Accommodation

Wajima is an extremely popular destination, but there is generally no shortage of accommodation except in July-August. In addition to youth hostels, it is reported that there are nearly 100 minshuku. One writer recommended Hegura minshuku (tel 07682 2-1018) near Sumiyoshi-jinja, but minshuku everywhere are usually good experiences. Near Sodegahama beach, there is a Kokumin-shukusha.

Festivals

There are annual festivals on 4-5 April and 23-25 August.

Getting There

Wajima is the terminal station for the JNR line from Kanazawa and farther south (Maibara). It is also served by the bus service that circles the peninsula.

Wajima to Sosoji

About 10 km inland on the road to Anamizu is a very picturesque village of farmhouses built on the hills surrounding the rice fields. I haven't seen it, but those who have say it is worth going out of the way to see.

Continuing along the coast east toward Sosogi, the coastline is pretty. There are two places worth watching for specially. One is Senkaida ('1000 terraces'), a poetic description of a very picturesque broad ravine in which paddies have been built in terraces from sea-level high up the side of the tall hill. Just before harvest time (late August-early September) would be the most colourful of all times to see this, for the rice then takes on a rich green-gold hue. (The same is true of all rice-fields, of course, but few are as beautifully located.)

A little farther on is a fine view of the kind that is comparatively rare these days as modernization takes over. Terraced rice-fields drop down to the sea, surrounding a small Shinto shrine. Its torii gate stands before the tiny building, and behind the shrine is a small, thick grove of trees. It is the very epitome of traditional Japan.

SOSOGI

At this town, a road branches inland from Route 249 toward Ushitsu. About 400 metres from the junction stand two of the largest traditional farmhouses in Japan. They are worth a visit for both their historic value and their aesthetic design. Both are thatched-roof buildings of the highest quality materials and traditional Japanese carpentry. The interesting story is that one of the highest-ranked court families (the Tokikuni) has lived in this area since the forces of the Taira clan (also called Heike) were defeated by the Genji (Minamoto) at the battle of Dan-no-ura (Shimonoseki) in 1185. This battle determined who would rule Japan for the following several decades, and the Taira fled to this area and the nearby inland mountain regions of the Shokawa river to escape extermination. Their descendants live in the Shirakawa-go/Gokayama area.

Tokikuni Houses

The house closer to Sosogi (they are a five-minute walk apart) is Shimo-Tokikuni-ke, and it is at least 300 years old. Inside its spacious interior are many relics of the past: foreign visitors are given a recorder with a taped explanation of the house, room by room.

The nearby Kami-Tokikuni-ke (Upper Tokikuni House; 'shimo' was the 'lower') is newer, having been built in the last century to replace the first house that had become unusable. It shows few signs of age, and the finest materials and workmanship were employed in its construction (it took 28 years to build). It is intriguing to find such a fine building and garden in such an out-of-the-way place, but it was built to suit a person of very high rank, a descendant of the Kyoto nobility. Visitors are given a notebook with a

handwritten explanation of the house's history, and a description of the high-points and exhibits, room by room. A story in the notes tells how one of the rooms was reserved for receiving guests only of Dai-na-gon rank or higher, which was higher than that of the local governor and many court officials, so they were not allowed to enter. On one occasion it was necessary to receive a person of lesser rank: for this occasion, the golden carving of a swallow-tailed butterfly (symbol of the Heike and indicating the resident's rank) had to be covered before he was allowed to enter.

Buses of Hokuriku Railway run from Wajima station to Kami-Tokikuni-ke bus stop in 45 minutes, and from Suzu station (farther east) in one hour.

Museums

There are two other museums in Sosogi. Wajima Minzoku Shiryokan, which houses local folk-art and items of daily use, is located between the Tokikuni houses. The other museum is Noto Shuko-kan, and is a more general art museum with no particular relation to the Noto area. It is south-east of Sosogi, and separate from the other attractions.

Accommodation

There are several minshuku and some hotels near the two old houses. There are, in fact, minshuku in virtually every town and hamlet along the coast.

AROUND THE COAST TO TAKAOKA

The coast east of Sosogi is pleasantly scenic, with outcroppings of eroded rock at intervals. Route 249 doesn't go out to the tip of the peninsula, but a good road does lead out to Cape Rokugo (Rokugo Misaki), near the town of Noroshi. An 11 km hiking trail (Misaki Nature Trail) begins at Takaya, and continues through Kinoura to Noroshi. At Noroshi, cape Rokugo and its light-house can be reached in 10 minutes on foot.

Below Noroshi, the uchi or inner (east) coast becomes much more placid and peaceful. While there are many pleasant views, there are not the outstanding scenic areas found along the outer coast.

Suzu
This hot-spring and port town has as its attraction a large old house (Kiheidon) that is a museum of local artefacts formerly owned by the Sakura family. It is a little different because it shows an exhibition of how salt was made from sea-water.

Koiji
There is a nice white beach here, 10 minutes walk from Koiji station or six minutes by bus from Iwatsunami station. A ferry leaves from here for Sado Island, and a coastal boat links it with Ushitsu and Noroshi.

Tsukumo
The name means '99 indentations', and indicates the attraction of this bay. It can be seen from any of the sightseeing boats that leave from Ogi (Noto Ogi station).

Ushitsu
Perhaps the main attraction of this fishing village is a large minshuku and garden, the Muroya (tel (07686) 2-0200). There is also a morning fish auction. (7-8 am). Nearby Toshimayama Park affords an excellent view of the bay. At the park (10 minutes by bus from Ushitsu station) are two old houses that act as local museums. Ushitsu has a festival, the Abare-matsuri, 7-8 July.

Kurokawa
Inland from Ushitsu is the attractive little village of Kurokawa, which contains a very interesting house, Nakatani-ke. The storehouse is com-

pletely lacquered inside, even the walls, doors and stairs.

Noto-Shima
Little fishing villages and nature (swimming, hiking and camping) are this island's main attraction. Access is by boat from Nanao (five per day), and the trip takes 30 minutes. This is a festival on the island on 31 July.

Wakura Onsen
This is a typical hot-spring resort of hotels and ryokan and rather expensive.

Anamizu
This town is also of negligible interest, but it has a festival on 22-23 July.

Nanao
Along Route 159 between Nanao and Hakui there are many beautiful old wooden houses, particularly between Nanao and Kue.

TOYAMA-KEN

TAKAOKA
Near eastern base of the Noto Peninsula is Takaoka. The city is noted for lacquerwork as well as copper and iron products, and is the main source of large cast bells. If you are interested in artistic foundry work, you might be able to arrange a visit to a workshop: try the town hall (shi-yaku-sho) for contacts.

Sightseeing potential in the city is limited. It does have the third-largest statue of Buddha (Daibutsu) in Japan, but although it is described as being of bronze, its appearance resembles greenpainted concrete and it cannot be compared with the serene beauty of the famous Daibutsu at Kamakura near Tokyo.

Zuiryuji
The nicest place to visit is in fact the

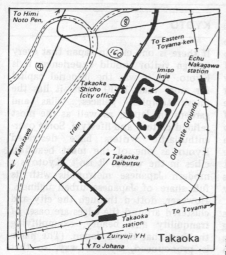

Keta shrines (jinja). The foundation of the old castle and its moats still stand. They are rather pretty during the cherry-blossom season, but the grounds have the buildings of the civic centre, etc, and are not otherwise very interesting.

Festivals

There are festivals on 14 January and 2-3 June, as well as the following:

1 May: procession of dashi (carved and decorated large wagons).

15 May: night processions of at least seven large floats lit by lanterns.

3-7 August: Tanabata, with pretty paper decorations on the streets, but negligible action.

23 September: Daibutsu festival.

Photos of the dashi used in the May procession show that they are old but not as fantastically elaborate as those of Takayama or Kyoto.

Around Takaoka

As well as using Takaoka as the starting point for trips around the peninsula, you can take Route 156 south to the very interesting Shokawa river valley and the old houses of the Shirakawa-go area described earlier. The scenery along the river is nearly always pleasant, and often pretty. There are buses from Takaoka station through the valley. There is also a JNR line as far as Johana, from which another road leads to and links up with 156 at Taira-mura, the northern extremity of the area of old houses mentioned above. The attractions of the Japan alps, south-east of Takaoka, are described in the sections covering Niigata-ken and the northern parts of Nagano-ken and Gumma-ken.

youth hostel (3207) because it is actually a large and venerable temple about 350 years old. Zuiryuji is a Zen temple of the Soto sect. The main building is large, as is the ceremonial entry gate; the spacious grounds are surrounded by a traditional wall. It is unusual to find such a splendid structure in such a remote area as this, and there is a peaceful feeling because there are no hordes of tourists. It is not worth a special trip, but for anyone who plans to stay overnight in the area it can be highly recommended. As a bonus, the wife of the priest speaks very good English, and can tell you a bit about the place.

Other

Other temples in Takaoka are Kokutaiji and Shokoji. Shrines include Imisu and

Kyoto, Osaka & Nara-ken

This is the most historic area of Japan. Not much is known of its prehistoric inhabitants, but it was settled quite early (first centuries AD) by the Yamato clan who went on to dominate all of Japan. Osaka was a trading centre by the fourth century, and the emperor had a palace there. Nara became the capital for 74 years in the latter part of the seventh century, followed by Kyoto (784) which then held the position until 1868. (It was the residence of the emperor — the imperial capital — but for several centuries the emperor was only a figurehead and real power lay elsewhere.)

So much of traditional Japan survives in this area that anyone truly wishing to know the country should devote a large fraction of a Japan visit to it. To the Japanese, Kyoto is known as 'Nihon no furusato' (the heart of Japan), an accurate assessment of its role in Japanese history and sentiment. However, Kyoto and Nara should really be considered as a whole, for there are several attractions lying outside but close to the two cities that can be easily visited, along with other interesting places that are the makings of interesting day excursions.

Kyoto and Osaka are not only the names of cities, but also of geo-political units, each of which is larger than some ken (prefectures). This section deals only with the cities and their immediate vicinity, and the larger northern part of Kyoto-fu is covered under Western Honshu. Osaka-fu, because the historic remains have either crumbled or were destroyed in the war, is of little interest, so not much more than survival information will be given for Osaka city.

This chapter also includes Nagoya which, although not an interesting city, conveniently forms the north-eastern end of a journey around the Kii peninsula.

KYOTO

If there is one city in Japan that every foreign visitor should experience, it is Kyoto. As it was the imperial capital for more than 1000 years, it has the finest temples, palaces, villas and gardens in Japan, as well as the most refined culture and lifestyle. Some over-enthusiastic writers have described Kyoto as one of the most beautiful cities in the world. It isn't. Kyoto is a modern Japanese metropolis with its full share of Japanese urban ugliness. However, dotted through the city and clustered around the edges are oases of tranquility and beauty, exemplifying the best that is/was Japan. (The name is pronounced, by the way, so that the 'y' acts as a consonant (as in 'yet'), not a vowel: the first syllable is 'Kyo', and does *not* rhyme with 'pie'). The name means simply 'capital city' (Tokyo, the successor capital, means 'east capital').

Getting There
Air
By air you can reach Kyoto easily from many points in Japan as well as overseas, for it uses Osaka International Airport. Buses run every 20 minutes through the day in each direction, making the rounds of several of the better-known hotels (the Miyako, Kyoto, JAL, International and Grand) as well as Kyoto station.

Trains
Kyoto is easily reached from Tokyo, Nagoya, etc to the north-east, or from Hakata, Hiroshima, etc to the west by Shinkansen services, as well as by slower (and less costly) JNR. The Shinkansen trip from Tokyo to Kyoto stations takes just over 2¾ hours, at speeds up to 210 km/h.

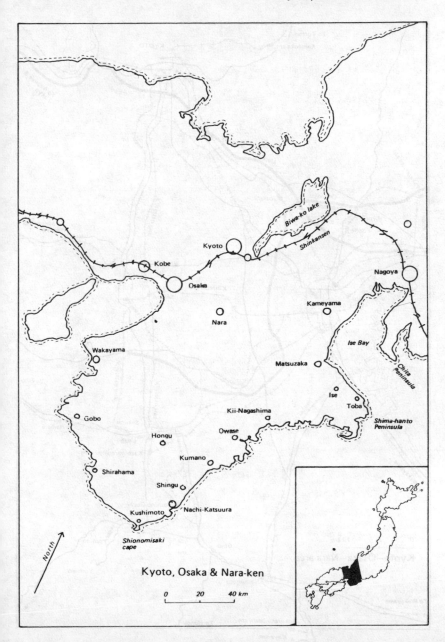

Biwa-ko lake

Shinkansen

Kyoto

Kobe

Osaka

Nagoya

Kameyama

Nara

Ise Bay

Wakayama

Matsuzaka

Chita Peninsula

Ise

Toba

Gobo

Kii-Nagashima

Owase

Shima-hanto Peninsula

Hongu

Kumano

Shirahama

Shingu

Kushimoto   Nachi-Katsuura

Shionomisaki cape

North

Kyoto, Osaka & Nara-ken

0   20   40 km

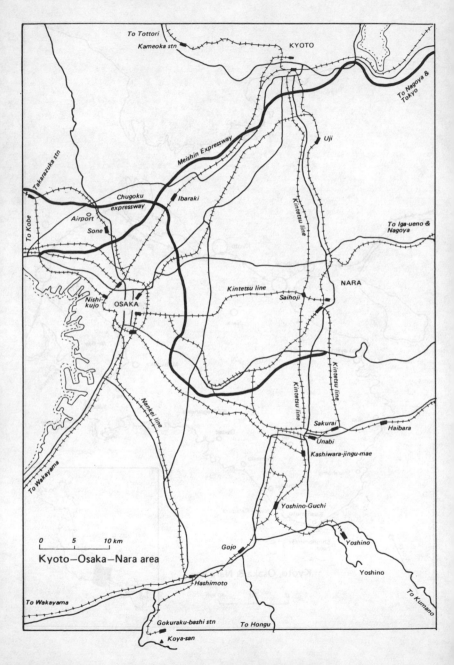

Kyoto–Osaka–Nara area

In addition to JNR services, several private railways link Kyoto with Osaka, Kobe, Nara, Ise and innumerable smaller towns and cities.

To Osaka The Hankyu, Keihan and JNR lines all run between Kyoto and Osaka. The first two (same fare) are cheaper than JNR; Hankyu is faster (46 minutes versus 54). The fastest Kyoto-Osaka service is the Shinkansen (18 minutes), but it does not reach its full speed in the short 43 km distance and costs three times the normal JNR fare (which is already about 75% higher than the private line fares). Also, it goes to Shin-Osaka station, a few minutes by local train from Osaka station, the one used by most JNR services and closer to the centre of Osaka. The fastest regular JNR service (compared with Tokaido and commuter services that make numerous stops en route) is the Shin-Kaisoku which leaves Kyoto every 30 minutes between 10.15 am and 3.45 pm. It runs non-stop to Osaka (29 minutes) before continuing beyond. All JNR trains leave from Kyoto station; the lines are well sign-posted in English, so it is easy to find the correct track. Hankyu trains leave from four underground stations along Shijo-dori, the easternmost of which is Hankyu-Kawaramachi. Keihan trains leave from Shijo-Keihan and Sanjo-Keihan stations (and a number of others north and south); the former is a little to the east of Hankyu-Kawaramachi station.

To Kobe and Himeji The Hankyu line and JNR services (Shinkansen, Tokaido and Shin-Kaisoku lines) continue to Kobe and Himeji. The Shin-Kaisoku gives the best balance of cost and speed, covering the distance to Himeji in less than two hours and costing no more than the slower Tokaido service. Shin-kansen trains are much faster, of course,

with fares to match; at Kobe they stop at Shin-Kobe station at the north end of the city. On the Hankyu line it is necessary to change trains at Osaka (Juso station); inquire at the TIC for details.

Buses
There is a bus service through the day to Nagoya, and from there to Tokyo. However, this is relatively slow and not particularly scenic unless the weather is clear while passing Mt Fuji. The most convenient service is the JNR 'Dream' bus that runs at night. It leaves Kyoto station at 10 pm and reaches Tokyo station the next morning at 6.45; from Tokyo, buses leave at 11 pm, arriving at Kyoto station at 7.45 am. This gives an early start on the day's activities, and also saves the cost of accommodation for a night. (You can sleep quite well for there are reclining seats.) The service is popular, so it is normally necessary to book in advance during months of temperate weather.

Hitching To hitch out of Kyoto to Nagoya, Tokyo or Hiroshima, take bus 19 or 20 from the station until signs for the entrance of the Meishin express-way (marked in English) come into view. Hold up a sign (in Japanese) showing your destination (Nagoya and Tokyo are to the east, Osaka and Hiroshima to the west). It is not possible to hitch on the freeway except at rest stops, so it is necessary to get a car going in the Hiroshima direction (which means switching freeways at Osaka).

Osaka is so close to Kyoto that it is not worth hitching; take the train.

To hitch toward Tottori (north coast), it is simplest to take the train to Kameoka and start there (according to one source), but you could also take one of several buses (or Hankyu train) to the Katsura area and hitch on Route 9.

Information

There is no shortage of information for seeing Kyoto. It is the only city other than Tokyo with a government-operated tourist information centre (TIC). Staff speak English well (plus other languages), and are absolute goldmines of information about any place, activity, art or craft in the Kyoto area and elsewhere in Japan. For this reason, the following section gives more emphasis to how-to-see and what-to-see than to detailed descriptions. Unless you arrive Saturday afternoon or Sunday, your first stop should be at the TIC to pick up one of their excellent maps of Kyoto and the booklet Kyoto Nara (also available at the Tokyo TIC), and to ask any specific questions you may have about travel-related topics. They have a great deal of other information on photocopied sheets and in printed booklets; particularly useful is *Walking Tours in Kyoto*, and some rail maps.

The TIC has information about accommodation in various price ranges, and will call to make reservations (unlike the Tokyo TIC). Low-cost places are listed later in this section, mostly for the benefit of those who arrive 5 pm on weekdays, Saturday afternoon or Sunday. The Tokyo TIC has a handout listing of accommodation that may be useful for making advance reservations, but it has occasionally omitted popular places (like Mrs Uno's house).

A very handy booklet is *Monthly Guide Kyoto*, which lists events of the month in good detail, and has descriptions of a large number of temples, shrines and palaces. (Much of the book may be in Japanese, but the English section is excellent.) It also lists the better hotels (with prices), tours and other useful information. The booklet is not available at the TIC, but may be obtained at the large hotels that cater to foreign visitors. It is also available in Japan by mail for a total of Y600 from:

Monthly Guide Kyoto
30-5 Chajiri-cho
Arashiyama
Nishikyo-ku
Kyoto-shi

The above should not be confused with another publication, *Kyoto Monthly Guide*, which is produced by the Kyoto city government. This one is much more detailed regarding events of the month. It is available at the TIC, or by mail in Japan on receipt of a Y50 stamp, from:

Tourist Section
Dept of Cultural Affairs and Tourism
Kyoto City Government
c/o Kyoto Kaikan
Sakyo-ku
Kyoto.

Both publications are very useful.

The Kyoto City Tourist Association publishes a worthwhile guide book simply called *Kyoto*. It contains useful information such as airline office phone numbers, etc, and is a steal at Y300. For a very good explanation of many of the attractions of the city and their significance in history, purchase a copy of *Kyoto, A Contemplative Guide*, by Gouverneur Mosher.

Another publication, more of interest to those staying long-term, is *A Resident's Guide to Kyoto*, a compilation of nearly every bit of information that one needs when arriving to stay in Kyoto for a while. It can be purchased at the YWCA for Y500, by domestic mail for Y1000, or by foreign airmail for Y1500, from:

YWCA Thrift Shop
Muro machi-dori, Demizu-agaru
Kamikyo-ku
Kyoto-shi 602

There is a thrift sale on the third Saturday of every month, a good place for bargains, exchanging information with other foreign residents, and even home-made Western-style munchies and crunchies.

Tickets and any other travel bookings are available (from English-speaking personnel) at the JTB offices near the north entrance of Kyoto station, and on Sanjo, east of Kawaramachi.

As described in the introductory section to this book, the better students of English of the Tesco company are willing to act as unpaid guides for English-speaking visitors to Kyoto: phone Mr Kira at 06 445-6116 (this is an Osaka number; Mr Kira coordinates the area).

Students of Kyoto and Doshisha universities, and Kyoto Women's College, are also willing to act as unpaid guides in return for the opportunity to practise English. You are expected to pay the expenses of the student, such as travel, meals, admittance charges, etc. Contact the TIC to make arrangements.

Social
Home Visit It is possible to visit a private home in Kyoto for a couple of hours in the evening to see what a Japanese home is like. Members of the participating families speak English or other foreign languages. Arrangements should be made as far in advance as possible (usually this can be done in a day, but more should be allowed). Travel agencies and large hotels can make arrangements; one can also contact the Kyoto City information office at Kyoto station (tel 371-2108). General information on this programme is given in the introductory section of this book.

Getting Around
Kyoto is covered by an extensive network of bus routes. The major ones are shown on a sub-map on the TIC Kyoto map. If possible, however, it is advisable to chat to the TIC staff because some of the buses are infrequent. In briefest terms, there are two loop bus lines, 206 and 214. The former goes along Higashi-

oji, Kita-oji and Karasuma streets on the way to and from the station, while the latter uses Kawaramachi, Kita-oji and Nishi-oji streets. The character following the number tells the direction. A one-day pass for unlimited travel on city buses is available, but you might not use it enough to justify the cost. There is also an '11 tickets for the price of 10' deal. Both are available at the bus centre, and further information can be obtained at the TIC.

Kyoto will have a subway in the early 1980s, running from Kyoto station north along Karasuma-dori to Kita-oji-dori. It will link with the Hankyu line at Shijo-Karasuma for east-west service along the Shijo-dori. Several railway lines, JNR and private, serve parts of the city; these are also shown on the TIC map.

Taxis are plentiful. There is no problem telling the driver your destination: if he doesn't understand your pronunciation, he can read it in Japanese on the TIC map.

Bicycles may be rented at the Bridgestone bike shop on the corner of Muromachi and Shimocho-jamachi streets. Most of Kyoto is flat, so this is a practical means of getting around, though the savings over bus fares might be negligible. The TIC can also give suggestions.

There is no problem whatever in finding your way around Kyoto on your own, even if you do not speak a word of Japanese. Kyoto is one of the few cities in Japan laid out on a rectangular grid (modelled on ancient Chinese capitals), transport facilities are well developed, and tourist information is readily available, as detailed above. I recommend that you pick up a TIC map and set out independently, which will give you a much better feel for this historic city. Even if you do get lost, you may well stumble across something more interesting than what you set out to find. One of the few commercial maps which is to the correct scale is the area map of Kyoto published by Shobunsha. The name is printed only in Japanese, so you will need to ask for it. Most streets and places are marked in English.

Bus tours are available, but virtually all go to the same destinations.

SIGHTSEEING
Kyoto Gosho Palace
This is only of moderate interest, but the office of the Imperial Household Agency is located at the entrance. You apply here for permission to visit some other places associated with the Imperial family.

Kyoto Gosho is the imperial palace, residence of the emperor in the days when he lived in Kyoto. The present building dates from 1855, replacing one destroyed in a fire. Although the capital was Kyoto from 794, this site was not used until 1788 when a palace was built to replace an older one that was also destroyed by fire. The main buildings are replicas of the former structures and are quite simple in design, though made with the finest materials and construction methods. A guide accompanies all visitors, so the details are explained.

To enter, you must fill in an application and show your passport, so arrive about 20 minutes before the tour at 10 am or 2 pm. (There are no tours on Saturday afternoon or Sunday). The palace is one of the most peaceful places in Kyoto because Japanese must wait for months to get permission to enter and few do.

Any Japanese accompanying you will have to wait at the entrance. Thus it is a privilege for foreigners to be able to visit so easily.

Before or after the tour, file your application to visit Katsura Imperial Villa, and Sento Imperial Palace, if desired. Permission will be given for a specific date and hour, usually within a day if requested, but you should apply soon after arriving in Kyoto to allow for delays. A permit is also required to visit Shugakuin Imperial Villa, but read the comments on it before applying.

Go-jinja
This little shrine, across from the west side of the Gosho, is not noteworthy except that, instead of the usual koma-inu guardian dogs/lions at the entrance, it has two pigs.

Sento Imperial Palace
There is another palace on the south-east side of the same grounds. In addition to the buildings (which have been re-built many times), there is a garden completed in 1630 and designed by Kobori Enshu, possibly the most famous of all landscape-garden designers. As mentioned above, advance permission is required to enter.

Nijo-jo Castle
Although called a castle, the main build-

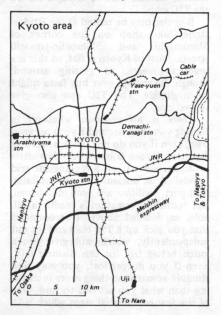

Kyoto area

Cable car

Yase-yuen stn

Demachi-Yanagi stn

Arashiyama stn

KYOTO

JNR

JNR

Kyoto stn

Hankyu

Meishin expressway

To Nagoya & Tokyo

To Osaka

0   5   10 km

Uji

To Nara

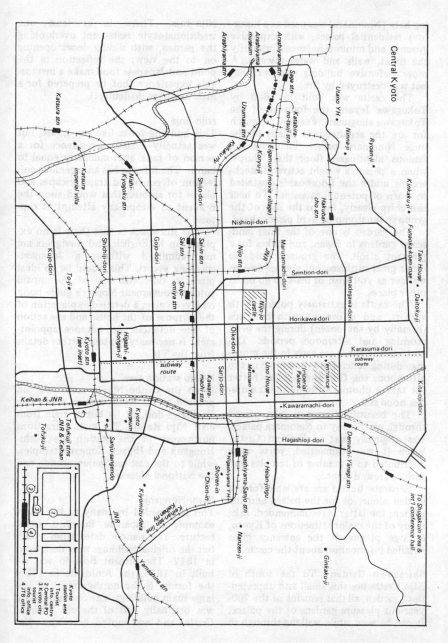

ing here (Ninomaru) was used as a luxurious residential palace, with expensive grounds and minimal defences (primarily the moat, walls and watch-towers). A more defensive building once existed, but was destroyed by fire.

The castle was built in 1603 by Tokugawa Ieyasu, the founder of the Tokugawa shogunate. Features to watch for are the architectural details of the huge Ninomaru palace, including the famous nightingale floor that 'chirps' when a person's weight activates mechanisms under the floorboards (installed to warn of potential assassins). To hear the chirp clearly, fall to the rear of the group so the stomping herd passes ahead.

The garden is one of the finer landscape gardens in Japan, and makes for a pleasant stroll. The grounds hold no other great surprises, but you are free to wander as you wish or leave to go on to other places.

The castle is extremely popular with visitors, and is overrun with busloads (literally by the dozen) during the peak morning and afternoon periods. The best visiting times are early in the morning, during lunch-time, and later in the afternoon; the first and last are better for taking photos, avoiding the featureless noon sun.

The beautiful Karamon gate, passed through on the way to Ninomara palace, was originally part of Fushimi Castle. When it was dismantled, parts were distributed to a number of temples and shrines around Kyoto.

Separate tickets are available for the garden alone, or for the palace and the garden; the latter is recommended. Like many of the major attractions of Kyoto, a large plaque at the entrance gives detailed information about the castle.

Shinsen-en Garden To the south of Nijo Castle lies this small and unpretentious garden, all that remains of the 700-year-old pleasure gardens of the palace. It can be seen while walking through to Nijo-jinja. There is at least one traditional-style restaurant overlooking the garden, with sliding doors opening on to the view: the reflection in the pond and Japanese food make a memorable experience (but be prepared for a little language difficulty!).

Nijo-jinja
This building looks like any house, but was actually a fortress-residence for a person of rank approximately equal to baron. The interior has an ingenious collection of concealed traps, escapes and places for ambush that would allow the resident to escape any attempt at capture.

The drawback is that there is no explanation in English, and foreigners are not admitted without a Japanese-speaking escort. This would be an ideal place to visit with one of the unpaid guides. Gouverneur Mosher's guide book on Kyoto gives a detailed explanation of the purpose of the house and the action of the defences. An advance appointment is necessary. Obtain further details from the TIC.

Kyoto station area
From the Gosho/Nijo-jo area, you can proceed to the Kyoto station area along Horikawa-dori, or by bus or train from JNR Nijo station. The main attractions north-west of the station are Nishi-Honganji and Higashi-Honganji temples, while to the east are Sanjusangendo and the National Museum.

Nishi-Honganji
This is regarded by many as the finest example of Japanese Buddhist architecture. The temple dates from 1592, but the original buildings were destroyed in 1617. The present Boei-do was rebuilt in 1636, the Amida-do in 1760; the former is the northernmost of the large main buildings. The Shoin building was originally part of the old Fushimi Castle, and was moved here when the

castle was dismantled. The carvings and other details in the north building are colourful, although difficult to discern in the gloom. Not to be missed is the very colourful Karamon gate in the south wall: of typically flamboyant Momoyama style, it has much gold inlay on the metal fittings and brightly coloured carved figures of animals and humans, many obviously of Chinese derivation.

There are four tours a day, at 10 and 11 am, 1.30 and 2.30 pm. Though lengthy (if the explanation is being given only to Japanese visitors), this is the only way to see the interior buildings, the two Noh stages, Komei-no-en (a pretty karesansui garden of rocks, gravel and greenery), and other glimpses of beauty such as verandahs made of a single plank of wood. Not open to the public, unfortunately, is the more beautiful Hyakka-en garden.

Costume Museum Close to Nishi-Honganji is an interesting museum with costumes, both original and replicas, worn in Japan over the past 2000 years. It is on the fifth floor of the Izutsu Building. There is an English-language pamphlet, and the costumes are also labelled in English.

Higashi-Honganji

This temple has the largest wooden structure in Kyoto. The temple was founded in 1602, but the present buildings date from 1895. It is worth a look around.

Kikokutei Garden

This large strolling-type garden is/was a villa of the abbot of Higashi-Honganji temple. Unfortunately it has been neglected and allowed to run down, but it is little visited and provides a haven of relative peace. An interesting scandal has been hovering around it, for the abbot transferred ownership to a private individual without consulting the 10,000

or so temples affiliated with Higashi-Honganji.

Toji

To the south-west of the station and thus a little off our track, this temple on extensive park-like grounds has the tallest pagoda in Japan (55 metres). The koda (lecture hall) is a simple building containing only a few large gilded statues. This was the first temple I visited in Kyoto: in the late afternoon, with the sun shining in the doorway and reflecting off the floor, the effect was quite mysterious (for lack of a better word). The first Europeans here must have been similarly impressed by the unfamiliar symbolism. The pagoda dates from 1644, the lecture hall from 1598, and the main hall from more recent times.

Sanjusangendo

The name means '33 bays', and refers to spaces between the pillars of this long, narrow structure dating from 1266. The spaces are filled with a huge and intriguing collection of 1001 life-sized statues of Kannon, Goddess of Mercy. (If they look small, remember that the Japanese were once very short: many old people in the countryside are no taller than these figures.) Some of the statues wear 'necklaces': the face of each statue is different, and if a visitor sees one that resembles himself, it is customary to donate such a decoration. The central figure is a seated 3.3 metre statue of 1001-handed Kannon (from 1254), and her 28 helpers. Also take time to look at the large (but dusty) sculpted wooden statues in the back corridor. Signs in English explain all attractions briefly. The temple is famous for its archery festival on 15 January.

National Museum

The National Museum is just across the road from Sanjusangendo, and is worth a visit for its large collection of Japanese artefacts from prehistoric to recent vintage. The pottery from about 2000 BC shows how little this craft has advanced since 'primitive' times.

Although the museum is conveniently reached from Sanjusangendo, it might be worth saving (literally) for a rainy day. Admittance is free on the 15th of each month (closed Mondays and at year-end).

Kawai Kanjiro Pottery

This is the house and workshop of the late Kawai Kanjiro, a noted potter. Those interested will find displays of his work, the workshop and a climbing kiln. (Closed Mondays, mid-August, and year-end.)

Chishaku-in

Of somewhat less interest, but pleasant to visit during a long Kyoto stay, this temple has an attractive garden with an unusual pond that extends under the porch of the main building. A special building is used to exhibit wall and door paintings from the 16th century, that survived fires in the main building. They are considered masterpieces of their type, but may not appeal to everyone. An English-language pamphlet gives further details.

Kiyomizu-dera Temple

This temple is also very popular with visitors and included on every tour. It is unusual for the main hall (honden), which is built out on pillars from a hillside. The grounds are especially lovely during the cherry-blossom season and autumn. The present buildings date from 1633, and include a picturesque Sanmon gate at the entrance and a three-storey pagoda as well as the famous pillar-supported verandah.

Access from the south is by walking up the long hill from Gojozaka bus stop, either through the cemetery (southernmost road) or up the shop-lined road. These shops, and those along the other approaches, have a large variety of pottery and other crafts as well as countless souvenirs and Kyoto-type nibbles.

Sannen-zaka

After exploring the temple, follow the northernmost road (Kiyomizu-zaka) downhill until the first turn-off to the right, (also downhill). This is Sannen-zaka (not marked in English), which passes more interesting little shops. On the east side of this street there is a fence with an entranceway to Saka-guchi, a lovely little garden teahouse with a pond. For a few hundred yen one can order soba (noodles) or tea and have them while enjoying the view. Pleasant, tinkly koto music provides the background and guarantees one of the most 'Japanese' experiences available. There is a similar garden restaurant a little farther on, on the left side as the road slopes down again, and another smaller one shortly before Ninen-zaka ends at a T-junction. All can be recommended.

Where Sannen-zaka ends and steps lead to Ninen-zaka, a road branches down to the west. Here you can see a pagoda, five-storey Yasaka Gojonoto, all that remains of a once-grand temple. However, the grounds are closed so it is not worth a walk to see. Photographers will find that the view along the road is ruined by numerous power-lines, but the little uphill road to the west shortly before the T-junction gives a good silhouette of the top four storeys (a telephoto lens will be needed to cut out foreground clutter).

Ryozen Kannon

The road forming the T-junction with Ninnen-zaka leads to Ryozen Kannon, a large seated figure of Kannon (after whom Canon cameras were initially named). The figure is of no historic importance, but the concrete structure is peaceful and reassuring. It is surrounded by a wall, but you can see through the entrance gate without paying the entry fee.

Yasaka-jinja

Not far away is Yasaka shrine. It has several photogenic brilliant-orange buildings as well as one of the largest granite torii gates in Japan (on the south side), dating from 1646. It is one of the best places in Japan to see people 'waking the gods': shaking and whipping a thick rope attached to a rattly gong at the eaves, then putting their hands together in prayer. It is said to be a favourite of geisha in the nearby Gion entertainment area.

Adjacent Karuyama-koen park has a pleasant little pond and Japanese style garden arranged around it. It is as much of interest to see how Japanese enjoy their leisure as for its own attractions. It provides a path to nearby Chion-in Temple.

Chion-in Temple

The huge Sanmon gate at the south (main) entrance to this hillside temple is the largest in Japan and dates from 1619. It also has the largest bell in the country. The main building is impressively large, and is best seen from the large open area in front. The interior is equally large and is an excellent place to examine the great range of Buddhist symbols and other ornate gilded decorations; it is a feast for the eyes. The temple is still functioning, so there is a good chance of observing priests chanting prayers for deceased members of visiting families.

The garden and large building behind the main temple are also worth visiting. Although there are always other visitors around, the temple is rarely overcrowded. An English-language pamphlet gives the history of the temple and serves as a primer on the Jodo sect, for which it is the head temple.

Shoren-in

This is one of my favourite temples. It is

off the beaten path enough for it not to be overrun with hordes of sightseers, so you can enjoy its lovely little garden, the peace, and the blending of the buildings (and their architectural details) with the setting at the foot of a hill. Birds can be heard in nearby trees. It is very pleasant in late afternoon (especially in autumn, when the trees are beautiful): 2-3.30 pm is good in November, later in summer when the sun is higher. After exploring the buildings and the views from there, return to the entrance, don shoes, and walk around the garden, which is entered by a tunnel under one of the corridors (to the right when exiting the building). An English-language handout gives the history of the temple.

Nanzen-ji

Another temple highly recommended for a visit, especially when the autumn leaves are at their peak. Nanzen-ji began as a villa for a retired emperor, and was made into a temple in 1291. The present buildings date from post-1600. The grounds have many tall, venerable cedar trees, so the approach to the entrance is canopied by nature. The buildings of the temple feature the finest construction techniques — rooms with exquisite details (some opening on to lovely little gardens), sliding doors with fine, treasured paintings, and several rock-and-sand Zen gardens. (Nanzen-ji means 'south Zen temple'.) A leisurely walk will be rewarding.

To the right inside the main entrance is a simple room where you can sip tea (Y200 extra). It is a good chance to appreciate the beauty of the tea ceremony, sitting in this simple room on tatami mats looking out at the little waterfall. An English-language pamphlet gives the history of the temple.

Toriyasu

Another peaceful and beautiful place for rest and refreshments is the teahouse/

restaurant/garden Toriyasu, just across from the right-hand corner of the grounds of Nanzen-ji. Koto music provides the background, and tall trees the shade.

Eikando

The grounds of this temple are gorgeous during autumn and pleasant at other times. A graceful stone bridge arches over the pond, and the temple buildings enclose small gardens, including one of rocks and sand raked into elaborate patterns. Unfortunately, loudspeakers babble incessantly and destroy any potential for peaceful exploration.

Kyoto Centre of Traditional Industry (Kyoto Dento Sanyo Kaikan)

This museum is worth a visit for beautiful lacquerware, masks and robes for bugaku dances, a reproduction of a typical, traditional Kyoto house with its long corridors (nicknamed unagino-nedoko, 'bedrooms for eels'), as well as exhibitions of hand-forging knives, and other traditional crafts. The museum is located to the right of the National Museum of Modern Art and can be recognized by its unusual architecture, with a curved wall up to the second floor and a traditional square form for the upper storey. The TIC map has only the English name, which no Japanese would understand to give help with directions. The Kyoto Municipal Art Museum, and the zoo, are nearby.

National Museum of Modern Art

This has many large and attractive works — note that 'modern' refers to the past century or so.

Heian-jingu shrine

A Johnny-come-lately among Kyoto's shrines and temples, Heian-jingu was built in 1895 to mark the 1100th anniversary of the founding of Kyoto as the capital of Japan. It is a threefifths' scale reproduction of the palace built in 794; the present buildings are large, so the imagination runs overtime picturing the originals. The present buildings do not date even to the last century: a mysterious fire in 1976 caused extensive damage, resulting in the reconstruction of the main hall and several other buildings. The shrine has an extensive and pretty garden, known especially for cherry blossoms in spring. It is a popular place for wedding parties, so keep your eyes open for brides in beautiful wedding kimono. Also, take bread crusts to feed to the carp in the pond. The huge torii at the front entrance is the largest in Japan (23 metres high).

Kyoto Handicraft Centre

Although a commercial establishment, this is a first-rate attraction. On its several floors, craftsmen may be seen using their traditional skills in damascene, wood-block print-making (carving the plates and actually making the prints), pottery (making and painting), doll-making and several other crafts. Work is in progress every day of the week, but some of the people take Sunday off. For a convenient one-stop look at a number of the traditional crafts, it can't be beaten. Like Heianjingu, it is on the route of almost every tour, although a visit on your own would be more enjoyable, allowing you to move at your own pace. The products being made are sold on the premises, along with a large variety of other good-quality souvenirs (plus some tourist rubbish).

Ginkaku-ji

North-east of the station, this temple was originally built in 1489 as a hillside retreat of a shogun and converted into a temple after his death. The intention was to cover the walls of the main building with silver foil; although this was never done, the name Ginkaku (Silver Pavilion) was given to it anyway. (In Japan, intention counts for a lot, a tradition carried on into many aspects of daily life.)

The effect of the buildings and the rock-and-sand garden (including some unusually-shaped piles of gravel), and careful use of greenery, is one of restrained elegance. It should perhaps be visited before the more flamboyant and spectacular Kinkaku-ji (Gold Pavilion Temple) for it may seem to suffer by comparison, although it is probably a better expression of Japanese taste and quietude (at least of the educated classes).

It is about two km away from Heian-jingu and the others, so a bus or taxi will save time. A plaque at the entrance gives the history in English.

This and the following shrines and temples are all north-west of the station.

Daitoku-ji

Daitoku-ji is a functioning Zen temple, made up of 22 separate temples of which eight are open to visitors. Each one is explained on the ticket (payment is separate for each). Three of the best-known are Daisen-in, Zuiho-in, and Koto-in.

Kinkaku-ji

This is probably the best-known temple in Kyoto (if not Japan) because its pavilion is covered with gold leaf. The pavilion, set beside a large pond in which it is reflected, is very beautiful and worth a visit (it is on the itinerary of virtually every full tour of Kyoto). The present building dates only from 1955, replacing the previous structure (1397) that was destroyed in 1950 when it was set on fire by a student-monk with deranged metaphysical notions. (Mishima based his well-known *Kinkaku-ji* on this story.)

Even though it is popular with every visitor to Kyoto and therefore crowded, a visit to this temple is recommended for the lovely views around the pond,

and the wooded grounds. It is especially beautiful when the leaves change colour in November. An English-language pamphlet tells the history of the temple and its high points. Access from other points of Kyoto is convenient by bus or taxi.

Ryoan-ji

This temple houses the most famous rock-and-sand seki-taki garden in Japan. It is an enigmatic arrangement of 15 rocks in groups of various sizes in a sea of grey-white gravel that is raked daily into set patterns. A tile-topped earthen wall surrounds it on three sides; the fourth is part of the temple where viewers may sit and admire it. The unknown designer in the 1470s left no explanation of the meaning of the garden (if any), so numerous interpretations have been concocted.

There's more to the temple than just the garden — small groves of trees, a pond, a giant *moku-gyo* (wooden gong that makes a 'tonk' sound when struck), a carved-stone well in the shape of a coin (the water is safe to drink), the paintings on the interior sliding doors, and many details of the buildings. Ryoan-ji is in walking distance from Kinkaku-ji.

Ninna-ji

The great gate of this temple fronts on to the street, and at each side of the entrance is a fearsome, huge Nio-sama guardian god. One has an open mouth, the other closed, like Koma-inu. These are some of the finer Nio-sama in Japan, and they are better lit than most (good for photos). The grounds are large, and at their best when the cherry blossoms are out; at other times the temple is only of moderate interest.

Kitano-tenmangu Shrine

Quite the opposite of the flamboyant Heian shrine, Kitano is old (1607) and of a restrained Japanese style in natural wood. Its size, and the beautifully coloured details and carvings, set this apart from most shrines.

Museums

There are many museums other than the few detailed here. If the following sound interesting, inquire at the TIC for more information: Japan Historical Museum (Nippon Rekishi-kan); Kiyotaki Folkcraft Museum (Kyoto Mingei-kan); Kyoto Ceramic Hall (Kyoto Tojiki-kaikan); Kyoto Folkcraft Museum (Kyoto Minzoku-kan); Kyoto Municipal Museum of Art; Kyoto National Museum of Modern Art; Kodai Yuzen (has old yuzen-dyed items); Steam Locomotive Museum (Umekoji Joki Kikansha-kan).

WEST OF KYOTO

Arashiyama

This area is on the western edge of the city, where the Hozu river emerges from a gorge and tree-covered hills spring up. Though it is often promoted as a tourist attraction, most of it will be of limited interest to short-term visitors unless nature walks are of particular appeal. (It *is* of great appeal to the Japanese, who are city-bound much of the time.) There is a pleasant park at the end of a picturesque footbridge across the river from Arashiyama station (Keifuku railway); it is at its prettiest in spring because of the many cherry trees on the grounds.

The area north and west of Arashiyama is shown on the TIC's *Walking Tour Courses in Kyoto*, but it does not detail east of the museum, so you will need to rely on the TIC Kyoto-Nara map or the one in this book.

Arashiyama Museum One of the better museums in Japan, this is located at the north end of the bridge near the station. Kyoto-Arashiyama Hakubutsu-kan, to give it its proper name, will be of greatest interest to war buffs, but also has general appeal. It has one of the best collections of ancient armour,

helmets, swords, halberds and other weapons, as well as incredibly ornate and fine lacquerware. What sets the museum apart from others, however, is its display of World War II weapons, including the only Zero fighter left in Japan (all were destroyed by American authorities, but this one was fished out of Lake Biwa in 1978), a midget suicide submarine (raised from off Izu Peninsula), and an enormous gun barrel from the sunken battleship *Mutsu*. This immense piece of steel is 19.3 metres long and about two metres wide at the breech end; it fired a shell weighing over 1000 kg up to 40 km.

Tenryo-ji Temple The landscape garden behind the abbot's quarters is well known, although the buildings are of recent vintage (about 1900).

Nison-in Temple The grounds of this temple, north-west of Tenryu-ji, are planted with maples which are famous for their autumn colour.

Ukai (Cormorant Fishing) Every night between 1 July and 31 August (except on nights of full moon or after heavy rains when the river is muddy), there is a performance of fishing using cormorants as the divers. (More details of this are given in the Gifu section in the chapter on Central Honshu.) The best view and the most fun is on a boat, but the river is not too wide, so the action can also be seen from shore or the bridge.

Eiga-mura The name means 'Movie Village', and is a studio used for making films that require a traditional Japanese setting. There are streets of buildings of the samurai era, others of later eras, and visitors are welcome to watch actual filming. There are several exhibits from Japanese film history, and frequent screenings of various films. All visitors have spoken well of it. Eiga-mura is north on the road passing Uzumasa (six stations before Arashimaya), or south of JNR Hanazono station.

Koryu-ji temple Another place to visit from Uzumasa station is Koryu-ji temple, noted for a number of carved figures dating from the 9th and 10th centuries. The lecture hall (kodo) is one of Kyoto's truly old buildings, dating from 1165.

Saiho-ji

Formerly very popular with visitors because of the unusual beauty of the 200 or so varieties of moss that have been planted in the garden, the hordes of sightseers caused neighbours of this temple to protest, with the result that the garden has been closed to general admittance since July 1977. Entry is still possible, but only to those who write for an appointment and are willing to pay Y3000, as well as fulfill some other obligations. I visited the garden several times before the closure: I found it nice, but not special, and consider the fee exorbitant. If you wish to check, send a reply-paid postcard, giving name, address, age, occupation and desired date of visit to:

Saihoji
56 Kamigatani
Matsuo
Nishi-kyo-ku
Kyoto-shi.

SOUTH-WEST OF KYOTO
Katsura Rikyu Imperial Villa

This villa was built for the brother of an emperor; it was finished in 1624. The buildings are of very simple design, but are made of the finest materials by the best craftsmen available. It is considered the zenith of restrained elegance, the highest point in purely Japanese architecture.

The villa is under the control of the Imperial Household Agency, and it is necessary to make an appointment in advance (details are given under Kyoto

Gosho at the beginning of this section). Although there may be a wait of two to three days, it is sometimes possible to go the same day. The villa is closed Saturday afternoons, Sundays, national holidays, and from 25 December to 5 January.

It can be reached from Arashiyama/Saihoji, or from central Kyoto (Shijo-dori area) by different branches of the Hankyu railroad.

SOUTH AND SOUTH-EAST OF KYOTO

The TIC has a small photocopied map that is useful for general orientation in this area as far south as Nara.

Tofuku-ji

This temple is at its best in November, when the maples in the ravine (crossed by picturesque Tsuten-kyo bridge) are at their best. Some of the architectural details of the buildings are noticeably different from those of most temples, and the karesansui garden of mixed greenery and raked sand has a beauty of its own.

Access is from Tofukuji stations of both JNR Nara line and Keihan hon-sen (main line).

Fushimi-Inari Taisha Shrine

This is the largest of the 32,000 Inari shrines found throughout Japan. They honour the patron deities of agriculture and business, two of the most important activities in the country, which ensures their continued popularity. (For this reason, you are likely to come across a family or members of a small business praying for success in a new venture.) The fox is the messenger of the shrine deities, which explains the large number of fox statues on the grounds.

The shrine is famous for the huge number of orange-painted torii erected over some of the paths that wind up the mountainside. There are somewhat over 1000 of them, so close together that they form a tunnel. They have been donated by worshippers whose supplications were answered.

At various shrines along the route one may see hundreds of miniature torii (sold at the entrance) that have been left by worshippers — they can be seen stacked like firewood at the end of the season.

Those energetic enough to climb to the top — there are many paths branching off, many leading considerable distances away — may find a stone monument engraved with the profile of Charles Bronson! He is used as the symbol of virility by a line of male cosmetics called 'Mandom'.

Inside the shrine there is a good chance of seeing some sort of ceremony at the main building; there may also be performances of the slow and graceful sacred Kagura dances by shrine maidens.

The shrine is reached easily from Inari station of the JNR Nara line, or Fushimi-Inari station of Keihan hon-sen line. It is one of very few in Kyoto with no admittance charge.

Daigo-ji

The oldest structure in Kyoto is the five-storey pagoda of this temple at the far south-east of the city; it dates from 951. Nearby Sambon-in has one of the finest landscaped gardens in Japan. There is no nearby train station; ask the TIC for access information.

Fushimi-Momoyama Castle

This is marked on the TIC map and you may be tempted to see it. It is a modern concrete reconstruction of a magnificent old castle that stood here centuries ago before it was torn down and many of its parts moved elsewhere. The modern version offers nothing that can't be seen better elsewhere (such as Himeji or Hikone, both relatively close to Kyoto). Some of the parts of the old castle may be seen at Nijo-jo and Nishi-Hongan-ji.

Manpuku-ji

This is the head temple of the Obaku sect of Zen, probably the least-known of the three Zen 'schools' in Japan. It was introduced from China in the mid-17th century, and until the mid-1700s was headed by a Chinese monk. Every attempt is still made to preserve Chinese traditions. The buildings are of Chinese architectural style, which makes them unique in Kyoto.

Access is from Obaku stations of JNR Nara line or Keihan main line (the former is closer).

Uji

For centuries this has been a resort for the wealthy and powerful of Kyoto. It is best known for Byodo-in temple, an elongated structure dating from 1053 that is meant to portray a phoenix-like bird of Chinese mythology. It is the building seen on a Y10 coin, and is considered the finest structure of the Fujiwara era. However, most of the painted details inside the main building have disappeared with time, and you may be somewhat let down by the temple and grounds.

A suggestion is to see it late in the afternoon, have an evening meal or a snack, and then watch the cormorant fishing which is held on the river at Tonoshima Island (very close to the temple) every night from 11 June to 31 August, except during full moon or after heavy rains. You can rent a boat only, or arrange for a party/supper with food and drink. (A person who speaks Japanese would be helpful for this; the TIC might be able to offer suggestions.) The actual fishing lasts only 20-30 minutes, so the Japanese watchers usually make a party out of it. The fishing takes place close to shore and can be seen quite well without taking a boat, but the latter can be more fun.

Access to Uji is by the JNR Nara line, or the Keihan line for which Uji is the terminus. Byodo-in is on the same side of the river as the JNR station; from the Keihan station, you cross the bridge and turn left.

NORTH-EAST OF KYOTO
Shugaku-in Rikyu Imperial Villa

This villa dates from 1629: the upper garden is built around a pond, and is considered the most scenic part of the grounds. The landscape is mostly lawn and rolling hills, and not worth a special visit to see, at least until after seeing most of the other places listed here. It is at its best in autumn. Advance permission must be obtained from the Imperial Household Agency (refer to the Kyoto Gosho details at the beginning of this section).

Kyoto International Conference Hall (Kokusai Kaigi-jo)

A source of civic pride, the Conference Hall is a six-storey building constructed in 1966 beside the Takara-ga-ike pond and used for many international gatherings. It can be reached from Kyoto station by bus 5, 36 or 65; it is about one km from Takaragaike station of the Keifuku line out of Demachi-Yanagi station (to the north-east of the city). When the subway is operational, the fastest access will be to take it north to Karasuma-Shakomae, which is linked to the hall by bus 36. From here it is simple to get into the city for sightseeing: the Ohara area is easily reached because the Conference Hall is close to the bus and rail connections to Yase-yuen and Ohara.

Enryaku-ji

This is a very large temple complex on Mt Hiei, the highest point in the ridge that separates Kyoto from Lake Biwa. Temples have stood here since 788, when Emperor Kammi (who founded Kyoto as the capital) ordered its construction to guard against 'evil spirits'

from the north-east. One theory suggests that the spirits were Ainu or another race who predated the ethnic Japanese (Yamato).

Enryaku-ji grew to an astounding 3000 temples, and its private army of several thousand armed monks was more powerful than any government force. They terrorized other Buddhist sects, and often attacked Kyoto itself if their wishes were not met. In 1571, Nobunaga Oda, who began the unification of Japan after the civil war, overcame the monks and destroyed every temple. After this, Enryaku-ji was limited to one-twentieth of its former size. Today there are still 130 temples on the mountain.

There are four possible routes to Enryaku-ji. The first two are either by Keifuku private railway from Demachi-Yanagi station, or by bus from Kyoto station to Yase-yuen and then cable

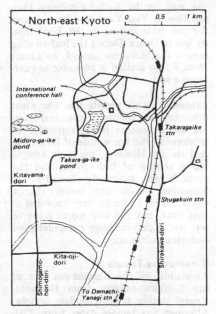

North-east Kyoto

0   0.5   1 km

International conference hall

Midoro-ga-ike pond

Takara-ga-ike pond

Takaragaike stn

Kitayama-dori

Shugakuin stn

Kita-oji-dori

Shimogamo-hon-dori

Shirakawa-dori

To Demachi-Yanagi stn

railway to the top. The third route is by Keihan train from Sanjo-Keihan station via Otsu along the shore of Biwa-ko to the terminus at Sakamoto. From there a cable-car runs up the east side of the mountains, offering good views of the lake. Fourth, there are also at least 10 buses a day from Kyoto station to the temple. The third is the most scenic route.

Ohara

This small village is well known for Yakko-in and Sanzen-in temples. The women of Ohara have long been famous for their characteristic costume and customs. Unusual in Japan, they carry loads on their heads. They may be seen on occasion in Kyoto selling produce from Ohara; in Ohara itself they may be working at souvenir stalls.

Access to Ohara is by bus which originates at Kyoto station and passes by Sanjo-Keihan and Yase-Yuen stations on the way, or by Keifuku railway Hiei-sen line to Yase-Yuen (the base station for the cable railway to Mt Hiei) then by bus to Ohara. During the leaf-viewing season the buses are packed, so a start from Kyoto station is advisable to guarantee a seat.

Sanzen-in This temple has, like most other temples, images of historical interest which become rather repetitive to westerners who know little of Buddhism and its art. However, the main temple has a setting of lush green, and the grounds are extremely beautiful in November when the leaves change colour. It is, naturally, very crowded at that time, but still well worth going to see. An English-language pamphlet gives historical information.

Kurama-dera Temple

Accessible by the Kurama-sen line of the Keifuku railway from Demachi-Yanagi station is Kurama-dara temple. Although the temple dates from 770,

the present main hall is only from 1971 so it is of little architectural interest. However, the grounds are very pretty in November, so this is the best time for a visit. There is also an interesting festival on 20 June.

There is a good hiking trail between Kurama-dera and Kibune-jinja shrine; it also is most recommended during autumn.

NORTH-WEST OF KYOTO

Takao

This is possibly the supreme area for maple-viewing, several km into the mountains north-west of the city. There are three temples to visit while admiring the foliage, Jingo-ji (at Takao), Saimyo-ji (at Makino-o), and Kozan-ji (at Togano-o); all are within walking distance of each other.

On the approach to Jingo-ji, tables and mat-covered areas are set up on level patches of ground and on platforms so visitors may lunch beneath the canopy of brilliant colours. The view of a Japanese family, with one or two of the women dressed in kimono, eating amidst such beauty is a memorable picture of Japanese civilization at its best.

Visitors may find a speciality of the season on sale, maple-leaf tempura: the batter tastes good, but the leaf is terrible.

Buses run as far as Takao; check with the TIC for schedules.

Shooting the Rapids

An enjoyable excursion, especially during the heat of summer, is to shoot the Hozu rapids. The starting point is Kameoka, accessible by JNR Sanin-sen line or bus from Kyoto station. The dock is at Hozu-ohashi bridge. The trip lasts about two hours and is exciting without being dangerous (it finishes at Arashiyama). The 'season' is 11 March to 30 November.

There are generally six boats a day,

so inquire at the TIC to be sure of getting a seat.

ENTERTAINMENT IN KYOTO

If you aren't worn out after a day's sightseeing, or if you want a break during the day from a seemingly endless round of temples and shrines, what else is there to do in Kyoto? There are many events that would fit into the 'cultural' category, performing arts that have been passed down through the centuries and represent some of the highest levels of achievement in these fields in the world. Naturally, these are not going to be everyone's cup of *o-cha*, but it would be a pity to ignore this side of Japanese life. Those looking for something less highbrow will discover that Japanese popular taste can be as earthy as that anywhere.

Dance & Theatre

Through the year, at various times and theatres, there are performances of the straditional arts Noh, Kabuki, Bunraku, Kyogen and others. As Osaka is only an hour away by train, performances of Kabuki and Bunraku (puppet theatre which originated in Osaka) given there are also in easy reach. These performing arts are explained in greater detail elsewhere in the book.

A highly recommended condensed version of all the major Japanese arts — dances by geisha, traditional bugaku dances, koto music, Bunraku, flower arrangement — can be seen between 1 March and 29 November twice daily at Gion Kaburenjo Theatre. The show is called Gion Corner and lasts an hour; performances begin at 8 and 9 pm: each 'act' is long enough to give a feel for the skill, but short enough not to be dull (most seem too short). Tickets can be bought at the door, but bookings or advance purchase may be advisable during busy seasons.

There are many performances of traditional dances at certain times of the year. Examples are Miyako-odori (Cherry Blossom Dance) throughout April, when numbers of beautifully-dressed maiko (apprentice geisha) perform traditional dances; and Kamogawa-odori in May, when geisha of the Pontocho area perform.

To check on what is happening, obtain the booklets mentioned earlier, and be sure to stop in at the TIC. They have a bulletin board listing all the events of that month, and can give further details of anything of interest.

Coffee Shops

For other innocent entertainment, there are many coffee shops. Some are only places to sit and chat; a coffee-shop 'date' is a common boy-girl activity, which helps explain the high prices — you're not paying for the coffee, but for the space. Many shops offer music, recorded or live: the latter is jazz, while recorded music may be jazz, classical or in-between. Because such shops come and go, it is pointless to list them here; the TIC people can give suggestions. It is often possible to meet people at such places, but it's all the luck of the draw.

Bars & Clubs

For drinking there is a huge number of places, as is true of any large city in Japan. Some are reasonable in cost and quite enjoyable to visit, but beware of what would be called 'clip joints' in any other country, but which are accepted in Japan because of the generous expense accounts. It is not unknown to be billed well over Y10,000 for a beer! There are many little pubs and 'stand-bars' (Japanese term), many of which are run by companies that make or distribute whisky. These reasonably-priced places can be identified after a little practice. Don't be embarrassed to ask prices — remember the possible consequences! Avoid any place that has touts in front enticing customers in, and places with hostesses, unless you are able to check prices for all services. Hostess charges can skyrocket. The TIC may be able to give suggestions.

Bars in international hotels will be safe from gouging (though not cheap), but will generally have an international atmosphere, not the Japanese one that visitors presumably have paid a lot of money to enjoy.

There are many lower-class clubs where strippers and similar entertainment may be found. Finding them on your own may be difficult, if not impossible, and a Japanese friend would be invaluable in locating one; also, a lone foreigner might well be refused entry. The cost of such a place would not be cheap: if a girl can earn Y10,000-30,000 for an 'all-nighter', she's going to expect a fair proportion of this for playing around in a club.

Seasonal Events

There are many seasonal sights and entertainments, some natural, some 'man-made'.

Cherry Blossoms The exact time of the blossoms varies over a range of several weeks from year to year, but is generally around early-mid April. The best places to see the blossoms are Kiyomizu-dera, Heian-jingu, Daigo-ji, Maruyama-koen park and Nanzen-ji. Yoshino (Nara-ken) is a mountainside planted with thousands of trees, and can be seen as a day trip from Kyoto. Also highly recommended is Hikone: its castle grounds are covered with cherry trees, and the moats are lined with them.

Maple Leaves The temples of Kyoto are among the most beautiful places in the world in autumn. The temple founders planted the grounds, which are generally located on the hills around the city, with maples. The leaves of these trees change colour in a fiery display of reds and oranges rarely matched anywhere else in the world (a difficult admission

for someone from eastern Canada!), and their beauty underscores the fine lines of the walls and roofs of the buildings. The peak period is usually early-mid November. Temples noted for their folliage are Eikan-do, Nanzen-ji, Kiyomizu-dera, Tofuku-ji, Sekiya-Zen-in, Kinkaku-ji and Ryoan-ji. Areas close to the city include Arashiyama, Sugino, Kiyotani valley, Yase, Ohara (Sanzen-in and Jakko-in), Mt Kurama and Kibune and Takao (Jingo-ji and Kozan-ji).

Markets

There are two monthly flea markets. One is at Kitano-jinja on the 5th of every month, and the other is at Toji on the 21st. For the best selection it is best to arrive early in the morning. Don't expect any valuable antiques, for these people know the worth of their goods. (Hint: Don't pick up any antiques; some unscrupulous dealers carefully assemble already broken items so that they 'break' when touched, obliging payment.)

Festivals

There are many festivals in Kyoto, but because information is so easy to obtain there is no need to list them all here. The JNTO pamphlet on Kyoto/Nara has a good listing, as do the monthly booklets listed earlier. The most famous festivals, worth making a point to see, are the following:

Aoi Matsuri (15 May) A procession of people in costumes of centuries ago passes through the streets from Kyoto Gosho Palace to Shimogamo and Kamigamo shrines.

Gion Matsuri (16-17 July) Probably the supreme Japanese festival. Huge festival carts are pulled through the streets on the 17th. There are 29 in all, of various sizes, all several tonnes in weight and build like miniature temples, small boats, etc, with the finest lacquer covering, gilded ornamentation, and some with European tapestries — they are a fantastic sight. The night before, they are on display in little sidestreets; many may be entered on payment of a fee. Also open are some of the old nearby houses where families display their treasures, such as suits of armour. The TIC can give information on the route and display sites. Accommodation is hard to find at this time, so it is necessary to book ahead, or to commute from a nearby city or town.

Daimonji (16 August) Five huge bonfires that trace out one Chinese character each light up five mountains surrounding Kyoto. City lights are doused to add to the effect. It is the culmination of the Bon season when the spirits of the dead are believed to return to earth. During this season, you may find neighbourhood dances with hundreds of people in kimono, moving in great circles and performing the slow and graceful movements of the dance. The best vantage points are Shogun-zuka hill (Hagashiyama) and Yoshida-yama hill, near Kyoto University.

Jidai Matsuri (22 October) The name means Festival of the Ages, and it is a procession of people in historical costumes of the 13 main periods of Kyoto's history.

Arts & Crafts

Kyoto is famous for a number of handicrafts of the highest quality, a legacy of its past as the capital for over 1000 years, a period when there was a continual demand for fine fabrics, lacquerware, etc. Many of these goods are still produced by the traditional methods evolved centuries ago, and you can see several types of craftsmen at work. As well as the crafts mentioned here, it is possible to arrange an introduction to other specialists through the TIC or City Information Office.

Kyoto Handicraft Centre Described earlier, this is well worth a visit to watch a variety of crafts in action. Goods may be purchased on the spot.

Tatsumara Silk Fine silks are on display here, and demonstrations are given on fingernail weaving. Inquire at the TIC for more details.

Inaba Cloisonne Demonstrations are given of making cloisonne ware. Inquire at the TIC.

Municipal Museum of Traditional Industry Described earlier, this has displays of many handicrafts of the very highest quality, along with live demonstrations of some crafts.

Yuzen An interesting and quite extensive live display here shows the historic process for producing the incredibly beautiful material used for one kind of (very expensive) kimono. Yuzen Bunka Kaikan is on the west side of the city near Nishi-Kyogoku station (Hankyu railway Kyoto-sen line). A leaflet and more information are available at the TIC.

Pottery There are several potteries in the area, but they do not encourage visitors because of the interruption of their work. An exception is Kotobuki Toshun, who has set up special facilities in the Kiyomizu-Yaki Danchi building so that visitors can see how pottery is made and even make some for themselves. This is usually only for group tours, so inquire at the TIC if you are interested.

Shopping

Kyoto probably offers the largest variety of traditional Japanese handicrafts of any city in the country. There are many shops near the station, and near many of the major temples and other tourist attractions. There are also several department stores, and the Kyoto Handicraft Centre. A commercial map, 'Shopping Guide Map of Kyoto', is useful for locating specialty shops. It should be available at the TIC and hotels. The TIC staff can also help you to find anything out of the ordinary.

I found that the tax-free shops along Kawaramachi-dori gave slightly less discount on photographic equipment than the lowest-price shops in Tokyo, but the difference wasn't enough to worry about. If it is to be a first camera, it is better to spend the extra yen and have it available to photograph the beauties of Kyoto.

Food
To help with the search for a good restaurant, the Kyoto Restaurant Association has printed a pamphlet, *Kyoto Gourmet Guide*, available at the TIC. Staff at the TIC would also probably be willing to suggest a good restaurant and perhaps even a sample menu if your visit was not at one of their busy times.

For budget diners, there are many little restaurants with realistic wax displays which show you the dishes available. A former student of Kyoto University recommended *Nakagima* for economical food (open Monday to Saturday). For a real bargain (of doubtful nutritional value), one can gorge on pizza at *Trecca Pizza:* all you can eat, between 11 am and 2 pm, Monday to Saturday, for about Y500. It is located on Kawaramachi-dori near Sanjo-dori on the second floor of the BAL Fashion building.

Accommodation
A large number of places offer reasonably-priced accommodation in Kyoto, along with hotels of the international luxury class, (plus some ryokan that are even more costly).

For the full listing of cheap accommodation, it is best to obtain photocopied sheets 'moderately-priced Accommodation in Kyoto' from the TIC in either Kyoto or Tokyo.

There are six youth hostels in the vicinity. Those nearest the station are Higashiyama (tel 761-8135) and Matsusan (221-5160). Because of their proximity to the city centre they are more likely to be booked. Also, the latter is run by a couple of suspicious older ladies. Both Utano Youth Hostel (462-2288/9) and Kitayama (492-5345) are about 50 minutes by bus to the north of the city (which will be reduced by the north-south subway line); the latter is more out of the way. Some distance into the country (more than an hour by bus) are Ohara Youth Hostel (744-2721) and Oharago Youth Hostel (744-2721).

Favourites with travellers who don't care for the restrictions of youth hostels are two private homes, Tani House and Uno House.

Tani House (492-5489) is a spacious, traditional-style house with several rooms, one each set aside for males and females, plus several smaller rooms suitable for couples or whoever happens to get there first. The only disadvantage is that it is the better part of an hour away from Kyoto station. Access is by bus 214, 204 or 222 to Funaokakoen stop: there is a small road across the main road from a tailor shop; follow this, and turn right at the third little side-street (it faces an earthen wall inset with tiles).

Uno House is conveniently located not far from the south-east corner of the Kyoto Gosho. Access from Kyoto station is by bus 4, 14, 54, 200 or 215 to Kawaramachi-Marutomachi stop. From the large intersection, walk west to the second small street on the south side and turn left (there's a bank on the corner). The house is on the east side and a very small sign announces 'Uno'. Travellers arriving in Kyoto by bus from Osaka airport should get off at Kyoto Hotel (on Kawaramachi-dori) a 20-minute walk to the south of Uno House. The house is something of a wonder and quite untypically Japanese, with so many added-on rooms and wings that it is a bit of a rabbit warren. It is advisable to ensure that payment of room charges is written down at once, as in my experience they have been forgotten and attempts made to collect them again. This slight disadvantage is outweighed by the convenience of simple cooking facilities and the closeness to the city. Mrs Uno is very good-hearted, and occasionally has a room for a long-term occupancy.

There is another private home run by another family named Tani. It is to the south of the city (681-7437). One of the benefits of staying at these two places is that the other travellers you meet there often have useful information and interesting stories.

The least expensive ryokan are *Ichiume* (tel 351-9385, Y1500), *Sanyu* (tel 371-1968, Y1500), and *Yuhara* (tel 371-9583).

Others in increasing order of cost are given below. Prices are for lowest-priced room.

Ryokan: *Rakutuso Bekkan* (tel 761-633, Y3900), and *Rakutuso Honkan* (tel 761-6336, Y8000 for two), both near Heian-jingu.

YWCA: *Kyoto YWCA* (tel 431-0351, Y3500, women only).

Western-style hotels: *Pension Utano* (tel 463-1118, Y3200); *Traveller's Inn Honkan* (tel 771-0225, Y3800), near Heian-jingu; *Traveller's Inn Hotel Sun Shine* (tel 771-0225, Y3800); *Hokke Club* (tel 361-1251, Y4000); *Kyoto Business Hotel* (tel 222-1220, Y4000); *Kyoto Central Inn* (tel 211-1666, Y5080); *New Ginkaku Inn* (tel 341-2884, Y5500); *Tokyu Inn* (tel 593-0109, Y5900); *Pension Shimogamo* (tel 711-0180, Y8200).

Those on large budgets who wish to sample a really fine ryokan in beautiful surroundings should enjoy *Rankyokan*,

which is on a hillside overlooking the Hozu river just above Arashiyama and set among tall trees. The price is over Y10,000 per person.

Miscellaneous Left-overs

Zen Those interested in Zen will be disappointed to learn that you cannot join meditation on a casual basis without an introduction. The reason is that many other foreigners joined in, didn't know what to do, would not conform to the customs, and distracted those who wanted to participate properly. Anyone who is seriously interested should contact the TIC or arrange an introduction through a previous teacher elsewhere. Those just becoming interested would be better advised to go to Tokyo, where there are facilities for teaching Zen in English (this is described earlier in the book).

Temple Accommodation Many people wish to stay at a temple in Kyoto. Unfortunately, as with Zen meditation, previous foreign guests have not conformed with customs and rules of the temples and soured any desire of temple staff to have foreign visitors. Anyone sincerely interested in staying at a temple and able to demonstrate both some genuine interest in the religious aspects and a willingness to conform to custom should contact the TIC for further information.

Post Office The Post Office offers basic services 24 hours a day, including mail pick-up from Poste Restante. A passport or other identification will be required. Postal rates are conveniently noted in English in the main section.

Day Trips Kyoto is close to many of the most interesting sightseeing territory in Japan. A number of places can be visited in a day using Kyoto as a base, or you can go out on circling routes and return after a few days. Day trips include Nara, Hikone, Himeji, Osaka, Ise and Yoshino (in cherry-blossom time). Extended trips would be Nara and area, and around the Kii-hanto peninsula. If you are not pressed for time, you should consider the Kiso area (described under Central Honshu).

NARA-KEN

The city of Nara is a very famous and popular destination for visitors to Japan, for it predates Kyoto as the imperial capital, and some temples from that period still survive. The Nara plain was one of the most important areas in the early history of Japan, and many remnants abound. There are also other attractions in the southern parts of the prefecture, and the adjoining Kii-hanto Peninsula. Included in this section is a patch of adjacent north-west Mie-ken that fits in with Nara-ken more conveniently due to historic links and accessibility, and also part of Wakayama-ken.

NARA

Usually mentioned in the same breath as Kyoto, Nara is another ancient capital of Japan, only 42 km from Kyoto and usually included in any tour of Japan. It was the first permanent capital of Japan, from 710 to 784, previous to which the capital was moved after the death of each emperor. Nara witnessed the introduction of Buddhism into Japan, with the far-reaching effects on culture and the arts that resulted. Amazingly, some of the temples and other structures from that period still stand. Although they were then in the city of Nara, the present city is considerably smaller, and many of them are now some distance out in the country.

Getting There

Nara is conveniently reached from both Kyoto and Osaka by Kintetsu private

railway (Kyoto and Namba stations, respectively). From both stations there is approximately one train an hour through the day. There is also service by JNR, but JNR Nara station is less conveniently located. The trip from either city takes about 50 minutes. There is also a convenient service to many other centres in the region, for it is intensively blanketed with railway lines: a few such cities are Nagoya, Toba and Wakayama.

At Kyoto station the Kintetsu service to Nara is reached by the entrance closest to the post office. Watch for the sign 'Kinkinippon tickets' for tickets for the line. Ticket in hand, go through the JNR wicket and take the overpass to the Kintetsu line tracks. Kyoto station is well signposted in English.

There is a non-stop express (tokkyu) to Nara with a Y300 surcharge. Tickets can be purchased at a kiosk on one of the platforms.

Information

The TIC in Kyoto has a useful pamphlet *Kyoto Nara* that has some sightseeing information to complement the following pages, and the JNTO Kyoto-Nara map is quite adequate for sightseeing in Nara city. The TIC in Tokyo also has a printed sheet 'Walking Tour Courses in Nara' but it is not quite as informative as others in the series. Finally, the Nara City Tourist Information Office is located on the first floor of the Kintetsu-Nara station.

Voluntary Guides

To make your visit more interesting and enjoyable, the Nara YMCA will introduce you to one or more English-speaking Japanese who will act as unpaid guides for sightseeing around Nara. (As in Kyoto, it is reasonably expected that you pay their transport, admittance charges, etc.) A programme like this is a superb way to meet 'everyday' Japanese, as distinct from those in the tourist business. During working

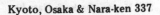

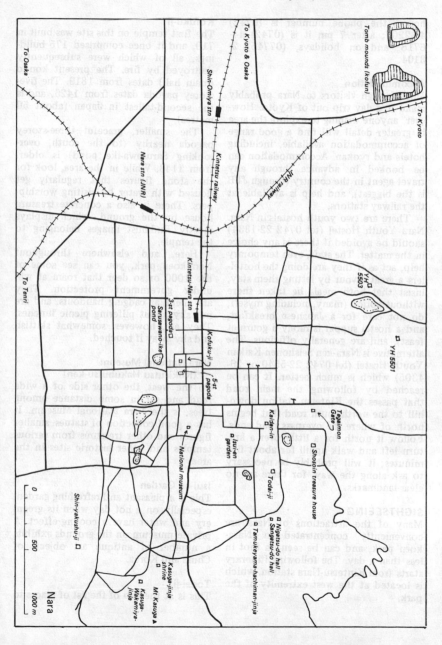

To Kyoto & Osaka

To Osaka

To Kyoto

Tomb mounds (kofun)

Shin-Omiya stn

Kintetsu railway

Kintetsu stn (JNR)

JNR railway

YH 5503

Kintetsu-Nara stn

3-st pagoda

Sarusawano-ike pond

Kofuku-ji

YH 5501

To Tenri

5-st pagoda

Kaidan-in

Tegaimon Gate

Iui-en garden

Shosoin treasure house

National museum

Todai-ji

Nigatsu-do hall
Sangatsu-do hall

Tamukeyama-hachiman-jinja

Isui-en garden

Shin-yakushi-ji

Kasuga-jinja shrine

Kasuga-Wakamiya-jinja

Mt Kasuga

Nara

0

500

1000 m

hours, the phone number is (0742) 44-2207; after 7 pm it is (0742) 44-6718; and on holidays, (07745) 2-3104.

Accommodation

Most foreign visitors to Nara probably make it a day trip out of Kyoto. However, anyone wishing to explore the area in greater detail will find a good range of accommodation available, including hotels and ryokan. Accommodation can be booked in advance through any travel agent in the country (though JTB is the biggest), and help is available at the railway stations.

There are two youth hostels in Nara. Nara Youth Hostel (tel 0742 22-1334) should be avoided if there is any choice in the matter. The staff, even temporary help, act as if they are doing the hostellers a great favour by letting them stay, insist that both meals be taken there without option (many, including myself, do not care for a Japanese breakfast, and a hostel supper is rarely a gourmet feast), and are generally officious. The alternative is Nara-ken Seishonen-Kaikan Youth Hostel (tel 0742 22-5540 or 26-4305) which is much better. It can be reached by following the main road that passes the Kintetsu station downhill to the north-south road that begins north of where the overpass road ends. Follow it north for a little over a km, turn left and walk uphill for about five minutes; it will probably be necessary to ask along the way, for there are no clear landmarks.

SIGHTSEEING

Many of the attractions of Nara are conveniently concentrated in Nara-koen park, and can be seen on foot in less than a day. The following itinerary starts from Kintetsu-Nara station, which is located at the west extremity of the park.

Kofuku-ji

The first temple on this site was built in 710, and it once comprised 175 buildings, all of which were subsequently destroyed by fire. The present kondo (main hall) dates from 1819. The five-storey pagoda dates from 1426, and is the second-tallest in Japan (about 50 metres).

The smaller, graceful three-storey pagoda nearby (to the south, overlooking Sarusawa-ike pond) is older, from 1143. While in the area, look for the stone figures that regularly get doused with water by visiting worshippers. There is also a concrete treasure house on the ground, which displays mostly Buddhist images belonging to the temple.

Here, and elsewhere throughout Nara-koen park, you can see some of the 1000 or so deer that roam at will under government protection. They are adept at cadging handouts, and are not shy about pilfering picnic lunches. They are, however, somewhat skittish and shy away if touched.

Nara National Museum
(Kokirutsu Hakubutsu-ken)

To the west, the other side of a wide road and set in some distance among trees, is the Nara National Museum. It has a good collection of statues, smaller figures and other treasures from various temples and other historic sites in the area.

Isui-en Garden

This is a pleasant and refreshing garden, especially on a hot day when its greenery and water have a cooling effect. A private museum on the grounds exhibits a number of antique art objects of China and Korea.

Todai-ji

This is at the top of the list of places to

visit in Nara. The main temple building, Daibutsu-den, houses Japan's largest bronze statue of Buddha. The building itself is the largest wooden structure in the world, even though its area is one-third smaller than originally. At the entrance to the temple is Nandaimon ('South Great Gate') dating from 1199. The eight-metre high Nio-sama (Deva kings, guardians of Buddhism) are national treasures (like the gate), and among the finest such carvings in Japan. The koma-inu in the rear niches are also highly regarded. Special biscuits for the deer are on sale in this area — no fools, the deer are also to be found here in the greatest numbers.

Daibutsu-den was built in 1709, the latest in a series from 752; it has recently had extensive renovations. The Daibutsu (Great Buddha) statue in its incense-filled interior was first cast in 749, but subsequent damage in fires has required replacing the head (at least twice), the right hand and other parts. Possibly as a result of this later work, the statue lacks the artistry and serenity of the Daibutsu at Kamakura (near Tokyo). The statue is 16 metres high and weighs 437 tonnes (further details are given on the admittance ticket).

The two large statues in front of the Daibutsu are Nyoirin-Kannon, who grants prayers and wishes, and Kokuzo-Bosatsu who possesses wisdom and happiness. The figure in the left-hand corner behind the statue is Komokuten, one of the four heavenly guardians who destroy all obstacles in the path of Buddhism. Another of the guardians, Tamonten, is found in the right-hand corner — he is trampling a demon.

Kaidan-in is a separate temple west of the Daibutsu-den; it contains clay images of the four heavenly guardians (all national treasures).

Sangatsu-do is the oldest structure of Todai-ji, dating from 733. Many statues of national-treasure merit are displayed.

Kasuga-taisha Shrine

One of the best-known places in Nara, Kasuga-taisha is famous for its forested setting and lanterns. There are approximately 3000 lanterns, some of stone and standing as tall as a man, others of bronze and hung from the eaves of the various buildings that make up the shrine. Seen against the bright orange and white of the buildings, the effect is very photogenic. Lanterns line nearly all the paths of the shrine grounds, and this is within the area roamed by deer, so one is quite likely to poke its head out between two of them for a very cute picture.

The lanterns are all lit twice a year, on the day of the Setsubun festival (variable: 2 or 3 February), and on 15 August. The annual festival of the shrine, Kasuga-matsuri, is held on 13 March and features a colourful procession.

In addition to the four shrines (surrounded by a gallery) that make up the main shrine, there is also Kasuga-Wakamiya-jinja to the south. Here it may be possible to see Kagura (sacred dances) in the Kagura-den, the southernmost of the three buildings. The annual festival of this shrine is the greatest in Nara, and is a procession of large numbers of people in costumes and armour of ancient times. It is held on 16-17 December.

Shin-Yakushi-ji

This temple is of modest interest, and is known primarily for its central seated image and 12 clay figures of 12 divine generals.

OUTSIDE NARA

The other attractions are somewhat outside today's city, which gives an idea of the size of the old capital.

Horyu-ji

This is one of the most important temples in Japanese history, art and culture. Its construction began in 607 under the direction of Prince Shotoku, the man depicted on Y10,000 notes and one of the great builders of the Japanese state. Amazingly, some of the original structures still stand; others were added or rebuilt in later eras. Easiest access is by bus from Kintetsu-Nara station, either directly to Horyuji-mae stop, or after a visit to Yakushi-ji and other temples (described below).

The temple is divided into Sai-in Garan and To-in Garan (west and east minsters). Sai-in is now the larger, since more of its structures have survived: a leaflet given on entry has a map that identifies the buildings. The following is a brief description.

Sai-in Garan Entry is via Nandaimon ('South Great Gate'), a national treasure dating from 1438 (rebuilt), a walled avenue, then Chumon (Middle Gate, also a national treasure and dating from the year of the temple's construction). The red deva king (guardian of Buddhism) in the gate symbolizes light; the black king, darkness. The five-storey pagoda is one of the oldest wooden buildings in the world, and incorporates the same timbers used in its original construction. It was dismantled during World War II for safety.

The open-fronted kodo (990) houses several important statues; the gilded main figures are Yakushi-Nyorai (2.6 metres and two attendants (1.7 metres). The kondo (main hall, another national treasure) is also one of the oldest buildings in the world and houses many important images, both sculptures and castings.

Shoryo-in has a statue of Prince Shotoku at age 45 (figure and building are national treasures), while Daihozo-den (two concrete buildings) have displays of many treasures of the temple.

To-in Garan Leaving the Sai-in area and passing through Chu-mon and Todaimon (Middle, and East Great Gates), you come to the To-in Garan precincts. The octagonal building in the central rectangle is Yumedono (Hall of Dreams, used by Shotoku for meditation), rated the most beautiful rectangular building in Japan. Dating from 739, it also contains a number of fine images, including several national treasures. There are several other buildings in the grounds, many of which also house historic images. Chugu-ji temple is a former nunnery attached to To-in Garan.

Horin & Hokki Temples

In the vicinity of Horyu-ji are two other historic temples, Horin-ji and Hokki-ji. They date from 621 and 638 respectively, and also house several treasured images. The pagoda at Hokki is believed to date from 685.

Nara-ken Museum of Ethnology
(Nara-ken Minzoku Hakubutsu-kan)

This museum features a number of traditional farmhouses from the early 18th century, that have been moved from various places in Nara-ken and re-erected. Inside them, items once used in daily life but obsolete for decades or centuries are displayed with photos or drawings to show how they were used. Exhibits represent the three main geographical/cultural areas of Nara-ken: Nara plain, the Yamato highlands, and the mountains of the Yoshino area. Most interesting are the full-size scenes with life-like models of farmers, lumberjacks, teapickers and others, all dressed in authentic garb. (Some of the dummies were actually dressed by people who still make their living in the way portrayed, so even the underwear is correct!)

Access is from Kintetsu-Koriyama station, from where you take a bus to Yoda-Higashiyama (15 minutes). It might be possible to go by bus directly

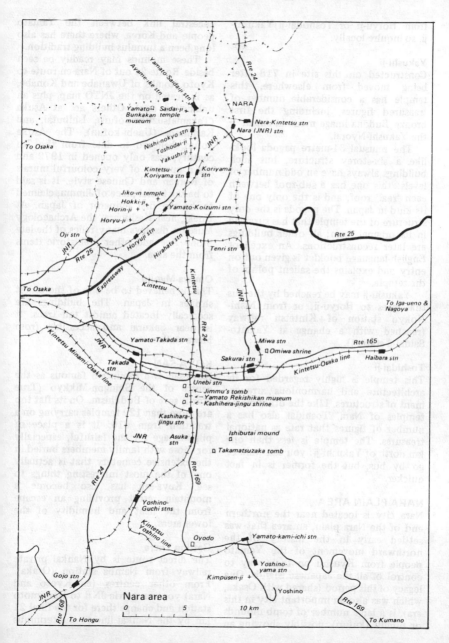

Nara area

0   5   10 km

from Horyu-ji or Toshodai-ji/Yakushi-ji, so inquire locally.

Yakushi-ji

Constructed on this site in 718 after being moved from elsewhere, this temple has a considerable number of treasured figures, including the first bronze Buddha image made in Japan — the Yakushi-Nyorai.

The unusual 34-metre pagoda looks like a six-storey structure, but such buildings always have an odd number of levels: this one has a sub-roof between each 'real' roof, and is the only one of its kind in Japan. The pagoda is the only structure of the temple that has survived in its original form; all other buildings are later reconstructions. An excellent English-language booklet is given out on entry and explains the salient points of the temple.

Yakushi-ji may be reached by the bus that goes to Horyu-ji, or from Nishi-Nokyo station of Kintetsu railway (reached with a change at Yamato-Saidai-ji station).

Toshidai-ji

This temple is highly regarded for its architecture and harmonious arrangement of structures. Like the other major temples of Nara, Toshidai also has a number of figures that rate as national treasures. The temple is less than one km north of Yakushi-ji: you can walk or go by bus, but the former is in fact quicker.

NARA PLAIN AREA

Nara city is located near the northern end of the Nara plain, an area that was settled early in the history of the northward movement of the Yamato people from Kyushu on their way to control of all the Japanese islands. One legacy of this period (shared with Osaka, which was also an important city in this era), is a large number of tomb mounds or tumuli (kufun), possibly showing an ancestral link between the Yamato people and Korea, where there has also long been a tumulus-building tradition.

These mounds may readily be seen beside Route 24 out of Nara en route to Kyoto (tombs of Uwanabe and Konabe, as indicated on the JNTO map, plus an unlabelled one). Others are at Asuka (Takamatsuzuka-kofun), Ishibutai, and Kashihara (Unebi-kofun). The Asuka kofun, believed to date from the 7th century, was only opened in 1972 and has a number of very colourful murals of Korean and Chinese style. It is said to be the burial place of Jimmu, claimed to be the first emperor of Japan. At Uneki, near Kashihara, the Archaeology Museum displays many relics of the late Stone Age and other prehistoric items from the area.

Omiwa-Myojin

This is believed to be one of the oldest shrines in Japan. The buildings are scenically located amidst tall trees. It is near Sakurai and accessible from Miwa station.

KOYA-SAN

Koya-san is a mountain famous as the centre of the Shingon-Mikkyo (True Word) sect of Buddhism. On its flat top are more than 120 temples carrying on a tradition from 816. It is a place of pilgrimmage for the faithful, especially for those with family members buried in the extensive cemetery that is actually one of the most interesting things to see. Koya-san has also become a mountain resort providing an escape from the heat and humidity of the lower areas.

Getting There

The direct route is by Nankai private railway from Namba station (Osaka). From other centres (eg Kyoto and Nara) you can go via JNR to Hashimoto station and change there for the final 21 km by the Nankai line to the terminus

at Gokuraku-bashi station. From there a cable-car runs to the top of Koya-san.

Sightseeing

Buses run from the upper cable-car station into the centre of the small community, or you can take a taxi or walk the three km or so into town. The road is pleasantly lined with tall cedars, and leads to the main temple at the west side of the community.

Gobyo

If a bus is available, it is better to go directly to Gobyo. This is the mausoleum of Kobodaishi, the founder of the temples and a great teacher of Shingon (he devised the hiragana syllabary for writing Japanese in a simpler form than using kanji). From Gobyo there is a very pleasant and peaceful walk through the great cemetery, where tombs and memorials are set amidst a forest of great cedar trees. The path leads to Ichinohashi (First Bridge), from where you can walk through the town and visit any of the large number of temples on the way. There is only one main street so it is impossible to get lost. At the intersection with the main road is an information office that can supply a map, some literature, and give assistance in finding a room.

Kongobi-ji Temple

Just a short distance beyond the town is Kongobu-ji (Temple of the Diamond Mountain, rebuilt in 1861), the chief temple of the sect and the best one to visit if time is limited.

Other

Nearby (downhill and across the road) is a large courtyard in which is located the pagoda Daito, of a style uncommon in Japan (rebuilt 1937). The interior features brilliantly coloured beams, and houses five sacred images of Buddha in different incarnations. Other buildings are the Golden Hall (for ceremonies) and Miedo.

Farther along the road below the latter cluster of buildings is Daimon (Great Gate), a large wooden structure from 1705; it is similar to such gates at other old temples.

Accommodation

There are 53 temples on the mountain that provide accommodation. Most, if not all, have been developed into attractive places to stay, with lovely little gardens. Each of these temples is virtually owned by its abbot, and then inherited by his son (natural or adopted). By charging about double the tariff of most temples elsewhere in Japan (about Y5000 a night), the abbots have turned them into a very lucrative business, and many are reputedly quite weak in the theology of their sect. Since wealth is required to advance in the religious hierarchy of the sect, this operation of the temples as money-making activities is encouraged. (Remember that these comments apply to the Shingon-Mikkyo sect only, and other sects are still close to the original tenets of their faith.)

Information

Koya-san is best visited for its symbolic value, being a community of temples.

But as an object of architectural study, it is not worth a special trip compared with the beautiful buildings of Kyoto. The Tokyo TIC distributes a single-page information sheet that gives some more details on Koya-san, although its map is (regrettably) not to scale.

Getting Around

From Koya-san you can go west to Wakayama and continue around the Kii-hanto Peninsula. From Gojo, Route 168 runs south to Hongu, Shingu and other attractions of the peninsula (described in the Mie-ken section), which area includes the more interesting parts of the peninsula. Three buses daily make the scenic run between Gojo and Shingu, and another two from Gojo to Hongu.

YOSHINO

The spring cherry blossoms on the side of Yoshino hill (north-east of Mt Koya) are famous throughout Japan. There are perhaps 100,000 trees planted at various levels; they mature at different times, so the blossom season lasts a month or so instead of the usual few days. The normal season is from early to late April.

From Yoshino station a cable-car leads up to Yoshinoyama. From there the road continues to rise steadily, lined with temples and shrines. The main structure of Kimpusen-ji temple is the second-largest wooden building in Japan (after the Daibutsu-den in Nara): it stands 34 metres high. Chikurin-in temple has a well-known landscape garden.

Yoshino station is the terminus of the Kintetsu line from Abeno-bashi station (Osaka); travellers from Kyoto transfer at Kashiwara-jingu-mae. You can also go most of the way by JNR, changing to the Kintetsu line at Yoshino-guchi.

To the east and south of Yoshino is a heavily-wooded wilderness area that would appeal to hikers. Accessible from the Nara-plain side of the mountains is a point on the flank of Mt Odaigahara (1695 metres), which is the starting point for hikes to Owase (on the east coast of Kii-hanto Peninsula) and Doro Gorge to the south, both of which are described in the section on Southern Kii-hanto Peninsula along with the rest of the coastal region. (The Odaigahara area is the wettest region of Japan, and the mountain top is often fog-bound.)

During many months of the year there are three buses a day to Odaigahara from Nara-Kintetsu station. The bus passes through Yamato-Kami-Ichi (two stops before Yoshinoyama station). There are also two buses a day between Nara and Kumano (on the south-east coast) which passes Wasabi-dani, the point where the toll road to Odaigahara branches off Route 169; it should be possible to get off there and transfer to the other bus (if schedules match) or hitch the rest of the way.

MIE-KEN

Mie-ken, east of Nara-ken, is divided by a coastal ridge of mountains. On the Nara side of this ridge is the area around Iga-Ueno. Most of the other attractions of Mie-ken are on the coastal side of the mountains. From there you can conveniently travel in a clockwise route around the Kii-hanto peninsula and up the west coast to Wakayama and Osaka.

IGA-UENO

This small city east of Nara has some unusual history, and an attraction almost unique in Japan. (The name means simply 'Ueno of the Iga region' to identify it from other places called Ueno which is a common name in Japan.)

Ueno Castle

Ueno has a small but picturesque castle. Although the present building dates only from 1953, it is a reminder of when the rulers of Iga had to defend their fertile lands against neighbouring, powerful Kyoto and Yamato. As part of their defences, they developed the Ninjutsu art of stealthy combat to defeat foreign armies in the mountains, beginning around the 1200s. Ninja, the practitioners, were trained in invisibility, poisons, sabotage, espionage, assassination and other genteel arts (ninja appear in the novel *Shogun*).

In the grounds of the castle is Ninja-Yashiki (Ninja House), an ordinary-looking building that actually has a number of hidden passages, hiding places, and weapons caches. These are demonstrated frequently during the day for visitors.

Elsewhere in the grounds is Ninjutsu Shiryo-kan, a museum of weapons, clothing, climbing devices and other ingenious items used by ninja in their work — such as an iron claw that would tear a victim as if by the claw of a bear, armour, and several kinds of throwing weapons. This is one of very few places in Japan with such a large display of items of this black 'art' (another is nearby at Akame 48 Falls).

Tenjin-matsuri festival is a 400-year-old Demon Procession held on 23 October. It features a procession of more than 100 'demons' in masks and costumes, as well as nine festival wagons, similar to but smaller than those of Kyoto's Gion-matsuri. Masks and other items from the procession are displayed at the museum beside the Ninja-Yashiki.

A pamphlet on Ueno in quite-good English is given out at the castle, and may also be available at the TICs in Kyoto and Tokyo. It also contains information on some other places of lesser interest.

The castle is reached by walking up the hill from Ueno-shi station of the Kintetsu line, which may be reached by transferring from the JNR Kansai hon-sen line at Iga-Ueno station, or by branching off the Kintetsu Osaka line at Iga-Kambe. The Kansai line runs between Osaka and Nagoya via Nara, the latter between Osaka and Matsuzaka. Both are easily reached from Kyoto and Nara.

Akame 48 Falls

Due south of Iga-Ueno is a very pleasant gorge known for 48 waterfalls. Many are rather small, especially higher up near the source, but the large ones are quite impressive. The riverside walk is a rare way to enjoy nature with no sound but the shrilling cicadas, some birds, and the rushing water. There is a good chance you will see some of the large and very colourful butterflies for which Japan is noted. Higher up the gorge, there is an inviting pool.

Just inside the entrance to the park is a very non-descript concrete cage containing some equally non-descript animals: they are giant salamanders, found only in this area.

Before the entrance to the park (on the left going in) is a small building that houses a good (if modest) museum of historic articles used in daily life. Possibly of greater interest is a sizeable collection of ninja weapons and devices. If you can't locate the building, ask for 'Ninja hakubutsu-kan'.

The entrance to the falls ('Akame Taki') is reached easily by bus (12-per day) from Akame-guchi station of the Kintetsu Osaka line, three stations west of Iga-Kambe station (the junction for Ueno city).

YOKKAICHI

There is nothing but industries in the city itself, except for its annual festival on 26-27 September, a procession of a feudal lord and townspeople in costumes of that era. Inland about 20 km is Yunoyama-onsen ('Hot Water Mountain Hotspring'), at the foot of Gozaisho-dake.

GOZAISHO-DAKE/YUNOYAMA-ONSEN

The main attraction (apart from the hot springs of the town, which are sufficient inducement for the Japanese) is the mountain Gozaisho-dake, 1210 metres. Its upper reaches rank among the three most famous among Japanese mountaineers. However, no climbing skills are needed to enjoy the views of the rock faces on the way up, for a cablecar system takes passengers to the top in 20 minutes. The very top of the peak is actually reached by separate lift.

At the top, one can see Biwa-ko lake (on a clear day), and there is a sanctuary near the top for Japanese serow, a kind of antelope.

There are three waterfalls in the area, Kugurido-no-taki, Ao-taki, and Hyakken-daki. Ao-daki is the most easily reached, by hiking from the base station of the cable car.

Getting There

From Yokkaichi Kintetsu station, by Kintetsu Yunoyama-sen (line) to Yunoyama-onsen station, and by bus to the hot spring town itself (and the base station).

Accommodation

There are about 30 hotels of varying prices in the onsen, and a Youth Hostel near the top.

SUZUKA

The largest motor racing circuit in the world is located near this industrial city.

ISENOUMI PARK

Between Yokkaichi and Tsu stretches the long beach of Ise-no-umi prefectural Park. Beach names include Tsutsumi-gaura, Chiyozaki, Akogigaura and Gotemba. Another, nearer Tsu, is Niezaki.

KII PENINSULA

The broad peninsula that projects southward between Nagoya and Osaka can be broken into three major areas for sightseeing convenience as well as for 'ranking' them in interest. The three are: 'Nara & Area' (described earlier in this chapter), 'Shima-hanto & Ise', and 'Nanki & Southern Kii Peninsula'.

'Shima-hanto & Ise' covers the small Shima-hanto peninsula area on the east side of the main peninsula. It is famous for pearl farming and is the home of Mikimoto pearls. The most important Shinto shrines in Japan are located at Ise. There are also other attractions.

'Nanki & Southern Kii Peninsula' describes all the rest of the peninsula south of Osaka, Nara-ken and the Shima-hanto area. It is best-known for natural attractions, like mountains, forests, gorges, waterfalls and rivers, although it is home to some very revered shrines as well.

MATSUZAKA

There is nothing of particular interest in Matsuzaka, but it is the starting point for an overnight ferry to Tokyo. The terminal is at the end of the road leading straight out from the front of the JNR station. The ferry is excellent for those who want to get to Tokyo at low cost and who wish to avoid the long and boring road trip up Route 1 along the south coast. (Those with the time would be advised to make the land trip via the Kiso region or up to the Noto Peninsula.)

The city gives its name to a type of beef, famous for its flavour, tenderness and price. It would appeal more to Americans, say, than Australians for it has a very high fat content, the meat being 'marbled' with almost equal amounts of fat. By all means try it if

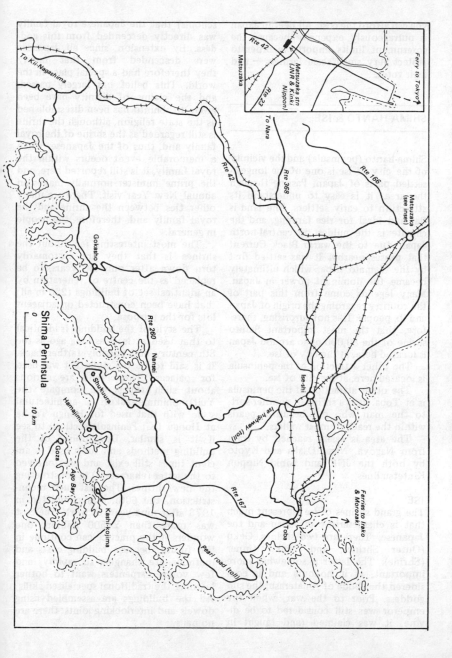

Shima Peninsula

0

5

10 km

To Kii-Nagashima

Gokasho

Rte 260

Nansei

Shukuura

Hamajima

Goza

Ago Bay

Kashi-Kojima

Pearl road (toll)

Rte 368

Rte 166

Matsuzaka (see inset)

To Nara

Rte 42

Ise-shi

Ise highway (toll)

Rte 167

Toba

Ferries to Irako & Morozaki

Ferry to Tokyo

Matsuzaka stn
(JNR & Kinki
Nippon)

Rte 42

Matsuzaka

Rte 23

you can afford the cost. All beef in Japan is outrageously expensive because the government limits imports in order to protect very small scale farmers — and their votes.

SHIMA-HANTO & ISE

Shima-hanto (peninsula) and the vicinity of the city of Ise is one of the longest-settled parts of Japan. Passing through the area, it is easy to understand its attraction to early settlers. The land is flat and ideal for rice farming, and the climate is the mildest in central-north Japan due to the warm Black Current that passes nearby. It was settled first by the Yamato tribe, which ultimately became the dominant power in Japan. Many legends come from this part of the country regarding the origin of Japan and its people. It is not surprising, therefore, that the most important Shinto shrine of the 80,000 or so around Japan is located here, at the city of Ise.

The other attraction of the peninsula is located here, at the city of Ise.

The other attraction of the peninsula is at Toba. It is a shrine of another sort, to the man who put beautiful pearls within the reach of most wallets.

The area is easily reached by train from Nagoya, Nara, Osaka and Kyoto by both the JNR and Kinki Nippon Kintetsu lines.

ISE

The grand shrines of Ise represent much that is characteristic of Japan and the Japanese. There are two shrines, Geku (Outer Shrine), and Naiku (Inner Shrine). The latter is somewhat more important, as it honours and is considered the abode of Amaterasu, the sun goddess. Prior to the war, when the emperor was still considered to be divine, it was claimed (and taught in schools) that the Japanese royal family was directly descended from this goddess. By extension, since all Japanese were descended from that family they therefore had a special place in the world. This belief has largely passed, and the claims of divinity have been given up. Shinto has been disestablished as the state religion, although the shrine is still regarded as the shrine of the royal family and, thus of the Japanese. When a memorable event occurs within the royal family, it is still reported here, and the prime minister normally makes an annual New Year visit. There are many other ties between the shrine and the royal family and, therefore, the people in general.

The most interesting fact about the shrines is that they are customarily torn down after only 20 years, to be replaced as the centre of veneration by an identical set of buildings (220 in all) that have been constructed on adjacent lots for the purpose.

The style of the buildings is identical to that used at least as long ago as the 8th century and possibly farther back. It is said to be the style that was used for palaces. Those who are curious about such things can compare the Yuitsu-Shimmei-zukuri architectural style with that used for Hongu Taisha at Hongu (Kii Peninsula section) to see if it is similar. Descriptions of the building methods and tools used in ancient times still exist and are followed to the letter (character?) in constructing the new shrines. The last such reconstruction, the 60th, was completed in 1973 after nine years of work. The cost was more than Y4500 million; one wonders if the practice can continue in the future, because building costs and methods are changing so rapidly, and few young carpenters want to bother learning the traditional specialised skills. All the buildings are assembled using dowels and interlocking joints; there are no nails.

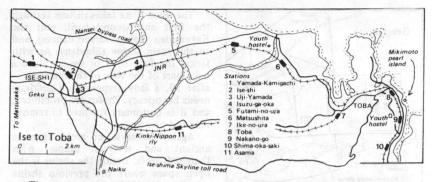

Ise to Toba

Stations
1 Yamada-Kamigachi
2 Ise-shi
3 Uji-Yamada
4 Isuzu-ga-oka
5 Futami-no-ura
6 Matsushita
7 Ike-no-ura
8 Toba
9 Nakano-go
10 Shima-oka-saki
11 Asama

There are two separate shrine complexes, Geku (Outer Shrine), located in Ise-shi (city), and Naiku (Inner Shrine), six km away, outside the city.

Geku (Outer Shrine)

Geku shrine is located within 15 minutes walk of the two stations (JNR and Kinki Nippon lines). It honours Toyouke-Omikami, Goddess of agriculture. Like those of Naiku, the buildings of Geku are built in the traditional style dating from the times before Chinese influence swept over the country. The shrine dates from 478 AD. Also, like Naiku, the grounds are covered with magnificent, tall, ancient cedars.

The main entrance is easily seen from the road. One follows the path under two torii (gates) and past the large Magatama-ike pond. To the right of the first torii are the Anzaisho and Sanshido, a combined building where the emperor and other members of the imperial family rest when visiting. Just past the second torii is the Kagura-den, where performances of sacred dances are performed (fairly frequently).

A bridge to the left leads to the shrines Kaze-no-miya, Tsuchi-no-miya, and Taka-no-miya. Continuing straight on leads to the main shrine. The architecture of the buildings is severely plain — unpainted, fine, hinoki (cypress) wood, with a thatched roof — but four fences surround the buildings and block much

of the view from ordinary eyes; only members of the imperial family and their envoys are permitted beyond the Tonotamagaki gate.

The sightseeing is far from spectacular. One should enjoy/appreciate the mood and atmosphere of the wooded grounds and take it for what it is, one of the two most sacred shrines in the country. Don't spend too long here, for there is still Naiku, the inner shrine, to visit and it is the more important of the two.

Naiku (Inner Shrine)

Naiku is easily reached from Geku by the regular bus that runs between the two shrines. The bus stop is 'Naiku-mae'.

Naiku is the sacred home of Amaterasu, the sun goddess, the highest deity in the Shinto pantheon. The importance of the sun in Japanese history/ mythology can be appreciated a little more by recalling that the name of Japan in Japanese is Nippon (or Nihon), which means 'origin of the sun'.

The shrine grounds are entered by crossing Isuzu-kawa river by Uji bridge, a picturesque structure. From here the faithful follow one of several paths to the riverside where they wash their hands and rinse their mouths as purification. The many tall cedars on the grounds give a peaceful mood, and the size of the grounds (over 66 hectares) swallows up the large number of people who visit.

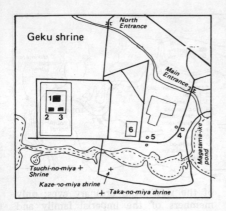

Geku shrine

North Entrance

Main Entrance

Magatama-ike pond

Tsuchi-no-miya + Shrine

Kaze-no-miya shrine

+ Taka-no-miya shrine

Legend for both maps

1 Shoden (main hall)
2 Saihoden (west treasure hall)
3 Tohoden (east treasure hall)
4 First torii
5 Second torii
6 Kagura-den (sacred dance hall)

Naiku shrine

Aramatsuri-no-miya shrine.

Isuzu-gawa river

Kazahinomi-no-miya shrine

The usual route takes visitors through the first and second torii, past the Kagura-den (hall of sacred dances), and to the main shrine (Shoden). As with Geku, the four rows of fences block a large part of the view of the buildings — after all, a lady (especially a goddess) needs her privacy. Photos are prohibited, and it is customary for men to remove hats and overcoats.

Again the style of architecture is ancient and severely simple, with thatched roofs. Beside the shrine is the open space where the previous shrine stood until 1973, when the present buildings were finished and consecrated and the goddess (along with her belongings) moved into her new quarters amidst very solemn ceremony. The accompanying map will be valid until 1993 or so.

On the same compound with the Shoden (main hall) are two treasure houses, Tohoden and Saihoden (East and West Treasuries) in which are housed about 2500 treasures of the shrine — fine clothing, lacquerware, swords, etc. These are made anew each time along with the buildings, and represent the finest of craftsmanship in the best Japanese tradition. In previous times these were destroyed when the new shrine was opened. But today, because of the great value of these objects as representations of the work of perhaps the last generations who were part of the 'old ways', they are preserved and displayed at Choko-kan, the museum of the history of the shrine.

Included among the treasures in the two treasure buildings (not on display) is the sacred mirror, one of the sacred treasures of the imperial throne. The others are the sword and jewel, which are kept elsewhere. A news item stated that some antique rickshaws (jin-riki-sha) where being operated at the shrines (entrances). If you wish to try one, keep your eyes open. Proceeds are for charity.

ISE TO TOBA

There are two main routes to Toba, Ise-Shima Skyline, and Route 167/railway.

Ise-Shima Skyline

From a point near Naiku, a toll road runs along and over a ridge of the Asama mountains to Toba-shi (city). The scenery is pretty, with distant views to the water and the indented coast (though it is not worth a special trip from elsewhere just to partake of the view). At the top of the ridge is Kongoshoji temple. Two buses an hour make the trip from Naiku to Toba station, (last bus in mid-afternoon).

Route 167/railway

Travellers by Route 167 or JNR from Ise to Toba might want to stop for a look at a sight dear to the hearts of the Japanese, Futami-ga-ura. This is a pair of rocks that jut out of the sea close to each other, not far from shore. In keeping with the traditional Japanese view of nature as representations of kami (spirits/gods), or other 'semi-animate' objects, the rocks have been regarded as male and female (exactly in the same manner as assigning gender to most or all mountains in the country). Being male and female, what could be more natural than for them to be wed? So, wed they are (their name, 'meoto-iwa', means wedded rocks) with thick ropes of twisted and braided straw of the type used to make the shimenawa rope often found between the uprights of many torii, especially after the harvest season. The ropes are replaced every 5 January in a colourful ceremony. The rocks are likened to Iaanagi and Izanami, the founders of Japan (in mythology, at least), who are honoured yearly by National Foundation Day, a national holiday.

Near the rocks is an aquarium, Sea Lion House, and Marine House where the women divers give demonstrations. There is a Youth Hostel (4404) that is also a temple, not far from the rocks.

The rocks are about a km from Futami-no-ura station (JNR). Buses from the station, as well as from Toba, Ise-shi, Uji-yamada, Naiku and Geku, go close to the stretch of beach (Futami-ga-ura), seawall and hotels that preceed the short walkway around the base of the cliffs to the lookout near the rocks.

TOBA

Toba is famous as the place where cultivating pearls was perfected. The Toba area is still one of the most important pearl-farming areas of Japan. Until Kokichi Mikimoto began his researches in the late 1800's, the only pearls were accidents of nature. If a grain of sand or other foreign material happened to find its way into the shell and iritate the oyster, the irritant would be covered with layers of nacre, forming a pearl. Mikimoto reasoned that it should be possible to introduce such an irritant artificially, and began experimenting in 1888. By 1893 he had succeeded in producing a pearl, though it was not spherical, but by 1905 he had succeeded in his quest.

Since then, he and his company (he died in 1954) continued to grow in size, and his name is well-known around the world. Always dedicated to top quality (and a bit of a showman), he once burned hundreds of kilos of pearls of inferior quality that he had rejected, but which his competitors would have sold. Such pearls are now used to decorate items of lesser value.

Tatoku-shima island, where he performed his experiments, is now the site of a very interesting museum where all stages of producing cultured pearls are shown, both as a static display of photos and materials (with flawless English text), and exhibitions by young women of how they insert the irritant, remove a pearl from a mature oyster, match pearls by colour and size, then drill and string them. Also on display are some fabulously valuable displays utilizing pearls, like a third scale model of the Liberty Bell in solid silver (16.9 kg), 336 diamonds and 12,250 pearls.

The complete process of making pearls begins with a pearl oyster, an inedible variety, of large enough size; this is usually about 2 years of age. Its shell is pried open, an incision is made in its body, and two spheres (the irritant) are introduced into the wound. For collectors of trivia, the irritant is made from the Pig Toe shell, a variety found along the Mississippi River. (After trying thousands of materials, Mikimoto found this to be the best). Along with the two spheres (about six mm in diameter) a small piece of tissue about a mm square is introduced from the body of another oyster. This piece is cut from the band of tissue at the juncture between the body of the oyster and its shell. This tissue excretes the nacre that deposits as Mother of Pearl. The oyster 'adopts' this and uses it to coat the irritant with layer after layer of nacre. By this method, one oyster can be used to produce two pearls.

The oysters are suspended in special ranks hung below rafts in the sea; these rafts can be seen in Ago Bay and other sheltered bodies of water in the region, where the temperature and other conditions are ideal. The nearby Black Current guarantees a plentiful supply of plankton, the food on which oysters thrive.

The racks are pulled up four to six times a year and the shells are cleaned of marine growths, then they are lowered again. After about three years they are lifted out a last time and the pearls are removed, sorted to remove imperfections and odd shapes, classified by colour, then drilled and strung. The range of colours is quite amazing to anyone who is not familiar with pearls, going from pink and gold through silver to a distinct blue tint.

Only about 50% of oysters produce pearls after all that effort, and only

about 5% of these are suitable as gems. In past years, the lifespan of oysters was six to seven years, with the seeds being implanted at age two, but pollution is raising its ugly head these days, and the pearls must now be harvested after only two to three years in the water instead of four to five years as before. The quality of the pearls is also said to be slipping.

There is, if it need to be said, absolutely no difference in composition between cultured and naturally-occuring pearls; the former just increases the harvest and guarantees consistent quality. Where do the oysters come from? They grow on trees. When females are spawning, they release thousands of larvae into the water, to come to rest where they may. Trees are lowered into the water and, with luck, larvae will cling to the branches. After two to three months they are raised and transferred to a better place where they can grow to sufficient maturity to allow the irritant implantation.

Every 40 minutes there is a display of women divers. Similar divers may be seen in action near Toba and in nearby sheltered bays and coves, like Ago Bay. Thre are still about 3500 of them actively diving, but this is only half the number who were diving a few years ago.

There is so much nonsense written about these white-clothed divers that it is time to put the record straight. They do not dive for pearls. Before Mikimoto's successful experimentation their ancestors did dive for the gems of the sea, but they could not make a living at it today. The whole idea of cultivating pearls is to sidestep the hit-or-miss (mostly miss) business of looking for

A Festival wagon (yatai) at Takayami Matsuri festival
B Furukawa Matsuri is famous for the procession of a large drum through the streets at night
C Sharing

natural pearls. Also, natural pearls are often misshapen and/or discoloured, while cultivating them gives a good yield of nearly-perfect spherical ones.

What the women do dive for is seafood, both shellfish, like abalone, and octopus, as well as edible seaweed. Any pearl oysters that they find can be used to grow pearls by implantation of a nucleus. But they do not dive for pearls, and publications and tour pamphlets that repeatedly refer to them as 'women pearl divers' are verging on dishonesty. Their activities are interesting enough, with their peculiar whistling breathing sound, that such publicity is uncalled for.

Other attractions of Toba

The aquarium at Toba is considered one of the best in Japan. Other related attractions are Dolphin Island (Irukajima) and the marine museum (Burajirumaru).

Accommodation

The Youth Hostel at Toba (4405) is a temple and has a good reputation. The drawback is that it accommodates only seven persons, so advance booking is usually needed.

Transport

There are regular boat excursions out of Toba to nearby islands, including Kamishima, scene of Mishima's story *Sound of Waves*.

There is a ferry service across the bay to Irako at the tip of the Atsumahanto peninsula (at least 13 times daily), as well as to Gamagori on the 'mainland' between the peninsulas (at least six times daily); these places are all on the east

side of the bay, below Nagoya, and offer a convenient way to bypass that city if someone is planning to travel to Tokyo via the south coast. (It should be said that this is the least desirable and interesting way to get there; routes via the Kiso region and the Noto peninsula are much more interesting.)

AGO BAY

This bay, sheltered from the ocean tumult and incredibly indented, offers the beauties of nature, the finest scenery of the Shima-hanto peninsula. A common sight is the number of rafts from which pearl oysters are suspended in the water. They should not be mistaken for even rows of poles protruding from the water near the shore; these have nets strung horizontally among them and edible seaweed grows on them. Ago Bay is ideal for pearl oysters because the water temperature is always between 17 and $22^{\circ}C$ and there is plenty of food.

KASHIKOJIMA

This is the main town on Ago Bay. From it, sightseeing boats leave regularly on excursions that circle the bay. It would be a good way for a closer look at the rafts, and there is a good chance of seeing ama (women divers) at work. Near Kashikojima station is Shima Marineland which houses an aquarium.

GOZA

This town affords a good view, from Kompira-san hill, of both the Pacific and Ago Bay. It can be reached from Kashikojima by boat or by bus.

Accommodation

There is a Youth Hostel (4406) not far from Kashikojima, at Isobe. It sits on a hill, giving a pleasant view over a smaller bay. However, it is a JYH hostel, and has some of the characteristics of one, since the housefather is a regional YH executive. The biggest drawback of the place is that the rooms are almost hermetically sealed and are very stuffy (the

A *Kintai-bashi (Bridge of the Brocade Sash), Iwakuni (Hiroshima-ken)*
B *Himeji-jo castle, Japan's finest*

Japanese never open windows at night, even in summer); a shame because it is so close to all that fine sea air.

Further information
The TIC in Tokyo has issued photocopied notes for travellers to the Ise-Shima National Park area. They have additional information on transportation.

NANKI & SOUTHERN KII PENINSULA

Travellers who plan to continue from the Ago Bay area to southern Kii peninsula destinations like Shingu by road (hitching or own transportation) might find it preferable to backtrack to Ise and beyond to connect with Route 42 (or railway) rather than following Route 260 along the coast. Few roads require more time to travel a given distance than this one. It winds in, out, up, down, over and around every combination of cape, ridge, hill and promentory imaginable. The scenery is pleasant, as it passes through fishing villages and coves of pearl rafts or seaweed 'frames', but it tends quickly to become variations on a theme rather than new melodies. From the YH at Isobe I followed the road by motorcycle for what seemed like hours and reached only Shukuura, at which point I gave up and headed back to Ise.

Getting around Southern Kii-hanto
JNR services loop around the entire Kii-hanto peninsula from Nagoya to Osaka, as well as branching off to Toba. The Kinki Nippon line runs from Nagoya to Kashikojima in the Shima-hanto peninsula. There are many local bus services. The northern part of the peninsula is intensively served by a number of railway lines.

Accommodation
As in all parts of Japan that are popular with tourists, there are accommodation facilities everywhere, including hotels, ryokans, minshuku and Youth Hostels. Some hostel locations have been mentioned.

NANKI
The Kii peninsula (Kii-hanto) is still relatively unpopulated due to its mountainous terrain. Two areas have been combined into a national park, the forest lands named for Yoshino, and the sea coast area, named after Kumano. Yoshino itself is in Nara-ken and is covered in the section on that part of the country.

The Japanese way of treating this area for tourist publicity purposes is a little peculiar, and is similar to the practice mentioned elsewhere for southern Toyama-ken. Mie-ken extends almost to Shingu, so literature issued by Mie-ken covers much of the south-east coast, while Wakayama-ken literature describes the rest of the south-east coast and all the south-west coast. This isn't of much use to travellers who are trying to see the whole region and who might have only one lot of literature. This book covers the Kii peninsula in what seems to be a logical manner, beginning from above Owase and continuing around to Wakayama, taking in inland areas conveniently reached from the coast.

USUGI-DANI
Inland from a point 10 km or so above Owase (just a short distance below Funa station), a road leads inland to Usugi-dani, considered one of the grandest valleys in Japan. A publicity photo shows a very pretty series of cascades and pools and a rustic suspension bridge.

The valley leads close to Mt Odaigahara, a mountain much more easily reached from Yoshino (and described in more detail in the section on Naraken).

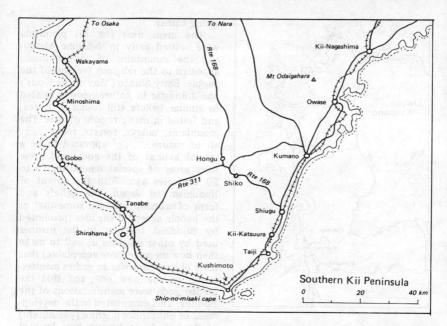

Southern Kii Peninsula

0   20   40 km

There are trails in the area between Odaigahara and Owase (32 km), and to Doro-kyo (described below). Serious hikers can obtain more detailed information on the spot.

Keep in mind that there is no scheduled transport in to Usugi-dani and that Odaigahara has the greatest rainfall of any area in Japan.

OWASE

The town is an important fishing centre but of limited touristic interest. Along the shore of Owase Bay are rock formations of columnar basalt, similar to those of Land's End in Britain, though smaller in scale.

KUMANO

The attractions of Kumano ('Bear Field') are the sea and cliffs. Two popular sights are Onigajo ('Ogre's Castle'), a large chamber in the cliffs. Near it, the rock has been weathered to an unusual text-

ure, slightly resembling the exterior of the brain. It is about a km east from the station, along the coast.

In the opposite direction, also along the coast is a rock formation known as Shishi-iwa ('Lion Rock') from its resemblance to a lion.

Kumano is the starting point for a trip by raft through the rapids of the scenic Doro-kyo gorge. Sightseeing information for the gorge, including this trip from Kumano, is given in the description of the area around Hongu.

SHINGU

The name Shingu ('New Shrine') reveals Shingu's attraction, Kumano-Hayatama Taisha (shrine), one of the three main shrines of the Kii-hanto peninsula. The others are at Hongu and Nachi. Unlike the weathered buildings of Hongu, those of Shingu are of a more recent 'tradition' and are more bright and colourful. Its festival is on 15 October.

Owase
·-Kumano

Owase

North

Rte 42

Rte 311

Odomari stn

Kumano

Kumano stn

Onigajo

5 km

INLAND FROM SHINGU

A short distance inland, up the valley of the Kumano River, are the Shingu and Doro-kyo gorge. Between Shingu and Hongu, the road passes through the Kumano-kawa valley. The pretty, relatively-unspoiled scenery makes the trip enjoyable. Hills rise on both sides of the valley, and the water is a beautiful emerald or jade green. In seasons of heavy rainfall, like the September-October typhoon season, several waterfalls thunder close to the road or can be seen clearly nearby.

Buses run from Shingu station to Hongu (70 minutes), and on to Gojo (four hours, 45 minutes).

HONGU

Hongu, which means 'Main Shrine', is the most important of the three great shrines of Kii. Nearby are a couple of typical mountain hot spring resorts (onsen) with rotemburo (open-air hot spring baths).

The areas near the Kii peninsula were settled early in Japanese histoy, and the mountains of the peninsula appealed to the religious feelings of the people. Early Shinto ('Way of the Gods') was animistic in nature, closely related to similar beliefs still found in Korea, and found in many regions of Asia. The mountains, valleys, forests, rocks . . . . all of nature . . . . appeared to be a special habitat of the gods, and these were areas of special veneration 15 to 20 centuries ago. With the advent of Buddhism to Japan, the beliefs and form of worship changed somewhat as the people accepted the idea (promoted by Buddhist teachers in the manner used by other religions as well to make their new message more acceptable) that their old religion was an earlier manifestation of the new one, and that the Shinto gods were manifestations of the Buddha. This culminated in the development of Shugendo; pilgrims (yamabushi) of this belief may be seen here (as well as at areas like Haguro-san near Tsuruoka, and elsewhere in Tohoku), dressed in white with unusual (and hard to describe) 'ornaments', perhaps ringing bells as they proceed. Such yamabushi indulge in ascetic practices like bathing under icy mountain waterfalls and other forms of corporal mortification. More information is included in the section on Tohoku.

The main shrine is at Hongu and is set in wooded land near the town of the same name. Access is via a long path attractively lined with tall cedars. This is not too far from the wettest place in Japan, so lush greenery can be expected. In other areas of the Kii peninsula there are still virgin forests with some trees 600 to 1000 years old. The name 'Kii' is a contraction of Ki-no-kuni, or 'country of trees'.

The present buildings are quite large and have a natural weathered colour. Their architectural style is an uncommon

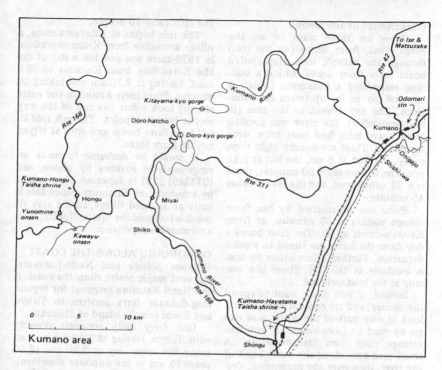

Kumano area

form used in the early 10th century for palaces. Its festival is 15 April.

YUNOMINE

In past days, yamabushi pilgrims included bathing at the hot springs of Yunomine as part of their devotions. These days it is more like a typical onsen, with visitors who indulge in the hot water for the same reasons as elsewhere, for health and pleasure. Along with hotels (large and small), and their private baths, there is also a rotemburo, a natural hot spring pool in the middle of the stream, surrounded by a simple wooden fence and an equally simple (and quite traditional) bathhouse.

KAWAYU

This is another hotspring resort town. It also has a rotemburo, hot water that appears in the river, open to all comers. There is a Youth Hostel (5612) here.

DORO—KYO

This gorge on the Kitayama-kawa river is considered the finest in Japan. Cliffs rise 50 metres vertically from the green water, nature-sculptured rocks decorate the way, and in June, azaleas and rhododendrons bloom on the cliff faces. The gorge stretches several km along the river with alternating rapids and wide, calm areas. The three major sections are Oku ('inner') doro, Kami ('upper') doro, and Doro-hatcho. Shimo-Doro ('lower Doro') is the entrance and not so noteworthy. Doro-hatcho means 'eight cho', signifying eight cho of tranquil water, a 'cho' being an old measurement of 109 metres.

There are three ways to see the gorge. First, from Shiko (on the road through the valley), long glass-roofed boats leave from docks behind a building resembling a restaurant (which it is), and go as far upstream as Kami-Doro. The day I went to the area (in mid-September), the river was swollen from heavy rains and boat trips were suspended. There are usually eight trips a day, the first at 8 am, the last at 3.15 pm. The trip up takes 50 minutes, there is a 20 minute rest, and the return takes 45 minutes.

Shiko can be reached by bus from Shingu station in 30 minutes, or from Kawayu-onsen in 20. The four buses a day from the latter are timed to meet a departure. Further information on that is available at the YH. There is a bus stop at the boat terminal.

Second, if you don't want to spend the money, and are content with a small look at only part of the gorge, you can go by road to Doro-hatcho if you can arrange your own transportation. A small road runs along the north bank of the river, then over the mountains, descending to a lookout over Doro-hatcho. Maps indicate future road construction to link this point with Kitayama-mura and an offshoot to join Route 311 to Kumano is also likely, but the completion date is uncertain.

The third way is much more thrilling, longer and costlier (Y5000 per person), and it begins at a place accessible from Kumano, not Hongu. This method is a ride through all the rapids on a long narrow raft. Passengers sit on lengthwise benches, have handrails to hold onto (on both sides, the full width of the raft being only arms' length), and must wear life vests. Swim suits or other 'wettable' clothing are advisable because the thrill-seekers' feet are always awash, and splashes while going through the rapids assure occasional drenchings. Waterproof cameras or bags are recommended!

The rafts carry 20 people.

The ride begins at Kitayama-mura, a village accessible from Kumano station. In 1979 there was one bus a day of the Mie Kotsu line from Kumano to Shimaoi, leaving at 7.10 am and taking 40 minutes. From there a minibus (no extra charge) took riders the rest of the way to the boarding point. The raft ride itself lasts three hours and ends at Miyai, not far from Shiko.

It would be desirable to make arrangements in advance by phone; call (073549) 2331 in Japanese. There might be minshuku at Kitamura. Since this is quite an isolated village, such a stay (if possible) should be quite 'folksy' and a memorable experience.

CONTINUING ALONG THE COAST

Between Shingu and Nachi-Katsuura, the next major centre along the coast, is the Nachi-Katsuura terminal for regular long-distance ferry services to Tokyo and Kochi (on the island of Shikoku).

One ferry daily connects directly with Tokyo, leaving at 1.50 am and arriving the same day at 2.20 pm (6.40 pm/8.10 am in the opposite direction). This ferry is actually travelling from Kochi (Shikoku). Ferries leave Nachi-Katsuura terminal for Kochi at 8.10 am and arrive at 3.40 pm (5.30 pm/1.50 am in the opposite direction). Ferries coming from Oita (Kyushu) stop at the terminal on the way to Nagoya, but not on the way to Oita.

The terminal ('ferry noriba') is close to Usui station, above Nachi. There are 12 trains a day between the two places, but note that the ferry leaves for Tokyo hours after the last train.

NACHI-KATSUURA

This is the collective name for the district between Nachi and Kii-Katsuura; both are station names. The several attractions of the area give it the most concentrated sightseeing of the southern part of the peninsula.

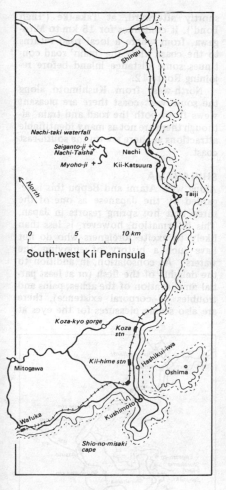

Nachi-taki waterfall

Seiganto-ji + Nachi-Taisha

Nachi

Myoho-ji +

Kii-Katsuura

Taiji

North

South-west Kii Peninsula

0   5   10 km

Koza-kyo gorge

Koza stn

Kii-hime stn

Hashikui-iwa

Mitogawa

Oshima

Kushimoto

Wafuka

Shio-no-misaki cape

There are Youth Hostels at Nachi, Katsuura, and Taiji.

Nachi-taki
The highpoint of the Nachi area is the 130 metres high Nachi-taki waterfall — one of the deepest plunges in Japan. The falls are reached by taking a bus from Nachi station, a short ride. From the stop, the falls are reached after a short and very pleasant walk down steps and between rows of tall and very old cedar trees.

Seiganto-ji
Immediately beside Nachi-Taisha is the temple Seiganto-ji.

Myoho-ji temple
At the top of the twisty toll road is the temple Myoho-ji.

Kii-Katsuura
From a place near Kii-Katsuura station one can take a boat ride around a group of pine-covered islands called Kii-no-Matsushima, the name implying a comparison with the 'real' Matsushima near Sendai, one of the scenic 'big three' that are supposed to send the Japanese into fits of ecstasy. The ones at Kii are scenic, one islet being perforated, another (visible from shore) resembling a camel in silhouette, while others come in a variety of other pine-covered shapes. A good lookout point is from the narrow peninsula on which is located Katsuura-onsen.

TAIJI
Taiji has been the centre of the whaling industry in the Kumano district. On a small peninsula a little more than a km from Taiji station, five minutes by bus, is Kujira-shama-koen (Whale Beach Park). Its main attraction is Geirui-hakubut-sukan (Whale Museum) — which has displays of articles associated with this now-criticised industry. As well, there are some full-size 'reproductions' of whales to show their immense size. Unfortunately, Japan is one of the few countries still hunting these behemoths of the deep.

KUSHIMOTO
This city is located at the base of the peninsula and is the entrance to the Shio-no-misaki cape. A short distance north-east from the city, and a little closer to Kii-Hime station, is the unusual

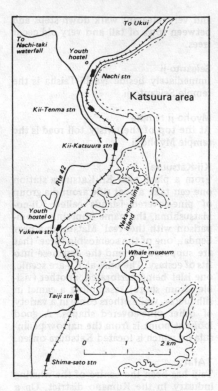

Katsuura area

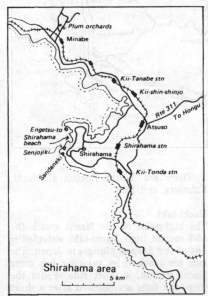

Shirahama area

5 km

shortly afterward, at Taka-ike ('High Pond'). It continues for 15 km to Mito-gawa, from where a local road returns to the coast while the 'main' road continues some distance inland before rejoining Route 42.

North-west from Kushimoto along the south-west coast there are pleasant views from both the road and train, although there are not as many identifiable attractions as there are on the south-east coast.

SHIRAHAMA

Along with Atami and Beppu this is regarded by the Japanese as one of the three best hot spring resorts in Japan. This information, however, is less than likely to excite foreigners who do not have such a history of enjoying 'the waters'. As consolation, in addition to the delights of the flesh (or at least partial amelioration of the aches, pains and troubles of corporal existence), there are also scenic pleasures for the eyes at

rock formation Hashi-kui-iwa, a row of about 30 large rocks spaced quite regularly in a line, stretching into the sea. They do resemble what their name means, 'bridge pillars'. Other writers likened them to a procession of hooded medieval monks.

KOZAKAWA-KYO

Inland a short distance from Kushimoto is a pretty gorge, Kozakawa-kyo. The Koza-kawa river has eroded rocks of its bed and flanks into interesting shapes and textures. Much of the rock was apparently formed with trapped bubbles; the water has removed the solid surface, leaving a strange perforated appearance.

The road through the gorge turns off Route 42 at Koza, and the gorge begins the water's edge and the enjoyment of a very good white sand beach; 'Shirahama' means 'White Beach'.

A short distance to the north of the beach is the islet of Engetsu-to, ('Round Moon Island') known for the hole in its middle. South of the beach are the layers of rock 'plates' of the Senjojiki formation, and just around the promentory are the cliffs of Sandaneki. The seascapes are considered among the best on the Kii peninsula, and a good view can be had from Heisogen hill, behind the town. A cablecar runs to the 130-metre summit from Shirahama. During the summer festival, large sand sculptures are built on the beach.

Accommodation

In addition to more than a hundred hotels of all types, some with floor shows at night, there is also a Youth Hostel at nearby Tanabe, very close to Kii-Tanabe station (third stop from Shirahama station).

TANABE

There are several good swimming beaches near this port city. The best known is Ogigahama. The name of the station is Kii-Tanabe.

MINABE

In late January to mid-February, Minabe-gawa-mura is a popular destination for tourists who flock to see the huge plum groves which have perhaps 300,000 trees on the surrounding hills and valleys. They are a couple of km inland from the station; buses are available from the station.

GOBO

There is a good white-sand beach, Enju-ga-hama, about half a km long, near this small city.

ARIDA (=ARITA)

On Arita-kawa river, there is nightly ukai (cormorant fishing). The usual type of ukai is described in the section

on Gifu, but there is a difference here. Usually the fishermen ride in boats which have a blazing fire in an iron grate at the bow. Here, however, the fishermen wade in the knee-deep water, holding a torch in one hand, and the leashes of the cormorants in the other. Sightseers watch from boats nearby. Further information for finding the exact site of the action can be obtained on the spot. Arida YH would be able to help; it is located near Yuasa railway station. There is no Arida station.

WAKAYAMA

This is the city for which the prefecture is named. Historically it was important as a castle town and residence of a very important daimyo. It is now a commercial and industrial centre of very limited touristic interest. Its 'trademark' is Wakayama-jo (castle) but, like many castles in Japan, it is a reconstruction (from 1958) of the historic one that stood on the spot from the late 1500's until it was destroyed in the war. The reconstruction is well done, and the

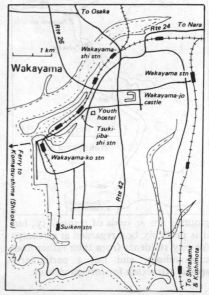

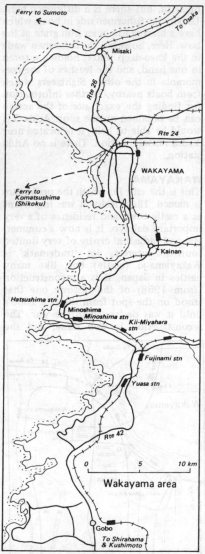

Ferry to Sumoto

To Osaka

Misaki

Rte 26

Rte 24

WAKAYAMA

Ferry to
Komatsushima
(Shikoku)

Kainan

Hatsushima stn

Minoshima
Minoshima stn

Kii-Miyahara
stn

Fujinami stn

Yuasa stn

Rte 42

0   5   10 km

Wakayama area

Gobo
To Shirahama
& Kushimoto

grounds are an oasis of tranquility, but it is probably best regarded as an escape for city residents from their rather drab surroundings, and not a particularly special attraction for foreign visitors.

OSAKA

Osaka is one of the important cities in Japan history, and was an important trading centre almost 2000 years ago. It is now a commercial and industrial city second in importance only to Tokyo, though it has slipped behind Yokohama into third position in population. Despite its history as a power centre (as narrated in *Shogun*), there is very little of historic interest within the city due to the passage of time and heavy bombing during the war. There are a few attractions north of the city, across the Shin-Yodo river.

However, Osaka is a recommendable international port of entry by air (the airport also serves Kyoto), and it is a transport centre used by many travellers passing through Japan: it serves as a hub for train services and several long-distance ferries leave here for a number of points. Most of this section will cover access and transport.

Getting There

Osaka airport is close to the city, and convenient to reach. Travellers who plan to visit Kyoto should consider landing at Osaka instead of Tokyo and beginning their travels there.

Clearing Immigration and Customs is straight-forward: the immigration officials there have a reputation for being among the most reasonable, and they seem more willing than those at other international ports of entry to give a 90-day entry period if you are entitled to it by bilateral agreement. Once out of the terminal building, buses are the most economical way to reach a variety of destinations; they leave from the front of the building. The most useful destinations for most travellers will be Shin-Osaka station (for Shinkansen trains), Osaka station (for most JNR services; posted as Osaka-Umeda, the name of the district in which it is

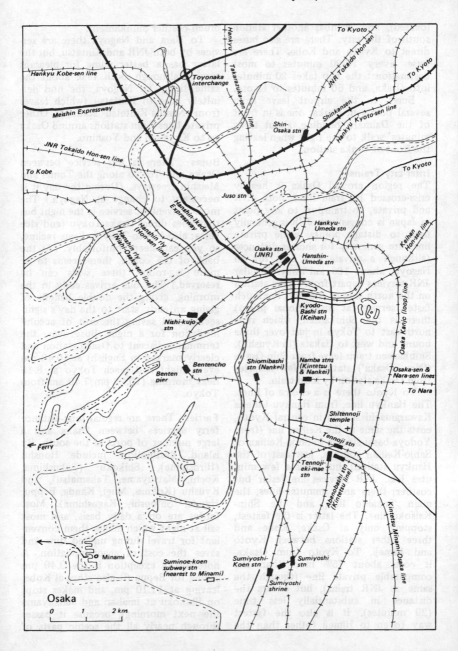

Osaka

0   1   2 km

located), and Namba, another station south of the city. There are also buses direct to Kyoto and Kobe. There are buses every 10-20 minutes to most destinations: the trip takes 20 minutes into Osaka, and 60 minutes to Kyoto.

Buses to the airport leave from several points in Osaka: one is in front of the Daimaru building, about three minutes' walk to the right when leaving the front of Osaka station.

Inter-city Trains

The region around Osaka is heavily criss-crossed by train lines, both JNR and private, so transport to any point in Japan is convenient. JNR is generally used to distant points, while private lines are generally for shorter distances (although a private line does run to Nagoya, about 180 km away). Regular JNR services depart from Osaka station on the north side of the city. For much faster service (at proportional prices) there is the Shinkansen, which runs north-east to Tokyo in just over three hours, and west to Hakata (in Kyushu). Shinkansen trains leave from Shin-Osaka ('New Osaka') station, a few minutes from Osaka station by local train.

To Kyoto there is a choice of lines. The Hankyu line, from Hankyu-Umeda Kawaramachi station in central Kyoto, costs the same as the Keihan line (from Yodoya-bashi station to Shijo-Keihan or Sanjo-Keihan stations, just east of the Hankyu station), but takes a few minutes less. JNR services are faster but costlier; there are commuter lines, the main Tokaido line, and the Shin-Kaisoku line. The latter is the fastest, stopping only at Osaka, Kobe and three other stations between Kyoto and Himeji. To Kyoto from Osaka, it costs about 75% more than the comparable private line (though the same as JNR trains), but covers the distance in substantially less time (29 minutes). It is also the fastest way to go to Himeji (other than the much costlier Shinkansen).

To Nara and Nagoya there are services by both JNR and Kintetsu, but the latter has a better name for pleasant service although both take about the same time. To Nagoya, the nod definitely goes to Kintetsu (which leaves from Namba-Kintetsu station). Other private lines from stations around Osaka go to Koya-san and Yoshino.

Buses There is bus service between Osaka and Tokyo along the Tomei and Meishin freeways. (During the day it is necessary to change at Nagoya.) The most convenient service is the night bus that goes direct Osaka-Tokyo (and vice versa; also Kyoto-Tokyo). Seats recline, so you can sleep comfortably. (At the back of the coach, there seems to be more leg-room; these seats can be reserved.) The bus arrives early in the morning, giving the double benefit of giving an early start to the day's sightseeing, and saving the cost of accommodation for a night. Buses leave the terminal (adjacent to Osaka station and clearly marked in English) at 10.40 pm every night and reach Tokyo at 8.15 next morning (10.20 pm/7.40 am from Tokyo.

Ferries There are regular long-distance ferry services between Osaka and a large number of ports to the south. By island, destinations include Honshu (Hiroshima), Shikoku (Tokushima, Kochi, Matsuyama, Takamatsu), and Kyushu (Kokura, Mogi, Kanda, Beppu, Hyuga, Shibushi, Kagoshima). Most ferries are on a daily basis, and most sail at night which makes them convenient for travel during unused time and saves the cost of accommodation. A noteworthy exception is the 9.40 pm sailing for Beppu (it also stops at Kobe, leaving at 11.10 pm, and makes stops on Shikoku at Imabari and Matsuyama the next morning), because it passes through nearly all the scenic parts of the Inland Sea during daylight hours.

Hitching Between Osaka and Kyoto, forget it. It takes too long to try to get a ride and back into the city at the other end. Take the train. For hitching to more distant points, it is necessary to reach the Meishin Freeway (between Kobe and Kyoto) or the Chugoku Freeway from Osaka to the Hiroshima area (Miyoshi, or beyond, actually, from where it is necessary to switch to regular highways until the freeway is extended). There is no simple way to get started, for the interchanges are all to the north of Osaka, and it is necessary to take a train or local road to the entrance, or start in Osaka itself and get a car that will switch to the exact road that you want to take (the latter requires a sign indicating where you want to go, for hitching is not allowed on the freeways themselves). One entrance is close to Osaka station, and leads onto the Osaka-Ikeda route which leads to Toyonaka interchange (Meishin), and Ikeda interchange (Chugoku); the latter is near the interchange for Osaka airport. Somewhat to the north-west is another entrance to a local freeway (Kinki Freeway) that becomes Chugoku and intersects the Meishin at Suita. The starting point is the Kadoma interchange, which is about a km from Kadoma station of the Keihan-Kyoto line. (Ibaraki, on the Meishin Freeway, is about two km from the Ibanaki JNR station, and there may be a bus passing close to it.) Alternatively, you can use the slower national highways which switch from Route 1 (from Tokyo) to Route 2 (to Shimonoseki, at the far west) in front of Osaka station. However, this is in the middle of Osaka, so hitching could be rather poor. If you are near the station, ask at the information office for a map and suggestions for getting to a better starting point.

Getting Around

A network of six subway lines laces Osaka, and the JNR operates a loop line (Osaka Kanjo-sen) with trains at frequent intervals in both directions. Although the subway and JNR lines intersect at several places, separate tickets are required for each system. A subway map (in English) is available at the information centre in Osaka station.

A large network of bus services exists, but destinations are written only in Japanese, making them difficult to use.

Information

At Osaka station there are two places giving information. The more important is in the main concourse, and is clearly marked: it is to the left when walking in the front central entrance. Its primary function is to assist travellers with transport information, but you can also arrange accommodation. They can give information for travel anywhere in Japan, and provide a serviceable map (in English) of the subway system. They do not, however, have tourist literature on Osaka. Any time I have been through, the staff on duty have spoken very good English and been models of helpfulness. It is open from 5.30 am to midnight.

The Osaka information office ('Osaka an nai sho'), provides literature on Osaka. Staff generally speak no English, but they do have a booklet, *Your Guide to Osaka*, and a map of the city, both in good English, which are adequate for getting around. There is also a large-scale map of Osaka on the back of the JNTO map of Japan, available at the TICs in Tokyo and Kyoto as well as overseas JNTO offices.

There is a lavish publication simply called *Osaka*, of 48 colour glossy pages, that has been distributed at the Tokyo TIC, and which should also be available at the Kyoto TIC and one of the offices in Osaka station. It is published by the Osaka government, and really makes a silk purse out of a generally pig's ear of a city.

Shopping

Because of the relatively small number of foreign visitors to Osaka, there is a correspondingly small number of tax-free shops for cameras, etc. Based on a very small sample, I found that discounts were smaller than those available in Tokyo, and about the same as (or a little less than) those in Kyoto, but it might be possible to shop around and do better than this. One place to look for would be Doi Camera, one of a chain of shops across the country; their Tokyo branch in Shinjuku has very favourable prices. Kimura Camera is another widespread chain, but their prices in Tokyo vary from branch to branch, so there is no assurance of matching Tokyo prices.

Accommodation

Because it is such an important business centre, Osaka has a large number of hotels of various prices, from luxury-class to business hotels, ryokan, etc. Help in finding a room is available at Osaka station; the information centre in the main concourse will help you find a place, make bookings on the spot, and give a voucher for the room. Most travel agents can make bookings at the larger hotels if you are arriving from another part of Japan. International hotels are not listed here because any overseas travel agent worth his salt has the same information and can make bookings in advance at little or no extra cost.

There are several youth hostels in and near Osaka. Osaka-Shiritsu-Nagai Youth Hostel (tel 06 699-5631/5632) is located in the municipal sports ground. It has 102 beds, is quite pleasant, and one of the cheapest hostels in Japan (Y400 in 1980). It is reached from Nagai station of either the JNR Hanwa line (south from Tennoji station) or Midosuji subway line. No card is required, only a passport. Hattori Ryoku-chi Youth Hostel (tel 06 862-0600) is located north of the city in the same park as the Farmhouse Museum. It has 108 beds, and is reached via Ryokuchi-koen station of Midosuji subway line. Sayama-Yuen Youth Hostel (tel 0723 65-3091) is small (24 beds) and located to the south of the city. It is reached by Nankai railway Koya-sen line via Sayama-yuen-mae station. Other hostels in the area can be located with the help of the information service at the station. Failing that, a Japanese person could ask for additional phone numbers by telephoning any of the hostels listed. The hostels of Kyoto and Nara are also within range of Osaka, but if Osaka hostels are full, they probably will be too.

Tescort

There are several people in Osaka who have competent English and wish to gain practice in conversation. Members of Tescort, a 'club' organized by a large private teaching institution, are willing to accompany foreign visitors as unpaid guides in exchange for the assistance it gives them with English. This is an ideal way to meet Japanese people, and it overcomes the problems of finding your way around an unfamiliar country. More details on the programme are given in the introductory section of this book. In Osaka, call Mr Kira at 445-6116.

SIGHTSEEING

Osaka is primarily a business city. Its day of political greatness and power is long past, and what relics were left from ancient times were obliterated during the war. Osaka reconstructed with little plan other than for commerce, with a notable lack of park space even by Japanese standards (which are lamentably low by Western standards). The following section gives information on the few attractions that are definitely worth seeing because they are unique or at least uncommon elsewhere in Japan. As mentioned in passing, the booklets *Your Guide to Osaka* and *Osaka* give information on everything that there is to see in the city.

Osaka Castle

The original castle was destroyed long ago. In 1931 a reproduction was built, in concrete, so it preserves a similar exterior though not interior (which even has lifts!). A visit gives much of the impression of its historic appearance. This was once the mightiest fortress in Japan (though it was captured in battle) and the huge foundation stones and the gates testify to its former strength. The municipal museum is in the castle grounds.

From Osaka station it is most easily reached by bus 2 (but check with the information centre to verify this route number). Because it is a reconstruction, the castle is of limited historical interest: the finest castle in Japan is only an hour or so away, at Himeji, and a visit there should be considered.

Sumiyosh-taisha Shrine

This was the only historic structure to survive the war. It is believed to date from 202, though the present four main buildings (all national treasures) are from 1810. Their architectural style is unique: the roofs, for example, are not tiled but covered with multiple layers of thin strips of wood. The grounds have many picturesque lanterns that have been donated by seamen, and an arched stone bridge.

It is easily reached from Sumiyoshi-koen station of the Nankai-sen line which begins at Namba station; another Nankai line begins at Tenno-ji station, but no sources agree on the station or even the route. Enquire locally.

Shitenno-ji

Often mentioned as an attraction of Osaka, this temple was totally destroyed during the war and the main buildings later reconstructed in concrete, a material which cannot begin to reproduce the qualities inherent in Japanese wooden temple construction design.

Keitaku-en Garden

Located beside the Municipal Art Museum (Bijustu-kan) in Tennoji-koen park, this very pretty garden is considered as an excellent example of the Japanese circular garden. It is open without reservation on Tuesdays, Thursdays and Sundays, and with reservation on Wednesdays, Fridays and Saturdays. It is easily reached from Tenno-ji stations of JNR or subway.

The Mint There is a museum of coins from around the world, but the main attraction is the cherry-blossom season when the grounds are open to the public.

Other

There are few unique sights in Osaka that can't be found elsewhere; if you have time to kill in the area, look through *Your Guide to Osaka* for more ideas. For combined shopping and sightseeing, the underground shopping centres are worth a look, for they are usually very attractive. They are generally located at the terminuses of the various private railway lines: that of the Hankyu line, at Umeda, has one section of the arcade that resembles the arched roof of a cathedral, with stained-glass windows.

Although Osaka is unlovely by day, with lots of large buildings, parts of it are quite pretty at night, particularly the Dotombori area where large multi-coloured advertising signs are reflected in the water of a canal. Fountain sprays in the canal serve the double duty of adding a note of beauty while helping to purify the water. Many shops and restaurants line the nearby streets.

NORTH OF OSAKA
Expo 70 & its Legacy

Osaka came to international attention by hosting the World Fair Expo 70. The use of the structures as pavilions ended in September 1970, but some of the buildings have been preserved and converted to other display purposes, and the famed garden has survived.

Japanese Garden A garden incorporating the elements for which Japanese gardens have become famous — the placing of rocks, water, 'hills', trees and other shrubbery — was created for Expo 70 and is one of the most pleasant places to see during a visit to Osaka.

National Museum of Ethnology This is located on the old Expo grounds and has been rated as very worthwhile by all who have visited — some who live in the area have returned several times. Exhibits include items of daily use, plus video tapes of festivals, music, etc, from a large number of countries. Most interesting and exotic to the Japanese is Spanish flamenco. Access to both the garden and museum is by bus from Ibaraki station of the JNR Tokaido line, or Ibaraki-shi station of the Hankyu Kyoto line. These stations are between Osaka and Kyoto (closer to the former) and can very easily be visited from Kyoto as a day trip.

Koriyama Honjin

This is in the same area. During the Edo era (1603-1867), feudal lords were compelled to spend part of their time in Edo (Tokyo) as virtual hostages, so there was much movement of their parties to and from Edo. To provide accommodation fit for people of such exalted rank, inns with the finest construction and facilities were set up along the route. Koriyama Honjin was one: it

looks much as it did then, and is open for inspection with many historical items on display. It is accessible from JNR Ibaraki station.

Japanese Farmhouse Museum (Nihon Minka Shuraku Hakubutsu-kan)

This open-air museum is an interesting collection of 12 traditional thatched-roof farmhouses of the type once common in Japan but now quite rare. They have been brought here to Hattori Ryoichi Pard and reassembled in a village-like arrangement. The buildings house exhibits of traditional furniture and items used in daily life (closed Mondays). There is an English-language pamphlet available. Hattori Ryoichi is accessible from Sone station (before Toyonaka) on the Hankyu Takarazuka-sen line from Hankyu Umeda station, or from Ryokuchi-koen subway station.

SOUTH OF OSAKA
Sakai Nintoku Tomb Mound

The greatest tomb mound in Japan, covering a larger area than the Great Pyramid (about 460,000 sq metres), is located a short distance south of Osaka. The keyhole-shaped mound is 478 metres long, 300 metres wide at the flat end, and as high as 35 metres. An immense amount of work went into its construction, involving the movement of 1.45 million cubic metres of earth. Three moats surround it.

After this description, it is only fair to say that it is not worth the effort (for most people) to see it, for there is no high point from which to view it and from ground level it looks like little more than a broad ditch surrounding a low hill. It's more interesting for what it represents. For several hundred years from the fifth century onward, the Osaka area was the residence of the rulers of Japan who had the power and resources to build these tombs. One theory was that this was the eastern tip of a crescent of peoples stretching to Kyushu and into part of Korea, and that the labourers who built the tomb were captives from wars on the Korean peninsula. This is only interesting speculation at this point, but would explain how so many people could be assigned to non-productive work. The practice of building these mounds seems to have died out in the seventh century.

Access is from Mozu station of the JNR Hanwa-sen line (from Tenno-ji station), or Mikuni-oka station of Nankai Koya-sen line (from Shiomi-bashi station of Nankai line, near Sakuragawa subway station).

Yoshimura House

This is a large farmhouse built in the 17th century and preserved in excellent condition. It is accessible from Takawashi station of Kintetsu Minami Osaka-sen line, which leads to Yoshino.

ENTERTAINMENT IN OSAKA
Food

While Osaka has few 'touristy' attractions, it has a well-deserved reputation for good dining. If you have no friends to act as guides, contact Tescort and inquire whether any Japanese members would be interested in dining out.

Home Visit

You can arrange a visit to the home of a Japanese family for a couple of hours in the evening. (For further details, see the introductory section of this book.) A day or more is usually required to arrange the visit, although if you are in Osaka for only a short time you might be able to arrange it on a same-day basis if you start early in the day. Contact Osaka Tourist Association (tel 261-3948) or Osaka Tourist Information Office (345-2189).

Bunraku

Osaka's contribution to the world's performing arts is Bunraku puppet theatre. The puppets are somewhat more than a metre tall, have realistic faces, and are beautifully costumed. ('Faces' rather than 'masks' is used because the mouths, eyebrows and eyes can move, making life-like expressions.) Each doll is manipulated by one to three persons standing behind it, moving the head, arms and legs in such a realistic manner that it seems to take on a life of its own. The master puppeteer is visible, and dressed in traditional costume, while his masked assistants are dressed in black. There is a narrator, and musical accompaniment by shamisen. Performances are given in the Asahiza Theatre, near Nihonbashi subway station. Information on performances is available at the information centres, large hotels, at the Kyoto TIC, etc.

Kabuki

Performances of Kabuki are also given at various times through the year: the theatre is Shin-Kabuki-za, near Namba station of the subway or Nankai line. Information is available from the same sources mentioned for Bunraku.

Takarazuka Girls' Opera

This is in the Kansai area, a music hall in which all performers are young women. Programmes include revues, musicals, and adaptations of light operas. The 4000-seat theatre, the largest in the Orient, is part of Takarazuka Family Land, a large recreation centre with cinemas, gardens, etc. Access is by Hankyu-Takarazuka line from Hankyu Umeda station.

Clubs & Bars

Being a large business centre, Osaka has all the nightclubs, cabarets, hostess bars, etc, found in any large Japanese city. The same warnings also bear repeating — that many (if not most) are aimed at expense-account spenders and can be *very* expensive. If prices aren't posted, ask before ordering anything. A safe and relatively inexpensive way around the problem is to take an evening tour that includes a nightclub and cabarets.

Festivals

9-11 January: Imamiya Ebisu-jinja (Niniwa-ku).

22 April: Shitennoji temple.

14 June: Sumiyoshi-taisha.

24-5 June: Tenmangu shrine (Tenjin matsuri).

30 July-1 August: Sumiyoshi-taisha.

11-12 August: Ikutama-jinja shrine (Osaka Takigi Noh performances at night).

NAGOYA

Nagoya, Japan's fifth largest city, is really just a transportation centre, a place to go through. It has some direct international flights, and could be a convenient place to first set foot in Japan because there are several attractions in the general region. The city itself is of very limited interest because it was a prime target during the war due to its concentration of industries and was flattened. As a result, virtually all historic relics such as the cast and Atsuta shrine were destroyed.

After the war, it was rebuilt as a city planner's dream. Streets run broad and straight, and everything is neat and tidy, and totally lacking in soul. It is as exciting as any commercial and industrial city. On the other hand, foreign residents say that it is a quite pleasant, though dull, city to live in.

The twin peninsulas of Chita and Atsuta, to the south-east, and the upper part of Mie-ken, to the south-west are

Information on areas immediately to the north is included under Gifu-ken in the previous chapter.

Information

Before setting off on the limited sightseeing of the city, stop at the Nagoya City Tourist Information Office at the JNR station and pick up a copy of the city map and other brochures. These give further information on the city. A full-colour 32-page booklet *Nagoya* gives greater information than space allows in these pages. The information centre is located inside the station to the left of the building when walking out (tel 052 541-4301). It is open daily 8.30 am to 7pm. The JNTO map of Japan has a usable Nagoya map on its back.

SIGHTSEEING

Nagoya Castle

Formerly one of the greatest castles of Japan in both size and importance, Nagoya-jo was destroyed during the war. The present building retains the original stone foundations and moats, but the building is a concrete reproduction completed in 1959. It preserves the grand external appearance of the original structure, but its interior is laid out as a museum, not in the original residential arrangement.

From late September to late November, there is an interesting display of 'dolls' made of chrysanthemum bushes that have been shaped so that the flowers form 'faces' and 'hands'. They are dressed in costumes and set out in tableaux of famous historic events. The building in which they are displayed is in the central castle grounds.

Visitors are given a brochure when entering the castle that describes its history and structural details extremely well. It is also available at the information centre at the station.

The castle is most easily reached (7 minutes) by city bus 5 or 17 from the station. The stop is 'Nagoya-jo-minami'.

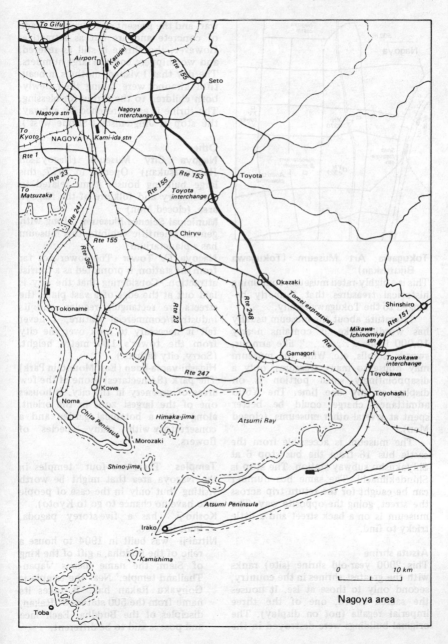

Nagoya area

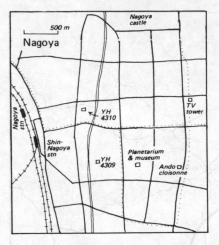

Nagoya

Tokugawa Art Museum (Tokugawa Bijutsukan)

This is a highly-rated museum, containing historical treasures that formerly belonged to the Tokugawa family.

Literature about the museum usually has wording like 'it contains nearly 10,000 items . . . .', like armour, swords, scrolls, etc. While the museum may house so many treasures, only a disappointingly small portion is on display at any one time. The Y500 admittance charge could be better spent at several other museums. (closed Mon).

The museum is accessible from the castle bus 16 from the bus stop 6 at Shiyakusho subway station. The stop is Shindekimachi. The same bus number can be caught for the return trip across the street, going the opposite way. The museum is on a back street and a little tricky to find.

Atsuta shrine

This 2000 year-old shrine (site) ranks with the greatest shrines in the country, second only to those at Ise. It houses the sacred sword, one of the three imperial regalia (not on display). The original buildings were destroyed in the war, and the present structures are made of concrete and are not as attractive. However, the shrine is still as revered, and worshippers come in large numbers. The day that I visited, mothers in beautiful kimono were taking their newly-born children to the shrine for blessing. The shrine is easily reached by subway; the stop is Jingu-nishi ('Shrine west').

Other

Nagoya City Museum (Nagoya-shi Hakubutsukan) Opened in 1977, this large building houses items related to the history and folklore of the Nagoya area. (closed Mon)

Municipal Science Museum Along with general scientific exhibits, this museum has a planetarium.

Nagoya TV Tower The tower not far from the station, is promoted as a tourist attraction. Considering that the city is laid out at the edge of a vast plain, the streets are rectangular-regular, and its industrial/commercial nature, I never felt it necessary to look over the city from the tower's 180 metre height. (Sorry, city fathers.)

Higashi-yama-koen (East Mountain Park) The park (84 hectares) is one of the few areas of greenery in the city. It houses one of the largest zoos in the orient, along with a botanical garden and a conservatory with many species of flowers.

Temples There are four temples in the Nagoya area that might be worth visiting (but only in the case of people who have no chance to go to Kyoto).

Kosho-ji has a five-storey pagoda, built in 1808.

Nittai-ji was built in 1904 to house a relic of the Buddha, a gift of the king of Siam; the name means 'Japan-Thailand temple.' Near the temple is Gohyaku Rakan hall. It takes its name from the 500 statues of Rakan, disciples of the Buddha. Each face and pose is said to be different.

Kenchu-ji has a historic two storey gate at the entrance, dating from 1651.

Ryusen-ji also has a large and picturesque gate at its entrance, though it is not historically noted.

Accommodation

There are many hotels and business hotels in Nagoya and three youth hostels. *Miyoshi Ryokan* (tel 052 583-0758) is a small ryokan, about 10 minutes from Nagoya station. It is shown on the map. Two other hostels in the city area are *Aichi-ken Seinen-Kaikan* (tel 221-6001) and *Nagoya Youth Hostel* (tel 781-9845).

The information office at the station can help in finding accommodation. It is also possible to stay at nearby places like Inuyama and Gifu.

Social

Home Visits You can arrange a visit to a Japanese home in Nagoya through the Home Visit Programme. Application can be made at the city information office at the station, JTB offices and major hotels. There is no charge for the service but a day is usually required to make arrangements.

Tescort Contact Mrs Okuzawa at 052 581-1872. Tescort will arrange an introduction with one or more Japanese people who speak English and wish to obtain practice.

Getting There — International

Travellers from Hong Kong, Seoul and Manila have the option of flying direct to Nagoya. Since the airport is only 30 minutes away from Nagoya station by bus (every 15 minutes) it is very convenient, especially when compared with the mess at Tokyo. Since there are few such international flights, one can expect quick processing.

The airport is not far from Kasugai station of the Meitetsu line that goes to Inuyama/Gifu, passing the shrines of

Tagata and Oagata on the way. There are several attractions in those areas, all of which are described under Gifu-ken.

Buses to the airport leave from Nagoya Bus Terminal, which is located in the Meitetsu Department Store, to the right when exiting the JNR Nagoya station.

Getting There — Domestic

Nagoya is a major stop on the Shinkansen, and is also a hub for several private lines as well as other JNR services. It is also served by many buses, and there are also some long-distance ferry runs.

Trains

JNR All Shinkansen trains stop at Nagoya. It is also on the Tokaido line to Tokyo, and the Chuo-hon-sen (line) to Shinjuku (Tokyo). Other lines run to Kyoto, Nara, Osaka, around the Kii Peninsula, and to the Shima Pen.

Private Lines The major private line is the Meitetsu-sen. Its Shin-Nagoyg station (downtown) is in the basement of the Meitetsu Department Store, to the right when exiting from the JNR station. From this station, trains run to Inuyama, Gifu, other points to the north, the Chita Peninsula, Osaka, Nara and Kyoto. (Private railways are generally cheaper than JNR trains to the same destinations, so should be considered when the option is given). Another private line is the Kinki-Nippon line that runs to the Shima Peninsula; its trains also leave from Shin-Nagoya station.

There is a second Meitetsu station at Kamiida, within the city limits, but some distance from Nagoya station. It can be reached by bus 1 from the latter, but it is simpler, for passengers who wish to use it (to Meiji-mura or Tagata/Oagata shrines), to go to Inuyama from Shin-Nagoya station, change trains at Inuyama and backtrack slightly along the other line.

This entire region is intensively

blanketed by railway lines and a complete listing can be found in the book of timetables *Jikokuhyo*, described in the Getting Around section.

Buses There are few intercity bus services in Japan but Nagoya is one city with connections, via the Tomei expressway, to Tokyo and several cities along the way. There are 15 day buses each day as well as one night bus in each direction, plus other buses that terminate at cities before Tokyo. The night buses leave each city at 11.20 pm (Nagoya station) and arrive at 6 am next morning. Similar services run between Osaka/Kyoto and Tokyo. They can all be recommended, for they are much more comfortable than the night train, and the cost is comparable.

Ferries Overnight ferries run to Sendai (Tohoku), Tomakomai (Hokkaido), and Oita (Kyushu). The respective sailing times and minimum fares are: 22½ hours/¥8400, 40¾ hours/¥13,700, and 21 hours/y6900. Ferries leave from Nagoya Ferry Terminal which can be reached by city bus from the station. It is not too far from Nagoya-ko subway station.

Hitching To hitch out of Nagoya along the Tomei expressway (to Tokyo or Kyoto/Osaka), take the subway from Nagoya station (platform 1) to Hongo. About half the trains terminate before Hongo at Hoshigaoka; if yours does, wait for the next one, which will terminate at Fujigaoka. Trains bound for Fujigaoka are shown in red on the timetable in stations. On ticket machines, the line is shown in yellow.

The entrance to the expressway is close to Hongo station. See the section on Hitching for further information.

Local Transport
City transportation services Nagoya has a subway system of two lines that run roughly north-south and east-west. It is easy to use, and has stations marked in romaji (although the station names on maps are not). The free handout map from the information centre shows the stations.

Crafts
World famous Noritake china is made in Nagoya and visitors may tour their factory at 10 am and 2 pm daily (except Sun & holidays). English-speaking guides are provided.

Visitors can watch the process of hand-painting cloisonne ware daily from 10 am to 12 noon and 1 to 5 pm (except Sun & holidays) at Ando Cloisonne. The workshop can be reached by subway to Sakae station. Ando is 10 minutes walk along Otaumachi-dori avenue.

Festivals
There are several festivals in the Nagoya area that could be worth seeing if you are in the area.

Jan 1	New Year's rites at Atsuta shrine
Jan 13 (lunar)	Naked Men's festival at Konomiya
Early April	Cherry Blossom festival at Nagoya castle
April 16-17	Toshogu jinja (shrine) matsuri (festival) — this is a small, local festival, but interesting nevertheless. On the 16th there are performances of Kagura, ancient sacred masked dances with equally ancient and strange gagaku court music.

(Contrary to what is written in both the JTB *Official Guide* and a guide issued by a well-known international writer of guidebooks, this is very much a local affair; people at the information office had trouble locating it!)

May 18	Toyokuni-jinja-matsuri yagumo koto and dances
June 1 (lunar)	Tenno-matsuri of Tsutsui-cho area (but celebrated throughout the city)
June 5	Atsuta shrine festival
July 20-21	Port festival (fireworks, etc.)
July 26	Shimono-ishiki-kawa (river) festival of Sengen-jinja. Three lantern-decorated boats sail on the Shinkawa river at night; there are also fireworks
late Sept to late Nov	Chrysanthemum Doll show (Nagoya castle)
Oct 7-8	Yobitsugi-jinja giant dolls three to four metres tall of Hotei (deity of children and symbol of happy life) and Jurojin (deity symbolic of longevity) also, a doll of Shojo (a drunken monster) appears at Hoshinomiya (at Hoshizaki) and at Maenowa-jinja at Narumi.
mid-October	Nagoya-matsuri numerous events of a cultural and folkloric nature (music, dancing, tea ceremony, folk songs/dances, kagura sacred dances/music) are scheduled, nearly all for the second Saturday and Sunday of the month. The high points are the procession of the Three Feudal Lords (both days), and the parade of eight dashi, elaborate wooden festival wagons of the type seen at the famous festivals at Kyoto, Takayama and Furukawa. A very interesting feature of these dashi is the display of mechanical dolls that are associated with some of the carts. These ingenious dolls, well over a century old, perform an amazing number of tricks and movements, all controlled by wires. Similar ones are to be seen at Takayama and Furukawa (Nagano-ken).

SOUTH-EAST FROM NAGOYA

To the south-east of Nagoya are the two peninsulas of Chita and Atsumi, looking like pincers poised to close on Mikawa Bay. Their attraction to Nagoya residents is a glimpse of nature, especially wildflowers in season but they are of limited interest to foreigners.

The Chita Peninsula can be reached by Meitetsu train from Shin-Nagoya station. The line ends at Noma, unless the extension to Minami-China is finished. Noma is a beach resort. From both places, buses run to Morozaki at the tip. The most exciting attraction here is the sight of buildings and other park facilities covered with sea shells.

From Morozaki, ferries cross eight times daily in both directions to Irako; fare is Y500. Ferries also cross Ise Bay to Toba five times daily. There is also a service to Toba from Irako 14 times a day. The fare is the same for both, Y750. There is a service to Toba from Gamagori as well, but at Y3000, it is much more expensive. There are also island-hopping services in the Mikawa Bay area, along the route Kowa (noted for beaches) — Himaka-jima — Shino-jima (considered the most attractive) — Gamagori. Morozaki is another starting point to Himaka-jima to pick up the route.

At Irako, bicycles can be rented at hours/Y8400, 40¾ hours/Y13,700, and 21 hours/Y6900. Ferries leave from

the service centre of the Toyotetsu railway (near the port) and at Irako Kokumin Kyuka-mura (vacation village). The Toyotetsu line itself does not begin until half-way along the peninsula, so it is just as easy to go by bus from Irago all the way to Toyohashi station.

Those wishing to hitch on the Tomei expressway to Tokyo or Kyoto/Osaka would find it easiest to take JRN from Toyohashi to Mikawa-Ichinomiya and backtrack a couple of km to the Toyohashi interchange ('inta' in Japanese). Route 1 passes through Toyohashi, but this road is very congested, slow to travel on, and the scenery is depressing nearly all the way to the Mt Fuji area.

Western Honshu

From the Kyoto area westward toward Kyushu lies the area known as Chugoku (Middle Country). It has several attractions, such as Himeji Castle and Hiroshima, but it would rank behind the major areas like Hokkaido, northern and central Honshu, and Kyushu as an area to explore in depth.

The north coast, Sanin-kaigan, has only a few specific places to visit, but it is one of the most pleasant areas to travel through for seascapes and peaceful landscapes of farms and (generally low) mountains. It is infinitely more pleasant than the heavily industrialized southern coast (Sanyo-kaigan) having little industrial build-up and an impression of greenness and general prosperity. The south coast is extremely crowded, and travel along Route 2 gives the impression (not too misleading) that the entire coast is one vast conurbation.

Travellers in a hurry will probably opt for a southern route (especially via the expressway, if hitching). Sightseeing from the main south coast road (without a stop) is negligible, and you would be well advised to take an overnight ferry if time is the main factor. You get occasional views of the Inland Sea, but to see it properly you need to stop at certain vantage points or take boats. This description of western Honshu moves westward via the north coast, returning via the south coast and centre.

NORTH COAST

WAKASA BAY

The Sanin coast is considered to extend from Amino to Tottori, but this description begins in the area just west of

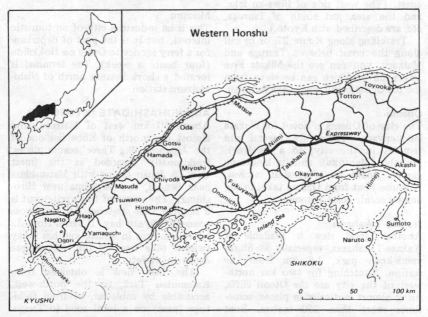

Western Honshu

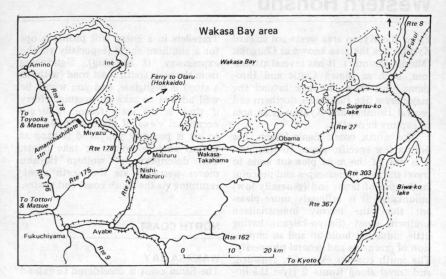

Wakasa Bay area

Tsuruga (Fukui-ken) because it fits in a little better with a trip along the Sanin coast. (The west side of Biwa-ko lake, and the area just south of Tsuruga, etc, are described with Kyoto.)

Travelling along Route 27, or by rail along the coast between Tsuruga and Maizuru, you can see the Mikata Five Lakes, all of which can be views from the top of Baijo Hill, near Lake Suigetsu.

Obama
The city of Obama is noted for Wakasa lacquerware. There are several old temples in the city; to a foreigner, probably Mantokuji and its landscape garden would be of greatest interest. A cruise boat from Obama takes in the nearby scenic coast Sotomo.

Wakasa-Takahama
Another good view is available at Wakasa-Takahama, especially at Shiro-yama-koen park, 1.6 km from the station. Stretching for two km north-west of the city are the Otomi cliffs, rising almost vertically in places, sometimes more than 250 metres. Boat

cruises lasting about two hours are available from Takahama.

Maizuru
This is an industrial city of no touristic interest, but it is the port of departure for a ferry service to Otaru on Hokkaido (four boats a week). The terminal is located a short distance north of Nishi-Maizuru station.

AMANOHASHIDATE (KYOTO-FU)
About 30 km west of Maizuru, and almost due north of Kobe lies one of the Japanese 'Big Three' scenic places, traditionally regarded as the finest view in Japan (along with Matsushima near Sendai, and Miyajima near Hiro-shima). The cause of this excitement is a sandbar that stretches 3.6 km across peaceful Miyazu bay. It varies from 35 to 110 metres in width, and has many twisted pine trees of the 'picturesque Japanese' variety.

The best view is obtained from Kasamutsu Park to the north-west, accessible by cable-car, or from Ochi-toge (pass) on a local road to Tango-

Omiya. The former can be reached by bus to Ichinomiya from Amanohashidate station (15 minutes), or ferry from Amanohashidate or Miyazu (15 and 25 minutes, respectively). The traditional way to look at the scene is by bending over and looking at it through your legs.

It should be noted that the scenery is, in fact, not spectacular, merely pleasant, and the modern generation of Japanese do not fall into raptures at the sight. It's worth a look for those passing through, but not worth a special trip for itself alone.

OKU-TANGO PENINSULA
A route taken by few travellers leads around the Oku-tango (or Yosa) peninsula, which begins at Amanohashidate. Friends of mine described a very picturesque fishing village, Ine, about 20 km from Miyazu and built right to the

water's edge around a semicircular bay.

Amino, a town on the other side of the peninsula, marks the beginning of the 'real' Sanin coast that continues to the sand dunes of Tottori. There are no single scenes that can be picked out, just a succession of very pretty views of small white beaches, rocks jutting out of the sea (often topped by one or more twisted pine trees), although the Kasumi and Yoroi areas are particularly highly regarded.

The road (and rail line) follow the coast quite closely, giving good views over the water which contrasts with the farms and mountains inland. This stretch of coast, and all of the north coast, have relatively few hills and can be recommended to cyclists, particularly as there is relatively little traffic.

TOYOOKA (NORTH HYOGO-KEN)
In the vicinity of this small city are the well-known basalt caves of Gembudo. Unlike limestone caves, these were formed by water erosion that dissolved the rock, but by a lava flow that cooled on the surface. Some still-liquid lava escaped, leaving caves or tunnels within the solid mass. Visible inside the caves are pillars six to nine metres in height, of five, six, seven and eight faces, some parallel, others growing at odd angles. There are five caves or grottoes, 23 to 30 metres or so in depth. They are located not far from Gembudo station, 5.3 km out of Toyooka.

TOTTORI (TOTTORI-KEN)
The best-known place along the Sanin-kaigan is the extensive area of sand dunes at Tottori, two km wide and 16 km long. They have a stark beauty all their own, their broad flanks rippled by the wind. Even though there are usually hundreds of sightseers on the dunes at any one time, they are swallowed in its expanse and the energetic can walk beyond the area usually tromped by the

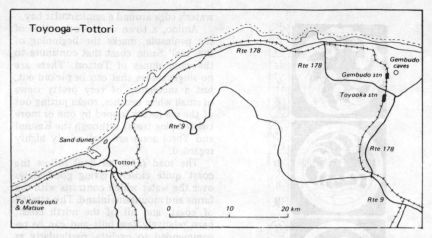

hordes. In the heat of the summer it is advisable to have a canteen of water or a few soft drinks, for the air is very dehydrating. The entrance of the dunes is easily reached by bus from town; the dunes are slightly to the east.

In the city of Tottori itself, Tottori Folk Art Museum (Mingei-hakubutsu-kan) may be of interest, along with the garden of Kannon-in temple.

West from Tottori, the coast becomes merely pleasant, with a succession of towns and cities, some fishing villages, and many farms. It is one of the better areas for observing unpolluted rural Japan. Foreigners are quite rare, so the people are even nicer than usual. An alternative route for those headed toward the south coast is via Tsuyama which is described in the Okayama-ken section.

Mt Daisen
For a considerable distance along the way, the form of Daisen is visible. It is interesting because although it presents a conical face from the west, it is seen as a succession of smaller peaks from the north or south. It may be climbed quite easily, and offers a good view over the coast (including the Oki Islands)

and nearby peaks. In clear weather it is possible to see Shikoku to the south. The climb begins at Daisen Temple, which is easily reached by bus from Daisenguchi station. The 5.5 km climb takes about 3½ hours going up and 1½ hours coming down. (The temple was founded in 718 and was once huge and powerful, but all its original buildings have been destroyed by fire.)

MATSUE AREA (SHIMANE-KEN)
Picturesquely located between a lake (Shinji) and a lagoon (Naka-umi), the city of Matsue is the proud possessor of one of the few original castles surviving in Japan, a small but attractive structure dating from 1611.

Near the castle is an old samurai residence that has been well preserved and opened to the public. Near it is the former residence of Lafcadio Hearn, an English writer who lived in Matsue during the 1890s and wrote a number of books about the Japan of that day. Close to his old house is a museum of manuscripts and other memorabilia.

Kaga
A stretch of picturesque coast may be found at Kaga, north of Matsue. The

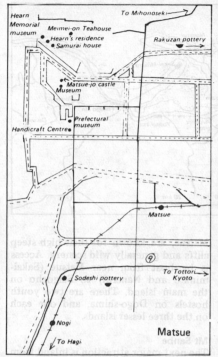

most interesting part is the cave Kagano-kukedo, which is entered by boat; the opening is small, but the interior is large. Access is by bus from Matsue, taking a little over an hour.

Fudoki Hill

The Matsue area was one of the regions settled before the Yamato conquest of the Japanese islands. There is an archaeological site of an ancient village to the south of Matuse at Fudoki-no-oka, with a museum displaying artefacts of this old civilisation. Inquire locally for information on how to get to the museum.

Izumo-taisha

Not far from Matsue is the oldest Shinto shrine in Japan, Izumo, which ranks only behind the grand shrines of Ise in

importance. It is most easily reached from Matsue by the Ichihata private railway line; the 40 km trip takes less than an hour, and 21 trains a day run from Matsue-onsen to Izumo-taisha-mae station. One can also go by JNR, transferring at Izumo-shi (city) to Taisha. In either case, turn right when leaving the station of either line and walk up the hill. If travelling by the private line, look for the tall trees grown as windbreaks on the windswept flat peninsula.

Typical of shrines in Japan, although the site is ancient the buildings are comparatively recent and date from 1874 (the main shrine from 1744). They are built in the oldest style of architecture known in Japan and are quite imposing. The grounds are covered with tall old trees, and the shrine is backdropped by Yakumo hill. There is a museum in the grounds.

By the old (lunar) calendar, the month of October was the time when all Shinto gods met at Izumo, so the month was known in the Izumo area as Kamiarizuki (month with gods), and Kaminazuki (month without gods) everywhere else in Japan.

Hirata

Between Matsue-onsen and Izumo is Hirata, where Gakuen-ji temple is noted for the brilliant autumn colours of trees in its grounds.

Inasano-hama

This is a beach close to Izumo-taisha shrine, about two km from the stations; swimming is good. About 6.5 km northwest of the beach is Cape Hino-misaki, site of ancient Hinomisaki shrine and a lighthouse, and with very pretty coastal scenery. Buses run to both the beach and the cape (35 minutes to the latter from the station).

Tachikue Gorge

Near Izumo-shi is the pretty one-km-long Tachikue-kyo, formed of cliffs,

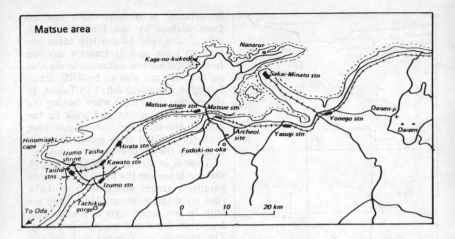

Matsue area

picturesquely eroded rock and basalt columns. It is easily reached from Izumu-shi station by train to Tachikue-kyo station in 30 minutes.

Festivals

Annual festivals at Izumo-taisha are on 14-16 May, 11-17 October (lunar calendar), and 22-3 November. October is also very popular for weddings at Izumo, so it should be possible to see gorgeous bridal kimonos against the backdrop of the shrine.

At Matsue, festivals are held in the first half of April (Castle Festival), and the last third of July (Matsue-odori dance and fireworks display); there is also the summer festival of Tenmangu-jinja shrine on 24-6 November.

On 16 August (Toro-nagashi), many paper lanterns on tiny boats are released on Shinji-ko lake. In the middle of the month is the Obon festival, and Takeuchi-jinja shrine festival is at the end. There are also various festivals on 3, 5 and 6 November.

BEYOND MATSUE
Oki Islands

These islands, almost due north of

Matsue, are known for their high steep cliffs and generally wild scenery. Access is by boat from near Matsue (Sakai-minato and Nanarui) to Saigocho on the main island. There are two youth hostels on Dogo-shima, and one each on the three lesser islands.

Mt Sanbe

The next major attraction is inland from Oda. The mountain can be climbed easily in an hour from Sanbe-onsen (hot-spring resort), which is accessible by bus (12 per day). Nearby is a large lava field and a lake, Ukinu-no-ike.

Easily reached from the area is the Dangyo-kei ravine that stretches four km along the Yagami-kawa river. The ravine is six km from Imbara, on the railway line passing close to Sanbe-onsen; a bus runs towards the ravine from Imbara.

Masuda

In the somewhat industrial city of Masuda, the attractions are Manpuku-ji and Iko-ji, both of which have noted landscape gardens. From Masuda Route 9 and the train cross diagonally to • Yamaguchi via Tsuwano, while Route

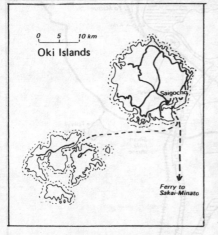

0   5   10 km

Oki Islands

Saigocho

Ferry to Sakai-Minato

191 and rail continue along the coast to Hagi and Shimonoseki at the western tip of Kyushu.

Tsuwano

The old castle town of Tsuwano has long been known for carp, and recently for steam as well. The former, of a variety of beautiful colours and in tens of thousands, measuring up to a metre in length, may be found in ponds of most business establishments, hotels, etc, and even in the channels passing beside the road in the Tonomachi district of the town.

Inari-jinja is the best known shrine in Tsuwano, and is noted for its huge, bright-orange torii gate. Near the shrine is a museum of historical items.

The other minor reason for fame is that Tsuwano is the north-east terminus of one of the two surviving steam train runs in Japan (originating in Ogori, Yamaguchi-ken). Further details are given in the section on rail transport in the introductory section of this book.

HAGI (YAMAGUCHI-KEN)

The city of Hagi is a very popular holiday destination for the Japanese. Its attract-ions result from its having been the castle town of the Mori clan. The castle stood from 1604 to 1871, when it was torn down — unfortunately, because the remaining walls and moats are quite picturesque.

Visitors will be most interested in the castle fortifications, the grounds (which now make up Shizuki-koen park, and house its historical museum as well as a shrine), and a pleasant beach, for Hagi is built on the delta of several rivers. The nearby attractions, good for an hour or two of exploration on foot or by bicycle (available at the youth hostel across the road from the castle), include the narrow streets, samurai barracks of the feudal days, and a number of old houses. Several are best known as the former residences of well-known figures in the history of Japan just prior to the Meiji restoration (and instrumental in it), but they can be appreciated just for their appearance as well. There are three potteries near the castle, Shiroyama, Shogetsu, and Hagi-jo.

The castle area is closest to Tamae station, one stop beyond Hagi station. Buses are also available, the closest stop being Shizuku-bashi.

Shoin Shrine

Another area of touristic interest centres around Shoin-jinja. In the grounds is a building that served as the village school where Shoin Yoshida taught; he was a loyalist to the emperor, and was executed by the Tokugawa government.

Near Shoin-jinja is Toko-ji, the family temple of the Mori family and famous for 494 stone lanterns erected by their subordinates over several generations. (Outside the city is Myojin-ike lake, built as a retreat by the Mori. The lake is connected with the ocean and follows its tides.)

Potteries   There are four potteries in

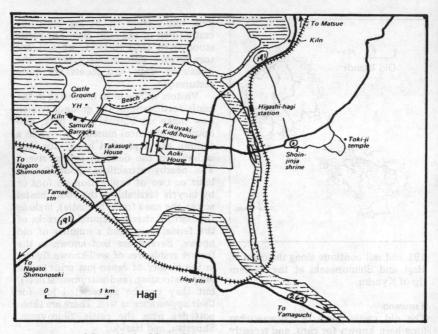

Hagi

the vicinity of Shoin-jinja: Miwa, Shodo, Renzokan and Hosen.

The Shoin-jinja area is easily reached by bus from Higashi-Hagi station (Naka-no-kura stop).

Other

Of lesser interest is a pretty little shrine to the right of the road when going into Hagi from Hagi station. I was interested by a stone turtle statue bearing a commemorative stone on its back, a common sight in Korea but almost unknown in Japan. It may have some relationship to the Korean potters who were brought here in the early 1600s by the Tokugawa following an invasion of Korea, or it may indicate earlier ties with that country.

Accommodation

There are numerous hotels, ryokan, etc, in Hagi, as well as a youth hostel

near the castle. Across the street from it is a Koku-minshu-kusha.

BEYOND HAGI

From Hagi one may continue along the north coast until it curves south toward Shimonoseki, at the western tip of Honshu. The scenery is mostly of lush green farms and prosperous-looking farmhouses. This was formerly something of a backwater with many mud-

A *Cherry blossoms and evergreens at Heian-jingu shrine, Kyoto*
B *Entrance of Sanzen-in temple, Chara (near Kyoto)*
C *Kinkaku ('gold pavilion') of Kinkaku-ji temple, Kyoto*

and-wattle houses, but when I returned there last they were replaced with modern aluminium-doored structures. There are some picturesque fishing villages along the way.

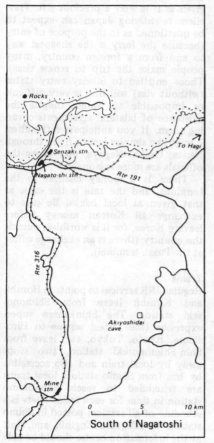

South of Nagatoshi

A *Blood-red waters of Chi-no-ike jig-oku, near Beppu (Kyushu)*
B *Carved stoned heads of Buddha, Usuki (Kyushu)*

Nagato

Off the end of Omi-shima island, near Nagato-shi city, is a picturesque prom-ontory of rocks, including twin pillars that jut more than 40 metres straight out of the sea. Access is by bus, and a cruise around the island is available.

Akiyoshi

An alternative route from Hagi is to travel inland to Akiyoshi plateau, then continue southward to the coast or branch back out to the north coast again. Clumps of limestone rocks dot this rolling tableland, looking (as many have expressed it) like thousands of sheep or tombstones. Although the rocks look small from a distance, many are as tall as a man.

Akiyoshi Cave

Beneath the plateau is Akiyoshi-do, the largest cave in the Far East. It extends several km into the ground, of which

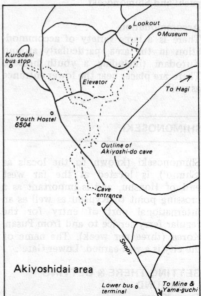

Akiyoshidai area

about one km is accessible to visitors. Electric lights and walkways made the expedition simple, and you pass typical features of limestone caves, like stalagmites and stalactites, as well as other fantastic forms that the limestone takes as it precipitates out of solution.

Well into the cave there is a lift that rises near Kurodani (Black Valley), which is located among the rocks of the plateau. A path leads up to a lookout (tempodai) and a museum of specimens associated with the cave and plateau. Buses run between the Kurodani area to the terminal near the entrance to the cave, so you can return to one entrance from the other bus or retrace your steps through the cave.

Getting Around
There are 11 buses a day between Higashi-Hagi and Akiyoshi-dai. Buses also (generally) run from the cave and the plateau to Ogori, Mine, Yamaguchi and Shimonoseki.

Accommodation
There is a large variety of accommodation in the area, particularly around Kurodani (including a youth hostel). There are places near the lower entrance as well.

SHIMONOSEKI

Shimonoseki (known to the locals as 'Shimo') is located at the far west end of Honshu, and is important as a crossing point to Kyushu as well as an international port of entry for the regular ferry service to and from Pusan, Korea (three per week). The name of the city is a well-earned 'Lower Gate'.

GETTING THERE & GETTING AROUND
From Korea
The dock for the ferry from Korea is a 10-minute walk from Shimo station.

For those arriving from Korea, the only problem is likely to be the immigration officials, who have a reputation for being the most unpleasant and officious in Japan: passports are rigorously scrutinized, and an entry stamp given as if it were a precious gift. Travellers re-entering Japan can expect to be questioned as to the purpose of entry (because the ferry is the cheapest way to and from a foreign country, many people make the trip to renew visas). Those entitled to 90-day entry status (without visa) will find it very difficult or impossible to obtain despite the existence of bilateral agreements covering them. If you anticipate difficulties, it might be simpler just to fly in through Narita, Osaka, Nagoya, etc, where the officials are more reasonable.

There is a money changer in the terminus, and the rate is the same as that given at local banks. Be sure to exchange all Korean money before leaving Korea, for it is worthless outside the country (there is an exchange office at the Pusan terminal).

Trains
Regular JNR services to points in Honshu and Kyushu leave from Shimonoseki station. The Shinkansen superexpresses (the fastest service to Hiroshima, Kyoto, Tokyo, etc) leave from Shin-Shimonoseki station, two stops away by local train and also accessible by bus from Shimo station; local trains are scheduled to reach Shin-Shimo station in time for each train. There is a schedule of all services posted in Shimo station in adequate English, and staff at the information centre should be able to give basic information. (As advised elsewhere, always speak slowly and clearly, avoid slang, and watch the person's face for signs of noncomprehension.) To cross to Kyushu, the simplest way is by train through the tunnel to Moji, Kita-Kyushu, etc.

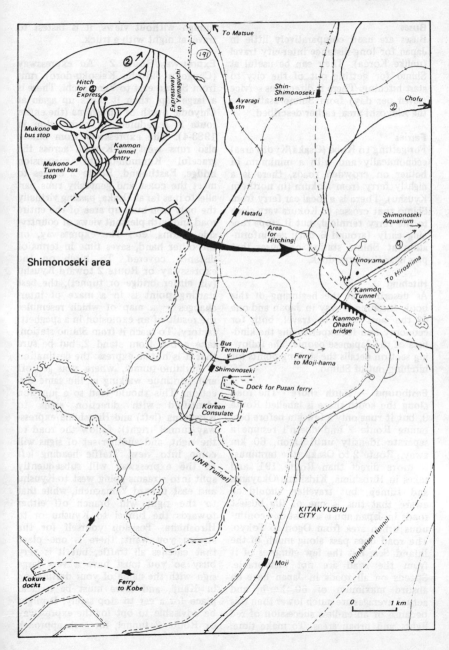

To Matsue

Ayaragi
stn

Shin-
Shimonoseki
stn

Chofu

Hitch
for Express

Expressway
to Yamaguchi

Mukono
bus stop

Kanmon
Tunnel
entry

Mukono
Tunnel bus
stop

Shimonoseki area

Hatafu

Area
for Hitching

Shimonoseki
Aquarium

Hinoyama

YH

To Hiroshima

Kanmon
Tunnel

Kanmon-
Ohashi
bridge

Bus
Terminal

Ferry
to Moji-hama

Shimonoseki

Dock for Pusan ferry

Korean
Consulate

(JNR Tunnel)

KITAKYUSHU
CITY

Shinkansen tunnel

Kokure
docks

Moji

Ferry
to Kobe

0   1 km

Buses

Buses are used comparatively little in Japan for long-distance inter-city travel (unlike Korea). They can be useful at Shimo for getting out of the city to start hitching. There is direct bus service (seven per day) from Shimo station to the Akiyoshi area, earlier described.

Ferries

For getting to Kobe (Osaka/Kyoto area) economically and with a minimum of bother on crowded roads, there is a nightly ferry from Kokura (in northern Kyushu). There is a local car ferry from Shimo that crosses to Kokura very close to the ferry terminal, but it stops running early (around 6 pm); get information at Shimo station on buses that pass near the ferry dock.

Hitching

As described at the beginning of this book, hitching is easy in Japan and one of the best ways to travel, both for economy and for experiencing the kindness of the Japanese people. The following section details the starting points for hitching out of Shimo.

Eastbound — south shore The road along the south shore is labelled Route 9, but it runs only a few km before becoming Route 2 and doesn't resume a separate identity until Ogori, 60 km away. Route 2 to Osaka (the terminus) is more direct than Route 191, and takes in Hiroshima, Kirishima/Okayama and Himeji, but travellers should be aware that this is one of the busiest roads in Japan and is almost one continuous urban area from Ogori to Tokyo. The road does pass along much of the Inland Sea, but the few glimpses of it from the road are not memorable. Speeds on all roads in Japan have an absurd maximum of 60 km/h, and actual averages are much lower than this because of an endless succession of red lights and urban areas. To make time,

though without views, it is fastest to travel at night with a truck.

Expressway/Route 2 An expressway (Chugoku Jidosha Kaisoku-doro) runs from Shimo east to Yamaguchi. There is a large gap, then it picks up again at Chiyoda, north of Hiroshima (the entire route is scheduled for completion in 1983-4). The expressway from Shimo also runs west to Kyushu across the graceful Kanmon-ohashi suspension bridge. Eastbound, Route 2 curves to meet the coast and generally runs parallel to it as far as Osaka, passing virtually the only non-built-up area of the entire road and with pleasant views of countryside, farms, etc. The expressway, on the other hand, saves time in terms of distance covered. To hitch on the expressway or Route 2 toward Kyushu (via either bridge or tunnel), the best starting point is in a maze of interchanges — a map of which resembles the result of an explosion in a spaghetti factory. To reach it from Shimo station, take a bus from stand 2, but be sure that it is not an express: the destination is Mukuno-tunnel, where you get off and continue walking in the same direction. This should lead to a junction identified with direction signs to Kawatana (left) and Hiroshima/expressway/tunnel (right): follow the road to the right, and another set of signs will come into view. Traffic heading left to the expressway will subsequently split into streams going west to Kyushu and east toward Yamaguchi, while that to the right will branch off either towards the tunnel to Kyushu or to Hiroshima. Position yourself for the stream you want; there is one place that catches all traffic, but it is very busy so you must have a very large sign with the name of your destination in Kanji, and there must be a clear place for a car to stop safely. It might be advisable to opt for the expressway or Route 2 tunnel, for each approach road offers better stopping places. If you want only the tunnel, it would be better to stand near the entrance quite close to the bus stop.

For those hitching to the Shimo area, a bus from Mukuno bus stop goes into the station, but quite infrequently during the day. If you are coming through the tunnel you should try to get out as soon as possible after clearing the tunnel exit. If crossing the bridge, get off at or before the Shimonoseki/Dannoura exit and scramble back to the road that leads back to the youth hostel.

ACCOMMODATION

Along with several hotels, etc, Shimo has a very pleasant youth hostel beautifully located overlooking the Kanmon Strait and the suspension bridge at one of the best vantage points in the city. The view is only second to that from the top of Hinoyama; the base station for the cable-car is only 100 metres away, and a 1.8-km walk (mostly downhill) to the Mukono bus stop. The house parents are very nice (the wife speaks some English), and only a passport is required. If Hinoyama Youth Hostel is full, there may be vacancies at others nearby at Toyota (tel (08376) 6-8271) or Akiyoshidai (tel (08376) 2-0341, or in northern Kyushu (see the Kyushu section).

SIGHTSEEING

If this is your first time in Japan, you can get a good idea of the prosperity of the country by a quick walk around either Daiei or Daimaru department stores on the square facing the station; the contrast with Korea will be quite striking (as will be some of the prices).

One of the major attractions of Shimonoseki is Akamon-jinja, a large and colourful shrine. It is made of concrete, not the traditional wood, and is named for its red gate, of uncommon Chinese shape. There are many shrines

in Japan that are more exciting. The shrine can be reached by the same bus that goes to the hostel.

The other attraction is view over the Kanmon strait from Hinoyama (Fire Mountain). This can be enjoyed from the youth hostel, or take the cablecar to the top of Hinoyama. The base station can be reached by bus from the station, either the hourly one from stand 3 to 'Koku-minshuku-sha-mae', which goes right up to and past the station; or any bus going past 'Ropeway-mae', where you get off and walk up the hill.

You may also see a sign pointing to the site of the battle of Dan-no-ura, but most of the action took place in the water and whatever beach might

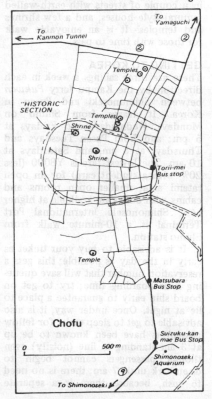

To Yamaguchi

To Kanmon Tunnel

Temples

"HISTORIC" SECTION

Temples

Shrine

Shrine

Torii-mei Bus stop

Temple

Matsubara Bus Stop

Chofu

Suizuku-kan mae Bus Stop

0   500 m

Shimonoseki Aquarium

To Shimonoseki

have existed has disappeared under the tall pillars of the graceful Kanmon-ohashi suspension bridge.

Shimonoseki Aquarium

An attraction of Shimo is its aquarium, claimed to be the largest in the Orient. It has a collection of some truly weird and wonderful creatures of the deep; dolphin and seal shows are part of the entertainment. The aquarium (suizuku-kan) is easily reached from Shimo station or by bus; the name of the bus stop is Suizuku-kan-mae.

Chofu

This is a separate town that is included as part of Shimo. Its claim to fame lies in a couple of streets with earth-walled samurai-style houses, and a few shrines and temples. It is an enjoyable walk for those with time to pass.

GETTING TO KOREA

There are three sailings a week in each direction by the Kampu ferry *Pukwan* between Shimonoseki and Pusan in Korea. It leaves from Shimo on Mondays, Wednesdays and Fridays at 5 pm; and from Pusan Tuesdays and Thursdays at 5 pm, and Saturdays at 10 am. The lowest fare is Y8000 (less 20% with a student card) for an open tatami area; smaller open rooms and cabins with bunks are available at higher cost. Shimonoseki International Port Terminal is a 10-minute walk from Shimo station.

It is advisable to buy your ticket as early in the day as possible; this gets a reservation number that will save queueing near boarding time; try to get on board ship early to guarantee a place to lie at night. Once under way, it is also advisable to get to sleep early, for fellow passengers have been known to be up at 3 am standing in line (noisily) even though passengers cannot begin to disembark until 7 am; there is no need to rush, because there is a separate

immigration line for aliens.

Changing Money

You can change money at banks in town or in the terminal itself; the rates are identical. The money-changer is beyond the barrier from the lounge area: US banknotes are available, and it is advisable to buy these even though yen can be exchanged in Korea, for there is an active black market in US money whereas the 'street' sometimes won't even pay the official rate for yen. The black market is well known, attacks on money-changers having been written up unabashedly in the newspapers; the premium is between seven and 10% over the official rate (Korean currency is not available in Japan). Large-denomination US bills ($50 and $100) may attract a rate slightly higher again.

Cameras & Films

Buy all your film in Japan. Except for Korean-made print film, colour film is generally not available even at the tourist hotels. In addition, a common racket is selling useless film in 'recycled' packages — even shops that seem to have film will often have nothing but piles of empty boxes (modern merchandising and display methods have not hit Korea yet). Safe places to buy would be the large department stores in Seoul, and at Sorak-san on the east coast.

Carry your film and cameras(s) through inspection at Pusan (and airports) for there is an X-ray inspection of baggage. It is claimed to be safe, but the minor bother of carrying them by hand guarantees that precious films will not be damaged: a polite (sometimes firm) request for a hand inspection is normally enough.

Valuables

Be careful of your money, cameras, etc in Korea. While the vast majority of Koreans respect honesty, there is a definite minority that doesn't. Never put anything valuable down for a moment, anywhere; one traveller had a bag of Nikon lenses stolen in the grounds of the National Museum in Seoul in one minute. Passers-by will seldom do anything to help. (Similarly, don't get into a fight, for you will be on your own; however, Koreans are usually content to fight amogst themselves, and normally do not bother foreigners.) Travel in Japan tends to relax your guard against theft, so be careful.

There is a continual demand for Japanese-made cameras, tape-recorders, etc (hairdryers are also popular). However, if it looks as if goods are being taken into Korea specifically for resale, the serial numbers may be written in your passport to guarantee their re-export. People have money to spend and cannot get the goods they want, hence the demand. No one wants to buy extra lenses, even though everyone wants an SLR camera. The only camera brands that are readily sold are Nikon, Canon, Pentax and Minolta. With a camera around your neck, it is difficult to enter shops anywhere without being solicited to sell it, especially in the Itaewon area.

Accommodation The most economical places to start are 'yogwon'; most are comparatively inexpensive (Y1500-2000), but prices have risen rapidly in the last few years, so Korea is no longer the bargain it once was. There are always some yogwon near bus and train stations.

Visas Visas are obtained with the least hassle at the visa annexe of the Korean embassy in Tokyo, but are also available at the consulate at Shimo, Fukuoka, Osaka and other cities.

In Shimonoseki the consulate is near the ferry dock. Here visas *can* be obtained within the day if applied for early in the morning, but more than one traveller has reported rather brusque treatment.

EAST OF SHIMONOSEKI

YAMAGUCHI
Formerly a castle town, this reached its zenith in the 1500s and declined when the daimyo found himself on the losing side in the civil war. Relics from those days include Ruriko-ji (from the 14th century) and its five-storey pagoda, a landscape garden by the famous designer Sesshu, Joei-ji temple, and the (modern) cathedral that commemorates the time spent in Yamaguchi by St Francis Xavier in 1551.

Chomon Gorge
About 20 km from Yamaguchi is the pretty gorge Chomon-kyo. It begins close to the station of the same name, and extends for 12 km to Uzugahara. The Abu-kawa river has sculpted the rock into fanciful shapes, pools, falls and Jacob's wells.

OGORI
There are no notable tourist attractions at Ogori other than its summer steam-train excursions to and from Tsuwaro.

HOFU
Here is located one of Japan's better-known shrines, Hofu-Tenmangu (Matsugasaki) shrine. The buildings are large, colourful and impressive.

IWAKUNI
The small city of Iwakuni is most famous for a very graceful and unusual wooden bridge of five arches, Kintai-Kyo ('Silver Brocade Sash'). It is unusual because not only does the understructure form an arch, but the actual walkway also rises and falls five times in its 193-metre length. The present bridge dates from 1953 and is an exact replica of the historic one that stood from 1673 to 1950, when it was swept away by a flood. No nails were used in its construction.

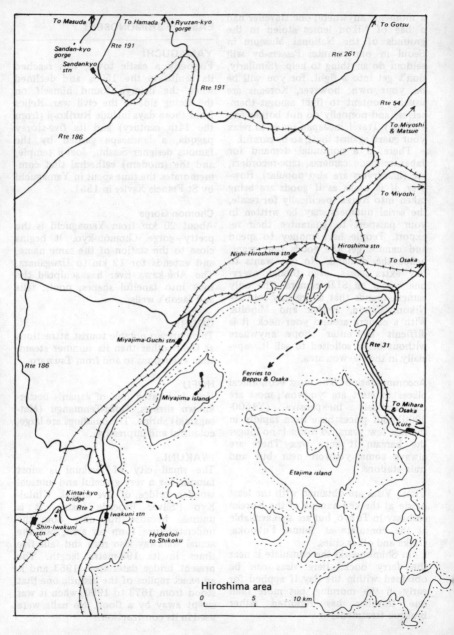

Hiroshima area

0   5   10 km

There is a hydrofoil service from Iwakuni several times a day across to Shikoku (near Matsuyama).

Cormorant Fishing
From June to August, ukai (cormorant fishing) is performed nightly at the bridge except on nights of full moon or after heavy rains when the water is muddy.

Nishimara Museum
Near the bridge is the excellent Nishimura Museum (hakubutsukan). Its collection comprises mostly samurai armour and weapons, along with other subjects used in daily life (especially of warriors), and is one of the best such collections in Japan, worth a special visit by anyone at all interested in how samurai warriors dressed, fought and lived (or died). The museum also has many pieces of superb lacquerware. The collection was put together over a period of 45 years from all over Japan, and was opened in 1963.

Shiroyama
On the top of Shiroyama, one of the hills overlooking the museum and bridge, is a novelty, a southern-European-style castle! A Japanese-style one stood here for the brief period, 1608-15, before being torn down. The present building was constructed in 1960. Easiest access is by the cable-car that rises from Kikko-en park (close to both the bridge and museum). All are easily reached from Iwakuni or Shin-Iwakuni (shinkansen) stations by bus.

Food
Because of the US military base near Iwakuni, there are several restaurants, fast-food joints, etc that serve US or pseudo-US food, which may be of interest to those suffering advanced junk-food withdrawal symptoms.

HIROSHIMA-KEN

MIYAJIMA
The major attraction of the Hiroshima area is Miyajima (Shrine Island). Its best-known feature is one of the most famous symbols of all Japan, the huge off-shore torii gate that is seen in every travelogue and book on Japan. The island is ranked traditionally as one of the three most beautiful sights in Japan (along with Matsushima, near Sendai, and Amanohashidate, on the north coast). There are many pleasant-to-beautiful scenes on and around the island, and a visit is sure to be enjoyed — for the famous shrine, the torii, the heavy woods and walks through them, tame deer, and other attractions. A half-day will take in a good number of the features of the island, but an overnight stay would allow greater relaxation and time to absorb the mood.

The ferry from Miyajima-guchi on the mainland arrives at Miyajima-ko in 10 minutes. In front of the building at the entrance to the dock is a large three-dimensional information board for orientation. Most visitors set off immediately to the right, to the main attraction of the island, Itsukushima-jinja shrine.

Itsukushima-jinja
The shrine is unusual because the buildings are built on piles over the shallows at the water's edge, and joined by narrow galleries. One explanation of the unusual construction is that the island has been regarded as sacred from ancient times, and Taira Kiyomori had the shrine built in this way in the 12th century so that it could be approached by boat without setting foot on land. (Earlier shrines had stood on the same spot since 593.)

The principle buildings of Itsuku-

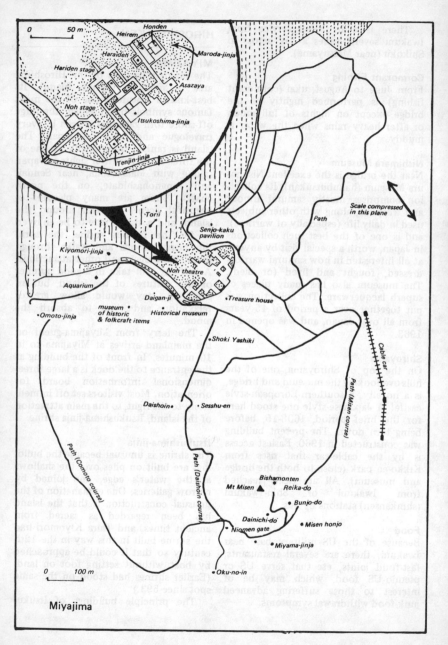

0   50 m

Honden

Heirem

Haraiden

Hariden stage

Asazaya

Maroda-jinja

Noh stage

Itsukoshima-jinja

Tenjin-jinja

Torii

Scale compressed
in this plane

Path

Kiyomori-jinja

Senjo-kaku
pavilion

Noh theatre

Aquarium

Daigan-ji

Treasure house

Omoto-jinja

museum
of historic
& folkcraft items

Historical museum

Cable car

Shoki Yashiki

Path (Misen course)

Daishoin

Sesshu-en

Path (Omoto course)

Path (Daishoin course)

Bishamonten

Mt Misen ▲

Reika-do

Bunjo-do

Dainichi-do

Misen honjo

Niomen gate

Miyama-jinja

Oku-no-in

100 m

Miyajima

shima Shrine are the honden (main hall), heiden (offering hall), haiden (hall of worship), and haraiden (purification hall). The public is allowed only as far as the outer sanctuary of the honden; all these buildings, plus the corridors, are ranked as National Treasures.

In the Asazaya (morning prayer room), dance costumes and masks, armour, etc are displayed. The great torii gate in the water (accessible on foot at low tide for those who don't mind mud) dates from 1875 and is the largest in Japan, 16.2 metres high and 23.3 metres wide. The large stone torii on the shore dates from 1905.

The first shrine structure seen when approaching from the ferry dock is Marodo-jinja, the largest shrine after Itsukushima-jinja itself.

Noh Theatre Most of the shrine buildings are of comparatively recent construction, but the Noh theatre dates from 1568, with a rebuild in Edo times; it is the oldest Noh theatre in Japan, and one of the only stages in the world where the audience is unlikely to crowd around and block the view, especially at high tide.

Dances The shrine is noted for performances of Bugaku and Kagura dances on the takabutai stage at the end of the shrine nearest the channel, and every brochure on Japan is likely to feature a photo of a masked dancer with the torii in the background. However, performances do not seem to be regularly scheduled but are performed according to the payment of a suitable fee, so seeing one may be hit-or-miss.

Treasure Hall On the shore near the shrine is the Treasure Hall (homotsukan), which contains over 3500 historical and cultural items including a number of national treasures. The building resembles a simple temple, but was built specifically for its purpose to replace an older wooden building. A folklore museum is located in an old, traditional-style house nearby.

Other
Apart from a visit to the shrine, there are several paths. A popular route passes a five-storey pagoda (goju-no-to), which dates from 1407, and Senjokaku, an old pavilion (1587) of little particular interest.

Farther inland, other attractions (besides the pleasant forest and semi-tame deer) await, including Momijidani maple-grove park and a number off lesser shrines scattered through the woods, and the cable-car to the top of Mt Misen. Near the upper station is a number of temple and shrine buildings, along with an observation platform (tempodai) that gives a good view.

Accommodation
Accommodation ranges from the Miyajima Youth Hostel (tel 08294 4-0328) to ryokan of high quality (and price).

Festivals
Colourful festivals are held on 17 June and 18 July of the lunar calendar the former, Kangen-matsuri is the biggest festival of the year. On 15 April and 15 November, monks walk on fire; and on 16-18 April a special Noh performance is given.

Getting There
Miyajima is easily reached (via Miyajima-guchi station) from Hiroshima by rail, both by JNR and by private line. The private line is shown on maps as starting at Higashi-Hiroshima station, but some trams from Hiroshima station go directly to Miyajima-guchi without transfer (inquire locally about the correct tram).

HIROSHIMA
The city of Hiroshima is known to the

inhabitants of every civilised country because of an instant in 1945 when it was flattened by an atom bomb. For this reason large numbers of persons visit the city during a stay in Japan, but be warned that there is relatively little else in Horishima city itself, for it is first and foremost an industrial city (which is why it was chosen as a target). It is built on the flat estuary of the Ota river and has little natural beauty, although this is more than offset by the beauties of nearby Miyajima Island. However, the relics and exhibits related to the A-bomb do make Hiroshima a recommended destination, for everyone should be made aware of the true horrors of nuclear warfare.

The bomb exploded almost directly over the Industrial Promotion Hall, formerly an architecturally noteworthy structure. It is the only ruined building still allowed to stand, its dome the symbol of the destruction. It is easily reached from Hiroshima station by tram 2 or 6, or bus 3 (but it is advisable to check on these routes).

Peace Memorial Museum

The area around the building has been made into Peace Park (Heiwa-koen), with a peaceful canal (row-boats for rent), greenery, etc. From the dome, it is an easy and pleasant walk through the park to the Peace Memorial Museum, a broad, low building standing on pillars; along the way, one passes the saddle-shaped cenotaph.

Every visitor to Japan should try to visit the museum (or its equivalent in Nagasaki -- this one is possibly a little better). Its purpose is to show the effects of the bomb on Hiroshima, and to serve as a warning to national leaders about the horrors of such weapons. It should be kept in mind that the terrific destruction was done by a bomb equivalent to about 20,000 tonnes of TNT: the average nuclear weapon in the world today is equivalent to 2000 Hiroshima bombs.

The museum has film showings (in English) at 10 am, 11.25 am, 12.50 pm, 2.15 and 3.40 pm, as well as a film of Hiroshima in wartime (in Japanese only) every hour from 9.30 am to 3.30 pm. There are signposts in the lobby.

Most visitors leave the museum in a sombre or depressed mood; it is a very sobering emotional experience, but not to be missed. An excellent book showing the effects of the bombing is worth looking for: the title is simply *Hiroshima-Nagasaki*. Two Hiroshima bookstores which have sold the book are Kinokuniya (Sogo Department Store, sixth floor), and Maruzen Department Store (third floor). The publishers are Hiroshima Heiwa Kaikan, 1-4-9, Shiba, Minato-ku, Tokyo.

Other

Shukkei-en Garden This landscape garden was originally designed in 1620, though its form has been changed. It offers a pleasant respite from the busy city, and is only about 700 metres from the station.

Hiroshima Castle The original castle stood here from 1589 until it was destroyed by the bomb. It was rebuilt in concrete, and preserves the external appearance of the former building. It is now a local museum, and gives some idea of the appearance of old Hiroshima. The late afternoon offers the best light for photographs.

Getting There

Hiroshima is one of the major stops of the Shinkansen: by the fastest service, Tokyo is just a little over four hours away and Kyoto less than 2½ hours. There are also slower and less expensive JNR services.

There are several boat services from Hiroshima to various places near and far. Hydrofoils cross several times a day to ports near Matsuyama (Shikoku), and offer a little chance to see part of the Inland Sea area. There is also a ferry service to Beppu and Hyuga (both on Kyushu) and Osaka. The dock area can be reached from Hiroshima station by tram or bus (the information centre can give assistance).

The ferry to Beppu leaves at 9 pm, arrives 5 am. The return ferry leaves Beppu at 3 pm, arrives 8.30 pm. Minimum fare is Y2800. The Hyuga ferry leaves at 10.50 pm from Hiroshima and 12.30 from Hyuga; the trip takes about nine hours each way; minimum fare is Y4000. The Osaka-Hiroshima ferry leaves at 8.20 pm from both ports and takes 11 hours; minimum fare Y3200.

Hitching along the south coast is very slow and unpleasant, although unavoid-

able if you are going to Okayama, etc. Route 2 passes through the city and can be intercepted by a tram 8 going south. To get back to Osaka/Kyoto quickly by thumb, the best way is north-east to Miyoshi and from there along the expressway.

Getting Around

The simplest way to get around Hiroshima is by tram; one goes to the A-bomb dome, and you can return by the same route or walk along Peace Boulevard (Heiwa Dori) and across the river, returning to the station by another line.

There are buses to Hiroshima station from various parts of the city. The bus station is in the Sogo Department Store; it serves both city buses and those to other cities. Any red or orange bus goes to the station; red-and-white striped ones pass by the castle.

Information

There is an information centre in front of the station, that supplies a good map and brochure in English. They should also be able to help with tram information, etc, but don't expect proficiency in English. Travellers starting from Tokyo can pick up information at the TIC there, including a printed pamphlet (MG-19).

Accommodation

There are many hotels, etc, in Hiroshima, as well as a youth hostel. The information centre may have directions on how to get to the youth hostel; if not, walk towards the post office (to the right at the front of the station), cross the street and turn right. A short distance along should be a sign '50 metres to Hiroshima Youth Hostel bus stop'. More than one bus uses the same stop so ask the driver before boarding and get off at Ushita-shin-machi or Ushita I-chome; signs from there should be clear guides up the hill to the hostel. It is one of the best-marked hostels in Japan, and is one of the more pleasant (apart from 6.30 am reveille); it is also an excellent source of travel information.

Another accommodation centre is the World Friendship Association; the information centre at the station should be able to help.

SANDAN-KYO GORGE

A pleasant excursion from Hiroshima is north-west to Sandan-kyo. Its 16-km length, covered on foot, takes in a number of waterfalls and scenery ranging from pretty to nearly spectacular. Access is by train to Sandan-kyo station (JNR) or by bus, both from Hiroshima.

MIYOSHI AREA

The inland areas of Chugoku have not gained a great name for tourist attractions but the scenery along the expressway from Miyoshi to Osaka is enjoyable.

Ukai (cormorant fishing) is carried out through June, July and August near the junction of three rivers, not far from Nishi-Miyoshi station.

TAISHAKU-KYO GORGE

This scenic gorge stretches about 20 km upstream from Taishaku-mura village along the Taishaku river. About 2.4 km from the village is Oni-wa-iwaya (Demon Cave), known for its stalactites. Farther along there are two natural rock bridges. The gorge is in one part of Hiba-Taishaku Quasi-National Park. Other attractions of the region include mountain, marsh and forest views. Taishaku-mura can be reached by bus in about 1 hour from Bingo-Shobara station.

KURE

Along the coast east of Hiroshima is the ship-building centre of Kure. During the war, the giant battleship *Yamato* was built here. The largest of its day, it was sunk by US aircraft without contributing to the Japanese war effort; in post-war days, Kure has produced many of the world's super-tankers that would dwarf the *Yamato*. If you want to visit the shipyards, inquire in advance; the city has no other attractions, being a typical industrial port city.

Nikyu Gorge

About 15 km north-east of Kure lies this scenic gorge, most noted for many waterfalls and Jacob's wells. It can be reached by bus from Kure in 40 minutes.

MIHARA & IKUCHI ISLAND

The industrial city of Mihara is the gateway to the island of Ikuchi, 12 km to the south. Setoda, on Ikuchi, is noted for its interesting temple Kosan-ji. Dating from 1946, the temple has several buildings modelled on those of famous temples elsewhere in Japan (eg the Hall of Dreams in Nara) as well as a collection of cultural and religious objects. Access is by ferry (50 minutes) or fast boat (20 minutes) from Mihara to Setoda; the temple is about 10 minutes on foot east from the dock.

Ferries also cross from Mihara to Imabari on Shikoku; the terminal is close to the station.

ONOMICHI

One of the best views of the Inland Sea may be had from the heights of Senko-ji temple. It is accessible in 20 minutes by direct bus, or by bus (five minutes) to Nagaeguchi, then by cable-car to the top. The park at the top is noted for cherry blossoms in season, and picturesque rocks.

The city was not touched by the war,

so many older houses and buildings have survived, and a walk around may provide some of the mood of olden times. The city is noted for a number of temples, such as Jodo-ji, Saigo-ji, Saikoku-ji and Tennei-ji (there are many others). A map of the city, showing the temples, is available at the station and can be used for a guide while strolling around.

Boats run regularly from Onomichi to Imabari and Matsuyama (on Shikoku); other boats run to nearby islands.

Mukai-shima
Located near Onomichi, and accessible by a bridge, Mukai-shima island has an observation post (tempodai) that features an excellent view of the Inland Sea and Onomichi.

FUKUYAMA
This industrial city is of little interest, although it has a 1966 reproduction of its historic castle. It is best known for the nearby town of Tomo-no-ura, regarded as one of the most picturesque places in the Inland Sea area (and Japan). The town of Tomonoura (port for Fukuyama) overlooks the islands of Sensui, Benten and Kogo.

Ferries cross from Tomo-no-ura to Tadotsu (Shikoku); Tomo-no-ura itself is easily reached from Fukuyama station by bus.

Abuto-Kannon Temple This temple to the Goddess of Mercy is built on a cape less than 30 metres above the water, and is noted for its superb view over the water. It is only four km from Tomo-no-ura, and is accessible from there by bus or boat, or from Fukuyama by bus to Abuto-guchi, from where it is a 20-minute walk.

OKAYAMA-KEN

KURASHIKI
This is possibly the most charming town in Japan (parts of it, at least). It was extremely prosperous in feudal days, for rice from the very productive inland region was shipped through here. Merchants built large and elaborate storehouses of dark stone and contrasting white mortar, which still stand in one section of the town. A canal (also stone-walled) passes by the buildings, and willows drop gracefully over the water. Although the architecture is Japanese, the mood of the area is almost that of old Europe. You can first enjoy just walking around, absorbing the appearance and atmosphere and possibly taking a short rickshaw ride along the narrow streets. I first saw the area late in the afternoon when the sun was low, and was quite captivated; but I could never recapture that mood exactly. May every visitor have such an opportunity. The area is not large, so a stroll of half an hour or so down the back streets will probably be enough before returning to the attractions along the canal.

The Warehouses
Several of the 'kura' (or warehouses, hence the name Kurashiki) have been converted into museums, and are worth a visit. They are described in the order that they are encountered along the canal bank.

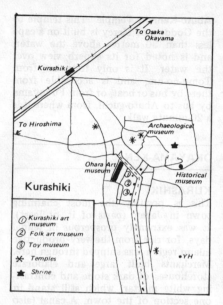

Kurashiki

① Kurashiki art museum
② Folk art museum
③ Toy museum
✳ Temples
★ Shrine

Toy Museum (Kyodo gangu-kan) This houses a collection of toys from all over Japan, including many no longer used and interesting for the simplicity of their designs (using local materials).

Folk-craft Museum (Mingei-kan) Several adjacent kura have been combined so that you can walk back and forth among them, up and down floors, while admiring a large collection of folk-craft, articles of daily utility made of indigenous materials. Most are of Japanese origin, but enough pieces have been brought from other countries and cultures to stress the similarities and individualities. (Closed Mondays.)

Kurashiki Art Museum (Bijutsu-kan) This museum houses mostly European art, including some ancient Mediterranean works.

Kurashiki Archaeological Museum (Koko-kan) Many relics excavated in the region are on display here to show the cultures that have flourished around Kurashiki and Okayama since ancient times, particularly the Kibi culture that survived into the fifth century and is known for a number of tomb mounds in the vicinity of the city. (Closed Mondays.)

Ohara Art Museum (Ohara Bijutsu-kan) No, not founded by an errant Irishman, but a wealthy Japanese textile manufacturer, Magosaburo Ohara, who collected Western art. To house his collection, he constructed a large Greek-style building complete with columns. The collection is interesting but not exciting, at least for those who have had access to the great western museums. In the grounds behind this building are other museums housing contemporary Japanese art, pottery, Chinese art and assorted other collections. Some regard these are more interesting than the main museum.

Kurashiki Historical Museum (Rekishi-kan) This museum is apart from the others and can be reached in 10-15 minutes on foot.

Ivy Square Built as a textile factory soon after the Meiji restoration in 1868, this ivy-covered red brick complex has been converted into a cluster of tourist attractions. It is of greatest interest to the Japanese (to whom such a brick structure is exotic), but there is a small museum of the Kurashiki textile industry, plus restaurants, coffee houses, an open square, and a hotel.

Information
The city has an information office near the Ohara Museum. If you are beginning your travels in Tokyo, you should pick up a copy of the photocopied information sheet on Kurashiki at the TIC.

Accommodation
In addition to the hotel in Ivy Square,

there are many hotels and ryokan of various price ranges, as well as a pleasant hilltop youth hostel. Assistance in finding a room is available at the railway station.

Getting There
Kurashiki is accessible by Shinkansen via Shin-Kurashiki station, but the connections make it simpler to transfer from Okayama station (also on the Shinkansen), which allows a short visit to Okayama as well.

NEAR KURASHIKI
Just north of Kurashiki is the Kibi plain, which was settled long before recorded history; many historic and prehistoric remains may be found in the area. Kibitsu-hiko-jinja shrine at the foot of a forested hill (near Bizen-Mikado station) is one of the attractions; its main building is built in an unusual Kibitsu-zukuri style, and dates from 1425 (a national treasure).

Tsukuriyama Tomb Mound
In the same area is the Tsukuriyama tomb mound, the largest such burial site in the Kibi area, and the fourth largest in Japan. Similar mounds are found in Kyushu, near Osaka (including the largest), and near Tokyo. The practice of building such mounds was also prevalent in Korea, so the question remains whether these people were Korean in origin, or if they were only influenced by the culture across the water. It is a keyhole-shaped mound of earth 350 metres long, 238 metres wide

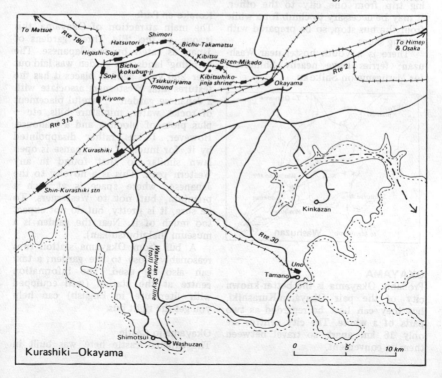

Kurashiki—Okayama

earth 350 metres long, 238 metres wide at the greatest point, and 25 metres high. It is of limited interest to most people, however, because it resembles nothing so much as another hill, even though man-made; its significance is more interesting.

Another attraction in the same area is Bichu-Kokubunji temple. It has a picturesque five-storey temple. To reach these attractions, make inquiries locally.

WASHUZAN

An excellent view over the Inland Sea is available at Washuzan, almost due south of Kurashiki. Buses run many times a day from Kurashiki station, taking about 80 minutes. Buses also run regularly from Okayama station (90 minutes), so you can make a looping trip from one city to the other. It may be necessary to climb for a while from the bus stop, so be prepared with walking shoes.

There is a youth hostel near Washuzan; ferries leave nearby Shimotsui for Marugame on Shikoku.

Washuzan

OKAYAMA

Probably Okayama is the better-known city of the pair Okayama-Kurashiki, but they can best be regarded as two parts of a whole. The city centres are only 16 km apart, so travel between them is convenient.

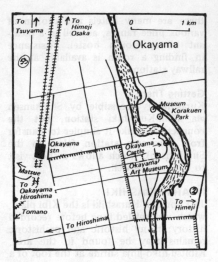

Okayama

Korako-en Park

The main attraction of Okayama, this is one of the 'Big Three' gardens of Japan as rated by the Japanese. The 'strolling' landscape garden was laid out over 290 years ago. In places it has the features that Westerners associate with a Japanese garden — careful placement of rocks, water, miniature hills, etc — plus plots of blooms, and a teahouse. However, I was rather disappointed by it, for much of its expanse is open lawn similar to that found in any Western park. This is a novelty to the Japanese, where space is at such a premium, but not to Westerners. To be sure, it is pretty, but do not expect too much of it. Near the garden is a museum (hakubutsu-kan).

A bus from Okayama station runs reasonably close to the garden; a taxi can also be used. The information centre at the station (well equipped with literature in English) can help you get the right bus.

Okayama-jo Castle

The original castle here was built in

1573, but subsequently destroyed. The present concrete reconstruction preserves the external appearance, and adds a traditional note to the Korako-en, which it overlooks. It is black, in contrast with the white of the castle at Himeji (Japan's finest); its nickname, 'Ujo' (crow) is a joke on the name of Himeji's pride, which translates as 'white egret'. The castle is only a short distance from Korako-en and is accessible by a bridge across the river. Nearby is Okayama Art Museum (Okayama Bijutsukan).

Kinkazan

An excursion from Okayama passes by Kojima Bay to Kinkazan hill. The bay is not spectacular, but is interesting for being the second largest man-made lake in the world (after one in Holland). It allowed the reclamation of a large area of farm land.

Kinkazan hill (403 metres) offers one of the best views of the Inland Sea. At the time of writing, there are three buses a day from Okayama station (8.08 am, 11.13 am and 2.53 pm), taking an hour for the trip. The return buses leave at 10 am, 1.20 pm and 4.10 pm. It would be wise to check if this schedule has been changed.

Festivals

On the night of the first Saturday in February, Saidai-ji is the scene of an interesting festival when loin-clothed young men vie to keep two sacred wands (shingi) that are thrown into their midst; the wands are supposed to bring lifelong happiness.

NEAR OKAYAMA
Shibukawa-hama Beach

One of the best beaches (white sand, etc) is about eight km from Uno station, accessible by train from Okayama to Uno station, and by bus from there in 25 minutes.

Tsuyama

Inland, due north of Okayama, lies Tsuyama. In cherry-blossom season the site of the old castle (destroyed in 1873) is very beautiful, for the grounds (now Kakuzan-koen) are planted with 8000 cherry trees. Of interest at any time to historians is the site of a Yogoi-era (pre-Yamato Japanese civilisation) pit-dwelling that has been excavated. Little is known of the people of that era, but their pottery and the remnants of their dwellings of 2000 years ago have been found in many parts of Japan. About 2.5 km north-east of Numa station, one Yayoi-type dwelling has been reconstructed and is open to the public.

BIZEN

The city of Bizen is famous in Japan for the pottery known as Bizen-yaki; numerous potteries and kilns are to be found in and around the city. The pottery is of a very old (1200 years) and simple style, obtaining its characteristic finish and patterns in the firing rather than the glazing.

An interesting sidelight of the pottery craft, it is reported, is a reduction in the number of birds in the coastal area. So many pine trees have (reportedly) been cut down that the roosts

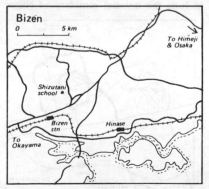

Bizen
0   5 km
To Himeji & Osaka
Shizutani school
Bizen stn
Hinase
To Okayama

and sources of insects have been reduced.

Shizutani School This historical school is unrecognizable as such to Westerners. It dates from 1666, and resembles classical schools of China and Korea. It was the first school in Japan for commoners. The white-walled buildings are roofed with Bizen-ware tiles, and surrounded with a rock-covered earthen wall that is broken by picturesque small gates. It is located at the foot of a tree-covered hill that is coloured in autumn. The appearance of the school is very uncommon in a Japanese setting.

HYOGO-KEN

HIMEJI

The city of Himeji is noteworthy for the finest castle in Japan. Begun on a modest scale in the 16th century, it was expanded by later daimyo until it reached its present form in the early 1800s, and was restored to nearly original condition in the 1960s. It is located on a hill not far from Himeji station, and its white form can be seen soon after leaving the station's front exit.

Other, lesser, attractions of Himeji include the unusual cemetery of Nago-

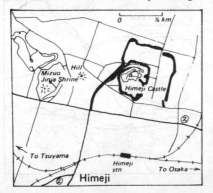

yama (15 minutes from the station by bus), and Enkyo Temple at the top of Shosha-san (eight km from the station). Access from Shosha station is by bus then a cable-car.

Himeji can be easily reached from Kyoto, Osaka and Kobe, and can be visited as a day trip from these cities. Regular train service (JNR) from Kyoto takes about 2¼ hours, a little over 1½ hours from Osaka. By Shinkansen (for those not counting pennies), Kyoto is only about one hour away, and Osaka (Shin-Osaka station) about 40 minutes.

Hakuro-jo Castle

Hakuro-jo (White Egret Castle) is made up of 78 individual buildings, the main one standing five storeys high. It is a defensive castle despite its aesthetic appearance, approached by narrow paths that can be showered with arrows from slits in the walls. In contrast, the upper part (which was unassailable) was designed for the best in gracious living, as defined by the tastes of the day; this can be seen in the delicate wood carving and bronze decorations around the rooms.

A couple of hours can easily be spent exploring the interior and exterior, observing the defensive details, racks for spears, the massive wooden pillars that support the upper storeys, etc.

The castle is easily reached on foot in 15 minutes from the station (less by taxi). The lighting for photos is most dramatic as the sun gets low in the sky. An interesting vantage point for those determined enough and with a telephoto lens, is the top of the hill where Mizuo-jinja shrine stands.

Festivals

At Hiromine-jinja, the Rice Planting Festival is held on 3 April, and the Spring Festival on 17-18 April. At Matsubara Hichiman-jinja (near Shirahama-no-miya station), Kenka-matsuri is held on 14-15 October.

AKASHI

Apart from the stone walls and two turrets remaining of the old castle, the main interest of Akashi is that it is one port for ferries to Iwaya on nearby Awaji-shima island; the trip takes 25 minutes.

KOBE

Kobe is an international port of entry to Japan, mostly for passengers of cruise liners, and also an industrial and commercial city. In a reversal of the old saying, it is considered a nice place to live, but you wouldn't want to visit there. Mt Rokko provides a view over the city, but there is relatively little else for a short-term visitor (new residents will learn the points of interest from old hands are soon after arrival). For this reason, most of the following information refers to getting to the nearby cities of Kyoto, Nara and Himeji.

Visiting liners docks at Pier 4. From there a wide road (known among foreigners as The Bund) goes straight to Sannomiya station, effectively the main station of Kobe. Bus 92 runs between the station and the port, and taxis are also available.

Trains

Kyoto and Osaka Trains for Kyoto leave Sannomiya station from track 2. The trip takes 60-70 minutes (depending on stops) and costs somewhat under Y1000. There are many trains throughout the day (between 8 am and 3 pm there are 41 trains); as well as commuter trains that make more stops and take closer to 90 minutes, running every 15 minutes or so. An alternative is a Shinkansen train from Shin-Kobe station (10 minutes from Sannomiya by bus 4); but the quick trip (under 40 minutes) is counterbalanced by the extra time to get to Shin-Kobe station,

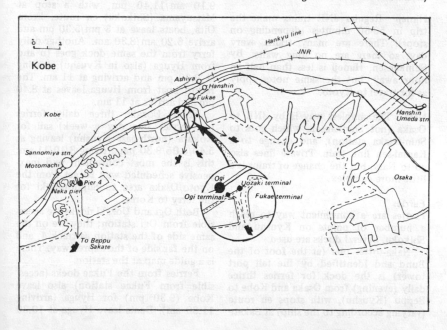

the smaller number of trains (20 during the same period, 39 for the day) which means a longer wait, and the fare which is more than 2½ times as high. Because of the stop at Osaka, and limitations to reduce noise in the urban area, the trains do not reach their top speed and the trip is less exciting than on other routes.

A new express service (the 'City Liner') has also been announced between Himeji and Kyoto, with stops only at Akashi, Sannomiya and Osaka; when operational, it will be the fastest practical service to use, so make inquiries.

There are also private lines on the same routes, which are generally less expensive than JNR but not as quick. The Hankyu line goes from Sannomiya station to Kyoto via Osaka (74 minutes Kobe-Kyoto by express), and to Takarazuka, while the Hanshin line (from Motomachi) goes only to Osaka.

Himeji Regular JNR trains make the trip in 50-60 minutes (depending on stops). There are many trains every day, so there are no long waits. By Shinkansen, Himeji is less than half an hour away, but the same notes apply as for travel to Kyoto.

Nara The simplest way is by JNR to Osaka (not Shinkansen, which goes to Shin-Osaka station), and change to a Kansai-sen line train. Private lines also go to Nara, but the change of trains is a little more complex.

Ferries

Ferries are a convenient way to reach a number of points on Kyushu and Shikoku. Several docks are used.

Naka-tottei pier (at the foot of the Bund and identified by the tall port tower) is the dock for ferries thrice daily (evening) from Osaka and Kobe to Beppu (Kyushu), with stops en route (varying according to the ship) at Sakate

(Shodo Island), Takamatsu, Imabari and Matsuyama (all on Shikoku). Boats leave Osaka/Kobe at 4.30/6 pm, 9/11 pm, and 9.40/11.10 pm, reaching Beppu at 8 am, 11.50 am, 12.40 pm (next day), respectively.

The other ferries leave from the area collectively known as Higashi-Kobe (East Kobe) which comprises Ogi, Uozaki and Fukae docks. The first two are reached most conveniently from Ogi station of the Hanshin line, the latter from Fukae station of the same line. Express trains do not stop at these stations, so you will need to take a local train from Kobe/Osaka, or an express from Osaka to Hanshin-Ashiya station, with a change to the local line. (Trains from Osaka leave Hanshin-Umeda station; from Kobe, Motomachi station.)

Ferries from Ogi docks sail daily to and from Oita (Kyushu), leaving Kobe at 6.30 pm/9 pm and arriving 9.10 am/11.40 pm, with a stop at Matsuyama (Shikoku) en route. From Oita, boats leave at 3 pm/5.30 pm and arrive 6.20 am/8.30 am. Another daily ferry from the same dock goes to and from Hyuga (also in Kyushu), leaving at 9.30 pm and arriving at 11 am. The return boat from Hyuga leaves at 8.40 pm and arrives at 11 am.

From Uozaki, three daily ferries (no service one day a week) sail for Kokura (north-east Kyushu) leaving at 5.40/8.05/9.30 pm arriving 8/10/11 am; this is the most convenient and inexpensive scheduled way to get from the Kyoto/Osaka area to Shimonoseki for the ferry to Korea.

Both Ogi and Uozaki docks are accessible from Ogi station; they are on the same side of the station as track 4, and on the far side of the expressway. There is a guide map at the station.

Ferries from the Fukae docks (accessible from Fukae station) also leave Kobe (9.30 pm) for Hyuga (arriving 11.30 am). Boats leave Hyuga at 10.30

pm and arrives at 12.30 pm. (This service is once every two days.)

If you plan to go by ferry between Osaka/Kobe and Kyushu, remember that the latest departure will give the most daylight hours in the morning for enjoying the sights of the Inland Sea (described below).

Social

Home Visit Programme A visit the home of a Japanese family (afternoon or evening) is an enjoyable experience and can be arranged by contacting the organizers (Sannomiya Kotsu Centre Building, 2F, near Sannomiya station; tel 391-4753), or through your hotel or shipping company.

Food

Kobe is famous for a type of beef that takes the name of the city. It is reputed to be delicious (and is very expensive, even more so than the already outrageous prices charged for beef of any kind in Japan), but it is very fatty and might not appeal if you are accustomed to lean beef.

Portopia '81

During 1981 (March-September) the Kobe Port Island Exposition, known more simply as Portopia '81, was held on the newly-completed artificial Kobe Port Island.

A new train line connects Sannomiya station (the main JNR station) with Minami-koen station at the south of the island, near the expo site. The trains are computer-controlled and require no operator.

There is also a bus from Shin-Kobe or Sannomiya station, and a ferry from Central Pier.

THE INLAND SEA

The Inland Sea (Seto Naikai) is one of

those areas in Japan about which travel writers have traditionally written in superlatives. The fact is that, while there *are* many very lovely views around this body of water, it has changed greatly since it first came to the notice of western eyes, and many fishing villages have been replaced by modern industries — substituting 'progress' and pollution for once-idyllic scenes. The waters are filled with large numbers of ships, and the peace and serenity of 20-30 years ago are gone. Anyone arriving with the expectation of charming views at every turn is doomed to disappointment, but time spent seeking out some or all of the places mentioned below will be rewarded.

Along the north shore of the sea, good views are available (from east to west) near Okayama/Kurashiki, Onomichi, Fukuyama and Itsukushima, as well as at Shimonoseki, which marks the western end of the sea. (Each vantage point is described under the appropriate city.) The most beautiful maritime views are in the area bounded on the east by Shodo Island, and on the west by Tono-no-ura (Honshu) and Tadotsu (Shikoku).

Four long-distance ferries pass through much or all of the area in daylight hours. The boat from Osaka/Kobe to Beppu reaches Imabari at 6.25 am, so it enters the most scenic part near daybreak in summer (since it is light as early as 4.30 am). The 10.30 pm ferry (every second day) from Hyuga (Kyushu) to Kobe passes the Hiroshima area around 7-8 am, so it takes the entire scenic area by daylight; as does the daily ferry from Hyuga to Kobe (leaving at 10.40 pm). The ferry from Shibushi (southern Kyushu) to Osaka arrives at 10.10 am, so it would likewise take in much of the most scenic area by daylight.

There are many more ferry runs across the sea between ports on Honshu and Shikoku, lasting from less than half an hour (by hydrofoil) to more than four hours. All the lines are listed in *Jikokuhyo*, the best of which include Shimotsui—Tomari—Marugame, Okayama—Tonosho—Takamatsu, Tomo-no-ura—Tadotsu, Onomichi—Setoda—Imabari, Hiroshima—Imabari, Onomichi—Matsuyama and Hiroshima—Matsuyama.

The best way to enjoy the mood of the Inland Sea (if you have time to spare) is to pick an island or two and spend some time there. Some have youth hostels, and an island of any size is sure to have a minshuku; an isolated area is the best place to enjoy the homely pleasures of minshuku accommodation.

AWAJI-SHIMA

This is the largest island in the Inland Sea and one of the most densely populated islands in Japan. It is relatively flat and agricultural, holding no fantastic visual delights. It serves as a bridge

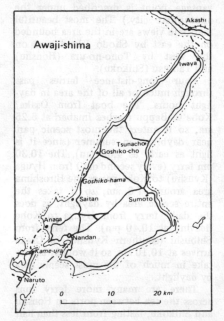

between the Kobe area (via Akashi) and Shikoku.

Puppet Theatre

Awaji appears to be the home of the oldest puppet theatre in Japan, more ancient though less famous than the Bunraku of Osaka. Short (about 30 minutes) performances of puppet plays are given daily at the small puppet theatre (Ningyo-za) by the ferry dock at Fukura at 11 am between 1 March and 30 November. At other times, you must be content with a look at the large number of puppets on display around the walls.

It was feared that the puppetry tradition would die out completely, for the 15 performers at Fukura are the only people left on Awaji, and their average age is close to 70. However, a renaissance seems to be in action, so there may be a return to the golden days of the start of the Meiji era, when there were 48 theatres on Awaji.

Naruto Whirlpools

The whirlpools are almost next door to Fukura. They are at their mightiest at high and low tide, when water swirls into or out of the Inland Sea through the narrow (1.3 km) Naruto Strait between Awaji and Shikoku. Like the famous Reversing Falls of the St John river in New Brunswick (Canada), rapids run in one direction at high tide and in the opposite at full ebb. It is necessary to catch either extreme to see the whirlpools at their greatest (over 20 metres across); tide tables are posted at touristed locales, and places of accommodation should also have the information. There is a lookout over the strait, accessible by toll road, a little to the north of Fukura and near the pier of the giant bridge going across the strait. Cruise boats from Fukura travel very close to the whirlpools, though without danger.

Other

Other sightseeing on Awaji-shima includes the beaches and sea views of Goshikihama and Kei-no-Matsubara. The former (meaning 'five-coloured beach') has multicoloured pebbles. Each stretches several km, and both are accessible by bus from Sumoto in less than an hour.

Accommodation

There are several hotels, ryokan and minshuku around the island, as well as a pleasant (temple) youth hostel at Sumoto, the major town.

Getting There

From Kobe, ferries cross to Sumoto; and from Akashi, ferries are available to Iwaya. At the south end ferries cross from Nandan to Naruto, and from Anaga to Kame-ura (both destinations on Shikoku).

SHODO-SHIMA

Everyone who visits Shodo Island has a good word for it. It is sufficiently off the beaten track not to be over-run with tourists, but it has adequate accommodation and travel facilities, as well as lots of beautiful scenery.

The main attraction of the island is Kanka-kei Gorge, near the east end (a cable-car descends through the most scenic part). There are also many fine views of unspoilt countryside, tidy terraced paddies up hillsides, mountains, farmers and fishermen; as well as quarries that supplied the giant stones for Osaka Castle. Other sights include groves of olives (in the south and central part of the island), a replica of a Greek temple (at Tayo-no-Oka Heiwa-koen) overlooking the sea and beautiful scenery; and a monkey park (friendly simians in the lower park, unfriendly higher): even a short-time visitor can get a feel for the social organization within their community.

Getting Around

Getting around Shodo is no problem, for buses run regularly — both special sightseeing coaches and scheduled public transport. The usual starting point is Tonosho, but tour buses also leave from Sakata, and possibly from other ports served by ferries (generally it seems that there is a tour bus waiting for each ferry arrival). More than one person has liked the relaxed pace of Shodo life and stayed for several days. You can get a good idea of its attractions by taking a bus tour upon arrival, then explore by public bus afterward.

Ferries connect the towns of Tonosho, Ikeda, and Fukuda (on Shodo) with Takamatsu, Ono, Okayama, Hinase, Himeji, Kobe and Osaka. Check the schedules in *Jikokuhyo*, or get help at an information centre or travel agency.

Accommodation

Accommodation is usually no problem, for there are many ryokan plus two youth hostels. Assistance in finding a roof is available at the information centre at both Tonosho and Sakate.

OTHER ISLANDS

From Shodo-shima, you can island-hop via Toyo-shima to Uno, near Okayama. Other pleasant, really off-the-beaten-track islands (some are listed below) are located between Imabari (Shikoku) and Mihara (Honshu), and accessible (along with nearby islands) from both places. Anyone really interested in this type of exploring might try to obtain a copy of Nancy Phelan's book, *A Pillow of Grass.*

Ikuguchi

The island offers views of orange groves, shrines, temples and, most important, an atmosphere of rural Japan. Besides the youth hostel overlooking a quiet village, there are also ryokan and minshuku.

Innoshima

This island is also pleasant, but has no

youth hostel. Ikuguchi Island is 'next-door', however.

Omishima

This island, 15 km off the north coast of the Kurushima-hanto Peninsula, is noted for the Oyamazumi-jinja shrine, dedicated to the guardian gods of sailors. In historic times it was visited by many warriors off to battle, and a large amount of the finest armour was donated in supplication for good fortune in battle. As a result, 80% of all the armour in Japan that has survived and been given the rating 'national treasure' or 'important cultural property' belongs to this shrine. The shrine is near Miyaura, the town where ferries dock. (Those interested in armous should inquire before making the trip to the island, to ascertain whether the armour is on display or 'preserved' there but out of sight.)

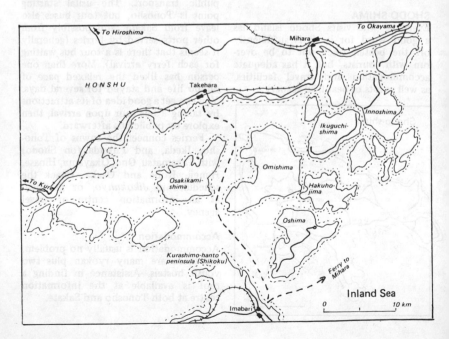

Inland Sea

0   10 km

Shikoku

Shikoku is the fourth main island of the Japanese group. It is generally rural and gets bypassed by most travellers, but it has a couple of unique attractions that could be of interest if you have a little extra time.

On Shikoku, you are almost sure to see large numbers of pilgrims dressed in white who are making a pilgrimage to the 88 temples related to the priest Kobo-Daishi. It should not be difficult to locate the temples, for they are marked by roadsigns (in Japanese only), but few are outstanding.

Getting There

There is a great variety of ship services to and from Honshu or Kyushu. There are also air services from the principle cities in each of the four prefectures that give Shikoku its name of Four Districts.

NARUTO (KAGAWA-KEN)

The great whirlpools of the Naruto strait have already been described in the section on Awaji-shima. From the Shikoku side, an excellent view is available from Naruto Park on Oge-shima Island (eight km north-east of Naruto city); buses run from Naruto station. The park is also accessible from Awaji-shima by ferry from Anaga (a little above Fukura), and there is also a ferry service from Fukura.

TOKUSHIMA

This city is known for a crazy dance, puppets, and a fine garden. One of the most famous festivals in Japan is the Awa-odori (15-18 August) when large numbers of celebrants dressed in traditional costume dance in the city streets through much of the night.

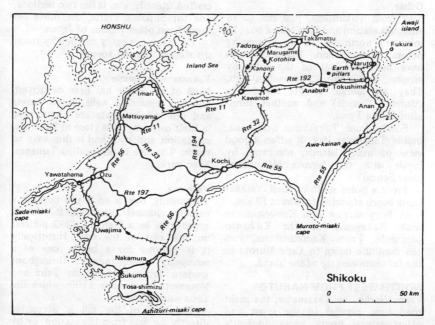

Shikoku

0   50 km

Getting There

There is a ferry service every few days between Tokyo and Kokura (Kyushu), stopping at Tokushima en route in the late morning/early afternoon.

Puppet Theatre

Along with Awaji-shima and Osaka, Tokushima has a tradition of puppet theatre. Performances are usually given by farmers, so they are more likely to be seen after harvest time and before planting; make inquiries locally.

Tokushima Park

This park contains a garden that was part of the mansion associated with Tokushima Castle (now ruined), and which dates from 1586. It is a landscape garden typical of the Momoyama period. The park is 400 metres east of the station.

Other

East from Tokushima, you can go to Anabuki station and then take a bus (15 minutes) north-east to an interesting natural phenomenon. Pillars of earth have been cut out of the earth by erosion, and stand 12-18 metres high. They are similar to the Hoodos in Alberta (Canada) and another formation in the Tyrol.

South from Tokushima lies Anan, beside Tachibana Bay. It offers a good view of many islands, compared by locals with the famous Matsushima (near Sendai).

From a point south of Mugi, Yasakahama beach stretches for about 10 km.

A ferry service links Komatsushima with Wakayama on the Kii-hanto peninsula. From Komatsushima, you can continue down to Cape Muroto at the far south-east tip of the island.

NORTH-WEST FROM NARUTO

From Naruto to Takamatsu, the main road runs parallel to the coast and offers several pretty views (lookouts are provided by the road). The rafts visible in the water are used to grow edible seaweed.

TAKAMATSU

Probably the most pleasant city on Shikoku, Takamatsu features one of the finest gardens in Japan as well as a number of other attractions.

Ritsurin-koen Garden

This is one of the finest gardens in Japan, superior (in my eyes) to at least two of the 'Big Three' gardens — those at Mito and Okayama — and at least the equal of Kenroku-en in Kanazawa. It is built around an interconnected series of ponds and concentrates a large variety of views, taking advantage of a large hill and natural forest in its plan. It dates from the mid-1600s.

A folk-craft museum in the park features an excellent collection of hand-crafted utensils, etc. It has two sections, one for Shikoku crafts, the other for those from other regions of Japan.

The garden is easily reached by tram: the stop is Ritsurin-koen.

Takamatsu-jo Castle

Most of the castle has been destroyed, but the remaining walls, three turrets and one original gate are picturesque in their own way. It is close to Takamatsu station and pier, and is thus easy to reach. The site is now called Tamamo-koen park.

Yashima

Technically this is an island because a narrow channel surrounds it, but it appears to be a high hill (292 metres) on the east of the city. Historically it is famous for a battle, one of a seemingly endless number throughout western Japan between the Taira and Minamoto in the late 1100s which the Taira usually lost.

The top of the hill is accessible directly by bus from the station, or by

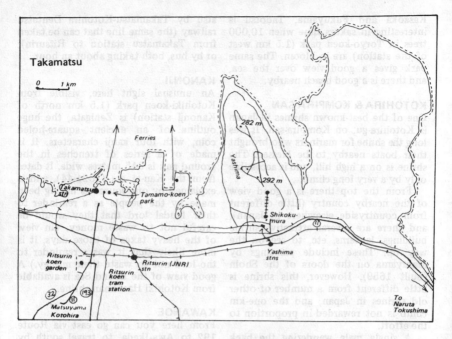

tram and cable-car to the south peak. At the top, Yashima-ji Temple has a display of relics from the battles, while the north peak offers a good view over the Inland Sea.

Shikoku-mura

This is a collection of typical, traditional buildings from various locations around the island, and includes a vine suspension bridge of the type once common in isolated valleys. It is interesting if you have not visited such a 'village' elsewhere, but could be a bit of a letdown if you have already been to Takayama.

Megishima Island

This tiny island (eight km in circumference) is famous to Japanese through the children's story of Momotaro, a boy who cleaned out a pack of demons. It offers a good view of the Inland Sea; it is only four km from the city, and

easily reached by ferry.

Accommodation

There are two youth hostels at Takamatsu, as well as ryokan, minshuku and hotels.

Getting There

Ferries link Takamatsu with Osaka, Kobe, Himeji, Shodo Island (Tonosho and Ikeda), and Uno (near Okayama).

MARUGAME

Of greatest interest for ferry connections to Honshu (Shimotsui, near Kurashiki, and Tomo-no-ura near Fukuyama), Marugame also has some gates and structures of Marugame Castle (built in 1597); the castle is about one km south of the station.

TADOTSU

In addition to ferry connections to

Kasaoka and Fukuyama, Tadotsu is interesting in sakura time when 10,000 trees in Toryo-koen park (1.5 km west of the station) are in bloom. The same park gives a good view over the sea, and there is a good beach nearby.

KOTOHIRA & KOMPIRA-SAN

One of the best-known shrines in Japan is Kotohira-gu, on Kompira-san. It was long the shrine for mariners who brought their boats nearby to be blessed. The shrine is on a high hill, and is accessible only by a very long climb.

From the top there is a good view of the nearby country (little different from countryside elsewhere in Japan), and there are several attractive shrine buildings, lanterns, etc, to see on the way up. These include paintings by Maruyama on the doors of the Shoin (built 1659). However, this shrine is little different from a number of other old shrines in Japan, and the one-km climb is not rewarded in proportion to the effort.

A single male wandering the back streets at night might get the impression that not all visitors to Kotohira come for a religious experience, as a woman in a dimly-lit window may beckon conspiratorially and offer 'Korean women'. (Koreans are widely believed by Japanese to have no morals.)

Accommodation

Of interest to anyone wanting to sample gracious ryokan living would be a small cluster of high-class (and price) inns at the foot of the hill where the path (and rows of souvenir stands) begins. Several have very ornate carved wooden panels, intimate gardens, and other 'typical' Japanalia (that are not seen so often, in fact). Of minor interest, just a little to the south, is an old-style bridge with a decorative roof.

Getting There

Kotohira is easily reached from Takam-atsu by Takamatsu-Kotohira Dentetsu railway (the same line that can be taken from Takamatsu station to Ritsurin), or by bus, both taking about an hour.

KANONJI

An unusual sight here, visible from Kotohiki-koen park (1.5 km north of Kanonji station) is Zenigata, the huge outline of an ancient square-holed coin, with four kanji characters. It is made of a series of trenches in the ground and is 345 metres wide. It dates from the Kan-ei era (1624-44), and is explained by one source as having been made by the people as a reminder to their feudal lord that they would be careful not to waste money. (In view of the heavy taxes of those days, it is more likely that it was a reminder to the lord not to waste their money.) A good view of the Inland Sea is available from Kotohiki Hachiman shrine.

KAWANOE

From here you can go east via Route 192 to Awa-Ikeda, to travel south by the (recommended) route described below. You can also travel west, but the north coast is relatively industrial and of little interest. The following description follows a route south from Takimatsu.

AWA-IKEDA TO KOCHI

South of Kompira lies some lovely inland scenery of the mountain and valley type. The starting point is Awa-Ikeda, not far below Kompira: you can either follow the main road (Route 32 and JNR), or branch inland for a while. Road and rail continue through the valley of the Yoshino river, passing the biggest gorge in Shikoku, which is particularly noteworthy for a 7.5 km stretch which includes two picturesque rock formations (Koboke and Oboke). There is a JNR station near each, both of which are accessible by train or bus from Awa-Ikeda station. From a

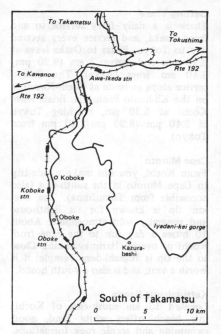

To Takamatsu
To Tokushima
To Kawanoe
Awa-Ikeda stn
Rte 192
Rte 192

O Koboke
Koboke stn
Oboke
Oboke stn
Iyadani-kei gorge
Kazura-bashi

South of Takamatsu

0   5   10 km

point two km north of Oboke, a boat is available for a descent of the river (30-40 minutes), ending about 3.5 km from Koboke station. A toll road links Oboke to Iyadani Gorge.

Iyadani-kei Gorge

This is a very lovely valley rather off the beaten track. The gorge extends from a point near Iyaguchi for about 45 km to Sugeoi. After only a few km a toll road branches west to rejoin Route 32, and a short distance past the junction is Iya-no-kazura-bashi, the last surviving original vine suspension bridge of the type once common in this region (they had the advantage of being easily cut to block the ingress of invaders). The inhabitants of the valley are believed to be descendants of the Taira who survived the defeat at Yashima and retreated here, much as other Taira descendants are found in the Shirakawa-

go area of Gifu-ken. (The bridge is of the same type as that at Shikoku-mura in Takamatsu; those in a rush can be content with the latter.) There is a fee for crossing the bridge, and the keeper becomes angry if you set foot on it without paying.

There are several buses daily running through the very pretty valley to Sugeoi. Beyond that the bus continues in a near-circle north to Sadamitsu station; an area where a foreigner is sure to be a rarity. From there it would be simple to return to Awa-Ikeda; alternatively, you can backtrack to the toll road (and out to Oboke to take the boat ride, or just continue south toward Kochi).

Jofuki-ji

On the way to Kochi, Toyonaga station is the landmark for Jofuki-ji. Not a famous 'sight', it is a temple cum youth hostel. The young priest speaks good English, is very friendly and well-travelled, and is happy to introduce guests to Zen, including meditation. One French girl stayed more than two weeks, and it is easy to understand why, for the surroundings are peaceful and beautiful. The temple is located high on the side of the valley among tall trees; it is 1.7 km from the station (ask for directions on arrival).

Buraku-ji

Located one km north of Otaguchi station, this temple is noted for the architecture of its main hall (hondo), Yakushido, which was built in 1151. It is a national treasure, and a good example of Fujiwara architecture (897-1192).

Ryugado Cave

Discovered only in 1931, this cave contains clay dishes of a prehistoric people. It features stalagmites and stalactites and other sights of a typical limestone cave. It is accessible in 20 minutes by bus from Tosa-Yamada station.

Oshino

The Kochi area is noted historically for the raising of roosters with incredibly long tail plumage, sometimes more than six metres in length. The village of Oshino is the centre where such birds are raised (said to be a fading interest). Oshino is a district in the city of Nangoku, accessible from Gomen station. Local inquiries in the city (or possibly in Kochi) would be required to track down such birds.

KOCHI

The main attraction of Kochi is its five-storey castle, the present buildings dating from 1748. It gives an open view of the city and surrounding hills (which I found to be of quite limited interest).

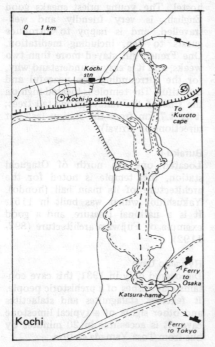

Kochi

Getting There

There is a daily ferry service to and from Osaka, and service every second day to Tokyo. Boats to Osaka leave at 9.20 pm and arrive 7 am (9.20 pm/ 6.40 am from Osaka). The Tokyo service stops en route at Nachi-Katsuura on the Kii-hanto Peninsula. Boats leave Kochi at 5.30 pm, reaching Tokyo at 2.40 pm (6.20 pm/3.40 pm from Tokyo).

Cape Muroto

From Kochi, you can make a side-trip to Cape Muroto in the south-east (also accessible from Tokushima). The five-km tip is known for its lighthouse and generally wild atmosphere. About 10 buses a day run to the cape from Kochi or nearby Harimaya-bashi. Close to the tip is Higashi-dera Temple; it is worth a visit, and is also a youth hostel.

Katsurahama Beach

Located 13 km south-east of Kochi, this beach offers white sand, good swimming and scenic rock formations. it is accessible in 35 minutes, by bus from Kochi station. Collectors of sea-shells will find a wide variety of beautiful specimens on sale at very reasonable prices.

Ino

This is a town noted for producing hand-made paper (local inquiries would yield directions to watch the process). The town is the last stop of the Kochi tram system.

ASHIZURI-MISAKI CAPE

The beauties of this cape and the surrounding area are reached from Tosa-Shimizu: three roads, each with its own bus service, run to the tip. The coastal road is adventurously narrow, while the central (toll) road — the Ashizuri Skyline — passes over the central ridge, skirting 433-metre Shiraou-san. (The name Ashizuri translates as 'leg-

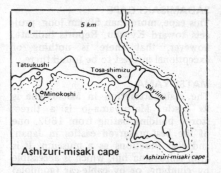

Ashizuri-misaki cape

grazing', quite possibly a reference to the narrowness of the paths of olden times.) Attractions of the tip are the wildness, the lighthouse, and Kongo-fuku-ji temple, close enough to the sea for you to hear the crash of the surf. Today's temple dates back 300 years, but there has been one on the site for more than 1100 years. The vegetation verges on tropical, with palms and banyan trees, and there are coral reefs to contrast with granite cliffs.

MINOKOSHI AREA

Continuing west from Tosa-Shimizu leads to the coastal area of Minokoshi that contains some of the most beautiful views of all. Glass-bottomed boats can be hired to see the colourful fish of the coral reefs. Beside the road are eroded limestone cliffs of wondrous shapes, which lead up to another strange rock formation at Tatsukushi. Tatsukushi means 'dragon skewers', a name taken from numbers of slim cylinders of stone.

The Hall of Shells At Tatsukushi town is a very interesting museum that displays nothing but seashells — about 50,000 of them, including many rare and beautiful types. The building is modern and the displays are well planned. Many typhoons pass through this area and stir up the sea bottom, bringing large numbers of shells.

NORTH FROM MINOKOSHI

The coast north from the Minokoshi area is also very scenic, although of the rias type (submerged fingers of land). There are views of the sea and the coast to the west, orange groves and other greenery to the east — sometimes in both directions when the road goes a little inland. From Sukumo there is ferry service to Saiki on Kyushu.

UWAJIMA

Uwajima has several attractions. Places of interest include Uwajima Castle (dating from 1665), and Atago-koen Park on a hill high enough to give a good view of the city and sea. The impression of this city and the entire coast is of unusually lush foliage. There is a fine landscape garden, ('Heavenly Forgiveness Garden'), two km south of the city.

Bull Fights Uwajima is famous for bullfights (togyu). These are not the kind that pit matador against animal with the result of hundreds of kg of beef, but are contests between two animals that lock horns and try to push the other backwards. Generally there is a fight every month; but, with the exception of Wareisai summer festival (23-4 July), dates vary from year to year. Information offices such as the TIC in Tokyo or Kyoto, as well as travel agencies, should be able to provide

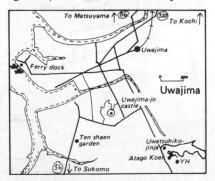

details. Ehime-ken also maintains an office in Tokyo and other large cities, so a friend can phone in Japanese for up-to-date information. The fights are held at 'Togyu-jo' at the foot of Tenman-yama, a 30-minute walk from Uwajima station.

OZU

There is ukai (cormorant fishing) on the river at Ozu from 1 June to 20 September.

YAWAWATAHAMA

The hillsides behind this port city are noted for the scenic appearance of their terraces as well as the many orange groves. Kinzan Shusseki Temple, at the top of Kinzan, gives an excellent view of the Inland Sea and as far away as Kyushu. Yawarahama is a convenient port for ferries to Oita and Beppu, both in Kyushu.

SADAMISAKI CAPE

This cape, more than 50 km long, projects toward Kyushu. Reports indicate, however, that there is nothing of exceptional interest to be found there.

MATSUYAMA

The main attraction in Matsuyama is its castle. Matsuyama-jo is a three-storey building dating from 1602, one of the best-preserved castles in Japan, and also functions as a museum. It is atop shiroyama hill, which is accessible by climbing, or by cable-car (gondola) from the east side (remote from the station).

Dogo-onsen

Matsuyama is famous among the Japanese for its nearby hot-spring resort, Dogo-onsen, which is known for the traditional architecture of its municipal bathhouse (Shinrokaku) and the variety

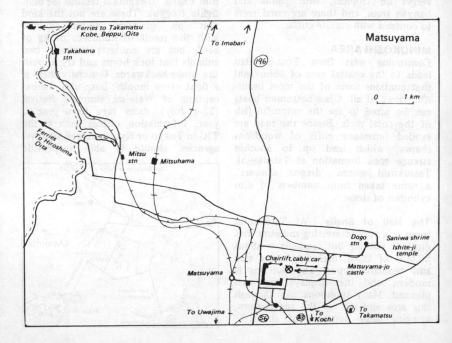

of waters available there. However, Japanese sources continually overstress hotsprings in tourist literature, so this one will be of limited interest to most.

Ishite Temple Near the hot spring, this is the only temple of note in the area. It dates back to 1318, and illustrates the Kamakura style of architecture of that day.

IMABARI

This is an industrial port city of no interest, located at the top of the Kurushima-hanto Peninsula. The nearby strait between Imabari and Oshima Island is famous for its whirlpools, that form at high and low tide like those at Naruto.

Getting There & Getting Around

There are many ferry services between Matsuyama and the ports of Kobe, Hiroshima, Onomichi, Iwakuni, Mihara, Yanai, Beppu and Oita. Oita is the terminus of a Kobe-Matsuyama-Oita (and reverse) service. Three ports near Matsuyama are used: Mitsuhama (accessible from Mitsu station of the local railway line), Matsuyama-kanko port, accessible from Takahama station of the same line, and Horie, on JNR north from the city. There are so many services that you should obtain details from an information service or the *Jikokuhyo*.

The Dogo area can be reached by bus or tram from Matsuyama.

Kyushu

Kyushu is the southernmost of the four main islands of Japan, and has many places of interest. It is the 'cradle of Japanese civilisation', for it was from here that the Yamato 'tribe' spread to the Kobe-Osaka-Ise area before subjugating the peoples already occupying other parts of the country. Kyushu has also been substantially influenced by continental civilisations, particularly Chinese and Korean, because it is the part of Japan closest to those countries. However, because of its antiquity (dating from about 600 BC) only archaeological remains are left, especially in the Usuki and Miyazaki areas. The main attractions of Kyushu are scenery, such as Mt Aso, the Yamanami Highway, Kagoshima/Sakurajima, Kirishima, various islands off the coasts, some interesting hot springs, and sightseeing (temples, shrines, Nagasaki, the anti-

Mongol wall, gardens, etc). The people of Kyushu also have a reputation for being more friendly than in most parts of Japan (although there can be no complaints about other people!).

The description begins at Kitakyushu in the north and follows an anti-clockwise circular route back. I also suggest some side-trips and shortcuts that will assist travellers with limited time, or those who begin their Kyushu travels at a different point.

FUKUOKA-KEN & SAGA-KEN

KITAKYUSHU
When crossing from Shimonoseki (on northern Honshu) to Kyushu, the first city encountered is Kitakyushu, a composite of five formerly separate

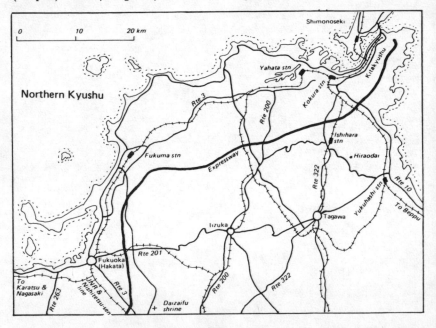

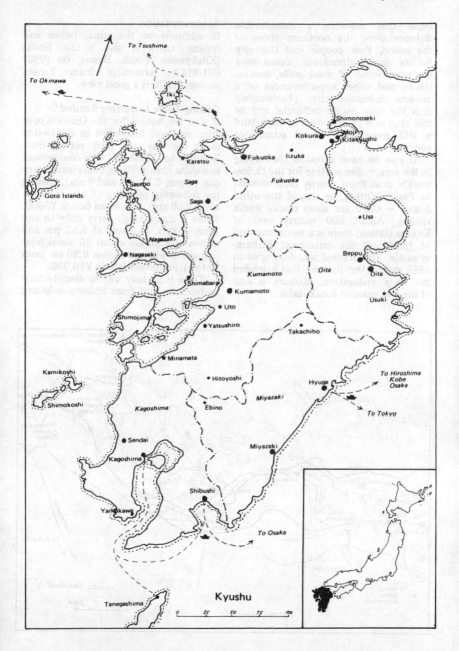

Kyushu

cities that stretches a considerable distance along the northern shore of the island. Few people visit this city for its tourist attractions, unless they are enamoured of steel mills, smokestacks and other appurtenances of a modern industrial city. (Fortunately it is the only major industrial city of this kind in Kyushu; most of the island is still green, and natural attractions abound.)

If you do have a reason for staying in the area — like waiting for the thrice-weekly boat from nearby Shimonoseki to Pusan (Korea), or one of the other ferries — there are some places worth visiting. About 500 metres west of Kokura station, there is a reconstruction of (parts of) the once-great Kokura-jo castle. The original was destroyed in 1866 during the fighting that attended the Meiji restoration. Kokura is one of the five cities of Kitakyushu.

Accommodation

In addition to the usual hotels and ryokan, there is also a nice hostel (Kitakyushu Youth Hostel, tel (093) 681-8142), accessible from Yahata station. It offers a good view.

Getting There & Getting Around

If you are bound for the Osaka/Kyoto area, and not interested in sightseeing along the way, the ferry service from Kokura to Kobe is very convenient and quite cheap. Three boats leave every day (4 pm, 6.30 pm and 9 pm), arriving the following morning (7 am, 9.30 am and 10.50 am), minimum fare is Y3600. There is also a single ferry daily to and from Tokyo. It leaves at 5.50 pm and arrives at 6.30 am about 36 hours later (departs 6 pm and arrives 6.30 am from Tokyo); minimum fare is Y10,000.

There is no easy way to describe how to hitch to and from Shimonoseki and

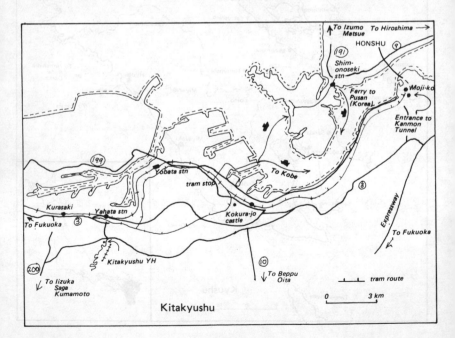

Kitakyushu

other points on Honshu, or other points in Kyushu. The city of Kitakyushu is the seventh-largest in Japan, and hitching from the middle of the city is not as easy as it is in the country. The simplest way to cross to Shimo is by JNR from Kokura or a nearby station, through the tunnel under the Kanmon Strait to Shimonoseki station. To hitch to other points in Kyushu you might try your luck at the entrance/exit of the Kanmon tunnel, which is not far from either of the last two stations of the tram line that runs through Kitakyushu. It is somewhat longer distance from Moji (JNR) station. The closest interchange for getting on to the freeway leading to the high and graceful Kanmon-hashi suspension bridge is some distance away, and you will need help to get to it.

HIRAODAI

An unusual geological feature that makes for a pleasant excursion and hike in open countryside (a rarity close to cities in most of Japan) is Hiraodai. This is a rolling plateau covered by weathered and rounded outcroppings of limestone, many taller than a person. To non-geologists (like myself), this is known as a karst tableland. At the east end of Hiraodai lies the limestone grotto of Sembetsu.

Hiraodai can be reached most easily by JNR (or Route 322) from Kokura to Ishihara, from where a local road leading to Yukuhashi passes Hiraodai. There might be direct transport from Kokura; make inquiries at the station.

FUKUOKA/HAKATA

The largest city of Kyushu, Fukuoka is also an international port of entry.

Fukuoka has a limited number of attractions worth looking at. If setting out from Hakata station, first stop at the travel centre and pick up a copy of their map of the Fukuoka area. Everything is marked in both Japanese and English, so it can be used to find your way almost anywhere. There are other information centres in the same station, but they don't have much useful information, so be sure to get the right one. (If you need film, Doi camera shop, near the station, has good prices.)

Getting There – International

If you are arriving from Korea, Fukuoka is a convenient starting point for travels in Japan. The flight from Pusan is the cheapest air route from Korea. Fukuoka airport is – with one caveat – a delight to use because it is only a short distance out of town, and connections are easily made by frequent bus service from the main JNR station (which is called Hakata, not Fukuoka). The warning, applicable mostly to budget travellers and those entitled to 90-day visas by reciprocal agreement, is that the immigration officials at Fukuoka have a reputation for vying with those at Shimonoseki for being the most unpleasant in Japan, and are reluctant to give any status other than 'Tourist', which is a nuisance if you plan to remain more than a couple of weeks. (See also the section on Immigration in the introductory part of the book.)

Getting There – Domestic

In addition to several flights a day to various points within Japan, there is good train service. Hakata is the western terminus of the Shinkansen, and the trip to or from Tokyo takes less than seven hours.

Sumiyoshi-jinja (shrine)

This shrine, less than one km from Hakata station, has buildings dating from 400 years ago. Its festival is held on 12-14 October.

Shofuku-ji temple

Also located not far from Hakata station, this temple was the first centre of Zen teachings in Japan (from 1195).

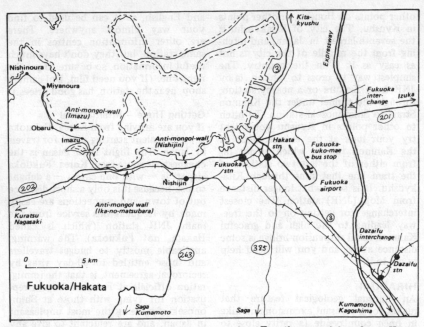

Fukuoka/Hakata

Potteries

There are several pottery-making centres in northern Kyushu. Some, if not all, are the legacy of Korean potters who came to Japan about 200 years ago. Within Fukuoka are the well-known towns of Agano and Koishiwara; less famous is the town of Onta, near Koishiwara, the last village of Japanese potters who work as a cooperative. There is usually no pottery for sale, because the climbing kilns are fired only occasionally and the production is generally spoken for in advance, but the methods used are traditional as is some of the equipment used. Of the 14 houses in the village, 10 produce pottery. On the Fukuoka city map is another pottery, indicated as Takatori Kiln (Famous Folk Pottery).

Other Information

There is a Korean consulate in Fukuoka, making it a convenient place to obtain a visa. For those arriving from Korea after a long time in South-East Asia, there is a Shakey's Pizza Parlour in Fukuoka. It is in the central business district: ask for directions at the travel centre.

Accommodation

There are many hotels, business hotels and ryokan in Fukuoka, as well as in nearby hot-spring resorts. Assistance is available at the information centre at Hakata station. Jodoji Youth Hostel is a temple, and temples are usually the nicest kind of hotel in Japan, but it has only 16 beds (tel (092) 751-3377). Daizaifu Youth Hostel is an alternative, but it has only 24 beds (tel (09292) 2-8740). Other hostels in the area include Kongo-kaku (45 beds, tel (09405) 2-0009) at Tsuyazaki (toward Kitakyushu), or Kitakyushu Youth Hostel (96 beds, tel (093) 681-8142). Both can be reached by JNR, the former from

Fukuma station, the latter from Yahata.

Festival
On 10-12 July is the Daiko (drum) matsuri, when over 100 floats carrying drums and drummers parade through the city. Japanese drumming is both complex and unexpectedly primitive, so such a festival is interesting.

SOUTH OF FUKUOKA
Dazaifu-Temmangu shrine
Less than an hour south of Fukuoka by train is the famous shrine Dazaifu-Temmangu, one of the highest-ranking shrines in Japan. The grounds and picturesque bright-orange buildings (dating from 1590) are attractive, and include an arched stone bridge. From the 7th to the 14th century, Dazaifu was the residence of the Kyushu governor. The shrine's annual festival takes place on 23-5 September, and features a procession.

The shrine is easily reached by the Nishitetsu line that leaves from Fukuoka station. At Futsukaichi it is necessary to change trains and go one stop to Dazaifu station, from which the shrine is about 500 metres away. (There is also a JNR Futsukaichi station, but there is no connecting train.) If you are coming from Hakata station, it is simpler to go by JNR to Futsukaichi and transfer to the other station there. Dazaifu Youth Hostel is near the shrine.

Close to Dazaifu-jinja are Komyo and Kanzeon temples, as well as the Fukuoka-ken Historical Museum. Komyo-ji has a very pretty Zen-style garden. Kanzeon-ji has a number of valued Buddhist images on display.

Pottery
If you are interested in pottery, it is worth visiting the kilns and potters in the towns of Hoju and Ichinose, all in the vicinity of Kurume.

Hot Springs
Two hot-spring resort towns, Harazuru (in southern Fukuoka-ken) and Hita (just across the boundary in Oita-ken) feature ukai (cormorant fishing) on the nearby river: May to September in Harazuru, and until the end of October in Hita.

WEST OF FUKUOKA
The major route westwards from Fukuoka takes you along the coast towards Nagasaki.

Anti-Mongol wall
To combine a swim on a white-sand beach with a bit of history, visit the remnants of the 20-km wall built around Hakata Bay to prevent the landing of the Mongol hordes in 1281. It was feared that the next wave of invaders would overpower the defenders, but a typhoon sank the Mongol fleet, thus saving Japan from the invasion until 1945 (which explains the great shock felt at the end of the last war). Because this wind saved Japan, it was named 'Kamikaze' (wind of the gods), a word revived in the last war but with less effective results.

Only traces of the walls (originally three metres high) remain. Near Imazu, one stretch of 100 metres or so has been excavated from the sand, and once you see this remnant (still nearly two metres high), you realize that the traces of rocks just beneath the sand through the groves of picturesque, twisted pine trees near the shore are the top of the wall. From here it is only a short walk to the beach. To take the bus from Hakata station, ask for the Nishi-no-ura yuki bus, which probably leaves from gate 3 on the second floor. The location is shown on the handout map in Japanese as well as English: the wall is marked as 'Genko Fort', but ask for 'boheki', which is its local name. The bus trip takes about two hours.

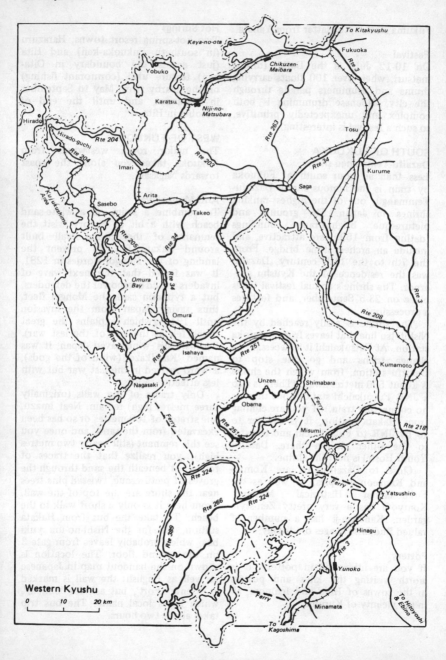

Western Kyushu

0   10   20 km

GENKAI PARK

The anti-Mongol wall at Imazu, and others (shown on the handout map, but said to be in much poorer condition), are part of Genkai Quasi-National Park that extends about 90 km along the north coast of Kyushu into Saga-ken. Other features are more white sand beaches, and more groves of gnarled pine trees (the best-known one is at Niji-no-matsubara).

Keya-no-Ota

The crowning glory of the park is 'the Great Cave of Keya', a rocky promontory at the western end of Itoshima Peninsula. It juts 60 metres out of the sea, and is formed of groups of parallel columns of basalt projecting at different angles (probably created as lava cooled in a large mass and formed giant crystals). The sea has eroded a cave nine metres high and 18 metres wide, that extends more than 50 metres into the rock.

Keya-no-Ota can be reached by bus either from Chikuzen-Maibara station (40 minutes) or directly from Hakata station (95 minutes).

Pottery

There are three famous pottery towns in Saga-ken: Karatsu, Imari and Arita. The pottery there is noted for its very colourful glazes, and is considered more artistic than that from the kilns of Seto (near Nagoya in central Honshu). You can get to the Imari potteries in 15 minutes by bus from Imari station, passing through pretty countryside with thatched-roof houses.

Festival

On 3-5 November, giant floats of papier-mache figures are drawn through the streets of Karatsu.

ISLANDS OFF THE NORTH-WEST COAST

There are three large islands off the north-west coast of Kyushu: Iki, Tsushima and Hirado. While none has any particular sightseeing attractions, nearly all are relatively isolated and visited by only a few foreigners. The people are thus 'unspoilt' and friendly, though even less able to communicate with outsiders than other Japanese, for they have still less incentive to learn foreign languages. Their dialects are usually incomprehensible even to other Japanese. Iki and Tsushima are both accessible from Saga-ken and Fukuoka-ken. For up-to-the-minute information on transport to these two islands, as well as scheduled services to a number of smaller islands not mentioned here, consult the *Jikokuhyo* (book of timetables).

Iki-shima

This island was recommended particularly by a cyclist friend who liked its flat terrain and beautiful beaches: the island is small, and the sea always close. There are several campsites, plus ryokan. There are four boats a day between Iki and Yobuko on the tip of the peninsula near Karatsu, as well as from Hakata. There are also three flights a day from Fukuoka.

Tsushima

Very close to Korea, this island is much larger and more rugged than Iki, and you will need a bus or car for transport. One traveller reported several quizzings by police during his visit, because foreigners are very rare and there is a lot of drug-smuggling from Korea. Just prior to his arrival, a smuggler had come out on the wrong side of police bullets, so the authorities were edgy.

In addition to ryokan, there is a Kokuminshuku and two youth hostels on the island (one a temple).

There is boat service to Kokura, as well as to Iki. There are also four daily flights to and from Fukuoka.

Hirado-shima

At the north of Nagasaki-ken is Hirado Island, accessible by bridge from Hirado-guchi (JNR station). The island is hilly, with many high cliffs.

Kujukushima

Between Hirado Island and Sasebo (on the coast of Nagasaki-ken) is Kujuk-ushima ('99 islands'), in fact a group of about 170 islets. A cruise boat makes two trips daily from Sasebo (Kashi-mae pier).

Goto-shima

This is the name of five islands west of Kujukushima. Like other islands in the area, they are mostly agricultural and fishing communities. The coast is rugged. Access is by boat from Nagasaki, Sasebo and other centres, as well as by air from Fukuoka. (Again, consult *Jikokuhyo* for more detailed information.)

NAGASAKI-KEN

NAGASAKI

So much has been written about Nagasaki that it is difficult for another travel writer to try to follow suit. However, while enjoying my visit to Nagasaki, I would not claim that it is the one and only place in Japan (or in Kyushu, for that matter) to visit. It certainly has several attractions, but reality should temper enthusiasm.

Nagasaki has an interesting history, and has long flourished as a port. During the period when Japan was closed to the outside world (the early 1600s to 1867), Nagasaki was virtually the only gateway open for trade. Formerly a point of contact with the Asian continent, it became the entry point for western knowledge and religion (Roman Catholicism).

Nagasaki might never have become so well known if it had not been the second city to be A-bombed, having been picked as a target because of the huge Mitsubishi shipyards across the harbour from the city.

Getting Around

The easiest way to get around the city is by tram, for the five lines pass near all points of interest and are clearly numbered. City buses cover much more extensive routes, but they are much more difficult to use because they are labelled only in Japanese.

The following route covers all the major places of interest. It is based on the tram routes, beginning and ending at the Dejima Pier/Nagasaki Station area.

Martyrs' Site

On 5 February 1597, 20 Japanese and six foreign Christians were crucified in an effort by Hideyoshi Toyotomi to stamp out Christianity. A church-like building of somewhat unusual features (dating from 1962) stands on the site.

A-bomb relics

Everything related to that fateful 1945 day are clustered within easy walking distance. From Nagasaki station, easiest access is by a northbound tram 1 or 3 (the stop is Matsuyama-cho, eighth from the station). After leaving the station, a short uphill walk leads to the main road. Across the road and a little to the right is a small park which marks the epicentre of the blast. Relics showing the force of the blast are on display, including a crumpled fire-tower and a bit of the wall of the old cathedral. (Photographers will be infuriated by lamp-posts and a pavilion that block all good photographic angles.)

Atop the hill behind the park (accessible by stairs) is the A-bomb museum, properly known as Nagasaki Kokusai Bunka-kaikan (International Cultural Hall). It houses an excellent display

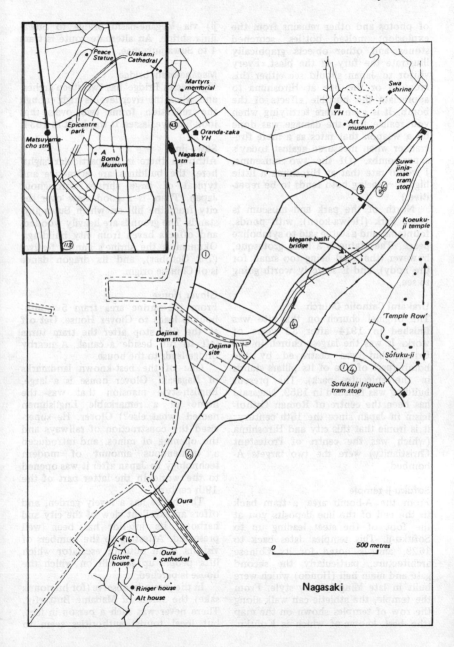

Nagasaki

0   500 metres

of photos and other remains from the explosion: melted bottles, scorched stones and other objects graphically illustrate the fury of the blast. Every visitor to Japan should see either this museum or the one at Hiroshima to appreciate the horrible effects of the bomb. It is even more terrifying when you realize that the damage was done by a weapon that rates as a mere firecracker when measured against today's super-bombs. (Of the two museums, I would rate that at Hiroshima a little higher — seeing both tends to be repetitive.)

North of the park and museum is Peace Park (Heiwa-koen), with ponds, fountains, and a statue said to symbolize peace. The statue is a little grotesque, however (the head being too small for the body), and is scarcely worth going to see.

Urakami Catholic Church

The original church on this site was finished in 1914 after 32 years of work. It was the largest church in the Orient, but was destroyed by the bomb (part of one of its pillars stands in the epicentre park). The present building was finished in 1959. Nagasaki has been the centre of Roman Catholicism in Japan since the 16th century: it is ironic that this city and Hiroshima (which was the centre of Protestant Christianity) were the two targets A-bombed.

Sofuku-ji temple

From the A-bomb area, a tram back to the end of the line deposits you at the foot of the steet leading up to Sofuku-ji. This temples dates back to 1629, and is noted for its Chinese architecture, particularly the second gate and main hall (Hondo) which were built in late Ming-dynasty style. From the temple, the athletic can walk along the row of temples shown on the map (the best known-of which is Kofuku-

ji) via Megane-bashi bridge to Suwa-jinja shrine. An alternate route is tram 4 to Suwa-jinja-mae.

Megane-bashi bridge

'Spectacles Bridge' has two steep arches, and when the river level is high enough the reflection forms two ovals that look like eyeglasses. It was built in 1634.

Suwa-jinja

Although there is no particular 'sight' here, the buildings are attractive and typical of large shrines throughout Japan. There is a good view over the city from the hill on which Suwa-jinja stands. The grounds are heavily wooded, and offer a haven from city buildings. Okunchi is the shrine's annual festival (7-9 October), and its dragon dance is of Chinese origin.

Glover House

From the shrine area tram 5 (south-bound) leads to Glover House. Get off at the first stop after the tram turns left to run beside a canal. A nearby bridge leads to the house.

One of the best-known landmarks of Nagasaki, Glover house is a large, English-style mansion that was the home of a remarkable Englishmen named (what else?) Glover. He supervised the construction of railways and the opening of mines, and introduced a tremendous amount of modern technology to Japan after it was opened to the world in the latter part of the 19th century.

The house has a lovely garden, and offers an excellent view of the city and harbour; its interior has been well preserved. Attesting to the numbers of visitors is an outdoor escalator which lifts people up the hill on which the house is perched.

In the grounds, observe (for humour's sake) the statue of Madame Butterfly. There never was such a person in fact, but local tourist authorities seem to be pushing the story for all it is worth.

Nearby are three other houses of the same era, two of which are also known for their former residents, Alt and Ringer. The third house ('No 16') has considerable quantities of Victorian bric-a-brac. In the bottom of the building is a museum of portable shrines, costumes and a dragon — all of which are carried in the annual Okunchi festival. A videotape shows scenes from the celebrations.

Oura Catholic Church
This is the oldest Gothic-style structure in Japan, dating from 1865. It was built in memory of the 26 Christian martyrs. From this area, tram 5 returns to Dejima Pier area.

Dejima
The pier at which visiting cruise ships dock is named for Dejima Island, a small body of land to which the Dutch traders were restricted during the 'closed' years when Japan's only connection with the rest of the world was through Nagasaki. The island no longer exists, for the harbour was filled in to make the pier (the dock area is now further out than the island used to be). A garden and reproduction of an old Dutch warehouse now stand on the site of the former island.

Nagasaki Aquarium
There is an aquarium about 12 km from the city. Access is by bus or taxi from station.

Views of the city
The best view of the city is from the top of Mt Inasa (332 metres). A cable-car runs from a point about one km from Nagasaki station. The view at night is especially attractive, somewhat resembling Hong Kong, although the lights are not so numerous nor bright.

Information
There is an information office at Nagasaki station, where maps and tourist literature in English are available. The Nagasaki Tourist Centre is on the second floor of the building opposite the station.

Getting There
Nagasaki is served by JNR lines, as well as air links with several other cities. The airport is 10 minutes from Omura station by bus, and 90 minutes from Nagasaki by bus. The train passes briefly along the shore of Omura Bay en route to Nagasaki; the main highway goes inland most of the way. Northward to Sasebo, both pass along the shore for most of the distance, giving pleasant views including the rafts of pearl farms (this is the second-largest pearl-producing area in Japan, after Ise). Inter-city buses leave from the terminal across from Nagasaki station.

If travelling by aid of the thumb, you will find it simplest to take a train or bus to Isahaya and start hitching from there.

Accommodation
As can be expected at a very popular destination for domestic travel, there is plenty of accommodation available, with many hotels and ryokan clustered near the station. There are three youth hostels: Nagasaki Oranda-zaka (across from Nagasaki station), and nearby Nagasaki-kenritsu Youth Hostel are in town; the third is quite far away.

FROM NAGASAKI TO KUMAMOTO
From Nagasaki, one of the most popular routes is via Obama and Unzen to Shimabara, from where frequent ferries ply to and from Misumi on the Uto Peninsula. From Misumi it is only a short distance north to Kumamoto or south to Kagoshima.

Unzen

In the days of the British Empire, Unzen used to be a favourite resort for colonial officials and old China hands, breeds now vanished. There are still some attractions, though most travellers stop only for a look around before continuing. Unzen has golf courses and other recreational facilities, but its raison d'etre is the hot-spring waters. These boil up — violently in places — in a steaming, desolate but colourful area near town. The waters are conducted to the various hotels for the baths (the claims of curative properties would get hotels into plenty of hot water of another kind if made in countries with strong consumer-protection laws). During the days of Christian persecution, these boiling waters were put to another use — disposing of those who refused to renounce their faith.

A toll road loops up between Nodake and Myoken mountains. The view from the road itself is not spectacular, but from the top cable-car station there is a beautiful view of the ocean and off-shore islands. Wildflowers are pretty in spring and summer, while leaves are the attraction in autumn.

Shimabara

Another place of some interest on the Shimabara Peninsula is Shimabara, with its reconstructed castle the original was destroyed in 1637 in an episode during the government's effort to eradicate Christianity. About 30,000 of the faithful captured the castle, but it was later retaken by the authorities and the defenders were slaughtered. The castle was ruined at that time, but the large reproduction built in 1964 re-creates the beautiful appearance of the white original and serves as a museum. Among the exhibits are fumi-e, ('trampling images'), images of Christian significance upon which people had to tread in order to prove that they were

not Christians. The castle is about 400 metres west of the station.

Misumi

From Misumi it is 27 km to the main north-south road (Route 3) at Uto, from where it is only 15 km to Kumamoto. An alternative is a visit to the Amakusa Islands.

KUMAMOTO-KEN

KUMAMOTO

Kumamoto is the third-largest city on Kyushu, and was one of the major military centres of Japan until the last century. It is best described as rather provincial: although it has modern buildings, shops, etc, it is not a metropolis. Some sections of the city could be described as delightfully seedy, and are worth seeing for that reason before they are conquered by the aluminum-and-glass that has transformed the traditional appearance of nearly all Japan.

The two major attractions of Kumamoto are Suizenji-koen and Kumamoto-jo castle, plus a shrine or two.

Getting There

In recent times, Kumamoto has joined the list of international ports of entry for air travellers. Although the connections are limited to Korea, it is a step forward and offers an alternative to, say, Fukuoka. The airport is located near the road/rail route to Mt Aso, so on arrival you have the option of taking the bus into Kumamoto, or proceeding directly to the Aso area. From the airport there is a possibility of direct bus service to Aso, or it might be necessary to go to Higo-Otsu station and take a train or bus from there.

Suizenji-koen park

This is a very attractive landscape gar-

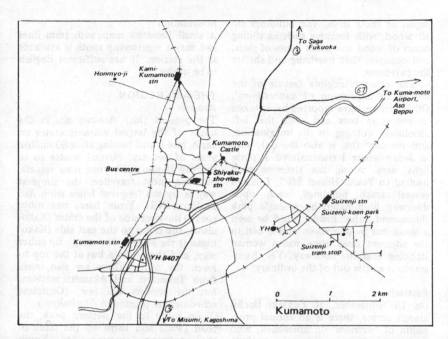

Kumamoto

den, larger than most in Japan. I would rate it ahead of two of the 'Big Three' gardens, behind only Kenroku-en in Kanazawa. The hills and water have been arranged to resemble famous natural features such as Mt Fuji and Lake Biwa, and there is a teahouse identical in every feature to one of the most famous of such buildings in Kyoto. The garden dates from 1632, so it is much older than the more celebrated ones mentioned above. It was part of a villa of the Hosokawa clan who once commanded the region.

The park is easily reached by tram from Kumamoto station (the stop is named 'Suizenji').

Kumamoto-jo Castle

Kumamoto was once of the principal castle towns of Japan, ranking only behind Osaka and Nagoya. The original castle was finished in 1607 and stood until 1867, when most of it was burned in a siege during the period of unrest following the Meiji restoration. In 1960 the structure was reproduced in concrete, and now houses a museum. I usually downplay such reproductions for their lack of authenticity, but this one is so large and set in such attractive surroundings of tall trees and stone walls that it is worth at least a look if you are passing through.

The castle is easily reached on foot or by tram from the station: the stop is 'Shi-yaku-sho mae' (town hall).

Other

Other attractions that can be singled out are Hommyo-ji temple and Tatsuta-koen park. The latter houses a folk-art museum as well as an attractive garden and teahouse from 350 years ago.

Undefinable attractions include several streets of shops that appear to have survived from pre-war times and preserve the appearance of the

Japan of those days. The buildings are all wood, with features such as sliding doors of wood and small panes of glass, and canopies that overhang and shelter the pavement.

The other intangible feature of the city is an impression of 'raunchiness'. Other writers have reported being taken to shows in bars and clubs that left absolutely nothing to the imagination, and sexually this is also the only city in Japan where I encountered a 'pink-light' area. Along the riverside road leading to Youth Hostel 8407, I passed several small buildings, each open doorway illuminated by a single pink fluorescent tube. Inside could be seen a small bar in one room and a bed in the adjacent one; there was a woman standing near the doorway. Yes, Kumamoto is a little out of the ordinary.

Festivals
On 15 September, at Fujisaki Hachimangu shrine, there is an annual procession of 'warriors' on horseback, who wear ancient armour to escort three portable shrines.

Accommodation
There are several hotels, minshuku, etc, in Kumamoto. Assistance in finding a room can be obtained at information centres at the airport, station, or travel agencies. There are also three youth hostels: Ryokan Shokaku (8407, tel (0963) 52-1468), a delightfully seedy old ryokan close to the station; Suizenji YH (8406, tel 0963) 71-9193), accessible in 25 minutes by tram from the station; and Kumamoto-Shiritsu YH (8408, tel (0963) 52-2441), a municipal hostel that is more difficult to reach. Details on hostels in the Aso area are given in that section: they can be considered as alternatives because of the short travelling time from Kumamoto (100 minutes by train).

Information
A small handout map with tram lines and major sightseeing spots is available at the station. It has sufficient English to be useful.

THE ASO REGION
Aso-zan
The present (Mt) Aso-zan sits in the midst of the largest volcanic crater on earth, and is still fuming after 80 million years of activity. Several routes go to the top if you have your own vehicle, but for most travellers the simplest way is by the frequent buses from Aso station (JNR). From here, one route goes to the west side of the crater (Kakonishi), the other to the east side (Kakohigashi) via Miyaji. One can go up either way, and then take a bus at the top to reach the other. There are also buses from Takamori and Akamizu stations, but the services are few. (Complete schedules are printed in *Jikokuhyo*.)

En route to the western peak, the road twists and turns up the flank of the mountain (passing Aso Youth Hostel just past the toll gate). At the lush meadows you may see Japanese tourists out of their cars photographing an exotic species of animal life, a cow. Clearly visible in the green are fingers of lava from prehistoric flows. The road also passes a smallish cone, Komezuka, an 'afterthought' of a later mini-eruption.

Eventually the road reaches the flattened top of Aso-zan. From the first lookout near the crest of the uphill road, you can finally see (on a clear day, at least) the enormity of the crater, for the cliffs several km away are in fact the walls of the original hole. Its dimensions are given variously as 23 or 32 km north-south, 16 km east-west, and 80 or 128 km in circumference. Any way you measure it, it's huge and the mind boggles at the amount of energy once set loose from

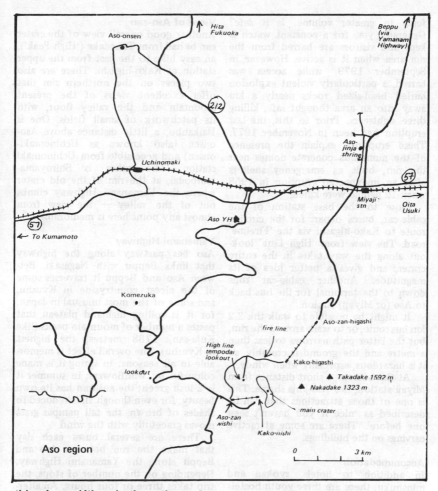

Aso region

this place. Although the volcano has been active for about 30 million years, the present form probably dates back a little more than 120 millenia.

The road circles around a lake before the bus reaches the base station of the Kako-nishi cable-car (four minutes to the top). A toll road also continues the short distance to the same place. The view from here is one of great desolation, mostly black ash thrown out over the centuries. A path leads to the very rim of the main crater (no guard rail — caution!) in the side of Nakadake, on the far side of which can be seen layers of ash and lava — mostly black, but with colourful streaks of dark red. In its own sombre way, it is very picturesque.

Far below, down in the deep black cavity, steam billows forth continuously, sometimes diminishing only to burst forth in greater volume. Is it safe? Generally yes, for a constant watch is kept and visitors are barred from the rim area when it is active. However, in September 1979, while access was barred, a particularly violent explosion hurled head-sized rocks nearly a km away into an area thought safe, killing three sightseers. Prior to this, the last eruption had been in November 1977. These eruptions explain the presence of the numerous concrete domes near the rim, built as emergency shelters after an unexpected eruption in 1958 when 12 people were killed.

Close to the base station of the cable-car, buses depart for the circling route to Kako-higashi via the 'Fireline' road. The view from 'High Line' lookout along the way takes in the entire crater, and gives a better idea of its magnitude. Another cable-car runs down to the terminal for the bus back to Aso (or Miyaji) station.

It might be possible to walk the 2.2 km bus route, or to walk around the rim, but the latter path narrows to less than a metre and the ground is crumbly, so it is hazardous, especially when windy.

At the bottom, a short distance from Miyaji station, lies Aso-jinja shrine. This is one of those attractions that can be described as 'nice if you haven't seen one before'. There are some attractive carvings on the buildings.

Accommodation

In addition to hotels, ryokan and minshuku, there are three youth hostels around the base of the mountain. I stayed at Aso Youth Hostel (8402, tel (09673) 4-0804) and found it pleasant: it can be reached by the bus to Kako-nishi, and is just beyond the toll gate. The others are Aso YMCA Camp Youth Hostel (tel (09673) 5-0124), and Murataya-Ryokan (tel (09676) 2-0066), though one traveller gave a low rating to the latter.

Views of Aso-zan

Another good overall view of the crater can be had from Takadake ('High Peak'), an easy hike to the east from the upper station at Kako-higashi. There are also two places on the northern rim that offer excellent views of the present mountain and the valley floor, with its patchwork of small fields. One is Daikanbo, a little distance above Aso-onsen (also known as Uchinomaki-onsen) and accessible from Uchinomaki station. The other is Shiroyama-tempodai, at the rim of the old crater where the Yamanami Highway climbs out of the valley — the view from almost any point here is memorable.

Yamanami Highway

Aso lies partway along the highway that links Beppu with Nagasaki. Between Aso and Beppu it traverses some of the nicest countryside in Kyushu, and some of the most unusual in Japan, for it is rolling highland plateau that passes a number of mountain peaks (like Kuju-san, 1788 metres, the highest in Kyushu). The overall effect is memorable in all seasons: in spring it is made colourful by wildflowers; in summer it is a lush green; the autumn has its own beauty, for even though all is reduced to shades of brown, the tall pampas grass moves gracefully with the wind.

There are several buses each day that make the run between Aso and Beppu along the Yamanami Highway. Depending on the number of stops, the trip takes three or four hours. An alternate route northward from Aso (for those in a rush) is via Hita, but the attractions of the Yamanami Highway make it preferable.

From Aso, another route is southeast through Takachiho Gorge, a very pleasant place to visit. Like Beppu, however, it lies in Miyazaki-ken and is described in that section.

KUMAMOTO TO KAGOSHIMA
Yatsushiro
This is an industrial city of little interest except for pottery addicts; it is the origin of Koda-yaki (or Yatsushiro-yaki) pottery, carrying on a tradition started by Korean potters who came here in the 16th century.

In late August-early September, strange lights can be seen in the sea late at night. Known as shiranui, it is caused by phosphorescence from a kind of marine life. (It is described in Japanese literature as occuring in late-summer/ early-autumn, but somehow the Japanese autumn begins on 1 September instead of 21 September as in other countries in other countries in the Northern Hemisphere.)

Hinagu
The view from the shore near this hot-spring resort is regarded as particularly appealing, taking in the Amakusa islands and the bay in front of them.

Minamata
Another industrial city of not touristic merit, but brought to world attention in the early 1970s for the illness caused by mercury poisoning known as Minamata disease.

Yunoko
The swimming is regarded as partially good here.

Hitoyoshi
Travellers descending from the Kumamoto area bound for Kagoshima could do far worse than to turn inland at Yatsushiro and travel through the pretty, wooded valley to Hitoyoshi by rail or road (Route 219). The Kuma river, flowing through the valley, is intensely green. At Hitoyoshi, both rail and road turn southward: the road (Route 221) to Ebino and Kobayashi, rail to Yoshimatsu and Kagoshima (a branch from Yoshimatsu goes to Ebino and Kobayashi).

From Hitoyoshi, one can shoot the rapids on the Kuma river for 18 km to Osakahama (on the JNR). The trip lasts 2½ hours, and the starting point is 1.5 km south-east of Hitoyoshi station, opposite the grounds of the former castle, Hitoyoshi-jo. The rapids are rated among the three swiftest in Japan, but there is no risk involved.

I was struck by the strange appearance of one town along routes 219-221 (possibly Hitoyoshi itself — memory fails), which looked as if every building along the main street had been built from the same pre-fab components with only the colours varying. It's nothing special, just a curiosity to look out for.

Kobayashi
This is one entry point for a trip through the very scenic Kirishima National Park. Several buses a day leave for Ebino-kogen, the changing point for the most scenic parts. (This same trip can be made in reverse from Kagoshima.) There are also buses to Kobayashi from Miyazaki many times a day (the trip takes 1½-2 hours).

KAGOSHIMA-KEN

KIRISHIMA AREA
The Kirishima area is well known for the two peaks Karakuni-dake (1700 metres), and Takachiho-no-mine (1574 metres) which are 16 km apart; between them stand 21 lesser peaks. Easily seen from the Kirishima Skyline toll road (along which the bus passes) are colourful caldera lakes, craters, and much other evidence of volcanic activity. It is unusual scenery and very much worth seeing.

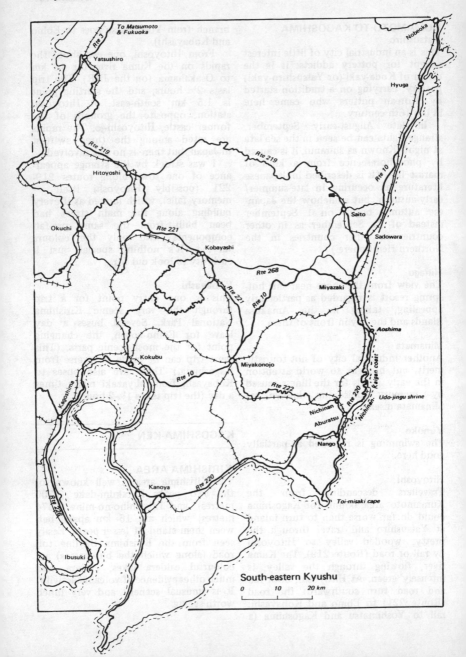

Rte 3
To Matsumoto
& Fukuoka
Nobeoka
Yatsushiro
Hyuga
Rte 10
Rte 219
Hitoyoshi
Rte 219
Saito
Okuchi
Rte 221
Sadowara
Rte 221
Kobayashi
Rte 268
Miyazaki
Rte 10
Rte 221
Kokubu
Aoshima
Keian coast
Kagoshima
Rte 10
Miyakonojo
Udo-jingu shrine
Rte 220
Nichinan
Nichinan
Rte 222
Aburatsu
Nango
Kanoya
Rte 220
Ibusuki
Rte 226
Toi-misaki cape

South-eastern Kyushu

0   10   20 km

Ebino-kogen

From Kobayashi, the local road passes under the freeway, twists along to the entrance of the toll road, then twists a great deal more up to Ebino-kogen (Ebino highland plateau). This is the terminus of the bus and the transfer point for another bus bound for Kagoshima.

At Ebino-kogen there are three small lakes (literally 'ponds'). They are volcano calderas, and quite round; all are of different colours, including one of the most intense green I have encountered. (Use a polarizing filter to photograph them, otherwise reflection from the water will wash out the colour.) There are several paths to follow for different views (Karakuni-dake is visible from here as well).

From Ebino-kogen southward, the most desirable route is along the toll road as far as Hayashida, then from there to Takachiho-kawara, which gives the best view of Takachiho-no-mine and is the starting point for hiking to the picturesque cratered cone. The problem is that only one bus a day runs from Hayashida (9.10 am), or two a day in the opposite direction from Kirishima station or shrine (10.05 am and 2 pm). There may be local buses not listed, or it should be possible to hitch. From Kirishima it is 7.6 km to Takachiho-kawara.

From Ebino-kogen to Hayashida-onsen, various views of Karakuni-dake unfold to the east. A short distance later you reach Onami-ike, a caldera lake even more circular than the others mentioned above (Shinsho lookout gives a good view). Here and there along the road, steam pours out of the ground, sometimes beside the road (or even through cracks in the pavement) — evidence of the potential geological forces underfoot.

A fork at the junction of the toll roads leads to Takachiho-kawara. From here, one has a good view of Takachiho-no-mine (1574 metres), an ugly-scenic still-active volcano. Its rim is red-brown heat-discoloured rock; the conical top vanished in prehistoric eruptions. The gaping crater, back-dropped by yet more craters and peaks, gives an other-worldly look to the area.

Kirishima

Kirishima-jingu shrine (in Kirishima town, which is 15 minutes from the JNR Kirishima-jingu station) is colourful with wood carvings and set amidst tall cedars. There is a youth hostel in the town, as well as ryokan and hotels. Buses run from Kirishima-jingu (both shrine and station) to Kagoshima several times a day, and an even larger number of trains connect Kirishima-jingu station with both Kagoshima and Miyazaki.

KAGOSHIMA

The largest city in southern Kyushu, Kagoshima is an international airport as well as a seaport for regular boats

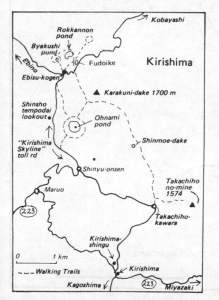

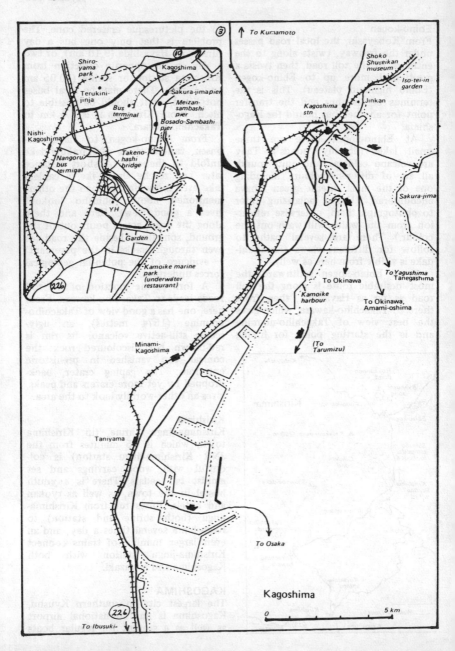

③ To Kumamoto

⑩

Shiro-yama park

Kagoshima

Shoko Shuseikan museum

Terukini-jinja

Sakura-jima pier

Iso-tei-in garden

Jinkan

Bus terminal

Meizan-sambashi pier

Kagoshima stn

Nishi-Kagoshima

Bosado-Sambashi pier

Nangoru-bus terminal

Takeno-hashi bridge

Sakura-jima

YH

To Yagushima Tanegashima

Garden

To Okinawa

Kamoike marine park (underwater restaurant)

To Okinawa, Amami-oshima

②②⑥

Kamoike harbour

Minami-Kagoshima

(To Tarumizu)

Taniyama

To Osaka

Kagoshima

To Ibusuki-

②②⑥

0   5 km

to and from Okinawa and other southern islands. It is also a stop-over point for some cruise ships.

There are only a few things to see in Kagoshima itself, but two to three days can be profitably spent looking around the nearby attractions.

Kagoshima is one of the few cities in the world where an umbrella is useful rain or shine. The cause is the most spectacular sight of Kagoshima, the massive smoking cone of Sakurajima across the harbour. Sakurajima has an awesome history of eruptions and its south peak is still active, regularly spewing fine ash into the air — with an unfavourable wind it blows over Kagoshima and covers streets with a thin layer, or drifts into shallow piles. A good view of Sakurajima may be had from the top of Shiroyama, the hill behind the city. Bus 25 runs close to the top, and you can also walk up from the tram stop. The park was formerly the site of a castle.

The main attractions of the city are located a little to the north, and are associated (like most history of Kagoshima up to the time of the Meiji restoration in 1868), with the Shimazu family who controlled the area for only five years short of seven centuries.

Getting There & Getting Around

Kagoshima is linked with Hong Kong and Nauru (South Pacific) by regular flights, which makes it a convenient port of entry for travellers from those areas who wish to start their Japan travels in the south. The airport is north of the city, and connections are convenient by bus (departures are every 20 minutes, and the trip takes about an hour). If you want to make your way immediately to the Kirishima area, try to get to Kajiki station, from where seven trains a day run directly to Kirishima-jingu station. Information can

be obtained at the airport about schedules.

Airport buses make more than one stop in Kagoshima: the best place to get off is Nishi-Kagoshima station (west Kagoshima), which is close to the post office and the central business district.

There are daily overnight boats to Osaka and a regular service to Okinawa. the former leave Kagoshima at 6.30 pm and Osaka at 6.50 pm, arriving approximately 20 hours later (minimum fare Y8700). There are two lines to Naha on Okinawa: their sailings are a little odd, sometimes every second day, sometimes at three-day intervals, and only occasionally does the ship of one line fill the gap of sailing dates of the other. Schedules are published in *Jikokuhyo*, so you can plan in advance. The ships of one line stop at several islands along the way, which adds 4½ hours to the trip. From Okinawa, there is regular boat service to Taiwan. Minimum fare to Okinawa is Y10150.

If you are arriving from Okinawa, take bus 20 to the station; the youth hostel is not too far from the dock.

Information

There is an excellent information centre at the station. The person on duty when I was there spoke excellent English and was very helpful. The office keeps generous hours (6 am to 11 pm), has literature in English, and can give any information required for further travel connections, access to boat docks for Okinawa, etc.

Even if you have studied Japanese and speak it well, you can expect great difficulties in speaking to people in Kyushu, especially around Kagoshima, for the local dialect is quite different from standard Japanese. The old dialect, Satsuma-ben, now spoken only by older generations, is totally incomprehensible to other Japanese. The story given (and apparently believed by most Japanese) is that a local feudal lord commanded that the people change their way of speaking so that spies from Honshu could be detected. However, the most likely explanation is that the accent is a carry-over from other languages in the general area, in the same way that accents in England reflect intonations brought by the various tribes and groups from the Continent. The dialect of Okinawa, for example, only a relatively short distance to the south, is virtually a separate language.

Home visit At the station you can arrange a visit to a private home. Families who speak English or other foreign languages have been selected for this programme. Arrangement can also be made by phone (24-1111).

Iso-tei-en

This is a large landscape garden over 300 years old, employing ponds and plants in artistic arrangement. It stretches along the coast, overlooking the magnificence of Sakurajima and overlooked by nearby Isoyama (to which a cable-car leads). In the midst of the garden stands a 13-room villa, and there is a good beach nearby. Iso-tei-en can be reached by city bus 1 in 20 minutes.

Shoko-Shuseikan Museum

This building was formerly a factory, built by Nariakira Shimazu, an exceptionally enlightened daimyo of the area in the second quarter of the 19th century. He introduced his people to a number of western skills, like photography, telegraphy, cotton-spinning, glass- and armaments-making, etc. The museum displays items from 700 years of the Shimazu family, and is located beside Iso-tei-en garden.

Ijinkan

A short distance back toward the city from the museum is Ijinkan ('foreigners' residence'), built for overseas advisors in the last century. It is a large wooden house of distinctively foreign architecture — probably early Victorian — and is an anomaly in Japan, especially when contrasted with the lovely and traditional villa in Iso-tei-en garden.

Other

Another (lesser) attraction of Kagoshima is the foundation stones and walls of the former Tsurumaru Castle. The northbound tram line passes by it, and the closest stop is also the most convenient for walking up to Shiroyama ('Castle Mountain'). The castle was built in 1602, but was destroyed in the 1870s when local Satsuma rebels under Saigo opposed the Meiji restoration. There isn't space here to describe Saigo's activities, but his battle was futile, and he committed sepuku (ritual suicide) in a cave near the castle. His name will be found in many places in Kagoshima, and Terukuni-jinja shrine at the foot of Shiroyama honours him.

Other attractions include the Tropical Plants Botanical Garden, and nearby Kamoike Marine Park with its underwater restaurant.

There are three potteries in Kagoshima area: Satsuma Toki, Urushima-Togei, and Chotaro-Yaki. You can arrange to visit them through the tourist office at the station.

Accommodation

There are many hotels in Kagoshima and nearby resort towns like Ibusuki and the hot-spring town of Furusato. Help in finding a room can be obtained at the station. There is a pleasant youth hostel (in a large, oldish, semi-western style building) in Kagoshima

(Kagoshima-ken Fujin-kaikan; tel (0992) 51-1087), as well as others on Sakurajima across the harbour (Sakurajima Youth Hostel, tel (099293) 2150), at Ibusuki (Ibusuki Youth Hostel tel (09932) 2-2758), and Tamaya Youth Hostel (tel (09932) 2-3553). Fujin-kaikan Youth Hostel is easily reached from Nishi-Kagoshima station by tram 1 (north-bound for Kagoshima station). One line branches off to the left after crossing a bridge; shortly afterward, another branches off to the right. Get off at the fourth stop (the second after crossing the large Takeno bridge. Buses 16 and 25 also pass close by.

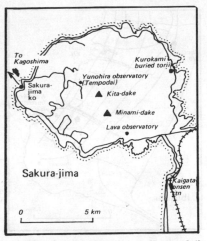

SAKURAJIMA

The cone of Sakurajima dominates the skyline of Kagoshima. The city is sometimes compared with Naples, and this is one time that the comparison is not far-fetched (as it often is elsewhere in Japan). Sakurajima was an island until 1914, when an immense eruption poured out an estimated 3000 million tons of lava and ash, and bridged the gap to the mainland on the side facing away from Kagoshima. The peninsula is virtually one large lava and ash field, and it is interesting to spend some time looking around the huge and jagged masses of ugly but fascinating black rock. You can take a sightseeing bus from the Kagoshima ferry dock; the trip takes 1¾ hours. The lava field begins only about 10 minutes walk away from the dock. Only Minami-dake (south peak) is still active; it occasionally ejects rock, so climbing is prohibited. Large clouds of smoke and fine ash are also quite common.

One of the interesting sights on the island is the torii (gate) of a shrine at Kurokami. It was once four metres high, but the eruption buried so much of it that only the top metre still shows above the ground.

There is a lava observatory (tempodai) on the south side of the island, giving a good view of the great expanse of lava hurled out during the 20 or so eruptions known during recorded history. On the peninsula are farms that produce the largest radishes in the world — some 50 cm in diameter and 45 kg in weight!

Ferries to Sakura-jima leave the Kagoshima side regularly; the dock (Sakurajima-sambashi) is close to the main Kagoshima station.

CHIRAN

This little town, a bit over an hour from Kagoshima by bus, preserves one corner much as it was two centuries ago. Several samurai houses are open to the public, and are worth visiting for a look at the lovely gardens and large residences of this formerly privileged class. Buses to Chiran leave Kagoshima from Yamagataya bus terminal (Yamagataya department store), and make trips in each direction 11 times a day.

IBUSUKI

About an hour south of Kagoshima by train or bus (from Nishi-Kagoshima

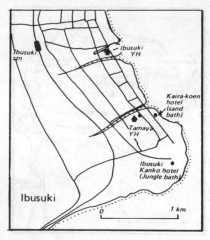

station), Ibusuki is a pleasant hot-spring resort town. Unlike most such towns, this one can be readily enjoyed by westerners as well as Japanese.

Information

At Ibusuki station, your first stop should be at the tourist information office to pick up a map of the area; it has enough English to be useful. The girls probably won't speak English, but they are friendly and helpful.

For the day's nibbles, try to find the Lotteria coffee shop near the station; a shop in the building sells a variety of tempura, good for a picnic lunch.

Sand Bath (Sunamushi)

One of the most unusual sensations of Japan (very pleasant!) is to be buried up to the neck in hot sand. This occurs when a hot spring surfaces near a beach, permeating the sand and heating it to a high but still bearable temperature. Go to the Kaira-kuen Hotel and ask for a sunamushi: you'll be directed to a small area on the beach behind the hotel next to the sea-wall, where the attendant will dig a hole and shovel you in. The experience is wonderfully relaxing, probably better left for the end of a

day's explorations lest all your energy be sapped at the start!

Jungle Bath (Junguro-furo)

After lying in the sand, move down the road a km or so to the huge Ibusuki Kanko Hotel, a very popular destination for Japanese honeymooners and recommended to anyone travelling on a non-budget basis. Its facilities are quite luxurious and on a grand scale.

The Jungle Bath is a building the size of an aircraft hangar, to the left of the main hotel building. It contains over 15 pools of hot-spring water of different temperatures, size, shape, and mineral content. Luxuriant growths of tropical plants decorate the room. Depending on the season, it may be crowded or you may have the place almost to yourself. The sensation of luxuriating in the various pools is marvellous, but it is best to go with a friend because the experience becomes boring without someone to talk to. (It doesn't matter if the friend is male or female, for this is one of the few easily-found mixed baths in Japan. There is a ladies-only section, but it only has two or three pools.) If you would like to try it, but are shy, remember that a towel can hide everything worth hiding, and the novelty wears off so that the whole experience seems quite natural. The baths are open from 7 am to 1 am, and entry costs about Y500.

There is also a sand bath adjacent to the pools, but it is indoors and the water is piped, so the beach area might be preferable.

Kaimon-dake

Another attraction of the Ibusuki area is the graceful conical shape of Kaimon-dake. Buses run from Yamagawa (near the Kanko Hotel) past the mountain to Makurazaki; from there, buses run to Kagoshima via Chiran, allowing a circular route around the bottom of the peninsula. Kaimon-dake can be climbed in about two hours, starting from Kaimon-dake bus stop. Another nearby feature is the round caldera lake, Ikeda-ko; and projecting below the body of the peninsula is the spit Nagasaki-bana (Long Cape Harbour), which offers an excellent view of Kaimon-dake and the sea.

Bus tours

Several bus tours begin at Ibusuki station, and make sightseeing in the area very easy. All but one begin in the morning; some return to Ibusuki, and some terminate in Kagoshima. The basic tours take in Kaimon-dake and Ikeda-ko, others take in destinations such as Ibusuki Skyline Highway, Chiran and Sakura-jima, while others cross the bay and travel to Sata-misaki Cape, ending at Kagoshima. Information on these tours, and others beginning at Kago-shima, is available from the information centres at Nishi-Kagoshima or Ibusuki stations.

SATA-MISAKI CAPE

Sata-misaki, across Kagoshima Bay, is the southernmost point of the main islands of Japan. Rugged rocks projecting out of the sea, blue water, and the first lighthouse in the counyry (built under the supervision of an Englishman soon after the country was opened to foreigners) are the attractions. The cape can be reached easily by tour bus from Ibusuki or Nishi-Kagoshima station.

MIYAZAKI-KEN

TOI-MISAKI CAPE

This is another scenic cape, north-east of Cape Sata, famed for small herds of wild horses that are allowed to roam free. It is most easily reached by bus from Aburatsu or Miyazaki; a sightseeing bus travels from the latter along the picturesque Nichinan coast.

NICHINAN-KAIGAN COAST

This is a very pretty stretch of coast extending about 100 km from Shibushi Bay to Miyazaki city. It has been compared with the Amalfi coast of Italy, and one cyclist friend said he was tempted to turn around and return the way he had come because he found it so pleasant. Because the climate is so mild, semi-tropical plants such as palms flourish.

Along the way is Udo-jingu shrine, perched on cliffs at the edge of the sea, partly in a cave.

Aoshima

Aoshima is a small island, now connected to the mainland by a causeway. It is covered with betel-nut palms, and the surrounding beach has many tiny sea-shells. It is famous for the Ogres' Washboard, formed over the ages when sedimentary rock became un-ended and eroded differentially, so that there are now separate ridges of rock. It is quite interesting when visible at low tide.

There is good swimming at Aoshima, and other places to visit are the Cactus Park (with a reputed million plants) and the Sub-tropical Plant Garden. Because it is a popular tourist destination, there are many hotels, etc. There is also a youth hostel close by.

MIYAZAKI

The city of Miyazaki sits in the middle of the area that was the centre of early Japanese civilisation (as we now know it). Because this period predated written history, much of its story is mythical, and no structures survive. However, some interesting remains have been excavated and are worth a look. The name Miyazaki means 'shrine promontory'.

Heiwadai Park

The city of Miyazaki is quite ordinary,

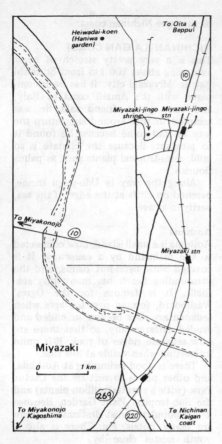

Miyazaki

Haniwa-niwa Haniwa are charming and attractive clay figures that have been excavated from the many burial mounds found in the vicinity. Reproductions of many of these have been artistically located around the park, surrounded by flowers, under shrubs, beside trees. Most of the figures are about a metre high, so the details are clearly discernable: most have very charming and humorous expressions. There are knights with horses, court ladies, even a vacant-faced village idiot — I thought it a most pleasant introduction to archaeology. Miniature reproductions of many of the figures are on sale at the administrative building near the garden. They can also be bought in Tokyo and other centres, but finding them can be a problem without time to look around, and the selection may not be as great.

Miyazaki-jingu shrine
The first emperor of Japan was Jimmu, a man known more from myths than actual fact. He was the ruler of this area of Kyushu about 600 BC; his descendants — the Yamato tribe — went on to conquer all of Japan, thus determining its culture. He is enshrined in Miyazaki-jingu, and in the grounds there is a museum of items excavated from nearby tombs.

Both Heiwadai and Miyazaki-jingu are accessible from Miyazaki station by bus; the first station north of Miyazaki (called Miyazaki-jingu) is also close to the shrine.

Saitobaru
The early settlers of this area brought with them the practice of building tomb mounds (kofun), which was carried on into at least the 7th century — culminating in the largest at Sakai, near Osaka (where the Yamato migrated in large numbers). Similar mound-building customs existed in Korea, especially in the Kyongju area, not too far from the

but you can spend your time profitably by visiting Heiwadai-koen park. Heiwa means 'peace', and it is somewhat ironic that the 36-metre tower was built in 1940. The tower is of little interest unless you look for the marker on the path leading to the main staircase. Standing there, clapping your hands loudly results in a strange, groaning echo. The main attraction of the park, other than the many flowers that bloom during the first five months, is Haniwa-niwa.

coast facing Japan. It would seem likely that the origin of the early settlers was Korea, but among scholars debates still continue. (Since many contemporary Japanese dislike Koreans (and vice versa), it would not please the national ego to admit that they are descendants of Koreans.)

This is intended as introduction to Saitobaru, where about 300 tomb mounds dot the flat countryside. They will probably be of limited interest to most visitors, because they are little more than grassy mounds of earth: some only a metre or so in height, others large enough to be mistaken for hills. They will be of greater interest to archaeologists, and items excavated from the tombs are displayed at the museums in Saito and at Miyazaki-jingu. The figures at Haniwa-niwa are reproductions of funerary items from this area.

The tomb area is close to Saito on Route 219, which leads to Hitoyoshi; the closest railway station is Tsuki, reached by branching off the main line at Sadowara.

HYUGA

The city of Hyuga is not special touristically, but it is connected with a number of cities by ferries: Hiroshima, Kobe, Osaka and Kawasaki (near Tokyo). Minimum fares, respectively, are Y4000, Y5800, Y5800 and Y11,600. The boat to Hiroshima is noteworthy because it leaves at 12.30 pm and arrives at 9.20 pm, so it passes through the western end of the Inland Sea during daylight; most other ferries run at night, so sightseeing is usually minimal. The other boats leave in the early evening (see *Jikokuhyo* for recent information).

TAKACHIHO-KYO GORGE

Inland from Nobeoka by road (Route 218) or JNR, or south-east from the Aso area by Routes 325 or 265/218, is the lovely Takachiho-kyo. The cliffs are formed by columnar basalt, lava that has cooled into parallel pillars of rock up to 80 metres high. The green water of the Gokase river passes through the narrow valley, and waterfalls splash down here and there.

Also of interest is Takachiho-jinja shrine. This sacred site is said to be the 'Crade of Japan', so the shrine is quite important. Of special interest is the sacred dance, Iwato Kagura, which is performed every day.

In addition to other accommodation in the area, there are three youth hostels. One traveller had nothing but the highest praise for the food at Yamatoya Youth Hostel; however, I tried three times to obtain accommodation there without success.

OITA-KEN

USUKI AREA

The attraction of the Usuki area is a number of statues of Buddha dating from the 10th to the 12th centuries. The most artistic and numerous of these are located near Usuki; several are largely intact, while elsewhere only the heads have survived (but these heads are well formed and some of the original colouring remains). The Usuki images (Seki-butsu) are displayed in a small ravine not far from Kami-Usuki station (JNR). A good descriptive pamphlet in English is given out when you enter.

Other rock sculptures are scattered through the valleys of the Oita and Ono rivers, at Motomachi, Takase, Sugao, Ogata and Fukoji, as well as on the Kunisaki Peninsula to the north. Motomachi has some of the best-preserved images, those at Magari are badly weathered, and those at Takase are so-so.

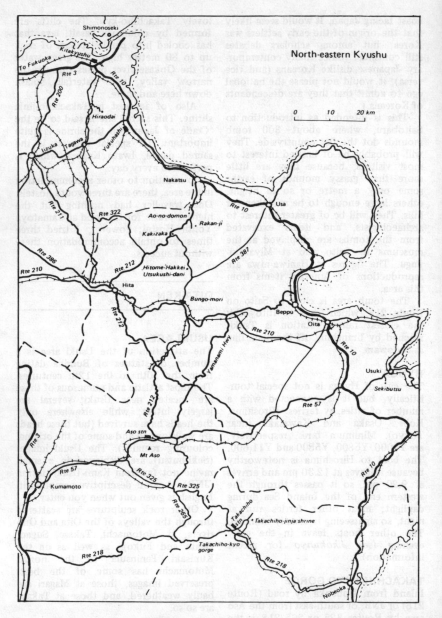

North-eastern Kyushu

0   10   20 km

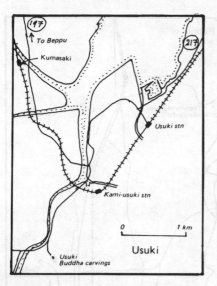

To Beppu
Kumasaki

Usuki stn

Kami-usuki stn

0   1 km

Usuki

Usuki
Buddha carvings

Takeda

Ogata and Fukoji are quite close to Takeda (Bungo-Takeda station), where Oka-jo castle once stood. The castle was destroyed in the late 19th century, and only its foundation stones and walls still stand, rising high up a hillside. It inspired the very famous composition Kojo-no-tsuki ('Moon over Castle Ruins'), one of the world's most hauntingly beautiful pieces of music, especially when played on the intended koto and shakuhachi. Its composer, Rentaro Taki, was influenced by western music so western ears will find it very beautiful. (A record of this composition would make a good souvenir of Japan.) Also in this area is Harajiki waterfall.

OITA

Ferries sail from this city to Kobe twice a day in each direction. Both leave in the evening. The boat stops at Matsuyama (Shikoku) en route.

BEPPU

Beppu is one of the best-known hot-spring resorts in Japan, ideal for sybaritic delights and interesting sightseeing. There are eight 'towns' with hot-springs within the bounds of Beppu; the total water outflow exceeds 100 million litres per day.

The hells (Jigoku)

For those not particularly interested in hot-spring bathing, however, there is another attraction — the jigoku or 'hells'. In several places around the city, subterranean water of boiling temperature comes to the surface, sometimes violently, sometimes quietly but colourfully — would you believe a pond of naturally red water? Other malevolent emenations include geysers and dark, malodorous, bubbling pools of mud.

The hells are located in two areas of Beppu. Several are clustered close together at Kannawa, about six km from Beppu station, and the other two are a couple of km farther away. The first cluster can be reached by Beppu station by bus 16, 17, 24, 25 or 27, getting off at Kannawa. A ticket for entry to most of the nine hells is available for the price of five (in fact, only about five of them are really worth visiting). The following list describes the hells from west to east, and then the separate ones.

Hon Bozu jigoku Not included on the multiple ticket, and some distance up a long hill (accessible from Hon Bozu bus stop, the second after Kannawa), this hell features a number of grey mud pools that plurp and plop in a humorous manner. Recommended more to those who will not have any other opportunity to see such boiling mud.

Umi jigoku The name means 'sea', and the water is a very picturesque green. It

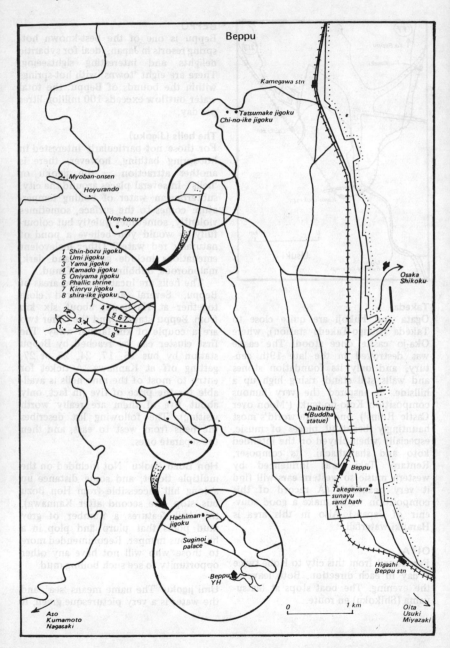

Beppu

Kamegawa stn

Tatsumake jigoku
Chi-no-ike jigoku

Myoban-onsen

Hoyurando

Hon-bozu

1 Shin-bozu jigoku
2 Umi jigoku
3 Yama jigoku
4 Kamado jigoku
5 Oniyama jigoku
6 Phallic shrine
7 Kinryu jigoku
8 shira-ike jigoku

Osaka
Shikoku-

Daibutsu
(Buddha
statue)

Beppu

Takegawara-
sunayu sand bath

Hachiman
jigoku

Suginoi
palace

Beppu
YH

Higashi
Beppu stn

Aso
Kumamoto
Nagasaki

0   1 km

Oita
Usuki
Miyazaki

is hot enough to boil eggs, as demonstrated by a basket of them suspended in the water. Around the grounds are torii gates. There is a second pond, also green, but cooler.

Yama jigoku This is of minimal proportions, and wild animals on display are the attraction. Their living conditions demonstrate an unfortunate Japanese trait of not caring for the comfort of animals. Not recommended.

Garden The garden on the corner between hells is pleasant, but not particularly noteworthy. Admittance is separate.

Oniyama jigoku The hell content here is negligible: the attraction is a number of crocodiles.

Phallic shrine Amidst the hells is this strange little shrine with a sizeable collection of carved phalluses. For those with an earthy sense of humour, very recommendable; for those easily shocked, to be avoided.

Kinryu jigoku The name means 'golden dragon'. There is nothing to see except for clouds of steam and gaudy faded Buddhist images. A waste of time.

Shiroike jigoku The attraction is a cloudy-white pond and several small aquaria of fish not native to Japan, including large ungainly pirarucu from the Amazon. The pond is similar to that at Hoyurando (described later), but of minor interest. The name, by the way, means 'white pond'.

Kamado jigoku One of the main attractions here is the noise, for steam jets non-stop out of the ground with a great roar. Also interesting is red-brown bubbling mud. If one dares to believe signs, the precipitated minerals on sale are good for the following interesting

collection of ailments: 'chronic mascular rheumatism, mascular rigidity, neuralgia, arthritis, gout, swelling of gland and syphilis, anaemia, weakness after illness, chronic gastroenteric catarrhs and fatigue, evidation after getting a wind, haemorrhoids, scabies, honeycomb ringworm, scaly tetter, moist tetter, leucodermia and other chronic skin diseases and ulcers'.

Chi-no-ike jigoku The name means 'blood hell', and comes from the surprising red of the water (due to ferrous oxide). It is worth seeing for its unusual colour. To reach this and the following jigoku, it is necessary to take a bus or taxi to Chinoike stop. The two hells are a short walk back up the hill.

Tatsumaki jigoku This is the only geyser of the Beppu hells. The name means 'waterspout hell', and it erupts frequently enough to be worth waiting for.

Tsurumi jigoku Not on the 'regular' route, this jigoku is close to the Suginoi Hotel. It also has a number of Buddha statues, said to be 'in good taste'.

Takasagi-yama
One of the other sightseeing 'targets', this mountain is known for its semi-wild monkeys (tame enough to have no fear of humans, but wild enough not to thrust). The mountain is most easily reached by bus from Beppu station; ask at the information centre for directions.

Daibutsu
This large concrete figure of Buddha is a rather unusual sight in Beppu, mostly of curiosity value. Unlike the usual benevolent visage, this Buddha scowls and looks generally unpleasant. Mixed into the concrete are the ashes of thousands of cremated Buddhists.

Hoyurando Hot-spring Baths

The best (perhaps only) outdoor hot-spring pools around Beppu are located at Hoyurando, a hotel-style resort: the name translates as either 'Recreation land' or 'Recuperation land'. Behind the hotel building are two outdoor pools of bluish-white water, strongly sulphurous to the nose. Bathing here is mixed, but there are segregated pools inside the buildings.

To use the baths, you enter the hotel lobby, pay the fee, then leave by the rear and follow the long covered walkway downhill to the baths. After disrobing and washing you then enter the chosen bath or pool. (Hints for proper decorum in mixed nude baths is given in the section on Noboribetsu-onsen, Hokkaido.) The outdoor pools are most enjoyable in warm, sunny weather although the warm water guarantees comfort in any season while submerged. There are also two kinds of mud bath.

Behind the hotel and to the left is the source of the hot water, marked by the bright colours of chemicals precipitated from the subterranean water as it cools. Most of the baths are for the use of hotel guests only, but the most interesting ones are open to the public.

Hoyurando is a couple of km beyond the jigoku of the Kannawa area, on the road that forks off to the right. There is bus service (en route to Ajimu), and the stop is Hoyurando. On the way, the bus passes through another of the eight active hot-spring areas, Myoban. Numbers of little tent-like grass huts have been built over the springs, and heat to form natural steam baths.

Suginoi Hotel

The huge Suginoi Hotel can be recommended for its annex, Suginoi Palace. Along with arcade games, it has a large stage with a nightly production of a play, mini-circus, or other act. In the same complex are two gigantic bath rooms, both the size of an aircraft hangar, one each for men and women (no mixed section). In each are several pools of different size and temperature: from two-people size to gigantic, from frigid to *very* hot. Decorations on the men's side include a waterfall, a slide, torii gate and a Chinese-style temple with heated marble floor. Tropical plants luxuriate. The ladies' side has a large and benevolent Buddha and equally lush greenery.

Oishi-so Bath

This smaller-scale bath is open to the public. It has tastefully decorated pools, with rock walls and floors. It is located a short distance down from the cluster of jigoku on the main road. (It also offers accommodation.) A sand bath is included in the amenities.

Hot-Sand Baths

Another activity to enjoy in Beppu is a sand bath, where one is buried to the neck in naturally hot, steaming sand. Public sand baths (suna) are found both on the beach and indoors at Takegawara. The latter is a large, oldish, wooden building, where you pay at the entrance, put your clothes in a locker, rinse at the small concrete tub, pick up your towel (or one of the many lying around) and follow one of the ladies to the hole she has dug for you in the sand. Lie down, put the towel where it will do the most good, and relax while she piles even more hot sand over your body. The feeling of infinite relaxation will overtake you as the warmth permeates. When your time is up, rinse off the sand, soap, rinse again, and it's all over (take your own soap and towel). Definitely worth while, and only costs a few hundred yen.

It's quite common to have your picture taken in the sand bath: pre-set your camera, and use sign language to explain to the 'burier' what you want.

It might be best to keep your camera in a plastic bag until it is time to take the picture.

There is also an open-air sand bath on the beach near Kamegawa station (ask for 'sunayu').

Information
There is an information centre at the station that gives out maps and other literature, some in English. As usual with Japanese maps, some may have only a superficial resemblance to true scale and actual locations.

Accommodation
In addition to countless hotels, ryokan and minshuku, there is also a Beppu Youth Hostel. The information centre should have instructions on how to get there (it is very close to the Suginoi Hotel).

Getting There
In addition to train service and flights from nearby Oita airport (which is actually north of Beppu, on the Kunisaki Peninsula), there are three ferries daily to and from Osaka. The departure times from Beppu are 5 pm, 5.30 pm and 9.30 pm, and the trip takes about 17 hours, making various stops on Shikoku en route. From Osaka, departure times are 4.30 pm, 9 pm and 9.40 pm, the trip taking 14-15 hours (minimum fare is Y4500). The last sailing from Osaka is one of the very few long-distance ferries that passes through a worthwhile portion of the Inland Sea during daylight hours. Since the sun rises as early as 4.30 am during the summer, a traveller to Beppu can see some of the scenery at the western end of the sea. Travellers from Beppu might also see some of the eastern end in daylight. There are also ferries to points on Shikoku. The dock is 10 minutes from the station by bus.

YUFUIN-ONSEN
This is another hot-spring resort town, not too far from Beppu. Accommodation is in the Y10,000 a night range, so not for budget travellers, but if you are not worried about money you would enjoy staying at one of the thatched-roof farmhouses that serve as inns. The town reputedly has the only free public bath in Japan. The setting is very scenic, with a mountain in the background. It can be reached by bus directly from Beppu, or indirectly via Oita by train.

YAMANAMI HIGHWAY
Beppu is the eastern terminus of this highway that crosses Kyushu via Mt Aso and Mumamoto, ending at Nagasaki. It passes through some of the prettiest countryside in Kyushu, and can be recommended. Four buses leave Beppu daily, one of which goes non-stop to Nagasaki, the others finishing at Kumamoto.

USA
To the north of Beppu lies the shrine city of Usa. The bright-orange shrine buildings are decorated with carvings; the style of the buildings is of the Heian era (1000-1100) but the shrine was founded earlier (725). The hill on which the shrine is built is an old burial mound.

Usa was once the political, economic and cultural centre of Kyushu. At one time there were 65 temples in the area, but through the years they have disappeared — only the carved Buddha heads and tombstones scattered around nearby Kunisake-hanto Peninsula testify to its former importance and strong Buddhist influence.

A story, probably dubious, reported that interest in Usa picked up in the immediate post-war occupation period by companies who wanted to be able to mark their manufactures MADE IN USA.

YABAKEI GORGE

Pleasant scenery may be found along the Yamakunikawa river in Yabakei Gorge. It is 'pleasant' rather than 'spectacular', for the cliffs on either side of the river (along which the road passes) are often far apart and do not soar skyward as do those of some other gorges in Japan.

The gorge is easily seen by bus from Nakatsu. The starting point of the gorge is near Ao-no-Domon, about 16 km out of Nakatsu, and continues for about 10 km to Kakizaka. Apart from the main gorge, (Hon-Yabakei) there are several gorges that branch off from it, the most attractive of which is Shin-Yabakei ('deep Yabakei'), beginning at Kakizawa. The main attractions begin about eight km into the valley and include Hitome-Hakkei ('one look — eight views') and Utsukushi-dani ('beautiful valley'). However, despite the fame and reputation of the valley, I was somewhat underwhelmed and would suggest it mostly for those with a little extra time.

From Nakatsu station, buses run at least as far as Kakizawa (23 a day): of these, three a day turn and go through Shin-Yabakei (with another four a day that originate at Kakizawa) as far as Bungo-Mori (on Route 210 and JNR). There are six buses a day returning from Bungo-mori to Kakizawa, and a much greater number from there back to Nakatsu (or on to Hita), so a one-day excursion out of Nakatsu is possible.

Nansei Islands

Below Kyushu and stretching to Taiwan are the Nansei (South-West) Islands. Some are mere atolls, while others support sizeable populations. As far as Yoron-shima is Kagoshima-ken, while Okinawa and all the islands south of it make up Okinawa-ken. Close to Kagoshima are Tanegashima and Yakushima, and further south the Satsuman group (which includes Amami-oshima, Tokuno-shima, Okino-erabu-shima, and Yoron-shima). Below them is the Ryukyu group (made up of Okinawa and the islands around it), the Saki group (around Miyako), and the Yaeyama group (Ishigaki, Iriomote, and Yanaguni). All offer a semi-tropical flavour not found in the main islands of Japan.

The culture of the Nansei islands is basically Japanese, but there is also a Chinese element. The islands closest to Kagoshima were most strongly influenced by the Satsuma culture, and the islands closest to Taiwan had the greatest Chinese influence. The unfortunate islanders had the misfortune of being squeezed between two powers, and had to pay tribute to both, causing much misery in olden times. Until quite recently there was a distinct Okinawan language, related to Japanese but quite incomprehensible to main-island Japanese, even to those of the Satsuma area. Many place names are local pronunciation of the kanji, used here as much as possible.

Snake Warning

Nearly all islands except Miyako are inhabited by a venomous snake — the habu. Every year about 300 people are bitten, four or five of whom die (prompt medical treatment from special clinics keeps the toll this low). The snakes are nocturnal, so be especially careful at night. Carry a bright light (which they dislike) and make lots of

Nansei Islands

0   100 km

noise, particularly walking heavily, for snakes are deaf. They are always found in pineapple plantations.

Getting There
There is boat service from Kagoshima to Okinawa that stops at all the major islands en route. The schedule is a little complex because more than one company operates boats, but the average is about four boats per week. Departure time from Kagoshima is 6 am, and Naha (Okinawa) at 6.30 pm. There is an air service to a number of the islands from Kagoshima and Naha. Details of these services may be obtained at any travel agent, TIC offices in Tokyo and Kyoto, and at the info office at Nishi-Kagoshima station. Further details of services to and from Okinawa are given below.

TANEGASHIMA
Both this island and Yaku-shima are close to southern Kyushu, and are easily reached by boat (two or more sailings a day to each island), or air from Kagoshima.

There is no special attraction on no single attractions (these islands are also basically agricultural, producing semi-tropical crops such as bananas, pineapples, sugar, etc), there are many good beaches for relaxation.

The scenery of Amami-oshima and

Tanegashima other than its relative remoteness; the island is flat and agricultural. There are campsites, and a bus service several times a day between the north and south. The main city and boat landing point is Nishino-omote.

YAKU-SHIMA
Whereas Tanegashima is quite flat, Yaku-shima has the highest mountain in Kyushu (Miyano-ura-dake 1935 metres), plus a number of lesser peaks. The island is well known for huge centuries-old cedar trees (yaku-sugi). Boats from Kagoshima dock at Miyano-ura, and there are several buses daily covering three-quarters of the distance around the island.

AMAMI ISLANDS
The Amami group comprises the main islands of Amami, Kikai-ga, Tokuno, Okino-erabu and Yoron. While there are

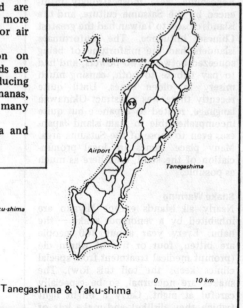

Tanegashima & Yaku-shima

the other islands is beautiful. There is a bus service through the island, or you can rent a bicycle or motorcycle. Camping is good. In contrast with the emerald of the coral sea around Okinawa, the water here is deep blue.

OKINAWA

The largest of all the south-west islands is Okinawa. From the 14th to the 19th century, this was a nominally independent kingdom with its own language and culture. Both were related to Japanese, but there was a strong Chinese influence. The rulers of both Japan and China maintained suzerainty of the islands, and the people were kept poor by having to provide tribute to both governments. In the last century the Japanese connection became dominant, but the people have generally been regarded as somewhat second-class citizens. After World War II the American military occupation continued, making travel there difficult until 1972 when it reverted to Japanese control.

Okinawa and the other islands of the Ryukyu group (south and west to Taiwan) are still economically disadvantaged relative to the main islands of Japan, and depend mainly on agriculture (especially crops like pineapple, sugar, etc) as well as tourism. All the islands offer a warm to hot climate very similar to the tropics, and most have good beaches and clear water, so they have become popular destinations for the main-island Japanese (especially in winter).

Getting There

Naha (the capital) is an international port of entry for flights from Manila and Taipei. There is a weekly boat between Naha and Keelung (Taiwan), leaving Naha on Friday, stopping en route at Miyazaki and Ishigaki islands, and arriving at Keelung the next day. A visa is required, and can be obtained in Tokyo. The company, Arimura

Sangyo, has offices in Tokyo (tel 562-2091), Osaka (345-7421) and Naha (68-2191). Reservations (which are obligatory) can be made by travel agents throughout Japan, though possibly not by JTB.

Naha is also the main sea port of entry. There are boat servies to and from Tokyo: two services, each every five or six days (46 hours direct, or 48 hours via Amami-oshima and Yoron-shima. There are two services to and from Osaka: one every three or four days, and one every four or five days: (30½ hours direct, or 41 hours via Kobe and Amami-oshima). From Hakata (Fukuoka), there is a boat every four days (27 hours). From Kagoshima there are boats about five days a week (24½ hours via Amami-oshima, Tokuno-shima, Okino-erabu-shima, and Yoron-shima.

There are air services from Tokyo, Osaka, Nagoya, Fukuoka, Nagasaki, Kumamoto, Kagoshima, Miyazaki and nearly all the other Nansei islands.

Information

Additional information on Okinawa is available from the TIC in Tokyo, including the booklet *Okinawa Japan*, and the photocopied sheets 'How to Get to Keelung' (Y20), as well as the Okinawa-ken office in the Kokusai-kanko-kaikan building in Marunouchi (Tokyo). It might be worthwhile ringing the latter (tel 231-0848) to see if they speak English.

Getting Around

There are several bus tours (in Japanese only) to different destinations on Okinawa lasting 4½ to 9½ hours. There is also a large number of local buses for the adventurous.

NAHA

Today the administrative centre of Okinawa-ken, Naha was the capital of the Ryukyu kingdom for about 400 years. Remnants of three major castles

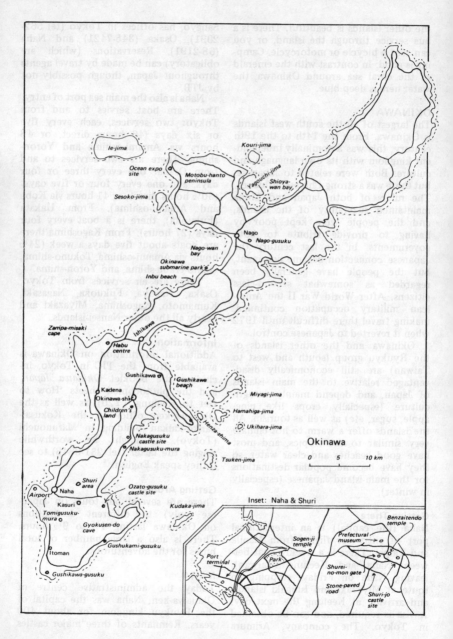

le-jima

Kouri-jima

Ocean
expo
site

Motobu-hanto
peninsula

Yagouchi-jima

Shioya-
wan bay

Sesoko-shima

Nago
Nago-gusuku

Nago-wan
bay

Okinawa
submarine park

Inbu beach

Zampa-misaki
cape

Ishikawa

Habu
centre

Gushikawa

Gushikawe
beach

Kadena

Miyagi-jima

Okinawa-shi

Hamahiga-jima

Children's
land

Ukihara-jima

Henza-shima

Nakagusuku
castle site

Nakagusuku-mura

Tsuken-jima

Okinawa

0   5   10 km

Shuri
area

Ozato-gusuku
castle site

Airport

Naha

Kasuri

Tomigusuku-
mura

Gyokusen-do
cave

Kudaka-jima

Inset: Naha & Shuri

Itoman

Gushukami-gusuku

Gushikawa-gusuku

Port
terminal

Sogen-ji
temple

Park

Benzaitendo
temple

Prefectural
museum

Shurei-
no-mon gate

Stone-paved
road

Shuri-jo
castle
site

and several lesser ones still stand for those days, along with some historic gates and other relics of Ryukyu design. Although the design of some of these structures appears Chinese, the architecture is an authentically Ryukyuan style that evolved through the centuries.

Information
A good first stop is the tourist information office, located on the city side of the harbour and river near the end of Meiji-bashi bridge. It is near the bus terminal and can be recognized by its red roof tiles. Staff there can provide ample information for getting around, and can also make hotel bookings.

The Boulevards
The main area of Naha is 1.6 km-long Kok'sai-dori (International Boulevard). It has several large department stores, as well as many shops catering to tourists with well-known Okinawa products like Bingata textiles, and shell and coral products. Near the end of Kok'sai-dori is Sogen-ji temple, known for the stone gates on two sides. Heavily damaged during the war, they were restored afterward. A uniquely Okinawan programme of classical and folk-dances and music is performed weekly at Oki-e theatre (near Mitsukoshi department store) and would be worth seeing.

Heiwa-dori (Peace Boulevard) runs off Kok'sai-dori and is the area of a typical Okinawa-style market. Women sit by their baskets of produce in a scene more like South-East Asia than Japan.

Shuri
Shuri is the former location of the castle of the kings of Okinawa during the zenith of the Ryukyu civilisation. The centrepiece, and symbol of this civilisation, is Shurei-no-mon gate. The original, dating from the founding of the castle, was destroyed during the war

and faithfully rebuilt afterward. Much of the original castle wall still stands, but a university now stands on the site of the castle itself.

Nearby is attractive Ryutan-ike pond and surrounding park, and not far away is Benzaitendo temple. The original dating from 1502, but it too was destroyed during the war and was rebuilt in 1968. On the north side of the pond is the very good prefectural museum (Kenritsu hakubutsu-kan) which is housed in the large and traditional residence of the Osho family.

A very charming walk goes along the stone-paved street of Kinjo ('silver castle') town. It leads down from the castle site to the harbour, and is lined by many fine traditional houses.

Other attractions of the area are Sone hiyan-utaki stone gate, Kankaimon gate of typical Ryukyu style (first built in the early 1500s, and rebuilt after the war), and Enkaku-ji somon temple (pre-1500s, and also rebuilt after war).

The Shuri area can be reached by bus 25 or 26 from the bus centre.

Arts & Crafts
A little farther away, you can find a workshop where Bingata textiles are produced. The dyes and patterns are very bright, quite different from the more subdued and restrained colours used on the main islands.

Another craft to look for is pottery. Tsuboya ware (named for the area where it is made) is quite simple ware intended mainly for use as storage vessels for water, etc. The forms and finishes owe more to Chinese and southern areas than to Japanese influences. The workshops are open to the public.

Tomigusuku
A castle once stood at Tomigusuku, south of Naha, but today only depressions in the ground indicate its site. More interesting, at least to those concerned

with events of World War II is the nearby headquarters of the Imperial Navy, easily reached on foot. The entire building was located underground, and was so well concealed that it was not discovered by the victorious Americans forces until three weeks after the landing. To their horror, they found that 4000 men and officers had committed suicide in the underground tunnels rather than surrender. The tunnels and rooms are now open to inspection, with no hint of that grisly occurence in 1945. Buses to Tomigusuku leave from the Naha bus centre.

Accommodation

As well as hotels and ryokan, there are three youth hostels in Naha. The Harumi-so has the best reputation; Tamazano is rated as OK; and the Maeda (north of the city) is also spoken of well.

AROUND THE COAST

As you travel south of Naha along town and country roads, a common sight is Okinawan houses with tiled roofs, all the tiles firmly cemented to guard against wind storms, and surmounted by a fierce shiisaa, the guardian lion that keeps evil spirits from the house. In former times, the tiles were formed and fired on site, and the shiisaa was sculpted of the same clay, but most nowadays are made in factories and lack individuality.

The south coast was the scene of the heaviest fighting of the landings of World War II — at Mabuni hill alone, 200,000 persons died. If you are interested in the various memorial sites, visit the tourist information office for further details. (*Note:* Residents still find live ordnance on the battlefields, and if you discover any you should notify the police or contact the USAF Kadena base.)

Gyokusendo

This is a limestone cave with a claimed 460,000 stalactites and other limestone configurations, many of which have interesting and lovely colours. About 800 metres of the cave are open for inspection.

Kasuri

If you are interested in weaving, visit the village of Kasuri (comprising Kiyan, Motobu, and Teruya) where the handwoven, vegetable-dyed Kasuri fabrics (mostly silk) are made.

Coastal Views

Continuing around the south coast and up the east, you are constantly in view of the deep-emerald sea. Along this coast and others you are likely to see uniquely Okinawan tombs — large structures set into the hillside overlooking the coast with a surrounding semicircular wall.

Nakagusuku Castle Site

Possibly the finest of such sites on Okinawa, the length and height of the remaining walls and three citadels give a good idea of the scale of the former buildings. From the ramparts you can see the Pacific Ocean in one direction, and the East China Sea in the other. It is located close to Nakagusuku-mura ('Central Castle Village').

Nakamura House (Nakamura-ke)

In the same area as Nakagusuku Castle, this is probably the finest residence on Okinawa. It was built in the mid-1700s by a wealthy farmer, and the five structures embody the best of traditional Okinawan building and decorative techniques.

OKINAWA-SHI

Much of this city is aimed at providing recreation for US airmen of nearby

Kadena Airforce Base. With its many clubs and bars, it has little resemblance to anything typically Okinawan or Japanese (other than an ability to make money). The mood is American, or at least the Japanese impression of American.

Of great interest to the Japanese is Plaza House Shopping Centre complete with large car park (an unaffordable luxury in most of Japan). The Tuttle Bookshop stocks a large number of books on Okinawa.

Okinawa Children's Land (Kodomo-no-Kuni)

To the south-east of the city, this aquarium raises more than 60 kinds of reptiles, and has exhibitions of over 200 kinds of tropical freshwater fish.

The Municipal Colosseum

At Gushikawa, near Children's Land, this is the venue of Sunday bullfights. These are not like the Spanish variety, but are 'bull sumo' — trying to force the opponent out of the ring by locking horns and pushing. Similar fights are found on several other islands of Japan and as far south as Indonesia.

The South-east Botanical Garden

This has a large variety and huge number of tropical plants, 600 kinds of flower, and 200 types of tropical fruit-tree intended to emphasize the island's nearly-tropical nature climate. A small lake and boats are also attractive.

HEDO-MISAKI CAPE

The view from this, the northern tip of Okinawa, is very pretty, and on a clear day you can see Yoron Island on the horizon. The view is definitely worth the trip, which passes a number of attractive villages along the way.

Until recently, only Route 58 on the west coast could be used to reach this northern tip, for the east-coast road was little more than a track. It has been improved, however, and completing a circle around the tip has become possible.

THE WEST COAST

Much of the west coast has been set aside as Okinawa Coast Quasi-National Park, which takes in the area from Hedo-misaki to the northern side of Motobu-hanto Peninsula, and resumes from the south side almost an equal distance to Zampa-misaki. The main attraction is the view of the coast and the beautiful colours of the water.

Motobu-hanto Peninsula

At the north-east neck of the peninsula, there is a beautiful view overlooking Yagachi and Okubo islands (large and small, respectively).

Ocean Expo In 1975 a mini World Expo was held near the north-west tip of the peninsula, based on the theme of using oceans. Although the exhibition lasted only six months, sufficient attractions have been carried over or added to give you an enjoyable day's outing.

The Okinawa Village Pavilion demonstrates the old culture of Okinawa, and has examples of houses in both traditional and modern styles. The Oceanic Culture Pavilion shows the rich variety of cultures found among the races and ethnic groups of the South Pacific. On the same site is the largest aquarium in the world, featuring three display areas that show tropical, ocean, and deep-sea fish as well as nine performing dolphins (at Okichan Theatre). Floating City is a science-fiction writer's delight, a large steel multi-columned structure in the water that supposedly represents the way we will live in the future (with appropriate phrases such as 'new era', 'producing harmony between science and nature', etc). It's interesting, but not to be taken seriously. (All attractions are closed on Mondays.)

At the northern end of the site is the graceful arc of beautiful Expo beach.

Accommodation in the vicinity of the Expo site is generally not inexpensive. Okinawa Resort Station is a resort village for young people, and uses retired JNR sleeping cars for accommodation. (They had to be brought to Okinawa, along with an idled steam engine, for there are no railways on the island.)

NAGO

Located at the southern neck of the peninsula, Nago was little damaged during the war and so you can still see several houses in the traditional Okinawan style. There are also tall gajyumaru trees 300 years old on the south-east approaches to the city. In late January and early February, the cherry blossoms are beautiful on the site of former Nago-gusuku castle, reached via a long stone staircase. At the top, you can enjoy an excellent view of the surrounding sea and land.

Okinawa Marine Park (Kaichu-koen)

Here a long walkway extends beyond the shallows of a reef to a column with underwater glass-windows, so visitors may look out from beneath sea-level. (Depending on conditions, the number of fish in view may be rather limited; visitors generally tend to visit Ocean Expo instead of here.)

In addition to the 'reverse aquarium' where fish can come to look at people, there is a museum showing may of the seashells found around the island. Glass-bottomed boats may be rented as well.

A short distance to the south are three fine beaches, beginning with Inbu Beach.

Habu Centre

Here you can see the venomous habu snake in perfect safety. A feature is a fight between a habu and a mongoose: the agile animal wins about 99% of the time, particularly because the nocturnal snake is at a disadvantage. The fights are staged relatively frequently, probably a reflection of the plentiful supply. (Recent research has shown that mature snakes can survive two to three years without any food whatsoever.)

Accommodation

In addition to several hotels of good quality, there are also many ryokan. Bookings may be made at the information centre.

OTHER RYUKYU ISLANDS

Ie-jima

Off the Motobu-hanto Peninsula, Ie island is easily traversed in a short time. There are many lovely views of the deep-blue sea. The Travel Village (on the side nearest Okinawa) is especially aimed at young travellers.

Minni-jima

This island is claimed to offer the most beautiful sunsets in Okinawa.

Kohama jima

Once bypassed by tourists, Kohama now has full-scale recreational facilities and is attracting more visitors to its fine beaches of white sand, and the coral reefs off-shore.

Kudaka-jima

The 'Island of the Gods' is quite sacred to Okinawans. There are many burials here, and funerary practices in the past were rather unusual. Many bodies were exposed to the elements in special places, and only after decomposition were the bones cleaned and buried. (This practice may still be found in mountain villages in the island of Bali in Indonesia.)

Especially on Kudaka, but true everywhere on Okinawa, foreigners are ill-advised to enter cemeteries. It will upset many of the local people, who believe that the presence of an outsider (especially a foreigner) will disturb the spirits of the dead with bad results for the living. It is worth reading up in advance of a visit to Kudaka to avoid misunderstanding. (The Tuttle bookstore in Naha has books on the subject.)

Others
Other islands that may be visited from Okinawa are Iheya, Izena, Kerama (a group of about 20 islands), and Kume. Information on how to get there can be obtained at the information centre or from travel agents.

MIYAKO
There are many beautiful views on Miyako, as well as fine beaches. Miyako-shima was not damaged during the war, so its appearance is more traditional than Okinawa. Most houses are surrounded by walls of coral as protection against the frequent typhoons. Unfortunately it can be a little difficult actually seeing the houses, because a screen of wood, rock, etc blocks the view through the gateway (its purpose is to keep out evil spirits, believed able to hop only in straight lines). Such superstitions are still strong, and a talisman will often be seen on a wall opposite the road that ends at a T-junction. Miyako-shima is at least as interesting for culture as its basically agricultural landscapes. It is one of the few islands free of the deadly habu snake.

Getting Around
The best way to get around is by bicycle or motorcycle rented from one of the shops near the harbour of the main city, Hiraro.

Accommodation
There are several minshuku, also near the harbour. A good one is Ueno-so.

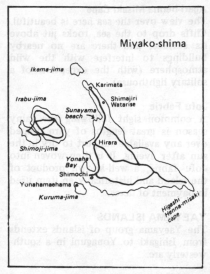

Miyako-shima

Ohonoyama-mura
Miyako Tropical Botanical Garden near here occupies 226 hectares of land, and houses 40,000 trees and over 1200 kinds of flowering plants from Central and South America, Africa, and the Philippines.

The 'poll stone' near Ohonoyama is a relic of harsh times in the past, when the islanders were little more than slaves, being taxed by both Chinese and Satsuma authorities. A person was compelled to pay taxes when his or her height equalled that of this stone. Its name is Jintozeizeki or Bubakariisu, depending on dialect.

Yonahamae Beach
Four km of white sand stretch along the blue waters, and offer excellent swimming.

Sunayama (Sand Mountain) Beach
Swimming is also good here, and nearby Miyako-jinja shrine is worth a look.

Agari-henna Misaki Cape
The view over the sea here is beautiful. Cliffs drop to the sea, rocks jut above its surface, and there are no nearby buildings to interfere with the wild atmosphere (with the exception of a solitary lighthouse).

Jofu Fabric
A common sight following the rainy season is great lengths of yarn draped over any available support to dry in the sun after dyeing. It is then woven into Jofu fabric, a well-known product of the island and historically an item used in payment of taxes.

YAEYAMA ISLANDS
The Yaeyama group of islands extends from Ishigaki to Yonaguni in a south-westerly arc.

ISHIGAKI-JIMA
The most important of the group,

Ishigaki is famed for its many beautiful beaches.

The main city and port is Ishigaki. Bicycles, motorcycles and cars can be rented from several shops near the centre of town (even by bicycle, it is possible to see the island in a day) and there is also a bus service.

Miyara Dunchi
This is a house of a noble of the old Ryukyu kingdom, dating from 1819. It follows the plan of houses of people of equal rank that were built around the castle at Shuri on Okinawa; here it is unique, the island's most valued cultural asset. (It may be described as a samurai house, but there were no true samurai in this region.) It houses a small museum of the period, and is also noted for its garden and stone wall.

Yaeyama Shiritsu Museum
Exhibits relating to the culture of the

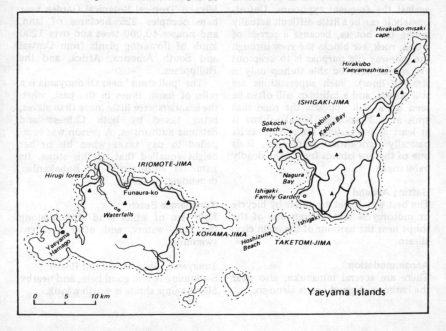

Yaeyama Islands

Yaeyama islands are on display at this very interesting museum. Labels, unfortunately, are only in Japanese, but most displays can be understood.

Chorin-ji
This temple has some beautiful old Buddhist sculptures.

Chinese Cemetery
The very Chinese-looking monument here commemorates 128 Chinese who were killed in a fight on a British ship in the last century, and is considered a general monument to peace.

Kabira-wan Bay
Most visitors consider this the most beautiful place on the island. Pearls are cultivated here, and are of an unusual (and thus very costly) black hue. They take the name of the island group, Yaeyama. The bay can be reached by bus.

The Beaches
Most visitors will want to enjoy the fine beaches of Ishigaki. Skindiving and scuba gear are available for rent, and since there are many types of incredibly and beautiful tropical fish in the waters around this (and all the other) islands diving can be recommended. Water-skiing and fishing are other potential activities.

Accommodation
Accommodation is plentiful, mostly in the form of minshuku, but there are two camping grounds as well.

Getting to Other Islands
Nearby Taketomi can be reached in about 10 minutes, and Iriomote is accessible by regular boat or hovercraft.

There is a boat service to and from Miyako and Naha every eight to 10 days; and the weekly boat from Naha to Taiwan stops at Ishigaki en route

(but not on the return trip). There is air service to and from Naha on Okinawa, as well as to Yonaguni, Tarama and Hateruma islands.

TAKETOMI-JIMA
Just a short distance west of Ishigaki, tiny Taketomi (11 km in circumference) can be explored easily in a day on bicycle (available near the boat dock). The island is very popular with day-trippers from Ishigaki, for its magnificent beaches virtually surround the island.

Because it was an untouristed backwater until only a decade or so ago, the pace of life and traditions on Taketomi are much as they always were. The people are friendly, and houses are still of the traditional style, surrounded by walls of coral. It is common to see people preparing the thread for weaving minsaori fabric, a craft going back to the 17th century: the yarn may be seen stretched by the side of the street. An exhibition of weaving may be seen at the Folk Art Museum in the village; small items are on sale.

Some water-buffalo may be seen in the island, either working in the fields or pulling carts for tourists.

Star Sand (hoshi-no-suna)
Taketomi's beaches are noted for 'star sand': what looks like ordinary white sand is actually the five-pointed skeletal remains of tiny sea creatures. Most of it has been collected by visitors (or souvenir-sellers), but it may be possible to find some in pockets in the coral, particularly on the south side of the island. The sand is stirred up from the depths by storms and washed ashore, so the supply is renewed periodically. (Not generally known is that this sand is found on all the Yaeyama islands.) If you find a 'deposit', remember the motto: 'Take a little and it will bring lots of happiness; take a lot and it will bring little happiness.' Leave some for the next person.

Accommodation

There are minshuku and a Youth Hostel in Taketomi.

Getting There

Taketomi is only 10 minutes from Ishigaki by boat; there are about 20 crossings a day.

IRIOMOTE

More than 80% of this island (plus nearby Kohama, Taketomi, Kuroshima and Aragusuka islands) forms Iriomote National Park, habitat of the primitive Triomote wildcat. Believed to be unchanged in five to 10 million years, this 'living fossil' is the size of a domestic cat and nocturnal, so it is seldom seen even by residents; in addition, there are only 30 to 40 still living, it is believed. Star sand is found on the island, but you are not allowed to collect it because Iriomote is a national park. The island also has habu snakes, so take care.

Ura-uchi-kawa

The best single excursion on the island is up the Ura-uchi river. Beginning at the mouth of the river, the boat usually carries about 12 people (there is no trouble making up a party, because many day-trippers cross from Ishigaki). After half an hour or so, you disembark and walk for about 40 minutes through canopied near-jungle to two pretty waterfalls, Mariyudo and Kampira. The first has three drops totalling 33 metres, ending in a deep pool; the latter is a long incline with numerous pot-holes.

Skin-diving

As on many of the other islands, skin-diving in the colourful coral beds among equally colourful fish is to be recommended. A barrier reef surrounds the island.

Accommodation

There are several minshuku, as well as two youth hostels at Funaura-ko. Of the latter, Irumote-so is the better, offering a nice view over the countryside and having pleasant staff.

Getting There & Getting Around

The boat and hovercraft/hydrofoil from Ishigaki (two hours and 30 minutes, respectively) dock at Ohara, from where a bus leaves soon afterward for the other side of the island and the trip up the Ura-uchi river. You can rent bicycles and motorcycles at a shop two minutes from Irumote-so Youth Hostel.

YONAGUNI-JIMA

This is the westernmost part of Japan, and on a clear day you can see Taiwan from Irizaki (West Cape). The main attraction is scenery, beaches and warm water, and the largest moths in the world. A beautiful view waits at the top of the 231-metre hill overlooking the village of Sonae.

Kubura-wari

One curiosity is this natural hole in the ground near Kubura. Legend is that anyone able to jump over it won't have to pay taxes, will have a long life, and women will give birth easily. It is wide enough that few are known to test the legend. It is surrounded by interesting rock formations, and is located behind Kubura school.

Getting Around

Bicycles and motorcycles may be rented for convenient transport.

Accommodation

There are only minshuku, no youth hostels.

HATERUMA-JIMA

This small island is the southernmost part of Japan and a pleasant place to visit. One good place to stay is a room adjacent to the Ishino-ume Restaurant.

Index

BIOGRAPHICAL NOTES

Ian L McQueen spent his earlier years in the port city of Saint John, New Brunswick, later graduating from the University of New Brunswick (Fredericton) in Chemical Engineering.

Travels to South America, Europe, Iceland and Trinidad were followed by a trip to Japan and South-East Asia. The planned three months in Japan stretched to fifteen, and over two years was spent in South-East Asia, Taiwan and Hong Kong. This was followed by nearly five years in Australia. He returned to Japan to write this book.

ACKNOWLEDGEMENTS

Many individuals and organizations have given information or other form of assistance in researching and producing this book.

The Japan National Tourist Organization, through both its head office and its Tourist Information Centres in Tokyo and Kyoto, have provided invaluable assistance of many kinds. The staff at the TICs deserve special thanks for their friendly helpfulness.

I would like to take special note of the kindness of the management of Canon Inc for the great contribution to preparing the manuscript and maps represented by the use of their high quality copying machines, and to thank various colleagues on staff for information and assistance, particularly K Sasaki and H Kawatsura.

Grateful acknowledgement is made to the Australian-Japan Foundation for supporting the research of this book.

The following individuals deserve specific mention for their assistance: D Britton, D Green, T Kaihata, N-J Kang, M Kira, K Matsumoto, R Morley, J Morris, N Nagayoshi, S Onda, J Pearce, D Petersen, H Suzuki, D Weber, W Wetherall, J Yamamoto, and Dr G Zobel.

Gilles Pineau was an invaluable source of most of the detailed information on Okinawa and other islands of southern Japan.

My apologies for not being able to single out everyone who has supplied useful information.

Lonely Planet travel guides

Africa on a Shoestring
Australia – a travel survival kit
Alaska – a travel survival kit
Bali & Lombok – a travel survival kit
Burma – a travel survival kit
Bushwalking in Papua New Guinea
Canada – a travel survival kit
China – a travel survival kit
Hong Kong, Macau & Canton
India – a travel survival kit
Japan – a travel survival kit
Kashmir, Ladakh & Zanskar
Kathmandu & the Kingdom of Nepal
Korea & Taiwan – a travel survival kit
Malaysia, Singapore & Brunei – a travel survival kit
Mexico – a travel survial kit
New Zealand – a travel survival kit
Pakistan – a travel survival kit kit
Papua New Guinea – a travel survival kit
The Philippines – a travel survival kit
South America on a Shoestring
South-East Asia on a Shoestring
Sri Lanka – a travel survival kit
Thailand – a travel survival kit
Tramping in New Zealand
Trekking in the Himalayas
Turkey – a travel survival kit
USA West
West Asia on a Shoestring

Lonely Planet phrasebooks

Indonesia Prasebook
Nepal Phrasebook
Thailand Phrasebook

Lonely Planet travel guides are available around the world. If you can't find them, ask your bookshop to order them from one of the distributors listed below. For countries not listed or if you would like a free copy of our latest booklist write to Lonely Planet in Australia.

Australia
Lonely Planet Publications, PO Box 88, South Yarra, Victoria 3141.

Canada
Milestone Publications, Box 2248, Sidney British Columbia, V8L 3S8.

Denmark
Scanvik Books aps, Store Kongensgade 59 A, DK-1264 Copenhagen K.

Hong Kong
The Book Society, GPO Box 7804.

India & Nepal
UBS Distributors, 5 Ansari Rd, New Delhi.

Israel
Geographical Tours Ltd, 8 Tverya St, Tel Aviv 63144.

Japan
Intercontinental Marketing Corp, IPO Box 5056, Tokyo 100-31.

Malaysia
MPH Distributors, 13 Jalan 13/6, Petaling Jaya, Selangor.

Netherlands
Nilsson & Lamm bv, Postbus 195, Pampuslaan 212, 1380 AD Weesp.

New Zealand
Roulston Greene Publishing Associates Ltd, Box 33850, Takapuna, Auckland 9.

Papua New Guinea
Gordon & Gotch (PNG), PO Box 3395, Port Moresby.

Singapore
MPH Distributors, 116-DJTC Factory Building, Lorong 3, Geylang Square, Singapore, 1438.

Sweden
Esselte Kartcentrum AB, Vasagatan 16, S-111 20 Stockholm.

Thailand
Chalermnit, 1-2 Erawan Arcade, Bangkok.

UK
Roger Lascelles, 47 York Rd, Brentford, Middlesex, TW8 0QP.

USA
Lonely Planet Publications, PO Box 2001A, Berkeley, CA 94702.

West Germany
Buchvertrieb Gerda Schettler, Postfach 64, D3415 Hattorf a H.

LONELY PLANET NEWSLETTER

We collect an enormous amount of information here at Lonely Planet. Apart from our research we also get a steady stream of letters from people out on the road – some of them are just one line on a postcard, others go on for pages. Plus we always have an ear to the ground for the latest on cheap airfares, new visa regulations, borders opening and closing. A lot of this information goes into our new editions or 'update supplements' in reprints. But we'd like to make better use of this information so, starting in November '81 we're going to produce a quarterly newsletter packed full of the latest news from out on the road. It will appear in February, May, August and November of each year. If you'd like an airmailed copy of the most recent newsletter just send us A$1.50 (A$1 within Australia) or A$5 (A$4 in Australia) for a year's subscription.